INTRODUCTORY ECONOMETRICS

This highly accessible and innovative text and accompanying CD-ROM use Excel workbooks powered by Visual Basic macros to teach the core concepts of econometrics without advanced mathematics. These materials enable Monte Carlo simulations to be run by students with a click of a button. The fundamental teaching strategy is to use clear language and take advantage of recent developments in computer technology to create concrete, visual explanations of difficult, abstract ideas. Intelligent repetition of concrete examples effectively conveys the properties of the ordinary least squares (OLS) estimator and the nature of heteroskedasticity and autocorrelation. Coverage includes omitted variables, binary response models, basic time series methods, and an introduction to simultaneous equations. The authors teach students how to construct their own real-world data sets drawn from the Internet, which they can analyze with Excel or with other econometric software. The Excel add-ins included with this book allow students to draw histograms, find *P*-values of various test statistics (including Durbin–Watson), obtain robust standard errors, and construct their own Monte Carlo and bootstrap simulations. For more, visit www.wabash.edu/econometrics.

Humberto Barreto is the DeVore Professor of Economics at Wabash College in Crawfordsville, Indiana. He received his Ph.D. from the University of North Carolina at Chapel Hill. Professor Barreto has lectured often on teaching economics with computer-based methods, including short courses with the National Science Foundation's Chautauqua program. The author of *The Entrepreneur in Microeconomic Theory*, Professor Barreto has served as a Fulbright Scholar in the Dominican Republic and is the Manager of Electronic Information for the History of Economics Society.

Frank M. Howland is Associate Professor of Economics at Wabash College. He earned his Ph.D. in Economics from Stanford University. He was a visiting researcher at the Fundación de Estudios de Economía Aplicada in Madrid, Spain. Howland has extensive experience designing spreadsheets and Visual Basic macros for intermediate microeconomics, statistics, and corporate finance courses. His academic research covers a variety of topics, including government crop support programs and the economics of higher education.

INTRODUCTORY ECONOMETRICS

Using Monte Carlo Simulation with Microsoft Excel®

HUMBERTO BARRETO

Wabash College

FRANK M. HOWLAND

Wabash College

CAMBRIDGE UNIVERSITY PRESS

CAMBRIDGE UNIVERSITY PRESS
Cambridge, New York, Melbourne, Madrid, Cape Town, Singapore, São Paulo, Delhi

Cambridge University Press
32 Avenue of the Americas, New York, NY 10013-2473, USA

www.cambridge.org
Information on this title: www.cambridge.org/9780521843195

First published 2006
Reprinted 2008 (twice)

Printed in the United States of America

A catalog record for this publication is available from the British Library.

Library of Congress Cataloging in Publication Data

Barreto, Humberto, 1960–
Introductory econometrics : using Monte Carlo simulation with Microsoft Excel /
Humberto Barreto, Frank M. Howland.
p. cm.
Includes bibliographical references and index.
ISBN-13: 978-0-521-84319-5 (hbk.)
ISBN-10: 0-521-84319-7 (hbk.)
1. Econometrics. 2. Monte Carlo method – Data processing. 3. Microsoft Excel (Computer file)
I. Howland, Frank M., 1958– II. Title.
HB139.B376 2006
330'.1'518282 – dc22 2005014585

ISBN 978-0-521-84319-5 hardback

Humberto Barreto
Para mi familia, Tami, Tyler, Nicolas, y Jonah

Frank M. Howland
To my parents, Bette Howland and Howard Howland

Contents

Preface

"I hear and I forget. I see and I remember. I do and I understand."

Confucius[1]

The Purpose of This Book

We wrote this book to help you understand econometrics. This book is quite different from the textbooks you are used to. Our fundamental strategy is to use clear language and take advantage of recent developments in computers to create concrete, visual explanations of difficult, abstract ideas.

Instead of passively reading, you will be using the accompanying Microsoft Excel workbooks to create a variety of graphs and other output while you interact with this book. Active learning is, of course, the goal of the Excel files. You will work through a series of questions, discovering patterns in the data or illustrating a particular property. Often, we will ask you to create your own version of what is on the printed page. This is made easy by the many buttons and other enhancements we have incorporated in the Excel workbooks.

You may be worried that learning econometrics will be a long, hard journey through a series of boring and extremely puzzling mathematical formulas. We will not deny that acquiring econometrics skills and knowledge takes real effort – you must carefully work through every Excel workbook and pay attention to detail – but introductory econometrics has little to do with complicated mathematics, nor need it be boring. In fact, the core of econometrics relies on logic and common sense. The methods presented in this book can be used to help answer questions about the value of education, the presence of discrimination, the effects of speed limits, and much more.

---

[1] This quote is frequently attributed to Confucius, but it is not in the *Analects* (a collection of excerpts and sayings), which were compiled by his followers after his death.

Our Goals

This book embodies a new approach to teaching introductory econometrics. Our approach is dictated by our beliefs regarding the purposes of a first course in undergraduate econometrics and the most important concepts that belong in that course; our frustrations with the traditional equation-laden, proof-oriented presentation of econometrics; and our experience with computer simulation as a tool that can overcome many of the limitations of traditional textbooks.

In terms of a student's educational development, there are short- and long-term reasons for including an introductory econometrics course in the undergraduate economics curriculum. Three major short-term goals for such a course stand out. A fundamental purpose of a first course in econometrics is to enable students to become intelligent readers of others' econometric analyses. To do so, they need to be able to interpret coefficient estimates and functional forms; understand simple inferential statistics, including the sampling distribution; and go beyond accepting all results at face value. A more ambitious introductory course should teach students to conduct creditable elementary econometric research. Students should be able to gather and document data, choose appropriate functional forms, run and interpret multiple regressions, conduct hypothesis tests and construct confidence intervals, and describe the major limitations of their analyses. Finally, an introductory course should prepare some students to take a second course in econometrics. Students who will take a second course ought to come to appreciate the method of least squares, the logic of the Gauss–Markov theorem, and the distinction between finite sample and asymptotic results.

In the long term, the learning that students carry with them throughout their lives should include two basic lessons: First, economic data should be interpreted as the outcome of a data-generation process in which chance plays a crucial role; second, because they typically deal with observational studies instead of controlled experiments, economists must always worry about whether the models they estimate and, more generally, the explanations they give for economic phenomena, are subject to confounding by omitted variables. Only a few students will go on to conduct econometric research in their future careers, but they all will benefit from these two fundamental ideas as workers and citizens who must evaluate the claims of business leaders, social scientists, and politicians.

An econometrics course that aims to teach these short- and long-term lessons must impart a very sophisticated message, which in its essence is something as follows: The data we observe must be interpreted as being produced by some data-generation process. Modeling that process requires both economic and statistical theory. To recover the parameters of the model, we use estimators. Every estimator has important properties relating to its accuracy (bias or consistency) and precision (standard error). Depending on what we know or conjecture about the data-generation process, we will want to use different estimators. Given the nonexperimental character of our data, we must always be on guard for the effects of omitted variables.

How do we convey this complicated message? Many textbooks employ mathematical formalism to teach the numerous abstract concepts in the basic story. The resulting mass of equations and theorems intimidates students, and, worse yet, hides the truly essential and genuinely difficult core logic of econometrics. In the traditional classroom format of a lecture accompanied by chalkboard or overhead projector, students lapse into desperate attempts at passive memorization. Furthermore, there is pressure to cram the course and textbook with as many of the results of modern econometric research as possible.

Our approach differs from that of the traditional textbook in three aspects: we emphasize concrete examples rather than equations to exemplify abstract concepts, active learning by using computers rather than passively reading a book, and a focus on a few key ideas rather than an attempt to cover the whole waterfront. We wholeheartedly agree with Peter Kennedy and Michael Murray, critics of the traditional approach, who have argued, first, that the crucial concept in introductory econometrics (and statistics) is that of the sampling distribution and, second, that students can only learn that concept by actively grappling with it.[2] On the basis of our teaching experience, we give a second crucial abstraction almost as much prominence as the sampling distribution: the way in which a multiple regression summarizes the relationship between a dependent variable and several independent variables, including especially the notion of ceteris paribus.

All of these pedagogical considerations led to our choice of Microsoft Excel as the central vehicle to teach econometrics. We use Excel's underlying programming language, Visual Basic, to create buttons and other tools to tailor the environment for the student. The key advantages of computer-based instruction are dynamic visualization and interesting repetition. A printed textbook may contain outstanding graphics, but on the page all charts and tables are of necessity static. In contrast, using Excel, a student can instantly redraw charts and tables after changing a parameter or taking another sample. Students can toggle through different charts depicting the same data set or go back and forth through a complicated exposition. The ability of spreadsheets to convey interesting repetition greatly increases the effectiveness of specific, concrete examples designed to illustrate general, abstract ideas. Students are able to associate the specific numbers on the screen with the abstract symbols

[2] Kennedy (1998) and Murray (1999a).

in equations and can see the workings of the general claim when the asserted result is shown to hold over and over again in specific examples.

The advantages of Excel and Visual Basic are perhaps best displayed in the numerous Monte Carlo simulations we use to approximate sampling distributions throughout the book. Visual Basic obtains the samples, computes the estimates, and draws the histograms. Students are invited to make comparisons by altering the parameters of the data-generation process or directly racing two estimators against each other.[3] We are under no illusions that students will immediately understand the sampling distribution. Thus, we employ Monte Carlo simulation whenever it is relevant and ask students to view the outcomes of Monte Carlo experiments from a variety of angles. Because it is easier to understand, we have used the fixed-X-in-repeated-sampling assumption in almost all of our Monte Carlo simulations. We also, however, demonstrate other, more realistic sampling schemes.

We also use Excel to compute regression estimates in numerous examples. Although Excel has been rightly criticized for its sloppy statistical algorithms, it is adequate for the relatively straightforward computations required in an introductory course. Where Excel is lacking, we have written add-ins – for example to draw histograms, compute Durbin–Watson statistics and robust standard errors, and obtain nonlinear least squares and maximum likelihood estimates in Probit and Logit models. We do not recommend Excel as a statistical analysis package; we use it instead as a teaching tool.

To sum up, our primary goal in writing this book was to bridge the gap between the traditional, formal presentation of econometrics and the abilities of the typical undergraduate student. Today's student is, on the one hand, uncomfortable with mathematical formalism, and, on the other, adept at visually oriented use of computers.

We take advantage of modern computing technology to teach introductory econometrics more effectively. The basic Microsoft Excel spreadsheet, as familiar to the student as pencil and paper, is augmented and enhanced by powerful macros, buttons, and links that easily facilitate complicated computations and simulations. Monte Carlo simulation is the perfect tool for conveying the fundamental concept in econometrics – the sampling distribution – to the modern audience. It produces concrete, visual output and permits exploration of the properties of estimators without sophisticated mathematics.

It is ironic that simulation- and computer-intensive numerical techniques figure prominently in frontier research in econometric theory, whereas the teaching of econometrics languishes in old-style, chalk-and-talk memorization and proof methods. Our goal is to bring the benefits of the computer revolution to the undergraduate econometrics textbook and classroom.

---

[3] See Murray (1999b).

Content and Level of Presentation

This book is divided into two parts: descriptive data analysis and inferential econometrics. The first part is devoted to methods of summarizing bivariate and multivariate data. We use the correlation coefficient and PivotTables to set up regression as an analogue to the average. Additional chapters on functional form, dummy variables, and multiple regression round out the first part.

In the second part of the book, we focus on the effects of chance in estimation and the interpretation of regression output. We begin with a chapter dedicated solely to Monte Carlo simulation. Throughout the second part of the book, we emphasize modeling the data-generation process. We explain the sampling distribution of the OLS estimator with Monte Carlo simulation to support the proof of the Gauss–Markov theorem. We also employ Monte Carlo simulation to demonstrate the effects of elementary violations of the classical linear model, including omitted variable bias, heteroskedasticity, and autocorrelation. Every chapter contains both contrived and real-world examples and data. Finally, we provide introductions to binary response (dummy dependent variable) models, forecasting, simultaneous equations models, and bootstrapping.

Although the entire book is essentially a study of regression analysis, our two-part organization enables us to emphasize that regression can be used to describe and summarize data without using any of its inferential machinery. When we turn to regression for inference, we are able to highlight the importance of chance in the process that generated the data.

Because we expect students to obtain and analyze data, we include detailed instructions on how to access a variety of data sets online. For example, the CPS.doc file (in the Basic Tools\InternetData folder) explains exactly how a student can extract data from the Current Population Survey (CPS) available at <ferret.bls.census.gov>. In addition, we include practical explanations of how to recode variables and construct an hourly wage variable. The CPS is an outstanding source and has provided the raw data for many excellent student papers.

Another advantage of online data resources is the ability to access the latest figures. Web links are included in our Excel files, and thus updating data is easy. Many of the workbooks have links to a variety of data sources. Online data resources have transformed our teaching and enabled students to access high-quality, timely data.

In presenting the material, we focus on getting a few key ideas exactly right and explaining these concepts as simply as possible. Instead of concisely writing a result in terse mathematical notation, we walk you through the commonsense logic behind the formula. We also repeat the same idea. Often, we will use hypothetical data to demonstrate a point and then use an example from the real world to show how it has been applied.

To read this book and use our materials, you need a working knowledge of elementary statistics. You should understand the standard deviation (SD) and be able to read a histogram. You should be familiar with the standard error (SE) of the sample average. To help those in need of a little brushing up, we have included a chapter that reviews inferential statistics and the explicit modeling of a data-generation process. Finally, this book will make more sense if you have had at least an introductory economics course.

Of course, you also have to know how to use Excel and work with files on a computer. You do not need to be an expert, but we expect you to be able to create formulas and make a chart. Our materials will introduce you to much more advanced uses of Excel, and it is fair to say that, by working through this book, you will become a more sophisticated user of Excel.

Conclusion

The installed base of Microsoft Excel (and Office) is staggering. At any given time, many different versions of Excel are in use. Exactly counting all of the versions in use, legally purchased, and pirated is impossible. Table 1 shows the Gartner Group's estimate of the breakdown of Windows Office versions in use in 2001.

The materials in this book require Excel 97 (or greater). Each version will have differences in functionality and, especially, display, but the files packaged in this book should work with versions of Excel from 97 to 2003.

- To determine the version of Excel you are using, execute Help: About Microsoft Excel.
- To find the previous versions of Excel, visit <www.microsoft.com/office/previous/excel/default.asp>.
- To find the latest version of Excel, go to <office.microsoft.com/home/>.
- To compare versions of Office products, see <www.microsoft.com/office/editions/prodinfo/compare.mspx>.
- To search Microsoft's extensive Knowledge Base for questions about Excel, visit <support.microsoft.com/> and click on the Search the Knowledge Base link.

Table 1. Estimated Microsoft Office installed base in 2001.
Source: www.infotechtrends.com/

Office 95	10%
Office 97	55%
Office 2000	35%
Yearly Upgrade	15%

Acknowledgments

This book is a collaborative effort of several professors in the Wabash College Economics Department. Humberto Barreto and Frank Howland are the principal authors of this book and share equal responsibility for its content. In addition, Kealoha Widdows made extensive contributions to the book, and Joyce Burnette revised many of the illustrations, examples, and computer files.

Michael Einterz provided excellent error checking and test drove many examples. He added clear instructions for data sources and improved our presentation greatly. Matthew Schulz helped us polish the exercises and answers. The book also reflects comments and reactions of several generations of Wabash College students. We thank them all.

Scott Parris of Cambridge University Press deserves our gratitude. He took a chance on an idea far outside the mainstream, and we hope it pays off. Thank you, Scott, for your support and helpful feedback. We are grateful to Katie Greczylo, our production manager at TechBooks, and John Joswick, our copy editor.

We also thank our Web site designer Jeannine Smith. Her ability to write sophisticated computer code combined with artistic flair resulted in an excellent Web site (www.wabash.edu/econometrics) that is functional and fashionable.

A major inspiration for our work is *Statistics* by David Freedman, Robert Pisani, and Roger Purves (W. W. Norton & Company, 3rd edition, 1998). We have tried to adapt the same approach to the study of econometrics that Freedman et al. use in teaching statistics. That is, we emphasize the importance of basic concepts and reject the memorization of boring formulas. We have taken the central metaphor of their book, the box model, and extended it to handle the classical linear model. Finally, we follow their visual and verbal approach to the material.

We would appreciate your criticisms and suggestions.

Humberto Barreto and Frank Howland   Crawfordsville, Indiana
barretoh@wabash.edu and   2005
howlandf@wabash.edu

References

Kennedy, P. (1998). "Teaching Undergraduate Econometrics: A Suggestion for Fundamental Change," *American Economic Review* **88**(2): 487–491.

Murray, M. (1999a). "Taking Linear Estimators Seriously in Introductory Economics." Conference on Teaching Undergraduate Econometrics: Does Monte Carlo Work?, Middlebury College.

Murray, M. (1999b). "Econometrics Lectures in a Computer Classroom." *Journal of Economic Education* **30**(3): 308–321.

User Guide

The introduction of Lotus's spreadsheet solver in 1-2-3/G motivated the other spreadsheet vendors to develop or acquire solvers of their own. In 1990 – well before the launch of Windows 3.0 – Frontline won a competition among third-party Solver developers to create a Solver on an OEM basis for Microsoft Excel 3.0.

Frontline Systems Company History

0.1. Conventions and Organization of Files

To gain the full benefit of this book, you must have access to the accompanying Excel workbooks. We make constant reference to a variety of objects in Excel, and you must actively work with Excel while reading this book. Because changing parameters and seeing the results are so crucial to our approach, we have adopted several conventions that will help you navigate through our materials.

In this book, a *figure* refers to a variety of graphics, including charts and pictures of portions of a sheet. We often display a chart or range of cells in a figure in the printed book, but we want you to look at the live version on your computer screen. Thus, in addition to a caption, many figures have a source line indicating their location in the Excel workbook. We follow Excel's naming convention for workbooks and sheets: [workbookname]sheetname. For example, if the source says, "[SimEq.xls]Data," then you know the figure can be found in the SimEq.xls workbook in the *Data* sheet. We will always italicize sheet names in the printed text to help you locate the proper sheet in a workbook. We might also refer to cell C7 in the *Female* sheet of the PairedXYBootstrap.xls workbook as [PairedXYBootstrap]Female!$C$7.

You may need to adjust your display or the objects in Excel. Use the Zoom button to magnify the display. You can also right-click objects such as buttons (Why Bias?) or scroll bars (◄ ▶) to select and move them. Once you open a workbook, you can save it to another location or name (by executing

Figure 0.1.1. Organization of the CD-ROM.

File: Save As...) and make whatever changes you wish. This is the same as underlining or writing in a conventional printed book.

In addition to the Excel workbooks associated with the printed book, we also provide important additional materials with this book. Figure 0.1.1 shows the contents of all of the materials included in the CD-ROM. The Chapters folder contains the book itself with the accompanying workbooks always located in an ExcelFiles folder.

The Chapters and Answers folders are paired with each other. For example, in Chapter 5 on interpreting regression, there are several Excel workbooks. Some of the workbooks have questions, which are always located in the workbook's *Q&A* sheet. The corresponding answers can be found in the Chapter 5 folder in the Answers folder. We think of the Q&A material in the Excel workbooks as self-study questions.

The book itself has other questions that we call Exercises. Readers do not have easy access to the answers to the exercise questions. To see these answers, you must register online as an instructor at <www.wabash.edu/econometrics>.

In addition to the Chapters and Answers folder, the Basic Tools folder contains software and additional material. The ExcelAddIns folder contains various supplementary programs that we have written for teaching and learning econometrics. Figure 0.1.2 lists the add-ins available with this book.

Each add-in folder has the add-in itself (with filename extension.xla) and a document with instructions on installing and using the software. As you work

Figure 0.1.2. Available Excel add-ins.

Figure 0.1.3. Internet data sources.

through the chapters in the book, you will have the opportunity to use these materials.

The HowTo folder in Basic Tools has a series of files that explain how to do a particular task in econometrics. For example, the DeltaMethod.xls workbook explains how to use the delta method to find the SE of an elasticity.

Figure 0.1.3 displays the contents of the InternetData folder. As you can see, we explain how to access, download, and import data from a variety of online sources. Each folder has detailed instructions and offers at least one example.

Finally, the RandomNumber folder (the last folder in Basic Tools in Figure 0.1.1) has extensive documentation on random number generation. Although this may seem an arcane, unimportant topic, we believe the increasing reliance on simulation means that every student of econometrics should understand the principles behind the creation of "random numbers" by a computer. Chapter 9 offers the basic explanation, and the RandomNumber folder provides more in-depth coverage.

Much of the value of this book lies in the Excel workbooks and additional materials. We hope you will read the book carefully and access the computer files as directed.

0.2. Preparing and Working with Microsoft Excel®

A working knowledge of Microsoft Excel is a prerequisite for this book. In other words, you must be able to open Excel files, write formulas that add cells together, create charts, and save files. As you will see, however, Excel is much more than a simple adding machine. It can be used to solve nonlinear optimization problems, run Monte Carlo simulations, and perform multiple regression analysis. In addition, we have packaged several add-ins with this book. They will provide additional features and functionality. Specific instructions for each add-in are provided as they are used.

In the next section, we provide a little background on Excel and explain how to configure your computer properly to enable you to work with the materials in this book.

A Brief History of Microsoft Excel

The first spreadsheet on a personal computer was called VisiCalc (short for "visible calculator") and was created by Daniel Bricklin and Bob Frankston in 1978. Bricklin, a Harvard Business School student, was looking for an easier way to conduct a case study. He envisioned "an electronic blackboard and electronic chalk in a classroom."[1] He recruited Frankston to help him write the code. VisiCalc was an instant success and was one of the first "killer apps."

By the early 1980s, Lotus 1-2-3 was the leading spreadsheet. Lotus had bought and then discontinued VisiCalc. Borland's Quattro Pro was another well-known product at that time.

In 1985, Microsoft Corporation came up with Excel for the Macintosh computer. This product was remarkable for its use of pull-down menus and a point-and-click device called a mouse. Other spreadsheets used a command line interface that required knowledge of cryptic DOS commands. "There is some controversy about whether a graphical version of Microsoft Excel was released in a DOS version. Microsoft documents show the launch of Excel 2.0 for MS-DOS version 3.0 on 10/31/87."[2]

When Microsoft named its spreadsheet software "Excel," it apparently did not know that Manufacturers Hanover Trust already had an automated banking program called Excel. As part of the settlement for trademark infringement, Microsoft agreed to refer always to its product as Microsoft Excel. In promotional materials, on its Web site, and even on the Windows Task Bar, Microsoft always calls its flagship spreadsheet program "Microsoft Excel."

The rest of the 1980s were marked by intense competition. Lotus 1-2-3, Quattro Pro, and Microsoft Excel battled for dominance. Microsoft's spreadsheet software pulled away from its competitors in the 1990s, and the product was marketed as part of a family of "office tools" that included Microsoft Word and PowerPoint.

Check Google results for entries related to "spreadsheet excel history" to learn much more about the fascinating history of how Excel came to be the dominant spreadsheet.

Excel Versions and Your Version

As Microsoft included new features and enhancements in Excel over the years, they released newer versions of the software. Excel 3.0, launched in 1990, featured the idea of many sheets in a workbook. Two years later, Microsoft gained market share with the release of Excel 4.0 along with

[1] <www.bricklin.com/history/sai.htm>.
[2] <dssresources.com/history/sshistory.html>.

Windows 3.1 – Microsoft's first graphical user interface (GUI) operating system for the PC. In December 1993, Microsoft's dominance was solidified with the release of Excel 5.0 because it was powered by Visual Basic instead of its own macro language (called Excel 4 Macro Language). Excel 7.0 for Windows95 debuted in July 1995. With Excel 8.0, in 1997, Microsoft changed the version pattern, for marketing purposes, to the year of release, calling the product Excel 97. Thus, Excel 2000 is Excel 9.0, Excel 2002 is 10.0, and in October 2003, Microsoft released Excel 2003 (Excel 11.0). As you would expect, Excel 2003 has new bells and whistles along with fixes and modifications of existing code, which includes a new set of algorithms for many statistical functions.

In addition to "major upgrades" that merit an entirely new version number, Microsoft occasionally releases slightly different versions to different market segments. For example, ExcelXP is actually a member of the Excel 10.0 family. You may also see references to Excel as Standard, Business, or Professional Editions.

Excel for the Apple Macintosh has a similar version history with new releases every few years, but you should be aware that Windows Excel and Mac Excel are not identical software and that there can be serious cross-platform compatibility problems. Our materials work with newer versions of Mac Excel, but buttons and dialog boxes may not display optimally. Mac Excel users should make sure to run Solver before using add-ins that require Solver.

Non–English-language versions of Excel should be fully functional with our materials (which have been tested with Spanish Excel). Excel (and other Office software) has several hundred different language versions, but it is only the front end that is in a different language. The Visual Basic engine that drives Excel is the same across all languages, and thus our workbooks and add-ins will work with foreign language versions of Excel. Of course, our text, buttons, and dialog boxes will be in English.

You can check the actual version of Excel on your machine by executing Help: About Microsoft Excel. Visit <office.microsoft.com/officeupdate/> to obtain the latest security patches and updates for your version.

Excel 97 (or Mac Excel 2001) or greater is required to use the materials in this book. Your screen may sometimes look a little different than the screenshots in the book, but the basic functionality will be the same.

Properly Configuring Excel

To make sure that Excel is able to access and run the Visual Basic macros in the workbooks, security must be properly set.

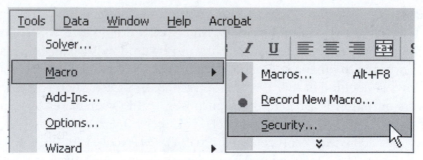

Figure 0.2.1. Accessing security options.

Step 1: From Excel, execute Tools: Macro: Security (see Figure 0.2.1).
At the Security Level tab, make sure that High is *not* selected (as shown
in Figure 0.2.2). Medium will always give you a warning that the file you are
about to open has macros, and then you can decide whether to run the macros
(or open the file). Low is (quite reasonably) not recommended because Excel
will automatically run all macros with no warning or prompt. Figure 0.2.2
shows the display from an older version of Excel. An additional option, Very
High, is included in Excel 2003. Click the Trusted Sources tab and, as shown
in Figure 0.2.3, make certain both boxes are checked to ensure that installed
add-ins will have access to your Visual Basic Projects (i.e., your workbooks).

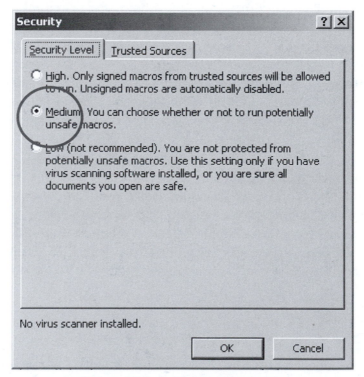

Figure 0.2.2. Setting security level.

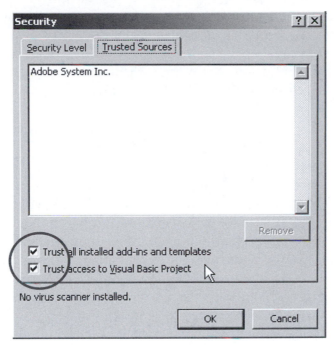

Figure 0.2.3. Setting trusted sources.

Security need be set only once because Excel will remember your settings. With Excel's security correctly configured, you are ready to open the Excel workbooks on the CD and install add-ins as needed.

Step 2: From Excel, execute File: Open in order to open a workbook.
When opening a workbook from the CD, always click the "Enable Macros" option (see Figure 0.2.4). For workbooks not included with this book, do not click Enable Macros unless you are completely confident that the workbook is safe.

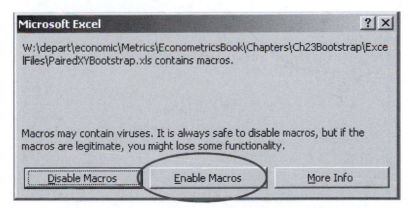

Figure 0.2.4. Opening a workbook with macros.

When you open a file from the CD, it will be read-only. Execute File: Save As and navigate to a folder on your hard drive or network space to save your work. You may drag the contents of this CD onto your hard drive and change the Attributes setting (by right-clicking on the file and choosing Properties) and checking off the Read-Only option.

Excel on a Macintosh

Macintosh users know that there can be problems working with Windows files, and Microsoft Excel does have some cross-platform compatibility issues. Fortunately, when opening our Windows-created workbooks, the content remains true. The display in Mac Excel, however, may not be optimal. Mac users may notice imperfections (such as cutting off text in buttons). We recommend adjusting the Zoom in Mac Excel to improve the display.

In addition, we have noticed that Solver in Mac Excel can be somewhat temperamental. Make sure you run Excel's Solver before attempting to open a workbook that uses Solver. If you have trouble opening a workbook (e.g., you get an error message that says, "Can't find project or library"), always try the following simple fix: quit Excel, open it, run Solver, and then open the workbook.

Troubleshooting

We guarantee that, at some point, something will go wrong while you are working with our materials. Your computer may freeze up or you will not be able to perform a particular task. The first step to overcoming difficulties is simply to start over. Often closing a workbook and reopening it is sufficient, but you may have to quit Excel or restart your computer.

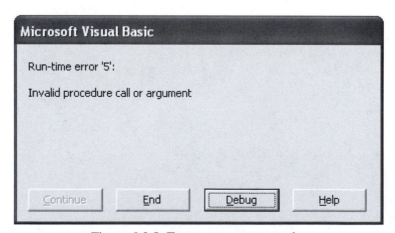

Figure 0.2.5. Error message example.

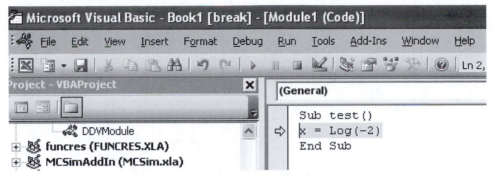

Figure 0.2.6. Debugging in Visual Basic.

We also suggest that you revisit the instructions and read carefully to make sure you are following each step closely. For example, in newer versions of Excel, you need to run Solver before accessing macros that use Solver. The instructions point this out, but it is easy to overlook this step.

An error message like that shown in Figure 0.2.5 may appear. If you click the End button, the message will disappear and you will return to where you were working in Excel. Clicking the Debug button takes you to Visual Basic and highlights the offending line of code, as displayed in Figure 0.2.6.

In some cases, you may be able to determine how to fix the error. In Figure 0.2.6, an attempt to take the log of a negative number has triggered an error in the subroutine named test.

We do not expect our readers to be proficient Visual Basic programmers, but with a little ingenuity you may be able to diagnose and correct the problem quickly. If not, we welcome your feedback, and we will try to fix problems associated with our workbooks.

We will keep an updated set of the latest versions of our workbooks and add-ins on the Web at <www.wabash.edu/econometrics>. If you have persistent problems with a workbook or add-in, please check the Web site to see if we have an updated, corrected version online.

1

Introduction

We find that a 10-percent permanent increase in the price of cigarettes reduces current consumption by 4 percent in the short run and by 7.5 percent in the long run.
Gary Becker, Michael Grossman, and Kevin Murphy[1]

1.1. Definition of Econometrics

In this chapter we discuss the contents of this book, including the basic ideas we attempt to convey and the tools of analysis used. We begin with our definition of the subject: *Econometrics* is the application of statistical techniques and analyses to the study of problems and issues in economics.

The term econometrics was coined in 1926 by Ragnar A. K. Frisch, a Norwegian economist who shared the first Nobel Prize in Economics in 1969 with another econometrics pioneer, Jan Tinbergen.[2] Although many economists had used data and made calculations long before 1926, Frisch felt he needed a new word to describe how he interpreted and used data in economics.

Today, econometrics is a broad area of study within economics. The field changes constantly as new tools and techniques are added. Its center, however, contains a stable set of fundamental ideas and principles. This book is about the core of econometrics. We will explain the basic logic and method of econometrics, concentrating on getting the core ideas exactly right.

We divide the study of econometrics in this book into the following two fundamental parts:

Part 1. Description
Part 2. Inference

In each part, *regression analysis* will be the primary tool. By showing regression again and again in a variety of contexts, we reinforce the idea that it is

---

[1] Becker, Grossman, and Murphy, (1994, p. 396).

[2] A good source for more on the life and work of Frisch is Bjerkholt (1995). By the way, Frisch also came up with another common term – macroeconomics. "Polypoly," however, never quite caught on. For more on the history of empirical analysis in economics, see <cepa.newschool.edu/het/schools/metric.htm>.

a powerful, flexible method that defines much of econometrics. At the same time, however, we describe the conditions that must be met for its proper use and the situations in which regression analysis may lead to disastrously erroneous conclusions if these conditions are not met.

In addition to regression analysis, we will use *Monte Carlo simulation* throughout the second part of the book to model the role of chance in the data generation process. The Monte Carlo method is an integral part of our teaching approach, which emphasizes concrete, visual understanding.

Section 1.2 uses the example of the study of the demand for cigarettes to illustrate the goals and methods of econometric analysis and how regression fits into this enterprise. We will further discuss the concept of Monte Carlo analysis in Chapter 9, the first chapter of Part 2 of the book.

1.2. Regression Analysis

Workbook: Cig.xls

We illustrate our discussion of the methods and goals of econometrics with a rich, complicated example. It will serve as a vehicle to demonstrate the uses of regression analysis and the difficulties inherent in quantitative analysis. Our aim is to provide an overview of how regression can be used, while introducing fundamental concepts that will be explained in greater detail throughout this book.

Economists, policymakers, health professionals, cigarette manufacturers, and citizens are all interested in the demand for cigarettes. Cigarettes were one of the major consumer product success stories of the first half of the twentieth century. Adult per capita consumption exploded, starting at under 3 packs per adult per year in 1900, rising to 33 packs in 1920, tripling to 99 packs in 1940, and finally peaking at 217 packs per adult in 1963. Since then, cigarette consumption has collapsed almost as dramatically as it rose. Per capita adult consumption fell to 107 packs per person in 1999. Figure 1.2.1 tells the story for the entire century.

As the source information in Figure 1.2.1 indicates, the data underlying the graph are available in the Cig.xls workbook in the *HistoricalData* sheet. The workbook can be found in the Chapters \ Ch01Introduction folder of the CD-ROM or the <www.wabash.edu/econometrics> Web site. Open up the workbook now. Upon opening the workbook you should be given a warning that it contains macros and therefore possibly viruses, as shown in Figure 1.2.2.[3]

---

[3] The User Guide explains how to configure Excel properly to use the materials in this book. Security must be set to Medium, and you should click Enable Macros when opening our workbooks.

12 *Introduction*

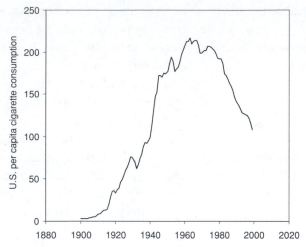

Figure 1.2.1. U.S. per capita consumption of cigarettes for persons 18 and over, 1900–1999.
Source: [Cig.xls] Historical Data.

We refer you to the Cig.xls Excel workbook at various points throughout this chapter. Notice that the Cig.xls workbook, like many of our workbooks, has extensive documentation, including clickable Web links. Think of the Excel workbooks as an extension of this printed book and do not hesitate to make notes, create charts, or otherwise modify the workbooks.

Even with the post-1960s collapse in per capita consumption, cigarettes have remained a very lucrative business. In the 1996 fiscal year, for example, consumers paid about $47 billion for 21.6 billion packs of cigarettes. Of that revenue, $5.2 billion went to federal taxes, $7.8 billion to state taxes, and perhaps $6.5 billion to profits for manufacturers.[4] Cigarettes, of course, are known to be addictive and damaging to people's health. The large increase in cigarette consumption led to millions of premature deaths, and the decline in consumption since the 1960s has undoubtedly reversed this trend. The cost to society of the health effects of smoking is staggering: A responsible estimate of the sum of the current medical costs of treating smoking-related illnesses and the lost earnings due to illness and death is $100 billion per year.[5]

This history and current reality make questions like the following very much worth asking: What will happen to sales of cigarettes if taxes on

[4] *The Tax Burden on Tobacco, 1999.* Price of cigarettes used in this computation is the nationwide average for January 1, 1996, on p. 269; tax collections are from pp. 5 and 8. Profit estimate of 30 cents per pack is from Harris (1998), p. 2.
[5] Chaloupka and Warner (2000).

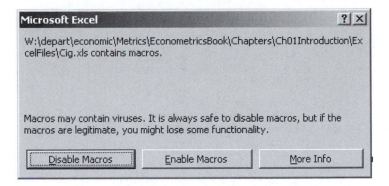

Figure 1.2.2. Message displayed when opening Cig.xls.

cigarettes are increased? How will adolescents change their smoking behavior if prices rise? What is the incidence of cigarette taxes? How will the effects of the cigarette tax increase differ between the short run and the long run? Econometric analysis can throw considerable light on these and many other questions.

In this section we show how the techniques of bivariate and multiple regression can be used to study the demand for cigarettes. Various research designs are discussed that can be used to examine this question. The aim of our discussion is to present general ideas and methods used throughout this book; details follow in later chapters.

A persistent theme of this book is that successful econometric analysis depends on economic and statistical theory as well as a careful reading of the data. Each element is considered in turn. Economic theory contributes the basic concept of a demand curve, which shows how the quantity demanded for cigarettes varies as the price of cigarettes changes if other factors are held constant. The demand curve provides a framework for statistical analysis by suggesting which factors affect demand and therefore posing questions that analysis must answer. Two crucial questions ask how responsive quantity demanded is to changes in the price of cigarettes and to the income of consumers. To fix ideas, let us suppose that quantity demanded falls as price rises and rises as income increases. If that is the case, then we might have market demand curves that look like those of Figure 1.2.3.

We have drawn curves in which a one-pack-per-person-per-year increase in quantity is associated with a 2-cent-per-pack decrease in price; the slope of both demand curves is –2. In this hypothetical diagram, the demand curve shifts to the right as per capita income rises. Specifically, a $5,000-increase in per capita income results in an increase in quantity demanded of 25 packs per person per year ceteris paribus. This shows up as a horizontal shift of

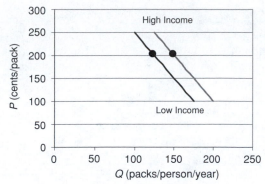

Figure 1.2.3. Hypothetical demand curves for cigarettes.
Source: [Cig.xls]HypotheticalData.

25 packs per person per year. For example, the two points highlighted in Figure 1.2.3 show how – when price is held constant at 200 cents per pack – quantity demanded rises from 125 to 150 packs per person per year when income rises by $5,000.

Econometricians modify this diagram in one significant respect – they reverse the axes. The reason is that the scientific and statistical convention is to draw the variable causing changes, the "independent" variable, on the *x*-axis, and the variable responding to changes, the "dependent" variable, on the *y*-axis. Economists believe that quantity demanded responds to changes in price, not the other way around. The conventional diagram of introductory economics classes, however, puts quantity demanded on the *x*-axis and price on the *y*-axis. In Figure 1.2.4, we redraw the data to reflect standard scientific practice.

Notice that the mathematical slope has changed. Before it was −2; now it is −0.5. Furthermore, shifts in the demand curve due to changes in income are read as vertical, not horizontal shifts. The two points we singled out in

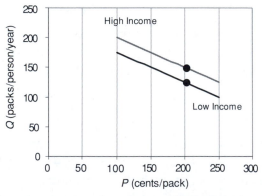

Figure 1.2.4. Demand curves redrawn to reflect standard practice.
Source: [Cig.xls]HypotheticalData.

Figure 1.2.3 are once again highlighted in this figure. They show that at a price of 200 cents per pack, the quantity demanded is 125 packs per person per year when per capita income is \$15,000, and 150 packs per person per year when per capita income is \$20,000. To review this discussion of demand curves, go to *HypotheticalData* in Cig.xls. Click on the buttons on the sheet to see the effects of price decreases and income increases.

Economists' standard instrument for measuring the responsiveness of behavior to changes in the environment is the concept of elasticity. Elasticity is the percentage change in an endogenous variable (e.g., quantity demanded) divided by the percentage change in an exogenous variable (e.g., price) with other factors held constant.

In this book we compute the point elasticity as follows, taking the price elasticity as an example and using obvious symbols:

$$\text{Price Elasticity of Demand} = \frac{\%\Delta\text{Quantity Demanded}}{\%\Delta\text{Price}}$$
$$= \frac{\Delta Q/Q}{\Delta P/P}$$
$$= \frac{\Delta Q}{\Delta P} \cdot \frac{P}{Q}.$$

The expression on the left, the change in Q over the change in P, is the slope of the demand curve when drawn in the standard scientific way. Thus, the elasticity at the point $Q = 200$ packs per person per year and $P = 125$ cents on the Low Income Demand Curve is

$$\text{Price Elasticity of Demand} = \frac{\Delta Q}{\Delta P} \cdot \frac{P}{Q}$$
$$= -0.5 \cdot \frac{125}{200}$$
$$= -0.625.$$

We repeat that the example above is entirely hypothetical. It is certainly possible that, as in this example, the quantity demanded of cigarettes does not change very much when price rises. After all, cigarettes are addictive. Furthermore, it is by no means guaranteed that cigarettes are a normal good. Econometric analysis aims to estimate the responsiveness of quantity demanded to price and income.

With the demand curve as our foundation in economic theory, we turn now to statistical considerations. Much of this book is devoted to a careful exposition of the statistical issues we must deal with when trying to estimate the demand curve. Two crucial ideas must constantly be borne in mind as we proceed. These are issues of design and the role of chance. This section covers the design of econometric studies; we defer study of the role of chance to Part 2 of this book.

All econometric studies rely on the method of comparison. The basic comparison in our example is how quantity demanded changes as the price changes. The design of a study refers to the way in which the data are gathered and which variables are employed in the study. Thus, the design dictates the way the comparison is undertaken. In principle, the best way to determine how quantity demanded for cigarettes changes as the price changes is to run a controlled experiment.

There are two major types of controlled experiments: field experiments and laboratory experiments. In field experiments, subjects are observed in their everyday lives, but the experimenter manipulates some part of his or her environment. In laboratory experiments, subjects are placed in an artificial environment under the complete control of the experimenter. Let us consider a possible field experimental design to learn more about the demand for cigarettes.

Divide a group of subjects into control and treatment groups using some method of random assignment. The control group can buy cigarettes at the normal retail price. The treatment group must pay a higher price designed to simulate a tax increase. Compare the behavior of the two groups to see if the price of cigarettes makes a difference in the amount of cigarettes they buy. Ideally, one would be able to identify two points on the demand curve by looking at the behavior of two groups facing two different prices.

Several obvious problems are inherent in this design. How can experimenters enforce the higher price for cigarettes? They typically cannot and so in such experiments it is common to give subjects in the treatment group a better deal than they can get on their own. The assumption is that decreases in price will produce effects opposite to those of price increases, and thus little is lost by cutting the price rather than raising it. But if the treatment group is allowed to pay a lower price, subjects may decide to resell the cigarettes they get through the experiment. Furthermore, because the experiment cannot last forever and cigarettes are easily stored, heavy smokers in the treatment group would have an incentive to stock up on the lower priced cigarettes. Both of these objections suggest that the treatment group's response will not be the same as it would be with an actual change in price. Finally, any experiment that might encourage people to smoke could be ethically suspect. For these reasons and others, to our knowledge there have been no studies that follow a design similar to the one we just outlined.

There have, however, been laboratory experimental studies that attempted to model the effect of price on the demand for cigarettes.[6] Behavioral

[6] See Bickel and Madden (1999).

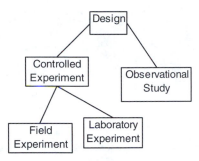

Figure 1.2.5. Classification of experimental design schemes.

economists have used one-pack-or-more-per-day smokers as subjects. Subjects "paid" for cigarettes by pulling and resetting a plunger before being allowed a puff from a cigarette. The quantity demanded is the number of puffs; the price is the number of required pulls on the plunger. In these experiments, quantity demanded falls as price rises.

Although laboratory experiments therefore help to confirm a basic finding in research on the demand for cigarettes, they have severe limitations. It is not easy to translate results on effort exerted in a laboratory to obtain another puff into estimates of the slope or elasticity of a real-world demand curve. Laboratory subjects are not entirely representative of the population because ethical considerations preclude using teenagers and alcoholics as subjects, and it is difficult to induce high-income people to participate in experiments. Also, these experiments tell us nothing about the effect of changes in price on the decision to start or stop smoking. Figure 1.2.5 summarizes the different types of experimental designs.

If one cannot conduct a controlled experiment, the alternative is to do an observational study. In such a study, the researcher looks for something in the actual economic environment that causes the variable of interest, here the price of cigarettes, to vary across subjects. Two possible directions are variation over time, which provokes time series studies, and variation across individual entities at the same point in time, which leads to cross-sectional studies. Economists who study cigarettes are fortunate because there has been substantial variation in the price of cigarettes in both dimensions. In fact, many studies use a hybrid approach, called a panel study (also known as a longitudinal study), in which many different consuming units are followed over time. Figure 1.2.6 classifies the different types of observational studies.

Because observational studies dominate empirical economic research, we consider an example involving cigarettes in some detail. We have chosen a cross-sectional study using data collected by each state on total cigarette sales. Residents of different states pay different prices for cigarettes largely owing to differing state taxes on cigarettes. We can think of each state as if it were a separate treatment group in our study.

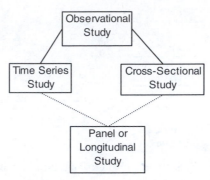

Figure 1.2.6. Different types of observational studies.

This type of study is called an aggregate-level cross-sectional study. It is conducted at the aggregate level because, rather than looking at individuals, we are examining the behavior of aggregates, or groups of individuals. The study is cross-sectional because the data are a slice of information gathered at one point in time across many different units of observation.

Our cross section focuses on the year 1960. (We will tell you later why we chose such old data.) We have data on the quantity and price of cigarettes in each state and the District of Columbia in fiscal year 1960. The quantity variable, Q per capita, is the number of cigarettes sold per capita in packs per fiscal year in each state. Price, P, is the average retail price per pack in January 1960 in each state (and the District of Columbia, which we will treat as a state).[7] The price is a weighted average price per pack in current cents, using national weights for the type of cigarette purchase (carton, single pack, and machine). The price variable includes all federal, state, and municipal excise and sales taxes imposed on cigarettes. We used per capita figures to adjust for the great dependency of total sales figures for a given state on its population. Figure 1.2.7 shows the data.

Notice that data on quantity are missing for four states: Colorado, North Carolina, Oregon, and Virginia. Because these states did not collect a tobacco tax back in 1960, there was no need for them to gather data on cigarette sales. A common problem in observational studies is missing data. Figure 1.2.8, which is a scatter plot of the data, gives an immediate visual summary.

Each point in the scatter plot represents a single state. Each point can be regarded as if it were the outcome of a different experimental treatment – namely, the quantity consumed on average by a group facing a particular price for cigarettes. We have provided summary statistics for the data and emphasized the meaning of the diagram by highlighting two rather different states. Utah had $P = 26.3$ cents per pack in 1960, which was just a shade over the average P in the data set, and yet it had sales of only 69 packs per person

---

[7] The fiscal year 1960 began July 1, 1959, and ended June 30, 1960. The January 1960 price fell right in the middle of this period.

State	P	Q p.c.	State	P	Q p.c.	State	P	Q p.c.
AL	28.4	87.2	KY	23.9	113. 6	ND	26.6	97. 6
AK	27.9	118.8	LA	30.2	108. 3	OH	25.9	127. 1
AZ	23.7	127.7	ME	25.9	141. 8	OK	26.1	112. 9
AR	27.2	89.2	MD	25	125. 6	OR	20.7	N/A
CA	25.4	142	MA	27.7	131. 1	PA	26.8	119. 2
CO	21.5	N/A	MI	26.5	125. 6	RI	26	143. 3
CT	24.3	153.7	MN	26.7	106. 6	SC	26.4	86. 7
DE	24.5	159.9	MS	27.3	8 4	SD	27.2	101
DC	22.2	186.7	MO	23.3	134	TN	26.1	98. 7
FL	25.8	138.9	MT	30.7	115. 7	T X	28.7	105. 3
GA	27.2	101.2	NE	25.3	111. 9	UT	26. 3	6 9
HI	27.9	71.3	NV	25.5	199. 3	V T	27.5	122. 8
ID	26.3	100.2	NH	23.9	190. 2	V A	2 1	N/A
IL	26.4	134.6	NJ	26.2	141. 1	W A	28.6	103. 4
IN	24	128.8	NM	26.4	105	WV	26.8	106
IA	26	107.6	NY	25.6	145	WI	25.9	112. 8
KS	24.6	106.7	NC	20.9	N/A	WY	25.6	129. 5

Figure 1.2.7. State-level average prices and per capita quantities sold of cigarettes, 1960.
Source: [Cig.xls]1960Analysis.

per year, which is very far below average. At the opposite extreme, Nevadans (and people visiting Nevada) paid on average 25.5 cents per pack but bought 199.3 packs per person in 1960.

We would like to interpret the data as if they were a series of points on a single demand curve, or, more generally, a series of points on parallel demand curves. Economic theory tells us that observed prices and quantities

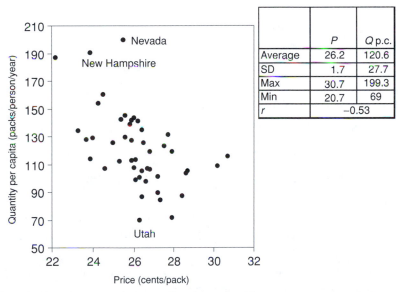

		P	Q p.c.
Average		26.2	120.6
SD		1.7	27.7
Max		30.7	199.3
Min		20.7	69
r		−0.53	

Figure 1.2.8. Scatter plot of per capita cigarette sales versus average price per pack in 47 States, 1960.
Source: [Cig.xls]1960Analysis.

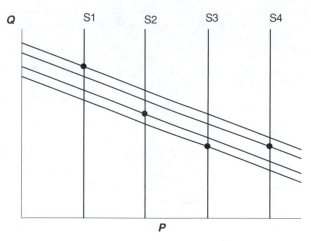

Figure 1.2.9. Assumptions about supply and demand that justify our interpretation of the state-level data on cigarette prices and quantities.

are equilibrium values resulting from the intersection of supply and demand curves. To justify our interpretation, we make two assumptions. First, we assume that the supply curves for different states are all perfectly elastic. In other words, we assume that each state's residents could buy as much as they wished at the observed price. Supply curves shift across states because of differences in shipping costs and state tax rates. Second, we assume that chance factors other than price cause the demand curve to shift from one state to another but that the shifted demand curves all share the same slope with respect to price. Figure 1.2.9 illustrates these two assumptions about supply and demand.

As you look at Figure 1.2.9, note that, because the axes have been reversed, perfectly elastic supply curves show up as vertical lines. Furthermore, you should convince yourself that if the demand curves did not shift, that is, if there were only one demand curve, then all the observed price–quantity combinations would lie on the single demand curve. It is clear from the figure that the observed price–quantity combinations conform more or less to a common demand curve.

Both of the assumptions we have just adopted may be misleading simplifications. Econometricians have made considerable progress in working with more general models that do not require such restrictive assumptions. For example, Chapter 24 describes techniques that allow us to dispense with the first assumption by taking into account the simultaneous determination of price and quantity.

The general shape of the scatter diagram and the negative correlation coefficient suggest a negative relationship between price and quantity – people in states with higher prices buy fewer cigarettes. But the correlation coefficient

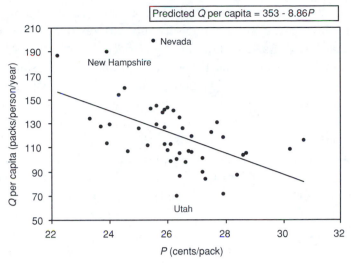

Figure 1.2.10. Regression of per capita sales on average price, 1960.
Source: [Cig.xls]1960Analysis.

does not tell us how much difference higher prices make. A regression line is one approach to answering this question. The regression line delineates the average value of the dependent variable associated with a given value of the independent variable. In Figure 1.2.10, we add a regression line to the graph.

The regression summarizes the data into a single, simple equation. All the points do not lie on the line, but the line clearly captures the general trend. The equation for the regression line is

$$\text{Predicted } Q \text{ per capita} = 353 - 8.86 \cdot P.$$

This regression is called a *bivariate* regression because it is an equation summarizing the relationship between two variables, Price and Quantity.

Quantity per capita is just the total quantity divided by the number of people in the population. Thus, to obtain the demand curve for the United States as a whole, simply multiply per capita demand by the population. There were about 179 million people in the United States in 1960. Thus,

$$
\begin{aligned}
\text{Predicted } Q \text{ for United States} &= 179 \, \text{million} \times (\text{Predicted } Q \text{ per capita}) \\
&= 179 \, \text{million} \times (353 - 8.86 \cdot P) \\
&= 63.2 \, \text{billion} - 1.59 \, \text{billion} \cdot P.
\end{aligned}
$$

Our regression analysis says that, across states in 1960, a one-cent-per-pack increase in the price of cigarettes was associated with an 8.86- pack-per-year decrease in per capita cigarette sales, which translates into a 1.59-billion-pack-per-year decrease in national cigarette sales.

Regression analysis can be employed either for description or inference. As description, the regression line concisely summarizes the observed relationship between per capita sales and average price across states. As inference, under appropriate assumptions, the regression line estimates a market-level per capita demand curve in which changes in price cause changes in quantity demanded. For this interpretation to be valid, we must regard the observed prices and quantities for each state as if they were the outcomes of individual trials of a controlled experiment. The failure of the points to fall exactly on the regression line would then reflect the influence of chance factors.

If it is possible to interpret our data as if they came from a carefully controlled experiment, then we have tentative answers to at least some of the questions one can ask about how taxes would affect cigarette smoking. For example, we can say that a rise in the cigarette tax that had the effect of increasing prices by one cent per pack (in 1960 prices) would reduce consumption by 8.86 packs per capita per year.

Is the estimated effect of price on quantity demanded large or small? According to the equation, a 5-cent increase in 1960 dollars (about a one-fifth increase in price) would reduce cigarette consumption by 44 packs per person per year, which is a very large effect because average consumption is about 121 packs per person per year. Another way to think about the responsiveness of quantity demanded to price is to work out the price elasticity of demand, which in this case can be estimated as about −1.9. Roughly speaking, this says that a 1-percent increase in price will lead to a −1.9-percent decrease in quantity demanded.[8]

We repeat that inference depends on claiming that the data are like the results from a controlled experiment. Perhaps we are not justified in making this leap. Observational studies suffer from two important difficulties that impair the analogy to controlled experiments. First, the relationship we observe may be a confounded version of the relationship we would like to study. Perhaps the differences in per capita cigarette sales between states are not due to differences in prices but rather to differences in other factors. Those other differences may be confounding the comparison we would like to make. Second, the variables used may not be the ones we would really like to measure. We examine each of these issues in turn.

Income is an important confounding variable in our analysis of cigarette consumption. It turns out that, in 1960, cigarettes were apparently a normal good, and thus people in higher per capita income states purchased more than people in lower per capita income states. It was also the case that prices in higher income states tended to be lower. In our regression we attributed the

---

[8] We are computing the point elasticity at the mean values of price and quantity demanded. The computation is in Cig.xls.

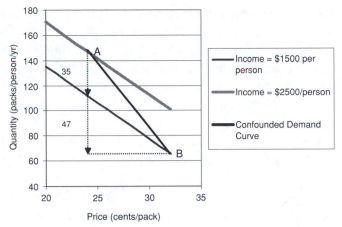

Figure 1.2.11. How changes in income confound the effect of price on quantity demanded.
Source: [Cig.xls]1960Analysis.

entire decrease in cigarette consumption as we moved from states with high income and low prices to states with low income and high prices to the change in prices. Part of the drop in cigarette consumption, however, was due to the fall in income, not the rise in prices. (We focused on 1960 because the confounding was most obvious then; cigarettes may well no longer be a normal good.)

Another look at the demand curves we drew in Figure 1.2.4 may clarify matters. In Figure 1.2.11, three different curves have been drawn. The two parallel curves are very similar to the curves drawn in Figure 1.2.4. They are demand curves corresponding to two different levels of per capita income. The third line shows how the bivariate analysis exemplified by the regression of quantity per capita on price is subject to confounding. Suppose that we observed only two states. One of them, State A, has a high per capita income (that is why it is on the upper demand curve) and a low price (24 cents per pack). The second state, State B, has a low per capita income – hence, it is located on the lower demand curve – and a high price for cigarettes (32 cents a pack).

A bivariate analysis focusing on the relationship between price and quantity alone would attribute the entire difference in quantity demanded between States A and B to the difference in price alone. In our example, a price increase of 8 cents is associated with a drop in quantity demanded of 82 packs per person per year. The slope of the line connecting points A and B is therefore about –10.2. In this example, however, the 82-pack-per-person difference in quantity demanded is actually the sum of two separate effects. If price is held constant, the $1,000 difference in per capita income reduces quantity demanded by about 35 packs per person per year. If income is held constant, the 8-cents-per-pack difference in cigarette prices reduces quantity demanded by about 47 packs per person per year.

A bivariate regression analysis alone cannot disentangle the separate effects of price and income on quantity demanded. The key weapon in the arsenal of econometricians is *multiple regression* analysis. By including a third variable into the regression model – namely per capita personal income – economists hope to remove confounding.

A multiple regression equation that attempts to control for the confounding created by income gives this result:

$$\text{Predicted } Q \text{ per capita} = 198 - 5.81P + 0.035 \text{ Income per capita.}$$

This equation can be interpreted as follows. With income per capita held constant, a one-cent per pack increase in price was associated with a 5.81-pack-per-person-per-year decrease in cigarette sales. With price held constant, a $100 increase in income per capita was associated with a 3.5-pack-per-person-per-year increase in cigarette sales. (Average per capita income was about $2100 in 1960.) Figure 1.2.11 and the numbers in our example of States A and B are based on the estimates from the regression of quantity per capita on price and income per capita. These results seem to show that a naive model in which price is regarded as the sole determinant of the quantity demanded of cigarettes substantially overestimates the reaction of consumers to changes in cigarette prices. The bivariate analysis estimates the price elasticity of demand as −1.9, whereas the multivariate analysis estimates price elasticity of demand as −1.3.

We cannot, however, be certain that including income in a regression equation will eliminate all sources of confounding. It is entirely possible that other variables are causing systematically incorrect estimates of the impact of price and income on the demand for cigarettes. (That of course is the reason why controlled experiments with random assignment are generally preferred to observational studies; the random assignment controls for confounding.) Furthermore, we have implicitly assumed that differences in supply have nothing to do with changes in demand. It is entirely possible, however, that states in which cigarette demand is lower are also ones that choose to impose higher taxes on cigarettes. Let us leave aside all these concerns for now. Is anything else potentially wrong with our analysis? Unfortunately, the answer is yes.[9]

Thus far, we have overlooked that the dependent variable employed sales per capita, is not exactly the one we want. In fact, we would like to use consumption per capita. The difference is important because there are large incentives for smuggling. Evidence of smuggling is apparent in the data for

[9] Although we highlight only two problems with the analysis, there are other difficulties. Most important, perhaps, is our using aggregate-level data to look at individuals' behavior.

New Hampshire. A quick look at Figure 1.2.10 shows that New Hampshire is well above the regression line. People in the Granite State seem to buy many more cigarettes than would be predicted from the regression line. Figure 1.2.7 throws more light on the issue. The price of cigarettes in New Hampshire was 14 percent lower than that in Massachusetts, giving smugglers ample opportunity to make profits by buying in bulk in New Hampshire and transporting the cigarettes to sell from the back of trucks in Massachusetts. The upshot is that consumption per capita in New Hampshire was probably considerably below the 190.2 packs per year recorded for sales, whereas consumption in Massachusetts was higher than 131.1 packs.

These discrepancies highlight the problem posed by proxy variables (i.e., variables that are stand-ins for the actually desired variable). Because of smuggling, there is almost certainly a definite pattern to the discrepancies – that is, consumption is underreported in high-price states and overreported in low-price states. Consequently, consumption appears to fall more with an increase in price than it actually does, and thus our estimate of the slope of the demand curve is probably overstated. Several studies of cigarette demand have attempted to adjust for smuggling.[10]

This concludes our introductory discussion of the estimation of the demand for cigarettes. If we have obtained a satisfactory estimate of the effect of price on quantity demanded, what do we do with it? Our result – that quantity demanded of cigarettes falls as price rises – has two principal uses. First, it supports economists' emphasis on price as a determinant of human behavior. Many people claim that, because of the addictive properties of nicotine, smokers do not respond to changes in price. This is not the case. Second, our estimate can be used to forecast future consumption of cigarettes under alternative scenarios about the level of taxes and other government policies.

Here is a quick tour of how forecasting works. We will confine ourselves to a very simple forecast based on the bivariate regression. Forecasting is essentially extrapolating. Recall that the bivariate regression results were as follows:

$$\text{Predicted } Q \text{ per capita} = 353 - 8.86 \cdot P.$$

At the 1960 average price of 26.2 cents per pack, predicted Q per capita is 120.6 packs per person per year. Suppose Congress decided to enact a 5-cent-per-pack cigarette tax increase effective in 1961. How would consumption have been affected? Assume that the tax increase translated one-for-one into a price increase. (This is a controversial issue, for some economists claim that, because the cigarette industry is oligopolistic, price rises will exceed the tax increases.) Forecast per capita quantity demanded is then obtained

[10] See Chaloupka and Warner (2000) for references.

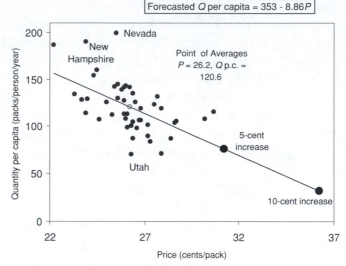

Figure 1.2.12. Forecasting 1961 quantity demanded using the bivariate regression equation.
Source: [Cig.xls]1960Analysis.

by simply substituting the new price of 31.2 cents per pack (i.e., 26.2 plus 5 cents) into Predicted Q per capita:

$$\text{Predicted } Q \text{ per capita} = 353 - 8.86 \cdot (31.2)$$
$$\text{Predicted } Q \text{ per capita} = 76.3.$$

Figure 1.2.12 illustrates forecasts for 5- and 10-cent increases in price.

Our forecasting procedure relies on the inferential assumption that the data for each individual state represent one trial of an experiment. The regression line summarizes all the different trials. Our best guess as to what would happen were we to conduct another experiment – for instance by setting the price at 31.2 cents – would be that quantity demanded would fall on the regression line at the point vertically above 31.2 cents on the *x*-axis (i.e., at the dot marked "5-cent increase"). Of course, it would be surprising if actual quantity demanded were exactly as predicted because chance factors will likely cause some deviation from the forecast just as none of the observations for the states in 1960 fell exactly on the regression line.

Figure 1.2.12 highlights an important problem with simple extrapolation: carried far enough, it produces absurd results. Extend the line to a price of 40 cents, and quantity demanded becomes negative, which is an impossible outcome. This in turn points to two flaws in our procedure. First, we have assumed that a straight line best describes the data. Second, we have no evidence on how consumers behave under extreme conditions. Common sense tells us that quantity demanded will fall considerably if cigarette prices are nearly doubled, but not to zero. We will return to these issues.

Summary

Much ground has been covered in this section, all of which will be considered more carefully later in this book. The main points include the following. Empirical researchers in economics must use economic theory to frame their research questions, and they must carefully consider the design of their studies. Although it is sometimes possible to conduct field or laboratory experiments, observational studies dominate econometric practice. The technique of regression is a key tool for dealing with observational studies for two reasons. First, it can be used to describe the impact of independent variables on dependent variables. Second, it can be used to address the problem of confounding. There are many possible designs for observational studies. We distinguished between cross-sectional and time-series studies and between studies based on aggregate-level data versus those based on individual-level data. We noted that economists must often use proxy variables, that is, variables that are not exactly the ones they want but that may be decent stand-ins for the desired variables. Finally, we gave a simple example of forecasting.

Thus far, we have slighted the role of chance in econometric analyses. Twice it has been noted that the observed data points do not all fall on the regression line. In other words the postulated demand curve does not completely determine the observed values of quantity demanded. The same phenomenon will recur in virtually all applications of regression analysis. Just as we drew on the established economic model of demand to come up with a regression equation, econometricians draw on a model of chance to complete the description of the process that generated the data. Much more is presented on this topic in Part 2.

The cigarette example made clear that estimating a demand curve is hard work. Simply fitting a line through a cloud of price and quantity points is a flawed procedure. We highlighted three reasons why this is poor practice. First, if both price and quantity are dependent variables, determined by the interaction of supply and demand, then the observed points do not lie on a single demand curve. We were forced to apply the restrictive assumptions of perfectly elastic supply curves and chance demand shocks in order to continue with our single equation analysis. Next, we explained the pervasive role of confounding in observational studies. If income is correlated with price and we leave income out of the regression, we end up with a biased estimate of the effect of price on quantity. Of course, including income does not protect us from the confounding effects of other omitted variables. The cigarette example also illustrated the issue of imperfect data. Since there is no data on actual consumption, we are forced to use sales data, even though we know that in some states, this is a problem.

Econometricians do the best they can under difficult conditions. You will learn, as you work through this book, that quantitative analysis can be frustrating and inconclusive. That does not mean, however, that we shouldn't bother. It means that we need to honestly, explicitly state the restrictive assumptions we are forced to make and properly weight these assumptions in evaluating the conclusions drawn from the data.

1.3. Conclusion

In Part 1 of this book you will learn exactly what regression is and how it can be used to describe and summarize data. Section 1.2 offers an example to explain why regression is so important: It is economists' main tool for analyzing data from observational studies. In Part 2, we will turn to inference. At that point, we will ask you to make an imaginative leap. We hope that you come to understand that regression estimates are random variables (i.e., numbers that bounce around).

Your intuition should tell you that there is only one regression line that best summarizes the data and that intuition is correct. But you should also see that, though we computed a slope of − 8.86 in the bivariate regression of quantity per capita on price, if we were to examine data from another year, a different slope would be obtained. This would happen even if cigarette demand had not changed at all and the prices in every state had not changed. Why? The cause is the inherent variability in human behavior. In some states, cigarettes might suddenly drop out of fashion among young adults; in others, rising unemployment and divorce might drive people to smoke and drink. An omniscient being might be able to pinpoint the exact reasons for the variation in the regression slope, but econometricians regard that variation as being due to chance.

We conclude this introduction by summarizing the main ideas students are expected to learn from this book. We realize that most students will not follow the path chosen by their professors to go on to make the study of economics or econometrics the focus of their career. The vast majority of readers of this book will never be required to deal with the most esoteric concepts presented in the following chapters. We believe nevertheless that an introduction to econometrics is a valuable learning experience. We hope that you will learn the following fundamental ideas in econometrics:

- There are many ways to summarize the same set of data. Tools like regression summarize data more compactly than tools like cross-tabs (known as PivotTables in Excel). Every summary is a compromise between giving all the details and giving a quick, compact description.

- How to interpret a regression. What the slope coefficients mean; what units are they measured in; how to change your interpretation if a nonlinear functional form is used in the regression equation; how to determine relevant elasticities; how multiple regression coefficients control for the presence of other variables besides the one of immediate interest; the meaning of confounding.

- That the data in your sample could have been different. If you take a second sample, you will get a different estimate of the average wage of the population or the support for a political candidate. This lesson has extremely wide applications.

- That without a convincing model of the data generation process, it is impossible to draw inferences about the population from your sample.

- The meaning of statistical inference: the concepts of population and sample, population parameter, and sample statistic. The ideas behind hypothesis tests and confidence intervals.

- The difference between statistical significance and practical importance.

- How Monte Carlo analysis sheds light on the concepts of the probability histogram and the standard error of an estimator.

- Important cases in which the standard model of the data generation process does not apply and what can be done in such situations to rescue statistical inference.

Some of these concepts are essential knowledge for anyone who deals with data in the social sciences. Thus, this book should play an important role in your economics curriculum in college. Some of these concepts will be applied repeatedly in your future careers. In other cases, you may not use the concept itself, but you will use related ideas; your having learned the concept will enable you to appreciate those ideas better. For example, you may never use Monte Carlo analysis again to think about a probability histogram. However, you may well use simulation in business or scientific applications.

1.4. Exercises

All of these exercises are based on material in Section 1.2.

1. Using the bivariate regression results forecast the impact of a 5-cent increase in price on quantity demanded. Assume prices start at 26 cents per pack and per capita income is $2,500 per person. To find out how much quantity demand changes owing to a price increase, do you need to know what price and per capita income you are starting from? Why or why not?

2. Assume that it is 1961 and Congress is for some bizarre reason considering a 50-cent cigarette tax. You are armed with the multiple regression analysis that includes price and income per capita as independent variables. Is it reasonable to use these results to forecast the response of smokers to such a tax increase? Why or why not?

3. Consider the research design of cross-sectional aggregate data based on state level sales and prices for 1960. Also assume (as the data appeared to show) that cigarettes are a normal good. Suppose, however, that states with higher per capita

income had higher prices rather than lower prices for cigarettes. How would that difference affect the bivariate regression of quantity sold per capita on average price? In your answer, draw a diagram similar to that of Figure 1.2.6.

4. There is a big difference between the Centers for Disease Control (CDC) figures for tobacco consumption, which underlie Figure 1.2.1, and the Tax Burden on Tobacco figures, which underpin Figure 1.2.7. For example the CDC figures show consumption of 208.6 packs per year in 1960, whereas the average value in Figure 1.2.7. for the year 1960 was 120.6 packs per year. What is going on? There are several reasons for the discrepancy. Name the one or two reasons that in your judgment are most important.

5. Suppose that supply curves are perfectly elastic and all demand curves are parallel but that states with lower demand for cigarettes are ones in which taxes are higher and therefore where supply is shifted to the right (with Price on the x-axis). Explain, using a supply and demand diagram, how this would cause the scatter of points and the regression line to give a misleading impression of the true shape of the demand curve.

References

Interesting biographical information on Ragnar Frisch can be found in

Bjerkholt, Olav (1995). "Ragnar Frisch, Editor of *Econometrica* 1933–1954," *Econometrica*, **63**(4): 755–766.

Data on state level cigarette consumption can be found in

The Tax Burden on Tobacco, 1999. Orzechowski & Walker, Arlington, VA.

Other references on cigarettes include

Bickel, W. K. and G. J. Madden (1999). "The Behavioral Economics of Smoking," in *The Economic Analysis of Substance Use and Abuse: An Integration of Econometric and Behavioral Economic Research*. F. J. Chaloupka, M. Grossman, W. J. Bickel, and H. Saffer, eds. The University of Chicago Press, pp. 31–61.

Chaloupka, F. J. and K. E. Warner (2000). "The Economics of Smoking," in *The Handbook of Health Economics*. J. Newhouse and A. Culyer, eds. North-Holland (Amsterdam) Volume 1B: 1539–1628.

Harris, J. (1998). "The Price of Cigarettes and the Profits of Cigarette Manufacturers with and without Federal Intervention, 1997–2006," A Report to the American Cancer Society, May 11, 1998.

The study of the determinants of the demand for cigarettes remains an important area of research. Significant papers in this literature include

Becker, G. S., M. Grossman, and K. Murphy (1994). "An Empirical Analysis of Cigarette Addiction." *American Economic Review* **84**(3): 396–418.

Sloan, Frank A., V. K. Smith, and D. H. Taylor. (2002). "Information, Addiction, and 'Bad Choices': Lessons from a Century of Cigarettes," *Economics Letters* **77**: 147–155.

Part 1

Description

2

Correlation

The invalid assumption that correlation implies cause is probably among the two or three most serious and common errors of human reasoning.

Stephen Jay Gould[1]

2.1. Introduction

This chapter begins the study of describing data that contain more than one variable. We will see how the correlation coefficient and scatter plot can be used to describe bivariate data.

Not only will you learn the meaning and usefulness of the correlation coefficient, but, just as important, we will stress that there are times when the correlation coefficient is a poor summary and should not be used. There is no such thing as a perfect summary measure of data.

In addition, we emphasize that correlation merely indicates the level of linear association between two variables and should never be used to infer causation. It is tempting to suppose that a high correlation implies some kind of causal connection, but this is wrong.

Although much of this material may be familiar to students of statistics, we conclude the chapter with a discussion of ecological correlation, which is often omitted from introductory statistics courses. We show that the correlation coefficient based on individual level data may be markedly different when computed with grouped data. In economics, this is called the aggregation problem, and it merits attention.

2.2. Correlation Basics

Workbook: Correlation.xls

The basic message of this section is that a good, standard method for describing the relationship between two variables is to present a bivariate scatter

---

[1] Gould (1996, p. 272).

diagram accompanied by summary statistics: the standard deviation (SD) and average of the two variables, the correlation coefficient, and the number of observations. To make this point, we first review the use of descriptive statistics in the univariate (single-variable) case and then develop analogies between the univariate and bivariate frameworks. The same example is used throughout the chapter to illustrate the use of the correlation coefficient and other summary statistics.

Many high school students in the United States take the Scholastic Aptitude Test, or SAT, as part of the college application process. For many years, the exam was composed of a series of multiple choice questions organized in two sections, Verbal and Math.[2] Scores ranged from 200 to 800 on each section.

One question that has been asked about the SAT is the degree of association between the Verbal and Math portions of the exam. In other words, do students who do well on the Math part also do well on the Verbal? You might think so, but perhaps people who are good at one thing, like English or reading, may not be so good at another, like mathematics.

Let us take a look at some SAT data to see how we can measure the degree of association between two variables. We will quickly review the univariate summary statistics and then focus on the correlation coefficient r as a measure of the linear association.

The Excel workbook Correlation.xls contains data on 527 applicants to Wabash College, a small liberal arts college in Indiana, from one year in the early 1990s. Open this workbook now and go to the *SATHist* sheet.

Univariate Analysis: Average, SD, and Histogram

When describing a list of numbers, the average and SD are usually the best descriptive statistics to present. The average provides information on the center of the list, and the SD communicates the spread in the numbers.

If the data are approximately normally distributed, one can use the average and SD to recreate a mind's eye histogram of the data. For example, suppose the data roughly follow the normal curve, the average is 18, and the SD is 2, as shown in Figure 2.2.1. Then roughly two-thirds of the numbers fall in the range from 16 to 20 (the average $-$ 1 SD to the average $+$ 1 SD), and about 95 percent of the numbers fall around 14 to 22 (average $\pm$ 2 SDs).

Notice that one does not need to provide the histogram. The average and SD can be used to recreate the histogram easily and to approximate the number of observations that fall in particular ranges.

---

[2] Beginning in 2005, the SAT included a written portion. For more, see <www.collegeboard.com/>.

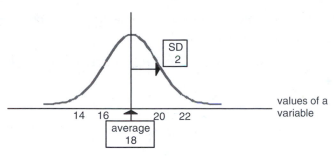

Figure 2.2.1. A mind's eye histogram.

The sheet *SATHist* reports that the average Verbal score of the 527 applicants was about 510 with an SD of roughly 90. Armed with that information, can you guess what the histogram of the list of 527 Verbal scores looks like? Draw a rough picture of the histogram. The same question can be asked for the Math scores, which had an average of around 595 and an SD of roughly 90. In the *SATHist* sheet, you can scroll down to row 37 to see the actual histograms. How did you do?

Although the average and SD are powerful descriptive statistics, they are inappropriate in some cases. Skewed distributions (with long left- or right-hand tails), truncated distributions, the presence of outliers, and other situations arise in which the average and SD alone can be quite misleading.

The usual strategy when the average and SD poorly represent the list of numbers is to provide additional descriptive statistics (such as the median and percentile information) along with the average and SD. If an accurate description is especially needed, a histogram of the values of the variable is an excellent solution. In fact, we recommend use of the histogram to describe univariate data whenever there is enough space.

Even though the average, SD, and a histogram are excellent summary measures, it should be obvious that these univariate tools are never going to indicate the degree of association between two variables because by their very nature, univariate descriptors are about a single variable. To measure association, we need bivariate tools.

Bivariate Analysis: The Scatter Diagram (or Plot) and Correlation Coefficient

The sheet *SATScatter* contains a scatter diagram or plot of the Verbal and Math data. It was created by making an *XYScatter* chart. The choice to place the Verbal variable on the *x*-axis and Math on the *y*-axis is arbitrary – we could just as well have reversed them. In addition to the averages and SDs, we report the correlation coefficient *r*. In this case, $r = 0.55$. This section will explain how this number is calculated and what it means.

The correlation coefficient is a summary statistic that measures the degree of clustering in the scatter diagram.

- The absolute value of the correlation coefficient tells us how tightly the data are clustered around the line.
- The sign of the correlation coefficient reveals whether there is a positive or negative linear association between the two variables
- The correlation coefficient always has a value between –1 and 1.

Take a quick look at the sheet *Extreme*. It contains three examples. The first is called perfect positive correlation ($r = +1$), the second is perfect negative correlation ($r = -1$), and the last is no correlation ($r = 0$).

Obviously, the Verbal and Math SAT data (in the sheet *SATScatter*) are not tightly clustered on a straight line. This fact is reflected by the correlation coefficient value of 0.55. But this raises a question: What is the line around which the correlation coefficient is measuring the degree of clustering? The answer is the *SD Line*.

The SD line passes through the *point of averages* and has a slope of

$$\frac{SD \text{ of } y}{SD \text{ of } x} \quad \text{if } r > 0 \text{ or } -\frac{SD \text{ of } y}{SD \text{ of } x} \quad \text{if } r < 0.$$

Note that the sign of r indicates whether the SD Line is positively ($r > 0$) or negatively ($r < 0$) sloped.

In the *SATScatter* sheet, click on the $\boxed{\text{SDLine}}$ button. This line is created by moving one SD Verbal to the right and one SD Math up from the point of averages. The point of averages can be seen by clicking on the $\boxed{\text{Average}}$ button. It is the very center of the cloud as measured by the average value of the x and y values. Click on the $\boxed{\text{Both}}$ button to combine the SD Line and the point of averages with the cloud of points. The SD Line orients the cloud, and r measures the degree of clustering around the SD Line. The tighter the clustering, the closer the absolute value of r is to 1.

The correlation coefficient says nothing about the numerical value of the slope of the SD line (around which the strength of clustering is being measured), nor does "tight" clustering occur until around 0.9 or more. Correlation coefficients of 0.5 or 0.6 reflect broad dispersion around the SD line. The Math and Verbal correlation coefficient is 0.55, and the data are clearly not tightly clustered.

You can see these attributes for yourself by going to the *Patterns* sheet. Change cell B3 to 0.95 and click the $\boxed{\text{Generate Y}}$ button to see how the data are much more tightly clustered. Experiment with other values (such as 0.99, -0.5, and -0.99) to see how the correlation coefficient and the graph are related.

Click on the sheet *Corr* to see how the correlation coefficient is actually calculated. The $\boxed{\text{Computing } r}$ button will take you to another sheet that shows you

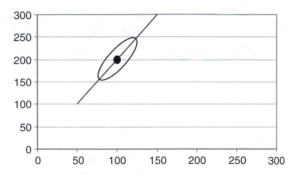

Figure 2.2.2. A mind's eye scatter diagram.

how r is numerically computed. Return to the *Corr* sheet and click on the Understanding Correlation button to walk through a demonstration of how each data point affects the correlation coefficient.

If the scatter plot is approximately football shaped, it is easy to recreate a scatter diagram for the variables. One needs the average and SD for both variables and the correlation coefficient between the two variables. For example, suppose you are given the following:

$$\text{Average } X = 100; \text{ SD of } X = 10$$
$$\text{Average } Y = 200; \text{ SD of } Y = 20$$
$$r = 0.8.$$

You use the averages to plot the point of averages ($x = 100$, $y = 200$) and the SDs to plot the SD line and therefore orient the cloud. In this case, the line has a slope of 2 because the SD of Y is twice the SD of X. Finally, r indicates the strength of clustering around the SD line and whether the line is positively or negatively sloped. Figure 2.2.2 shows a good mind's eye rough sketch of the scatter diagram given the summary statistics.

Notice that, just as in the univariate case, you do not need to provide the graph for a "well-behaved" relationship. The average and SD of each variable combined with the correlation coefficient can be used to recreate the scatter diagram easily and to approximate the number of observations that fall in particular ranges.

Let us look at a real-world example. We obtained the yearly data from the Penn World tables for the country of Costa Rica for the period 1950–1992.[3] The consumption share of gross domestic product (GDP), or C/GDP, averaged 68 percent with an SD of 4 percent. The investment share of GDP (I/GDP) averaged 16 percent with an SD of 3 percent. The correlation coefficient was −0.7. Create a mind's eye scatter diagram using this information.

---

[3] See Basic Tools\Internet Data\Penn World Tables for more on how to access this excellent data source.

The *CRExample* sheet contains the actual scatter plot and correlation coefficient. How did you do? Check your scatter diagram against the one in the Excel workbook to make sure that

- it is oriented correctly,
- the point of averages is correct, and
- the SD line is correct.

Be sure you understand that each point corresponds to a different year in the data set. That is, the label we give to each observation is a year (e.g., 1975).

Given our emphasis on the similarities between the histogram in the univariate case and the scatter diagram in the bivariate case, you might conclude that these are analogous graphs. In fact, they are not. They are not on the same level. Consider the four different panels in Figure 2.2.3. All four are created from the same underlying data in the *SATHist* sheet.

A scatter plot does not provide information on the number of observations at a particular coordinate. In the top right panel of Figure 2.2.3, there is no way to tell the difference between a point with a single observation and one with many repeated observations.

Unlike a histogram, a scatter diagram may be misleading if many values are repeated because it does not tell you how many dots are superimposed over each other. One way of getting around this problem is to put the number of repeated values next to each dot on the scatter diagram. Sometimes, however, as in the Verbal/Math SAT scatter, this is impractical.

Summary

In this section, we introduced the scatter diagram and correlation coefficient as two basic ways of describing the relationship between two variables.

We have emphasized that univariate data are summarized and described by the average, SD, and histogram. Bivariate data can be summarized by each variable's univariate summary statistics and by two methods that emphasize the relationship between the two variables: the scatter diagram and the correlation coefficient r.

The correlation coefficient is a standardized measure of clustering around a line; r ranges from -1 to $+1$. Here are some guidelines for interpreting the value of the correlation coefficient:

- r close to -1 means that the data cloud exhibits a tight cluster around the negatively sloped SD line;
- r is close to 0 when the data cloud is a formless blob;
- r close to $+1$ means the data cloud is an upward-sloping, cigar-shaped cloud;
- $|r|$ around 0.5 shows a definite pattern, albeit with substantial spread around the SD line (remember that $r = 0.55$ for the Math and Verbal SAT); and
- $|r|$ above 0.9 is a rather tight cloud.

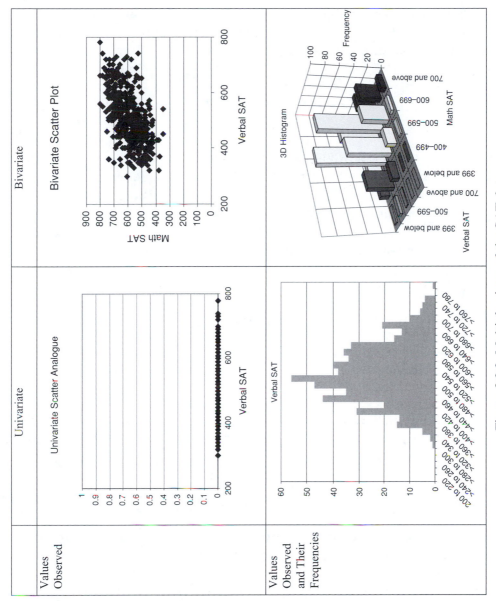

Figure 2.2.3. Multiple views of the SAT data.
Source: [Correlation.xls]SATHist.

Finally, the SD line is the line around which the points cluster (where the degree of clustering is measured by the correlation coefficient). The SD line goes through all of the points that are an equal number of SDs away from the average for both variables. The absolute value of the slope of the SD line is (SD of y)/(SD of x).

Although it is a powerful descriptor, r is not without its limitations. The next section is devoted to exploring the weaknesses of the correlation coefficient as a summary measure of bivariate data.

2.3. Correlation Dangers

Workbook: Correlation.xls

The previous section showed how the correlation coefficient r can be used to summarize a bivariate relationship. This section turns the tables and focuses on the limitations of the correlation coefficient. Unfortunately, as a general rule, there is no such thing as a perfect descriptive statistic, and r is no exception.

We begin by noting that one problem with the correlation coefficient is that it is not as intuitively understood as the average. Three things to keep in mind about the correlation coefficient are

(1) Twice the r *does not* mean twice as much clustering.
(2) $r = 0.60$ *does not* mean that 60 percent of the points are tightly clustered.
(3) r says *absolutely nothing* about the value of the slope of the relationship; r is a measure of the tightness of clustering around a line that may have any slope.

Misunderstanding aside, two principal dangers are associated with the correlation coefficient. Because it is a measure of linear association only, it will poorly describe nonlinear relationships. In addition, it is often misinterpreted as indicating causation.

The Correlation Coefficient as a Poor Descriptor of the Data

We will make the shortcomings of the correlation coefficient clear by working with the *Patterns* sheet in Correlation.xls. When you open the *Patterns* sheet, it should look like Figure 2.3.1.

The Parameters box allows you to set the average and SD of the y variable and the degree of correlation between the x and y variables. For now, make sure that r is 0, the Average of y is 20 and its SD is 20, and that the three buttons appear as in Figure 2.3.1. If not, hit the Reset button. Next, click on the Generate Y button several times to see patterns consistent with no

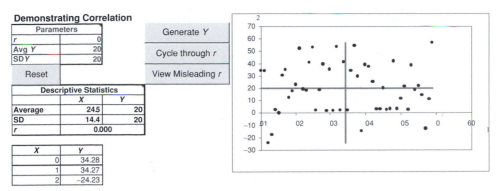

Figure 2.3.1. Understanding how *r* can be misleading.
Source: [Correlation.xls]Patterns

correlation. The *x* values stay fixed, and so the average *x* value remains constant at 24.5. The vertical pink line records this average. Meanwhile, the *y* values bounce around, but the average *y* line does not change and the spread of the *y*'s remains the same.

Click on the Cycle through *r* button and watch how the scatter plot changes. The average and SD for both *x* and *y* stay constant, but the shape of the cloud changes. The Descriptive Statistics box records the average and SD of the data. If you manually change one or more of the parameters in the Parameters box but do not hit the Generate *Y* button, then the Descriptive Statistics will be different from the parameter values. Once you hit the Generate *Y* button, a new data set will be drawn that conforms to the parameter values in cells B3 to B5.

Next, click on the View Misleading *r* button. Several new options will appear. We will explore each one in turn.

Click the Cycle through *r* button until the correlation coefficient equals 0.8. Select the Linear, Homoskedastic radio button if it is not already selected. Click on the Generate *Y* button a couple of times again to see a typical "well-behaved," pattern. The term *Homoskedastic* means that the spread of the *y* variable remains constant as the *x* values change.

Now, select the Linear, Heteroskedastic radio button. *Heteroskedasticity* means that the spread of *y* varies as *x* changes. Click on the Generate *Y* button several times. You will observe the first problem with the correlation coefficient as a descriptive statistic: The correlation coefficient does not warn you about changes in the vertical spread of the data.

We have rigged the linear heteroskedasticity option so that the vertical spread of the points in the scatter plot is much greater for large values of *x* than it is for small *x*. Yet, the average of the *y* values and the correlation coefficient is exactly what it was before, 20 and 0.8, respectively.

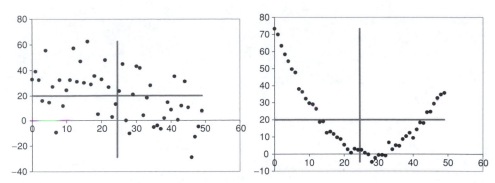

Figure 2.3.2. Two data sets with the same summary statistics.
Source: [Correlation.xls]Patterns.

Next, choose the Nonlinear Deterministic radio button. Click $\boxed{\text{Generate Y}}$. A pretty curve results. You clearly see a second shortcoming of *r*: the correlation coefficient does not warn you of deterministic patterns in the data.

Now, steadily change the value of *r*, using the $\boxed{\text{Cycle through } r}$ button. Next, change the value of the (somewhat mysterious) Free parameter (in cell E16) from 0.5 to 50 and watch for a different set of pretty curves as you repeatedly click the $\boxed{\text{Cycle through } r}$ button. This should prove the point that, corresponding to every possible value of *r* (except –1 and 1), there is an infinite number of different deterministic patterns that the data might take for the same given average values of *x* and *y*. (You should think about why $r = 1$ and $r = -1$ are exceptions to this rule.)

Finally, choose the Nonlinear radio button and set the Free and Nonlinear parameters both to 2. Click on the $\boxed{\text{Generate Y}}$ button and then cycle through the *r*'s. You will see deterministic patterns with a small amount of noise. There are many real data sets that look more or less like these pictures.

In Figure 2.3.2, we display two data sets, both of which share exactly the same summary statistics in terms of averages of *x* (24.5) and *y* (20), SDs for *x* (14.4) and *y* (20), and correlation coefficients (−0.5); yet there is a very big difference between the two.

Our mind's eye reconstruction, given the summary statistics, would probably give us a picture like the scatter plot on the left in Figure 2.3.2. Providing only the summary statistics (without the scatter diagram) for data represented by the right-hand graph would be misleading. The reader would be left with an incorrect impression about the data without the scatter diagram.

Do not rely on the average or the correlation coefficient (or any other descriptive statistic) as a foolproof means of communicating information. Judgment is needed when the data are not represented accurately by a single statistic. In such cases, a graphical display may well be required.

If the data are truly continuous, measured precisely, and far enough apart from each other, plotting values in a scatter diagram is an excellent way to display the relationship between two variables visually. Annotate the graphic display with carefully labeled axes, source information, and descriptive statistics (the average and SD of each variable along with the correlation coefficient) and you will have an outstanding display of the information.

Association Is Not Causation

A second problem with the correlation coefficient involves its interpretation. A high correlation coefficient means that two variables are highly associated, but association is *not* the same as causation.

This issue is a persistent problem in empirical analysis in the social sciences. Often the investigator will plot two variables and use the tight relationship obtained to draw absolutely ridiculous or completely erroneous conclusions. Because we so often confuse association and causation, it is extremely easy to be convinced that a tight relationship between two variables means that one is causing the other. This is simply not true.

The fundamental reason that association is mistaken for causation lies in the notion of confounding. A prototypical example of confounding involves three variables: x, y, and z. Typically, z is a third confounding variable that is causing or driving both x and y, and thus a simple plot or correlation of x and y will make it seem like x causes y when, in fact, x and y are caused by the underlying missing z. The problem with observational studies is that the confounding z variable is often deeply hidden in such subtle ways that the investigator is unaware confounding is present.

Examples of misinterpreting correlation as causation abound. Do private schools cause better students? A quick look at the data shows that students from private schools do better on SATs and in college than those from public schools – there is a correlation between type of school (the x variable) and educational success (the y variable). Private schools would have you believe that they are responsible for this. Some reflection on the matter should convince you that there are other differences that may be responsible for the observed correlation. Candidates for the z or confounding variable include parental support, family income, nutrition, and student motivation. This is not to say that private schools do not matter – they may, in fact, have a positive effect on their students' education. The point is that a correlation of type of schooling and educational success should not lead one to conclude that type of schooling causes educational success. It does not matter how tight the relationship is; even if $r = 0.99$, such a conclusion would be unwarranted. To determine if private schools really do cause better student performance would take much more work than a high correlation coefficient.

No matter how tight the relationship between two variables, the correlation coefficient alone can never prove causation. The correlation coefficient can only tell you about linear association. Association, however, is not causation.

Summary

The correlation coefficient can fail as a summary of a bivariate relationship if the data exhibit nonlinearity, heteroskedasticity, or other patterns in which the cloud is not nicely distributed around the SD line. A second potential problem with the correlation coefficient lies in its interpretation. It is easy to confuse a degree of linear association with causation. This is a mistake.

The next section shows a more subtle way in which the correlation coefficient can be misleading.

2.4. Ecological Correlation

Workbooks: EcolCorr.xls; EcolCorrCPS.xls

The previous section warned that the correlation coefficient is not a perfect statistic. Including a scatter diagram along with r and the basic summary statistics (average and SD of x and y) is good practice. The scatter diagram is a must if r alone will mislead the reader.

This section extends the idea that r may be misleading by exploring an important issue in using correlation to describe empirical data. *Ecological correlation* is the practice of using a correlation coefficient based on grouped or aggregated data. The difficulty with ecological correlation is that researchers often are interested in correlation at the individual level but must instead content themselves with exploring correlation at the group level. Ecological correlations are typically, though not always, bigger in absolute value than individual-level correlations. Researchers can thus be fooled into thinking they have found something important when the correlation they are really interested in is much smaller. Sometimes the problem is even worse: The ecological correlation is of opposite sign to the individual-level correlation.

Statisticians refer to any incorrect inference about individual behavior from grouped data as the *ecological fallacy*. Economists call this same phenomenon the *aggregation problem*. Although this section will focus on the effects of grouping on the correlation coefficient, aggregating data can cause problems for other descriptive statistics and strategies for summarizing data.[4] Because much social science data comes in grouped form, the aggregation problem

---

[4] For example, Simpson's paradox occurs when the averages of subgroups show a different result than average of the entire group. The *Example* sheet of EcolCorr.xls has more on Simpson's paradox.

is extremely common. It is hard to spot, however, and even more difficult to correct or work around.

A good example of the motivations that lead economists to use grouped data is the analysis of cigarette demand discussed in the previous chapter. Because states tax cigarette sales, state-level data on cigarette purchases are readily available. Average prices are easy to obtain for the same reason. Good individual-level data is much harder to find. It is much more expensive to gather data on individual consumption of cigarettes. Surveys require trained workers and a good deal of planning for usable data to be obtained. For surveys in general, individuals do not necessarily tell the truth, nor do they always remember exactly what they did. In the case of cigarettes, people may not wish to reveal their vices, though they probably have a good idea of how many cigarettes they consume because consumption is a habitual action. Thus, given that it is much more difficult to obtain individual data, which can be less reliable, until recently almost all papers on the demand for cigarettes in the economics literature have used state or national data on cigarette purchases.[5] The problem is that these researchers are really interested in the behavior of individuals, not groups.

Why should we worry? For example, suppose that the demand for cigarettes does depend on price. If the price of cigarettes is higher on average in California than it is in North Carolina, will that not mean that people in California smoke less on average than individuals in North Carolina? Would we not be able to see the results of individual behavior in the aggregate data? The answer is in general yes, but the strength of the association between price and quantity will usually be overstated at the aggregate level; sometimes the aggregate results will give a completely misleading picture of the story at the individual level. Applying a group-level correlation coefficient to draw conclusions about individual-level data exposes researchers to the ecological fallacy. We will demonstrate the ecological fallacy by first looking at a hypothetical example and then examining real data.

A Hypothetical Example

Grouping removes individual variation because a single number, usually the average, is used to represent the entire group. This typically results in a group-level r that is greater than the individual-level r. The problem arises when we make a judgment about individual-level correlation based on group-level data. Usually, the correlation at the individual level seems to be much stronger than it actually is when the group-level correlation is used as an estimate of

---

[5] See the references at the end of the first chapter for important articles on the demand for cigarettes.

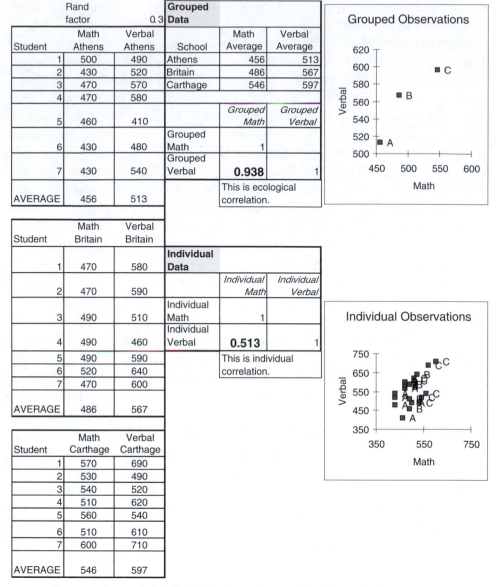

Figure 2.4.1. Individual- and group-level correlation.
Source: [EcolCorr.xls]Example.

the individual-level correlation. Although this is difficult to understand in the abstract, it is rather easy to see with a simple numerical demonstration.

Open the Excel workbook called EcolCorr.xls. The *Example* sheet contains the data used to generate Figure 2.4.1. There are seven students, each at three different high schools (Athens, Britain, and Carthage). They have just taken the SAT. We want to know the correlation between the Math and Verbal SAT scores. We can look at the data at two levels: individual and high school.

At the group level, the correlation coefficient is 0.938. There appears to be a strong association between Math and Verbal SAT scores. But, in fact, the association between Math and Verbal SAT using the individual-level data is only 0.513.

Why is the group-level *r* so much greater? The scatter diagrams reveal the answer. The individual variation in the bottom scatter diagram weakens the association between Math and Verbal SAT. When the data are viewed at the high-school level, we group the seven students in each high school into a single number, the average. The three group-level observations exhibit a much higher correlation.

Of course, this could be an artifact of the particular 21 pairs of Math and Verbal SAT scores in this example. The *Live* sheet in the EcolCorr.xls workbook allows you to generate your own set of observations. Hit F9 to have the 21 students take the SAT again. Every time you hit F9, the SAT is retaken and the average score for each high school is recalculated. You can then compare the group- and individual-level correlation coefficients. If both graphs do not fit on your screen, use Excel's Zoom tool to shrink the display. The parameter in cell B1, Rand_factor, is not an important parameter. It just ensures that the SAT scores stay between 200 and 800.

As you hit F9 and examine the results, you should notice that the group-level *r* is almost always higher than its corresponding individual-level correlation coefficient. Keep your eye on the graphs as well. Do you see how the grouped scatter plot removes the individual variation? That is why the correlation coefficient at the group level is so much higher. If you look closely at the formulas generating the data in the *Live* sheet, you will discover how we ensure that the Carthage High School students will score on average higher than the Britain and Athens students and how we build in a correlation between the Verbal and Math scores. Because the data are generated using random numbers, the extent to which the group-level *r* diverges from the individual-level *r* will vary in every case.

Here is the lesson: Beware of correlation coefficients based on grouped data! Unfortunately, caveats are hard to follow. You need considerable practice in the form of many different examples before you can spot the danger yourself. Try to remember that the use of averages (or any other constructed measure) might paint a very misleading picture of what is really going on at the disaggregated level.

There is one important exception: the investigator may really be interested in the group level. If so, the correlation coefficient based on grouped data is correct. Note once again that the danger lies in making statements or drawing inferences about individual behavior from grouped data. If you really want to make inferences about the behavior of aggregates, grouped data are appropriate.

Correlation Table			
	Educ	Age	Earnings
Educ	1		
Age	−0.17	1	
Earnings	0.63	−0.30	1

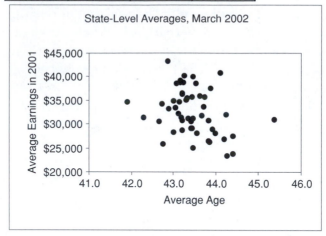

Figure 2.4.2. Group-level correlation analysis.
Source: [EcolCorrCPS.xls]State.

An Actual Example

Let us now consider an actual example of ecological correlation. The Current Population Survey collects data on a wide array of variables via a monthly survey. In March, the survey is augmented with a series of economic and financial questions. We obtained data from the March 2002 Current Population Survey on 23,187 people between the ages of 30 and 60.[6] Open the EcolCorrCPS.xls workbook to access the data (The file CPS.doc in the Basic Tools/InternetData folder explains how to access the CPS online, download data, and import it into Excel. We discuss CPS data in detail in Chapter 3.)

We have information on each person's age, education, and annual earnings for the year 2001. We are interested in the association between pairs of these variables. You might expect a strong association between earnings and education, but what about age and earnings or age and education?

At the group level, in this case the state level, the data show the expected strong positive correlation between education and earnings and a negative correlation between age and earnings. The results in Figure 2.4.2

[6] Actually, we obtained data on 92,400 people between the ages of 30 and 60 and then took an approximate 25 percent sample, resulting in the 23,187 observations in the data set. More details are in the *Intro* and *Codebook* sheets of the file, EcolCorrCPS.xls.

Correlation Table			
	Educ	Age	Earnings
Educ	1		
Age	0.003	1	
Earnings	0.336	0.040	1

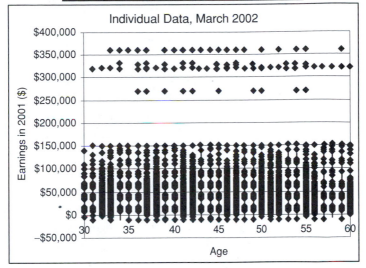

Figure 2.4.3. Individual-level correlation analysis.
Source: [EcolCorrCPS.xls]Individual.

present a correlation matrix and a scatter diagram of the age and earnings variables.

The results for the Age and Earnings variables are curious and thought provoking. The graph in Figure 2.4.2 and the fact that $r = -0.30$ point to a negative relationship between age and earnings. Is a powerful force at work here? It looks like older people earn less. Perhaps, but remember that the correlation coefficient is based on grouped data. The 51 observations represent the average age and average earnings in each state (and the District of Columbia). Grouping data by using the average, as we learned in the hypothetical example in the previous section, may mislead us. In this case, we have the underlying observations, and thus we can find the individual-level correlation coefficients.

When we calculate the individual-level correlation between personal earnings, age, and education, the results are markedly different. Figure 2.4.3 shows the same variables as Figure 2.4.2 except that we now use the individual-level data. The positive association between education and earnings is still present, but it is weaker. The negative association between age and earnings has completely disappeared.

Figure 2.4.3 is ugly and hard to read. Note that, although there are 23,187 people in the data set, 23,187 dots are not in the scatter plot. Many of the dots in the graph stand for numerous individual observations.[7] The correlation coefficient helps us to make sense of what is going on. For the people aged 30 to 60 that were sampled in the March 2002 survey, there is a definite positive association between earnings and education, but there is no strong association between age and earnings or age and education.

Summary

So which level of analysis is correct? It depends on the question you want to answer. Economists typically are interested in how personal characteristics (e.g., age and education) affect earnings. Thus, the individual level of data is the appropriate one to use. The danger posed by ecological correlation is that researchers will use the aggregate data to reach conclusions about questions at the individual level. In our example incorporating actual data, concluding that age and earnings were strongly negatively associated at the individual level based on a group-level r of -0.3 would be quite wrong.

Unfortunately, many times (as in the cigarette example we cited at the beginning of this section) group-level data are the only data available. The choice then is to proceed with caution or not to proceed at all. When the former path is taken, conclusions should be presented carefully and the reader should be told that the ecological fallacy or aggregation problem is a concern.

2.5. Conclusion

The correlation coefficient r is a commonly used measure of linear association between two variables. Often, reporting the averages and SDs of the two variables along with r is enough to enable the reader to create a rough, mind's eye representation of the scatter diagram.

In many cases, the bivariate data will exhibit a nonlinear association or heteroskedasticity, contain an unusual number of extreme values, or have a peculiar characteristic that cannot be captured by the averages, SDs, and correlation coefficient alone. Providing the scatter diagram is then recommended.

Good econometric practice also requires vigilance with respect to the process that generated the data. Ecological correlation, also known as the aggregation problem, is a common concern in the social sciences because we often do not have data at the individual level. Unfortunately, by aggregating

---

[7] Notice as well that the earnings variable is "top-coded." For confidentiality purposes, earnings above \$150,000 are replaced by values between \$270,000 and \$361,000, which represent the average values of earnings for those who earned more than \$150,000 in different demographic groups. (See <www.bls.census.gov/cps/ads/2002/sfiledif.htm.>) Earnings include income from self-employment, which sometimes can be a loss. Losses greater than \$9,999 were apparently "bottom coded."

individual units into groups, the loss of dispersion within the group tends to generate a stronger correlation at the group level compared with the individual level. The lesson to avoid the ecological fallacy is complicated by two factors. First, it may be difficult to see that the data are, in fact, grouped. In addition, grouping individual observations into categories is not always a bad idea.

The correlation coefficient can be a powerful statistic for summarizing bivariate data, but its limitations force us to use additional techniques. The next chapter explains how the data can be tabulated in a variety of ways and provides the foundation for regression analysis.

2.6. Exercises

Click the | Data for Exercises | button near cell J1 of the *SATHist* sheet in the Correlation.xls workbook.

1. Provide a conventional description of the data, including averages and SDs for the two variables, the correlation coefficient, and a scatter diagram.
2. Is the scatter diagram needed for effective description in this case? Why or why not?
3. Is the correlation coefficient an appropriate summary statistic in this case? Explain.
4. Compute r on a subset of the data for Verbal scores between 400 and 600, inclusive. Report your answer.
5. Compare the correlation coefficient of the 44-observation data set to the $r = 0.55$ value from the original 527-observation data set. Given that the former data were created from the latter, why are we not getting the same correlation coefficient?

References

Francis Galton invented the concept of correlation. Karl Pearson developed the conventional formula. Our presentation leans heavily on Freedman, D. R. Pisani, and R. Purves (1998). *Statistics*, 3d edition (New York: W. W. Norton), Chapters 8 and 9. Freedman et al. use the terms *point of averages* and *SD line*, and, unlike most introductory statistics books, they discuss ecological correlation. Our demonstration of how the same summary statistics can arise from very different data sets is inspired by Tufte, E. (1983). *The Visual Display of Quantitative Information* (Cheshire, CT: Graphics Press), pp. 14–15. Tufte's discussion in turn is based on Anscombe, F. J. (1973). "Graphs in Statistical Analysis," *American Statistician* **27**: 17–21.

A nice example of Simpson's paradox is given by Morrell, C. H. (1999). "Simpson's Paradox: An Example from a Longitudinal Study in South Africa," *Journal of Statistics Education* **7** (3). This is available on the Web at <www.amstat.org/publications/jse/secure/v7n3/datasets.morrell.cfm>.

A textbook discussion of another real-world example can be found in Freedman et al., pp. 17–20. A much more sophisticated discussion is Samuels, M. L. (1993). "Simpson's Paradox and Related Phenomena," *Journal of the American Statistical Association* **88** (421): 81–88. Simpson's original article is Simpson, E. H. (1951).

"The Interpretation of Interaction in Contingency Tables," *Journal of the Royal Statistical Society*, Ser. B, **13**: 238–241.

To learn more about the demand for cigarettes, see the papers listed in the references for Chapter 1. All those papers on the demand for cigarettes rely on aggregated data at either the state or national level.

The introductory quote by Stephan Jay Gould is from *The Mismeasure of Man*, revised and expanded edition (New York: W. W. Norton & Company, 1996, originally published 1986), p. 272. Gould was a paleontologist who wrote on a wide range of topics for the general public, focusing especially on evolution and the role of science in society. For more, see <www.stephenjaygould.org/>.

3

PivotTables

Not everything that can be counted counts; and not everything that counts can be counted.

Albert Einstein[1]

3.1. Introduction

This chapter focuses on summarizing and describing patterns in data via tables. Tables efficiently convey basic summary information such as counts and averages. Tables can also be a powerful device with which to explore complicated relationships in data. Thus, the work on tables in this chapter will enable you to understand the concepts of the conditional average and regression analysis better. Tables make clear that a particular value can be viewed as the result of a conjunction of conditions or categories. That is a crucial aspect of regression analysis.

A powerful way to tabulate data is Excel's PivotTable feature. A PivotTable enables the user to try a variety of different views of the data. PivotTables, combined with Excel's formatting and charting, facilitate effective and clear data description.

3.2. The Basic PivotTable

Workbooks: IndianaFTWorkers.xls; Histogram.xla(Excel add-in)

Open the Excel file called IndianaFTWorkers.xls (available in the folder Basic Tools\InternetData\CPS) to begin learning about PivotTables and tabulation. The file contains information on 598 people from the March 1999 Current Population Survey (CPS). The *Doc* sheet describes how the data were

---

[1] Einstein had this saying on a sign hanging in his office at Princeton. See "Some Quotable Quotes for Statistics" at <www.ewartshaw.co.uk/>.

Table 3.2.1. *Univariate Summary Statistics for Indiana March 1999 CPS*

Usual Hours Worked		Age		Total Personal Income	
Mean	42.5	Mean	41.0	Mean	$37,174
Median	40	Median	41	Median	$30,000
Mode	40	Mode	42	Mode	$15,000
SD	14.0	SD	10.9	SD	$33,560
Range	144.0	Range	67	Range	$324,731
Minimum	0	Minimum	18	Minimum	–
Maximum	144	Maximum	85	Maximum	$324,731
Sum	25398	Sum	24494	Sum	$22,229,813
Count	598	Count	598	Count	598

Education	Total	% of Total
No HS Gra	60	10.0
HS Grad	233	39.0
Some Coll	174	29.1
Coll Grad	131	21.9
Total	598	100.0

Race	Total	% of Total
AsianPI	1	0.2
Black	31	5.2
IndEsk	7	1.2
White	559	93.5
Total	598	100.0

Sex	Total	% of Total
Female	258	43.1
Male	340	56.9
Total	598	100.0

Source: [IndianaFTWorkers.xls]DescStat.

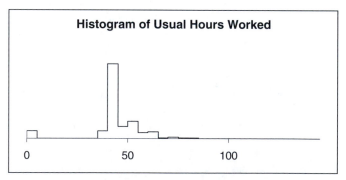

Figure 3.2.1. Usual hours worked histogram.
Source: [IndianaFTWorkers.xls]Histogram.

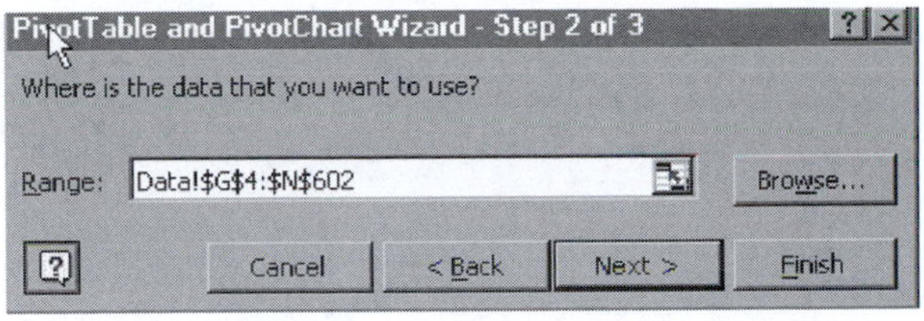

Figure 3.2.2. PivotTable Wizard Step 2.

obtained, and the file CPS.doc in the same folder contains detailed instructions on downloading data from the CPS.

We do not approach the data in a vacuum. Prior questions guide our exploration of the data. For example, we might want to find out if more education is associated with higher income and, if so, how much more. Additionally, we might want to look for evidence of income disparities between whites and blacks or men and women.

We begin our analysis of the data by reporting univariate summary statistics using the Data Analysis Excel add-in. The *DescStat* sheet in the IndianaFTWorkers.xls workbook explains how to use the Data Analysis tool to get univariate summary statistics like those in Table 3.2.1.

Another way to get univariate summary statistics is by using the Histogram add-in included in the BasicTools\ExcelAddins\Histogram folder.[2] In the case of Usual Hours Worked, a histogram greatly helps in summarizing the data. Usual Hours Worked looks to be a problem. The minimum is zero, even though these are full-time workers. The maximum is 144 hours, or 6 full days of nonstop work. Neither of these two extreme values makes much sense for the usual hours of a full-time worker. Puzzling values are a common part of analyzing real-world data. (Apparently, some people are on call all the time, which is their justification for saying they work 24 hours a day.)

Let us explore the Usual Hours Worked variable further with a one-dimensional PivotTable. Execute Data: PivotTable Report.[3] In the first step of the PivotTable and PivotChart Wizard, select the Microsoft Excel list or database option and then click Next. In step 2, you should see a screen like Figure 3.2.2.

By clicking on the icon, you can collapse the Wizard display to find the range you wish to select more easily. Select the data range Data: G4:O602 (or whatever range contains your data). Step 3 is the heart of the PivotTable feature. It is depicted in Figure 3.2.3. Choose New Worksheet as the place

---

[2] See Histogram.doc in Basic Tools\ExcelAddIns\Histogram for instructions on installing and loading the Histogram add-in.

[3] The PivotTable interface we describe is that for Excel 2000. It should be easy to figure out the appropriate moves in other versions (e.g., Excel 97 or more recent versions).

Figure 3.2.3. PivotTable Wizard Step 3.

you want to put the PivotTable. Then click on the Layout button. You will see something like Figure 3.2.4.

The basic idea is to drag the variable or field buttons to the row, column, or data areas. In the data area, you determine the operation you want done. Once the PivotTable is created, you return to this step each time you want to reorganize the data.

To continue, click on the Usual Hours Worked field button and drag it to the row area. Then click on the Usual Hours Worked field button again and drag it to the data area. Double click on the "Sum of Usual Hours Worked" tile that appears and change it so that it is summarized by the Count (instead of the Sum). The PivotTable settings should now look like Figure 3.2.5. Notice for future reference that there are two types of counts to choose from: Count and Count Nums. The former counts all observations; the latter counts just those observations with numerical values.

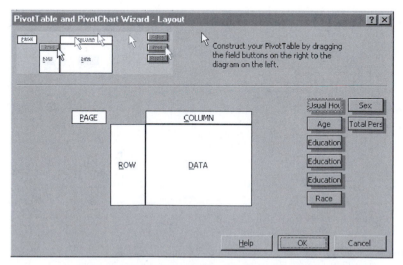

Figure 3.2.4. PivotTable Wizard – Layout.

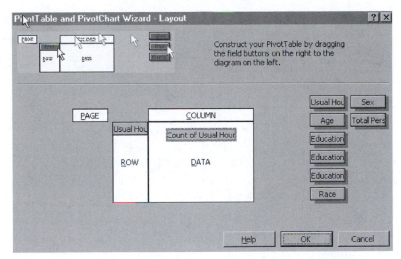

Figure 3.2.5. PivotTable Wizard – Final layout for Usual Hours Worked.

Click OK when you are ready, and then click Finish. The beginning of your PivotTable on the newly created worksheet should look like Figure 3.2.6.

You should rename the sheet created by the PivotTable to keep the workbook well organized and easy to understand. You may also see the PivotTable toolbar, which looks like Figure 3.2.7.

This toolbar can be dragged and parked with the other Excel menus at the top of the display. The toolbar changes appearance when you select any cell inside the PivotTable itself, as shown in Figure 3.2.8. In Excel 2003, a PivotTable Field List appears.

You can drag variables from the toolbar into the PivotTable row or column areas and thereby add more information to the table. One of the more important icons in the display is the exclamation point, !, which refreshes the PivotTable if you change the underlying data.

	A	B
1	Drop Page Fields Here	
2		
3	Count of Usual Hours Worked	
4	Usual Hours Worked	Total
5	0	33
6	35	18
7	36	8
8	37	2
9	38	5
10	39	1
11	40	314

Figure 3.2.6. Frequency Table of Usual Hours Worked.

Figure 3.2.7. PivotTable toolbar.

Excel's PivotTable can create a variety of different tables. We will concentrate on just two of the many different types of tables: (1) Frequency tables that show counts and (2) Crosstabs that contain conditional averages. Each type has a dimensional attribute. Figure 3.2.6 displays a one-dimensional frequency table analogous to a histogram.

The tabulation of the number of people for a given value of usual hours worked reveals that there are 33 people who answered yes when asked if they are full-time workers working 35 or more hours per week but are also reported as having a usual workload of 0 hours. In addition, there are three people who report that they usually work 102 hours or more per week.

A nice feature of the PivotTable is that values can be hidden while the data set continues to be explored. To illustrate this procedure, click on the down arrow in the right-hand edge of the Usual Hours Worked tile (in cell B4 in Figure 3.2.6). This brings you to a window in which you can determine via a check box which values of observations are to be included or removed from the table, as shown in Figure 3.2.9.

Click on the 0, 102, 120, and 144 values, thereby deselecting them. Click OK. The PivotTable is recreated without the corresponding observations. Note that there are now only 562 values. PivotTable computations are based on only the remaining observations.

Note also that the hidden observations have not been deleted but merely temporarily removed. Another analysis based on the same data set would contain all 598 observations. Whether these observations should be permanently removed from the underlying data set is a difficult question that depends on the objective of the analysis. The point here is that PivotTables allow you to view the data with and without observations selected according to their value for a variable of interest.

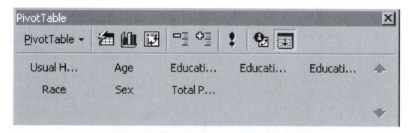

Figure 3.2.8. Active PivotTable toolbar.

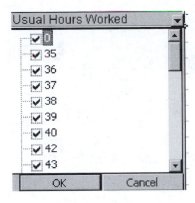

Figure 3.2.9. Choosing values to display in a PivotTable.

Summary

This introduction to the basics of PivotTables has demonstrated how to explore a single variable with a PivotTable and how to hide values. Of course, this merely scratches the surface of what you can do with PivotTables. The next section focuses on creating two-dimensional tables or crosstabs.

3.3. The Crosstab and Conditional Average

Workbook: IndianaFTWorkers.xls

Continuing with the Excel file called IndianaFTWorkers.xls, which you have now augmented with a PivotTable sheet as described in the previous section, we demonstrate how to create a crosstab (which is short for crosstabulation) and is also known as a contingency or cross-classification table. Unlike a frequency table, which shows the distribution of counts, a crosstab displays conditional information. By including another dimension to the table and tabulating the averages in various subgroups, the crosstab can quickly summarize and reveal patterns in the data.

Begin by clicking on any cell in the PivotTable. Execute View: Toolbars: PivotTable if the PivotTable toolbar is not visible. Click on the PivotTable Wizard button ( ) or click on the PivotTable pull-down menu and select the PivotTable Wizard to return to Step 3 of the PivotTable Wizard. Click on Layout. Note that, when you select a cell in the PivotTable, a right click accesses a pop-up menu.

We want to explore the relationship between Education and Total Personal Income via a table. Remove the Usual Hours Worked tiles by clicking and dragging them away. Move the Education General field button (let your cursor rest over an Education field button to see the full name) to the Row area and put Average of Total Personal Income in the Data area as in Figure 3.3.1.

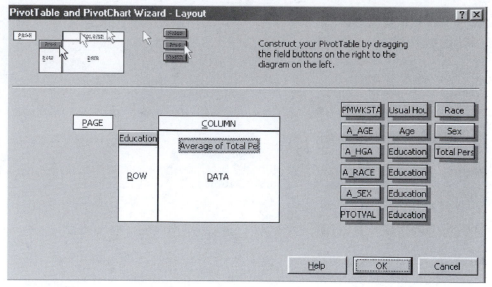

Figure 3.3.1. PivotTable layout for education and total personal income.

Click OK and then Click Finish. You have a one-dimensional crosstabulation depicting the relationship between education and income. The *Pivot-
Table* sheet explains how to format the cells. Click and drag to reorganize the
groups in order of ascending education in order to create Figure 3.3.2. Instead
of showing how many people are in each group, the PivotTable reports the
average total personal income for each educational group.

This crosstab or contingency table displays the conditional average. For
each educational category, the PivotTable reports the average total personal
income of the individuals with that level of education. The Grand Total is the
overall average. As expected, as education increases, so does average total
personal income.

To see how many people are in each group, return to the PivotTable Wizard
and add the Count of Total Personal Income to the data area. The PivotTable

Average of Total Personal Income	
Education General Categories ▼	Total
FirsttoEighthGrade	$ 21,037
SomeHighSchool	$ 25,647
HighSchoolGrad	$ 28,624
SomeCollege	$ 34,555
CollegeGrad	$ 60,295
PostGraduateStudy	$ 63,076
Grand Total	$ 37,174

Figure 3.3.2. Income as a function of Education crosstab.
Source: [IndianaFTWorkers.xls]PivotTable.

Race	Data	Total
Black	Average of Total Personal Income	$ 30,228
	Count of Total Personal Income	31
White	Average of Total Personal Income	$ 37,303
	Count of Total Personal Income	559
Total Average of Total Personal Income		$ 36,931
Total Count of Total Personal Income		590

Figure 3.3.3. Income as a function of Race crosstab.
Source: [IndianaFTWorkers.xls]PivotTable.

is recreated and the counts are added, but the counts are formatted as dollars. To remedy the formatting problem, select a cell in the data area of the PivotTable report that contains one of the counts. On the PivotTable toolbar, click Field Settings, which is this icon: ▣. Click Number. In the Category list, click the format category you want, which in this case is Number, and then choose zero decimal places. Click OK twice. Note that there are 598 total observations. We are working with the entire data set (without hiding the Usual Hours Worked = 0 values).

Continue exploring the data by making one-dimensional crosstabs of the average of Total Personal Income by Sex and Race. We chose to hide the AsianPI and IndEsk categories in Figure 3.3.3 but used the entire data set in Figure 3.3.4. Your results should be similar to these figures.

Note that Figures 3.3.3 and 3.3.4 mix frequency and average information. Both PivotTables report conditional averages. That is, the tables report average values given Race (black or white) or Sex (female or male). The totals are overall averages and overall counts.

Before we begin to explore the relationship between total personal income and race and sex, note the seeming error in the race table. If African-Americans have, on average, a total personal income of $30,228 and whites come in at $37,303, how can the overall average be $36,931? After all, the average of $30,228 and $37,303 is about $33,765. The answer is contained in the count information. There are many more whites than blacks. The Pivot-Table is correctly computing the overall average as a weighted average. The basic idea is captured by Figure 3.3.5.

Sex	Data	Total
Female	Average of Total Personal Income	$28,880
	Count of Total Personal Income	258
Male	Average of Total Personal Income	$43,467
	Count of Total Personal Income	340
Total Average of Total Personal Income		$37,174
Total Count of Total Personal Income		598

Figure 3.3.4. Income as a function of Sex crosstab.
Source: [IndianaFTWorkers.xls]PivotTable.

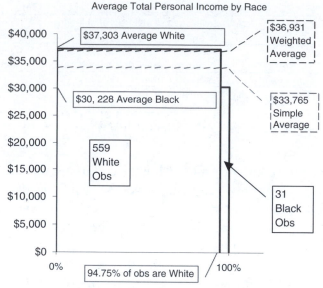

Figure 3.3.5. Understanding the weighted average.
Source: [IndianaFTWorkers.xls]WeightAvg.

Notice that Excel's PivotTable is correctly using a weighted average in its Average of Total Personal Income. The sheet *WeightAvg* in IndianaFTWorkers.xls explains the concept and calculation in more detail.

Wage or income discrimination occurs when otherwise identical workers are paid different amounts. To explore the evidence for income discrimination, we can create a crosstab. The simple comparison of average of total personal income against sex or race suffers from potential confounding. After all, perhaps the difference in incomes is due to some hidden factor that happens to be correlated with race or sex.

A PivotTable can help analyze additional factors by creating an additional dimension in the table. Return to the PivotTable sheet and Step 3 of the PivotTable Wizard. Make a PivotTable with Race in the row area, Education in the column area, and Average of Total Personal Income in the data area. Our table is Figure 3.3.6.

Average of Total Personal Income	Education General Categories						
Race	First to Eighth Grade	Some High School	High School Grad	Some College	College Grad	Post Graduate Study	Grand Total
Black		$8,921	$27,770	$33,268	$27,097	$62,500	$30,228
White	$21,037	$26,947	$28,662	$34,502	$61,974	$61,254	$37,303
Grand Total	$21,037	$25,821	$28,624	$34,416	$60,138	$61,302	$36,931

Figure 3.3.6. Income as a function of education and race.
Source: [IndianaFTWorkers.xls]PivotTable.

Figure 3.3.6 is a two-dimensional crosstab (or contingency table). Each cell in the interior represents the average of Total Personal Income for given combinations of categories. Note how the Grand Total row and column represent the one-dimensional view. By comparing more similar people, or more homogeneous groups, one obtains a better analysis. The conditional average reported in each cell is now a combination of two categories: race and education.

Figure 3.3.6 should pique your curiosity. It shows that African-Americans in Indiana from the March 1999 CPS sample had about $7,000 less income on average than whites. The table contains two possible explanations. First, notice that African-Americans and whites in the Some High School and College Grad categories have the greatest differences in average income. We could then argue that wage gaps in these categories largely account for the observed $7,000 gap in the overall average. A second consideration, however, concerns the frequency distribution across the groups. Perhaps there are relatively more African-Americans in the lower educated groups, whereas whites are concentrated in the higher education groups. The table does not provide enough information to determine an answer. You can, however, use Excel's PivotTable feature to add a count and percent of row information, as we did in Figure 3.3.7.

As you do this, you are using PivotTables as a dynamic data exploration tool. The easy movement of variables and quick retabulation of data is a powerful feature of Excel's PivotTable.

Notice that adding variables to the table makes it messier and harder to read. The low counts for Black should make us wary. We simply have too few observations to reach any definite conclusions. Furthermore, notice that we know nothing about the kinds of jobs these workers are doing nor about any other dimensions on which workers might differ. We cannot conclude that blacks are suffering from income discrimination absent much more information on these workers and their jobs.

Return to the PivotTable Wizard and add Sex to the table into the columns section. Once one starts to consider more than two variables, tables become particularly difficult to interpret. This is one of the reasons researchers use multiple regression analysis. For one- or two-way presentations of relationships, however, tables are a good initial step.

The last feature of Excel's PivotTable is the ability to group numerical values. Create a one-dimensional PivotTable of Age and Usual Hours Worked. The table is too long. Right-click on the Age tile in the table and select the Grouping option. Go ahead and group the ages by 10-year categories. The table is now easier to read. Get a count on each category. It would probably make sense to hide the last two categories. Our table is presented in Figure 3.3.8.

Race	Data	First to Eighth Grade	Some High School	High School Grad	Some College	College Grad	Post-Graduate Study	Grand Total
Black	Average of Total Personal Income		$8,921	$27,770	$33,268	$27,097	$62,500	$30,228
	Count of Total Personal Income		3	10	12	4	2	31
	Percent of Row	0.00%	9.68%	32.26%	38.71%	12.90%	6.45%	100.00%
White	Average of Total Personal Income	$21,037	$26,947	$28,662	$34,502	$61,974	$61,254	$37,303
	Count of Total Personal Income	8	45	223	161	72	50	559
	Percent of Row	1.43%	8.05%	39.89%	28.80%	12.88%	8.94%	100.00%
Total Average of Total Personal Income		$21,037	$25,821	$28,624	$34,416	$60,138	$61,302	$36,931
Total Count of Total Personal Income		8	48	233	173	76	52	590
Total Percent of Row		1.36%	8.14%	39.49%	29.32%	12.88%	8.81%	AZZ

Education General Categories

Figure 3.3.7. Income as a function of education and race with counts and percentages.
Source: [IndianaFTWorkers.xls]PivotTable.

Age	Data	Total
18–27	Average of Usual Hours Worked	41.84
	Count of Usual Hours Worked	69
28–37	Average of Usual Hours Worked	41.93
	Count of Usual Hours Worked	162
38–47	Average of Usual Hours Worked	42.79
	Count of Usual Hours Worked	192
48–57	Average of Usual Hours Worked	44.30
	Count of Usual Hours Worked	133
58–67	Average of Usual Hours Worked	38.46
	Count of Usual Hours Worked	39
68–77	Average of Usual Hours Worked	55.00
	Count of Usual Hours Worked	2
78–87	Average of Usual Hours Worked	0.00
	Count of Usual Hours Worked	1
Total Average of Usual Hours Worked		42.47
Total Count of Usual Hours Worked		598

Figure 3.3.8. Usual hours worked as a function of age in groups. *Source:* [IndianaFTWorkers.xls]PivotTable.

Summary

PivotTables are a powerful way to analyze data. They help indicate patterns and relationships, but they can get messy when more than two or three variables are considered. Using PivotTables to display the conditional average can be an excellent way to summarize the data and highlight a relationship in the data.

3.4. PivotTables and the Conditional Mean Function

Workbook: EastNorthCentralFTWorkers.xls

The information in data sets must be summarized in order to perform description and analysis. So far in this chapter, we have looked at an example of a data set from a recent year of the March CPS and used various tables to summarize the data via Excel's Data Analysis: Descriptive Statistics and PivotTable features.

In this section, we will consider a similar but larger data set. As in the previous Section, we will use Excel's PivotTable for data exploration. In addition, we will utilize the PivotTable to introduce the conditional mean function. This will lay the foundation for understanding regression analysis.

A New Data Set

The workbook EastNorthCentralFTWorkers.xls contains information on the following variables for the full-time workers in the March 1999 Current Population Survey sample who lived in the five East North Central states:

Usual Hours Worked
Education
Yearly Earnings
Race

Illinois	Average of Yearly Earnings	$ 37,328
	Count of State	2064
Indiana	Average of Yearly Earnings	$ 33,124
	Count of State	598
Michigan	Average of Yearly Earnings	$ 39,317
	Count of State	1489
Wisconsin	Average of Yearly Earnings	$ 34,497
	Count of State	630
Ohio	Average of Yearly Earnings	$ 40,051
	Count of State	1585
Total Average of Yearly Earnings		$ 37,796
Total Count of State		6366

Figure 3.4.1. Average yearly earnings by state with counts.
Source: [EastNorthCentralFTWorkers.xls]Tables.

Sex
Usual Weekly Earnings
State
Month in Sample

See the *Intro* sheet to learn how to get more information on the data sets and how they were constructed. We are interested in describing the yearly earnings of the 6,366 workers in the data set. In fact, yearly earnings will become the dependent variable in our analysis, and we will identify explanatory, or independent, variables that may determine yearly earnings. Figure 3.4.1 is one quick summary of the data.

In Figure 3.4.1, the Count of State values indicate how many observations there were for each state. For example, there were 1,585 full-time workers in the sample in Ohio, and their average yearly earnings were $40,051. It should be obvious from what we did in the previous section that Figure 3.4.1 is just one of the many possible tables we can produce from this data set.

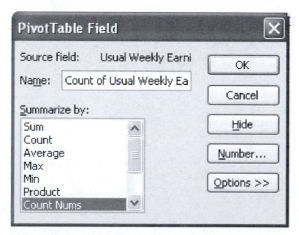

Figure 3.4.2. The Count Nums summary option.

Count of Education	Yearly Earnings						
Education	0–19999	20000–39999	40000–59999	60000–79999	80000–100000	>100000	Grand Total
8	101	34	10	2			147
9	34	9	5	1		1	50
10	70	46	7	2	1		126
11	84	58	12	2			156
11.5	27	23	6	1			57
12	769	994	358	92	20	14	2247
13	415	603	326	103	34	22	1503
14	45	94	61	16	2	3	221
16	163	420	310	171	88	68	1220
18	54	113	188	117	69	98	639
Grand Total	1762	2394	1283	507	214	206	6366

Figure 3.4.3. Frequency distribution of yearly earnings for different levels of education.
Source: [EastNorthCentralFTWorkers.xls]Tables.

There is another variable in the data set that measures income – namely, Usual Weekly Earnings. In the Current Population Survey, households are surveyed for a total of 8 months. Questions pertaining to Usual Weekly Earnings are asked only of people in households that are in their fourth and eighth months of being in the survey. Thus, there are numerous missing values (indicated by a "." in the workbook) for this variable. To count the number of observations with nonmissing values, one needs to use the Count Nums option, as illustrated in Figure 3.4.2.

Rather than exploring differences in annual or weekly earnings across states, we will examine the association between yearly earnings of full-time workers and their education in these five Midwestern states in March 1999. First, let us look at a frequency table in which earnings levels have been grouped, as depicted in Figure 3.4.3.

Here is an example of how to read this table: 358 people in the data set had completed 12 years of education and earned between $40,000 and $59,999. Grouping values helps create tables that are easy to read. To group, select the variable to be grouped (by clicking on its label on the worksheet) and right-click. Select Group and Outline and choose the desired ranges.

You can practice grouping by creating a PivotTable of Yearly Earnings by Sex. From the Data sheet, create a PivotTable for which the layout looks like Figure 3.4.4. After you have created the PivotTable, right-click the Yearly Earnings variable and group the values in ranges of 20,000. There are few values beyond 100,000; therefore group them into one category. If you cannot figure out how to do this, go to the *Grouping* sheet for instructions.

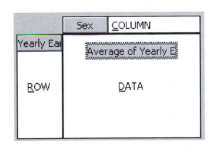

Figure 3.4.4. Grouping practice layout.

Average of Yearly Earnings	Yearly Earnings							
Education	0-19999	20000-39999	40000-59999	60000-79999	80000-100000	>100000		Grand Total
8	$ 10,605	$ 27,252	$ 47,860	$ 60,000				$ 17,662
9	$ 10,966	$ 26,222	$ 45,326	$ 60,000		$ 306,731		$ 24,044
10	$ 10,508	$ 27,968	$ 44,500	$ 70,503	$ 94,000			$ 20,386
11	$ 9,795	$ 27,427	$ 47,674	$ 65,300				$ 19,976
11.5	$ 6,980	$ 28,279	$ 48,269	$ 60,000				$ 20,851
12	$ 10,629	$ 27,857	$ 46,957	$ 65,797	$ 89,654	$ 160,494		$ 27,934
13	$ 10,857	$ 28,375	$ 46,917	$ 66,117	$ 88,765	$ 190,624		$ 33,888
14	$ 10,012	$ 28,760	$ 46,568	$ 65,937	$ 92,000	$ 217,745		$ 35,687
16	$ 7,803	$ 29,496	$ 48,072	$ 66,878	$ 89,280	$ 173,702		$ 48,907
18	$ 6,974	$ 31,011	$ 49,097	$ 68,316	$ 89,997	$ 218,059		$ 76,187
Grand Total	$ 10,198	$ 28,441	$ 47,512	$ 66,783	$ 89,512	$ 197,001		$ 37,796

Figure 3.4.5. Average yearly earnings for yearly earnings intervals by education. *Source:* [EastNorthCentralFTWorkers.xls]Tables.

Next, look at Figure 3.4.5, which shows average yearly earnings for different levels of education and different intervals of Yearly Earnings. For the group that had 12 years of education and earned between $40,000 and $59,999, average yearly earnings were $46,957. We would fully expect these people to earn on average something in the $40s or $50s, though it is somewhat surprising that the average is only $46,957 (instead of closer to $50,000).

Finally, Figure 3.4.6 is a collapsed version of Figure 3.4.5. Figure 3.4.6 is just the extreme right- and left-hand columns of Figure 3.4.5. The values in this table can be computed from Figures 3.4.3 and 3.4.5. The overall ("Total") average yearly earnings by education level are weighted averages of the average earnings in Figure 3.4.5.

Figure 3.4.6 takes information on all 6,366 people in the sample and collapses it into 10 pairs of numbers and an overall average ("Grand Total") figure. This table provides a powerful way of thinking about the relationship between yearly earnings and education in our sample. It can be used to answer the following question: Given that a particular observation has a certain value of Education, what is the value of Yearly Earnings we expect to see for that observation? Questions of this type are fundamental to the empirical analysis of multivariate data sets.

Average of Yearly Earnings	
Education	Total
8	$ 17,662
9	$ 24,044
10	$ 20,386
11	$ 19,976
11.5	$ 20,851
12	$ 27,934
13	$ 33,888
14	$ 35,687
16	$ 48,907
18	$ 76,187
Grand Total	$ 37,796

Figure 3.4.6. Average yearly earnings by education. *Source:* [EastNorthCentralFTWorkers.xls]Tables.

Figure 3.4.6 reports a value of Yearly Earnings we expect to find for people at each level of education. This value is the average level of Yearly Earnings for all people in the data set who have the given level of education. The technical name for the information in the table is the *conditional mean function*. To understand this concept, look at each word in turn. *Function* says we are going from one variable – Education – and moving to a second variable – Yearly Earnings. *Mean* signifies we are looking at averages. *Conditional* denotes that we are reporting the mean level of Yearly Earnings conditional on the level of Education.

The conditional mean function is one way of answering the general question, Given that a particular observation has a certain value of the "independent" variable, what is the value of the "dependent" variable that we expect to observe for that observation? Of course, not every observation will have the same yearly earnings given a level of education. There is dispersion around the conditional average. The conditional mean function, however, gives us a measure of the center of the values of yearly earnings for a given level of education.

If the average is a poor measure of the center, another statistic may be more appropriate. For example, instead of using the average of yearly earnings for each education level, we could have reported the median. Tables published by the U.S. Census and Bureau of Labor Statistics from data from the Current Population Survey very often do exactly that – their tables report the *conditional median function*. This makes sense because yearly earnings tend to have long right-hand tails in their distribution, and this property holds also for yearly earnings conditional on education.

Summary

The crosstab of average income as a function of education is an example of the conditional mean function. This is an important building block in understanding regression as a data summary tool. We will soon show that the conditional mean function is one step away from the regression line. Before we can do that, however, the next chapter will explain exactly how the regression is calculated.

3.5. Conclusion

This part of the book is about developing tools to describe data and the relationship between variables. Recall that the average and standard deviation of a list are key summary statistics in the univariate (single variable) case. With two variables, the correlation coefficient can be quite useful. This chapter showed how tables may be used to summarize data.

Tables can be simple frequency counts or more sophisticated compressions of the data. A crosstab displays the conditional average or, more technically, the conditional mean function. By viewing the average of one variable given a value of another variable, the reader quickly picks up information about the relationship between the two variables.

Excel's PivotTable feature makes creating crosstabs and exploring data with tables easy. By moving tiles in and out of the table and enabling the display of a variety of queries (e.g., average, count, or SD), one can generate interesting and sophisticated tables.

Finally, this chapter has emphasized that summarizing the relationship between two variables is often guided by answering the question, Given that a particular observation has a certain value of the independent variable, what is the value of the dependent variable we expect to observe for that observation?

Chapter 4 introduces the least squares regression line and explains how it is computed, and Chapter 5 shows how the regression line answers the same basic question emphasized in this chapter.

3.6. Exercises

1. Many college seniors interested in law school anxiously scan a special kind of crosstab called the law school admissions grid. The grid shows, for a particular school and year of application, the fraction of students admitted according to the range of college cumulative GPA and LSAT score that they fall into. The upper-left-hand corner of such a grid is shown below.

	LSAT Scores	
GPA	175–180	170–174
3.75–4.00	92%	85%
3.50–3.74	83%	84%
. . .		

   Draw a picture of what the spreadsheet table containing the original data set used to construct the law school admissions grid looks like. Give a few rows and the relevant columns (variables).

2. (Hypothetical.) Fill in the missing cells in the table below on the body weights of students at a small university.

	Average Weight	Number of Observations
Males	182	
Females	135	
Total	153.8	3000

3. Using Figure 3.4.3, what can you determine about the median yearly earnings for people with 8 years of education as compared with the median yearly earnings of people with 18 years of education for the people in the sample of full-time workers in Midwestern states? Explain your answer.

Percent under—	Cumulative Percentage
4′8″	-
4′9″	-
4′10″	-
4′11″	-
5′..	0.1
5′1″	0.1
5′2″	0.5
5′3″	1.3
5′4″	3.4
5′5″	6.9
5′6″	11.7
5′7″	20.8
5′8″	32.0
5′9″	46.3
5′10″	58.7
5′11″	70.1
6′	81.2
6′1″	87.4
6′2″	94.7
6′3″	97.9

Figure 3.6.1. Cumulative height distribution of men 20–29.
Source: U.S. Census Bureau, Statistical Abstract of the United States: 2002, Table 189.[4]

4. (A followup to Question 3.) You should have found that the two medians are well below the averages even if their precise value is unknown. Explain why median yearly earnings are below average yearly earnings in the East North Central full-time workers data set.

5. The data in Figure 3.6.1 on the Cumulative Percent Distribution of the Population of Young Men Aged 20–29 in the United States comes from the U.S. National Center for Health Statistics. It is based on unpublished sample survey data collected between 1988 and 1994. Convert the data in this table into a tabulation of the percentage distribution of height to the nearest inch. As an example of how to read Figure 3.6.1, the figure 3.4 in the 5′4″ row means that 3.4 percent of the males in the sample had a height below 5 feet 4 inches.

References

Tabulation has a long history in statistics. Early practitioners include Adolphe Quetelet in the 1820s and Francis Galton starting in the 1860s, though useful tables were constructed as long ago as the 1690s by Edmond Halley. Galton's work with crosstabs led directly to regression, the topic considered in the next two chapters. A major breakthrough occurred in the 1890s when Herman Hollerith perfected electronic means of cross-tabulating data for the U.S. Census. See Stigler, S.M. (1986) *The History of Statistics: The Measurement of Uncertainty before 1900* (Cambridge, MA: The Belknap Press of Haward University Press). Goldberger discusses the conditional mean function in his two textbooks; his discussion inspired ours. See Chapter 5 References for citations to the two books.

---

[4] Available at <www.census.gov/prod/www/statistical-abstract-03.html>.

4

Computing the OLS Regression Line

Of all the principles which can be proposed for that purpose, I think there is none more general, more exact, and more easy of application, that of which we made use in the preceding researches, and which consists of rendering the sum of squares of the errors a minimum.

Adrien-Marie Legendre[1]

4.1. Introduction

Chapters 4 and 5 introduce the concept of regression, the fundamental analytical tool of econometrics. The regression line summarizes the relationship between two variables. Chapter 4 covers the mechanics of regression. We discuss the theory behind fitting a line, present an algebraic exposition of the ordinary least squares (OLS) regression coefficients, and show several ways to have Excel report regression results. We note that OLS is not the only way to fit a regression line. Chapter 5 focuses on interpreting what OLS regression does and the results it produces. Of course, these two chapters are only an introduction to regression analysis. The remainder of this book is dedicated to ever more powerful and sophisticated applications of the method of regression.

4.2. Fitting the Ordinary Least Squares Regression Line

Workbook: Reg.xls

In this section, we use an artificial data set to demonstrate how the OLS (also abbreviated LS) regression line summarizes a bivariate scatter plot. We will describe the optimization problem behind the OLS regression procedure and show that OLS is only one of many varieties of regression analysis.

---

[1] See the references at the end of this chapter for the source of this quotation and suggestions for further reading on the history of the least squares method.

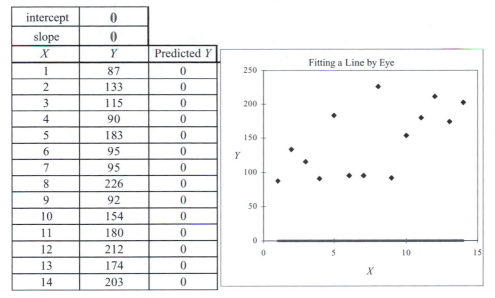

intercept	**0**	
slope	**0**	
X	Y	Predicted Y
1	87	0
2	133	0
3	115	0
4	90	0
5	183	0
6	95	0
7	95	0
8	226	0
9	92	0
10	154	0
11	180	0
12	212	0
13	174	0
14	203	0

Figure 4.2.1. An artificial data set.
Source: [Reg.xls]ByEye.

We emphasize throughout the book that there are many possible ways to summarize the relationship between variables.

Figure 4.2.1 contains a table and a scatter plot of the 14 points in the data set. We want to draw a straight line summarizing the relationship between X and Y. The simplest way to draw such a line is to use one's own judgment (i.e., to draw "by eye"). For the data above, go ahead and roughly draw in a straight line you think best fits the data – whatever you think that means. Write down the approximate value of your line's intercept and slope.

Next, open the Excel workbook Reg.xls to try out the values of your line of "best fit." The first sheet, called *ByEye*, permits experimentation with different values for the intercept and slope variables. Input your intercept and slope choices in cells B3 and B4. Excel immediately updates the chart. (Hit F9 to recalculate the workbook manually if the chart does not automatically refresh.) The red line shows how the intercept and slope you have chosen fit the data. You might experiment somewhat in an effort to find the best-fitting line.

Figure 4.2.2 is one possible graph you might draw. Figure 4.2.2 contains much information. The regression line captures the upward-sloping relationship between the X's and the Y's. The line goes more or less through the middle of the data cloud. The equation of the proposed regression line is

$$\text{Predicted } Y = 50 + 10\, X.$$

intercept	**50**	
slope	**10**	
X	Y	Predicted Y
1	87	60
2	133	70
3	115	80
4	90	90
5	183	100
6	95	110
7	95	120
8	226	130
9	92	140
10	154	150
11	180	160
12	212	170
13	174	180
14	203	190

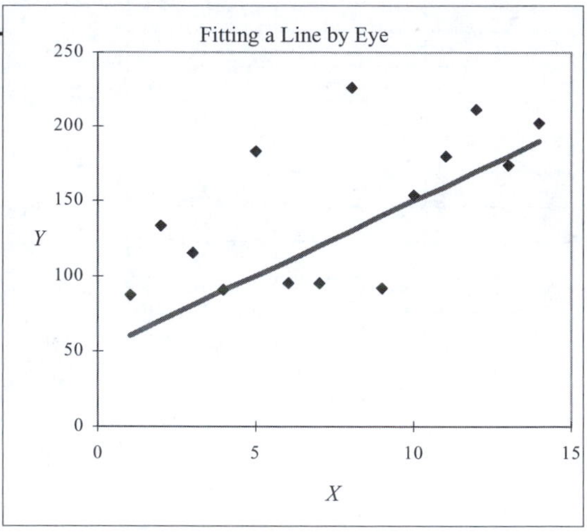

Figure 4.2.2. A by-eye regression line.
Source: [Reg.xls]ByEye.

The intercept of this proposed regression line is 50; this is where the line cuts the y-axis. It is the value of Predicted Y we would obtain if we were to substitute a value of 0 for X. The slope of the regression line is 10. The slope tells us that, for every one-unit increase in X, the value of Predicted Y rises by 10. The proposed regression line passes through all the points whose coordinate pairs are given by the values in the first and third columns of the table in Figure 4.2.2.

Perhaps most important, the proposed regression line tells us the predicted value of Y for a given value of X. In other words, the graph is read by taking any given X, moving vertically up to the line, and then moving horizontally to the y-axis and reading off the value as our prediction of Y for that given X.

You may think that your by-eye regression line is better than the one displayed in Figure 4.2.2, but how could you determine whether it really is? And, what is the OLS regression line? To answer these questions, we need to learn about residuals.

The Residual

The predicted value of Y given X is the value of Y that lies on the regression line for that given value of X. One finds the predicted value by plugging the value of X into the equation of the regression line. Using the equation and the specific values of Intercept and Slope for our by-eye regression line, you can

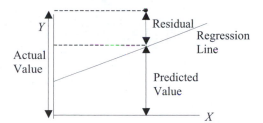

Figure 4.2.3. A positive residual.

compute that when X is 5, Predicted Y is 100. (Verify this by looking at the table and graph in Figure 4.2.2.) The actual value of Y in our data set, however, is 183, and so we are off by 83. Eighty-three is the value of the residual associated with the data point (10, 183) and our by-eye regression line. In general, the vertical distance of the actual observed Y from its predicted Y value is called the residual:

$$\text{Residual} = \text{Actual value of } Y - \text{Predicted value of } Y.$$

Every observation (or point in the scatter diagram) has a residual. We can also consider all of the residuals together as a list of numbers and chart them, creating a residual plot.

Residuals can be either positive or negative (the residual is zero only when predicted equals actual Y). Figures 4.2.3 and 4.2.4 depict the positive and negative residual cases, respectively.

Each observation has an actual (or observed) value of Y and X, a predicted value of Y given X, and a residual. The units of the residual are the same as the units of the Y variable. Because the residual is always the difference between the actual value of Y and its predicted value, a positive residual means that the actual (or observed) value of Y is above its predicted value. Whenever actual Y less predicted Y is negative, that observation's residual is negative.

Let us observe residuals in our example on the *minSSR* sheet in Reg.xls. This sheet contains two new columns, one that computes the residuals and a

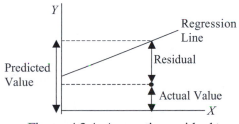

Figure 4.2.4. A negative residual.

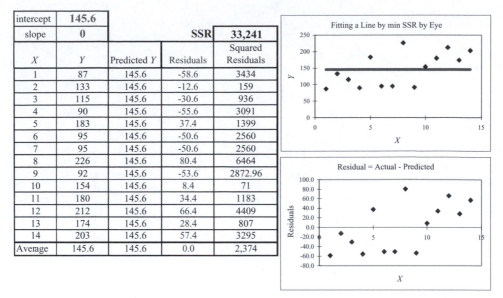

intercept	**145.6**			
slope	**0**		**SSR**	**33,241**
				Squared
X	*Y*	Predicted *Y*	Residuals	Residuals
1	87	145.6	-58.6	3434
2	133	145.6	-12.6	159
3	115	145.6	-30.6	936
4	90	145.6	-55.6	3091
5	183	145.6	37.4	1399
6	95	145.6	-50.6	2560
7	95	145.6	-50.6	2560
8	226	145.6	80.4	6464
9	92	145.6	-53.6	2872.96
10	154	145.6	8.4	71
11	180	145.6	34.4	1183
12	212	145.6	66.4	4409
13	174	145.6	28.4	807
14	203	145.6	57.4	3295
Average	145.6	145.6	0.0	2,374

Figure 4.2.5. The Average *Y* line.
Source: [Reg.xls]minSSR.

second that squares those residuals. The sheet initially displays a horizontal line whose *y*-intercept is equal to the average value of *Y* in the data set. Thus, the value of the Intercept is 145.6 and the Slope is 0. Figure 4.2.5 shows the data, scatter diagram, and residual plot. We call this line the Average *Y* line because, no matter what *X* is, Predicted *Y* equals the average value of *Y* in the data set. Take a look at the residual in the table and residual plot.

The residuals are sometimes positive, sometimes negative, but in this case they average out to zero. That is not a coincidence. Look at the bottom row of the table. Just as each individual residual is the difference between *Y* and predicted *Y*, the average of the residuals is the difference between the average *Y* (145.6) and the average of the Predicted *Y*'s (also 145.6). We hope this reasoning is intuitively attractive; using mathematical tools to be introduced in Section 4.3, it is very easy to make the argument rigorous. A regression line in which the residuals average to zero is appealing because that means on average Predicted *Y* is correct.

Although the Average *Y* regression line is on average right, it suffers from a systematic flaw. When *X* is small, this regression line tends to overpredict *Y*; when *X* is large, the average *Y* line tends to underpredict *Y*. This is obvious both from the scatter plot with the regression line superimposed and the residual plot in Figure 4.2.5.

At this point, we have several contenders for the line of best fit. In addition to your suggested line, we have Predicted *Y* = 50 + 10*X* and Predicted

$Y = 145.6$ (the line of Average Y). We need a way to judge and evaluate the how well these lines fit the data.

The Sum of Squared Residuals

The most commonly used criterion for best fit focuses on the sum of squared residuals or SSR. Every possible contender (including your line fitted by eye) has a value for the sum of squared residuals.[2] This sum is found by determining the residual for each observation, squaring each residual, and then adding up the values of all of the squared residuals.

In the Reg.xls workbook, go to the *minSSR* sheet and enter the values for your line of best fit in cells B3 and B4. One of the important advantages of a spreadsheet is that you can see exactly how a number is computed. Click on cells in the table (e.g., C6, D6, and E6) to see how a squared residual is calculated. To facilitate your understanding of the table, the cells have been named in the relevant columns. You can more closely examine the computations by clicking in the formula bar on the spreadsheet. The formulas in cells D6 and E6 show how the residual and squared residual for each observation are computed.

The reason the residuals are squared is to prevent the negative residuals (that lie below the regression line) from canceling out the positive residuals.[3] Observations far off the line are being poorly predicted – it does not matter if they are above (positive) or below (negative) the line. Squaring makes sure that negative residuals are properly accounted for in fitting the line.

Cell E4 in the *minSSR* sheet sums the squared residuals. This cell represents our measure of fit. The lower the number, the better the fit. Try to see if you can improve your line of best fit by eye by keeping track of the SSR. Adjust your intercept and slope values in cells B3 and B4 so that you improve the fit. You are trying to minimize, or make as small as possible, the SSR.

It is important that you recognize that the line changes as the intercept and slope change, resulting in a new SSR. The idea behind the actual fitting of the least squares regression line is that it is the line with the SSR-minimizing intercept and slope combination.

Minimizing the SSR Using Excel's Solver

Sophisticated Excel users will recall that Excel contains a powerful numerical optimization algorithm called the Solver add-in. (If Solver is not available on

---

[2] The sole exception would be a completely vertical line.
[3] This is nothing new. In calculating the SD, we find the root-mean *squared* deviations from the mean.

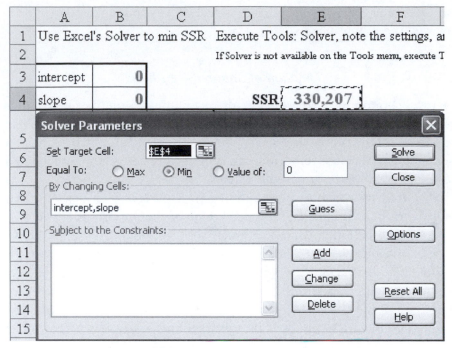

Figure 4.2.6. Using Solver to find the regression line.
Source: [Reg.xls]Solver.

the Tools menu, execute Tools: Add-ins and select the Solver add-in. If it is not listed, you must install it from your Office CD.) Click on the sheet called *Solver* in Reg.xls and use Excel to solve the optimization problem by executing Tools: Solver. The Solver dialog box has been preconfigured for you, as shown in Figure 4.2.6

The Target Cell, E4, contains the SSR. The ⊙ Min radio button indicates we wish to minimize this sum. Excel will attempt to do so by changing the named cells "intercept" and "slope." Hit the Solve button, and you will obtain an answer very close to the exact least squares solution.[4] How does the fitted line look now?

Another View of the Least Squares Optimization Problem

We further underscore the fact that the OLS regression line chooses the intercept and slope combination that minimizes the SSR by having you take a look at the sheet called *Table* in Reg.xls. The table displays the SSR for different regression lines with varying combinations of slope and intercept.

---

[4] It will be close but not exactly the answer. Solver stops when it gets "close enough" to the solution. In the next chapter we will discuss a method that produces the exact solution (within limits of computer precision).

Intercept	Slope	
	0	**1**
0	329,956	296,974
20	254,033	225,251

Figure 4.2.7. A portion of the *Table* sheet. *Source:* [Reg.xls]Table.

The table makes clear that there are many possible combinations of intercept and slope. Each intercept–slope pair yields a sum of squared residuals. The upper-left-hand corner of the table is reproduced in Figure 4.2.7.

The entry for Slope $= 0$ and Intercept $= 20$ tells us that the SSR for that combination is 254,033. The combination of intercept and slope that yields the smallest number in the interior of the table is the optimal least squares solution. Click on the Take me to the chart button in the table to see a three-dimensional (3D) representation of the problem. The graph is reproduced in Figure 4.2.8. Seeing the SSR in three dimensions makes a striking impression. The 3D graph makes clear the optimization problem of minimizing the SSR by choosing an intercept and a slope.

The *MoreSSR* sheet in the Reg.xls workbook offers a set of controls that you can adjust, and the effect of these controls can then be seen on the SSR 3D graph. Figure 4.2.9 shows how the sheet is organized. The spread controller adjusts the amount of variability in Y. When the spread controller is drawn all the way to the left, there is no variability in Y and the data lie on the line. The SD X controller allows you to adjust the spread of the X variable from a low spread of 1-unit increments in X to a high spread of 10-unit increments. When you change the SD X controller, it may appear that nothing has happened, but the x-axis scale reveals that the SD of X does affect the problem. Finally,

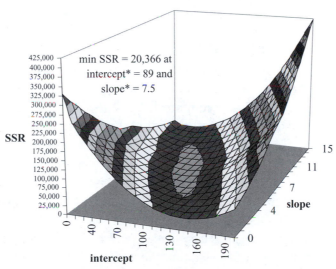

Figure 4.2.8. The SSR surface. *Source:* [Reg.xls]3DView.

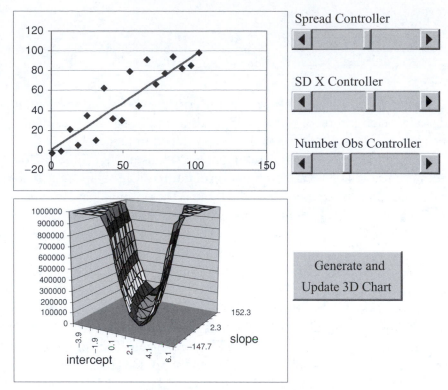

Figure 4.2.9. The SSR surface.
Source: [Reg.xls]3DView.

you can determine the number of data points by setting the Number Obs controller.

The scatter diagram updates immediately when you change one of the slider controls, but the 3D chart does not. To update the 3D chart, you must click the Generate and Update 3D Chart button to refresh the chart and display the 3D graph given the controller settings.

Explore a variety of combinations. What happens when the spread controller is low and the SD X and Number Obs is high? With the spread and SD controllers set in the middle, compare the results of the highest and lowest values of the number of observations. What do you see?

Clearly, the shape of the SSR objective function depends on the data. The dispersion of the Y values, spread of the X values, and the number of observations affect the clarity of the minimum. It is easier to find the minimum when the SSR function forms a sharply descending bowl than when it has a gradual descent and a flat bottom.

In fact, there is a pathological case, called perfect multicollinearity, in which a unique minimum does not exist, and therefore a regression line of best fit, defined as the line that minimizes the SSR, cannot be found. We discuss this case in Chapter 7.

Other Objective Functions

The conventional way to fit a regression line is to choose the intercept and slope that minimize the SSR. This is often called Least Squares or Ordinary Least Squares (OLS). There are, however, many other ways to fit a line. First, there are many different objective functions to use when fitting a line. With the standard minimize-the-SSR objective, residuals are squared because deviations from the line in positive or negative vertical directions mean the same thing. But the absolute value function also eliminates the importance of the sign. Minimizing the sum of the absolute values of the residuals (instead of the sum of the squared residuals) is called least absolute deviation or LAD. Another approach, called orthogonal regression, minimizes not the vertical distance of the residuals but the distance at a right angle to the regression line.

A third alternative approach to fitting the line accepts the squaring of vertical deviations from the line as the basis of the objective function but changes the recipe applied to the squared residuals. Instead of summing the squared residuals, this method finds the median of the squared residuals. The least median of squares, or LMS, approach to fitting a line is said to be a robust regression technique because it is not as sensitive to outliers as the conventional least squares approach.

Least absolute deviation, orthogonal regression, and LMS are only three examples of the many sophisticated techniques that have been implemented in fitting a regression line. Although these methods are beyond the scope of this book, you should understand that any line of "best fit" is determined according to a particular objective function.

Because there are different objective functions when fitting a line, you might wonder why minimizing the SSR is the most commonly used. This is an excellent question with a complicated answer that we cannot provide at this time. In the second part of this book, after we understand the role of chance in the data generation process, we will be able to explain the desirable properties of a line fit by minimizing the SSR.

Summary

Although there are many ways to fit a regression line, the LS or OLS algorithm chooses the intercept and slope that together minimize the SSR. The resulting line is said to be the "best linear fit" for the data.

Although this section used Excel's Solver to fit the OLS line in order to demonstrate the optimization problem that OLS solves, in practice no one computes regression lines that way. Instead, there are analytical solutions for the OLS line. In the next two sections we will discuss the formulas for the OLS regression line and ways to compute the slope and intercept in Excel.

4.3. Least Squares Formulas

Workbook: Reg.xls

The previous section showed that the OLS regression line is based on solving an optimization problem. We used Excel's Solver to find a numerical approximation to the optimal intercept and slope, but this is not the usual way to obtain the regression coefficients. Because an analytical solution to the minimization problem exists, it is simply a matter of applying a formula for the OLS solution to a particular data set. In this section we present mathematical notation for general representations of the OLS solutions and the formulas for the OLS intercept and slope. We show how to derive the formulas in an appendix to this chapter.

Notation

We first present the standard algebraic notation for the OLS model. We use the data in the *minSSR* sheet reproduced in Figure 4.3.1 as an example. There are n observations in the data set, and thus $n = 14$ in our example. Each row is an observation. Observations are labeled or indexed by a subscript.

The data in our example are $X_1 = 1, X_2 = 2$, and $X_3 = 3$, whereas $Y_1 = 87.3$, $Y_2 = 133.4$, and $Y_3 = 115.4$. To refer to an observation in general, without specifying which one it is, we use the subscript i. Thus (X_i, Y_i) are the

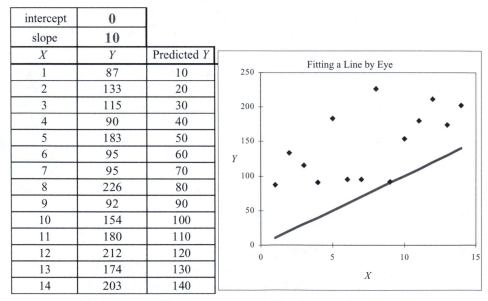

intercept	**0**	
slope	**10**	
X	Y	Predicted Y
1	87	10
2	133	20
3	115	30
4	90	40
5	183	50
6	95	60
7	95	70
8	226	80
9	92	90
10	154	100
11	180	110
12	212	120
13	174	130
14	203	140

Figure 4.3.1. Table and graph of data points and fitted line.
Source: [Reg.xls]minSSR.

coordinates of the ith observation. In this special example, the X values are the same as the index, and so $X_i = i$.

The intercept and slope coefficients for a regression line are designated with a letter b. Subscripts identify the coefficient: the intercept is b_0, and the slope is b_1. (Notice that the subscripts in this case index regression coefficients, not observations.) Thus, the general equation for Predicted Y given X is

$$\text{Predicted } Y_i = b_0 + b_1 X_i.$$

The residual is defined as the actual minus the predicted value:

$$\text{Residual}_i = Y_i - \text{Predicted } Y_i = Y_i - (b_0 + b_1 X_i).$$

For now, we will designate the OLS coefficients by a special superscript: b_0^{OLS} and b_1^{OLS}. To better understand what is going on, let us make the connections between the table in the Excel sheet and the abstract symbols. We set the values of b_0 and b_1 to 0 and 10, respectively, in the *minSSR* sheet and obtained Figure 4.3.1.

The choices of the intercept $b_0 = 0$ and slope $b_1 = 10$ are clearly not optimal – that is, they are not the best possible choices of intercept and slope. The fitted line you see in Figure 4.3.1 is not the OLS regression line. When working with the *minSSR* sheet, if at any time you want to see the symbols corresponding to a portion of the table, select the cell or cells you are interested in and click the Show Symbols button. To clear the symbols, click the Clear Symbols button.

The Predicted Y column contains values of $b_0 + b_1 X_i$ for each i. Thus, in the ninth row, $i = 9$, we have a predicted Y of $b_0 + b_1 X_9 = 0 + 10 \cdot 9 = 90$. The fitted line passes through all the predicted Y's, which are not separately identified in Figure 4.3.1. The residuals are formed by subtracting the Predicted Y for each X_i from the actual corresponding Y_i. For example, because $Y_9 = 92$ and $X_9 = 9$, the ninth residual is $92 - (0 + 10 \cdot 9) = 2.0$. In the graph in Figure 4.3.1, the ninth data point stands out because it is by far the closest point to the regression line. The tiny residual shows up as a slight vertical distance between the ninth data point and the regression line.

Each squared residual is displayed in column E. The ith squared residual is $[Y_i - (b_0 + b_1 X_i)]^2$. Thus, the ninth squared residual is

$$[Y_9 - (b_0 + b_1 X_9)]^2 = [92 - (0 + 10 \cdot 9)]^2 = 4.0.$$

In our abstract notation, the SSR becomes $\sum_{i=1}^{n} [Y_i - (b_0 + b_1 X_i)]^2$. The capital sigma, Σ, tells us that we are going to sum all the terms immediately to the right (the squared residuals); the $i = 1$ underneath the sigma says that each term is indexed by i and that we are starting with 1, and the n on top of the sigma signifies that there are n terms in total.

The OLS Formulas

Having developed the needed notation, we can now state the optimization problem. We want to find that combination of b_0 and b_1 that minimizes the sum of squared residuals: $\sum_{i=1}^{n} [Y_i - (b_0 + b_1 X_i)]^2$. We show how to solve this problem in the chapter appendix. For now, we simply give the formulas containing the solution.

The formulas for the OLS slope and intercept, b_0 and b_1, can be written in many ways, but we prefer the following:

$$b_1^{OLS} = \sum_{i=1}^{n} w_i \cdot Y_i$$

$$b_0^{OLS} = \bar{Y} - b_1^{OLS} \bar{X},$$

where the weights are given by

$$w_i = \frac{(X_i - \bar{X})}{\sum_{i=1}^{n} (X_i - \bar{X})^2}, i = 1, \ldots, n.$$

The formula for b_1 says that the OLS slope is computed as a weighted sum of the Y_i's. The weight (w_i) for each observation is the deviation of the corresponding value of X from the average value of all n X's divided by the sum of the squared X deviations. We can immediately see that X values farther from the average X have a greater weight. The OLS intercept is determined by solving for the Y-intercept using a point-slope approach in which the regression line goes through the point of averages. In the appendix we show how to derive these formulas using calculus.

Summary

Although the previous section showed how Excel's Solver can be used to find the least squares solution, this section has presented the formulas associated with the optimal solution. These formulas are used by computer software to report the coefficients for the OLS regression line. The next section explains the various ways Excel can be used to fit a regression line.

4.4. Fitting the Regression Line in Practice

Workbook: Reg.xls

The previous sections have shown that the regression line is based on solving an optimization problem. We used Excel's Solver and an analytical approach employing calculus and algebra to find the optimal intercept and slope. Of course, with modern statistical software, the user need not manually compute

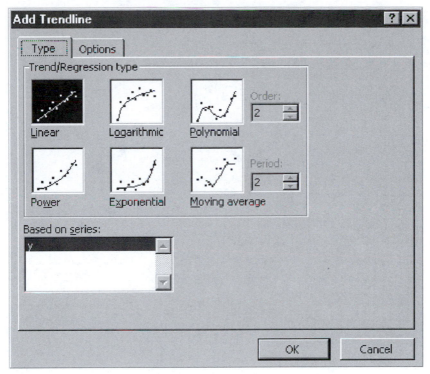

Figure 4.4.1. Adding a trendline to a scatter plot.

the optimal coefficients. A few clicks here and there are usually all that is required to generate a wealth of regression results.

Although Excel is not a full-fledged statistical package, it does offer several ways to run a regression. The *FourWays* sheet in Reg.xls explains four different methods and invites you to apply each of them.

The first and easiest way to fit a line is to create a scatter plot and then add what Excel calls a Trendline (see the *FourWays* sheet starting at row 12) by right-clicking on the plotted points and selecting the Add Trendline option. Figure 4.4.1 displays the "Add Trendline" dialog box in Excel.

Clicking the Options tab provides a variety of choices. Displaying the equation on the chart places a $y = mx + b$ text box on the chart. Unfortunately, displaying the equation with the variable names y and x is a poor default. You can (and should), however, edit the text box to provide more information about the variables

Although the Trendline approach is easy and fast, it is limited to bivariate regression. If more than one X variable is included, then Trendline cannot be used.

A second way to obtain regression results from Excel is to use the Data Analysis add-in. Execute Tools: Data Analysis and select the Regression option (see the *FourWays* sheet starting at row 43). Input the necessary

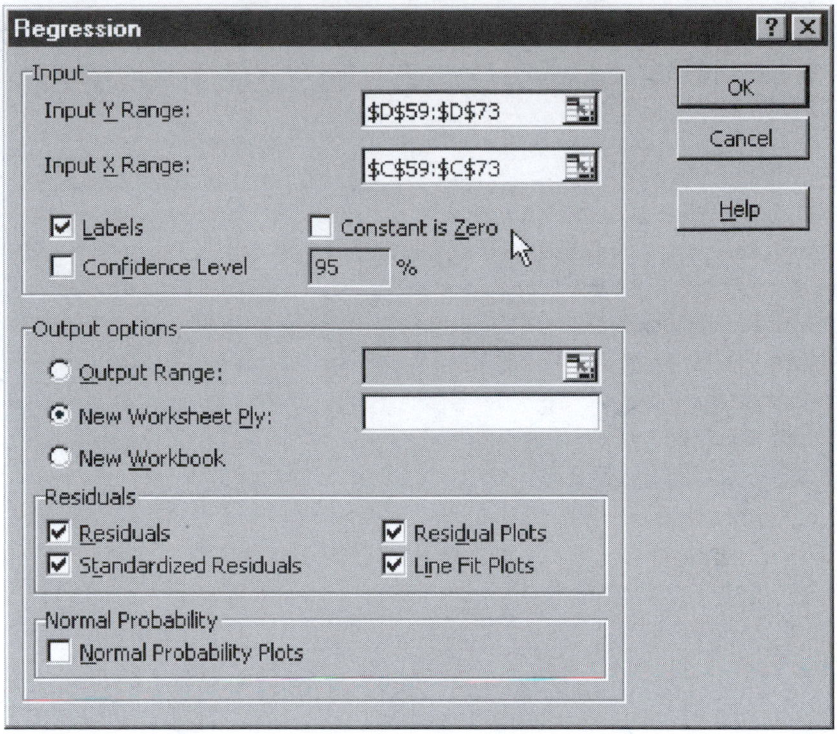

Figure 4.4.2. Data analysis: regression input.

information and click OK. Figure 4.4.2 displays a typical Data Analysis: Regression input.

Excel creates a new sheet with basic regression information, like the intercept and slope, and generates additional output that does not make much sense right now. The next chapter explains a few of these numbers, whereas others are explained in later chapters. A sample of the output reported is depicted in Figure 4.4.3.

In versions before Excel 2003, the Data Analysis: Regression approach has a known bug. Checking the Constant is Zero box generates incorrect results. This box should never be checked. Unless you are working with Excel 2003 or later, if you need to run a regression through the origin, forcing the intercept to be zero, you need to use another method.

One disadvantage of the Data Analysis: Regression approach is that it does not dynamically update the results if the underlying data change. Click on individual cells in the results to see that all of the cells are text and numbers – no formulas.

A third, and more powerful, way to run a regression in Excel is to use the LINEST array function (see the *FourWays* sheet starting at row 81). In Excel, arrays span more than one cell, and the results are put down in more than one cell. Because LINEST is a formula, Excel will update the results

SUMMARY OUTPUT						
Regression Statistics						
Multiple R	0.622631494					
R Square	0.387669977					
Adjusted R Square	0.336642476					
Standard Error	41.19700068					
Observations	14					
ANOVA						
	df	*SS*	*MS*	*F*	*Significance F*	
Regression	1	12894.04136	12894.04	7.597275	0.017397527	
Residual	12	20366.31438	1697.193			
Total	13	33260.35574				
	Coefficients	*Standard Error*	*t Stat*	*P-value*	*Lower 95%*	*Upper 95%*
Intercept	89.11337376	23.25647567	3.831766	0.002388	38.44186708	139.7848804
x	7.528419813	2.731334549	2.756316	0.017398	1.577353157	13.47948647

Figure 4.4.3. Sample data analysis: regression output.

after every recalculation. Unfortunately, LINEST is much more difficult to work with than the user-friendly interface of the Data Analysis: Regression approach.

The LINEST function has four parameters, each separated by a comma. The formula to be entered into an appropriate cell range is "=LINEST(*Y* value cell range, *X* value cell range, TRUE (or 1) to include an intercept in the regression or FALSE (or 0) if you want the line to go through the origin, TRUE (or 1) to report other regression results besides the slope and intercept or FALSE (or 0) to suppress additional regression output)." An example of the function (in cell range A148:C152 of the *FourWays* sheet) looks like this: =LINEST(E121:E140,B121:C140,1,1).

To use LINEST, you must select the appropriate cell range in which to place the output. The number of columns selected should equal the number of coefficients to be estimated. The number of rows to select depends on the output you want. If you just want the regression equation coefficients, the selected range should contain only one row. If you would like the full set of regression results, then the range must be five rows deep. Figure 4.4.4 shows two possibilities.

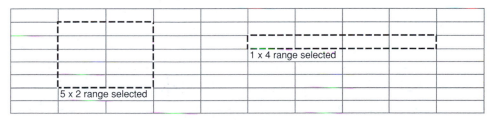

Figure 4.4.4. Possible LINEST output ranges.

Figure 4.4.5. LINEST error message.

With the appropriate cell range selected, you are ready to type in the LINEST function and input the necessary information. Type "=LINEST(" and then select the cell range with the *y* data. Then type a comma and select the *x* data. After selecting the cell range with the *x* data and typing in the 0 (FALSE) or 1 (TRUE) intercept and statistics options, finish the formula by closing the parentheses, but do not do anything else just yet.

The last step is to hit the keyboard combination Ctrl-Shift-Enter. This is the way all array functions are entered in Excel. The results are displayed throughout the cells that contain the LINEST array function. Once the LINEST array formula is entered, all of the cells in the range have the same formula within a pair of curly brackets, { }.

Because LINEST is an array formula that spans several cells, you cannot edit the formula by working with a single cell and hitting Enter. If you want to change the array formula, you must type in the change, and then press Ctrl-Shift-Enter. Failure to correctly edit the array formula can be quite frustrating because Excel will continue to flash the dialog box depicted in Figure 4.4.5. If this happens, remember that you need to enter the Ctrl-Shift-Enter combination to actually enter the formula. You can always hit the aptly named escape, ESC, key to get out of a cell.

Having correctly entered the LINEST function, you must now interpret the output. Unlike the Data Analysis: Regression approach, LINEST has no descriptive titles whatsoever. The user simply has to know the format of the output. Figure 4.4.6 displays two examples of the results that make the organization of the LINEST output clear.

$Y = b_0 + b_1 X$					
b_1	b_0				
SE(b_1)	SE(b_0)				
R^2	RMSE				
F	df				
RegSS	SSR				

$Y = b_0 + b_1 X_1 + b_2 X_2 + b_3 X_3$			
b_3	b_2	b_1	b_0
SE(b_3)	SE(b_2)	SE(b_1)	SE(b_0)
R^2	RMSE	#N/A	#N/A
F	df	#N/A	#N/A
RegSS	SSR	#N/A	#N/A

Figure 4.4.6. LINEST output organization.

On the left of Figure 4.4.6 is the output arrangement of a bivariate regression, and a multiple regression is depicted on the right. Both show all of the statistics reported. Notice that the coefficients are reported in "backwards" order. Although we have yet to explain some of the displayed statistics, they are standard regression output and will be covered in later chapters. The output itself might look like Figure 4.4.7.

You interpret the output in Figure 4.4.7 by matching the cells to the organizational map in Figure 4.4.6. For example, the number 17 is the df (or degrees of freedom) in the regression. The #N/A indicates that no value is available.

If the same output is provided by the Data Analysis: Regression approach, why use the more difficult LINEST strategy? The primary advantage of LINEST is that it is a formula that is recalculated if the underlying cells change. Thus, unlike Data Analysis: Regression, which has dead output, the LINEST output dynamically updates if the Y or X cell ranges are changed.

The final way to run a regression with Excel is even more primitive, and powerful, than LINEST. Excel has a series of linear algebra array functions that can be used to compute the coefficient vector via matrix algebra. This approach is beyond the level of this introductory econometrics book, but the interested reader may explore this advanced strategy beginning in row 159 of the *FourWays* sheet.[5]

With four ways to run a regression in Excel, which method is best? The answer depends on the type of regression, output needed, and whether the data will be changed. For a bivariate regression without the full set of statistical output, the Trendline method is quick and easy. The Data Analysis: Regression add-in provides a simple user interface and a full set of regression results for multiple regression. If the underlying data are going to be changed or you would like to display the results immediately next to the data in compact fashion, LINEST can be a good approach. Because of its array function nature and raw output, LINEST can be difficult to master. Finally, the matrix algebra approach is even more complicated to implement than LINEST but permits sophisticated calculations such as generalized least squares. Ironically, the simplest method, using the Trendline, is the only one that can handle missing data. If one of the values is replaced with a "." indicating

10.011404	5.045904	99.04957
0.0100483	0.050703	0.654067
0.9999843	1.282514	#N/A
541082.06	17	#N/A
1779989.2	27.96232	#N/A

Figure 4.4.7. A possible LINEST output.

[5] In Visual Basic macros in Excel workbooks, we employ both of the two final approaches, LINEST and matrix algebra, to run regressions; however, these operate behind the scenes. The OLS Regression add-in, introduced in Chapter 19, uses Excel's matrix capabilities for advanced regression procedures. It is yet another way to run a regression in Excel.

a missing value, all the other methods will fail, but the Trendline method will still produce a regression line based on the remaining observations.

Summary

This section demonstrated a variety of ways to run a regression in Excel. LINEST is our usual method. Remember to hit the ESC key if you have trouble editing LINEST or any other array function.

Finally, note that we employ Excel as a teaching tool and do not recommend its use for serious work in econometrics. Excel can usually (not always!) be relied on to provide correct results for simple analyses such as would be found in the typical term paper in introductory econometrics classes. To be assured of accuracy, however, it is best to use a specialized software package.

4.5. Conclusion

This chapter has introduced the regression line and focused on the computation of the OLS regression line. Although regression is understood geometrically as a fitted line, the theoretical foundation of OLS regression is the idea that the coefficients of the line are computed as the solution to an optimization problem. If the objective function of the optimization problem is to minimize the SSR, then the OLS line is the result. To actually fit a line to data, computer software relies on formulas that can be derived via calculus from the minimize-SSR problem. Excel, although not a full-fledged statistical package, offers rudimentary regression capabilities.

This chapter has shown how to obtain a fitted line. In the process, you have seen a bewildering array of information such as R^2 values, SEs, and much more. This has made clear that there is much more to regression analysis than simply fitting a line. The next chapter is the beginning of our explanation of regression output. The first step is to understand how to interpret the regression line.

4.6. Exercises

1. For one observation, $X = 5$ and $Y = 10$ and Predicted Y is 8. For another observation, $X = 9$ and $Y = 17$ and Predicted Y is 16. Both Predicted Y's are on the same regression line. Find the Intercept (b_0) and Slope (b_1) and the residuals.
2. Suppose that Joe proposes a zero-sum-of-residuals regression line. Joe says, "Just pick the unique straight line that produces a sum of residuals equal to zero." Susan says, "That is guaranteed to be the average Y line." What is wrong with Joe's reasoning? What is wrong with Susan's reasoning?
3. The formula for the OLS slope is sometimes written as follows:

$$b_1^{\text{OLS}} = \frac{\sum_{i=1}^{n} x_i y_i}{\sum_{i=1}^{n} x_i^2},$$

where $y_i = Y_i - \bar{Y}, i = 1, \ldots, n$, and $x_i = X_i - \bar{X}, i = 1, \ldots, n$. This is in fact completely equivalent to our formula

$$b_1^{\text{OLS}} = \sum_{i=1}^{n} w_i \cdot Y_i,$$

where

$$w_i = \frac{(X_i - \bar{X})}{\sum_{i=1}^{n} (X_i - \bar{X})^2}, i = 1, \ldots, n.$$

Show this using algebra. (See Q&A #3 in the Reg.xls workbook for a concrete version of the same problem.)

4. The one case in which the formula for the bivariate OLS regression line does not work arises when all of the X's take on the same value. Explain what goes wrong mathematically.

5. Recall that the formula for the OLS intercept is $b_0^{\text{OLS}} = \bar{Y} - b_1^{\text{OLS}} \bar{X}$.

    Show that the formula for b_0^{OLS} guarantees that the point of averages is on the regression line no matter what the formula is for the OLS slope b_1^{OLS}.

References

The history of fitting a line based on minimizing the SSR is complicated. In the late 1700s and early 1800s, Carl Friedrich Gauss in Germany, Adrien-Marie Legendre in France, and Robert Adrain in the United States independently developed the method of least squares to varying degrees of completeness. For more on this development, we recommend Stigler, S. M. (1986) (full reference in Chapter 3). In the abstract to "Gauss and the Invention of Least Squares," *The Annals of Statistics* **9**(3): 465–474, Stigler states his opinion on "the most famous priority dispute in the history of statistics": "It is argued (though not conclusively) that Gauss probably possessed the method well before Legendre, but that he was unsuccessful in communicating it to his contemporaries."

The quotation at the beginning of the chapter is an excerpt from "Sur la Méthode des moindres quarrés" in Legendre's *Nouvelles méthodes pour la détermination des orbites des comètes*, Paris 1805 translated by H. A. Ruger and H. M. Walker and taken from D. E. Smith (1929, 1959). *A Source Book in Mathematics*, McGraw-Hill and Dover, Volume II, pp. 576–579. Our source was <www.york.ac.uk/depts/maths/histstat/legendre.pdf>.

Appendix: Deriving the Least Squares Formulas

In this appendix we derive the OLS formulas for the intercept and slope using calculus.

The Optimization Problem in Abstract Notation

Choosing an intercept and slope to minimize the SSR can be written in mathematical form as follows:

$$\min_{b_0, b_1} \sum_{i=1}^{n} [Y_i - (b_0 + b_1 X_i)]^2.$$

Many readers will find the preceding expression intimidating. To understand what it means, start by noting that b_0 and b_1 are choice variables. The goal is to find the unique combination of these two variables that minimizes the sum of the n terms. Those solutions will be b_0^{OLS} and b_1^{OLS}. This way of stating the problem is just an abstract version of what you have already seen in the *minSSR* sheet of Reg.xls. The abstract expression is perfectly general – it applies to any number of data points, any values of X's and Y's, and any intercept and slope.

To solve the optimization problem, $\min_{b_0, b_1} \sum_{i=1}^{n} [Y_i - (b_0 + b_1 X_i)]^2$, first take derivatives with respect to both of the choice variables:

$$\frac{\partial}{\partial b_0}\left[\sum_{i=1}^{n}(Y_i - b_0 - b_1 X_i)^2\right] = -2\sum_{i=1}^{n}(Y_i - b_0 - b_1 X_i)$$

$$\frac{\partial}{\partial b_1}\left[\sum_{i=1}^{n}(Y_i - b_0 - b_1 X_i)^2\right] = -2\sum_{i=1}^{n}(Y_i - b_0 - b_1 X_i)X_i.$$

Then set the derivatives equal to zero:

$$-2\sum_{i=1}^{n}(Y_i - b_0^* - b_1^* X_i) = 0$$

$$-2\sum_{i=1}^{n}(Y_i - b_0^* - b_1^* X_i)X_i = 0.$$

The asterisks (*) in this second set of equations indicate that b_0^* and b_1^* are the optimal values of the slope and intercept, respectively.[6] Dividing each equation by –2 and rearranging terms, we obtain the following equations:

$$\sum_{i=1}^{n} Y_i = nb_0^* + b_1^* \sum_{i=1}^{n} X_i$$

$$\sum_{i=1}^{n} Y_i X_i = b_0^* \sum_{i=1}^{n} X_i + b_1^* \sum_{i=1}^{n} X_i^2.$$

We need to solve these two equations for b_0^* and b_1^*, the intercept and slope, respectively, of the least squares regression line. Despite their seeming complexity, we have two equations in two unknowns. We begin by solving for b_0^* using the first equation:

$$b_0^* = \frac{\sum_{i=1}^{n} Y_i - b_1^* \sum_{i=1}^{n} X_i}{n}$$

$$= \frac{\sum_{i=1}^{n} Y_i}{n} - b_1^* \frac{\sum_{i=1}^{n} X_i}{n}$$

$$= \bar{Y} - b_1^* \bar{X}.$$

Here $\bar{X}$ is the average value of the X_i's in the data set, and $\bar{Y}$ is the average value of the Y_i's in the data set. Next, substitute for b_0^* in the second equation and

---

[6] We will not bother to examine the second-order conditions to be sure that we are finding a minimum, but they can be shown to be satisfied.

solve for b_1^*:

$$\sum_{i=1}^{n} Y_i X_i = (\bar{Y} - b_1^* \bar{X}) \cdot \sum_{i=1}^{n} X_i + b_1^* \sum_{i=1}^{n} X_i^2$$

$$b_1^* \cdot \left(\sum_{i=1}^{n} X_i^2 - \bar{X} \sum_{i=1}^{n} X_i \right) = \sum_{i=1}^{n} Y_i X_i - \bar{Y} \cdot \sum_{i=1}^{n} X_i$$

$$b_1^* = \frac{\sum_{i=1}^{n} Y_i X_i - \bar{Y} \cdot \sum_{i=1}^{n} X_i}{\sum_{i=1}^{n} X_i^2 - \bar{X} \sum_{i=1}^{n} X_i}.$$

This not-too-appealing formula can be written in several equivalent ways. The way we prefer to think about the OLS regression formula is to regard the OLS slope, b_1, as a weighted average of the Y's. That is, we write the OLS formulas for slope and intercept as

$$b_1^{OLS} = \sum_{i=1}^{n} w_i \cdot Y_i$$

$$b_0^{OLS} = \bar{Y} - b_1^{OLS} \bar{X},$$

where the weights are given by

$$w_i = \frac{(X_i - \bar{X})}{\sum_{i=1}^{n} (X_i - \bar{X})^2}, i = 1, \ldots, n.$$

We will use this expression in the next chapter when we take a closer look at the properties of the OLS regression method.

To see where we get the formula for the slope, you need to realize that both the numerator and denominator in the equation

$$b_1^* = \frac{\sum_{i=1}^{n} Y_i X_i - \bar{Y} \cdot \sum_{i=1}^{n} X_i}{\sum_{i=1}^{n} X_i^2 - \bar{X} \sum_{i=1}^{n} X_i}$$

can be rewritten. Take a look at the numerator $\sum_{i=1}^{n} Y_i X_i - \bar{Y} \cdot \sum_{i=1}^{n} X_i$. Replace $\bar{Y}$ with $\frac{1}{n} \cdot \sum_{i=1}^{n} Y_i$. We then have the following expression for the numerator:

$$\sum_{i=1}^{n} Y_i X_i - \left(\frac{1}{n} \cdot \sum_{i=1}^{n} Y_i \right) \sum_{i=1}^{n} X_i.$$

The three terms after the minus sign can be interchanged. Move the sum $\sum_{i=1}^{n} X_i$ to the second position, recognizing that $\bar{X} = \frac{1}{n} \sum_{i=1}^{n} X_i$, and we end up with the numerator rewritten as

$$\sum_{i=1}^{n} Y_i X_i - \bar{X} \sum_{i=1}^{n} Y_i.$$

In this expression, each Y_i term is multiplied by $X_i - \bar{X}$, and so we can write the numerator as

$$\sum_{i=1}^{n} Y_i (X_i - \bar{X}).$$

Now let us tackle the denominator $\sum_{i=1}^{n} X_i^2 - \bar{X} \sum_{i=1}^{n} X_i$. We can show that this is equivalent to $\sum_{i=1}^{n} (X_i - \bar{X})^2$ simply by expanding the latter expression:

$$\sum_{i=1}^{n} (X_i - \bar{X})^2 = \sum_{i=1}^{n} \left(X_i^2 - 2X_i \bar{X} + \bar{X}^2 \right)$$

$$= \sum_{i=1}^{n} X_i^2 - 2 \sum_{i=1}^{n} X_i \bar{X} + n\bar{X}^2$$

$$= \sum_{i=1}^{n} X_i^2 - 2\bar{X} \sum_{i=1}^{n} X_i + n\bar{X}^2$$

$$= \sum_{i=1}^{n} X_i^2 - 2\bar{X} \sum_{i=1}^{n} X_i + \bar{X} \cdot n\bar{X}$$

$$= \sum_{i=1}^{n} X_i^2 - 2\bar{X} \sum_{i=1}^{n} X_i + \bar{X} \cdot \sum_{i=1}^{n} X_i$$

$$= \sum_{i=1}^{n} X_i^2 - \bar{X} \sum_{i=1}^{n} X_i.$$

Notice that in going from the first line to the second we use the fact that each of the n terms in the summation has an $\bar{X}^2$ in it, and this leads to the $n\bar{X}^2$ term. Farther down, we make use of the fact that $n\bar{X} = \sum_{i=1}^{n} X_i$. Finally, put the numerator and denominator together, and we end up with

$$\frac{\sum_{i=1}^{n} Y_i X_i - \bar{Y} \cdot \sum_{i=1}^{n} X_i}{\sum_{i=1}^{n} X_i^2 - \bar{X} \sum_{i=1}^{n} X_i} = \sum_{i=1}^{n} \left[\frac{(X_i - \bar{X})}{\sum_{i=1}^{n} (X_i - \bar{X})^2} \right] Y_i,$$

which is what we wanted to show because the portion in the brackets is just w_i.

5

Interpreting OLS Regression

When Mid-Parents are taller than mediocrity, their Children tend to be shorter than they. When Mid-Parents are shorter than mediocrity, their Children tend to be taller than they.

Francis Galton[1]

5.1. Introduction

In the previous chapter, we introduced the OLS regression line. This chapter is about interpreting regression in several different senses of the word. Section 5.2 interprets what regression does by exploring the way in which it compresses information about a scatter diagram. We then go on to compare the regression line to the SD line. Another interpretation, in Section 5.3, takes advantage of regression's historical roots. We show how regression was first used and point out that there are in fact two regression lines for summarizing the relationship between two variables. Section 5.4 examines regression from another angle, interpreting the regression slope as a weighted sum of the Y values. This will make clear that regression coefficients are closely related to the sum (and average). Next, Sections 5.5 and 5.6, demonstrate how to interpret the output from a regression, including the residuals and two new statistics called the RMSE and R^2. We show how regression output can be used to reveal important characteristics about the underlying data. Finally, Section 5.7, examines some of the limitations of regression analysis as a descriptive tool. Regression is not always appropriate and may mislead the reader.

5.2. Regression as Double Compression

Workbooks: DoubleCompression.xls; EastNorthCentralFTWorkers.xls

Regression answers a question about the relationship and movement between variables. Given a value of X, the regression line predicts Y. This section shows

---

[1] Galton (1886, Plate IX after p. 248).

how the prediction from the regression line can be understood as a double compression of the data.

In the first compression, the scatter diagram is replaced by the conditional mean function (discussed in Section 3.4). The conditional mean function (CMF for short) corresponds directly to a table showing the average of a variable at different levels of a second variable. Its graphical representation is the *graph of averages*. The second compression linearizes the CMF. In other words, the regression line smoothes out the squiggly relationship generated by plotting the conditional average of Y given X.

Let us examine each of the two steps in the double compression with an actual numerical example. Open the file called *DoubleCompression.xls* and note we are using the SAT example from the chapter on correlation. In addition to the univariate statistics, we report the correlation coefficient r. The correlation coefficient, however, does not reveal much about the movement of the two variables. Indeed, because r is positive, a higher than average Verbal score indicates a higher than average Math score is likely, but how much higher the Math score will be is unclear. The correlation coefficient does not help you answer that question.

First Compression

The first compression generates the CMF. Click on the *VerticalStrip* sheet to see what this means. The idea is that, within each category or range of the X variable, Verbal SAT, a vertical strip can be created. The average value of Y, Math SAT, given X, Verbal SAT, can then be computed. Click on the scroll bar to see this. If you place the cursor over an observation and leave it there for a moment, the Excel will report the value of predicted Math SAT. Figure 5.2.1 depicts one such point.

The example shows that when the Verbal SAT score is in a range around 470, the average Math SAT score is about 560. In fact, because SAT scores are reported in intervals of 10, the SAT range around 470 includes only individuals who scored 470 on the SAT. You can inspect the observations within each vertical strip by looking at columns J and K of the *VerticalStrip* sheet.

After playing with this example for a while, click on the *Accordion* sheet. The idea here is that the first compression of regression is like an expanding accordion. Start with No Intervals, which is like a completely compacted accordion. This situation says, predict the Math SAT score of a person in the data set given no information about that person's Verbal SAT score. The best prediction you can make in this case is the average Math SAT score for all the people in the data set.

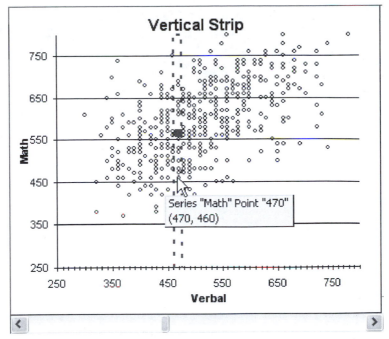

Figure 5.2.1. A point on the CMF (or graph of averages).
Source: [DoubleCompression.xls]VerticalStrip.

Now, click on the ⟨Two Intervals⟩ button. The accordion has been slightly pulled apart. If you know whether a student has a high or low Verbal SAT, you can use this information to predict that student's Verbal SAT better.

Clicking on the ⟨Four Intervals⟩ button provides even more information. When you click on the ⟨Many Intervals⟩ button, the accordion is almost fully opened – nearly every possible Verbal score is represented on the graph.[2] This is the graph of averages or CMF, as shown in Figure 5.2.2. Notice how the relationship between the two variables is emphasized. Individual variation (above and below the average) is hidden. Each point tells you the typical Math SAT given a particular Verbal SAT.

The graph of averages can be used as follows: Suppose you know that a particular individual in the data set has a Verbal SAT score of 430. Starting from 430 on the x-axis, travel straight up to find that the corresponding point has coordinates (430,495.9). The 495.9 is derived from the Verbal SAT = 430 vertical strip. It tells you that the average Math SAT score of all the people in the applicant pool who received a 430 on the Verbal SAT was 495.9. You could use this fact to make a prediction of the individual's Math SAT – 495.9 – based on your knowledge that this person received a Verbal SAT score of 430.

[2] To make the picture prettier, we have hidden some of the really low and high Verbal SAT scores.

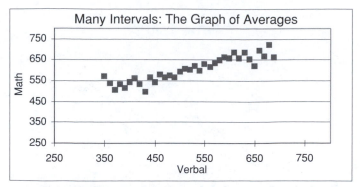

Figure 5.2.2. Average Math SAT given Verbal SAT.
Source: [DoubleCompression.xls]Accordion.

The graph of averages is the graphical equivalent of the PivotTable in the *AccordionPivot* sheet, only part of which is displayed Figure 5.2.3.

Note that, because Verbal SAT scores in this data set are reported to the nearest 10, the range 345–354 actually contains only people with scores of 350 on the Verbal SAT. The graph of averages conveys the same information by plotting a point with x-coordinate 350 and y-coordinate 568.33.

So far, we have taken roughly 500 observations on Verbal and Math SAT and summarized them with 35 points. This is a large compression of the data; however, one more compression is required before we have a regression line.

Second Compression

The graph of averages, which is obtained by a first compression of the data (hiding the individual points), is not yet the regression line. To obtain the regression line, we perform a second compression, linearizing the graph of averages. Click on the ⟨Regression Line w/ Averages⟩ button in the *Accordion* sheet to see how this works.

The graph in Figure 5.2.4 should make it clear that the regression line is a smoothed linear version of the graph of averages. The process of smoothing the graph of averages is the second compression. This line can be represented by the following simple single equation:

Predicted Math SAT $= 318 + 0.54$ Verbal SAT.

Average of Math	
Verbal ▾	Total
345–354	568.33
355–364	537.78
365–374	502.00
375–384	531.11
385–394	512.00

Figure 5.2.3. Average Math SAT given Verbal SAT – The PivotTable.
Source: [DoubleCompression.xls]AccordionPivot.

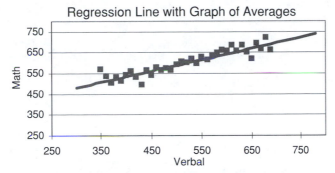

Figure 5.2.4. The second compression.
Source: [DoubleCompression.xls]Accordion.

This equation should be read as follows: Given a particular Verbal SAT score, multiply it by 0.54 and add 318. The result is the predicted Math SAT score. The regression line takes about 500 observations and summarizes them with just two numbers: the slope and intercept of the line. Algebraically, 318 is the *y*-axis intercept of the line and 0.54 is the slope of the line.

The benefit from regression can be great. In one quick look, hundreds of observations are summarized by a line or by the corresponding single, simple linear equation. Given Verbal SAT, the predicted Math SAT is easily computed. No recourse to a complicated table is needed. This makes regression a powerful descriptive tool.

As with every summary, the gain in brevity comes at a cost. In this case, the second compression hides the movement in the squiggly graph of averages. Not only are the individual observations hidden, but so too are the average-*Y*-given-*X* summaries. Regression is a severe double compression of the data.

Yearly Earnings Regressed on Education

Here is another example of how regression can be used to summarize data based on the EastNorthCentralFTWorkers.xls data set.[3] We are interested in answering the following question: Given that a particular observation has a particular value of the independent variable, Education, what is the value of the dependent variable, Yearly Earnings, that we expect to observe for that observation? Figure 5.2.5 presents the vertical strips/PivotTable method of summarizing the data and answering the question.

We can use this table to make predictions of an individual's yearly earnings based on what we know about his or her level of education. For example, if we know that the person has 12 years of education, we can use the average

---

[3] Data for this example come from the *Regression* sheet in the file, which is contained in Ch03PivotTables \ ExcelFiles folder. To view the data, you must unhide the *Regression* sheet.

Education	Average Yearly Earnings
8	$ 17,662
9	$ 24,044
10	$ 20,386
11	$ 19,976
11.5	$ 20,851
12	$ 27,934
13	$ 33,888
14	$ 35,687
16	$ 48,907
18	$ 76,187

Figure 5.2.5. Average yearly earnings by education level.
Source: [EastNorthCentralFTWorkers.xls]Regression.

yearly earnings of all those in the data set with 12 years of education as our prediction of the yearly earnings of such a person. In this case, that prediction would be $27,934.

Regression provides another way of summarizing the data. Here is the equation we obtain for our regression with the yearly earnings data:

$$\text{Predicted Yearly Earnings} = -47325 + 6310 \cdot \text{Education}.$$

Figure 5.2.6 shows the scatter plot, the regression line, and the graph of averages. Almost all the data points are plotted here, though we cut off some of the really high-earnings people. Thus, there are about 6,200 dots, but they blur into each other. You see vertical strips because Education comes in discrete jumps. The squiggly line is the graph of averages, which corresponds to

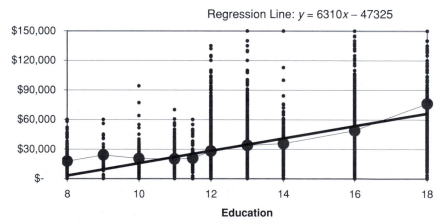

Figure 5.2.6. Regression of yearly earnings on education.
Source: [EastNorthCentralFTWorkers.xls]Regression.

Slope	Intercept	
6310	−47325	
	Predicted Yearly	Average Yearly
Education	Earnings	Earnings
8	$ 3,155	$ 17,662
9	$ 9,465	$ 24,044
10	$ 15,775	$ 20,386
11	$ 22,085	$ 19,976
11.5	$ 25,240	$ 20,851
12	$ 28,395	$ 27,934
13	$ 34,705	$ 33,888
14	$ 41,015	$ 35,687
16	$ 53,635	$ 48,907
18	$ 66,255	$ 76,187

Figure 5.2.7. Predicted yearly earnings at different education levels via regression.
Source: [EastNorthCentralFTWorkers.xls] Regression.

the table in Figure 5.2.5. The straight line is the regression line. The figure shows that the regression line approximates the graph of averages. Figure 5.2.7 displays this approximation in tabular form. By simply evaluating the line at the given values of Education, the table of conditional averages can be approximated as it is in Figure 5.2.7.

Because the CMF and regression lines do not give the same predicted Y (Yearly Earnings) given a value of X (Education), how do we decide which one to use? Economists typically prefer regression. It provides an instant read on the relationship between the two variables via a single, simple equation. Not only is the CMF harder to appreciate, but economists often believe that the underlying relationship is a smooth function better approximated by the straight regression line than the meandering line of the CMF.[4]

Regression versus the SD Line

Having explored the connection between the CMF and the regression line, we need to clear up a potential confusion over another pair of lines – the regression and SD lines. In a Chapter 2, we introduced the correlation coefficient as a summary measure of the association between two variables. We saw that the points cluster around the SD line (with slope SD_Y/SD_X). Could the regression and SD lines be the same?

They could for a special case, but they are almost always different. It turns out that the SD line fails miserably as a predictor of y given x. If we were to use points on the SD line as predictors of the value of the dependent variable given particular values of the independent variable, we would make systematic mistakes.

---

[4] Careful observers will question how well the regression does at summarizing the relationship for lower levels of education.

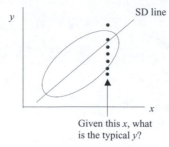

Figure 5.2.8. Poor prediction with the SD line.

Figure 5.2.8 shows why the SD line does not accurately report the typical value of Y given the value of X. You would not choose the point on the SD line. Instead your prediction would be below the SD line somewhere in the middle of the points in the vertical strip. Using the value of Y from the SD line leads to poor performance in predicting Y because most of the points, including the average Y given that X, are below the SD line.

A numerical example based on the SAT data will demonstrate this concept. The SD Line overpredicts above the average Verbal SAT and underpredicts below the average Verbal SAT. Figure 5.2.9 presents this example (scroll down to row 50 in the *SATData* sheet to see the figure).

Notice that both the SD line and the regression line go through the point of averages, and thus at the average level of the X variable both give the same answer to our question about predicting the Math SAT value for a person having a particular Verbal SAT score.

But what accounts for the difference in the two lines when we are not at the average X? It is a mathematical fact that the slope of the regression line is simply the correlation coefficient r multiplied by the slope of the SD line. This explains the conditions under which the two are the same: $|r| = 1$ and $r = 0$. Whenever $0 < r < 1$, as in the SAT example, the regression line will have a smaller slope (and a flatter shape) than the SD line because the SD line's slope is being multiplied by a positive number smaller than 1. You can work out the relationship between the two lines for r between -1 and 0.

Of course, by far the usual case is a nonperfect and nonzero correlation coefficient. Then the extent to which the SD line and the regression line diverge from one another is dictated by the value of the correlation coefficient. The bigger in absolute value the correlation coefficient, the tighter the clustering of the data around the SD line and the closer the SD and regression lines are to each other.

Finally, we point out that the mathematical fact that the slope of the regression line is equal to $r \frac{SD_Y}{SD_X}$ means that the SD line and the correlation coefficient together provide a handy way to compute the regression line. Thus, suppose

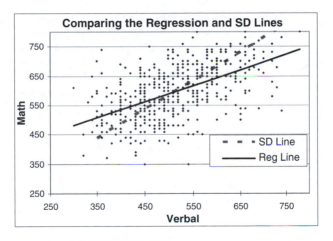

	Slope	Intercept
Reg Line	0.539465	318.9403
SD Line	0.977853	94.59735

Verbal SAT	Reg Line Pred Math SAT	SD Line Pred Math SAT
350	508	437
450	562	535
550	616	632
650	670	730
750	724	828

Figure 5.2.9. Regression and SD lines with SAT data.
Source: [DoubleCompression.xls]SATData.

you have the five basic bivariate summary statistics (averages and SDs of X and Y along with r). You can then create a mind's eye scatter diagram of the cloud of points, SD line, and even the regression line. It is also immediately obvious that the slope of the regression line will have the same sign as the correlation coefficient.

Summary

In Chapter 4, we saw that the OLS regression line is computed as the solution to an optimization problem (i.e., as the choice of intercept and slope that minimize the sum of squared residuals). This section has pointed out that a fitted regression line can also be interpreted as a double compression of the data. The double compression proceeds by first generating the graph of averages or conditional mean function and then linearizing that graph. The regression line thereby provides a quick and concise summary of the relationship between two variables.

5.3. Galton and Two Regression Lines

Workbook: TwoRegressionLines.xls

This section discusses some of the work of Francis Galton (1822–1911), the British polymath who discovered regression in the 1870s and 1880s. Galton hoped to discover universal laws of heredity. He was specifically interested in the extent to which children inherit characteristics of their parents. A crucial data set, for example, contained data on parents' heights and their sons' heights. Galton came up with the regression line as a way of summarizing the average height of children born to parents of differing heights.[5] In the course of his research, he obtained three key insights regarding regression:

1. For many data sets, the graph of averages can be well approximated by a straight line, the regression line.
2. The regression line always has a slope less than or equal to (in absolute value) the slope of the SD line.
3. There are in fact two regression lines as determined by the variable you are trying to predict.

We have already discussed the first two points in the previous section. Galton chose the term *regression* because the slope of the regression line is always shallower than that of the SD line. He found that sons of taller-than-average parents tended to be shorter than their parents (and, thus, closer to the mean), whereas sons of shorter-than-average parents tended to be taller than their parents (and, once again, closer to the mean). Thus, there was a tendency for children to revert to the average or mean. Eventually, Galton changed reversion to regression, and the latter name stuck.

Galton's third insight, the phenomenon of two regression lines, is a striking fact that at first seems counterintuitive. In theoretical discussions, a single line generally summarizes the relationship between two variables. In basic economics, supply and demand are good examples. The ceteris paribus relationship between price and quantity demanded is a single line. It does not matter which variable goes on the x-axis, for the same line describes the theoretical relationship. (Of course, one must be careful about the slope and y-intercept.) With regression lines, however, it is not possible to solve simply for X in terms of Y – there really are two separate regression lines.

The key to understanding that there are indeed two lines is to realize that each line is the answer to a different question. The Excel file TwoRegression-Lines.xls gives an illustration, using the SAT data set. The *SATData* sheet contains the data, the Verbal and Math SAT scores for 527 applicants to

---

[5] Galton used the average of the parents' heights. It is of interest to note that Galton experimented with other means of central tendency besides averages (e.g., the median).

Graphs of Averages: Verbal on *X*-Axis

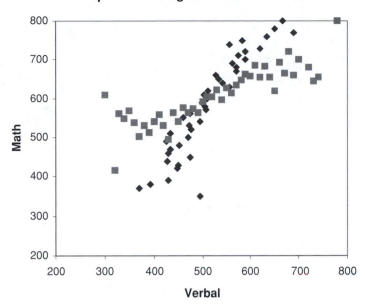

Figure 5.3.1. Two graphs of averages for the SAT data.
Source: [TwoRegressionLines.xls]PivotTables.

Wabash College and shows a scatter plot with Verbal scores arbitrarily displayed on the *x*-axis and Math scores on the *y*-axis. Go to the *PivotTables* sheet, which displays two pivot tables. The left table shows the average values of Math at different levels of Verbal. The graphical analogue of this table is the pink graph of averages. This first pivot table answers the question, Given that a student's Verbal score is such and such, what Math score do we predict for that student? The second pivot table answers a different, though related, question: Given that a student's Math score is such and such, what Verbal score do we predict for that student?

Take a moment to read the last two sentences again carefully. The two questions are different because they start from different places. Figure 5.3.1 shows the two graphs of averages.

The squares are the answers to the question, Starting from the Verbal score, what Math score do we anticipate? The squares are the averages inside vertical strips. This is the graph of averages presented in the previous section. The diamonds are the answers to the question that begins instead from the different Math scores and answers with the expected Verbal score. The diamonds are the averages of horizontal strips because the Math scores are plotted on the *y*-axis. The button beneath the graph is a toggle that will switch the axes.

So far, only the graphs of averages have been displayed. The *TwoLines* sheet illustrates the two regression lines that summarize their respective

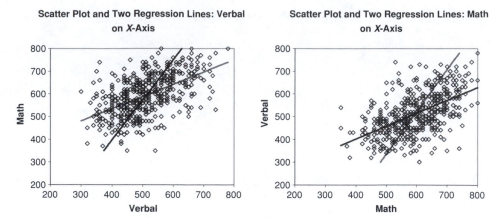

Figure 5.3.2. The two regression lines plotted both ways.
Source: [TwoRegressionLines.xls]TwoLines.

graphs of averages. The two buttons below the graph toggle. One controls
the axes and the other switches the display from the regression lines superimposed on the original scatter plot to the graph of averages. Figure 5.3.2
displays the two scatter plots.

Notice that in each case the regression line describing how the predicted
value of the *y*-axis variable varies as the *x*-axis variable changes is the shallower line. The other regression line, the one that describes how the predicted
value of the *x*-axis variable varies as the *y*-axis variable changes, is the steeper
line. You should be able to convince yourself that, in each case, the shallower
line is a much better approximation to the graph of averages (based on *vertical*
strips) than the other line would be. However, the very same line, when trans-
posed to the other graph as a result of the switch in axes, becomes the steeper
line and does a poor job of predicting the *y*-variable based on the *x*-variable.
The two lines agree only at the point of averages for the entire data set.

Understanding that there are two regression lines requires the ability to
interpret regression as a conditional average. Because regression answers
the question Given *X*, what is predicted *Y*? a regression line cannot be algebraically manipulated to solve for *x* in terms of *y*. For example, Predicted
Math = 318.9 + 0.5395 Verbal cannot be used to predict Verbal given Math.
Solving for Verbal yields – 591.2 + 1.8537 Predicted Math, and this is not the
same as the regression line Predicted Verbal = 176.1 + 0.5642 Math (see cell
H28 in the *TwoLines* sheet for the calculations). Note that the variable names
are not the same – Verbal is not Predicted Verbal and Math is not Predicted
Math. This is merely another way of saying that there are two regression lines,
which means that you cannot simply flip the axes from a single equation to
shift from using *X* to predict *Y* to using *Y* to predict *X*.

Finally, the *SDLine* sheet shows the SD line and its relation to the two
regression lines and the scatter plot. Each regression line is shallower than
the SD line; this is the regression effect noted by Galton. Therefore, the

SD line is an inferior predictor of SAT scores. The slope of the regression line is the correlation coefficient multiplied by the slope of the SD line. The mathematical slope of the SD line in turn depends on which variable is on the x-axis. When Verbal is on the x-axis,

$$\text{Slope of SD Line} = \frac{\text{SD(Math)}}{\text{SD(Verbal)}} = \frac{87.2}{89.1} = 0.98,$$

and, when Math is on the x-axis,

$$\text{Slope of SD Line} = \frac{\text{SD(Verbal)}}{\text{SD(Math)}} = \frac{89.1}{87.2} = 1.02.$$

The toggle button can be used to switch the axes. Notice that when you click on the toggle button, the SD line seems to shift as do the two regression lines and the points in the scatter plot. In both graphs, however, they are depicting exactly the same points with the coordinates reversed. For example, the point Verbal = 400, Math = 450 is displayed with coordinates (400,450) on one graph and coordinates (450,400) on the other.

All of these ideas are perfectly general. Galton's insight about the two regression lines applies to all data sets in which there is less than perfect correlation between the two variables. Only when $|r| = 1$, signifying perfect positive or perfect negative correlation, do the two regression lines and the SD line all coincide.

Summary

We conclude this section with a note on terminology. When one refers to a regression of Y on X, X is the variable we are starting with and Y is the variable being predicted. Thus, the regression of Math on Verbal treats Verbal as the X-variable and Math as the Y-variable. The regression line in this case would be read from a given Verbal score vertically up to the line and horizontally over to the predicted Math score.

Galton would say that predicting Math from a given Verbal score demonstrates regression to the mean because higher than average Verbal scores are associated with higher Math scores, but not by as much as the SD line would predict. Someone who is 89 points (one SD) above the mean in Verbal score is only predicted to be 0.55×87 ($r \times \text{SD}_{\text{Math}}$) or 48 points above the mean Math score. This is the regression to the mean effect that gave regression its name.

5.4. Properties of the Sample Average and the Regression Line

Workbook: OLSFormula.xls

The previous sections interpreted regression as a double compression of the data. The least squares regression line is an example of an estimator – that

Y_i	Sample Average w_i	Sample Average w_iY_i
97.70	0.1	9.770
108.65	0.1	10.865
108.66	0.1	10.866
97.63	0.1	9.763
100.69	0.1	10.069
96.10	0.1	9.610
87.30	0.1	8.730
101.76	0.1	10.176
99.30	0.1	9.930
96.13	0.1	9.613
993.92	1	**99.392**

Figure 5.4.1. The sample average is a weighted sum.
Source: [OLSFormula.xls]SampleAveIsOLS.

is, a recipe for describing data. In this section we will interpret least squares estimators in general as weighted sums of the data. We begin with a simpler statistic computed from sample data, the sample average. Like the regression line, the sample average is a least squares estimator. Furthermore, both the sample average and the regression line are weighted sums of the data. This section concludes by demonstrating some general properties of the OLS regression line with a simple data set.

The Sample Average

We first show, by example, that the sample average is a weighted sum and that it is the least squares estimator of central tendency. Open the suggestively titled sheet *SampleAveIsOLS* in OLSFormula.xls. Begin by looking at the first three columns in the table shown in Figure 5.4.1.

The Y_i column displays the 10 observed values in the data set. The sum of the 10 observations is, in this specific case, 993.92. With 10 observations, the average is 99.392, the number in bold in the lower right-hand corner. The general recipe for the sample average with n observations is, of course

$$Sample\ Average = \frac{\sum_{i=1}^{n} Y_i}{n}.$$

The symbol $\sum_{i=1}^{n}$ indicates that we are summing up all n of the terms to the right (the Y_i's).

Via the auditing arrows, however, Figure 5.4.1 invites us to think about the computation of the average in a slightly different way. Take each observation (Y_i), multiply it by a weight (w_i), and sum up the products (the w_iY_i's). In the

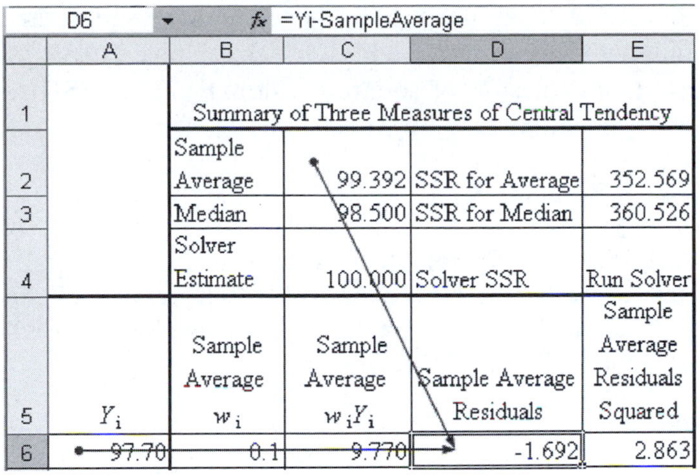

Figure 5.4.2. Computing the sample average residual.
Source: [OLSFormula.xls]SampleAveIsOLS.

specific case at hand,

$$Sample\ Average = 0.1 \cdot 97.70 + 0.1 \cdot 108.65 + \cdots + 0.1 \cdot 96.13$$
$$= 9.770 + 10.865 + \cdots + 9.613$$
$$= 99.392.$$

More generally, the sample average can be represented as follows:

$$Sample\ Average = w_1 \cdot Y_1 + w_2 \cdot Y_2 + \cdots + w_n \cdot Y_n$$
$$= \sum_{i=1}^{n} w_i Y_i,$$

where the w_i's are all equal to $\frac{1}{n}$. Note, for future reference, that the weights sum to 1.

If this exposition seems overly pedantic, we assure you that there are good reasons for the detailed approach. First, we want to show that most of the important recipes for summarizing data amount to weighted sums of the data. Second, the fact that the sample average and regression slope are weighted sums will come in very handy when we come to statistical inference.

Next, we show that the sample average is that recipe for summarizing the central tendency that produces the smallest sum of squared residuals (i.e., that the sample average is the least squares measure of central tendency). We show this first by example. Figure 5.4.2 demonstrates how the residuals for the sample average are computed. Notice from the formula bar that we use named cells to make it easier to understand the Excel formulas. The first residual is the observed value, 97.7, less the Sample Average, 99.392, or -1.692. This residual is squared, and the result is put in Column E. All the residuals and their squares are computed in the same way. The squared residuals are summed, and that sum goes into cell E2, which is labeled "SSR for Average" (where SSR stands for sum of squared residuals). The "SSR for Median" is computed in a similar fashion in columns H, I, and J and displayed in cell E3.

This worksheet demonstrates two important related facts:

1. The Average SSR is never greater than the Median SSR.[6]
2. More generally, the Sample Average is the least squares recipe for a measure of central tendency – that is, the SSR produced by the sample average is the minimum possible SSR for an estimator of central tendency.

The first fact is just a consequence of the second; we chose the Median to compare with the Average because it is the most important alternative estimator of central tendency.

We will use Solver to demonstrate by example that the average yields the lowest possible sum of squared residuals. Solver can quickly find that estimate of central tendency that minimizes the SSR. Our objective is to show that the OLS estimate is the same as the Sample Average estimate.

We will have Solver begin with an estimate of 100 in cell C4.[7] The residuals based on this estimate are displayed in the Solver Residuals column of the table (column F). The formula for each of these residuals reads "=Yi-SolverEstimate." Notice that if the Solver Estimate is 100, the Solver Residuals sum to −6.08. This is not an accident, for the sum of the observations (the sum of the 10 *Y*'s) is 993.92 and the sum of the Solver Estimates (10 each equal to 100) is 1,000. Now activate Solver by executing Tools: Solver. Solver should already be set up as shown in Figure 5.4.3. In this example, the initial value of Solver Estimate is set at 100.00. With this value, it is easy to see that the residuals for the first two observations will be −2.300 and 8.650, respectively. In this initial setup, the Solver SSR is 356.266, the value in cell G16, which is the sum of the squared Solver residuals. Solver will systematically change the value of Solver Estimate to minimize the SSR. We ran Solver and obtained the results shown in Figure 5.4.4.

You can try this yourself. Click on the [Draw Another Data Set] button and then run Solver. You will find that the Sample Average estimate corresponds to the minimum SSR estimate found by Solver. Of course, another name for the minimum-SSR estimate is the OLS estimate. This demonstration does not prove conclusively that the Sample Average is the OLS recipe for measuring central tendency. In the appendix to this chapter we use calculus to prove that the estimator of central tendency minimizing the SSR is the Sample Average.

---

[6] The two are only equal when the median equals the average.
[7] If there is a different value in cell C4, change it to 100.

	Y_i	Sample Average w_i	Sample Average $w_i Y_i$	Sample Average Residuals	Sample Average Residuals Squared	Solver Residuals	Solver Residuals Squared
4	Solver Estimate	100.000	Solver SSR	Run Solver			
6	97.70	0.1	9.770	-1.692	2.863	-2.300	5.29
7	108.65	0.1	10.865	9.258	85.711	8.650	74.82
						8.660	75.00
						-2.370	5.62
						0.690	0.48
						-3.900	15.21
						-12.700	161.29
						1.760	3.10
						-0.700	0.49
						-3.870	14.98
						-6.080	356.266

Solver Parameters

Set Target Cell: $G$16

Equal To: ○ Max ⦿ Min ○ Value of: 0

By Changing Cells: SolverEstimate

Subject to the Constraints:

Solve | Close | Guess | Options | Add | Change | Delete | Reset All | Help

Figure 5.4.3. Solver set up to find the minimum SSR estimate of central tendency. *Source:* [OLSFormula.xls]SampleAveIsOLS.

The Regression Line

So far we have shown that the Sample Average, an estimator of the central tendency of a single variable, is a weighted sum and the least squares estimator of central tendency. We turn now to the regression line, which is an estimator of the relationship between two variables. Here are the formulas for the Slope and Intercept of the regression line from Section 4.3:

$$b_1^{OLS} = \sum_{i=1}^{n} w_i \cdot Y_i$$

$$b_0^{OLS} = \bar{Y} - b_1^{OLS} \bar{X},$$

where the weights are given by

$$w_i = \frac{(X_i - \bar{X})}{\sum_{i=1}^{n} (X_i - \bar{X})^2}, i = 1, \ldots, n$$

Summary of Three Measures of Central Tendency			
Sample Average	99.392	SSR for Average	352.569
Median	98.500	SSR for Median	360.526
Solver Estimate	99.392	Solver SSR	352.569

Figure 5.4.4. The minimum SSR estimate is the sample average estimate. *Source:* [OLSFormula.xls] SampleAveIsOLS.

Mean X	30.00	Slope	16.00
Mean Y	560.00	Intercept	80.00
Denominator	1000	n	5

i	X_i	Y_i	X_i-Mean(X)	$(X_i$-Mean(X)$)^2$	w_i	$w_i Y_i$
1	10	300	−20	400	−0.02	−6.00
2	20	400	−10	100	−0.01	−4.00
3	30	500	0	0	0.00	0.00
4	40	600	10	100	0.01	6.00
5	50	1000	20	400	0.02	20.00
Sum	150.00	2800	0.00	1000.00	0.00	**16.00**

Figure 5.4.5. Computing the OLS slope and intercept in a simple example. *Source:* [OLSFormula.xls]Example.

in which n is the number of observations, $\bar{X}$ is the average value of the X_i's in the data set, and $\bar{Y}$ is the average value of the Y_i's in the data set. We see immediately that the OLS Slope (b_1^{OLS}) is a weighted sum of the Y_i's and the weights are a complicated function of the X_i's. We have demonstrated that these formulas produce the least squares estimator of the regression line.

We will now use another simple data set to help you better understand the formulas for the OLS slope and OLS intercept. Go to the *Example* sheet in OLSFormula.xls. This sheet conveys the following lessons:

- The OLS regression line goes through the point of averages.
- The OLS slope is a weighted sum of the Y's.
- The weights get bigger in absolute value the farther away an observation is from the average value of X.
- The weights sum to zero.
- A change in the Y value of an observation has a predictable effect on the OLS slope and intercept.

The *Example* sheet contains the table displayed in Figure 5.4.5. This example presents five observations. The table shows the steps involved in constructing the weights. First, each observation's deviation from the mean of the X's is calculated. These computations are in the $X_i - \text{Mean}(X)$ column. For example, the first observation, with an X value of 10, has a deviation of − 20 from the mean of 30 for the X values. (Note that we are using Mean(X) instead of $\bar{X}$ because of the difficulty in writing the latter symbol in Excel.) Next these deviations are squared, and the resulting squared deviations are summed. The first observation's squared X deviation is 400. The sum of the squared X deviations is 1,000. This sum of squared deviations goes into the denominator of each observation's weight w_i.

The weight for the first observation is − 0.02, which is −20 (the X deviation for that observation) divided by 1,000 (the sum of squared X deviations). The weights get bigger in absolute value as the X values of the observation move farther from the center of the X's. Finally, each observation's contribution

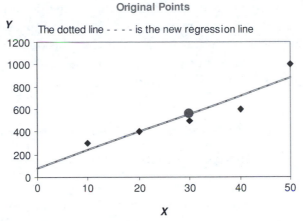

Figure 5.4.6. Simple example showing regression line, observations, and point of averages.
Source: [OLSFormula.xls]Example.

to the slope is the product of its Y value and its weight. The sum of the $w_i Y_i$ terms is the Slope, which in this case is 16. Notice that the weights sum to zero and that the regression line goes through the point of averages. These facts are always true when OLS is used to find the regression line and are a consequence of the mathematics behind the underlying optimization problem.

The OLS Intercept is the value of the Y-intercept for a line that has the computed Slope and passes through the point of averages. The coordinates of the latter are (30, 560), the Mean X and Mean Y. Figure 5.4.6 shows the regression line and point of averages.

In the *Example* worksheet you will see a second table and graph immediately below the first table and graph. You can use this second table to change the Y values of the five observations in order to see how the OLS regression line shifts as the observations move around.

The *Q&A* sheet contains suggested exercises designed to give you geometric and algebraic intuition. We have put buttons on the Example sheet to help you answer those questions.

Summary

In this section we have compared the mathematical algorithms for computing the Sample Average and the OLS regression slope. It is important to see that there are both similarities and differences in the weighted averages used to compute these statistics. Both the Sample Average and regression slope are weighted averages of the Y values, but the weights are constant and sum to one for the Sample Average while they are varying and sum to zero for the regression slope.

We now have three different ways of looking at the OLS regression line: as the solution to an optimization problem, as a double compression of the data, and as a weighted average of the data. In Part 2 of this book we demonstrate that the weighted average perspective is very useful for working out the inferential properties of the OLS method.

5.5. Residuals and the Root-Mean-Square Error

Workbooks: ResidualPlot.xls; RMSE.xls

Thus far in this chapter we have viewed OLS regression from two perspectives: as a method, given an X value, to predict Y and as a weighted average of the data. We next examine graphical and numerical ways to evaluate how the OLS regression summarizes the data. This section concentrates on descriptions of the residuals. Section 5.6 covers a single, very commonly used statistic R^2, which purports to describe how well the OLS regression fits the data.

Residual Output

We return to the familiar Math and Verbal SAT data from 527 recent applicants to Wabash College. The Excel workbook ResidualPlot.xls has the data and the results from a regression of Math on Verbal via the Data Analysis: Regression approach. The *Data* sheet shows how selecting the four choices in the Residuals section of the Regression dialog box generates information about the residuals from the regression.

In Section 4.2 we defined the residual as Actual Y – Predicted Y. The predicted value of Y given X is the value of Y that lies on the regression line

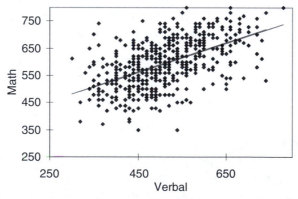

Figure 5.5.1. Scatter plot of Verbal and Math SAT with the Predicted Math SAT regression line.
Source: [ResidualPlot.xls]Output.

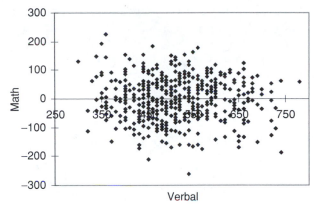

Figure 5.5.2. Residual plot from the regression of Math on Verbal SAT in Figure 5.5.1.
Source: [ResidualPlot.xls]Output.

vertically above the given value of X. Algebraically, you find the predicted value of Y by plugging the value of X into the equation for the regression line. The distance of the actual observed Y from its predicted Y value is called the residual. In general, the residuals are nonzero – not all points lie on the regression line. We can use the resulting pattern of residuals as a diagnostic device.

In Figure 5.5.1, which shows the scatter plot of the SAT data and the Predicted Math SAT regression line, the vast majority of the points are off the regression line. Positive residuals lie above the regression line, whereas negative residuals correspond to those Math scores that fall below the regression line. In Figure 5.5.2 we have drawn a residual plot for the data in which the residuals are graphed as a function of the X variable, Verbal SAT. In the residual plot of Figure 5.5.2,

- The average of the residuals is zero. This is always true.[8]
- There are just about as many residuals above zero (underprediction) as below zero (overprediction). This is not always the case.
- The size of the residual does not seem to be systematically related to the value of the *x*-variable. In other words, the spreads of the residuals in vertical strips for a given Verbal score are about the same. This is the desired attribute of homoskedasticity (as opposed to heteroskedasticity). Again, this is not always the case.

The residuals should not display a discernible pattern. If there is a pattern, then it is possible that linear regression is an inappropriate method of describing what is going on in your data.

To make clear exactly what the residual plot shows, examine a single point in the data set. One individual scored 370 on the verbal and 750 on the Math.

---

[8] True, that is, whenever the regression contains an intercept term.

Locate this individual on the scatter diagram in Figure 5.5.1. Calculate the residual associated with this observation:

First, substitute the value of X into the regression equation:
Predicted Math $= 319 + 0.54 \times [370]$.
Compute predicted Y:
Predicted Math $= 519$.

The residual is easily found by applying its definition:

$$\text{Residual} = \text{Actual value} - \text{Predicted value}$$
$$= 750 - 519$$
$$= 231.$$

Of course, computer software can rapidly do this calculation for each observation. For example, if you use the Regression tool in Excel's Data Analysis add-in, you can request a report of the residuals and a residuals plot (as in the *Output* sheet of ResidualPlot.xls).

One can see that the regression line is doing a poor job of predicting this particular observation. It is unexpected, given the other observations in the data set, that a student with a 370 Verbal score would do so well on Math. You should now locate this point on the residuals plot in Figure 5.5.2 and circle it.

Figure 5.5.3 shows that, given a Verbal score of 370, the regression line greatly underpredicts, by 231 points, the y-coordinate in the observation (370, 750), which stands for this particular student's Math score. The regression line is a measure of the center of a vertical strip (for the entire cloud) given a value of X. It is not surprising that some points may be far off the regression line. In this case, there are a few students who do much better on the Math SAT than would be predicted by their score on the Verbal SAT.

The Root-Mean-Squared Error (RMSE)

For a single list of numbers, the center is often measured by the average (or mean). The spread in the list is usually represented by the standard deviation (SD). We have shown how the bivariate regression line is a conditional average: it tells us, given X, what is the average Y. We need a way to indicate spread around the regression line that is analogous to the SD.

The root-mean-square error (RMSE) measures the dispersion of the data around the regression line. You can think of the RMSE as the typical vertical distance of an observation from the regression line – in other words a measure of the typical size of the residuals. It is a single number that measures spread just as the standard deviation measures spread for univariate data.

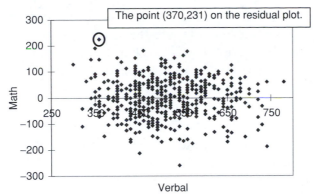

Figure 5.5.3. Identifying a particular residual.
Source: [ResidualPlot.xls]Output.

Calculating the RMSE

To understand how the RMSE is computed, all you have to do is to look carefully at the name and to remember how the standard deviation is computed.

- Root-Mean-Squared is a conventional method used for computing the average size of a deviation. For example, "Root-mean-squared deviations from the mean" describes the method for calculating the standard deviation of a list of numbers. You read it backwards to find the method: SQUARE the differences between each value and the mean, take the MEAN, and then take the ROOT.
- Error is the difference between the actual and predicted value of *y*.

Of course, we have been calling the difference between the actual and predicted values of **Y** *residuals*, and so the correct name for the size of the typical residual should be *root-mean-squared residual*. Unfortunately, by historical accident, this concept is called root-mean-squared error. The use of Error in place of Residual is a source of serious confusion for anyone trying to understand regression analysis. *Error* is an important concept in inferential statistics and econometrics that is different from the *residual*. We will be discussing error in later chapters of this book. Keeping residual and error straight requires concentration, and the RMSE misnomer makes things worse. In addition, the RMSE is also known as the *Standard Error of the Regression* and the *Standard Error of the Estimate*. You might see this terminology in the economics literature or reported by software, but we will use the RMSE throughout this book.

The close tie between the SD and RMSE is evident in the calculation and use of these statistics. Both rely on root-mean-square computations and both are used to measure spread. Furthermore, like the SD (which has the same units as the list of numbers), the RMSE has the same units as the dependent variable.

Although there are a variety of shortcuts for calculating the RMSE,[9] we will rely on the computer to compute the RMSE easily. The Computation sheet in the Excel workbook RMSE.xls has a simple numerical example of how the RMSE is actually calculated. You can change the spread parameter (cell B2) to see how that affects the dispersion of the five observations around the regression line and the resulting value of RMSE. The sheet also explains a subtle difference in the way most statistical packages compute the RMSE, adjusting it for degrees of freedom.[10] This is analogous to the difference between the calculations of the SD of a sample versus the SD of a population. With large data sets, this distinction is not important.

Interpreting the RMSE

The RMSE is essentially the SD of the residuals – a measure of the dispersion in the residuals. We can take advantage of the fact that what we are doing has a direct parallel with the univariate case. The RMSE plays the same role and is used in the same way as the SD. The RMSE conveys the likely size of the typical residual off the line. Thus, the RMSE can be thought of as a measure of the vertical spread of the observations around the regression line. It even turns out that the same rough approximation used in connection with the SD for lists of numbers also applies for the RMSE. Figure 5.5.4 shows an example in which the rule of thumb that 68 percent of the observations fall within ± 1 SD roughly holds: 10 of the 14 observations fall in the ± 1 RMSE band.

Similarly, the rule that about 95 percent of the values fall within ± 2 RMSE, also applies to many data sets. Of course, there are data sets for which the approximation does not hold.

Example: Wabash College SAT Scores

We can demonstrate the interpretation of the RMSE by returning to the Wabash College Math and Verbal SAT scores data set. For the Wabash College SAT data, the RMSE is about 73 Math points.

In the data set, approximately 69 percent of the points are within ±1 RMSE from the regression line. Approximately 94 percent of the points are within 2 RMSEs from the regression line. The rule of thumb works very well for the Wabash College SAT data.

---

[9] One useful shortcut is that the $RMSE = \sqrt{1 - r^2} \times$ SD of the Y's.

[10] In regression, the number of degrees of freedom is the number of observations less the number of coefficients being estimated.

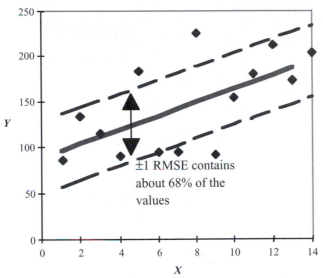

Figure 5.5.4. Applying the ± 1 SD rule of thumb to a bivariate regression.

Why does our approximation work for the SAT data? To answer this question, let us make sure we understand what we mean when we talk about the distribution of the residuals. Figure 5.5.6 shows three views of the residuals.

In Figure 5.5.6 the top diagram shows a scatter plot of the data and the regression line. The middle diagram reveals the scatter plot of the residuals. The two share the same *x*-axis, but for each point on the residual plot, the

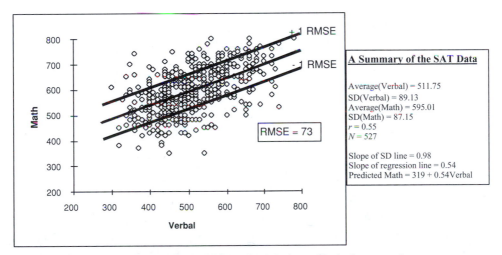

Figure 5.5.5. The RMSE in the Math on Verbal regression.
Source: [RMSE.xls]Accordion.

Regression of Math on Verbal SAT

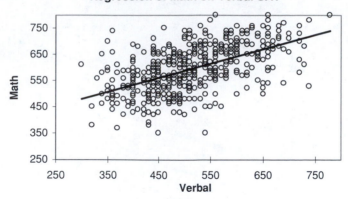

Residuals versus Verbal SAT

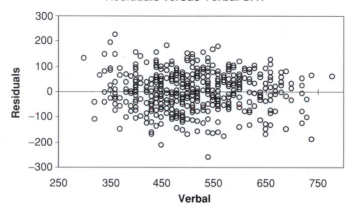

Histogram of Residuals for Math on Verbal SAT

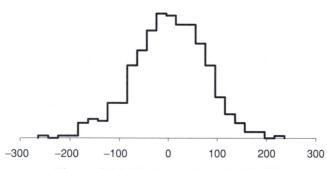

Figure 5.5.6. Understanding the RMSE.
Source: [RMSE.xls]Pictures.

y-value no longer measures the Math SAT score; instead the vertical distance between the Math SAT score and the score predicted by the regression equation is measured. For example, the person with the lowest verbal score had a Verbal SAT of 300 and a Math SAT of 610. This observation can easily be located on both of the two top diagrams. It is a point northwest of most of the

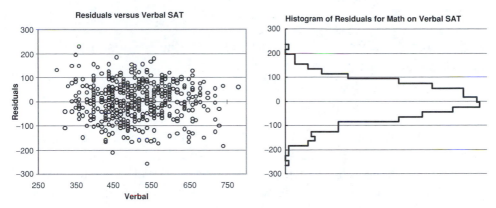

Figure 5.5.7. Another view of the relation between the residuals and their histogram. *Source:* [RMSE.xls]Pictures.

rest of the data. The coordinates of this observation on the middle diagram are Verbal SAT of 300 and residual of 129.2. You can also find this individual in the *SATData* sheet in the RMSE.xls workbook. Because the data have been sorted, it is the first observation.

The histogram, to drive home exactly what it is showing us, is displayed once again in Figure 5.5.7 tipped on its side to facilitate comparison with the scatter plot of residuals.

One thing to note about the residual plot is that some of the points in the scatter plot stand for many observations. For example, there are five people in the data set who scored 500 on the Verbal SAT and 600 on the Math SAT. Every one of them has a predicted score of 588.7 on the Math SAT and therefore a positive residual of 11.3. The center of the histogram is tall in part because many of the points represent more than person in the data set. There are simply more people with residuals close to zero than people with residuals far away from zero.

The histogram of the residuals bears more than a passing resemblance to the normal curve. The rule of thumb for the RMSE depends on the fact that many histograms for residuals look like normal curves. Also note that a spread of 73 is very plausible for this histogram.

A final way to grasp the concept of the RMSE is to consider an extension of the intervals idea of Section 5.2. The sheet *Accordion* in the RMSE.xls workbook provides not only the average in an interval but also the SD within an interval. Compare the displays produced by the Many Intervals and RegressionLine w/ +/- 1 RMSE buttons.

Just as the regression line is a linearization of the graph of averages, the RMSE is an overall single measure of spread across all of the intervals. The sheet *PivotTable* makes clear that, for this data set, computing a weighted average of the SDs in each interval comes fairly close to the RMSE.

Summary

Here is the regression equation that describes the Math and Verbal SAT scores and the RMSE:

$$\text{Predicted Math} = 319 + 0.54 \text{ Verbal}$$
$$\text{RMSE} = 73.$$

Suppose that you are asked to predict the Math score of a student who earned a 500 on the Verbal part of the exam. You should calculate and report the Predicted Math score of 580 ($= 319 + 0.54 \times 500$) along with the RMSE of 73. The RMSE tells the reader that there is considerable spread around that predicted score, which is valuable information.

The RMSE is the SD of a particular list of numbers – namely the residuals in a regression. The RMSE provides information on the size of the typical residual. As such, it is ideal for improving the information conveyed by the regression line.

Just as a summary of a univariate list of numbers should always include at least the average and SD, a bivariate summary should include the five basic summary statistics (average X and Y, SD of X and Y, and r), the regression equation, and the RMSE. This will enable the reader to reconstruct the scatter plot. Of course, if the resulting reconstruction misses crucial details of the scatter plot, then the summary information is misleading and should be augmented by the scatter diagram. Section 5.7, presents several cases in which the summary is misleading.

5.6. *R-Squared* (R^2)

Workbook: RSquared.xls

Suppose you had information on Math SAT scores for a group of students. You pick one of the students at random and want to guess his or her Math SAT score. The best guess you could come up with would be to use the average Math SAT score for the group, which is 595. How far off would the typical guess be? The answer is given by the SD of the Math SAT scores.

Now suppose you had additional information – namely, each student's Verbal SAT score. You now are to guess a random student's score not only knowing that he or she comes from the group of 527 students with average Math SAT score of 595, but also this student's Verbal score. Our work in previous sections has made clear that the best guess of the Math SAT score given a Verbal SAT score would be to use the regression line of Math SAT score on Verbal SAT score for the group. How far off is your guess likely to be? The answer is given by the RMSE.

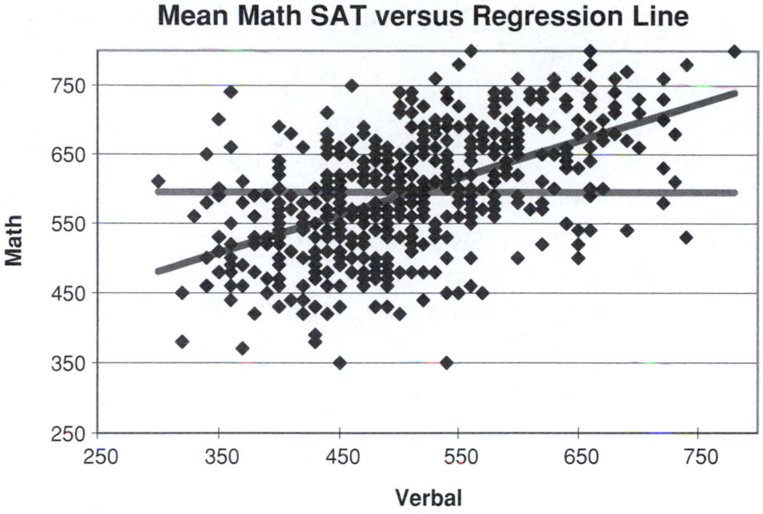

Mean Math SAT versus Regression Line

Figure 5.6.1. Two ways to predict Math SAT.

You might want to know how much better your guess would become when you had made use of the additional information. This section explains the *R*-Squared (R^2) statistic.[11] It measures the improvement in prediction accuracy gained by using the regression line instead of the average value of the dependent variable.

After providing some intuition behind the concept of R^2, this section will show how the statistic is actually computed. We conclude the presentation of R^2 with a warning on the misuse of this common statistic.

The Logic of R^2: The Guessing Game

Because R^2 is concerned with measuring the improvement in prediction, we first need to come up with a procedure to quantify how good the predictions are.

Imagine that every time you make a guess you are penalized for guessing incorrectly. The size of the penalty is the square of the difference between your guess and the actual Math score of the student. How big is the penalty likely to be? If you use the mean Math SAT score as your guess every time, then the penalty will on average be the square of the SD of the Math scores. If you use the regression line, then the penalty will on average be the square of the RMSE of the regression.

The *GuessingGame* sheet in the RSquared.xls workbook puts the ideas in this section to work. Play a few times and see if you can do better than

---

[11] The R^2 statistic is sometimes called the coefficient of determination.

guessing the average Math SAT or the Predicted Math SAT from the regression equation.

R^2 is a statistic that answers the question of how much better the regression predicts each Y value than the process of using the average alone, which is the simplest possible way to predict the value of Y. In other words, the R^2 statistic is a way of computing how much better the regression is at the guessing game we have just described. In essence, R^2 measures the percentage improvement in prediction over just using the average Y. A quick presentation of the accounting of the sums of squares in regression will make the computation of R^2 clear.

Computing R^2

If we subtract the average Y from each Y and square the resulting deviations from the average, the result is called the total sum of squares (TSS). The formula for the TSS is

$$TSS = \sum_{i=1}^{n} (Y_i - \bar{Y})^2,$$

where i indexes observations and n denotes the number of observations. This is a measure of the total variation in the Y values. With regression, we can compute the sum of squared residuals (SSR). The SSR is the variation left unexplained by regression. The amount left over, total variation minus SSR, must be the explained variation. The explained variation is also known as the regression sum of squares (abbreviated RegSS in our workbooks) or the explained sum of squares (ESS). The accounting identity being used here is

Total Variation = Explained Variation + Unexplained Variation.

SSR is the unexplained variation by regression. The smaller the SSR, the better the performance of the regression.

The most direct and clear definition of R^2 is that it is the ratio of the explained variation (which can be found by computing the total variation minus the SSR) to the total variation. The *Computation* sheet in the Rsquared.xls workbook presents an example. Change cell B2 to see how more variation in Y affects R^2. The formula for R^2 is

$$R^2 = \frac{TSS - SSR}{TSS}$$
$$= 1 - \frac{SSR}{TSS}.$$

It should be clear that R^2 ranges from 0 to 1. At one extreme, if regression offers absolutely no improvement in predicting Y compared with using the average Y, then R^2 is 0. The scatter plot would be the ultimate formless blob with no correlation whatsoever between X and Y. On the other hand, if regression has 0 SSR, then R^2 is 1. In this case, the points would all lie on the line.[12]

Could it be a simple coincidence that the correlation coefficient is the letter r and the measure of prediction improvement via regression is capital letter R^2, or is there a tie between these two concepts? It turns out that in a bivariate regression the two are easily related. The square of the correlation coefficient is the R^2 statistic!

The Use and Misuse of R^2

The R^2 statistic is often provided as a quick summary measure of the regression. It is true that, as R^2 approaches 1, the regression better explains the variation. This statistic, however, is somewhat controversial. Many authors, in our opinion, put too much emphasis on getting high R^2's as an important goal of empirical analysis. We are skeptical of using R^2 as a tool to judge empirical work. One reason is that R^2 is guaranteed to improve if more independent variables are added to the regression (Chapter 7 explains regression with more than one X variable). The push to maximize R^2 leads some researchers to throw the kitchen sink into their models. When we turn to regression for inference, we will see that this is a bad strategy.

Many software packages (including Excel's Data Analysis: Regression add-in) report an Adjusted R^2 statistic designed to penalize the addition of variables. Although the adjustment is potentially useful, we believe it is better to understand that R^2 is not a perfect statistic and should thus not be used to reach immediate conclusions about a particular regression model.

Summary

The R^2 statistic is a measure of the improvement in prediction provided by regression compared with predicting with average Y alone. It is a commonly used descriptive statistic. Excel's Trendline, for example, offers R^2 as an option (but not RMSE). Although it serves a useful purpose as an indicator

---

[12] There is one exception to this logic: the case in which the regression does not include an intercept term – that is, where

$$\text{Predicted } Y = \text{Slope} \cdot X$$

instead of

$$\text{Predicted } Y = \text{Intercept} + \text{Slope} \cdot X.$$

The *ZeroIntercept* sheet demonstrates why the standard formula for R^2 is inappropriate in this case and presents the alternative used by Excel 2003.

of the predictive performance of the regression line versus simply using average Y to predict Y, R^2 should never be interpreted as a definitive measure of a regression's validity.

The next section addresses the limitations of regression as a data-summarizing strategy. It will be clear that, for some data sets, irrespective of the value of R^2, regression is simply inappropriate or at best inadequate.

5.7. Limitations of Data Description with Regression

Workbooks: Anscombe.xls; IMRGDPReg.xls;
SameRegLineDifferentData.xls; HourlyEarnings.xls

This section offers several examples of data sets for which linear regression is inappropriate. Scatter plots with regression lines, plots of residuals, and analyses of the RMSE are used to understand the limitations of linear regression better. We discuss two main problems when using linear regression to describe the relationship between two variables: nonlinearity and heteroskedasticity.

Example 1: The Anscombe Data

Clear examples of nonlinearity can be found in four well-known data sets produced by Anscombe. They are artificial and have been used to test the accuracy of regression algorithms. They also have special characteristics that are rather remarkable. These four data sets are displayed in Figure 5.7.1.

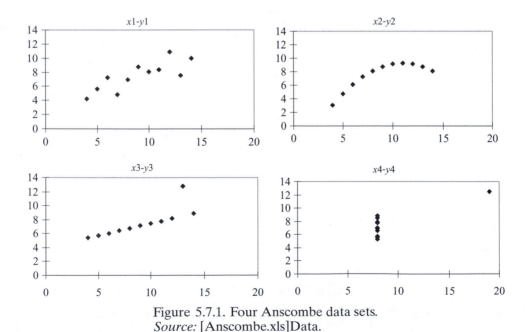

Figure 5.7.1. Four Anscombe data sets.
Source: [Anscombe.xls]Data.

Table 5.7.1. *Your Estimates*

Data Set	Intercept by Eye	Slope by Eye
$x1-y1$		
$x2-y2$		
$x3-y3$		
$x4-y4$		

By eye, fit regression lines to each of the four data sets. The x- and y-axes are similarly scaled, and thus you should be able to read off approximate intercept and slope coefficients for each of the four graphs and report them in Table 5.7.1.

Now open the Anscombe.xls workbook and fit the regression line to each of the four data sets. In the Options tab of the Add Trendline dialog box, make sure you select the options displayed in Figure 5.7.2.

How did you do? Were you able to see that the four data sets have the same regression line? That is remarkable, is it not?

Obviously a linear regression line does not do justice to the curvilinear relationship between $x2$ and $y2$ in the Anscombe example. A completely vertical line would summarize all but one point in the graph of $y4$ versus $x4$; whether the vertical line would be better than the regression line depends on where we think the anomalous point came from. For both the graphs of $(x3, y3)$ and $(x4, y4)$ it seems in each case that if we could somehow separate the outlier (by identifying what went wrong when it was measured or why it is so odd), then a regression line that fits the remaining points well would be better than the simple regression line.

Anscombe's data sets are prepared so that not only are the regression lines the same, but numerous other summary statistics are also almost exactly the same, as shown in Figures 5.7.3 and 5.7.4.

Anscombe wanted to show that summary measures (both univariate and bivariate, including regression) might be flawed and misleading. His four-data–set example is a good way to remember that scatter diagrams can reveal what is obscured by summary statistics.

Example 2: Nonlinearity in the Real World

Although Anscombe's $x2-y2$ data set is an obvious example of the inappropriateness of regression when the data exhibit a marked nonlinear pattern,

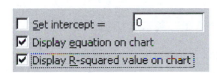

Figure 5.7.2. Adding a trendline to Anscombe data.

				Summary Statistics						
N	11	11		11	11		11	11		11	11
mean	9.00	7.50		9.00	7.50091		9.00	7.50		9.00	7.50
SD	3.16	1.94		3.16	1.94		3.16	1.94		3.16	1.94
r	0.82			0.82			0.82			0.82	

Figure 5.7.3. Univariate summary statistics from Anscombe data sets.
Source: [Anscombe.xls]Data.

it is an artificial example. There are many real-world data sets in which non-linearity is present. In such cases, a straight line summary is misleading.

Figure 5.7.5 shows the residuals from a regression of infant mortality on GDP per capita. The residuals show a marked pattern. Contrast this figure with the residual plot for the regression of Math on Verbal SAT scores. The data are contained in the workbook IMRGDPReg.xls.

Notice that, below a per capita GDP of 2,500 dollars per year, the residuals seem to be scattered more or less equally above and below zero. However, for higher income countries, especially those with per capita GDP's above 5,000 dollars a year, there is a definite pattern: the higher the per capita GDP, the greater the residual. Figure 5.7.6 displays the scatter plot and linear regression line for the same data.

It is easy to see that the regression line does not very accurately depict the relationship between the two variables, which appears to be nonlinear. The regression of IMR on GDP is an inappropriate tool for describing the relationship between the variables. Clearly, using the regression line to describe this scatter diagram is a mistake because much information is lost by trying to describe this relationship as a linear one. Here are two lessons from this example:

- Nonlinear scatterplots should not be summarized with a regression line. Predictions made from a regression equation will be systematically off (higher in one part of the line and lower elsewhere).
- Nonlinearity can often be diagnosed by looking at a plot of residuals. The residuals should show no discernible pattern. If they do, regression may be inappropriate.

LINEST OUTPUT		x1-y1			x2-y2			x3-y3			x4-y4	
slope	intercept	0.50	3		0.50	3		0.50	3		0.50	3
SE	SE	0.12	1.12		0.12	1.13		0.12	1.12		0.12	1.12
R^2	RMSE	0.67	1.24		0.67	1.24		0.67	1.24		0.67	1.24
F	df	17.99	9		17.97	9		17.97	9		18.00	9
RegSS	SSR	27.51	13.76		27.50	13.78		27.47	13.76		27.49	13.74

Figure 5.7.4. Regression results from Anscombe data sets.
Source: [Anscombe.xls]Data.

1998 IMR and 1992 Per Capita Real GDP Residuals

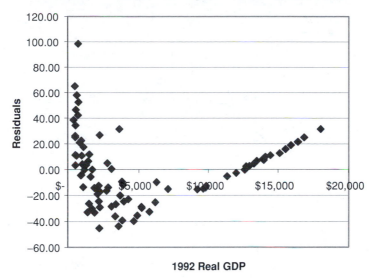

Figure 5.7.5. Residuals from a regression of infant mortality rates on GDP per capita in U.S. dollars, selected countries, 1990s.
Source: [IMRGDPReg.xls]

Example 3: A New Pattern in the Residuals

Regression may also be misleading if the scatter plot exhibits a hornlike pattern. We demonstrate this point by contrasting two very similar data sets.

1998 IMR and 1992 Real GDP

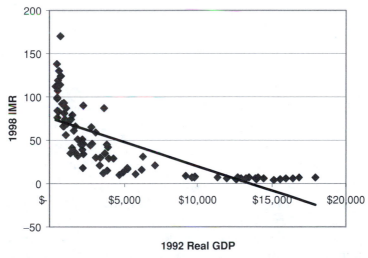

Figure 5.7.6. Regression of infant mortality rates on GDP per capita in U.S. dollars, selected countries, 1990s.
Source: [IMRGDPReg.xls]

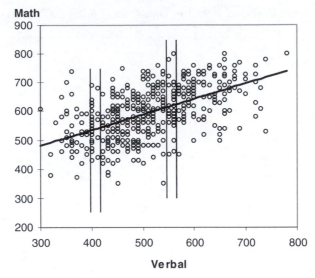

Figure 5.7.7. Homoskedasticity in the SAT example.
Source: [SameRegLineDifferentData.xls]SAT.

The first is our familiar SAT example illustrated on this occasion in the Excel workbook SameRegLineDifferentData.xls.

Upon opening the workbook and going to the *SAT* worksheet, you should see the chart in Figure 5.7.7. If the scatter plot does not look like this figure, click on the Restore SAT Data button.

When all the vertical strips in a scatter diagram show similar amounts of spread, then the diagram is said to be homoskedastic. The scatter plot for the regression of the SAT Math score on the SAT Verbal score, shown in Figure 5.7.7, exhibits a homoskedastic pattern. In this case the RMSE does a good job of summarizing the typical residual for all values of the independent variable. The spread in the two vertical strips is just about the same.

If the vertical strips do NOT show the same amount of spread around the regression line, then the residuals are said to be heteroskedastic. To illustrate heteroskedasticity, we constructed a fanciful example in which the Verbal scores are the same as before but the Math scores have been deliberately chosen in such a way that, though their average and SD are the same as in the original data, something is amiss. We obtained a picture like Figure 5.7.8 and statistics like those in Figure 5.7.9 by selecting the ⊙Linear, Heteroscedastic option and clicking on the Generate Y button.

The regression line in this case is exactly the same as for the actual data, the *R*-square is the same, and the RMSE is the same. In fact, all summary statistics are identical – they are given in Figure 5.7.9. What is wrong? Although linear

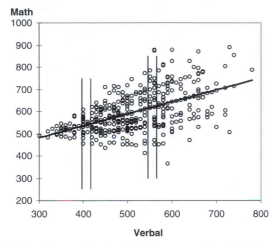

Figure 5.7.8. Heteroskedasticity in a contrived SAT example.
Source: [SameRegLineDifferentData.xls]SAT.

regression gives exactly the same results with this new data set, we have built in heteroskedasticity: the spread of the residuals rises as Verbal score rises. We have drawn in red vertical strips to highlight the difference between the actual homoskedastic data and the artificial heteroskedastic data. Of course, an infinite number of data sets exist that would produce exactly the same regression line. Every time you click on the Generate Y button, another data set will be obtained that shares exactly the same summary statistics. To see especially wild examples, click the ⊙ Nonlinear, Deterministic radio button and then generate a new set of *Y*'s. You can generate different patterns by using the nonlinear slide control.

Example 4: Heteroskedasticity in Earnings Data

To illustrate a typical real-world case of heteroskedasticity, we went back to the EastNorthCentralFTWorkers.xls database and created a new variable called Hourly Wage, which is defined as Usual Weekly Earnings

Descriptive Statistics			LINEST output			
	X	Y	slope	0.53947	318.94	intercept
			SE(slope)	0.03559	18.4892	SE(int)
Average	511.7	595.0	R^2	0.30435	72.7582	RMSE
SD	89.0	87.2	F	229.695	525	df
Corr(*X,Y*)	0.55		Reg SS	1215950	2779225	SSR

Figure 5.7.9. Summary statistics for both SAT data sets.
Source: [SameRegLineDifferentData.xls]SAT.

	Slope	Intercept	
Estimate	1.92	$ (9.42)	
SE	0.11	1.49	
Rsquared	0.19	$ 9.01	RMSE
F	310.7	1336.0	df
RegSS	25213.8	108416.8	SSR

Figure 5.7.10. Excel's report of regression of hourly wage ($ per hour) on education (years). *Source:* [HourlyEarning.xls] HourlyWagebyEduc.

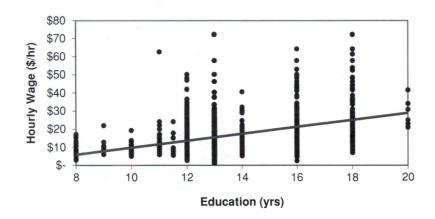

Hourly Earnings on Education

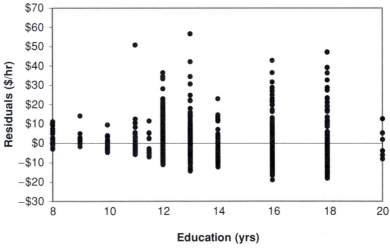

Residuals of Hourly Earnings on Education versus Education

Figure 5.7.11. Regression of hourly earnings on education from HourlyEarnings.xls and corresponding residuals plot.
Source: [HourlyEarning.xls]HourlyWagebyEduc and [HourlyEarning.xls]Residuals.

divided by Usual Weekly Hours. The workbook HourlyEarnings.xls contains the revised data set and shows the results from a regression of Usual Weekly Earnings on Education. Figure 5.7.10 is a picture of the regression output.

The estimates for slope and intercept are given in the estimate line. They tell us that, for each additional year of education, predicted Hourly Wage rises by $1.92 per hour. According to the RMSE, the size of the typical residual is $9.01. You could use this information to recreate the scatter diagram of the data.

Scatter diagrams of the data and residuals are depicted in Figure 5.7.11. Look at the residual plot on the bottom first. Notice that the spread of the residuals increases as education rises. This is an example of heteroskedasticity. You can see the same pattern in the scatter diagram with the regression line in the top half of Figure 5.7.11.

By examining the residual plot and scatterplot, you can see that the RMSE is not a good summary description of the size of a typical residual. The typical size of a residual depends on the value of education. You cannot use a global measure of dispersion around the regression line because the dispersion varies along the line. Once again, we are dealing with heteroskedasticity, though it is not as noticeable as it was in the contrived SAT example.

The heteroskedastic pattern is confirmed by a closer look at the vertical strips (that is, the observations within a single education level). In Figure 5.7.12, we calculated the means of the residuals for different values of the X variable (education). If the data were homoskedastic, one would expect the SD of the residuals to be similar across different values of the variable education.

Yet another way to see the inappropriateness of the RMSE as a means of summarizing the spread of the residuals is to examine a histogram of the residuals within two different education levels as in Figure 5.7.13. The lesson is that, with a heteroskedastic scatter plot, the RMSE does not provide a good idea of what the typical residual looks like.

Summary

The regression line can be a powerful tool for describing a bivariate relationship. Often the scatter diagram, regression line, and RMSE can adequately and succinctly provide a great deal of information about the relationship between the variables.

At times, however, linear regression is inappropriate or incomplete as a descriptive tool. For example, when the relationship is nonlinear, simple

Education		Data	Total
	8	StdDev of Residuals	$3.97
		Average of Residuals	$3.83
	9	StdDev of Residuals	$4.90
		Average of Residuals	$2.29
	10	StdDev of Residuals	$2.95
		Average of Residuals	-$1.14
	11	StdDev of Residuals	$10.71
		Average of Residuals	$1.22
	11.5	StdDev of Residuals	$6.12
		Average of Residuals	-$1.78
	12	StdDev of Residuals	$7.02
		Average of Residuals	-$0.09
	13	StdDev of Residuals	$8.34
		Average of Residuals	-$0.20
	14	StdDev of Residuals	$7.60
		Average of Residuals	-$1.19
	16	StdDev of Residuals	$10.92
		Average of Residuals	-$0.27
	18	StdDev of Residuals	$14.02
		Average of Residuals	$1.37
	20	StdDev of Residuals	$7.82
		Average of Residuals	$0.20
Total StdDev of Residuals			$9.00
Total Average of Residuals			$0.00

Figure 5.7.12. Summary statistics for vertical strips of residuals.
Source: [HourlyEarning.xls]Residuals.

linear regression does not accurately represent the relationship between the variables. When the residuals exhibit heteroskedasticity, the RMSE does not correctly summarize the spread of the data around the regression line.

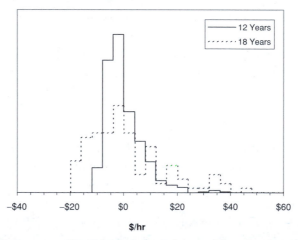

Figure 5.7.13. Histograms of residuals in hourly earnings on education regression.
Source: [HourlyEarnings.xls]Residuals.

5.8. Conclusion

This chapter has introduced several fundamental ideas:

1. Regression is a simplified conditional mean function and therefore an extremely compact summary of the relationship between two variables.
2. Regressions produce intercept and slope coefficients that summarize the relationship between the y and x variables. Using the slope and intercept, given a value of the x variable, one can predict the y variable's value.
3. For any bivariate data set, there are two regression lines determined by which variable is treated as the X variable and which as the Y variable.
4. The OLS regression slope is a weighted average of the values of the Y variable.
5. The RMSE and R^2 are additional summary statistics for OLS regressions and are helpful for evaluating regression results.

In this chapter we have emphasized visualizing the data. For example, it is extremely helpful to think about regression as proceeding by dividing the data into vertical strips, finding the points of averages, and then fitting a line to those points.

The last section showed that fitting a straight line to a nonlinear pattern is a big mistake. But if the straight-line regressions produced so far are obviously flawed when the data are nonlinear, how do we deal with curvilinear relationships between variables? Is regression worthless in such cases?

The answer is a resounding no. The next chapter will show that regression is, in fact, powerful and flexible. Through differing manipulations and transformations, regression can handle a variety of patterns in the data.

5.9. Exercises

1. A student scored 660 on the Verbal SAT and 800 on the Math SAT. Use the regression results from Section 5.3 to answer these questions.
   a) What were his or her Predicted Math SAT from the bivariate regression of Math SAT on Verbal SAT and the corresponding Residual?
   b) What were his or her Predicted Verbal SAT from the bivariate regression of Verbal SAT on Math SAT and the corresponding Residual?
2. Despite the positive correlation coefficient between A and B, the regression of A on B has a negative slope. Could this situation occur? Explain why or why not.
3. In an analysis of the SAT data, 1,000 is mistakenly added to every math score. For example, a Math score of 650 becomes 1650. What impact will this have on the slope coefficient in a bivariate regression of Math SAT on Verbal SAT as compared with the slope coefficient from the same biavariate regression using the original correct data? What impact will this mistake have on the slope coefficient in the regression of Verbal SAT on Math SAT? Explain your reasoning. (Hint: Think about how the graph of averages is affected.)
4. If the slope in a bivariate regression is zero, what is the value of the R^2?
5. If the RMSE in a bivariate regression is zero and the slope is not zero, what is the value of the R^2?

References

Although the least squares method was developed around 1800, the concept of regression was not formulated until the 1870s and 1880s by Francis Galton. To learn more, we once again recommend Stigler (1986) – the full citation appears in the Chapter 3 References section.

The epigraph for this chapter is from:

Galton, F. (1886) "Regression Towards Mediocrity in Hereditary Stature" *The Journal of the Anthropological Institute of Great Britain and Ireland* 15: 246–263.

We are indebted to Freedman, D. R. Pisani, and R. Purves, *Statistics* 3d edition (1998), (New York: W. W. Norton), whose Chapters 10 and 11 cover the graph of averages, the RMSE, the relationship between the regression line and the SD line, the regression phenomenon, and the two regression lines. We have drawn on their treatment of these topics in constructing our examples and in our exposition. We have also drawn ideas from two textbooks by Arthur Goldberger that give very clear discussions of the conditional mean function and regression: *A Course in Econometrics* (1991) and *Introductory Econometrics* (1998), which were both published by Harvard University Press.

Appendix: Proof that the Sample Average is a Least Squares Estimator

This appendix proves that the sample average is the least squares estimator of central tendency of a univariate data set. Suppose c is an estimate of central tendency for n observations, each called Y_i. Then the sum of squared residuals is

$$SSR = \sum_{i=1}^{n}(c - Y_i)^2.$$

The optimization problem is

$$\operatorname*{Min}_{c} SSR = \sum_{i=1}^{n}(c - Y_i)^2.$$

To find the solution, differentiate with respect to c and set the derivative equal to zero. After some algebra we will find that the estimate that minimizes the sum of squared residuals is the sample average. First take the derivative of the sum of squared residuals with respect to c:

$$\frac{\partial SSR}{\partial c} = \sum_{i=1}^{n} 2(c - Y_i).$$

In this case it is very easy to show that the second-order condition for a minimum is satisfied. The second derivative is clearly greater than zero:

$$\frac{\partial^2 SSR}{\partial c^2} = \sum_{i=1}^{n} 2$$

$$= 2n > 0.$$

Next set the first derivative equal to zero and solve for c^*, the SSR-minimizing estimator of central tendency:

$$\sum_{i=1}^{n} 2(c^* - Y_i) = 0$$

$$2\sum_{i=1}^{n} (c^* - Y_i) = 0$$

$$\sum_{i=1}^{n} c^* - \sum_{i=1}^{n} Y_i = 0$$

$$n \cdot c^* = \sum_{i=1}^{n} Y_i$$

$$c^* = \frac{\sum_{i=1}^{n} Y_i}{n}.$$

This is the sample average.

6

Functional Form of the Regression

This result can be summarized in the following statement: Annual earnings corresponding to various levels of training differing by the same amount (d) differ, not by an additive constant, but by a multiplicative factor (k).

Jacob Mincer[1]

6.1. Introduction

This chapter shows that the technique of linear regression is an extremely flexible method for describing data. That flexibility derives from the possibility of being able to replace the variables in the regression equation with functions of the original variables. As examples, instead of fitting the equation

$$\text{Predicted } Y = a + bX,$$

we can fit

$$\text{Predicted } Y = a + bX^2,$$

or

$$\text{Predicted } \ln Y = a + bX,$$

where ln stands for the natural log function. Applying polynomials, multiplying or dividing variables by each other, applying logarithms and exponentials, and taking reciprocals are just a few of the variable transformations available to generate nonlinear fits.

Even though variables may be transformed so that the equation is nonlinear in the original units of the variables, as long as the equation remains in the form of an intercept plus a slope multiplying a (possibly transformed) X variable, it remains a linear regression. In other words, linear regression means linear in the parameters, not the variables. For example, Predicted

---

[1] Mincer (1958, p. 285).

$Y = 1/a + b^2 X$ is a nonlinear regression model because the parameters themselves enter into the equation in a nonlinear way. This model cannot be fit using the usual least squares intercept and slope formulas. We will review a specific kind of nonlinear regression model in Chapter 22 but otherwise confine ourselves to linear regression in this book.

This chapter begins with an example of a famous nonlinear equation from the physical sciences. The example will allow us to explore theoretical and practical reasons for using different functional forms. Next, we return to the infant mortality and GDP per capita data set to demonstrate the double-log and reciprocal specifications. The fourth section is devoted to the semilog functional form, which has dominated empirical work in labor economics since it was introduced in the late 1950s. Finally, we explain how elasticities are computed from fitted lines and show how the functional form impacts the elasticity. The appendix to this chapter contains a catalog of functional forms commonly used by economists listing advantages and disadvantages of each specification.

6.2. Understanding Functional Form via an Econometric Fable

Workbook: Galileo.xls

In this section we peek into the laboratory of Galileo Galilei, a famous Italian scientist who was interested in how objects fall to Earth. The year is 1610. The story told here is an econometric fantasy. In fact, Galileo did solve this problem but in a much more clever way than in our story.

Galileo had made careful measurements from the leaning tower of Pisa of the distance traveled by a ball dropped from the top of the tower. He wanted to determine how the distance the ball falls depends on the amount of time it falls. He used a good flash camera and accurate (though not perfect) devices for measuring time and distance. Figure 6.2.1 is a schematic representation of what is going on.

The *DataGeneration* sheet in the Galileo.xls workbook brings Figure 6.2.1 to life and explains how each observation (as a time and distance traveled pair of numbers) is created. Use the [Get an Observation] button to create five observations for Time = 1, 2, 3, 4, and 5. In other words, as you are prompted for the time elapsed from when the ball dropped, enter a "1" for the first observation, a "2" for the second observation, and so on.

Suppose that Galileo gathered 40 observations on Time and Distance, proceeding in tenth of a second intervals. The data are available in the *OurData* sheet. You can create your own data set by clicking on the [Get 40 Observations] button. Galileo then ran a regression on the data. We say, "he regressed distance on time." Galileo used Excel's LINEST function to obtain the results in

For example, after 5 seconds, Galileo would measure the distance the object has fallen.

5 s...

398 ft

Figure 6.2.1. The data generation process: One observation in Galileo's data.

Figure 6.2.2. Written as a regression equation, Galileo's fitted line looks like this:

$$\text{Predicted Distance} = -124.82 + 96.83 \times \text{Time}$$
$$\quad\quad\text{(ft)}\quad\quad\quad\quad\quad\text{(ft)}\quad\text{(ft/s)}\quad\text{(s)}$$

In this equation, the units are below each variable and coefficient. At first blush, the descriptive regression appears to fit the data well. The RMSE is acceptably small: a little less than 20 ft with an average Distance of about 170 ft. The R^2 is a very high 0.97. The slope coefficient represents how fast Predicted Distance changes as Time changes. On the basis of this work, Galileo might conclude that a good description of the relationship between Time and Distance Traveled is that objects fall to the earth at roughly 97 ft/s.

In fact, Galileo abandoned the idea that distance traveled is a linear function of time. Galileo had some theoretical reasons for believing that bodies accelerate as they fall toward the Earth. This suggested that the relationship between time and distance is nonlinear. He thought the relationship might look more like a parabola. Galileo also thought he had better take a look at the data to see whether a linear functional form made sense. He plotted the residuals from the regression of distance on time and obtained the results in Figure 6.2.3.

Figure 6.2.2. Galileo's regression of distance on time.
Source: [Galileo.xls]OurData.

Regression Results		
Predicted Distance = $b_0 + b_1$Time		
slope	96.83	−124.82 **intercept**
R^2	0.97	19.40 **RMSE**
		38 **df**
Reg SS	499719	14299 **SSR**

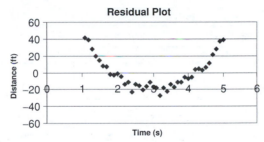

Figure 6.2.3. Residuals from regression of distance on time.
Source: [Galileo.xls]OurData.

Immediately, Galileo knew that the linear model was not a good description
of the data. A pattern in the residual plot is a signal that something is wrong.
He turned to the scatter diagram in Figure 6.2.4 of the original data for
additional confirmation.

The fitted regression line is plotted as well as the actual data. Clearly, the
data do not really follow a straight line. They follow some sort of curve, as
Galileo's theory suggested.

It was back to the computer for Galileo. For both theoretical reasons and
on the basis of analyzing the data, he changed the functional form of his
descriptive model. The functional form is nothing more than the hypothesized
way in which the variables are related to each other. The first equation was a
linear functional form, so-called because it assumed time and distance to be
linearly related. Galileo instead decided to estimate a nonlinear relationship
between distance and time, using the following equation (with units given
below):

$$\text{Predicted Distance} = \text{Intercept} + \text{Slope} \times \text{Time}^2$$
$$\text{(ft)} \qquad \text{(ft)} \qquad \text{(ft/s}^2) \quad \text{(s}^2)$$

The nonlinear equation can be estimated via linear regression because it is
linear in the parameters Intercept and Slope. It will result in a straight line fit
between the variables Predicted Distance and Time^2. When the coefficients

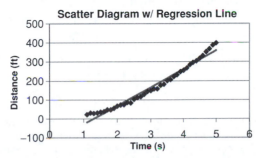

Figure 6.2.4. Regression of distance on time.
Source: [Galileo.xls]OurData.

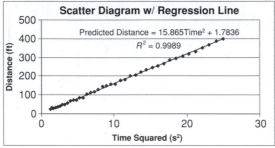

Regression Results		
Predicted Distance = $b_0 + b_1$Time²		
slope	15.86	1.784	**intercept**
R^2	0.9989	3.88	**RMSE**
		38	**df**
Reg SS	513445	573	**SSR**

Scatter Diagram w/ Regression Line

Predicted Distance = 15.865Time² + 1.7836
R^2 = 0.9989

Figure 6.2.5. Regression of distance on time squared.
Source: [Galileo.xls]OurData.

are used in a graph of Predicted Distance and Time (not Time²), the relationship will be nonlinear.

To use the quadratic functional form, we must transform the Time variable into Time². To do this in Excel, Galileo creates a new variable, Time Squared. Thus, if a single observation previously contained the two variable values: Distance = 22.85 and Time = 1.10, now this observation contains an additional variable, Time Squared = 1.21. See column Q in the *OurData* sheet.

When Galileo ran this regression in Excel, he obtained the results in Figure 6.2.5. This new nonlinear functional form is a much more satisfactory description of the data. The graph in Figure 6.2.5 makes clear that the fit is obviously better. The coefficient on the squared term is the estimated rate of acceleration.[2]

You might be wondering exactly what is nonlinear about Figure 6.2.5. It appears that the 40 observations have a strong linear relationship. In fact, they do. Distance and Time² are linearly related – that is why the linear regression summarizes the data so well. The nonlinear relationship is between Distance and Time (not Time²). If we use the regression coefficients to compute Predicted Distance and then plot the predicted and observed values

---

[2] For calculus students: The derivative of Predicted $D = 1.78 + 15.86 \times T^2$ with respect to T is $2 \times 15.86\, T$ ft/s, where d Predicted D/dT is velocity, which is an increasing function of time. The second derivative, 31.72 ft/s², is the rate of acceleration. Your physics book will tell you this constant is 32 ft/s². Galileo's data suffered from measurement error. (We should know because we cooked the data!)

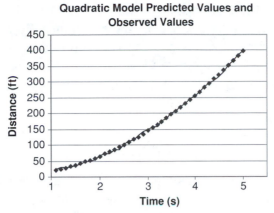

Figure 6.2.6. Predicted distance as a function of time.
Source: [Galileo.xls]OurData.

of distance against Time (not Time^2) on the *x*-axis, we obtain the nonlinear pattern displayed in Figure 6.2.6.

How is a *linear* regression able to generate a *curve*? This is possible because the linear regression works with nonlinear transformations of the variables and then employs the fitted intercept and slope coefficients in predicting the dependent variable (in this case, Distance). When the predicted *Y* variable values are plotted against the *X* variable in its original (untransformed) units, the relationship becomes nonlinear.

Not only does the curve fit the data well, but Figure 6.2.7 reveals that the residual plot also looks like the formless blob it is supposed to. Unlike the residual plot in Figure 6.2.3, there is no obvious pattern in this graph. Notice that the residuals are computed and graphed against the Time variable in this case.

The RMSE (about 3.9 ft for the quadratic model versus 19.4 ft for the linear model) and the scatter plots tell us that the nonlinear model does a

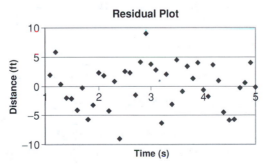

Figure 6.2.7. Plot of residuals from distance on time squared.
Source: [Galileo.xls]OurData.

much better job of describing the data than the linear model. Notice also that the intercept coefficient is also much more plausible with the quadratic functional form. Finally, Galileo noted that the quadratic regression does a much better job of predicting "out of sample" than the linear regression model (by extrapolating either to times shorter than 1 s or to times longer than 5 s).

Summary

In the first equation, Galileo assumed a linear relationship existed between Time and Distance. In the new transformed equation, he assumed a linear relationship between Distance and $Time^2$, but that implied a nonlinear relationship between Distance and Time. Galileo used linear regression of Distance on $Time^2$ to generate a nonlinear fit of Distance on Time. This strategy, applying linear regression to nonlinear transformations of variables, makes linear regression extremely flexible.

Our econometric fable is almost at an end, but a few points need to be emphasized. In this example, we have hinted at one way to model the data generation process. We argued that the data do not fit exactly on a mathematical curve because Galileo's measuring devices are not perfect. Galileo's measurements are subject to error. This idea will be further pursued when we consider inference in the second part of this book.

Second, we can improve on our model. Our estimate of the intercept term is still unsatisfactory. We know that the ball does not really start out 1.8 ft on its way at time 0. The improvement is to impose the requirement on the regression that the intercept be exactly zero. This will make our predictions more plausible at the cost of an RMSE which is slightly higher than it was in the unrestricted regression.[3] Scroll to column AK of the *OurData* sheet in Galileo.xls to see the results of the restricted model.

Finally, Galileo's quadratic functional form is just one of many nonlinear transformations. The next section offers two other examples of nonlinear functional forms.

6.3. Exploring Two Other Functional Forms

Workbook: IMRGDPFunForm.xls

This section examines a real data set that has been seen before – the World Health Organization data on infant mortality rates and per capita GDP in

---

[3] We follow up on this idea in Chapter 17, which covers ways to test claims about the true value of parameters in models of the data generation process.

different countries – and applies two new functional forms to describing the relationship between the two variables.

As we work through these transformations, we continue the key idea of this chapter: linear regression is extremely flexible and can be used to describe nonlinear relationships. This seeming contradiction is possible because the word "linear" in linear regression refers to linearity in the parameters. Although the regression line is a straight line when drawn in the coordinates of the transformed variables, this is no longer true when we graph the regression line in terms of the original units of the data.

The *AlternativeModels* sheet in the IMRGDPFunForm.xls workbook contains a data set with observations on Infant Mortality Rate (IMR) in 1998 and GDP Per Capita in 1992 in 87 different countries. We fit three different regression models to the data:

The Linear Functional Form

$$\text{Model 1}: \text{Predicted } IMR_i = b_0 + b_1 \cdot GDPpc_i, i = 1, \ldots, 87.$$

The Reciprocal (or Inverse) Functional Form

$$\text{Model 2}: \text{Predicted } IMR_i = b_0 + b_1 \cdot \frac{1}{GDPpc_i}, i = 1, \ldots, 87.$$

The Double-Log Functional Form

$$\text{Model 3}: \text{Predicted } \ln(IMR_i) = b_0 + b_1 \cdot \ln(GDPpc_i), i = 1, \ldots, 87.$$

Proceed to the *AlternativeModels* sheet in the IMRGDPFunForm.xls workbook to see how the data are transformed to fit the reciprocal and double log models. Click on cell I20, for example, to see that $1/GDPpc$ is one divided by cell B20 (which is *GDPpc*). Similarly, cells in column M and N (M20 and N20, for example) use Excel's LN function to take the natural log of the IMR and GDP per capita values.

Once the data are transformed, the usual least squares fitted line is found. In terms of the transformed data, the linear regression produces straight lines like those displayed in Figure 6.3.1. We used Excel's Trendline to fit the line but edited the $y = mx + b$ display in the chart on the right. This is good practice.

To see the fit of the regression on the original data, simply take the Predicted Y values and plot them against the X values instead of the transformed X values. In the case of the double log model, because the Predicted *IMR* units are the natural log of the original data, transforming back to the original Y values by taking the antilog is also required. Column P (click on cell P20, for example) shows how the formula EXP is used to calculate $e^{\text{Predicted } IMR}$ to

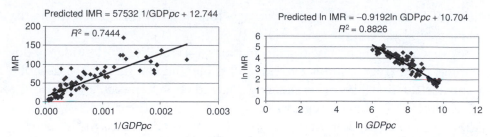

Figure 6.3.1. Linear regression on transformed data.
Source: [IMRGDPFunForm.xls]AlternativeModels.

compute *IMR* in its original units. Figure 6.3.2 shows how the two nonlinear models fit the data.

The primary purpose of this chapter is to convey the important idea that nonlinear transformations of the *X* and *Y* variables make linear regression extremely flexible. This means that linear regression can be used to summarize a very wide variety of nonlinear relationships between variables effectively.

Of course, once we admit the possibility of many curved fits, deciding on the best summary becomes difficult. In the IMR–GDP per capita example, most would agree that the reciprocal and double log models are vastly superior to the linear model, but how do we choose between the two curved fits?

One inappropriate approach is simply to compare the R^2 statistics. R^2 measures how much of the total variation in the dependent variable is explained by the regression. This means that the dependent variable must be the same when comparing the R^2's from two different regressions. Because the double log model has transformed the dependent variable, the R^2 of the double log model, 0.88, cannot be compared with the R^2's of the linear or reciprocal models, 0.54 and 0.74, respectively. Similarly, the RMSEs cannot be compared because the vertical scale is different.

We can, however, compute the residuals and squared residuals from the double log model in the original units of the dependent variable (i.e., after taking the antilog of Predicted lnIMR). Columns Q and R (click on cells Q20

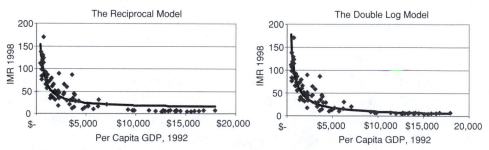

Figure 6.3.2. Two nonlinear regressions plotted against original variables.
Source: [IMRGDPFunForm.xls]AlternativeModels.

Comparing the Three Models		
Model	RMSE	SSR
Linear	26.77	62,354
Reciprocal	19.96	34,677
Double Log	21.35	39,658

Figure 6.3.3. Residual performance measures.
Source: [IMRGDPFunForm.xls]Alternative Models.

and R20, for example) show the calculation. Figure 6.3.3 displays the results once we have the residuals and squared residuals in the original units of the dependent variable.

It looks like the reciprocal model wins on the basis of a smaller spread in the residuals and smaller sum of squared residuals, but the residuals plots in Figure 6.3.4 reveal more information.

The reciprocal model overestimates all of the high-income countries, whereas the double log model is dead on for those richer countries (a characteristic you may have noticed from the regression fit chart in Figure 6.3.2).

There are no clear recipes for deciding which summary is the best. From this example we can state without any doubt that the linear model is a poor summary of the data. Furthermore, we can see that the reciprocal and double log models are much better summaries than the linear model. Unfortunately, although the curved fits do a much better job of summarizing the IMR and GDP per capita data, there does not appear to be a clear victor between the reciprocal and double log models in this case. Economists might prefer the double log model because of a special feature of that model: along the regression line, a constant percentage change in the X variable always translates into a constant percentage change in the Predicted Y variable with the constant of proportionality equal to the slope coefficient.

Sometimes, a strong theoretical framework, such as the one Galileo had, enables identification of the correct best-functional form. Usually, however, econometricians have theories with qualitative predictions that do not point to a particular functional form. We will continue to stress that theory and data must be combined to produce quality econometric analysis.

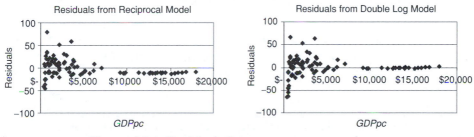

Figure 6.3.4. Residual plots.
Source: [IMRGDPFunForm.xls]AlternativeModels.

Summary

Although the first two sections of this chapter have introduced you to three nonlinear functional forms, that does not begin to exhaust the possibilities. The next section demostrates a common nonlinear functional form in labor economics.

6.4. The Earnings Function

Workbook: SemiLogEarningsFn.xls

This section introduces the semilog functional form

$$\text{Predicted } \ln Y = a + bX,$$

where ln stands for the natural log function. Unlike the double-log specification, where we transform both X and Y by taking natural logs, the semilog form applies the natural log only to the dependent variable.[4]

The semilog functional form is extremely common in labor economics. An *earnings function* is an equation that explains wage, salary, or other remuneration as a function of relevant factors such as education, experience, and demographic characteristics. Typically, economists have data on some measure of earnings that we regress on a variety of independent variables. We routinely take the natural log of the measure of earnings before running the regression. There are strong theoretical reasons for the use of the semilog functional form in the case of the earnings function.

This section is organized in two parts. First, we will explain the theoretical underpinnings of the use of the natural log of earnings. We then apply the theory to an example using data from the Current Population Survey.

Human Capital Theory

Why do some jobs pay more than others? Anyone who has taken an introductory economics course knows the answer: supply and demand. Higher paying jobs must have some combination of greater demand or lesser supply than lower paying jobs.

Let us take this simple truth and make it a little more rigorous. Economists argue that, in equilibrium, the gap, or difference in pay between two jobs, must be such that the next entrant into the labor market would be indifferent

---

[4] Because we are applying the ln transformation to the dependent variable, this is sometimes called a log-linear functional form. If we take the natural log of the X variable and not the Y variable, we would have another version of the semilog functional form called the lin-log model.

Length of working life (training included)	discount rate		Amount of training needed for job	Constant annual earnings	Present value of lifetime earnings
years	%/yr		ears	$/yr	$/yr
L	r		n	a_0	PV
41	7%	Job 1	1	$ 30,000	$ 399,951
		Job 2	3	$ 34,000	$ 391,805
				$ 4,000	$ (8,146)

IRR 5.69%

Figure 6.4.1. The two-job-choice model.
Source: [SemiLogEarningsFn.xls]TwoJobsModel.

between the two jobs. If not, people would flood into the more attractive job, reducing its pay, and avoid the less attractive job, increasing its salary and pushing the difference in pay toward equilibrium. Although labor markets equilibrate slowly, to demonstrate the logic behind the semilog functional form we will build a model that assumes that we are in equilibrium.

Notwithstanding that there are many sources of differences between jobs, let us concentrate on just one: training. No one would disagree that jobs that require more training should pay more. After all, when someone is busy training (going to medical school, for example), he or she is foregoing income from working at a job that does not require as much training. Clearly, we have to compensate doctors for the opportunity cost of training in order to entice people to become doctors.

Open the SemiLogEarningsFn.xls workbook and proceed to the *TwoJobsModel* sheet. A part of this sheet is reproduced in Figure 6.4.1. It depicts a person deciding between two jobs that require different years of training. The person can count on a working life of 41 years, and the pay received in each year is discounted by 7 percent per year. Job 2 requires 2 more years of training than Job 1, but it pays $4,000 more per year.

On your screen, to the right of this information, the sheet displays the earnings streams from the two jobs. Notice how we have simplified by assuming constant annual earnings. In other words, if the worker chooses Job 1, he or she will make $30,000 per year for 40 years, or $1.2 million over his or her entire lifetime. Scroll down to cell J61 to see the sum of the total dollars received over time.[5] To the right, in cell L61, you can see that Job 2 yields $1,292,000 because it pays $34,000 per year for 38 years. Notice that the difference between jobs is $92,000 and not $160,000 ($4,000 per year times 40 years)

[5] You might notice that the top nine rows remain visible while you scroll down. We did this by using Excel's Freeze Pane feature (available under the Window menu). This enables the user to see the labels when the data set is bigger than the screen.

because Job 2 requires 3 years of training. Scroll back to see (in cells L10:L12) that there are no earnings for the first 3 years for Job 2.

Of course, comparing the total dollars earned is pretty silly because a dollar today is worth more than a dollar tomorrow. With a dollar today, you could invest it and, as long as the interest rate was positive, it would return more than a dollar tomorrow. Using this logic, we compute the *present value* (PV) of future payments. In other words, we ask how much would be needed today to become a given amount in the future. Columns K and M show the present values of the annual salaries for the two jobs. Consider Year 20, for example. The present value of $30,000 at a 7-percent discount rate is $7,753. Click on cell K30 to see the formula. The idea is that if you had $7,753 right now and invested it at a 7-percent interest rate, it would grow to $30,000 in 20 years. You can change the discount rate in cell B11. Try 10 and 2 percent. The higher the discount rate, the lower the present value because it takes less money right now to become the target amount in the future. Click the Reset button before proceeding.

By enabling dollars received at different points in time to be valued at the same moment in time, present value ensures that we are making the correct comparison of the pay differential between the two jobs. Instead of saying, "Job 2 is worth $1.292 million and provides $92,000 more than Job 1," we say, "Job 2 has a present value of $391,805 at a discount rate of 7 percent and this is $8,146 less than Job 1's present value."

It is decision time. If all else is equal, should the worker choose Job 1 or Job 2? Job 2 does indeed pay more, but is the differential high enough? The negative *net present value* (NPV) computed in column O tells you that the PV of Job 1 is greater than the PV of Job 2. Thus, $4,000 extra per year is not enough to compensate for the lost 2 years of income due to training. A quick look at the earnings stream data shows that $4,000 far in the future really is not that much money in present-value terms and that those 2 lost years of income occur early on. On the basis of present values, this worker would choose Job 1 over Job 2.

In addition to comparing the present values of two income streams and choosing the bigger one, there is a second way to make this decision. We could compute the *internal rate of return* (IRR) generated by the $4,000 pay differential. Column N shows the difference between the Job 1 and Job 2 earnings streams. Cell F15 uses Excel's IRR function to compute the discount rate that sets the net present value equal to zero. You can confirm this by simply copying cell F15 and then clicking on cell B11 and executing Edit: Paste Special: Values. Click the Reset button before proceeding.

Once we have the IRR, the decision is easy: If IRR $> r$, then take Job 2. In this case, the IRR is 5.69 percent, which is less than the 7-percent discount rate, and thus the worker would not choose Job 2. For simple projects, with

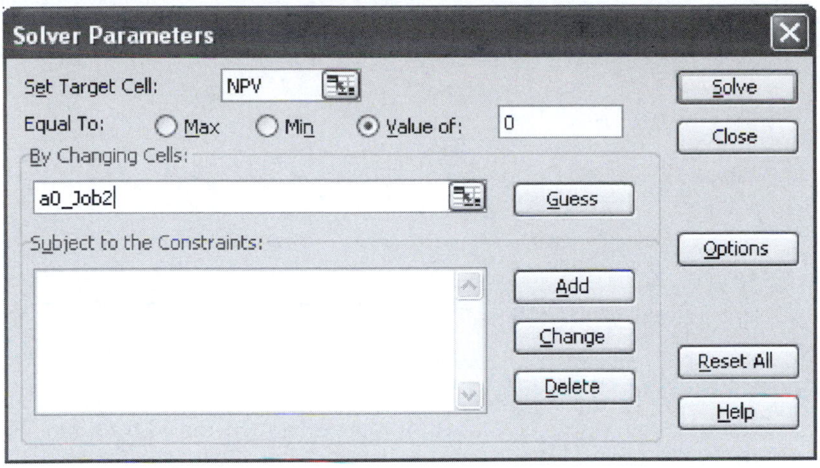

Figure 6.4.2. Using Solver to find the equilibrium pay gap.

upfront costs and future returns, the IRR method is reliable and always agrees with the NPV approach. For more complicated projects, the IRR method may fail, and so NPV is preferred. We explain the IRR method because, when we apply the semilog functional form to an earnings function we are actually estimating the internal rate of return to schooling.

Now that we know that $4,000 is not enough and that the worker will choose Job 1, we know that this will push the differential higher. Although the process would include Job 1's salary falling (as people entered that occupation) and Job 2's pay rising (as workers retired and no one entered), we will simplify the story somewhat by focusing only on Job 2's pay. We need to find that dollar gap that, for the project of choosing Job 2 over Job 1, makes the NPV = 0 and the IRR = r. Although we could hunt and peck, entering trial values in cell E12 by hand, this is clearly a job for Excel's Solver.

Execute Tools: Solver and you will see the dialog box displayed in Figure 6.4.2. We will have Solver change cell E12 (named a0_Job2, the annual earnings from Job 2) so that cell F13 (named NPV) is set equal to zero.

Click Solve and then OK to place Solver's answer in the sheet. The equilibrium difference in annual pay is $4,707. This sets the present values of both streams equal to each other and the IRR equal to the 7-percent discount rate. If all else is equal, a worker facing these two jobs would be indifferent between them. Job 2 does indeed pay more, but it has higher training requirements that exactly cancel out the higher pay.

We know the equilibrium pay differential when Job 2 requires 3 years of training. But what would be the equilibrium pay differential for jobs that required even more training? Change cell D12 from 3 to 4. We are back to the situation in which the differential is too low. We need to run Solver to find the equilibrium gap for this new Job 2 that requires 4 years of training.

Required Training	Job 2 Salary	Ratio Job1/Job2
3	$34,707	116%
4	$37,353	125%
5	$40,218	134%
6	$43,325	144%
7	$46,695	156%
8	$50,356	168%
9	$54,338	181%
10	$58,674	196%
11	$63,403	211%
12	$68,567	229%
13	$74,216	247%
14	$80,407	268%
15	$87,207	291%

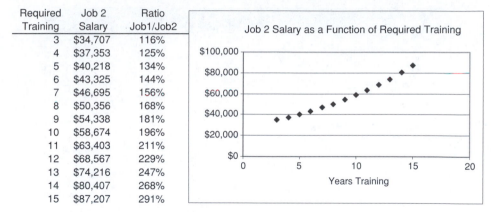

Figure 6.4.3. Job 2's equilibrium salary as a function of training.
Source: [SemiLogEarningsFn.xls]Job2(n).

After doing so, we see that the equilibrium difference in annual earnings has grown to $7,353.

We are now ready to make the leap that will explain why the semilog functional form is routinely applied to the dependent variable in an earnings function regression. By exploring the relationship of the equilibrium gap as a function of *n*, we can immediately see that differences in pay for jobs with differing required training are not linear. Proceed to the *Job2(n)* sheet, a portion of which is displayed in Figure 6.4.3, for a clear demonstration of this point.

The first two observations confirm our earlier work for the equilibrium salary for Job 2 when the required training was 3 and 4 years, respectively. We simply applied the same method, using Solver to find the equilibrium Job 2 salary, for various years of training.

Figure 6.4.3 shows that the salary differentials for jobs with differing training requirements are not constant. In fact, Jacob Mincer's brilliant insight was to realize this and, furthermore, to see that the function is following an exponential path. This is the heart of the matter: Equilibrium pay differentials for jobs with differing levels of training are constant *multiples* of each other.

The next and last step to the semilog functional form is trivial. By taking the natural log of the Job 2 equilibrium salaries, we linearize the exponential curve, as Figure 6.4.4 shows.

You might notice that the slope coefficient is 7.7 percent, which is a little off from the 7-percent discount rate in the model. This is because the earnings stream has a finite length. The longer the working life of the individual, the closer the slope coefficient will get to the discount rate. The *Q&A* sheet has a question that invites you to confirm this result by changing cell A11 in the *TwoJobsModel* sheet and running Solver for several values of *n*.

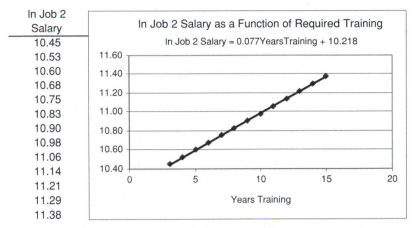

In Job 2 Salary
10.45
10.53
10.60
10.68
10.75
10.83
10.90
10.98
11.06
11.14
11.21
11.29
11.38

Figure 6.4.4. Linearizing via the natural log transformation.
Source: [SemiLogEarningsFn.xls]Job2(n).

By working through a numerical example, we have shown that salary depends on years of training or schooling in an exponential way. By taking the natural log of the dependent variable, we convert the curve into a line. This is the theoretical explanation for why earnings functions utilize the semilog functional form. We conclude this section by providing a real-world example of this approach.

The Earnings Function in Practice

Proceed to the *EducWageData* sheet in the SemiLogEarningsFn.xls workbook. The data are in columns A and B. If we regress Wage on Education, we obtain the results shown in Figure 6.4.5.

Wage is measured in $/hr and Education in years of schooling, and so we interpret the 1.65 slope coefficient as telling us that wages rise by $1.65 an hour for every additional year of schooling.

But our theoretical argument tells us that wages do not rise at a constant linear rate. In fact, we have strong theoretical reasons for believing that the difference in wages for those with higher levels of training (or schooling) is a nearly constant percentage or multiple. Thus, we are in the same position as

Regression Results

Wage = b_0 + b_1Education

slope	1.65	−7.13	intercept
R^2	0.20	7.63	RMSE
		1139	df
Reg SS	16,133	66,251	SSR

Figure 6.4.5. The linear model.
Source: [SemiLogEarningsFn.xls] EducWageData.

Regression Results			
ln Wage = b_0 + b_1Education			
slope	0.102	1.22	intercept
R^2	0.20	0.47	RMSE
		1139	df
Reg SS	61	247	SSR

Figure 6.4.6. The semilog model.
Source: [SemiLogEarningsFn.xls]
EducWageData.

in the second section of this chapter in which Galileo had strong theoretical reasons to believe that the functional form is not linear.

Because our theory explains that the relationship between earnings and training is exponential, it also supplies the needed transformation. By taking the natural log of the wage, we can linearize a function we believe to be exponential. Figure 6.4.6 shows the OLS estimates for the semilog functional form.

Before doing anything else, it is important to be certain we understand how to interpret the slope coefficient. We cannot say that wage rises by 10.2 cents an hour for every year of schooling. That would be absurd. In a 2,000-hour work year, would one more year of college give about $200 more income? That makes no sense. If we take the derivative of the fitted line, we can see what is going on:

$$\frac{d \ln Wage}{d Educ} = 0.102.$$

The coefficient is telling us not the change in the wage but the change in the natural log of the wage as Education changes. The change in the natural log is approximately equal to the percentage change. Thus, we interpret the slope coefficient in a semilog functional form as giving the percentage change in the wage given an additional year of schooling. For this data set, one more year of Education increases the wage by about 10.2 percent. Because the average wage in the data set is $16.85, an additional year of schooling from the average level of schooling will raise the wage by approximately $1.68 per hour. An extra year of schooling, from the average level of schooling, in this data set gives about $3,360 more per year. That is reasonable.

Just as we did with the other functional forms in this chapter, we can predict the wage using the semilog model by transforming the data back into their original units. Column T in the *EducWageData* sheet shows that we can predict the wage given a particular value of Education by taking the antilog, $e^{(1.22+0.102Educ)}$.[6] Figure 6.4.7 shows the nonlinear relationship between

---

[6] In the second part of this book, we show how, in some cases, a correction is applied to this computation.

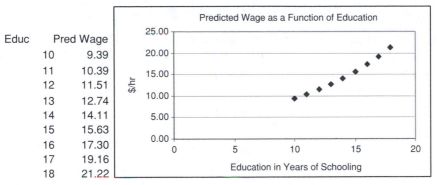

Educ	Pred Wage
10	9.39
11	10.39
12	11.51
13	12.74
14	14.11
15	15.63
16	17.30
17	19.16
18	21.22

Figure 6.4.7. Predicted wage from the semilog model.
Source: [SemiLogEarningsFn.xls]EducWageData

Predicted Wage and Education that resulted from the linear regression of ln Wage on Education.

Summary

This section has explained why the semilog functional form is standard operating procedure in regressions based on earnings functions. Although our two-job example made the theoretical argument clear, you should know there are some complications to the story. Jobs are different in many more ways than simply the amount of training required, and it is a source of debate among labor economists if we should interpret the world as being at, or even near, equilibrium. Evidence for these complications is provided by the regression results of the semilog functional form. Unlike the theoretical example, in which we obtained a perfect fit after applying the natural log transformation, the R^2 of 0.2 tells us that other factors besides education influence wages.

Later chapters demonstrate that labor economists improve the explanation of the variation in observed salaries by including more explanatory variables in the regression. The second part of this book also shows that there is a second reason for using the semilog functional form on earnings data – it reduces heteroskedasticity.

6.5. Elasticity

This section reviews the concept of elasticity and shows how the functional form of the regression affects elasticity. We show how elasticity is computed at a point or a finite distance from one point to another and offer a few examples.

Reviewing the Concept of Elasticity

Elasticity is a fundamental concept in economics used to express the sensitivity of the response of one variable given a change in another. Elasticity is the percentage change in the dependent variable (Y) given a percentage change in the independent variable (X) with other variables held constant.

The computed value of a measured elasticity depends on the size of the change in the X variable. We will use the following formula when we are considering a *discrete* change in the X variable:

$$\frac{\%\,\Delta Y}{\%\,\Delta X} = \frac{\frac{\text{change in } Y}{\text{initial } Y}}{\frac{\text{change in } X}{\text{initial } X}} = \frac{\text{change in } Y}{\text{change in } X} \cdot \frac{X}{Y}.$$

Economists sometimes use an arc, or midpoint, elasticity in which the change in the variables is measured relative to the average value of X and the average value of Y over the range under consideration as opposed to the initial values of X and Y, respectively.

Elasticities are more commonly computed and reported as point elasticities. Instead of considering a discrete change in X, *infinitesimally small* changes are used. In this case, the concept of elasticity can be expressed via the derivative:

$$\lim_{\Delta X \to 0} \frac{\%\,\Delta Y}{\%\,\Delta X} = \lim_{\Delta X \to 0} \frac{\frac{\Delta Y}{Y}}{\frac{\Delta X}{X}} = \lim_{\Delta X \to 0} \frac{\Delta Y}{\Delta X} \cdot \frac{X}{Y} = \frac{dY}{dX} \cdot \frac{X}{Y}.$$

We proceed by demonstrating these formulas with a concrete example and then discussing why economists focus on the ratio of percentage changes.

Suppose you are interested in the responsiveness of Y given changes in X. You fit a line to a scatter diagram and obtain an equation of the fitted line in the usual form, $Y = mX + b$. How can this equation be used to compute the X elasticity of Y? You have several options.

Because elasticity changes along a straight line (with a nonzero intercept), you must decide the value of X to be used as your reference point. Typically, but not always, the average X is used.[7] Once you have determined the value of X to be used, you can compute an elasticity with a discrete change in X or via the derivative.

To use the discrete change approach, you need to consider two separate points on the fitted line – for instance, $Y = 0.33X + 3$. Then, when X is 3, Y is 4, and when X is 6, Y is 5. Thus, when X moves from 3 to 6, Y goes from 4 to 5. The change in Y is 1 ($= 5 - 4$), and the percentage change in Y is 25 percent (because $1/4 = 0.25$ or 25 percent). Similarly, the change in X is

---

[7] In our introduction to regression in Chapter 1, we computed the price elasticity of demand at the average price.

3 (= 6 – 3), and the percentage change in X is 100 percent (= 3/3 = 1 = 100 percent). The X elasticity of Y from $X = 3$ to 6 is then 25%/100% or 0.25.

Instead of moving from one X value to another, you could measure the elasticity at a single point. To do this, we examine a change in X that is infinitesimally small. We use the derivative to find the change in Y for a given infinitesimally small change in X:

$$\frac{\%\Delta Y}{\%\Delta X} = \frac{dY}{dX} \cdot \frac{X}{Y},$$

where dY/dX is simply the slope of the function at the point (X,Y). For $Y = 0.33X + 3$, dY/dX is 0.33; thus, the point X elasticity of Y at $X = 3$ is simply 0.33 times 3 divided by 4, or 0.25.

The derivative approach, computing a point elasticity, is a shortcut. It is a way of calculating the percentage change in Y for a given percentage change in X without having to evaluate Y at the initial X, then evaluating Y at a new value of X, and then calculating percentage changes of Y and X.

The two approaches give the same answer in this case because the slope is constant. If the relationship is nonlinear, an elasticity at a point will differ from one based on a movement from one point to another on the curve.

The idea behind elasticity is to use percentage changes as a measure of responsiveness because we get a relative unitless measure of the sensitivity of one variable as another changes. In the example above, we could simply say that Y responds 1 unit as X increases 3 units but that measure is dependent on the units of Y and X. If X is measured in pounds, we could switch to ounces and say, "As X increases 48 units (ounces), Y increases 1 unit." Unlike the simple change, percentage changes remove the effect of scale. The percentage change in X from 3 to 6 (pounds) or 48 to 96 (ounces) or 0.0015 to 0.0030 (tons) is 100 percent. The scale used does not matter. This is a powerful, desirable property.

In our experience, we have found that many students have great difficulty appreciating that elasticity is a "local phenomenon" – to speak of an entire curve as having a certain elasticity is usually wrong ("usually" because some curves do have constant elasticities!). When you think of elasticity, think of it as representing the responsiveness of Y at a particular X value.

For example, consider the equation $Y = 100 - 5X$. You want to measure the elasticity at $X = 10$ (which implies $Y = 50$). Because the elasticity is being measured at a point, you use the derivative approach

$$\frac{\%\Delta Y}{\%\Delta X} = \frac{dY}{dX} \cdot \frac{X}{Y} = -5 \cdot \frac{10}{50} = -1.$$

At the coordinate $(10, 50)$, the X elasticity of Y is -1 (which is said to be unit elastic). We interpret this number by saying that a 1 percent change in X causes a 1 percent change in Y in the opposite direction.

You can check this for yourself by noting that a 1-percent increase in X from $X = 10$ to $X = 10.1$ leads to a movement in Y from 50 to 49.5 $(= 100 - 5 \times 10.1)$. Notice that the movement from 50 to 49.5 is -1 percent $[= (49.5 - 50)/50]$.

On the other hand, the X elasticity of Y at $X = 15$ (which implies $Y = 25$) is

$$\frac{dY}{dX} \cdot \frac{X}{Y} = -5 \cdot \frac{15}{25} = -3.$$

At $X = 15$, an infinitesimally small percentage increase in X will lead to threefold percentage decreases in Y.

Thus, in summary, elasticity depends on the value of X; it is a local phenomenon. The elasticity is always calculated as the percentage change in the Y variable caused by a given percentage change in the X variable. In practice, using the derivative approach, this reduces to the formula

$$\frac{\% \Delta Y}{\% \Delta X} = \frac{dY}{dX} \cdot \frac{X}{Y}.$$

Calculating the elasticity of a point on a line is simple: multiply the slope of the line times the ratio of the coordinates of the point. Given an estimated regression equation, the elasticity at a particular X (which is often chosen to be the average X) can be computed using the formula immediately above.

Although the formulas make this clear, we point out another common confusion: Elasticity is not the same as the slope. The slope is simply dY/dX, and the elasticity is dY/dX *times* X/Y. Thus, elasticity cannot be the slope because it contains the slope and then something more. Slope is just the rate of change, whereas elasticity is based on the percentage change. Do not confuse these two different ways of measuring change.

Elasticity with Different Functional Forms

Having reviewed the concept of elasticity, we are ready to tie it to the main topic of this chapter, the functional form of the regression. We have seen how elasticity is computed with the standard linear model, but what happens when other functional forms are chosen?

The general answer is that we simply apply the basic formula. For example, in Section 6.2, we have the nonlinear fit, Predicted Distance $= 1.784 + 15.86$ Time^2. We would compute the Time elasticity of Predicted Distance at

Time $= 3$ by applying the usual elasticity formula:

$$\frac{\%\Delta Y}{\%\Delta X} = \frac{dY}{dX} \cdot \frac{X}{Y} = 31.72X \cdot \frac{X}{Y} = 31.72\,(3) \cdot \frac{3}{144.164} = 0.22.$$

In the case of the Double Log specification, we obtain a neat result. Recall from Section 6.3 that we obtained Predicted ln $IMR = 10.704 - 0.9192$ln $GDPpc$. The change in the natural log is approximately equal to the percentage change

$$\frac{d\ln Y}{d\ln X} \approx \frac{\%\Delta Y}{\%\Delta X}.$$

Thus, in the case of the Double Log functional form, the estimated slope coefficient, in the IMR example, -0.9, is interpreted as an elasticity. Furthermore, in the case of the Double Log transformation, the elasticity is constant all along the fitted curve.

The fact that the slope coefficient immediately displays the elasticity and that the Double Log functional form imposes a constant elasticity on the relationship helps explain why you will see many applications of the Double Log functional form.

Summary

Elasticity is a fundamental concept in economics. Econometricians often use regression coefficients to compute elasticities or apply a particular functional form to estimate an elasticity.

6.6. Conclusion

One would think, because it is *linear* regression, that curvilinear relationships would render linear regression useless. In fact, because *linear* refers to linearity in the parameters, a wide variety of nonlinear transformations of the variables enable linear regression to produce an infinite array of nonlinear fits. Linear regression is extremely flexible.

This raises a new question, How do we decide which nonlinear transformation or curve to use? Here are some general pointers:

- When choosing functional forms for the relationship between two variables, it is important to consider *theory* and *data*.
- The linear model is a good place to start.
- The scatter plot of the data and the residuals as well as the RMSE and SSR (used correctly) will tell you how well a particular functional form fits the data.
- You cannot compare R^2's across functional forms that transform the dependent variable (such as linear versus log linear models).

- A variety of functional forms might be considered if the linear model does not work very well.
- You need to think about appropriate functional forms for the relationships between variables before running a regression. You should pay attention to what other researchers have done with similar data.
- Calculating slopes and elasticities is the same in every case. Compute dY/dX and $(dY/dX)(X/Y)$ and evaluate them at the average X and average Y or a particular value of X and corresponding predicted Y that is of interest. It is especially easy to compute the elasticity with the Double Log functional form.

6.7. Exercises

1. Open the Galileo.xls workbook and go to the *Q&A* sheet. This data set was constructed with a different gravitational constant. It appears our fictional Galileo has traveled to another, bigger planet. Use the data set to answer the following questions:
   a. Run regressions for the linear and quadratic models. Report your results in the standard Predicted $Y = b + mX$ format.
   b. Is the quadratic model still better? Explain why.
   c. For the quadratic model, compute the derivative of Predicted Distance with respect to Time.
2. Use the results of the reciprocal and double log models in Section 6.3 to compute the Per Capita GDP elasticity of IMR at a Per Capita GDP of $2,500.
   HINT: For the reciprocal model, apply the point elasticity formula to the equation of the fitted line.
3. Open the SemiLogEarningsFn.xls workbook. Click the Reset button to return the sheet to its default values. Change the length of working life L (in cell A11 of the *TwoJobsModel* sheet) to 31 and answer the questions below.
   a. Because L fell from 41 to 31 years, what will happen to the present values of the earnings streams from the two jobs? Why does this happen?
   b. Why does the PV of the Job 2 earnings stream fall by more than the PV of Job 1's earnings stream?
   c. Run Solver to create a data set of four observations that tracks Job 2's equilibrium salary for $n = 3, 6, 9$, and 12.
   In other words, create a data set similar to the *Job2(n)* sheet.
   d. Draw a chart of Job 2's salary as a function of n.
   e. Create a new variable, ln Job 2 Salary, which takes the natural log of the Job 2 salary at each value of n. Draw a chart of ln Job 2's salary as a function of n.
   f. Use the data set to estimate the rate of return to training. Report your regression results and calculations in coming up with your answer.
   g. In the book, we estimated the rate of return to training as 7.7 percent per year even though the true IRR is 7 percent per year. Your answer (from the previous question) is even farther away from 7 percent. What is going on?

References

On the argument that earnings across jobs are driven to equilibrium by the forces of supply and demand, one need look no further than Adam Smith:

The whole of the advantages and disadvantages of the different employments of labour and stock must, in the same neighbourhood, be either perfectly equal or continually tending to equality. If in the same neighbourhood, there was any employment evidently either more or less advantageous than the rest, so many people would crowd into it in the one case, and so many would desert it in the other, that its advantages would soon return to the level of other employments. This at least would be the case in a society where things were left to follow their natural course, where there was perfect liberty, and where every man was perfectly free both to chuse what occupation he thought proper, and to change it as often as he thought proper. Every man's interest would prompt him to seek the advantageous, and to shun the disadvantageous employment.

This is the first paragraph of Book I, Chapter X of Adam Smith, *An Inquiry into the Nature and Causes of the Wealth of Nations*, 1776. An excellent online source is <www.econlib.org/library/Smith/smWN.html>.

Jacob Mincer is the person responsible for the application of the semilog functional form to the earnings function. In a classic paper, published in 1958, which was a part of his doctoral dissertation, Mincer showed that salary differences in jobs with different amounts of training or schooling would be multiplicative instead of additive. Rosen's tribute in the 1992 *Journal of Economic Perspectives* is an accessible account of Mincer's contributions to economics.

Mincer, J. (1958). "Investment in Human Capital and Personal Income Distribution," *The Journal of Political Economy* **66**(4): 281–302.

Rosen, Sherwin (1992). "Distinguished Fellow: Mincering Labor Economics," *The Journal of Economic Perspectives*, **6**(2): 157–170.

Appendix: A Catalog of Functional Forms

Workbook: FuncFormCatalog.xls

This appendix presents a catalog of functional forms that can be used to model relationships between variables. Each functional form has its own advantages and disadvantages. Here are things you want to look for:

1. How do you interpret the coefficients? For example, in the linear form, one of the parameters is an intercept, which you can usually ignore, and the other is a slope, which tells you very simply how the dependent variable changes as the independent variable changes. Recall that this is merely a summary of a particular data set. Only with a model for the data generating process can you begin to attach causation to an interpretation of the regression results.
2. Are the variables restricted in the value they can take? For some functional forms it makes no sense to have a negative dependent variable.
3. How flexible is the functional form? This depends in part on the answer to the previous question but also has to do with other aspects of the shape of the function. For example, in the linear form, values of X and Y are unrestricted but the slope of the regression line is constant.
4. Does the functional form imply a constant elasticity or changing elasticity when the regression is used to characterize how one variable responds when another changes? This question is only valid when a model of the data generating process has been employed.

5. What are typical applications of the functional form in papers written by economists? This will help you in trying to decide whether a functional form is appropriate for your problem.

The remainder of this appendix presents a catalog of different functional forms that have wide applications in the social sciences. For each functional form, we describe its characteristics in terms of slope and elasticity, any restrictions on the values that the independent and dependent variables can take, and types of applications in which it has proved useful.

The Excel workbook FuncFormCatalog.xls demonstrates each one of the functional forms described below.

The Linear Form
$$\text{Predicted } Y = b_0 + b_1 X$$

- Constant slope;
- Changing elasticity of Y with respect to X (if b_0 is not equal to zero);
- X and Y are unrestricted in the values they can take;
- Flexible to the extent that the slope can take on any value;
- A good starting point.

The Double-Log Form
$$\text{Predicted } \ln Y = b_0 + b_1 \ln X$$

Note: **ln** denotes the natural log, which is preferred by economists over the logarithm to the base 10.

- Changing slope between Y and X;
- Constant elasticity approximately equal to b_1[8];
- Neither X nor Y can be negative;
- Quite flexible – it can describe many shapes;
- Applications for demand curves, production functions, cost functions. For production functions, this form produces sensible isoquants.
- Note that an equivalent way of writing the same model by taking the antilog is

$$\text{Predicted } Y = \exp(b_0) \, X^{b_1}.$$

Semilog: Log-Linear or Log-Lin
$$\text{Predicted } \ln Y = b_0 + b_1 X$$

- Y cannot be negative;
- Changing slope;
- Changing elasticity;
- When X is time, this is a constant-growth-rate model;
- This functional form is very frequently used in models for wages; if X is education, then b_1 is the rate of return to education (the percentage change in wages from one more year of education)
- In its equivalent nonlinear form, we have[9]

---

[8] The approximation is based on the fact that $d\ln Y/d\ln X = b_1$ and $d\ln Y/d\ln X$ is approximately equal to $\%\Delta Y/\%\Delta X$.

[9] When we turn to inferential statistics, it will become apparent that there is an additional correction factor that must be applied to compute Predicted Y.

$$\text{Predicted } Y = \exp(b_0)\exp(b_1 X).$$

Semilog: Lin-Log

$$\text{Predicted } Y = b_0 + b_1 \ln X$$

- X cannot be negative;
- Changing slope;
- Changing elasticity;
- The semilog form has applications to consumption functions because, if b_1 is greater than 0, Y (consumption) increases at a decreasing rate as X (income) increases.

Note that there are two kinds of semilog functional forms, depending on whether the ln transformation is applied to the X or the Y variable.

The Polynomial Form

$$\text{Predicted } Y = b_0 + b_1 X + b_2 X^2$$

- One can add terms of higher degree (X^3, for example) or omit particular terms;
- Changing slope;
- Changing elasticity;
- Flexibility;
- Applications to wages as a function of experience; with X as experience, negative b_2 means that human capital eventually depreciates as one stays longer in the job.

The Reciprocal (or Inverse) Form

$$\text{Predicted } Y = b_0 + b_1 \frac{1}{X}$$

- Changing slope;
- Changing elasticity;
- Sometimes used without an intercept (b_0) term.

7

Multiple Regression

As early as 1897 Mr. G. U. Yule, then my assistant, made an attempt in this direction. He fitted a line or plane by the method of least squares to a swarm of points, and this has been extended later to n-variates and is one of the best ways of reaching the multiple regression equations...

Karl Pearson[1]

7.1. Introduction

This chapter introduces the concept of multiple regression, which in many ways is similar to bivariate regression. Both methods produce conditional predictions, though multiple regression employs more than one independent X variable to predict the value of the Y variable. Just as before, the predicted value of the dependent variable is expressed in a simple equation, and in the case of least squares regression the RMSE summarizes the likely size of the residual and the R^2 statistic measures the fraction of total variation, which is explained by the regression. Once again, the OLS regression coefficients are those that minimize the SSR.

Multiple regression introduces some new issues, however. Some of the complications are purely mathematical. Although it is relatively easy to move back and forth between the algebraic expression and the pictorial (geometric) representation of the regression line in the bivariate case, most people have difficulty translating the algebraic formulation for a multiple regression into its geometric representation as a plane (in trivariate regression) or hyperplane (when there are more than two independent variables). Furthermore, the formulas for the OLS regression coefficients become very unwieldy (we discuss them in the appendix of this chapter).

To help you deal with the additional complexities of multiple regression, we will try to keep you focused on the main issues. The central goal is still

---

[1] Pearson (1920), p. 45. Yule was the first to apply multiple regression to social science problems and to emphasize that multiple regression makes it possible to control for confounding factors.

doing a good job of conditional prediction of values of the Y variable based on our knowledge of values of the X variables. Just as with bivariate regression, multiple regression can again be interpreted as a compression of a (more complicated) graph of averages. The OLS regression coefficients are still weighted sums of the Y variable. Finally, running a multiple regression on a computer is no more difficult than running a bivariate regression.

In addition to the more involved mathematics, multiple regression highlights two important conceptual issues: confounding and multicollinearity. Confounding is so important that it was already introduced in Chapter 1. We suggest that you reread the discussion of separating out the influence of price and income in the demand for cigarettes in Section 1.2.

This chapter makes extensive use of a single artificial example with data on the demand for heating oil. Section 7.2 explains how least squares multiple regression is the solution to the familiar optimization problem of minimizing the SSR, where the Predicted Y variable is now based on more than one X variable. Section 7.3 comes back to the artificial example to explain the concept of confounding. Section 7.4 treats multicollinearity, which is a technical issue you need to be aware of when running your own regressions. The appendix shows how all OLS regression coefficients can be obtained from an analytic formula, which we go on to derive in the trivariate case. The appendix also states the omitted variable rule, which is a simple mathematical relationship explaining the magnitude of confounding.

7.2. Introducing Multiple Regression

Workbook: MultiReg.xls

This section begins with a general discussion of the mathematical problem of fitting a (hyper)plane to a multivariate data set. We introduce some terminology and attempt to help you to visualize the regression plane. A hypothetical data set is then presented concerning the demand for heating oil. The data set is designed especially to make specific points about multiple regression. Four different least squares methods are explored to summarize the relationship between the dependent variable and the independent variables in the data set.

Terminology and Visualization

Multiple regression means that a single dependent variable is regressed on more than one independent variable. Often, econometricians refer to a multiple regression equation just as regression or regression analysis. In addition to multiple, you will also see multivariate used as an adjective to describe regression equation systems with more than one independent variable.

When doing regressions, it is important to keep dependent and independent variables distinct. In the bivariate case, we had one dependent variable (Y), and one independent variable (X). In the multivariate case, there are more than one independent variables. They are labeled X_1, X_2, X_3, and so on in this discussion to emphasize that they are all independent variables.

In the bivariate case, we calculated a regression line in two-dimensional space. The line was represented by

$$\text{Predicted } Y = b_0 + b_1 \cdot X.$$

Here, the b_0 coefficient is the Y-intercept and the b_1 coefficient is the slope, which tells us how fast Predicted Y on the regression line changes as X changes. In the trivariate case, we will calculate a regression plane in three-dimensional space. The equation for the regression plane is

$$\text{Predicted } Y = b_0 + b_1 \cdot X_1 + b_2 \cdot X_2.$$

The b_0 coefficient is still the Y-intercept, but now there are two slopes, b_1 and b_2, each of which tells how Predicted Y changes as the respective X variable changes with the value of the other variable held constant.

In multiple regression, the definition of the residual does not change. It remains the difference between the actual value and the predicted value. For example, for the trivariate case,

$$\text{Residual} = \text{Actual } Y - \text{Predicted } Y$$
$$= \text{Actual } Y - (b_0 + b_1 X_1 + b_2 X_2).$$

In the trivariate, three-dimensional case, we can visualize the residual as a vertical distance as we did in the bivariate situation. Now, however, the residual is the vertical distance between the actual value and the regression plane, as in Figure 7.2.1.

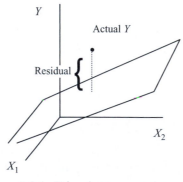

Figure 7.2.1. Trivariate regression plane.

Students often have considerable difficulty with the concept of a regression plane. Several conceptual leaps need to be made to appreciate the plane fully:

- It is easy to appreciate that an extra dimension is required when we add an independent variable.
- It is harder to see how one graphs a predicted value: First locate the X_1 and X_2 coordinates to map out the values of the two independent variables being used to predict Y and then move straight up to the height of the predicted Y value.
- It is harder still to understand that the collection of predicted values will all fit into a single plane.
- The hardest task is to visualize exactly what the plane will look like given the regression slopes.

The key to making this last conceptual leap is to realize that the regression slope of an independent variable tells whether the plane slopes upward or downward and how steeply it does so *in the direction of that independent variable*. For example, in Figure 7.2.1, travel in the plane is in the direction of increasing X_1, moving parallel to the X_1 axis. You are moving out of the page, and the value of X_2 is being held constant. Note that you are not moving upward – that is, the value of Y is not changing. Thus, the slope associated with X_1 (b_1) is in this case zero. Now move in the plane in the direction of increasing X_2, traveling parallel to the X_2 axis. You are moving left to right, and the value of X_1 is being held constant. Note that the value of Y is increasing. Thus, in this case, the slope associated with X_2 (b_2) is positive.

Computer graphics make it easier to visualize data plotted in three dimensions. Provided that you have Java enabled to work with your Web browser, you will be able to spin a 3D object and see the plane clearly.

From your browser, execute File: Open, navigate to the 3DScatterPlot folder in this chapter's Excel files folder, and open the file ScatterPlot.htm. If you prefer, you can navigate to the folder and simply double click on the ScatterPlot.htm file. You should see a 200-observation data set displayed in your browser that looks like the graph on the left in Figure 7.2.2. The X_1-, X_2-, and Y-axes are all perpendicular to each other; the Y-axis is the vertical axis when you open up the file. Use the mouse to spin the data set. As you spin the data, you can better appreciate that each observation lives in three-dimensional space and has associated with it X_1-, X_2-, and Y-coordinates. Spin the plot until you clearly see the points line up in a plane. If you do not like where you are, you can always click your browser's Refresh button to return to the original position.

You should be able to see that what first looked like a formless cloud of points becomes a well-defined pattern of points clustered around a plane. Figure 7.2.2 shows the beginning and (one possible) end of this transformation. Your final placement need not be exactly like the graph on the right of

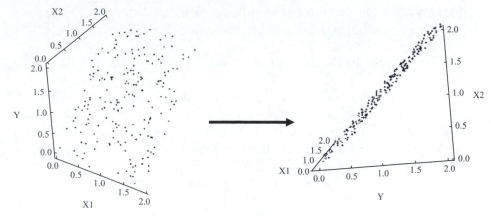

Figure 7.2.2. A three-dimensional swarm of points.
Source: 3DScatterPlot.htm.[2]

Figure 7.2.2, but you should be able to discern a clear pattern. Put another way, from the right perspective it is possible to appreciate that, in this specially constructed example, all the points fit into a fairly thin slab in space. The trivariate regression takes that slab and compresses it into a plane. The equation for the plane that best summarizes the data in 3DScatterPlot.htm is

$$\text{Predicted } Y = -0.001 + 0.005\,X_1 + 0.998\,X_2.$$

The regression plane in this example is very similar to the one of Figure 7.2.1 because changes in X_1 have almost no effect on the predicted value of Y, whereas Predicted Y is a positive function of X_2. In this example the residuals are relatively small, and the regression plane does an excellent job of predicting the value of Y based on the values of X_1 and X_2; the RMSE is 0.06 and the R^2 is .99.

Example: The Demand for Heating Oil

Next we introduce a hypothetical data set designed to illustrate important issues in multiple regression. Open the MultiReg.xls workbook in order to follow the presentation below.

Our purely fictional and quite unrealistic data pertain to the consumption of heating oil during the winter months for 24 towns in northern Canada. We have information on the average quantity of heating oil consumed per

---

[2] We thank our colleague Bob Foote for giving us this example. Foote used the software packages *Mathematica* and *LiveGraphics3D* to create the Web page. For more on *LiveGraphics3D*, go to <www.vis.informatik.uni-stuttgart.de/~kraus/LiveGraphics3D>.

Table 7.2.1. *Hypothetical Heating Oil Data Set*

Observation number	Price of heating oil (cents/gallon)	Income per household (thousands of dollars/year)	Quantity Demanded per household (hundreds of gallons/month)
1	50	9	7.1
2	50	9	5.7
3	50	10	10.3
4	50	10	11.8
5	50	11	11.9
6	50	11	13.9
7	60	11	5.7
8	60	11	6.6
9	60	12	11.5
10	60	12	12.6
11	60	13	16.8
12	60	13	14.4
13	70	13	13.2
14	70	13	9.7
15	70	14	16.0
16	70	14	9.3
17	70	15	19.0
18	70	15	21.5
19	80	15	11.3
20	80	15	15.6
21	80	16	15.6
22	80	16	15.8
23	80	17	21.7
24	80	17	20.9

Source: [Multireg.xls]DemandCurve.

household (in hundreds of gallons per month) in each town. We also have information on the price of heating oil (in cents per gallon) and per household income (in thousands of dollars per year). The price varies across towns owing to differing tax rates. This means that the supply curve is shifted upward in towns with higher taxes. As we did in the cigarette example of Chapter 1, let us assume that supply is perfectly elastic in every town.

Thus, in two towns in which the price of heating oil is different but per household income is the same, the difference in quantity consumed mainly results from movements along a single demand curve. In two towns in which the price of heating oil is the same but per household income differs, the difference in quantity consumed mainly results from a shift in the demand curve. The data are contained in Table 7.2.1.

Multiple Regression

Regression Coefficients	
b_0 (Intercept)	13.246
b_1 (Price)	0.000
b_2 (Income)	0.000
Sum of Squared Residuals	514.7

Figure 7.2.3. The univariate prediction of quantity demanded.
Source: [Multireg.xls]MinSSR.

Univariate, Bivariate, and Multivariate Least Squares Regressions

There are four different ways to use least squares techniques to summarize the relationship between the dependent variable, Quantity Demanded, and the independent variables, Price and Income:

1. Use Average Quantity Demanded to Predict Quantity Demanded for every observation.
2. Use a regression of Quantity Demanded on Price to predict Quantity Demanded.
3. Use a regression of Quantity Demanded on Income to predict Quantity Demanded.
4. Use a regression of Quantity Demanded on both Price and Income to predict Quantity Demanded.

To compare these four procedures, go to the *MinSSR* sheet of Multireg.xls. Cells A8 through D33 contain a table with the data. Regression coefficients can be chosen in cells B3 through B5. Using these regression coefficients, we can compute Predicted Quantity Demanded as follows:

$$\text{Predicted Quantity Demanded} = b_0 + b_1 \text{Price} + b_2 \text{Income}.$$

Armed with Predicted Quantity Demanded (recorded in column D), we can obtain the Residuals and the Squared Residuals (see columns E and F). We report the resulting SSR in cell B6. Let us consider the four methods of predicting Quantity Demanded in turn.

1. Use Average Quantity Demanded to Predict Quantity Demanded for Every Observation

Click on the Average Y button. This will generate the output in Figure 7.2.3.

The button sets b_0 equal to 13.246 (the average value of Y in the data set) and the coefficients b_1 and b_2 equal to zero. The algebraic equation for the Average Quantity Demanded method of predicting Quantity Demanded is thus very simple:

$$\text{Predicted Quantity Demanded} = 13.246.$$

As demonstrated in Section 5.4, the average value of the dependent variable is the least squares estimate of the center of the data set. In other words, of all estimates for Quantity Demanded that are just a single number, the Average Quantity Demanded is the one that has the smallest SSR. Holding the values of b_1 and b_2 constant at 0, type in any value for b_0 other than the Sample Average and you will increase the SSR.

2. Regress Quantity Demanded on Price to Predict Quantity Demanded

Click on the [Bivariate Regression of Q^D on Price] button. This fits a least squares regression line corresponding to the following equation:

$$\text{Predicted Quantity Demanded} = -2.105 + 0.236\,\text{Price}.$$

As you can see, the SSR falls to 347.4. This bivariate regression line generates a better fit (i.e., does a better job of predicting Quantity Demanded than the univariate average method). There is no surprise here: As economists, we believe that price has something to do with quantity demanded, and so knowing the price helps us to predict how much a consumer will buy.[3] The *DemandCurve* sheet contains the output from Excel's LINEST function for this regression. From that source, we learn that the R^2 is about 0.3 and the RMSE is about 4.

3. Regress Quantity Demanded on Income to Predict Quantity Demanded

Click on the [Bivariate Regression of Q^D on Income] button. This fits a least squares regression line corresponding to the following equation:

$$\text{Predicted Quantity Demanded} = -6.531 + 1.521\,\text{Income}.$$

As you can see, the SSR falls to 199.9, which is an even better fit than that produced by the regression of Quantity Demanded on Price. The *Demand-Curve* sheet tells us that in this case R^2 is about 0.6 and the RMSE is about 3. In terms of predictive power, this regression does a better job than the other bivariate regression. There is no economic reason why basing our prediction of Quantity Demanded on Income should do better than basing the prediction on Price, and fortunately there is no reason why we need choose between the two bivariate regressions.

4. Regress Quantity Demanded on Both Price and Income to Predict Quantity Demanded

Our economic intuition tells us that the Quantity Demanded of heating oil is probably related to both the Price and to per household Income. A trivariate least squares regression summarizes this more complicated relationship by

---

[3] You may be puzzled by the increase in Predicted Quantity Demanded as Price rises. We rigged the data set so that this would happen and will explain what is going on in Section 7.3.

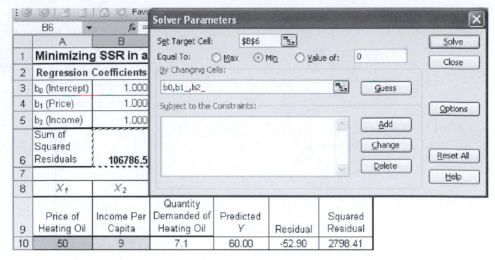

Figure 7.2.4. Running Solver.
Source: [Multireg.xls]MinSSR.

fitting a plane to the data. We want to find coefficients b_0, b_1, and now b_2 in this equation for a plane:

$$\text{Predicted Quantity Demanded} = b_0 + b_1 \text{Price} + b_2 \text{Income},$$

where b_0, b_1, and b_2 are chosen to minimize the SSR. Up to now, we have restricted the predicted values of Quantity Demanded to fall on a single line by zeroing out one or two of the preceding coefficients.

Multiple least squares regression does exactly the same thing as bivariate least squares regression: find the combination of parameter values that minimizes the SSR. Figure 7.2.4 shows the setup of the optimization problem as presented in the *MinSSR* sheet: This sheet starts with the coefficient values for the intercept and two slopes, b_0, b_1, and b_2. These are used to compute Predicted Y for each observation. In this example, each parameter has been set equal to 1. Thus, for the first observation (listed at the bottom of Figure 7.2.4),

$$\text{Predicted Quantity Demanded}_1 = b_0 + b_1 \cdot \text{Price}_1 + b_2 \cdot \text{Income}_1$$
$$= 1 + 1 \cdot 50 + 1 \cdot 9$$
$$= 60.$$

Note that the "1" subscripts on Predicted Quantity Demanded, Price, and Income tell us we are dealing with the first observation. Because the observed value of Quantity Demanded is 7.1, the first residual is –52.9 and the first squared residual is about 2,798. The objective function computed in the Target Cell of Solver is the sum of the squared residuals for all 24 observations. Solver

Minimizing SSR in a Multiple Regression

Regression Coefficients	
b_0 (Intercep)	-2.105
b_1 (Price)	-0.579
b_2 (Income)	4.075
Sum of Squared Residuals	81.7

Average Y

Bivariate Regression of Q^D on Price

Bivariate Regression of Q^D on Income

Results of Trivariate LinEst

	Slope$_2$ (b_2)	Slope$_1$ (b_1)	Intercept (b_0)
Coefficients	4.075	-0.579	-2.105
R^2	0.841	1.972	RMSE
		21	df
Reg SS	433.014	81.666	SSR

Figure 7.2.5. Solver's solution compared with LINEST.
Source: [Multireg.xls]MinSSR.

will choose values of b_0, b_1, and b_2 to minimize this sum. Run Solver and you will obtain results given in Figure 7.2.5

We generally use LINEST to fit a multiple regression in Excel.[4] The syntax is very similar to the bivariate case. To see the regression results for the heating oil example, go to the array in cells G3 through I7 in the *MinSSR* sheet in Multireg.xls. This array contains the function

$$\{= \text{LINEST}(C10\!:\!C33, A10\!:\!B33, 1, 1)\}.$$

The braces indicate that this is an array function with results contained in a rectangular bank of cells (an array), not a single cell. The Y data are located in cells C10 through C33; the X values are contained in two columns, A and B, in rows 10 through 33. The last two arguments (the 1's) indicate that an intercept is to be included in the model and that additional statistics besides the slope and intercept coefficients should be presented in the result array.

The notations on the cells bordering the array label the statistics. The slope coefficients are in reverse order across the top beneath the labels. The R^2 and regression sum of squares (Reg SS) are to the right of their respective labels, whereas the RMSE, degrees of freedom, and SSR are two cells to the left of their respective labels. The resulting regression equation could be written:

$$\text{Predicted Quantity Demanded} = -2.1 - 0.58 \cdot \text{Price} + 4.1 \cdot \text{Income}$$

$$\text{RMSE} = 1.97$$

$$R^2 = 0.841.$$

Both the RMSE and R^2 statistics tell us that the multiple regression does a better job predicting the dependent variable than the other methods. This

---

[4] You can also use the Data Analysis:Regression tool. The only difference is that you now select two or more columns of data for the X Range. See the *DataAnalysis* sheet in Multireg.xls for an example.

is not surprising because all four methods minimize the SSR and the trivariate regression makes use of more information in doing so than the other methods.

Summary

This section has emphasized the similarities between multivariate least squares regression and bivariate least squares regression. For both types of regression, the OLS regression coefficients are those that minimize the SSR; the predicted value of the dependent variable is expressed in a simple equation; the RMSE summarizes the likely size of the residual; and the R^2 statistic measures the fraction of total variation explained by the regression. Because it makes use of more information, the trivariate regression does a better job than the bivariate regressions in predicting the dependent variable. It is more difficult to visualize multiple regression than bivariate regression. To gain more understanding of exactly what multiple regression accomplishes, we take a closer look at how multiple regression makes conditional predictions of the value of the dependent variable.

7.3. Improving Description via Multiple Regression

Workbook: MultiReg.xls

In this section we tackle the key conceptual difference between bivariate and multiple regression, using our artificial data set to exemplify the points we wish to make. We stress that the truly new feature of multiple regression is that the regression coefficients show how the predicted value of the dependent variable changes as a single independent variable changes with the other independent variables included in the regression held constant. Crosstabs are another way to make conditional predictions; we explore the close relationship between crosstabs and multiple regression.

A simple example conveys three basic lessons.

Lesson 1: *You can improve your prediction of Y if you use more information*. We have already seen that using one piece of information (a single X variable) improves our prediction. In the same way, using two pieces of information instead of one yields an even better prediction.

Lesson 2: *Confounding may mislead us*. A bivariate analysis may lead us to think that there is a certain relationship between two variables with the other variables held constant. It may be, however, that a multiple regression analysis, taking into account movements in a third variable, gives us a different picture of the relationship between the first two variables.

Summary Statistics			
	Price (cents /gal.)	Income ($1000s/ person)	Q^D (100s gals. /Month)
Mean	65.00	13.00	13.25
SD	11.42	2.43	4.73

Figure 7.3.1. Means and SDs for each variable in hypothetical data set. *Source:* [Multireg.xls]DemandCurve.

Lesson 3: *We can correct (or "control for") confounding in two ways*:
- Comparing smaller, more homogenous groups.
- Statistically controlling for confounding using multiple regression to hold other variables constant.

In sum, using multiple regression gives a more precise prediction of the independent variable because it uses more information. In addition, multiple regression produces a more refined description of the relationship between a particular independent variable and the dependent variable because it controls for the confounding influence of other included independent variables.

We now return to our heating oil example, using the Excel workbook MultiReg.xls.

Predicting Quantity Demanded Using Univariate and Bivariate Approaches

We want to summarize and describe this data set. The univariate and bivariate approaches to analyzing data are reviewed as preparation for explaining the multivariate method of analysis. First, we report the means and standard deviations for each variable in Figure 7.3.1.

Predicting Demand in the Univariate Case

In the absence of any information on price and quantity, our best guess of the demand for hearing oil is simply the average quantity demanded. The SD tells us how far this guess is likely to be off. From Figure 7.3.1, if we had to predict the quantity demanded of heating oil, our best guess would be about 1,325 gallons per month give or take roughly 470 gallons per month.

Bivariate Cases

Given information on either price or income, we can form a better guess of the quantity demanded of heating oil. This can be done via a PivotTable and

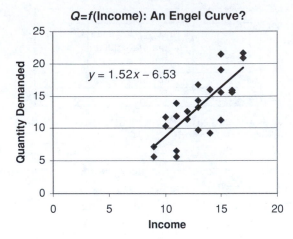

Figure 7.3.2. Bivariate regression of quantity demanded on income.
Source: [Multireg.xls]DemandCurve.

the graph of averages or, in more compressed form, a bivariate regression. For now, we concentrate on bivariate regression. Given the value of some independent variable, the bivariate regression line tells us the best guess of the quantity demanded of heating oil. The RMSE tells us how far off this guess is likely to be. The *DemandCurve* sheet uses LINEST and the trend line feature to run bivariate regressions of Quantity Demanded (Q^D) on Income and Quantity Demanded on Price.

Income

If we know per household income, we can predict the quantity demanded of heating oil. We get the regression line and use it to predict the Quantity Demanded of heating oil given Income.

The regression result is

$$\text{Predicted Quantity Demanded} = -6.53 + 1.52\,\text{Income}$$
$$\text{RMSE} = 3.01.$$

If per capita income is $15,000 per year, the predicted quantity demanded of heating oil is about 16.29 hundreds of gallons per month give or take about 300 gallons per month. This prediction is better than in the univariate case because the spread around the prediction is a little lower.

Price

If we know the price of heating oil, we can predict the Quantity Demanded of heating oil given its Price. The results are shown in Figure 7.3.3. The regression

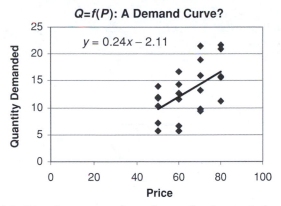

Figure 7.3.3. Bivariate regression of quantity demanded on income.
Source: [Multireg.xls]DemandCurve.

result is

$$\text{Predicted Quantity Demanded} = -2.11 + 0.24\,\text{Price}$$
$$\text{RMSE} = 3.97.$$

The regression of quantity demanded on income is consistent with economic theory. If heating oil is a normal good, the people should buy more of it. It makes sense that heating oil would be a normal good – richer people generally live in larger dwellings. The regression of quantity demanded on price, however, is inconsistent with economic theory because, if the price of heating oil rises and the demand curve slopes downward, then people ought to buy less heating oil, not more.

Using the information from an independent variable in a bivariate regression allows us to improve our prediction of the quantity demanded of heating oil. With either Price or Income as an independent variable, we obtain a lower spread around our prediction (RMSE) than when we use just the average of the quantity demanded of heating oil and its SD.

Unfortunately, the bivariate regressions may be misleading because of confounding. This is true of both of the bivariate regressions. In the case of Price as an independent variable, the presence of confounding is obvious because we are getting an upward-sloping relationship between Price and the Quantity Demanded of heating oil. Our understanding of the relationship between Income and the Quantity Demanded of heating oil is also confounded. In this case we will see that the confounding is merely a matter of magnitude, not sign.

Ways to Deal with Confounding

The relationship between price and quantity demanded does not fit our economic theory because the relationship is confounded by income. Somehow,

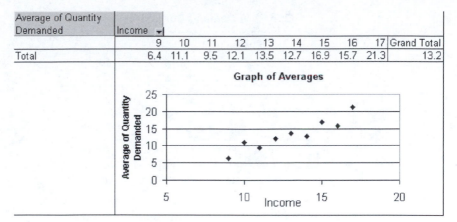

Average of Quantity Demanded	Income									
	9	10	11	12	13	14	15	16	17	Grand Total
Total	6.4	11.1	9.5	12.1	13.5	12.7	16.9	15.7	21.3	13.2

Figure 7.3.4. PivotTable showing average quantity demanded at different income levels.
Source: [Multireg.xls]PivotTable.

the Price coefficient is being calculated as a mixture of Price and Income. There are two ways to understand and deal with this confounding: using either smaller, more homogenous groups or multiple regression.

Both strategies use essentially the same method: they hold one variable (e.g., income) constant while analyzing the relationship between the other two variables (price and the quantity demanded of heating oil).

Controlling for Confounding: Smaller, More Homogenous Groups

One way of looking at the relationship between price and quantity demanded, with income held constant, is to break up the data into smaller, more homogeneous groups. Let us look at the data with PivotTables to see how this strategy works.

We begin with the graph of averages of quantity demanded for different levels of income in Figure 7.3.4. The 24 original data points have been compressed into 8 points. This figure corresponds to the bivariate regression of Quantity Demanded on Income, which summarizes the relationship between the two variables with two parameters, a slope and intercept in the equation Predicted Quantity Demanded $= -6.53 + 1.52$ Income. A second PivotTable (in Figure 7.3.5) shows average Quantity Demanded at each of the four levels of Price in the data set.

The graph in Figure 7.3.5 portrays an upward-sloping relationship between price and quantity demanded. The bivariate regression of the previous section, Predicted Quantity Demanded $= -2.11 + 0.24$ Price, is a perfectly straight-line further compression of this graph of averages.

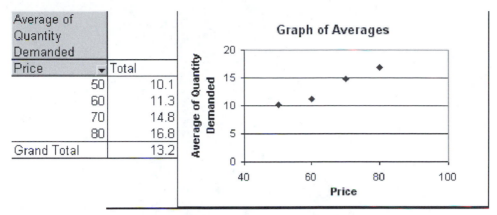

Figure 7.3.5. PivotTable showing average quantity demanded
at different price levels.
Source: [Multireg.xls]PivotTable.

Each of the two bivariate approaches to the data summarizes too much,
thereby hiding important patterns. The strategy of working with smaller,
more homogeneous groups splits data into groups that have the same level
of one variable, and thus the manner in which quantity demanded varies as
the second variable changes can be isolated. To see how this approach works,
we need to create an expanded PivotTable, as in Figure 7.3.6.

Notice how the bottom row and right-most column, Grand Totals, in
the expanded PivotTable are equivalent to the respective bivariate Pivot-
Tables. The crosstab reveals important phenomena obscured by the bivariate
summaries.

To implement the homogeneous groups strategy, read either vertically or
horizontally within the table. Let us start by making *vertical* comparisons. At
an income value of 11, a price increase from 50 to 60 corresponds to a decrease
in average quantity demanded from 12.9 to 6.15. We can also investigate
the impact of price increases, holding income constant for two other sets of
towns. In each of these three cases, holding income constant, price increases
of 10 cents per gallon correspond to roughly 400- to 700-gallon decreases in

Average of Quantity Demanded	Income									
Price		9	10	11	12	13	14	15	16	17	Grand Total
50		6.4	11.1	12.9							10.1
60				6.15	12.1	15.6					11.3
70						11.5	12.7	20.3			14.8
80								13.5	15.7	21.3	16.8
Grand Total		6.4	11.1	9.5	12.1	13.5	12.7	16.9	15.7	21.3	13.2

Figure 7.3.6. Crosstab of average quantity demanded given income and price.
Source: [Multireg.xls]PivotTable.

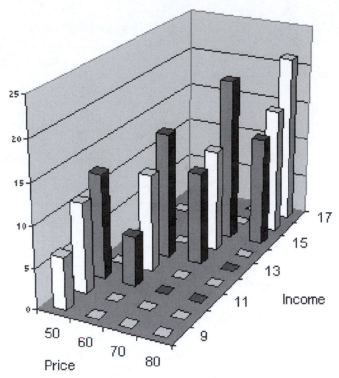

Figure 7.3.7. Quantity demanded versus price and income as summarized by
crosstab: a three-dimensional graph of averages.
Source: [Multireg.xls]PivotTable.

average quantity demanded. Similarly, to analyze how quantity demanded
changes as income rises, with price held constant read *horizontally* across
the crosstab. For each of the four price levels (50, 60, 70, and 80 cents per
gallon), income increases of $2,000 correspond to increases of roughly 650 to
900 gallons of average quantity demanded.

A graphic version of the crosstab conveys the same relationships. Figure 7.3.7 is a translation of the information in the crosstab of Figure 7.3.6; it
is the best Excel can do at drawing a three-dimensional graph of averages.
The height of each column tells the average Quantity Demanded for observations with the given Price/Income combination. If there is only a footprint but
no column, there are no observations for the particular Price/Income combination (and no entry in the PivotTable). Just like the crosstab, the graph
can be read in two directions. The negative relationship between Quantity
Demanded and Price, with Income held constant, can be observed in the
three pairs of darker columns marching across the page. The positive relationship between Quantity Demanded and Income, with Price held constant,
is visible in the four triplets of upward-progressing columns marching into
the page.

Average of Quantity Demanded	Income									
Price	9	10	11	12	13	14	15	16	17	Grand Total
50	6.4	11.1	12.9							10.1
60			6.15	12.1	15.6					11.3
70					11.5	12.7	20.3			14.8
80							13.5	15.7	21.3	16.8
Grand Total	6.4	11.1	9.5	12.1	13.5	12.7	16.9	15.7	21.3	13.2

Figure 7.3.8. Crosstab of average quantity demanded given income and price. *Source:* [Multireg.xls]PivotTable.

Pause for a moment to think about the difference between the bivariate and trivariate PivotTable/graph of averages approaches. Let us look at what each says about the relationship between Quantity Demanded and Price. The bivariate graph of averages shows Quantity Demanded rising as Price rises with a slope of roughly 0.24 hundred gallons per month per cent per gallon. The trivariate crosstab shows, with Income held constant, Quantity Demanded falling as Price rises with a slope of around –0.55 hundred gallons per month per cent per gallon. That is a big difference! What is going on? Take a look at the crosstab again in Figure 7.3.8.

We have circled the Price = 50 and the Price = 80 observations in the interior and margins of the table to emphasize that, in the bivariate analysis, when Quantity Demanded is compared at two different prices, we are not holding Income constant. In fact, Income is much higher for the high Price observations. The bivariate approach ignores this variation in Income when making the comparison. All that the bivariate graph of averages shows us is that the average Quantity Demanded was higher when Price was higher. It hides the fact that Income has changed.

The sheet *DemandCurve* in the MultiReg.xls workbook makes this same point in a slightly different way. Scroll over to column T and use the color coding to pick out points with the same level of income. You can discern three separate sets of points and therefore three demand curves. We compute slopes for the three curves by running three regressions on four data points each (see cells W22, W28, and W34).[5] The units on the slopes are hundreds of gallons of heating oil per month per cent per gallon. The analogous procedure, in which price is held constant, can be found starting in column AC.

Holding income constant via smaller, more homogeneous groups reveals that the relationship between price and quantity demanded, with income held constant, is negative instead of positive. Conditioned on price alone, the average quantity demanded does indeed rise as price rises, but that is

[5] We use the Excel function SLOPE (*Y* values, *X* values) to compute the regression slope.

because income is also changing. Once we remove the effect of income, the expected downward-sloping relationship emerges. The homogenous-group approach also more subtly corrects the bivariate analysis of the quantity demanded–income relationship. The bivariate regression slope is about 1.5, whereas the slopes of the four separate regressions for constant price levels range from 3.25 to 4.725.

Controlling for Confounding: Multiple Regression

Multiple regression is a statistical technique that follows the more homogeneous-group approach by applying a second compression to the multivariate graph of averages. As already noted, when we run the trivariate least squares regression of Quantity Demanded on Price and Income, the resulting regression equation is

$$\text{Predicted Quantity Demanded} = -2.1 - 0.58 \cdot \text{Price} + 4.1 \cdot \text{Income}$$
$$\text{RMSE} = 1.97$$
$$R^2 = 0.841.$$

The multiple regression results imply that

- If income is held constant, a 1-cent-per-gallon increase in the price of heating oil is associated with a decrease in quantity demanded of roughly 58 gallons.
- If price is held constant, a \$1,000 increase in per capita income is associated with an increase in quantity demanded of roughly 410 gallons.

  In addition, notice that, by using two independent variables instead of one, we have improved the accuracy of our prediction. The likely size of the error of our predicted quantity demanded is the RMSE, which has dropped from 4.0 and 3.0 in the bivariate regressions to 2.0 in the multiple regression.

  Multiple regression is similar, but not identical, to the homogeneous-groups approach. The multiple regression coefficients are close to the averages of the slopes in the smaller, more homogeneous groups. For example, the slope for price is –0.58, whereas the slopes within constant income groups vary between –0.415 and –0.68 (see column W in the *DemandCurve* sheet). The slope for income is 4.08, whereas the slopes within constant price groups vary between 3.25 and 4.725 (see column AF in the *DemandCurve* sheet). As will be seen in more detail in the next section, the multiple regression makes use of all the data points, but in our analysis of the smaller, more homogenous groups that held income constant we left out some of the data.

  Just as was the case with bivariate regression, multiple regression can be considered a second compression of the data. The first compression groups the data in the crosstab of average quantity demanded by income and price; visually this resulted in a series of vertical pillars in the 3D graph of

Figure 7.3.7. In the second compression, the regression further smooths the predicted values of the Y variable by putting them into a single plane.

Confounding

It is very important to be clear on one point: Multiple regression does not necessarily solve the problem of confounding. Just because we have controlled for the influence of income in describing the relationship between quantity demanded and price does not mean that all confounding has been removed. Why not? The reason is we have not held *everything else* constant. For example, our data do not include average winter temperatures, which presumably have a big influence on the quantity demanded of heating oil. It may well be the case that lower temperatures were accompanied by higher prices. Our regression, which does not include temperatures, would then tend to attribute the influence of temperature variation to variations in price.

The lesson is that multiple regression coefficients should always be interpreted as the effect of X on Y, with the other X's included in the regression held constant but with the left-out X's not necessarily held constant.

To drive home the point about confounding, we have drawn on your knowledge of basic economic theory. You know that demand curves have a downward slope, and so something must be wrong with the bivariate analysis. The multivariate analysis leads to a more theoretically satisfying summary of the data. However, we must caution you not to conclude that the multivariate analysis is automatically better in every case for three reasons. First, a bivariate analysis might answer the question you are asking. If all you know is the price of heating oil, the bivariate regression line is what you require to predict the quantity demanded. Second, the multivariate analysis may be confounded by a left-out variable, just as was true for the bivariate relationship. Third, the functional form in the multivariate analysis may be inappropriate (this will be an ongoing theme, for we continue our exploration of different functional forms in Chapter 8).

There is a great temptation to believe that adding more variables makes a regression better. Very often, however, what is needed instead is more careful consideration of the data generating process. Economic theory should be one's guide in determining what variables belong in a regression and whether the tools being used are appropriate.

Summary

In introducing multiple regression, we chose to stress the notion of confounding. We did so because researchers usually turn to multiple regression to avoid confounding; moreover, the concept of confounding highlights the holding-other-things-constant way in which multiple regression coefficients must be interpreted.

Multiple regression allows us to control for the influence of confounding variables (i.e., variables that may mislead us about the true relationship between the dependent variable and the independent variable in question). We interpret the slope coefficient as the change in the dependent variable associated with a one-unit change in the independent variable in question *with the other included independent variables held constant.*

To remove the effects of confounding variables, you need not run separate regressions on smaller, more homogenous groups. Instead, simply include the variable as part of a multiple regression to control for confounding statistically.

To understand the coefficients, remind yourself that multiple regression is an extension of the way the bivariate regression line compresses the graph of averages into a line. In a similar fashion, a crosstab is compressed into a single equation that represents how the variables in the data set are related. In the trivariate case, this equation can be visualized as a plane; with more than two independent variables, it becomes much harder for most people to visualize the relationship between the variables.

Remember that your multiple regression will only control for the effects of *included* variables. That is different from the economic theorist's usual ceteris paribus, or everything-else-held-constant, assumption.

The sheet *Conversation* in the MutiReg.xls workbook tries to tackle the confusing results generated in this section. There are two important issues: the relationship between the bivariate and multiple regression coefficients and the way to think about how multiple regression handles confounding.

7.4. Multicollinearity

Workbook: Multicollinearity.xls

This section deals with an important practical issue in multiple regression analysis: multicollinearity. We will tackle this subject by examining made-up data from the heating oil example. Multicollinearity comes in two forms: perfect, in which there is an exact mathematical relationship (e.g., perfect correlation) between the independent variables, and near, in which there is almost an exact mathematical relationship between the independent variables. We will mainly discuss the case of perfect multicollinearity in as much as its consequences are easier to understand than those of the more common situation of near multicollinearity and because you need to be warned about perfect multicollinearity when you start to run regressions.

Change b_1 and then use Solver to find a least squares solution

b_0 (Intercept)	3.405
b_1 (Price)	1
b_2 (Income)	−4.273

SSR	27.109

Price of Heating Oil	Income Per Capita	Quantity Demanded of Heating Oil	Predicted Y	Residual	Squared Residual
50	10	10.3	10.68	−0.38	0.14
50	10	11.8	10.68	1.12	1.25
60	12	11.5	12.13	−0.63	0.40
60	12	12.6	12.13	0.47	0.22
70	14	16.0	13.59	2.41	5.81
70	14	9.3	13.59	−4.29	18.40
80	16	15.6	15.04	0.56	0.31
80	16	15.8	15.04	0.76	0.57

Figure 7.4.1. Multiple regression with perfect multicollinearity.
Source: [Multicollinearity.xls]Example1.

A Heating Oil Example

An altered version of the heating oil example should give you valuable intuition about multicollinearity. Go to the *Example1* sheet in Multicollinearity.xls. You will find a small data set accompanied by two bivariate analyses. A careful comparison of the two bivariate analyses ought to tip you off that something strange is going on. Many of the summary statistics are identical: the estimates of the intercept coefficient are both 3.405; the SSR and Reg SS and therefore the R^2 are all the same. Furthermore, the value of the slope coefficient in the Quantity Demanded on Income regression is exactly five times that of the slope coefficient in the Quantity Demanded on Price regression. Looking back at the data table, note that in every observation the value of Price is always exactly five times that of Income.

Scroll right to reach a crosstab of the data set and a scatter diagram of Price and Income in the data set. Note from both the table and the scatter plot that Price and Income always move in lockstep. It is impossible to execute the smaller, more homogeneous groups strategy because we can never hold one variable constant and watch what happens as the other variable changes. At every level of Price, there is just one value of Income and vice versa.

Because multiple regression is a smoothed version of the graph of averages (and thus the crosstab) and the crosstab has essentially collapsed, we have good reason to suspect that regression will run into problems. Scroll right until the material in Figure 7.4.1 appears on your screen. This will

b_0 (Intercept)	3.405155
b_1 (Price)	2
b_2 (Income)	−9.27251

Figure 7.4.2. Solver's new solution.
Source: [Multicollinearity.xls]Example1.

show you exactly how multiple regression analysis fails in the face of perfect multicollinearity.

In Figure 7.4.1, the top left corner shows that we have used Solver to find a set of coefficients that minimize the SSR for this data set. In general, the consequence of perfect multicollinearity is that there are an infinite number of possible solutions to the problem of finding the coefficients that produce the minimum SSR. In this case, all the solutions share the same SSR of about 27.109 and the same intercept coefficient (roughly 3.405). There are, however, an infinite number of combinations of b_1 and b_2 that produce these outcomes.

To see that this is indeed the case, change the value of b_1 from 1 to 2 and then run Solver. We are trying to minimize the SSR (located in cell AB5) by changing the values of b_0 (the intercept, located in cell X3) and b_2 (the slope on Income in cell X5). Solver should quickly find the solution depicted in Figure 7.4.2.

Notice that b_0 has not changed and that b_2 has decreased by 5 in value. Change b_1 to 0 and run Solver again. Now you will have exactly reproduced the bivariate regression of Quantity Demanded on Income: Quantity Demanded no longer depends on Price and the value of b_1, and the Income slope is the same as the corresponding slope in the bivariate regression.

To gain further insight into multicollinearity, turn to the *Table* sheet in Multicollinearity.xls. Figure 7.4.3 shows a 3D graph of the SSR.

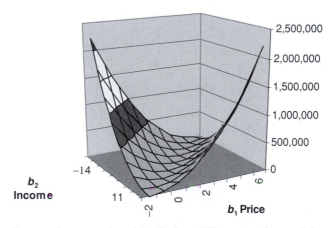

Figure 7.4.3. Sums of squared residuals for different values of b_1 and b_2 in the Example1 case of perfect multicollinearity.
Source: [Multicollinearity.xls]Table.

	11	6	1	−4	−9	−14	−19	−24	−29
−2	27	34,827	139,227	313,227	556,827	870,027	1,252,827	1,705,227	2,227,227
−1	34,827	27	34,827	139,227	313,227	556,827	870,027	1,252,827	1,705,227
0	139,227	34,827	27	34,827	139,227	313,227	556,827	870,027	1,252,827
1	313,227	139,227	34,827	27	34,827	139,227	313,227	556,827	870,027
2	556,827	313,227	139,227	34,827	27	34,827	139,227	313,227	556,827
3	870,027	556,827	313,227	139,227	34,827	27	34,827	139,227	313,227
4	1,252,827	870,027	556,827	313,227	139,227	34,827	27	34,827	139,227
5	1,705,227	1,252,827	870,027	556,827	313,227	139,227	34,827	27	34,827
6	2,227,227	1,705,227	1,252,827	870,027	556,827	313,227	139,227	34,827	27

Figure 7.4.4. Sums of squared residuals for different values of b_1 and b_2 in the Example1 case of perfect multicollinearity.
Source: [Multicollinearity.xls]Table.

Figure 7.4.3 depicts the values of the SSR for different combinations of b_1 and b_2. The key feature of this figure is the crease running down the middle of the surface. Everywhere along this crease, the value of the SSR is the same, − 27.11, which is the lowest achievable value. The table that produced the graph is in Figure 7.4.4.

The diagonal of Figure 7.4.4 shows several pairs of (b_1, b_2) combinations that reach the minimum attainable value for the SSR. These combinations clearly form a line. In the case of perfect multicollinearity, there is no unique solution to the optimization problem of minimizing the sum of squared residuals. For this specific case, any combination of b_1 and b_2 on the line $b_1 = 0.7275 - 5 \cdot b_2$ will minimize the SSR for this data set.

Note importantly that no matter which least squares solution you find, the Predicted Y values will be the same. This is a general feature of multicollinearity in regression: If all you care about is predicting Y, then any one of the solutions will work and multicollinearity is not really a problem. If, on the other hand, you are interested in the regression coefficients, multicollinearity poses a serious problem.

This particular case of multicollinearity arises because, for every observation, Price and Income are related by an exact formula:

$$Income = 0.2 \cdot Price.$$

More generally, whenever there is an exact linear relationship between two or more independent variables, perfect multicollinearity is present and there is no unique set of OLS regression coefficients.

When confronted with multicollinearity, Excel's multiple regression tools, the LINEST array function and the Data Analysis: Regression tool, will behave differently as determined by the version being used. In Excel 2003, both regression tools will "zero out" one of the variables – that is, set the value of its slope coefficient to zero and proceed to estimate the regression of the remaining variables. The careful student will realize that multicollinearity is present because of the zero slope. In addition, the estimate of the Standard

Error (to be discussed in Part 2 of this book) is also zero, which suggests that something is amiss. In previous versions of Excel, the regression tools sometimes failed completely when confronted with a perfectly multicollinear set of X variables and in the process reported an array of #VALUE!'s instead of numbers (see copies of output in the *Example1* sheet).[6]

A second example shows that multicollinearity can arise from more complicated linear relationships between explanatory variables.[7] Go to the *Example2* sheet. In this case, Price and Income are related by a slightly more involved formula:

$$\text{Income} = 0.2 \cdot \text{Price} - 1.$$

As in the first example, both bivariate regressions succeed in obtaining the minimum possible SSR. Unlike the first example, it is not the case that every solution to the least squares problem serves up the same value for the intercept coefficient. Scroll right through the sheet to column W, where you will find the material in Figure 7.4.5.

Two very different solutions to the problem of minimizing the sum of squared residuals are displayed. Solver has found that, when b_1 is set to 4, an intercept of –26.5 and a slope on income of –18.7 minimize the SSR. In the 2003 version of Excel, LINEST has found an entirely different set of parameters that attain the same minimum value for the SSR. The LINEST function does not warn the user of the existence of other solutions (nor for that matter does the DataAnalysis:Regression tool which is based on LINEST). However, LINEST has zeroed out b_2; the 0 value for the Standard Error of b_2 is also a tip-off that Income has been dropped from the regression owing to multicollinearity. The *Example2* sheet shows how previous versions of Excel dealt with this form of multicollinearity.

Of course, these are just two of the infinite number of possible solutions to this optimization problem. Change the value of b_1 in cell X4 to 3 (or any other number that suits your fancy) and use Solver, and another solution will result. Note that the Predicted Y's will not change. We should note that perfect multicollinearity arises when there is any exact linear relationship between explanatory variables.

For example, labor economists often argue that workers' wages depend on age, years of education, and experience in the labor force. Experience is often estimated by constructing a variable as follows:

$$\text{Experience} = \text{Age} - \text{Education} - 6.$$

---

[6] Unfortunately, Excel 2003 is unable to handle multicollinearity with large data sets. In experiments, we discovered that when there are 2,120 observations or more, LINEST no longer drops a variable from the regression in cases of multicollinearity.

[7] In this example, multicollinearity is a problem only if an intercept is included.

Change b_1 and then use Solver to find a least squares solution

b_0 (Intercept)	−26.507
b_1 (Price)	**4.000**
b_2 (Income)	−18.678

SSR	27.119

Price of Heating Oil	Income Per Capita	Quantity Demanded of Heating Oil	Predicted Y	Residual	Squared Residual
50	9	7.1	5.40	1.70	2.91
50	9	5.7	5.40	0.30	0.09
60	11	5.7	8.04	−2.34	5.48
60	11	6.6	8.04	−1.44	2.07
70	13	13.2	10.68	2.52	6.33
70	13	9.7	10.68	−0.98	0.97
80	15	11.3	13.33	−2.03	4.12
80	15	15.6	13.33	2.27	5.15

LINEST

	b_2	b_1	Intercept	
Coefficients	0.000	0.265	−7.830	
Estimated SE	0.000	0.067	4.434	
R^2	0.721	2.126		RMSE
		6		df
Total SS	69.960	27.119		SSR

Figure 7.4.5. Two OLS solutions.
Source: [Multicollinearity.xls]Example2.

For this equation it is assumed that education begins at age 6 and that the worker has been in the labor force ever since ending his or her education (e.g., a 25-year-old with a high school education is assumed to have 7 years of labor force experience). Unfortunately, if an intercept term is included in the regression, the exact relationship between the three variables induces perfect multicollinearity. The practical, though imperfect, solution is to include only two of the three variables in the regression.

Near-Perfect Multicollinearity

The last example of this section involves a case of near-perfect multicollinearity, which is a situation much more common in practical work than the case of perfect multicollinearity. Open the *NearMulti* sheet in Multicollinearity.xls. The data table and OLS solution are displayed in Figure 7.4.6.

We have highlighted the Income value for the last observation, which is the only difference between this data set and that of the first example (compare with Figure 7.4.1). The very slight difference in Income for one observation

b_0 (Intercept)	4.3925
b_1 (Price)	−2.1856
b_2 (Income)	11.5686

Price	Income	Y	Fitted Y	Residuals	Squared Residuals
50	10	10.3	10.8	−0.5	0.2
50	10	11.8	10.8	1.0	1.0
60	12	11.5	12.1	−0.6	0.3
60	12	12.6	12.1	0.5	0.3
70	14	16.0	13.4	2.6	7.0
70	14	9.3	13.4	−4.1	16.5
80	16	15.6	14.6	1.0	0.9
80	**16.1**	15.8	15.8	0.0	0.0
				SSR	**26.232**

Figure 7.4.6. Near-perfect multicollinearity.
Source: [Multicollinearity.xls]NearMulti.

guarantees that there is a unique solution to the problem of minimizing the SSR – that is, a unique set of least squares regression coefficients. The important things to note in this example are the graph of the sums of squared residuals for different (b_1, b_2) combinations and the corresponding table in Figure 7.4.7.

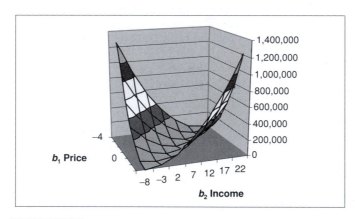

b_1 (Price)	b_2 (Income)						
	22	17	12	7	2	−3	−8
−4.2	27	34,747	139,228	313,469	557,470	871,232	1,254,755
−3.2	34,987	26	34,827	139,388	313,709	557,791	871,634
−2.2	139,546	34,906	26	34,907	139,549	313,951	558,113
−1.2	313,705	139,385	34,826	26	34,988	139,710	314,192
−0.2	557,464	313,464	139,225	34,746	27	35,069	139,872
0.8	870,824	557,144	313,224	139,065	34,667	28	35,151
1.8	1,253,783	870,423	556,823	312,984	138,906	34,588	30

Figure 7.4.7. The SSR near-perfect multicollinearity.
Source: [Multicollinearity.xls]NearMulti.

The graph and the table look very much like those in the case of perfect multicollinearity. All the (b_1, b_2) combinations in the crease of the graph are almost as good as the actual solution. There is really very little difference in how well these combinations fit the data, and so the other solutions might be regarded as being just as plausible as the least squares solution.

Once again, if the goal is simply to predict Quantity Demanded, near-perfect multicollinearity does not pose a real problem. If the goal, however, is to disentangle the separate influences of Price and Income on Quantity Demanded, near-perfect multicollinearity is almost as damaging as perfect multicollinearity. Many different descriptions of the data are almost equally valid, and thus it is hard to choose between them. The issue of multicollinearity is addressed again in Chapter 17.

Summary

Perfect and near-perfect multicollinearity pose difficulties for the ordinary least squares algorithm. Perfect multicollinearity arises when a linear function exactly summarizes the relationship between one or more explanatory variables. In this case, there is no unique solution to the problem of predicting the dependent variable. In Chapter 17, we will discuss the implications of near multicollinearity in an inferential setting.

7.5. Conclusion

For simplicity's sake all the examples in this chapter have referred to trivariate regression. All the ideas, however, apply to regression with any number of independent variables. The crucial concept in multiple regression is the idea of seeing how the dependent variable changes as one independent variable changes with other included independent variables held constant. With an understanding of this basic concept, you can properly interpret multiple regression results and will have some chance of visualizing the trivariate regression plane.

In attempting to understand multiple regression, all of the intuition you have developed for appreciating bivariate regression can be drawn upon. Multiple regression is once again a smoothed version of a graph of averages; the OLS parameters are obtained by minimizing the distance (as measured by the SSR) between the actual and predicted Y values. A simple equation allows you to compute predicted Y based on the values of that observation's independent variables.

A central concept of this book is that of confounding. Multiple regression is an important tool because it allows us to control for confounding variables and thus gives a more refined answer to the question, What is the relationship between X and Y ceteris paribus? Although multiple regression will help us obtain a clearer picture by removing the influence of *included* confounding variables, we will never be able to truly hold *everything* else constant. Thus, multiple regression provides a better, but not perfect, picture of the relationship between a dependent variable and two or more independent variables.

7.6. Exercises

1. Suppose that growing corn requires only two inputs: land and labor. A researcher obtains data on 100 farms of varying sizes located on roughly equally fertile land. In a bivariate regression of corn output on land (measured in acres), the slope is 40 bushels per acre. How do you think the coefficient on land will change when the researcher runs a trivariate regression, including hours of labor, as a second regressor? Will the coefficient increase or decrease? Explain your answer.
2. A researcher investigating the production function for corn is interested in the question of whether this production function exhibits constant returns to scale. (Constant returns to scale means that if we multiply the amount of all inputs by the same constant factor s, then output will increase by that same multiplicative factor s.) The researcher wants to choose between two different functional forms:

$$(1)\ \text{Corn Output} = b_0 + b_1 \cdot \text{Land} + b_2 \cdot \text{Labor},$$

and

$$(2)\ \text{Ln Corn Output} = g_0 + g_1 \cdot \text{Ln Land} + g_2 \cdot \text{Ln Labor}.$$

Comment on the different implications each functional form has for returns to scale.
HINT: Experiment, using Excel to implement the two functional forms.
3. Figure 7.6.1 is a PivotTable of the residuals from the bivariate regression of Quantity Demanded on Price from the Heating Oil example of Section 7.3. The equation for the bivariate regression is

$$\text{Predicted Quantity Demanded} = -2.105 + 0.236\ \text{Price}.$$

Explain the pattern that you observe in the table as you move from left to right.
4. In Figure 7.6.2, the interior of the table and the heights of the bars indicate the value of a variable Z as a function of variables X and Y. All of the points in the table and in the corresponding bar graph lie in a single plane. What is the equation for the plane?
5. In Figure 7.6.3, the interior of the table and the heights of the bars indicate the value of a variable Z as a function of variables X and Y. Write down the equations for three different planes that could fit the data in Figure 7.6.3. What phenomenon does this example illustrate?

Average of Residuals	Income									
Price		9	10	11	12	13	14	15	16	17	Grand Total
	50	-3.303333	1.347	3.197							0.41333333
	60			-5.92	-0.01	3.535					-0.7983333
	70					-2.98	-1.78	5.823			0.35666667
	80							-3.34	-1.09	4.512	0.02833333
Grand Total		-3.303333	1.347	-1.36	-0.01	0.279	-1.78	1.243	-1.09	4.512	0.00000

Figure 7.6.1. PivotTable of bivariate residuals.
Source: [MultiReg.xls]Residuals.

X/Y	10	20	30	40	50
10	120	140	160	180	200
20	100	120	140	160	180
30	80	100	120	140	160
40	60	80	100	120	140
50	40	60	80	100	120

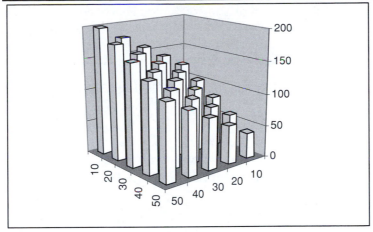

Figure 7.6.2. Three-dimensional data that lie in a plane.

X/Y	10	20	30	40	50
10					200
20				160	
30			120		
40		80			
50	40				

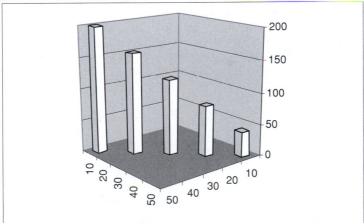

Figure 7.6.3. Three-dimensional data that lie in an infinite number of planes.

References

Multiple regression was first used by astronomers. The first application to social science problems, however, was made by G. U. Yule. He describes early developments in

Yule, G. Udny (1897). "On the Theory of Correlation." *Journal of the Royal Statistical Society* **60**(4): 812–854.

Yule's paper contains a clear discussion of the problem of confounding and demonstrates that adding variables to the equation may help to deal with confounding. See

Pearson, Karl (1920). "Notes on the History of Correlation." *Biometrika* **13**(1): 25–45, and
Stigler (1986), Chapter 10, for more details on the historical development of multiple regression.

Appendix: The Multivariate Least Squares Formula and the Omitted Variable Rule

In this appendix we derive the least squares estimates more formally using calculus and algebra. We point out that the multivariate OLS estimator is a weighted sum of the Y values, though that weighted sum is considerably more complicated than was the case for the bivariate regression. Finally, we look at the algebraic connection between bivariate and multiple regression coefficients, which is summarized by the omitted variable rule.

Using Calculus and Algebra to Obtain the OLS Formulas

Excel does not use an optimization routine to find the OLS coefficients in multiple regression. Instead, all regression software relies on analytic formulas. In the next few pages, which are based on Goldberger (1998, pp. 90–93), we show how the formulas are obtained in the trivariate case. Previously, we saw that the bivariate regression line is found by minimizing the SSR. The multiple regression coefficients are found the same way; there are just more choice variables. In the trivariate case, the regression chooses the values of the intercept and slopes that minimize the SSR.

Recall that bivariate regression solves the following optimization problem:

$$\min_{b_0,b_1} \sum_{i=1}^{n} (Y_i - b_0 - b_1 X_i)^2.$$

Trivariate regression solves this problem:

$$\min_{b_0,b_1,b_2} \sum_{i=1}^{n} (Y_i - b_0 - b_1 X_{1i} - b_2 X_{2i})^2.$$

Notice the subtle but important difference in the way the X variables are labeled. There are two independent variables, and thus X_{1i} means the ith observation on the

X_1 variable. The mathematical solution to this trivariate problem is very similar to that for the bivariate case. We begin by taking derivatives with respect to all three choice variables:

$$\frac{\partial}{\partial b_0}\left[\sum_{i=1}^{n}(Y_i - b_0 - b_1 X_{1i} - b_2 X_{2i})^2\right] = -2\sum_{i=1}^{n}(Y_i - b_0 - b_1 X_{1i} - b_2 X_{2i})$$

$$\frac{\partial}{\partial b_1}\left[\sum_{i=1}^{n}(Y_i - b_0 - b_1 X_{1i} - b_2 X_{2i_i})^2\right] = -2\sum_{i=1}^{n}(Y_i - b_0 - b_1 X_{1i} - b_2 X_{2i})X_{1i}$$

$$\frac{\partial}{\partial b_2}\left[\sum_{i=1}^{n}(Y_i - b_0 - b_1 X_{1i} - b_2 X_{2i_i})^2\right] = -2\sum_{i=1}^{n}(Y_i - b_0 - b_1 X_{1i} - b_2 X_{2i})X_{2i}.$$

Then we set the derivatives equal to zero:

$$-2\sum_{i=1}^{n}(Y_i - b_0^* - b_1^* X_{1i} - b_2^* X_{2i}) = 0$$

$$-2\sum_{i=1}^{n}(Y_i - b_0^* - b_1^* X_{1i} - b_2^* X_{2i})X_{1i} = 0$$

$$-2\sum_{i=1}^{n}(Y_i - b_0^* - b_1^* X_{1i} - b_2^* X_{2i})X_{2i} = 0.$$

The asterisks (*) indicate that b_0^*, b_1^*, and b_2^* are the optimal values of the intercept and slopes, respectively. Dividing each equation by –2 and rearranging terms, we obtain

$$\sum_{i=1}^{n}Y_i = nb_0^* + b_1^*\sum_{i=1}^{n}X_{1i} + b_2^*\sum_{i=1}^{n}X_{2i}$$

$$\sum_{i=1}^{n}Y_i X_{1i} = b_0^*\sum_{i=1}^{n}X_{1i} + b_1^*\sum_{i=1}^{n}X_{1i}^2 + b_2^*\sum_{i=1}^{n}X_{1i}X_{2i}$$

$$\sum_{i=1}^{n}Y_i X_{2i} = b_0^*\sum_{i=1}^{n}X_{2i} + b_1^*\sum_{i=1}^{n}X_{1i}X_{2i} + b_2^*\sum_{i=1}^{n}X_{2i}^2.$$

These equations can be solved to find an analytical solution for the intercept and the two slopes, b_0^*, b_1^*, and b_2^*. As you can see, the notation becomes rather daunting. The path to a solution, however, is fairly straightforward. Use the first equation to solve for b_1^*; then, substitute the result into the other two equations. Solve for b_1^*, substitute again, and then find b_2^* as a function of the various sums of X's and Y's; then, use the result to solve for b_1^* and b_0^*.

The final result involves sums of squared terms and sums of cross products. We need some notation to make the result comprehensible. Define a series of (empirical) variances and covariances:

$$s_{11} = \frac{\sum_{i=1}^{n} \left(X_{1i} - \bar{X}_1 \right)^2}{n}$$

$$s_{22} = \frac{\sum_{i=1}^{n} \left(X_{2i} - \bar{X}_2 \right)^2}{n}$$

$$s_{12} = \frac{\sum_{i=1}^{n} \left(X_{1i} - \bar{X}_1 \right) \left(X_{2i} - \bar{X}_2 \right)}{n}$$

$$s_{1y} = \frac{\sum_{i=1}^{n} \left(X_{1i} - \bar{X}_1 \right) \left(Y_i - \bar{Y} \right)}{n}$$

$$s_{2y} = \frac{\sum_{i=1}^{n} \left(X_{2i} - \bar{X}_1 \right) \left(Y_i - \bar{Y} \right)}{n}$$

$$D = s_{11}s_{22} - s_{12}^2.$$

We have seen these quantities before in slight disguise. The bar above a variable indicates a sample average. The sample variances s_{11} and s_{22} are simply the squares of the standard deviations of X_1 and X_2, respectively. The covariances s_{12}, s_{1y}, and s_{2y} tell us how the X's "covary" with each other and with the Y variable. The covariances appear in the formula for the correlation coefficient. For example, a little algebra will convince you that the correlation between X_1 and X_2 can be written as

$$r_{12} = \frac{s_{12}}{\sqrt{s_{11}} \cdot \sqrt{s_{22}}}.$$

The least squares regression coefficients are given by these equations:

$$b_1 = \frac{s_{22}s_{1y} - s_{12}s_{2y}}{D}$$

$$b_2 = \frac{s_{11}s_{2y} - s_{12}s_{1y}}{D}$$

$$b_0 = \bar{Y} - b_1\bar{X}_1 - b_2\bar{X}_2.$$

You should take away the following from these equations. First, as was the case with bivariate regression, the OLS coefficients are weighted sums of the Y values. Second, things can go awry if D equals zero. This will happen whenever there is perfect positive or negative correlation between the X variables, which you can check by working out what happens when the correlation between X_1 and X_2 is 1 or –1, making use of the formulas for r_{12} and D just presented. We discussed this possibility in Section 7.4.

The Omitted Variable Rule Relating Bivariate and Multiple Regression Coefficients

There is one important general consequence of all this algebra. It can be shown that if we run two regressions,

Multivariate: Predicted $Y_i = c_0 + c_1 \cdot X_{1i} + c_2 \cdot X_{2i}$ and

Bivariate: Predicted $Y_i = b_0 + b_1 \cdot X_{1i}$,

in which the Y_i's and the X_{1i}'s are the same in both, and then run a third, auxiliary, regression,

$$\text{Predicted } X_{2i} = d_0 + d_1 \cdot X_{1i},$$

the coefficients must have the following relationship,

$$b_1 = c_1 + d_1 \cdot c_2.$$

In other words, the slope coefficient on X_1 in the bivariate regression reflects both the direct contribution of X_1 in the multiple regression (c_1) and the indirect contribution of X_2 (the product $d_1 \cdot c_2$). The coefficient c_2 tells how much Y depends on X_2, whereas the coefficient d_1 reveals how X_2 changes as X_1 changes. An example of this omitted variable rule is discussed in the *Conversation* sheet in the MutiReg.xls workbook

Summary

This appendix has demonstrated that the OLS multiple regression plane is the solution to a familiar optimization problem – that of minimizing the SSR. That optimization problem has an analytic solution in which the regression coefficients are weighted sums of the Y values. The omitted variable rule shows how one can relate bivariate to multiple regression coefficients via an auxiliary regression.

8

Dummy Variables

The dummy variable is a simple and useful method of introducing into a regression analysis information contained in variables that are not conventionally measured on a numerical scale, e.g., race, sex, region, occupation, etc. The technique itself is not new but, so far as I am aware, there has never been any exposition of the procedure. As a consequence students and researchers trying to use dummy variables are sometimes frustrated in their first attempts.

Daniel B. Suits[1]

8.1. Introduction

Dummy variables (also known as binary, indicator, dichotomous, discrete, or categorical variables) are a way of incorporating qualitative information into regression analysis. Qualitative data, unlike continuous data, tell us simply whether the individual observation belongs to a particular category. We stress understanding dummy variables in this book because there are numerous social science applications in which dummy variables play an important role. For example, any regression analysis involving information such as race, marital status, political party, age group, or region of residence would use dummy variables. You are quite likely to encounter dummy variables in empirical papers and to use them in your own work.

This chapter first defines dummy variables, then examines them in a bivariate regression setting, and finally considers them in a multiple regression setting. We stress the interpretation of coefficient estimates in models using dummy variables; discussion of issues related to inference is deferred until the second part of this book.

Dummy variables are another way in which the flexibility of regression can be demonstrated. By incorporating dummy variables with a variety

---

[1] Suits (1957, p. 548).

of functional forms, linear regression allows for sophisticated modeling of data.

8.2. Defining and Using Dummy Variables

Workbook: Female.xls

A *dummy variable* is an indicator variable that reveals (indicates) whether an observation possesses a certain characteristic. The value of the dummy variable is 1 if the observation possesses the characteristic and 0 if it does not.

For example, Female is a dummy variable if it is defined like this:

$$\text{Female} = 1 \text{ if the individual is a female}$$
$$= 0 \text{ if the individual is a male.}$$

In this case, the unit of observation is the individual and the other variables in the data set will contain other information on each individual.

Open the Female.xls workbook and proceed to the *Data* sheet. The first five columns contain the original variable names and data used by the CPS. PESEX takes on the value of 1 for males and 2 for females. Column F contains a dummy variable recode for the variable Female. The formula used in cell F2 is "=IF(C2=2,1,0)." If C2 has a PESEX value of 2, then F2 will have a value of 1 (which means the observation is female); otherwise, F2 = 0.

Here is another example of a dummy variable:

$$\text{Large City} = 1 \text{ if the city has one million or more inhabitants}$$
$$= 0 \text{ if the city has fewer than one million inhabitants.}$$

Here the unit of observation is cities, and the other variables in the data set will contain other information on the cities.

Some dummy variables (e.g., Large City) correspond to continuous variables. For other dummy variables, like Female, no underlying continuous variable exists. Dummy variables are often called qualitative variables because they reveal qualitative information about the observation.

We suggest naming dummy variables for the characteristic indicated if the value of the variable is 1. Sometimes dummy variables are named after the characteristic itself as follows:

$$\text{Sex} = 1 \text{ if the individual is a female}$$
$$= 0 \text{ if the individual is a male.}$$

We think that Female is a more informative name for this variable.

A data set might contain dummy variables such as Nonwhite, Hispanic, Female, and Married. Although coded as 0 or 1, dummy variables are so named because the numbers "0" and "1" by themselves are meaningless. Rather, they are stand-ins, or "dummies" that merely indicate the presence or absence of some underlying characteristic. The word "qualitative" is often associated with dummy variables, but this adjective has a broader meaning. A crucial feature of dummy variables, as opposed to qualitative variables in general, is that they can only take on two values, 0 or 1. The following variable is a qualitative variable:

$$\text{Race} = 1 \text{ if individual is white}$$
$$= 2 \text{ if the individual is black}$$
$$= 3 \text{ if the individual is of Asian descent}$$
$$= 4 \text{ if the individual belongs to a different race.}$$

In this case the variable Race reveals qualitative information about the individual, but it is not a dummy variable. Note that it would be easy to create dummy variables by using the categorical Race variable. For example, we could define four new dummy variables, one for each category:

$$\text{White} = 1 \text{ if Race } = 1$$
$$= 0 \text{ if Race not } = 1,$$
$$\text{Black} = 1 \text{ if Race } = 2$$
$$= 0 \text{ if Race not } = 2,$$
$$\text{Asian} = 1 \text{ if Race } = 3$$
$$= 0 \text{ if Race not } = 3,$$
$$\text{Other} = 1 \text{ if Race } = 4$$
$$= 0 \text{ if Race not } = 4.$$

Using Dummy Variables in a Regression

Once the dummy variables have been created, one would expect simply to put them all into the regression equation. This is a big mistake. If both Female and Male or all four of the racial dummies are included in a regression with an intercept term, perfect multicollinearity will have been introduced into the regression. For example, if both Male and Female are included in a regression, there is an exact linear relationship between those two variables: Male = 1 – Female. This is perfect multicollinearity.

If the regression has an intercept term, there is no determinate solution to the least squares optimization problem. Your regression software will complain. You may get an error message or a display that certain parameters have

b_3	b_2	b_1	b_0	
0.95733711	−7.898E+12	−7.898E+12	7.8982E+12	
0.04046112	7.6067E+12	7.6067E+12	7.6067E+12	
R^2 0.07960924	7.00604713	#N/A	#N/A	RMSE
246.280209	8542	#N/A	#N/A	df
Reg SS 36265.7679	419281.477	#N/A	#N/A	SSR

Table title (spanning): Predicted Wage = $b_0 + b_1$Female + b_2Male + b_3Education

Figure 8.2.1. Excel's LINEST with both Female and Male included.
Source: [FemaleA.xls]Data.

been dropped from the regression. In Excel, the behavior depends on your version. You may see a coefficient that is zeroed out, or LINEST may display #NUM values. The worst behavior by Excel is that it may report a solution, although you can usually tell that it is wrong. Figure 8.2.1, from the answer key file for Female.xls, shows an example of this.

The most common way to avoid blowing up the regression is simply to drop one of the dummy variables arbitrarily from the regression.[2] In the case of the gender category, we would include either Male or Female, but not both. For the race variable, we would drop one of the categories and include the other three in the regression. The variable omitted is called the base case. The next section will show that which variable is omitted is irrelevant.

We conclude this section with another example. Suppose you have data on sales and one of the variables, called Season, takes on four values: Winter, Spring, Summer, and Fall. The Season variable cannot be included directly in a regression. It is nonnumerical.

This information, however, can be included in a regression by the method of dummy variables. Four dummy variables are created to indicate the four seasons, and each one is named for its season. All four are not included in the regression. Instead, one of them is dropped. Your base case might be Winter and, therefore, you would include only the three dummy variables Spring, Summer, and Fall in the regression. If all three dummies equal zero for a particular observation, then we know we are dealing with a Winter observation.

Summary

Having defined dummy variables and explained how qualitative information can be incorporated in a regression via dummy variables, we are ready to

---

[2] Another approach is to suppress the intercept. We do not use this strategy in this book, but you may see regression results in which all of the dummy variables are included. If there is no intercept term, the least squares fit can be obtained. Both approaches work because we are imposing an additional constraint (the coefficient on the omitted category is set equal to 0 or the intercept is set equal to 0).

show how dummy variables are used to allow regression greater flexibility in describing a data set. The next section focuses on a few basic properties of dummy variables, and then the rest of the chapter demonstrates dummy variables in regression with several examples.

8.3. Properties of Dummy Variables

Workbook: Female.xls

That dummy variables take on a value of 1 if the individual observation possesses the characteristic and 0 if the individual observation does not possess the characteristic gives dummy variables very useful mathematical properties. Here are three of the most important:

1. The average value of a dummy variable tells what fraction of all observations in the sample possesses the characteristic in question.
2. In a regression model with a dummy variable,

$$\text{Predicted } Y = b_0 + b_1 \cdot \text{Dummy Variable},$$

the b_1 coefficient tells you the difference in the average Y between those observations for which Dummy Variable $= 1$ and those for which Dummy Variable $= 0$.
3. It does not matter which category you omit as the base case. The fitted coefficients will, of course, be different, but the interpretation of the data is the same.

There are other helpful rules for using and interpreting dummy variables in regressions – See HowToUseDummyVariables.doc in the BasicTools \ HowTo folder. Let us consider each of these three properties more carefully.

1. Averages of dummy variables equal the percentage of all observations sharing the characteristic.

Here is an explanation of this fact via a hypothetical example. Suppose that in a data set of 500 adults, 210 are men. Then, if there is a dummy variable Male, 210 observations have Male $= 1$, and 290 observations have Male $= 0$. The sum of Male therefore is $210 \cdot 1 + 290 \cdot 0 = 210$. Thus, average value of Male is 210/500, or 0.42 or 42 percent. But this is exactly the calculation needed to find the percentage of males in the sample.

2. In a bivariate regression with a dummy variable, the b_1 coefficient tells you the difference in the averages of the dependent variable between those observations that share the characteristic and those that do not.

This requires somewhat more explanation, but it should make sense if you recall the interpretation of regression as a double compression and visualize how regression with a dummy variable can be seen as partitioning the data into two vertical strips. Suppose we had a data set of 478 workers, 276 of which are between 25 and 29 years old, whereas the rest are 45–49 years of

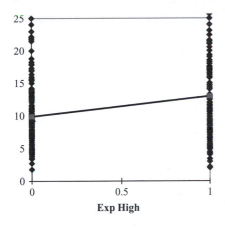

Figure 8.3.1. Regression of hourly wage on Exp High.
Source: [Female.xls] Exp Dummy.

age. Suppose we wanted to compare the average wage of the 25–29 year old workers to the average wage of 45–49 year olds.

An obvious approach is simply to compute the average wage of each group. It turns out the average wage of the young workers is $9.89 per hour. The older workers earn $12.98 per hour on average.

Another alternative, however, that will demonstrate how the coefficient of the dummy variable can be interpreted is to run a regression of wage on a dummy variable. The dummy variable is defined as

$$\text{Exp High} = 1 \text{ if the worker is aged } 45\text{–}49$$
$$= 0 \text{ if the worker is not aged } 45\text{–}49.$$

The idea is that there are two types of workers in the data set: experienced workers and inexperienced workers. The dummy variable Exp High tells us which group an individual worker belongs to.

Now let us run the following regression:

$$\text{Predicted Wage} = b_0 + b_1 \cdot \text{Exp High}.$$

The results are

$$\text{Predicted Wage} = 9.89 + 3.09 \cdot \text{Exp High}.$$

Figure 8.3.1 is a picture of the scatter plot and the regression line in which we have cut off a few of the really high-wage workers to make the line easier to see. The crucial features of the graph are these:

1. The Y-axis measures the hourly wage.
2. The X-axis measures the dummy variable. That variable has only two possible values, 0 and 1. Hence, the scatter diagram is composed of two vertical strips.
3. The regression line connects the two points of averages of the two vertical strips. That is, when Exp High = 0, the regression line reaches a vertical height of $9.89 per hour, which is the average wage of 25–29 year olds; when Exp High = 1,

the regression line reaches a vertical height of $12.98 per hour, which is the average wage of 45–49 year olds.

4. Therefore, the value of the b_1 coefficient in the regression is $3.09 per hour. This slope is simply the rise ($12.99 per hour – $9.89 per hour) over the run (1 – 0). Note that dummy variables are unitless.

5. The RMSE of this regression measures the average spread of the vertical distances around the two predicted values in the regression. That RMSE is in essence a weighted average of the standard deviations of the hourly wage for the two separate groups, inexperienced and experienced workers.

6. Although the regression line has been drawn in, it does not make any sense to predict the wage for a value of Exp High = 0.5. The only two possible values of Exp High are 0 and 1, and thus these are the only values we would use as given in order to predict the wage.

The final property of dummy variables in regression may seem like magic, but remember that if you have two categories, not being in one means you are in the other. This mirror reasoning will be used when we explain the third property of dummy variables.

3. Which category is omitted as the base case is irrelevant because the final interpretation of the data remains the same.

We proceed by example. Here are two regression results using the same data. The only difference is that we omitted Female in one regression and Male in the other:

$$\text{Predicted Wage} = 10.99 - 2.03\text{Female}$$
$$\text{Predicted Wage} = 8.96 + 2.03\text{Male}.$$

The coefficients are obviously different, but regardless of whether we use the first or the second fitted line, we say the same thing: males, on average, earn $2.03 more per hour than females in this data set. We can also use the first equation to say the males earn, on average, $10.99 per hour because they are the base case in the first equation. The second equation yields the same number, albeit in a slightly different way: we add 8.96 and 2.03 to get 10.99. Of course, the same holds true for the average Female wage. It is $8.96 per hour no matter if you use the first or second fitted line.

The first equation says that being female lowers your average wage, compared with males, by $2.03 per hour. The second equation says that being male raises your average wage, compared with females, by $2.03 per hour. This makes clear that the dummy variable dropped from the regression is not really excluded from the analysis at all. Instead, the included dummy variable coefficient is measured relative to the base case. This is why it is absolutely arbitrary which category is dropped from the regression.

Summary

This section demonstrated how dummy variables can be used in a regression to incorporate qualitative characteristics. Remember to leave out a base case to avoid perfect multicollinearity.

The next section extends our analysis of dummy variables by considering a multiple regression example. We show that there is no problem mixing conventional variables measured on a numerical scale with dummy variables.

8.4. Dummy Variables as Intercept Shifters

Workbook: Female.xls

This section shows how dummy variables are used in multiple regression via another example. Suppose we are interested in studying labor discrimination against women. We want to know if women are disadvantaged in the labor market in the United States today. One way in which discrimination might manifest itself is in lower earnings for women.

We begin our empirical work by getting data from the February 1994 Current Population Survey. The Excel workbook Female.xls has data on 8,456 people. For this section, we concentrate on the following variables:

Education = highest grade completed; in years (via the numerical Education recode)

Female = 1 if female; otherwise 0 (the dummy variable)

Wage = reported hourly wage; in $/hr (the computation of this variable is explained in the CPS folder)

Cell D13 in the *PivotTables* sheet of Female.xls shows that the average wage of women is $2.03 per hour less than that of men in the data set. This "raw differential" can also be found via regression. The *Data* sheet has the data that were used by the *PivotTables* sheet.

The regression, *Predicted Wage$_i$ = $b_0 + b_1 \cdot$ Female$_i$, $i = 1, \ldots 8{,}456$, yields the results displayed in Figure 8.4.1.

As was shown in the previous section, the slope of a bivariate regression with a dummy variable is the same as the differential between the two groups.

Predicted Wage = $b_0 + b_1$Female			
b_1	−2.03	10.99	b_0
R^2	0.019	7.231	RMSE
		8544	df
Reg SS	8781	446766	SSR

Figure 8.4.1. Regression of wage on Female.
Source: [Female.xls]Data.

Predicted Wage = $b_0 + b_1$Education + b_2Female			
b_2	b_1	b_0	
−2.263	0.956	−0.858	
R^2 0.079	7.006	#N/A	RMSE
	8543	#N/A	df
Reg SS 36213	419334	#N/A	SSR

Figure 8.4.2. Regression of wage on Education and Female.
Source: [Female.xls]Data.

In this case, the negative $2.03 per hour slope coefficient means that, on average, women in the data set earned $2.03 per hour less than men.

There are two possible reasons we would not conclude, from these results, that gender wage discrimination existed in the United States in 1994:

1. The presence of confounding variables in the analysis. What if there are other variables correlated with gender that explain the wage differential? Suppose, for example, that women have less education than men. The bivariate regression is picking up the correlation between education and wage and making it seem like gender is the causal factor.
2. Because the data are but a sample of the population, the observed wage differential could be due to chance. Perhaps in this sample we just happened to draw many low-wage women and high-wage men. This issue is important but will be postponed until the second part of this book.

In an effort to improve our empirical analysis, we attempt to control statistically for the confounding effect of education. We estimate Model 2:

$$Predicted\ Wage_i = b_0 + b_1 \cdot Education_i + b_2 \cdot Female_i.$$

Figure 8.4.2 contains the regression results for Model 2.

Let us interpret these results. For males, we do not need to worry about the b_2 coefficient because for males, Female $= 0$. Therefore, the regression equation for males is

$$Predicted\ Wage_M = -0.858 + 0.956\ Education.$$

Thus, if you are male with 10 years of education, the predicted wage is

$$= -0.858 + 0.956 \cdot 10,$$
$$= \$8.70/hr.$$

For females, we know that the Female variable has to equal 1. Thus, the regression equation for females is

$$Predicted\ Wage_F = -0.857 + 0.956\ Education - 2.263.$$

Average of HrlyWage	Female		
Education	0	1	F-M Differential
8	$ 7.83	$ 6.14	$ (1.69)
9	$ 9.30	$ 5.89	$ (3.41)
10	$ 7.71	$ 5.58	$ (2.13)
11	$ 7.88	$ 6.48	$ (1.40)
11.5	$ 7.83	$ 7.38	$ (0.45)
12	$11.14	$ 8.46	$ (2.68)
13	$11.14	$ 8.85	$ (2.28)
14	$12.69	$ 11.05	$ (1.64)
16	$13.75	$ 12.55	$ (1.20)
18	$17.94	$ 16.67	$ (1.28)
Grand Total	$ 10.99	$ 8.96	$ (2.03)

Predicted Wage from Regression of Wage on Education and Female

Education	0	1	F-M Differential
8	$ 6.79	$ 4.53	$ (2.26)
9	$ 7.75	$ 5.48	$ (2.26)
10	$ 8.70	$ 6.44	$ (2.26)
11	$ 9.66	$ 7.40	$ (2.26)
11.5	$10.14	$ 7.87	$ (2.26)
12	$10.62	$ 8.35	$ (2.26)
13	$11.57	$ 9.31	$ (2.26)
14	$12.53	$ 10.27	$ (2.26)
16	$14.44	$ 12.18	$ (2.26)
18	$16.35	$ 14.09	$ (2.26)

Figure 8.4.3. Comparing the graph of averages and regression.
Source: [Female.xls]PivotTables.

We can simply add the two constants to obtain

$$= -3.12 + 0.956 \, \text{Education}.$$

Thus, if you are female with 10 years of education, the predicted wage is

$$= -3.12 + 0.956 \cdot 10,$$
$$= \$6.44/\text{hr}.$$

Comparing the male and female regression equations shows that one way of interpreting the regression equation with a dummy variable is to think of the dummy variable as an intercept shifter. The base case, male, is the one without the presence of the dummy variable. If the dummy variable value is 1, which means the observation is a female, the only difference is that the intercept shifts by the amount of coefficient on the dummy variable. Figure 8.4.3 shows this interpretation. The thicker line, which is the regression equation for females, is shifted down relative to the thinner line.

By including a dummy variable, a single regression equation is flexible enough to incorporate qualitative information such as gender. We could continue this approach, adding dummy variables for other qualitative characteristics, to allow the regression equation to paint a fuller description of the data.

It is important to note that, given this specification of the model, an extra year of education is assumed to increase a male's wage and a female's wage by the same amount. According to our results, a year of education increases everyone's hourly wage by $0.956 per hour. In other words, the two lines relating education to wages for males and females are parallel, as shown in Figure 8.4.3.

This is an important restriction for our regression model – one that may not be borne out by the data. Fortunately, dummy variables can be used to estimate more flexible functional forms. That is the subject of the next section.

Summary

The simplest use of a dummy variable in a regression is an intercept shifter. The coefficient on the dummy variable is added to the intercept if the observation has the given characteristic. The next section demonstrates a more sophisticated application of dummy variables in regression analysis.

8.5. Dummy Variable Interaction Terms

Workbook: Female.xls

Section 8.2 showed how regression analysis easily incorporates qualitative data into the regression equation via a dummy variable. The example in Section 8.3 showed how including a dummy variable allows the regression to fit different intercepts for each qualitative characteristic. But what if the relationship is more complicated than that? What if the effect of being female is not a one-time negative number tacked on to your base wage but instead depends on the amount of education? The idea here is that discrimination works in various ways. One way is through lower wages for women across the board, but another way is through lower wages for women versus men as education increases.

If an additional year of education matters more to a male than to a female in terms of increased wages, we might illustrate this possibility as Figure 8.5.1. Note that the slopes of the two regression lines are different as well as the intercepts. The slope of the male line is steeper than that of the female line, meaning that an additional year of education is associated with a higher increase in the average male's hourly wage than his female counterpart. Of course, this is only one possibility, for the slope on Education for Females may be larger. The point is that we need to allow for the greater flexibility of nonparallel lines.

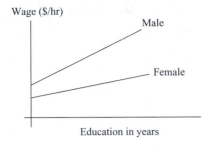

Figure 8.5.1. Different slopes on Education.

A simple dummy variable in a regression equation cannot capture such a sophisticated different-slopes story. But regression analysis is nothing if not an extremely flexible tool. How can we allow for different slopes as well as different intercepts in a regression with a dummy variable? We can relax (that is, drop) the assumption of parallel slopes or equal returns to education for men and women by introducing a new variable, called an *interaction term*, defined as follows:

$$\text{Female} \cdot \text{Education} = \begin{cases} 0 \text{ if the person is Male} \\ \text{Education if the person is Female.} \end{cases}$$

The interaction term is a new variable that is the product of the value of the dummy variable, Female, and the number of years of education. We would say that the variables Female and Education are *interacted* with each other to produce the new variable.

The new, expanded model with the interaction term is then

$$Predicted\ Wage_i = b_0 + b_1 \cdot Education_i + b_2 \cdot Female_i$$
$$+ b_3 \cdot Female \cdot Education_i.$$

The results are reported in Figure 8.5.2. We interpret the coefficient estimates in this model in the same way as the previous section. The basic strategy is to predict the wage for males and females.

Suppose that you want to predict the hourly wage for a male. We know the value of the dummy variable Female is 0. Therefore, the male regression

Predicted Wage = $b_0 + b_1$Education + b_2Female + b_3Female*Education				
b_3	b_2	b_1	b_0	
0.161	−4.278	0.881	0.076	
R^2	0.080	7.005	#N/A	#N/A	RMSE
	8542	#N/A	#N/A	df
Reg SS	36406	419141	#N/A	#N/A	SSR

Figure 8.5.2. Wage regression including interaction terms.
Source: [Female.xls]Data.

equation is easy to produce because the Female and Female·Education terms simply drop out.

$$\text{Predicted Wage}_M = 0.076 + 0.881\text{Education}$$

Thus, if you are male with 10 years of education, the predicted wage is

$$= 0.076 + 0.881 \cdot 10$$
$$= \$8.88/\text{hr}.$$

For females, the regression equation can be found by substituting a "1" for the Female variable and then combining like terms:

$$\text{Predicted Wage}_F = 0.076 + 0.881\text{Education} - 4.278 + 0.161\text{Education}$$
$$= -4.202 + 1.042\text{Education}.$$

Thus, if you are female with 10 years of education, the predicted wage is

$$= -4.202 + 1.042 \cdot 10$$
$$= \$6.22/\text{hr}.$$

Because the value of the variable Female is 1, both the intercept and the slope terms change in the female equation relative to the male equation. The Female dummy variable acts like an intercept shifter, and the Female· Education interaction term allows the slopes to be different.

We can interpret the coefficient on the interaction term, b_3, as being the adjustment to the slope attached to the education variable because of being female. Thus, to obtain an estimate of how much wage would go up with an additional year of education for a male, you look only at b_1, the slope coefficient for education. For females in this data set, however, the effect of an additional year of education is the sum of b_1 and b_3.

In this data set, an additional year of education is worth more to females because b_3 is greater than 0. An additional year of education is worth about \$0.88 per hour to males but \$1.04 per hour to females. Figure 8.5.3 shows how the addition of the Female · Education interaction term to the regression equation affects the Predicted Wage as a function of Education fitted lines.

Summary

This section has shown that including an interaction term in a linear regression with a dummy variable allows for more flexible modeling and summarizing of the data. The slope is allowed to vary as determined by whether the observation has or does not have a particular characteristic.

It is important to realize that the approach to interpreting an interaction term is the same as in the simple dummy variable case. We create two separate

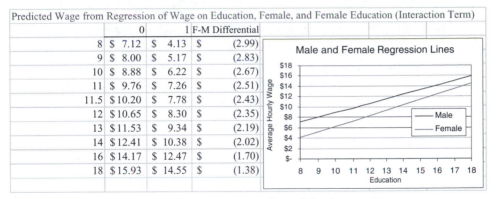

Figure 8.5.3. Graphical interpretation of the interaction term.
Source: [Female.xls]PivotTables.

equations based on whether the dummy variable is present (1) or not (0). Then we predict the dependent variable in the two equations.

Finally, we point out that economists routinely use the semilog functional form when working with earnings as the dependent variable.[3] In this section, we have used the wage in its original units as the dependent variable to facilitate the explanation of dummy variables. Of course, dummy variables can be used with a variety of functional forms.

8.6. Conclusion

This chapter introduced so-called dummy variables and showed how they can be used in a regression equation. Dummy variables are commonly used to include qualitative information in regression analysis.

We have stressed that you should choose the name of your 0–1 variable with some care. The best approach is to set the name equal to the observation having the characteristic. For example, Rookie (if the player is in his or her first year) and Retired (if the person is retired) are good names, whereas Gender and Ethnic are not.

In a regression with an intercept, it is mandatory that one of the categories be omitted from the regression, and this is called the base case. If all of the categories are included, your software will complain.

Including a single dummy variable acts as an intercept shifter, but dummy variables can also be multiplied against continuous variables to allow the slope to vary across the categories represented by the dummy variables. This ability to generate different lines of best fit for subcategories of the data is a powerful feature of dummy variables.

---

[3] See Chapter 6 for an explanation of why the natural log transformation is so common.

Whether a regression has a dummy variable as a simple intercept shifter or more complicated interaction terms, the procedure for interpreting the model and results is the same: create a predicted dependent variable for each category of the dummy variable.

The last several chapters have delivered an important message: Linear regression is remarkably flexible and can be used to describe a wide variety of nonlinear relationships in the data. Do not be misled by the word *linear* in linear regression, which refers to linearity in the parameters.

With this chapter, we end our presentation of regression as description. In the first eight chapters of this book, we have seen how regression lines are computed and interpreted. We have provided a variety of examples to show how regression can describe a data set. We now turn to the second fundamental use of regression analysis – inference.

8.7. Exercises

Copy the *Data* sheet in the Female.xls workbook.

1. Create the dummy variable UNION, using the CPS variable PEERNLAB. Fill your formula down.
2. Compute the average of the UNION dummy variable and interpret the result.
3. Regress Wage on UNION and Education. Report your results and interpret the coefficient on UNION.
4. Create a new dependent variable, ln Wage. Regress ln Wage on UNION and Education. Report your results and interpret the coefficient on UNION.
   HINT: See HowToUseDummyXVariables.doc (in Basic Tools \ HowTo) on how to interpret dummy variables in a semilog functional form regression.
5A. Add an Education*UNION interaction term to your semilog earnings function. Report your results.
5B. Use the regression results to create a graph that compares the predicted wages of Union and Nonunion members as a function of Education.

References

The various names used for dummy variables hint at the complicated history behind the idea. A JSTOR (<www.jstor.org>) search for "dummy variable" in the areas of economics and statistics yields over 6,000 hits. The term popped up in the late 1950s in the journals searched by JSTOR, but it was in use before that time.

Mathematicians would argue for *indicator variable* as a much better name (especially because *dummy variable* has a well-established meaning in mathematics as a placeholder variable) – and many economists would agree – but dummy variable seems to have stuck in the econometrics literature.

Daniel B. Suits (1957). "Use of Dummy Variables in Regression Equations," *Journal of the American Statistical Association* **52**(280): 548–551.

Part 2

Inference

9

Monte Carlo Simulation

Anyone who considers arithmetical methods of producing random digits is, of course, in a state of sin.

John von Neumann[1]

The one thing about Monte Carlo is that it never gives an exact answer.

Stanislaw Ulam[2]

9.1. Introduction

The chapters in the first part of this book make clear that regression analysis can be used to describe data. The remainder of this book is dedicated to understanding regression as a tool for drawing inferences about how variables are related to each other. The central idea in inferential statistics is that the data we observe are just one sample from a larger population. The goal of inference is to determine what evidence the sample provides about the relationship between variables in the population.

This chapter explains how we will use the computer to draw random samples to evaluate the performance of a variety of sample-based statistics. We will review basic theory behind random number generation with computers, offer a simple example of Monte Carlo simulation, and introduce a Monte Carlo simulation Excel add-in.

Like regression analysis, Monte Carlo simulation is a general term that has many meanings. The word "simulation" signifies that we build an artificial model of a real system to study and understand the system. The "Monte Carlo" part of the name alludes to the randomness inherent in the analysis:

The name "Monte Carlo" was coined by [physicist Nicholas] Metropolis (inspired by [Stanislaw] Ulam's interest in poker) during the Manhattan Project of World

---

[1] von Neumann (1951).
[2] Ulam (1991, p. 199).

War II, because of the similarity of statistical simulation to games of chance, and because the capital of Monaco was a center for gambling and similar pursuits. Monte Carlo is now used routinely in many diverse fields, from the simulation of complex physical phenomena such as radiation transport in the earth's atmosphere and the simulation of the esoteric subnuclear processes in high energy physics experiments, to the mundane, such as the simulation of a Bingo game or the outcome of Monty Hall's vexing offer to the contestant in "Let's Make a Deal."

(Drakos, 1995)

Monte Carlo simulation is a method of analysis based on artificially recreating a chance process (usually with a computer), running it many times, and directly observing the results.

We will use Monte Carlo simulation to understand the properties of different statistics computed from sample data. In other words, we will test-drive estimators, figuring out how different recipes perform under different circumstances. Our procedure is quite simple: In each case we will set up an artificial environment in which the values of important parameters and the nature of the chance process are specified; then the computer will run the chance process over and over; finally the computer will display the results of the experiment.

The next section explains the fundamental principles behind random number generation, which is the engine that drives a Monte Carlo simulation. Section 9.3 is a practical guide to generating random numbers in Excel. Section 9.4 demonstrates Monte Carlo via a simple example, and the last section introduces an Excel add-in that can be used to run a Monte Carlo simulation in any Excel workbook.

9.2. Random Number Generation Theory

Workbook: RNGTheory.xls

Because Monte Carlo simulation is based on repeatedly sampling from a chance process, it stands to reason that random numbers are a crucial part of the procedure. This section will briefly explain the theoretical principles behind random number generation.

We begin with a simple but important claim: Excel, like all other computer software, cannot draw a true sequence of random numbers. At best, Excel's random draws can mimic the behavior of truly random draws, but true randomness is unattainable. The inability of computer software to generate truly random numbers results from a computer program's having to follow a deterministic algorithm to produce its output. If the previous number and the algorithm are known, so is the next number. Because the essence of randomness is that you do not know what is going to happen next, numbers produced by computer software are not genuinely random. Thus, Monte Carlo simulation

Random Number Generation Theory 217

	A	B	C	D	E	F	G
1	An LCG in action. Set the A, B, and m values to control the LCG						
2	A	100					
3	B	3					
4	m	5					
5							
6	seed	0.5	NextNumber = MOD(B*PreviousNumber+A,m)				
7					1.5		
8					4.5		
9					3.5		
10					0.5		
11					1.5		
12					4.5		
13					3.5		
14					0.5		

Figure 9.2.1. An LCG demonstration.
Source: [RNGTheory.xls]LCG.

with Excel is based on pseudorandom number generation. Throughout this book, when we say random number, we actually mean pseudorandom number.

The random number recipe used by all versions of Excel before Excel 2003 is called a linear congruential generator (LCG).[3] Starting from an initial value, called the seed, the LCG simply puts a number through a formula

$$\text{NextNumber} = (B \cdot \text{PreviousNumber} + A)\, \text{Mod}\, m,$$

to generate the next number. In the formula above Mod means Modulus. The expression x Mod y yields the remainder when a number x is divided by another number y.

To see the simple logic behind this algorithm, go to the LCG sheet in RNGTheory.xls. Figure 9.2.1 is a picture of a portion of the LCG sheet. Starting from a seed of 0.5 and $A = 100$, $B = 3$, and $m = 5$, the next number is 1.5 (cell E7). The steps in the calculation are (1) $3 \times 0.5 = 1.5$, (2) $1.5 + 100 = 101.5$, (3) $101.5 \text{ Mod } 5 = 1.5$. The output of the Excel function $\text{MOD}(x, y)$ is x Mod y.

The LCG $(3 \cdot \text{PreviousNumber} + 100)$ Mod 5 is an unsatisfactory random number generator (RNG). After all, we will see 1.5 followed by 4.5, 3.5, 0.5 (the first number), and then the numbers simply repeat themselves. One way to judge a random number generator is by its period or the number of values generated before returning to the first value and recycling through the list.

[3] As part of a massive revision of statistical functions, Excel 2003 uses a new algorithm to generate Uniform(0,1) random numbers. Unfortunately, as of this writing, the new algorithm has a problem and can give negative numbers. A patch is available from Microsoft at <office.microsoft.com>. As this section will explain, we recommend using our own built-in random number generator. Execute Help: About Microsoft Excel to see what version of Excel you are using. See the Basic Tools/RandomNumber folder for more information about Excel 2003's random number generator.

By changing the parameters, A, B, and m, you change the performance of the generator. For example, set $m = 7$ (in cell B4). The generated sequence of numbers changes and the period lengthens to 6. The period, however, is a simple, and potentially misleading attribute of a random number generator. There are many other desirable attributes in a random number generator, and many different tests have been devised to judge randomness.

We are now ready to examine Excel's random number function, RAND as implemented in versions prior to Excel 2003. Click the $\boxed{\text{ShowRAND}}$ button to see the Excel LCG. For the LCG used by RAND, Microsoft programmers chose $A = 0.211327$, $B = 9821$, and $m = 1$. The numbers generated are always between 0 and 1. Excel's RAND function simulates a uniform distribution on the interval from 0 to 1 (known as the Uniform(0,1) distribution). The idea is that we are drawing random numbers from the interval 0 to 1 with every number equally likely to be chosen.[4] This is not as limiting as you might think. For example, we can obtain numbers uniformly distributed between 0 and 10 by multiplying the original numbers by 10. In addition, we can add 50 to make them range from 50 to 60. In fact, starting from numbers drawn from the Uniform(0,1) distribution, it is possible to generate numbers that are random draws from almost any desired statistical distribution.

You will not see a repetition in the 15 numbers generated in column E – the Excel RAND function has an extremely long period.[5] However, it is shown below that, its long period notwithstanding, Excel's RAND is not a good random number generator. Visual Basic, the programming language behind Excel, has its own LCG random number algorithm called Rnd. It is preferable to Excel's RAND. Rnd uses $B = 1{,}140{,}671{,}485$, $A = 12{,}820{,}163$, and $m = 2^{24}$. Its period is $16{,}777{,}216$ (2^{24}), but, like Excel's RAND, it is still a fairly crude RNG.

The problem with both RAND and Rnd is that the sequences of numbers they produce have too much structure, meaning they are not "random enough" when seen from certain perspectives. Figure 9.2.2 offers a simple example of the undesirable structure embedded in RAND and Rnd. The three graphs in Figure 9.2.2 were created by trapping the next number in the sequence whenever the previous number fell between 0.7 and 0.7001. Each graph has 1,000 data points. Excel's RAND function graph is the least random of the three. Whenever a number between 0.7 and 0.7001 is visited, the next number is guaranteed to lie on one of the two lines in the graph. That is not very random. Visual Basic's Rnd fills the graph, but the points are still too

---

[4] Well, not every number. Because it uses binary arithmetic and has finite memory, Excel can only recognize 2^{54} points on the number line between 0 and 1.

[5] In fact, because of complicated floating-point precision issues, Excel's RAND function does not exactly repeat itself after 1,000,000, the period for the LCG 9821*x_{-1} + 0.211327. For more on this issue, see the information in the BasicTools/RandomNumber folder.

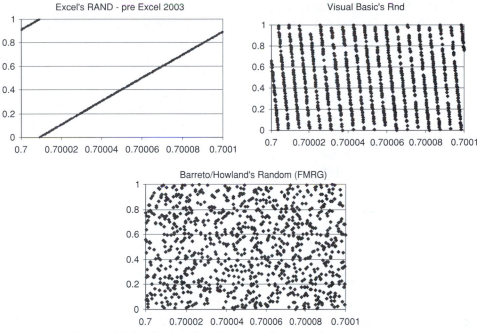

Figure 9.2.2. Comparing three random number generators.
Source: [RNGTheory.xls]Graphs.

systematic – they fall on straight lines. The bottom graph looks like the best of the three: there does not appear to be a systematic relationship between successive numbers in the sequence.

The bottom graph in Figure 9.2.2 is derived from an implementation of a random number algorithm based on a fast multiple recursive generator (FMRG) (Deng and Lin 2000). Multiple recursive generators are like LCGs in that they use the previous output to generate the next number, but instead of using just the previous number like an LCG, an MRG uses a linear combination of the past k random numbers generated.

$$x_i = (a_1 x_{i-1} + \ldots + a_k x_{i-k}) \bmod m$$

The formula above says that the ith number in the sequence is a linear combination of the previous k numbers. As with an LCG, the parameter choices (the a's and m) in an MRG are critical components of the quality of the random numbers generated. Our implementation of the MRG is the simplest one available (hence the F as in fast in FMRG) based on using only the last two random numbers generated ($k = 2$) and choosing the a_1 and a_2 coefficients from a special list of numbers. Deng and Lin, the developers of FMRG, report the period as 4,611,686,014,132,420,608. You will probably not revisit the same number.

Figure 9.2.2 might appear to paint FMRG as a perfect random number generator. This is not true. Although FMRG is better than RAND and Rnd, it too will exhibit structure when examined under higher magnification. The details of our implementation of Deng and Lin's FMRG are beyond the scope of this book, but additional information and complete documentation are available in the Basic Tools/RandomNumber folder.

Summary

This section has provided a basic review of the principles of random number generation and highlighted an important fact: Not all random number generators are the same. A Monte Carlo simulation based on a poor random number generator is a poor Monte Carlo simulation. The hidden structure in the pseudorandom sequence may completely invalidate the simulation.

The linear congruential random number generators employed by Excel (the RAND function in versions before Excel 2003) and Visual Basic (Rnd) are relatively unsophisticated and exhibit too much structure when successive pairs are plotted. This book will use a more sophisticated random number generator that has an extremely long period and possesses other desirable properties.

This is not to say that the FMRG generator in our RANDOM function is ideal or perfect. It turns out that random number generation is a complex, difficult task. There are many other generators out there (with such colorful names as the Mersenne Twister) and a great deal of debate in the computational science community about the best ones. If you are interested in the details of our random number generator or want references for a more in-depth study of random number theory, please see the Basic Tools/RandomNumber folder.

You should never trust a Monte Carlo simulation without knowing the random number generator used. You should always report the random number generator used in a simulation. We recommend avoiding Excel's RAND unless the application is rudimentary or a simple demonstration. The next section explains how to use RANDOM, the random number generator supplied with this book.

9.3. Random Number Generation in Practice

Workbook: RNGPractice.xls

Although previous section focused on the theory behind random number generation, this section will provide a guide to the practical issues of how to actually get Excel to provide random numbers. In addition to reviewing

	RAND	NORMINV(RAND(),0,1)	
	Uniform	Normal	
Average	0.50019275828668	0.00288489306875	
SD	0.29027807011725	1.00048089727527	
Max	0.99953004104712	3.30795409112160	Note how draws near 0 or 1 are
Min	0.00059867432756	−3.23954051612582	translated into numbers like −3.7 or +4.2

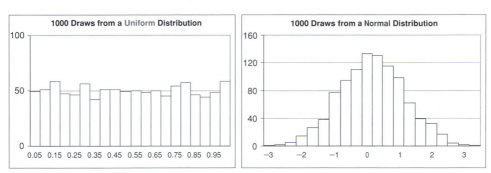

Figure 9.3.1. Output from RAND and NORMINV(RAND(),0,1).
Source: [RNGPractice.xls]NormalRand.

the different formulas available for uniform and normal distributions, this section also reviews how Excel calculates cells.

Before explaining the options available, we warn against generating random numbers with the Data Analysis add-in provided with many versions of Microsoft Excel. Regrettably, not only does the add-in simply provide "dead" values that do not change when the sheet is calculated, but the properties of the random number generator are bad. The Data Analysis add-in should never be used to generate random numbers.

To generate uniformly distributed random numbers with Excel, use either Excel's RAND function or, if the functions packaged with this book are available, use the RANDOM function. Both functions require formulas that use parentheses without any arguments: = RAND() and = RANDOM().

Open the RNGPractice.xls workbook and go to the *Uniform* sheet. Examine the formulas and results in columns A and E. Hit F9 to draw more random numbers. (If it takes a long time for the sheet to draw new random numbers, hit the Recalculate this Sheet Only button instead. There are thousands of cells containing random numbers in the workbook, and every time you hit F9, the workbook must compute formulas to replace every one of them.)

As with the uniform case, there are two ways to obtain normally distributed random numbers. The first approach uses intrinsic Excel functions RAND and NORMINV. The *NormalRand* sheet uses the formula "= NORMINV(RAND(), 0, 1)" to draw 1,000 random numbers from a normal distribution with mean zero and standard deviation one. Hit F9 to draw another 1,000 numbers. The summary statistics and histogram (see Figure 9.3.1) show that NORMINV is working as advertised.

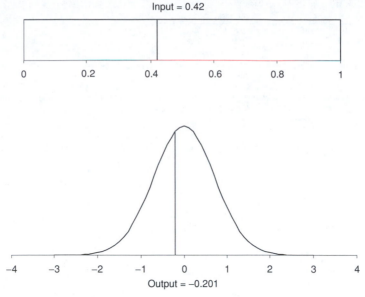

Figure 9.3.2. Converting from uniformly distributed random variables to normally distributed random variables.
Source: [RNGPractice.xls]UniformToNormal.

The *UniformToNormal* sheet explains how the NORMINV function maps numbers that are uniformly distributed into normally distributed numbers. It begins by taking a random number from the Uniform(0,1) distribution – for example, 0.42. Figure 9.3.2 shows that when we graph 0.42 on the Uniform(0,1) distribution, we see that 42 percent of the area under the entire curve lies between 0 and 0.42. We want to translate that number into a normally distributed random number. This is done as follows. Moving down to the Standard Normal curve (with mean 0 and SD 1), we find that value of x such that 42 percent of the area under the standard normal distribution lies between negative infinity and x. This turns out to be −0.201. That is what NORMINV does: given inputs, 0.42 for the area under the curve, 0 for the mean of the normal distribution, and 1 for the SD, NORMINV(0.42,0,1) yields a value of −0.201. Each time you hit F9, the *UniformtoNormal* sheet will draw another uniformly distributed random number and show how that number is converted into a normally distributed random number. The sheet also explains how to obtain numbers that follow a normal distribution other than the Standard Normal distribution.

The *NormalRand* sheet uses the NORMINV and RAND functions to generate normally distributed random variables. Although all seems well, our review of the theory behind random number generation in the previous section explained that RAND is not a great random number generator. In addition, it turns out that NORMINV in versions before Excel 2002 has a rare but serious problem. It can return the nonsensical value of minus 500,000 (or 500,000) whenever the first argument, *y,* is too close to 0 (or 1). NORMINV fails to report the error value #NUM (an indication that the computation is invalid) for values very close to 0 or 1. More modern versions of Excel have partially corrected the badly erroneous results, but testing has shown NORMINV still has problems in Excel 2002 (and XP).[6]

We therefore recommend using the second approach to generating normally distributed random numbers: the NORMALRANDOM function included with this book. The sheet *NormalRandom* shows how to use the formula, "=NORMALRANDOM(mean, SD)" to draw 1,000 numbers quickly and correctly from a normal distribution with given mean and SD.[7]

Although the results of the two sheets are superficially quite similar, remember that RANDOM and NORMALRANDOM are superior to Excel's intrinsic, analogous functions. Of course, you must have these functions properly installed on the computer you are using. Our workbooks come fully prepared with these functions, but you cannot simply type =RANDOM() on a blank spreadsheet because Excel may not have access to the function. You must either open a workbook with the function available or install one of the add-ins packaged with this book (such as the Monte Carlo Simulation add-in described later in this chapter). If =RANDOM() is entered in a cell and Excel displays #NAME?, then the function is not available. Finally, because RAND is a core Excel function, it is somewhat faster than RANDOM and NORMALRANDOM.[8] We believe the trade-off of lower speed for computational superiority is worth it.

You should be aware that if RANDOM or NORMALRANDOM is used on a computer with our software properly installed and you then try to open the workbook from a different computer, an update links notification will be received, as shown in Figure 9.3.3.

If you click the Don't Update button, when the workbook calculates, cells using the RANDOM or NORMALRANDOM functions will display a #NAME? error. If the Update button is clicked, it is possible to change the source to an add-in on the computer you are currently using that has the functions available.

[6] See articles listed in Section 9.8 for more details.
[7] NORMALRANDOM does not make use of the inverse cumulative function. See the Basic Tools/RandomNumber folder for more details on the Box–Muller algorithm used by our function.
[8] Testing has shown that NORMALRANDOM is quite a bit faster than NORMINV(RAND()).

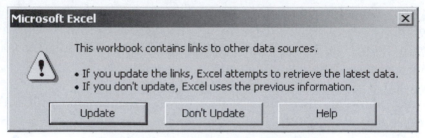

Figure 9.3.3. Update links notification.

We end this section with a brief review of calculation issues in Excel. You may have noticed, as determined by the speed of your computer, that Excel pauses for a few seconds when you hit F9 in the RNGPractice.xls workbook. This is because thousands of cells are being recalculated.

Excel's default calculation setting is to recalculate every cell with a formula in every open workbook automatically whenever any cell is modified. Excel reports its progress in the status bar at the bottom left-hand corner of the screen. Automatic recalculation can be quite cumbersome and tedious when you have a large spreadsheet with many formulas because it is necessary to wait for Excel to finish recalculating after every new entry or change in a cell.

In many of our workbooks, we change the calculation setting to manual by executing Tools: Options and clicking on the Calculation tab (displayed in Figure 9.3.4). Try this now in the RNGPractice.xls workbook. After changing

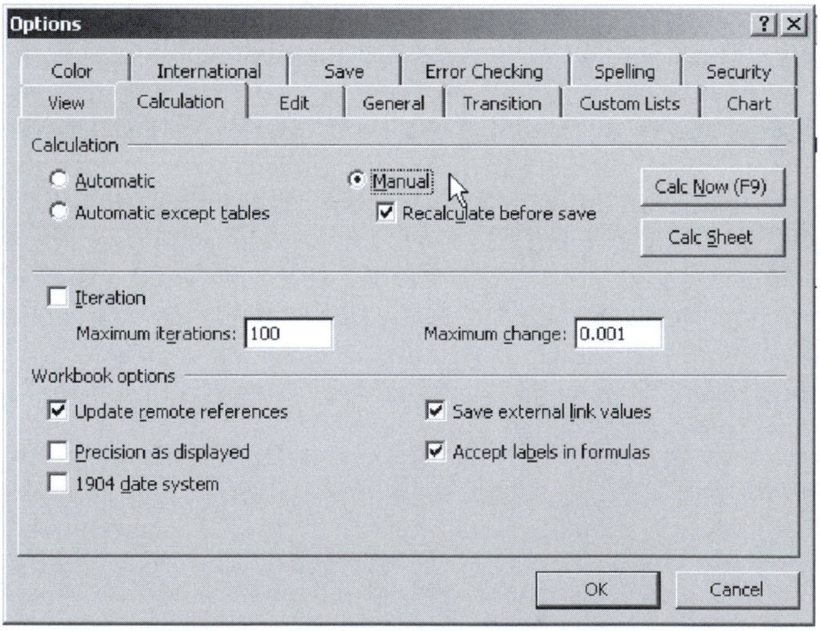

Figure 9.3.4. Controlling calculation.

the calculation setting to manual, enter a number in a blank cell and hit enter. Notice that the sheet does not recalculate and Excel displays the word "Calculate" in the status bar (on the bottom of your screen). This is the signal that the spreadsheet has been altered but the cells have not been recomputed and updated. You can continue to make changes and new entries in cells without pausing for recalculation because Excel is set to manual calculation. You can force calculation when in the manual calculation mode by hitting F9.

Manual calculation is a useful feature with large spreadsheets. Remember that the values displayed in the cells may be wrong, however, when the "Calculation" signal is displayed because the cells have yet to be recalculated.

Summary

This section has shown how to get uniformly and normally distributed random numbers from Excel. The Excel functions RAND and NORMINV can be used for this purpose. This book also provides software with our own functions, RANDOM and NORMALRANDOM, that we recommend and have used under a wide variety of applications.

When a spreadsheet is populated with many thousands of cells with formulas, automatic recalculation can really slow you down. Change the setting to manual calculation and use F9 to recalculate as needed.

Having reviewed the theory of random number generation in the previous section and covered how to generate random numbers within Excel in this section, we now turn to the heart of this chapter: Monte Carlo simulation.

9.4. Monte Carlo Simulation: An Example

Workbook: MonteCarlo.xls

This section presents a concrete example of how Monte Carlo simulation can be used. Suppose we know that Larry Bird, the legendary basketball player, is a 90-percent free-throw shooter. That is, the chance of his making any given free throw is 90 percent regardless of whether he made or missed his previous free throw.[9]

Suppose further that we want to know how well the sample percentage will perform as an estimator of Bird's free-throw accuracy if we have a sample of 100 free throws. Put another way, assume we have Bird, whom we know is truly a 90-percent free-throw shooter, take 100 free-throw attempts. What

---

[9] According to the Web site <www.larrybird.com/stats.html> Bird's lifetime NBA free-throw percentage was 88.6 percent in the regular season (3,960 made out of 4,471 attempts) and 89.0 percent in the playoffs (901 out of 1012).

percentage of the 100 attempts will he be likely to hit? We know that we should see something around 90 percent because that is his true long-run performance. However, because chance plays a role in free-throw shooting, we may well get something different from 90 percent.

Now, the possibilities are anywhere from 0 to 100 percent, but what are the likely or typical results? Is it plausible that we could see him make only 72 out of 100 attempts for a sample percentage of 72 percent? Is making every shot (100 straight free throws), giving him a 100-percent sample percentage, something that we might see every once in a while? Or, are results like 72 and 100 percent so extremely rare as not to be worth worrying about?

In statistics, "rare" and "likely" are important words, whereas "possible" is not too interesting.[10] If results like 72 percent were quite common, we would conclude that a single sample percentage of made shots out of 100 free throws would be a bad way to gauge Bird's true skill. After all, if we did not know his true percentage and had only one sample with which to guess his true, but unknown, shooting percentage, we might get a result like 72 percent and be way off. If, on the other hand, we consistently get a sample percentage within, for instance, 1 percentage point of 90 percent, then it could be argued that the sample percentage of made shots out of 100 free throws is a good gauge of Bird's true skill.

What we are trying to do, of course, is to evaluate the likely size of the spread in the sample percentage of a sample of 100 free throws. Each free throw has some chance built into it, and thus the sample percentage of 100 free throws also has a chance component. We need to figure out how much variation there is in the sample percentage of 100 free throws. In other words, we need to find the SE (standard error) of the sample percentage. A small SE of the sample percentage is good – it means that the observed sample percentages are unlikely to stray far from 90 percent.

There are two routes to figuring out the variation in the sample percentage. The first is statistical theory.[11] The second route is the Monte Carlo approach, which entails producing a simulation of the data generation process, generating a series of replications of that process, and analyzing the results of the experiment. This section shows how to implement this strategy.

The *OneFreeThrow* sheet in the MonteCarlo.xls workbook explains how to use the RANDOM() and IF functions to simulate the result from a single free throw. If the random number drawn is below 0.9, the free throw is made; otherwise, it is missed. Excel registers a "1" for a hit and "0" for a miss.

---

[10] It is "possible" that a 90-percent free-throw shooter would miss 100 in a row. The likelihood of this outcome, 0.1^{100}, is so remote that we ignore it completely. The chances of making every shot are not so great either – $0.9^{100} = 0.00266$ percent.

[11] We review exactly how statistical theory can be used to solve this problem in the next chapter.

To simulate Bird's shooting 100 free throws is simple: just repeat the formula in 100 cells as we show in the sheet called *Sample*. Call the results from 100 "shots" a single *repetition* of the simulation. The key information from a single repetition would be the sample percentage of 1's. You should press F9 per the instructions in the *Sample* sheet to make sure you understand that the sample percentage of 100 attempts varies; press F9 again and again and watch how the sample percentage bounces around. Sometimes Larry does exceptionally well, maybe 94 or 95 percent, but every once in a while he does quite badly – well, never as poorly as Shaq,[12] for instance. Badly for Larry is 85 percent, and below 80 percent is really rare. You might repeatedly press F9 for 20 minutes and not see 79 percent.

Now that you understand how the success or failure of a single free throw is determined via the RANDOM function and IF statement and how we calculate the sample percentage from 100 free throws, we can turn to actually creating and interpreting Monte Carlo simulation results.

To figure out the spread of the sample percentage in the Larry Bird example, we simply conduct many repetitions and examine the resulting empirical histogram of the results. Let us say we perform 1,000 repetitions. Now we have 1,000 sample percentages. We can find the mean of these sample percentages and their SD (standard deviation). You are guaranteed to get an average close to 0.90 (90 percent). The question is, How much spread is there in the 1,000 sample percentages? The SD of the 1,000 sample percentages is a Monte Carlo–generated approximation to the true, exact SE of the sample percentage. Similarly, the empirical histogram of the 1,000 sample percentages approximates the exact probability histogram (or sampling distribution).

Monte Carlo simulation will always be an approximation to the exact truth because the exact truth in a sampling context is based on an infinite number of repetitions. One thousand repetitions will usually generate a fairly good approximation, but 10,000 would be even closer to the truth. No finite number of repetitions, no matter how large, will give the exact answer. Monte Carlo simulation cannot be used to obtain the exact right answer, but it can give an increasingly good approximation as the number of repetitions rises.

We ran a Monte Carlo analysis of the sample percentage of 100 attempts with our simulated Larry Bird shooting free throws. Figure 9.4.1 shows the results.

The bars in the histogram show how many samples of 100 free throws made a particular percentage. Of the 10,000 repetitions of 100 free throws, the lowest sample percentage was 79 percent and the highest was 99 percent. In almost 1,400 samples, the computer simulation of Larry Bird made exactly 90 out of 100 free-throw attempts. The mean of the 10,000 sample percentages

---

[12] Shaquille O'Neal is a tremendously gifted 7-foot-1-inch athlete in the NBA.

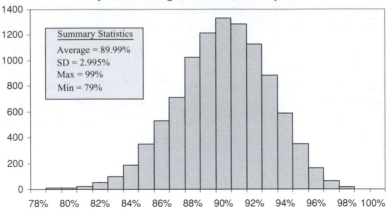

Figure 9.4.1. Monte Carlo simulation of percentage made.
Source: [MonteCarlo.xls]MCSim.

was 89.99 percent with a standard deviation of 2.995 percent. This analysis
says that the likely size of chance error for the sample percentage of 100 free
throws is about 3 percentage points. Thus, we should not be surprised to find
that Larry Bird sinks 87 or 93 percent of his free throws when he makes 100
attempts. It would be very surprising, however, if he hit all 100, or if he hit
only 80 out of 100, because these values are more than 3 standard deviations
away; in most cases that means such outcomes are rare indeed.

Now it is your turn. From the *Samples* sheet, click on the [Run Monte Carlo Simulation] button.
A new sheet appears in the workbook called *MCSim*, and you are looking at
the results of a previous Monte Carlo simulation of the sample percentage
of 100 free throws. There is one extremely important difference between
Figure 9.4.1 and the graph on the *MCSim* sheet, for the former is "dead"
and the latter is "alive." That is, the graph on the Excel sheet will change as
the values in column B change. That means you can run your own Monte
Carlo simulation as many times as you wish. Simply click on the [Run Monte Carlo Simulation]
button.

A dialog box like the one in Figure 9.4.2 will appear. After clicking the OK
button, you will be able to watch the progress of the simulation. So, how did
your simulation turn out? Is your histogram similar to ours?

A more subtle implication of the Monte Carlo analysis just performed is
that the empirical histogram of the Monte Carlo simulation for Larry Bird
appears slightly skewed to the left, which you can see by looking closely at
Figure 9.4.1. This is not an accident of our particular run. Look at your simulation results carefully. Is the left tail a little longer than the right? Is the
histogram symmetrical around the expected value of 90 percent? In other
words, is the fraction of samples with 91 percent made free throws roughly

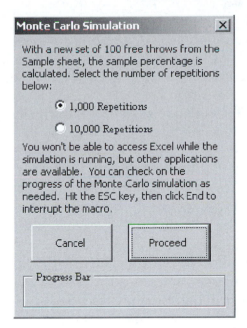

Figure 9.4.2. Running a Monte Carlo simulation.
Source: [MonteCarlo.xls]MCSim.

equal to the fraction of samples with 89 percent? How about the fraction of samples with 88 percent free throws made versus that for 92 percent? Two points can be made here. First, it is not possible to do better than 100 percent, whereas 79 percent and below are possible outcomes. Second, statistical theory tells us that, although the histogram of the sample percentage of 100 free throws ought to follow the normal distribution approximately, it will not be distributed exactly normally. This point is discussed in Chapter 10, in greater depth. For now, we remind you that the central limit theorem tells us that the sampling distribution of the sample percentage comes to resemble the normal distribution more closely as the sample size increases.

Let us summarize the Larry Bird free-throw shooting example. We wanted to know how much spread there was in the sample percentage. Instead of traditional analytical methods based on the theory of probability and statistics, we adopted the Monte Carlo simulation strategy. We resampled repeatedly and thereby obtained an approximation to the SE of the sample percentage of 100 attempts. Our run gave us a value of about 3 percent. What did you get? The formula for the SE of the sample percentage gives us precisely 3 percent.[13] It is, of course, no accident that Monte Carlo experiments yield results close to the standard formulas of statistical theory.

[13] The appropriate formula is

$$\text{SE for sample percentage} = \frac{\sqrt{\text{Probability of 1} \times \text{Probability of 0}}}{\sqrt{\text{Sample size}}}.$$

If Monte Carlo simulation will simply reproduce already known answers, why bother? First, it enables you to see clearly the source of chance error and variation in a problem. Formulas often make it difficult to see what is really going on. Although some people quickly understand and accept the notion of randomness and variation, we believe most people learn much better when they actually see variation. We believe many more people will really understand when they hit F9 to draw another sample and see that sample percentage bouncing around. By hitting F9, you are doing and understanding instead of passively reading or listening.

Second, Monte Carlo simulation focuses your attention on the details of the data generation process. The method requires that you set up and implement a chance process. This requires careful thought about the source of the randomness and how it is to be modeled.

Finally, Monte Carlo techniques drive home the concept of the SE, which is surely one of the most difficult ideas in statistics and econometrics for beginning students. The SE measures the spread of outcomes of chance processes. Visually, it is the spread of the probability histogram of the different outcomes of the chance process. The Monte Carlo method allows us to approximate the probability histogram and therefore the SE just by running numerous repetitions of the same data generation process.

Although our primary purpose in using Monte Carlo is to teach you econometrics, we also would like to point out that there are many random variable problems with no analytical solution. That is, traditional statistical theory cannot solve them. This happens in econometrics often when small sample sizes are under consideration. The advent of extremely fast computers has opened a new avenue for solving these problems. Thus, it is not merely a question of a neat alternative to a tried and true approach – Monte Carlo methods offer approximate solutions to previously impossible problems.

To see another example of the Monte Carlo method, click on the `Streak Finder` button (on the *Sample* sheet near cell D17) a few times. Each time, the longest run of consecutive free throws made in one set of 100 attempts is reported (see Figure 9.4.3).

Streaks in sports are the subject of much debate. Although no one disputes that streaks occur, there is an argument over whether observed streaks are caused by something other than chance.[14] The streaks exhibited by our virtual Larry Bird are due to chance alone because we draw random numbers to determine if a free throw is made.

There is variation in the longest streak of free throws made in each sample of 100 attempts. What is the average longest streak in 100 free throws? What is the spread in the distribution of the maximum streaks? What does the

---

[14] See the Hot Hand in Sports Web page: <www.hs.ttu.edu/hdfs3390/hothand.htm>.

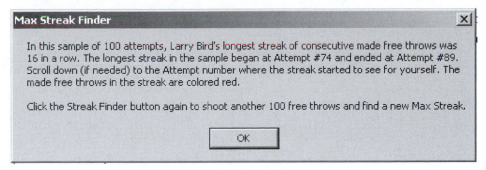

Figure 9.4.3. Maximum streak report.
Source: [MonteCarlo.xls]Sample.

sampling distribution of the maximum streak look like? As before, we forego analytical solutions to these questions in favor of Monte Carlo analysis.[15]

Click on the | Monte Carlo Simulation Max Streak | button (on the *Sample* sheet near cell D22) to see a demonstration of how a Monte Carlo simulation can be used for approximate determination of the average and spread of the Max Streak sampling distribution. As before, a new sheet, this time named *Streak*, appears in the workbook with results from 1,000 repetitions available for your inspection. Notice that Max Streak is not normally distributed – it has a long right-hand tail.

You might want to try your own Monte Carlo analysis by clicking the | Run Monte Carlo Simulation | button. Once again, the dialog box will describe the simulation and the progress bar will keep you updated on where the simulation stands. The progress bar is more useful this time because the simulation takes longer (calculating the longest streak in a stretch of 100 free throws is much harder than calculating the percentage made). You can do other work while the simulation is running, but this may slow down the simulation itself (after all, your computer will be busy doing other tasks instead of grinding out the next repetition). If your screen saver comes on, this will also slow down the simulation. You can interrupt the simulation by pressing the Esc (escape) key on the upper left-hand corner of your keyboard. Excel will prompt you with a dialog box, and you can click the End button to stop the simulation. Of course, if you happen to be running on the latest-generation chip, these suggestions are moot because the simulation will fly through 10,000 repetitions.

Summary

The free-throw shooting example in this section demonstrates how Monte Carlo simulation works. We will use Monte Carlo analysis repeatedly to

---

[15] For an analytical approximation to the exact distribution of the maximum streak problem, see William Feller, *An Introduction to Probability Theory and Its Applications*, Vol. 1, 3rd edition, revised printing, New York: John Wiley and Sons, p.325. Our Monte Carlo results agree with Feller's approximation.

examine the properties of statistical estimators and to explain a variety of ideas and concepts in econometrics.

With the computer generating random numbers, it will be fast and easy to draw many random samples and then examine the resulting distribution. This will provide a visual, concrete demonstration of difficult, abstract ideas. In addition, with Excel, you will be able to run your own simulations and compare your results to ours. If a point is unclear, you can always run the simulation again.

9.5. The Monte Carlo Simulation Add-In

Workbooks: MonteCarlo.xls; MCSim.xla (Excel add-in); MCSimSolver.xla (Excel add-in)

The previous section introduced Monte Carlo simulation using a workbook that was especially designed for that purpose. This section shows how to use an Excel add-in packaged with this book that will enable you to run a Monte Carlo simulation from any Excel workbook. The add-in allows you to easily and quickly run Monte Carlos of your own models and chance processes.

The first step is to install the Monte Carlo simulation add-in. The software is in the Basic Tools/ExcelAddIns/MCSim folder. Open the MCSim.doc file in that folder for instructions on how to install the add-in. Having installed the MCSim.xla file, open the MonteCarlo.xls workbook (from the previous section) to test drive the Monte Carlo Simulation add-in. Go to the *Sample* sheet (because this is where the free-throw shooting chance process is implemented in Excel) and execute Tools: MCSim . . . to get the dialog box shown in Figure 9.5.1.

Enter cell B1 (which is the sample percentage) and click the Proceed button; the MCSim add-in will then go to work. It simply recalculates the sheet for as many repetitions as requested and keeps track of the value of cell B1. When finished, it adds a worksheet to the workbook displaying the first 100 repetitions along with summary statistics and a histogram of the complete results (see Figure 9.5.2).

Comparing the results of the Monte Carlo Simulation add-in to the Monte Carlo built into the workbook shows the same substantive results, but the display in the workbook is more readable. The Monte Carlo Simulation add-in does not recognize that the sample percentage from 100 free-throws is not a continuous number (0.91 and 0.92 are possible, but 0.915 is not) because it is built for any chance process. Thus, in many of our workbooks that feature Monte Carlo simulation, we will include the simulation in the workbook and tailor it to the specific problem at hand.

The Monte Carlo Simulation add-in is ideal, however, for exploring problems in greater detail or running Monte Carlos on your own chance processes.

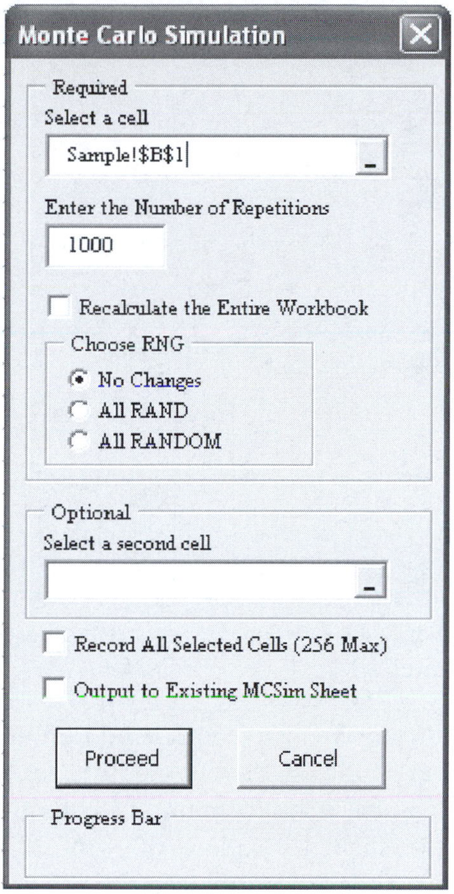

Figure 9.5.1. Preparing to run a Monte Carlo simulation.

For example, in the free-throw shooting model, you might wonder what happens to the spread in the sample percentage as the number of free throws changes. There is no way to explore this question in the MonteCarlo.xls workbook because we did not build in this option. You can easily, however, modify the sheet and use the MCSim add-in to explore this question.

To see how the SE of the sample percentage varies as the sample size changes, create a new cell in the Sample sheet that computes the sample percentage of a different number of free throws. In cell C1 of the *Sample* sheet, we entered the formula, "=AVERAGE(B4:B53)" to obtain the sample percentage of 50 free throws. Now, run the Monte Carlo Simulation add-in using cell C1. You should see that the SD of the 1,000 repetitions (which is our approximation to the true standard error) is larger and the histogram is more spread out and looks even less normally distributed.

You might worry about the bounce in the standard deviation. Remember that a Monte Carlo is never going to give the true, exact answer because that would require an infinite number of repetitions. To obtain a closer approximation to the exact SE of the sample percentage, however, you can increase

Summary Statistics		Notes
Average	0.900	
SD	0.0316	
Max	0.990	
Min	0.790	

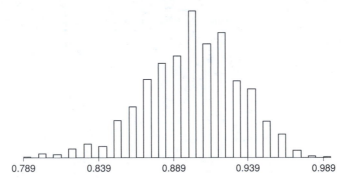

Histogram of Sample!$B$1

Figure 9.5.2. Results from the Monte Carlo Simulation add-in.
Source: [MonteCarlo.xls].

the number of repetitions. We also recommend that you get in the habit of running and rerunning Monte Carlos if you have doubts about the results. After all, you are just a few clicks away and the computer never gets tired.

You can modify the sheet to explore the sample percentage made of 200 free throws. Simply extend the formula in cell B103 (search for "fill down" in Excel's Help if you do not know how to do this) to cell B203; then find the average of the cells from B4 to B203. Run the Monte Carlo Simulation add-in to see the effect on the standard error. Note that you can compare two cells and the results will be displayed on the same histogram. Run a Monte Carlo that compares the sample percentage of 100 free throws to the sample percentage of 50 free throws.

The pattern is clear: As n (the number of free throws) increases, the SE of the sample percentage falls. In other words, the sampling distribution becomes more tightly concentrated around the true shooting percentage. You have demonstrated that the sample percentage is a consistent estimator of Larry Bird's true shooting percentage, which is an important property of the sample percentage in this chance process. (We study consistency in more depth in Chapter 15.)

Summary

Many of our workbooks will have Monte Carlo simulations that are configured especially for the chance process being discussed. By clicking a button, you can display the results. The Monte Carlo Simulation add-in is a more flexible, general tool. It permits resampling from any chance process that has been modeled in an Excel workbook. Use it to explore advanced ideas and to analyze your own problems via the Monte Carlo method.

Once you use Monte Carlo methods on your own models, you may find a second Monte Carlo add-in that is part of this book especially helpful. The Monte Carlo Simulation with Solver add-in uses a special, non-volatile cell formula, RANDOMNV(), to draw random numbers. After loading the MCSimSolver.xla add-in, you can enter RANDOMNV() as part of a cell formula. Use RANDOMNV() instead of RAND() or RANDOM() as you implement the optimization problem on a worksheet.

The volatility of RAND() and RANDOM() works in our favor when doing conventional Monte Carlo simulation (with MCSim.xla) because we can easily recalculate the sheet, then track the results. However, a Monte Carlo based on running Solver each repetition (e.g., to find a nonlinear least squares fit as discussed in Chapter 22) cannot be implemented with volatile random number formulas because each time Solver puts down a trial solution, the sheet recalculates and gets a new random number. For more information on this advanced Monte Carlo simulation tool, please open the MCSimSolver.doc file in the Basic Tools \ ExcelAddIns \ MCSim folder.

9.6. Conclusion

Random number generation is the heart and soul of Monte Carlo simulation. This chapter has briefly reviewed the theory behind the generation of pseudorandom numbers via linear congruential generators and explained how to obtain random numbers on a spreadsheet with either Excel's own RAND function or the RANDOM function packaged with this book.

Once random numbers are generated on a sheet, it is a short jump to a full-fledged Monte Carlo simulation. By repeatedly resampling and keeping track of the results, we create a concrete, visual representation of sample-based statistics. Our workbooks in the book may have built-in Monte Carlos, or we may use the Monte Carlo Simulation add-in that was introduced in the previous section. We hope the latter will stimulate your creativity and encourage you to model chance processes in a wide a variety of applications.

Econometricians have known that Monte Carlo simulation is an effective way to teach sophisticated concepts involving chance, but actually running a resampling procedure requires writing code, including loops, and storing results. We have completely removed this barrier in our materials. This book will use Monte Carlo methods extensively to race estimators and learn sophisticated concepts that once were accessible only through advanced mathematical means.

9.7. Exercises

1. Change the setup in the *Sample* sheet of MonteCarlo.xls to simulate the free-throw shooting behavior of Shaquille O'Neal, who shoots 50 percent from the free-throw line. Run a 1,000-repetition Monte Carlo simulation of 100 free throws by O'Neal. Of course he will make fewer free throws on average than Bird, but what happens to the spread in the number of free throws made per 100 attempts?

2. Change the setup in the *Sample* sheet of MonteCarlo.xls to simulate a more complicated process. On the very first shot that a player takes, he or she has an 80-percent chance of hitting the free throw. On every subsequent shot, the chances of hitting depend on what happened on the previous attempt. In taking a given shot, if the player missed the previous time, his or her chances of hitting are 70 percent; if the player hit, his or her chances are 90 percent. Run a 1,000-repetition Monte Carlo simulation of 100 such free-throw attempts. What are the Monte Carlo estimates of the expected percentage of free throws made and the SE of the percentage of free throws made?

3. Open the EcolCorr.xls workbook used (in Chapter 2) and run a Monte Carlo simulation (from the *Live* sheet) with 10,000 repetitions that tracks both the individual- and group-level correlation coefficients. Take a picture of your results. Copy and paste the picture in your Word document. Comment on your results.

4A. How do the average and SD reported by the Monte Carlo simulation relate to the expected value and SE?

4B. As the number of repetitions increases, what happens to the expected value and SE?

5A. Use the Record All Selected Cells option and run another 10,000-repetition Monte Carlo. In your 10,000 samples, how many times was the group-level r negative? HINT: Use an IF statement like this: =IF(D3 < 0,1,0), then add the entire column. (Do not forget to hit F9 to calculate the sheet if needed.)

    If individual-level $r > 0$ and group-level $r < 0$, then you have an example of the worst form of the ecological fallacy – association reversal.

5B. It is also possible to obtain a negative individual-level r with a positive group-level r. Use your Monte Carlo results to demonstrate this. HINT: Use the IF statement method used in part A.

References

The sources below provide an introduction and serve as an excellent starting point for studying random-number generation. The BasicTools/RandomNumber/ ExcelRNGDocumentation folder contains links to a series of Microsoft Knowledge Base articles available online.

Deng, Lih-Yuan and Dennis K. J. Lin (2000). "Random Number Generation for the New Century," *The American Statistician* **54**(2): 145–150.

L'Ecuyer, Pierre (2001). "Software for Uniform Random Number Generation: Distinguishing the Good from the Bad"; available at <www.iro.umontreal.ca/ ~lecuyer/> and <www.informs-cs.org/wsc01papers/prog01.htm>.

Marsaglia, George, *DIEHARD Battery of Tests*, available online at <stat.fsu. edu/pub/diehard>.

Matsumoto, Makoto and Takuji Nishimura, *Mersenne Twister*, available online at <www.math.sci.hiroshima-u: ac.jp/~m-mat/MT/emt.html> (free Excel implementation available online at <www.numtech.com/NtRand/>).

There is a literature critical of Microsoft Excel's statistical routines. We agree that Excel is not a full-fledged statistical program, but it has served us well in developing examples for teaching econometrics. Different versions of Excel behave differently. To learn more about Excel's statistical performance, we recommend the following:

Knusel, L. (1998). "On the Accuracy of Statistical Distributions in Microsoft Excel 97," *Computational Statistics and Data Analysis* **26**: 375–377 and available online at <www.stat.uni-muenchen.de/~knuesel/elv/excelacc.pdf>.

Knusel, L. "On the Reliability of Microsoft Excel XP for Statistical Purposes," n.d., available online at <www.stat.uni-muenchen.de/~knuesel/elv/excelxp.pdf>.

Knusel, L. (2004). "On the Accuracy of Statistical Distributions in Microsoft Excel 2003." *Computational Statistics & Data Analysis* **48**(3): 445–449.

McCullough, B. D. and Berry Wilson (1999). "On the Accuracy of Statistical Procedures in Microsoft Excel 97." *Computational Statistics & Data Analysis* **31**(1): 27–37.

McCullough, B. D. and Berry Wilson (2002). "On the Accuracy of Statistical Procedures in Microsoft Excel 2000 and Excel XP." *Computational Statistics & Data Analysis* **40**: 713–721.

McCullough, B. D. and Berry Wilson (2005). On the Accuracy of Statistical Procedures in Microsoft Excel 2003." *Computational Statistics & Data Analysis* **49**(4): 1244–1252.

Streaks in sports make for fun examples and can arouse intense debate. In addition to Alan Reifman's Web site on the hot hand in sports (<www.hs.ttu.edu/hdfs3390/hothand.htm>), we suggest the following journal articles:

Albright, S. C. (1993). "A Statistical Analysis of Hitting Streaks in Baseball," *Journal of the American Statistical Association* **88**(424): 1175–1183.

Gilovich, T., R. Vallone and A. Tversky (1985). "The Hot Hand in Basketball: On the Misperception of Random Sequences," *Cognitive Psychology* **17**(3): 295–314.

Additional sources for this chapter include the following:

Drakos, Nikos (1995). Computer Based Learning Unit, University of Leeds. *Introduction to Monte Carlo Methods*, <csep1.phy.ornl.gov/mc/node1.html>.

Ulam, Stanislaw (1991). *Adventures of a Mathematician*, originally published in 1976, University of California Press; p. 199.

von Neumann, John (1951). "Various Techniques Used in Connection with Random Digits," in U.S. Department of Commerce, National Bureau of Standards, *Applied Mathematics Series 12, Monte Carlo Method*. A 42-page booklet on number-generation methods and applications of the Monte Carlo method.

10

Review of Statistical Inference

One famous difficulty in teaching elementary statistics is getting across the idea that the sample average is a random variable. Randomness, after all, is quite a complicated idea. It is easily overwhelmed, either by the definiteness of the data, or by the arithmetic needed to calculate the average.

David Freedman, Robert Pisani, and Roger Purves[1]

10.1. Introduction

The goal of statistical inference is to use sample data to estimate a *parameter* (a statistic about the population) or determine whether to believe a claim that has been made about the population. We never actually observe the parameter we are interested in; instead we use an estimate of the parameter based on data from a sample. The sample estimate is almost always different from the claimed value of the parameter. There are then two possibilities: the difference (between the estimate and the claim) may be real or it may be due to chance. Thus, the fundamental question of statistical inference becomes, Is the difference real or due to chance?

To answer the fundamental question, we require a model for the *data generation process*, or DGP. The DGP describes how each observation in the data set was produced. It usually contains a description of the chance process at work. Given a DGP and certain parameter values, we can calculate the probability of observing particular ranges of outcomes.

In this chapter, we try to clarify these complicated issues by reviewing basic concepts of inference from introductory statistics. Our approach is somewhat unusual in that we downplay the mathematical formalism and instead emphasize the logic of statistical inference. We borrow the extremely useful metaphor of a box model from Freedman, Pisani, and Purves (1998). The

---

[1] Freedman et al. (1998b, p. 20).

10.3. The Coin-Flip Box Model

Workbook: BoxModel.xls

This section applies the box model metaphor to a basic chance process we call the coin-flip box model. After making the box model, we will implement it in Excel and use Monte Carlo simulation to examine the properties of the data generation process. We proceed by example.

Making a Coin-Flip Box Model

A coin is flipped 100 times. How many heads can we expect to get? How much spread will there be in the outcomes?
The box model recipe can easily be applied to this problem.

- What numbers are on the tickets in the box?
  We use "1" for heads and "0" for tails. Rather than "H" and "T" because letters cannot be added. Heads is 1 (instead of tails) because the question asks about the number of heads we expect to get in 100 flips.
- How many tickets of each kind?
  One of each. There is a 50-percent chance of getting heads.
- How many draws from the box?
  One hundred. One hundred flips of the coin is like 100 draws from the box.
- Are the draws with or without replacement?
  Because the chances of obtaining heads or tails stay constant, the contents of the box stay constant after each draw; hence, the draws are with replacement.
- What is done to the tickets after they are drawn from the box?
  We add up the numbers on the tickets to obtain the number of heads.

The box model for the data generation process of the number of heads in 100 flips of a coin looks like Figure 10.3.1. The box model says that the 100 coin flips can be interpreted as if they were 100 draws with replacement from a box with 2 tickets in it. One ticket is a 0, the other a 1. Because the draws are made with replacement, the contents of the box are the same every time a ticket is removed from the box. After the 100 draws, we add up the numbers on the tickets. The coin is never anywhere near a box and there are no tickets, but that does not matter. The data generation process at work can be

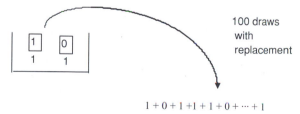

$$1 + 0 + 1 + 1 + 1 + 0 + \cdots + 1$$

Figure 10.3.1. Box model for sum of 100 coin flips.

box model is a way of concretely representing a random variable. In this chapter, we will distinguish between two basic types of box models – we call them coin-flip and polling box models. Though these models differ in important respects, it turns out that we can answer the fundamental question of inference in the same way with both models.

In subsequent chapters, we will develop additional box models that are designed to handle the more complicated situations arising when one examines data from observational studies. We will, however, be able to use the basic strategy outlined in this chapter to answer the question of whether the difference is real or due to chance.

The next section introduces the box model as a metaphor for handling chance processes. Sections 10.3 and 10.4 introduce the two fundamental box models and demonstrate how they work. We then present a review of hypothesis testing and follow up with the concept of a consistent estimator. Finally, we explain the algebra of expectations – a set of rules that are useful for computing the expected value and standard deviation of random variables.

We will call on the box model metaphor over and over again throughout the rest of this book. We will almost always employ Monte Carlo analysis to demonstrate properties of the various box models. On occasion, we will make use of results from the algebra of expectations to provide an alternative, more rigorous derivation of these properties.

Although the experienced statistics student may wish to skip this review chapter, we recommend a quick perusal of the material if only to ensure that the box model metaphor makes sense. Of course, every student can benefit from a detailed review to sharpen the crucial skills and concepts learned in an introductory statistics course.

10.2. Introducing Box Models for Chance Processes

A powerful way of explaining the elements of a process that contains chance as a driving force is a *box model*, which is nothing more than a visual description of the data generation process at work. Figure 10.2.1 shows a box model for the sum of 10 rolls from a single die. After each roll of the die, the number of spots on the side of the die facing up are counted.

As you can see, the actual act of tossing a die 10 times and recording the results of each roll is represented by drawing at random from a box with tickets representive the outcomes of the 6 different possible rolls. There is 1 ticket for each outcome because they are equally likely. The arrow symbolizes a toss of the die. We always include the number of draws from the box, whether it is with or without replacement, and a description of what is done with results of the sample. "With replacement" means that after a ticket is drawn from

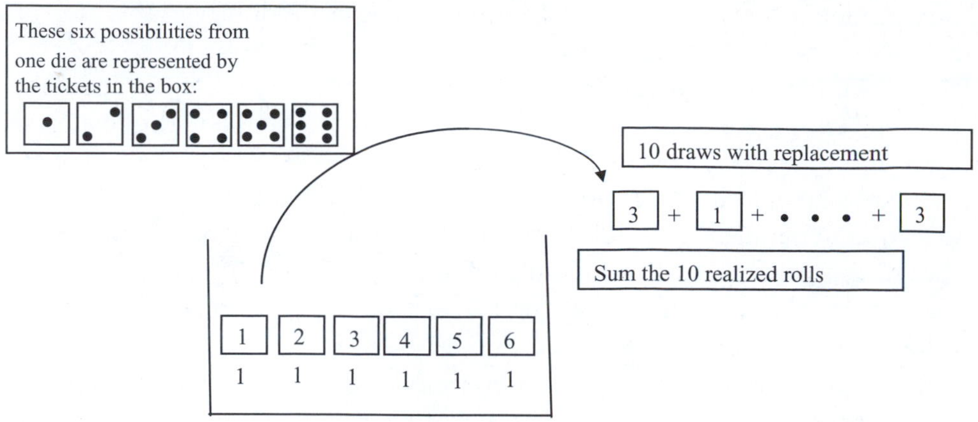

Figure 10.2.1. Box model for the sum of 10 rolls of a die.

the box, it is returned. Thus, the contents of the box are the same for every draw.

Given this simple data generation process, there are obvious conclusions you can immediately see. For example, the lowest possible sum is 10 and the highest is 60. It can also be easily imagined that there will be variation in the outcome. Repeat the experiment – that is, roll the die 10 times and sum the results; you might get 40 one time and 36 the next time. Statistical theory provides formulas for describing the distribution of the outcomes. The next section explains this in more detail.

The box model has several outstanding benefits:

- It forces an explicit model of the data generation process.
- It makes the underlying similarities between seemingly different phenomena clear.
- It facilitates understanding of sophisticated statistical concepts without quantitative jargon or symbols.

In short, the box model is a great way to learn about probability. We owe the box model metaphor to Freedman, Pisani, and Purves (1998). We will use it extensively throughout the rest of this book.

To build a box model, we follow a simple recipe composed of five questions. We used this recipe to construct the box model in Figure 10.2.1. Below each question, we report the answer as it applies to the example of the sum of 10 rolls of a single die.

- *What numbers go into the box?*

The numbers one through six because these are the six different possible results.

- *How many of each kind?*

One of each kind because each result is equally likely.

- *How many draws?*

Ten draws because that is how many times you roll the die.

- *Are they drawn with or without replacement?*

With replacement because, when you pick up the die to roll it, all six possibilities are always available.

- *What is done with the tickets after they are drawn from the box?*

We sum them because that was the original description of the chance process.

Here are general principles that go into constructing the box:

- The different types of tickets in the box correspond to the different possible outcomes in an individual realization of the data generation process.
- The chance of drawing any particular type of ticket from the box must equal the chance of obtaining the corresponding outcome in an individual realization of the data generation process.
- The number of draws from the box equals the number of realizations in the data generation process under consideration.

There are two ways of determining the properties of a data generation process. The first relies on statistical theory and uses formulas and formal mathematics. We offer a taste of this approach at the end of this chapter. The second approach, Monte Carlo simulation, was explained in the previous chapter. It relies on an artificial recreation of the DGP and then uses computers for resampling. This is our main tool in exploring the properties of a DGP.

Summary

A data generation process can be described by an appropriately configured box model. Put another way, a sample is like the draws from an appropriately configured box. Although not all chance processes can be represented with a box model, many important chance processes can be so represented. As determined by the chance process, creating the box model by answering the five questions in the box model recipe may or may not be easy. Box models can become rather sophisticated.

In the next two sections, we review two generic types of box models commonly discussed in introductory statistics courses. In the next few chapters of this book, we introduce additional box models.

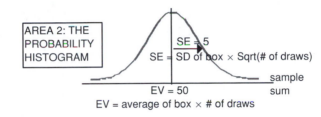

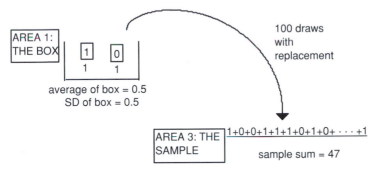

Figure 10.3.2. Three conceptual areas for the box model.

modeled as Figure 10.3.1 describes it, and the outcome can be interpreted as the sum of 100 draws from the box.

We can analyze this chance process by recognizing that there are three separate conceptual areas associated with the box model:

- Area 1. The box itself. Sometimes, this is also called the *population*.
- Area 2. The *probability histogram* of the sample statistic. This is also called the *sampling distribution*. Unlike a regular (or empirical) histogram that describes data, the probability histogram represents chance.
- Area 3. A single set of outcomes of the data generation process. This is called the *sample*. In the 100 coin-flip data generation process, with our sample of 100 individual outcomes, perhaps we got a total of 47 (or maybe 52). This sample sum is an example of a sample statistic.

It is obvious that we will usually get around 50 heads when we set the data generation process running. That is, 50 is the *expected value* of the sum of the draws for this chance process. Much less obvious is that the spread of the sample sums around the expected value, called the *standard error* (or *SE*), is five heads.

These two statements, about the expected value and SE, are statements about the probability histogram for the infinite number of outcomes that would be generated if the data generation process were repeated forever (i.e., if we took an infinite number of repetitions). The center and spread of this special long-run histogram are found by applying probability theory to the random process. A more elaborate picture of what is going on looks like Figure 10.3.2.

Many fundamental ideas in statistical inference are captured in Figure 10.3.2. In addition to the box itself and the sample, we have added another area: the probability histogram. It represents the distribution of the sample sum.

An extremely important concept is that the sample sum is, in fact, a random variable. If repeated, the data generation process will produce a new (and probably different) sample sum because a whole new set of individual outcomes will be generated. Thus, even though a particular sample sum (for instance, 47) may be realized, we understand that there is variability in the sample sum.

The center of the sample sum's distribution is called the expected value (or EV) of the sample sum. It can be calculated by taking the average of the box multiplied by the number of draws. In our coin-flipping example, we have $0.5 \times 100 = 50$ heads. The spread of the distribution of the sample sum is captured by its SD. Because we are dealing with a sampling distribution (a probability histogram for a sample statistic), it is given the special name SE. Basic statistical theory tells us that the SE of the sample sum of 100 draws can be found by multiplying the SD of the box times the square root of the number of draws (or $0.5 \cdot \sqrt{100} = 5$ in our example).[2]

Every statistics student struggles mightily with the SD versus the SE. The SD is used to describe the spread of a list of numbers (whether that list consists of tickets in the box or observations in the sample). The SE, on the other hand, is only about the spread of the sampling distribution. The SE is a type of SD, but it is the SD of a very special list – the list of the possible outcomes of the chance process, a list depicted as the sampling distribution.

Monte Carlo Simulation of the Coin-Flip Box Model

Open the BoxModel.xls workbook to see how the coin-flip box model can be implemented in Excel. Click on the [Make a Box Model] button to display the Ticket Creator form (as shown in Figure 10.3.3). The number of tickets is already set to 2, as desired, and we want to draw tickets with replacement, which is already specified. For the number of tickets, you can type in any integer between 2 and 10, inclusive. A box with only one type of ticket is trivial (you will always obtain whatever is on that ticket), whereas we set 10 as an upper limit owing to space limitations.

Next click the OK button. A second tab, Types of Tickets, appears in the form. It allows you to indicate what number should be on each type of ticket and how many there should be of each type. Fill in a "1" and a "0" for the

---

[2] The SD of the box is computed by taking the root-mean-square deviation of the value of each ticket from the average of the box. In the next subsection we will show how the computation is made.

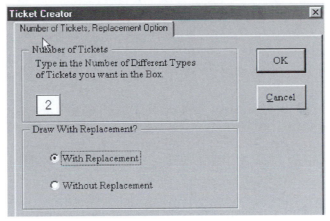

Figure 10.3.3. Ticket creator form.
Source: [BoxModel.xls]Setup

numbers on the tickets. (The program will only accept integer values for the numbers on the tickets; if you had typed in 1.1 and 0.234, you would still get tickets with values 1 and 0 on them.) Next, specify that there is one of each type of ticket. Figure 10.3.4 shows what the screen should look like.

Click the OK button; a new screen will pop up asking you to indicate the quantity of draws from the box and whether you are summing or averaging the results. Enter "100" for the number of draws and leave the option button for Sum selected. The screen should look like Figure 10.3.5.

Click OK and observe in Figure 10.3.6 that two areas of the original Setup worksheet now describe the box model. Cells shaded in yellow describe the

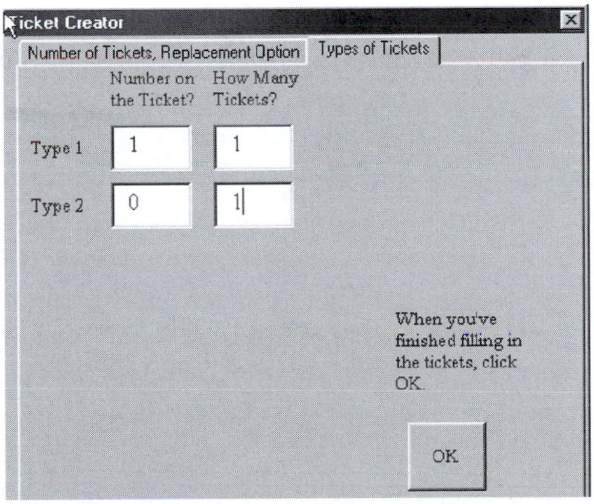

Figure 10.3.4. Ticket creator with types of tickets for coin-flip box model.
Source: [BoxModel.xls]Setup.

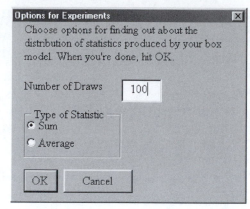

Figure 10.3.5. The number of draws and type of statistic choices.
Source: [BoxModel.xls]Setup.

contents of the box. Several rows below, summary statistics describe the contents of the box: In this case, the average and the standard deviation of the box are both 0.5.

The cell range I1 through M15 in BoxModel.xls contains the computation of the SD of the box. Note that the SD of the box is based on a weighted sum of the squared deviations of each ticket from the average of the box. The weights are the probabilities of obtaining each type of ticket, i.e. the number of tickets of that type divided by the total number of tickets in the box.

The space between the two displays allows room for up to 10 different types of tickets. Green-shaded cells show what is done with the tickets in the box. We are going to take 100 draws with replacement and sum them. We have answered all five questions in the box model recipe and are ready to explore the properties of the coin-flip box model.

The Draw a Sample from the Box button does exactly that: Click it to see that it takes you to the *Sample* worksheet and displays the outcome a single sample. Figure 10.3.7 is one potential sample. Yours is probably different.

The Contents of the Box	
Number of Types	2
Number on Ticket How Many Tickets	
0	1
1	1
Average	0.500
SD	0.500

Draws from the Box	
Number of Draws	100
Statistic	Sum
Draws	With Replacement

Figure 10.3.6. The coin-flip box model implemented.
Source: [BoxModel.xls]Setup.

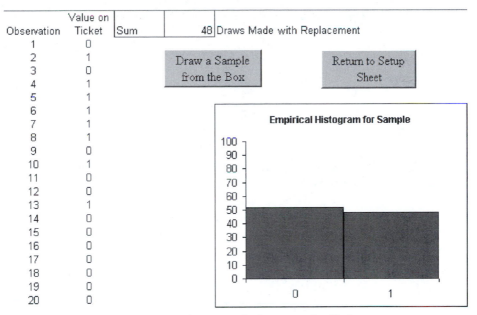

Observation	Value on Ticket	Sum	48	Draws Made with Replacement
1	0			
2	1			
3	0			
4	1			
5	1			
6	1			
7	1			
8	1			
9	0			
10	1			
11	0			
12	0			
13	1			
14	0			
15	0			
16	0			
17	0			
18	0			
19	0			
20	0			

Figure 10.3.7. One sample from a coin-flip box.
Source: [BoxModel.xls]Sample.

The empirical histogram displayed shows that, in the sample drawn in Figure 10.3.7, the number of 0's drawn slightly excceded the number of 1's. In fact, the sample sum displayed in the top center is 48. You can draw repeated samples by clicking the Draw a Sample from the Box button (in the *Sample* sheet) again and again. The sample sum will bounce around, usually falling in the 45 to 55 range. To get a better idea of the chances of obtaining particular outcomes, click the Return to Setup Sheet button.

The probability histogram tells you the exact, long-run probability of obtaining a particular outcome to a chance process. Suppose we want to know the chances of obtaining exactly the expected value – a sample sum of 50. On the *Setup* sheet, hit the Draw Probability Histogram button. You will get a chart that looks like Figure 10.3.8. Notice that the probability histogram strongly resembles the normal curve. This diagram shows that 50 outcomes is the most likely outcome. To see the exact probability of this outcome, click the Show ProbHist Sheet button, which takes you to a new sheet called *ProbHist*.

If you scroll down to cells A48:B54, you will see that the probability of obtaining a sum of exactly 50 is 7.96 percent. This is an exact result to two decimal places. If we took an infinite number of sets of 100 draws, we would find that 7.96 percent of the sets summed exactly to 50.

In addition to the exact probability histogram, the BoxModel.xls workbook allows you to run Monte Carlo simulations. Let us draw 10,000 samples from this box and look at the results. To do so, return to the *Setup* sheet and click

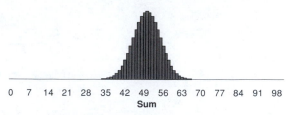

**Probability Histogram for Sum of 100 Draws from Box
Containing 2 Tickets**

0   7   14   21   28   35   42   49   56   63   70   77   84   91   98
Sum

Figure 10.3.8. Probability histogram for the coin-flip box model.
Source: [BoxModel.xls]Setup.

on the ⌗Run Monte Carlo Experiment⌗ button. An hourglass appears, and a short time later (how short depends on your computer), you are taken to the *MonteCarloResults* worksheet. There is much information on this sheet. Begin with the upper-left-hand corner shown in Figure 10.3.9.

The yellow (bottom) section of Figure 10.3.9 shows the contents of the box, and the green (middle) section tells what is done with the draws from the box. The blue (top) section summarizes the Monte Carlo results. In this case, we ran 10,000 repetitions of the chance process. The average of the 10,000 sample sums was 50.002, whereas the spread (SD) of the sample sums was about 4.964. You will obtain different results, but they should be pretty similar. Finally, the sample sums from the first 100 repetitions are displayed in the lower left beneath the yellow box with the contents of the box (you will need to scroll down to see all of them).

More information on the outcome of the Monte Carlo experiment is contained in the middle of the worksheet. The histogram on top shows the distribution of the 10,000 sample sums. The table below the histogram gives the exact number of repetitions that produced each of the possible sample sums.

Monte Carlo Experiment Results	
Number of Repetitions =10,000	
Average of the Sample Sums = 50.002	
SD of the Sample Sums = 4.964	
Draws from the Box	
Number of Draws = 100	
Statistic = Sum	
Draws Are with Replacement	
The Contents of the Box	
Number of Types	2
Number on Ticket	How Many Tickets
0	1
1	1

Figure 10.3.9. Monte Carlo results for coin-flip box model.
Source: [BoxModel.xls]MonteCarloResults.

The probability histogram gives the long-run chances of obtaining given outcomes of the chance process. The Monte Carlo experiment approximates the long-run probability distribution. How well does the Monte Carlo experiment conform to the probability histogram? To find out, click on the Show Data from Probability Histogram button. With 10,000 repetitions, the Monte Carlo does pretty well.

The probability histogram shows the exact long-run probability of obtaining a given result from the chance process. As the number of repetitions in the Monte Carlo experiment is increased, the empirical histogram showing the results of the experiment comes to resemble the probability histogram more and more closely. To put it loosely, the more repetitions, the closer we are to the long run.

There are two more important points to make about this example before we move on to the next box model. First, the spread of the Monte Carlo sample sums is measured by the empirical SD. The SE is the standard deviation of the probability histogram and is approximated by the empirical SD; the approximation improves as the number of repetitions in the Monte Carlo simulation increases.

The second point relates to the shape of the probability histogram. Using BoxModel.xls, you can demonstrate to yourself that, as the number of draws increases, the probability histogram converges toward a normal curve (as shown on the right). To see this in the context of our example, go back to the *Setup* sheet and take a shortcut to setting up a new DGP. Change cell D2, which currently lists the number of draws as 100 to 4 and then click on the Draw Probability Histogram button. Repeat this process, changing the number of draws to 10 and then 100. The resulting probability histograms are shown in Figure 10.3.10. It is easy to see that the probability histogram is converging toward a normal curve as the number of draws from the box increases. Notice that the expected value of the data generation process rises from 2 to 5 to 50 as we increase the number of draws from 4 to 10 to 100. This is a reminder that the probability histogram is a function of the number of draws.

Summary

This section introduced the coin flip model, which can be adapted to a variety of situations that may initially seem quite far-removed from a coin flip. By exploring how the coin flip model works, we gain general insight because all box models, no matter how complicated the data generation process, are organized similarly. There are three conceptual areas: the box itself (sometimes called the population), the sample of draws from the box, and the probability histogram or sampling distribution for sample statistics created from the sample draws. The center of the probability histogram is the expected value;

Probability Histogram for Sum of 4 Draws from Box Containing 2 Tickets

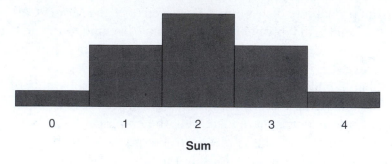

Probability Histogram for Sum of 10 Draws from Box Containing 2 Tickets

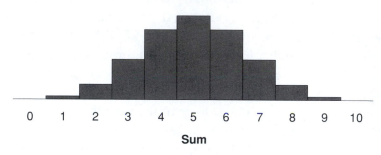

Probability Histogram for Sum of 100 Draws from Box Containing 2 Tickets

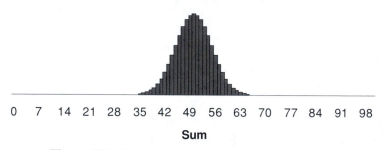

Figure 10.3.10. Convergence to the normal curve.

its spread is called the SE of the sample statistic. This section also showed that Monte Carlo simulation can be used to approximate the probability histogram.

In the specific case of recipes based on summing the draws (as in the coin flip model), we demonstrated the convergence of the probability histogram toward the normal curve as the number of draws increases. This is an important result.

The next section covers a different type of box model, one with an actual, finite population. Fortunately, much of the work in this section carries over to this new box model.

10.4. The Polling Box Model

Workbook: PresidentialHeights.xls

Unlike the coin-flip box model, in the polling box model the contents of the box represent an actual population. In a poll, the box represents potential voters with the tickets registering who they would vote for. The polling box model is useful in social science applications in which researchers wish to know about the characteristics of a population. We will begin with an artificial example in which the characteristics of the population are actually known.

Suppose we were interested in the trivial question of the average height of U.S. presidents through the year 2005 and we are about to obtain a random sample of 10 presidents' heights. What can we say about the types of samples we could get? What are the expected value and the SE? To answer these questions, we model the data generation process.

Open the PresidentialHeights.xls workbook and proceed to the *Setup* sheet. Column B contains the heights of the 43 presidents of the United States in inches (to the nearest half inch). These 43 values will serve as our population. We are interested in the sampling distribution of the sample average under a variety of sampling schemes including the following: if we sample with or without replacement, the number of draws (or size of the sample), and if we decide to take a shortcut and use consecutive presidential heights to construct the sample.

When sampling without replacement, the box model looks like Figure 10.4.1. The box contains 43 tickets, but the summary of the population in the *Setup* sheet makes clear that there are only 17 unique values. For example, 8 Presidents were 73 inches tall. Each ticket is stamped with the president's height. We will draw out 10 tickets, without replacement, and average the 10 observations. This completes our description of the box model.

Figure 10.4.1 adds population statistics and shows a single sample outcome. It also includes the probability histogram of the sample average. Each time we sample, we will get a different sample average. The probability histogram tells us the chances of getting a particular result. For example, we might want to know the chances of getting a sample average that is 72 inches or higher.

Make sure the controls in the *Setup* sheet are set to take 10 draws without replacement and click the `Draw Sample` button. You will be taken to a new sheet called *Sample*, where your sample will be displayed. In the *Sample* sheet, click the `Draw Sample` button a few times to see that the sample average bounces around, because a new set of presidents is being included in each new sample.

We are interested in the expected value and SE of the sample average. Although, in principle, we could find the exact probability histogram using analytical methods, we will proceed with the Monte Carlo approach. We

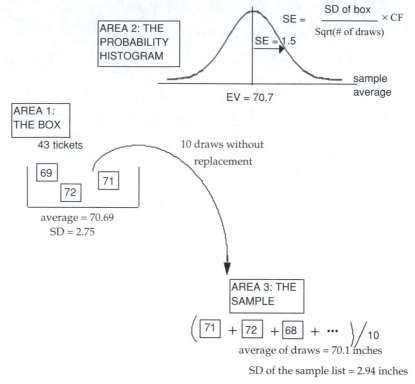

Figure 10.4.1. Box model for presidential heights.

could write down the sample average every time we click the button, but why not let the computer keep track of this for us?

Verify that the *Setup* sheet options are "without replacement" and "10 draws," then go to the *MonteCarloResults* sheet. We ran a 10,000 repetition Monte Carlo by clicking the Run Monte Carlo Simulation button and got the results shown in Figure 10.4.2.

Monte Carlo Experiment Results	
Number of Repetitions =10,000	
Average of the Sample Averages = 70.68	
SD of the Sample Averages = 0.770	
Draws from the Box	
Number of Draws = 10	
Statistic = Average	
Draws Are without Replacement	
The Contents of the Box	
Average	70.67
SD	2.72
No. Tickets	43

Figure 10.4.2. Monte Carlo results.
Source: [PresidentialHeights.xls] MontecarloResults.

Your results should be similar. Notice that the average of the 10,000 repetitions is close to the expected value (the average of the 43 presidential heights) and the SD of 0.77 approximates the exact SE of the sample average (computed in cell H28).

An alternative approach would have been to use the standard formula for the SE of the sample average, derived from statistical theory. Knowing the SD of the box, one could compute the SE of the sample average as

$$\frac{SD(\text{Box})}{\sqrt{n}} = \frac{2.72}{\sqrt{10}} = 0.86.^3$$

This is quite different from the Monte Carlo result. Something is wrong. In fact, it is our analytical work. The formula is good only for sampling with replacement or when the sample is very small compared with the size of the population. Neither of those conditions is met here. We need to use the correction factor (CF in Figure 10.4.1) to compute the SE correctly. The CF is based on the fraction of tickets taken out of the box:

$$CF = \sqrt{\frac{PopulationSize - SampleSize}{PopulationSize}}.$$

Once we multiply the SE with replacement by the CF (as shown in cells H25:I28 of the *MonteCarloResults* sheet), we obtain 0.75, which agrees much better with our Monte Carlo approach.

With the Monte Carlo results, we can directly answer the question regarding the chances of obtaining a sample average that is 72 inches or greater. The documentation at the top of the frequency table says that the right endpoint is not included; thus, simply scroll down column E until you find the cell that says 72.0 to 72.1. Add up all of the repetitions for which the sample average is 72.0 or greater. In our Monte Carlo simulation, there are 464 out of 10,000 repetitions with an average of 72.0 or greater, and so we would approximate the chances of this happening as about 4.6 percent.

The conventional statistical approach would be to use the normal approximation to compute the relevant area. See the appendix to this chapter for a refresher lesson on the mechanics of the normal curve. We would find that 72 inches is $(72 - 70.67)/0.273 = 1.76$ standard units. The area under the normal curve from 1.76 standard units to positive infinity is about 3.9 percent.

Note that neither the Monte Carlo approximation nor the calculation using the normal curve is exactly right. The former suffers from the fact that we did not run an infinite number of repetitions, whereas the latter is using the

---

[3] We do not use $n-1$ because we know the SD of the box. If we estimated the population SD with the sample SD, then we would use $n-1$.

normal curve as a rough stand-in for the true probability histogram (that is not exactly normally distributed).

Finally, return to the *Sample* sheet and click the [Draw Several At Once] button. Enter 5 (the default) when prompted. This sampling scheme is a little more complicated than taking 10 individual tickets from the box. It takes a random number from 1 to 43 but then includes in the sample the next 4 presidential heights (in the chronological order in which they served). To see what is going on, compare the presidents in your sample with the list in the *Setup* sheet. If the first President is near the end (for instance Clinton, #42), then the list wraps around, taking George W. Bush (#43), George Washington (#1), John Adams (#2), and Thomas Jefferson (#3). Note that this is sampling with replacement because you can get multiple observations of the same president. For example, if the next draw was Washington, we would repeat Washington, Adams, and Jefferson. Two batches of five in a row will give us a total of 10 draws.

What effect does this sampling scheme have on the sampling distribution of the sample average? We will use the Monte Carlo technique to answer this formidable question. Before running a Monte Carlo, however, click the [Take a Picture of the Results] button to compare the consecutive draws scheme to the simpler 10 draws without replacement scheme. Click the [Run Monte Carlo Simulation Consecutive Draws] button and run a Monte Carlo with the same number of repetitions as before. What do you get?

Our results show that this sampling scheme is apparently unbiased (because the average of the sample averages is very close to the population average), but the SE, 0.87, is higher than the "without replacement scheme." The SE is quite close, however, to the simple random sample with replacement SE. What happens when we take longer sets of consecutive draws? This is left to the reader as an exercise in the *Q&A* sheet.

Why would we explore the properties of such a crazy sampling scheme? Well, consider the Current Population Survey (CPS) – a household is chosen at random, but the individuals in the household are all surveyed. This is called *cluster sampling*. If we are interested in, for example, educational attainment, it matters that the husbands and wives in a given household are included together in the sample. The SE from this type of sampling is different than a sample where individuals are drawn.

The presidential heights example is unrealistic in that we know the population average and SD. Let us explore a second example of the polling box model that will demonstrate the typical situation encountered by the social scientist.

Suppose we were interested in knowing the average weight of adults (those people 18 years of age and older) in the United States. We do not have the weight of every single adult in the United States, but suppose we did have a simple random sample of the weight of 400 adults.

We are now firmly in the land of inference. We cannot compute the sum of the weights divided by the number of people because we do not have that information. Instead, we have limited information about a sample of people from which we will *infer* a corresponding value for the population.

This example seems far removed from flipping coins or rolling a die, but it is not. This problem shares a crucial similarity with flipping coins and rolling dice – *chance is present in the observed outcome*. In this case, chance is working at the level of the particular 400 individuals who were randomly chosen to be in the sample.

The word "simple" in the phrase "simple random sample" does not mean "easy." In fact, simple random samples are extremely difficult to come by. For example, it is almost impossible to obtain a simple random sample of 400 adults from the U.S. population. The word "simple" means that each individual had an exactly equal chance of being chosen. If we assigned a number to every single adult and then drew 400 numbers out of the 190 million or so numbers in that list in such a way that each number had an equal chance of being selected, then we would have a simple random sample. No such numbering system exists – even Social Security numbers would not work because not every adult in the United States has a Social Security number!

But if we had such a precious sample, we would be in position to answer the question about the average weight in the United States. We would calculate the sample average and use it as our estimate of the population average. We would next immediately embark on a procedure to determine the SE of the sample average. Although the sample average seems to be a fixed number, we would interpret it as a random variable. It is simply one realization of the chance process. If we drew another sample of 400, we would almost surely get a different group of 400 people and, thus, a different sample average. How much spread is there likely to be in the sample average? That is exactly what the SE would tell us.

The box model for this example looks like Figure 10.4.3.

The box model in the figure is a pictorial representation of the problem faced by the investigator trying to *infer* the average weight of the 190 million adults in the United States from a simple random sample of 400 adults.

If we had the list of 190 million weights, we would have the population and there would be no need to do any estimating. But if we only have a simple random sample of 400 weights (that is Area 3: The Sample), we are forced to guess the population parameter. We use the sample average as our best estimate of the population average.

We know the sample average has a probability histogram (or sampling distribution) and we would like to include a measure of the variability by calculating the SE of the sample average. Unfortunately, we cannot reconstruct the true probability histogram for two reasons. First, and more important, we

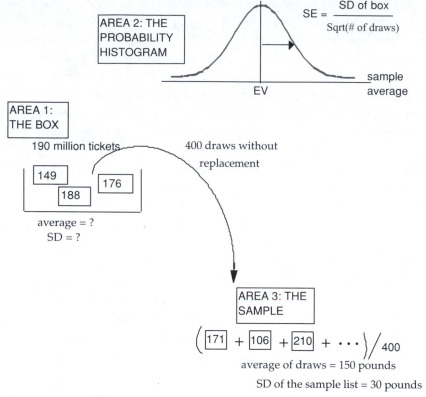

Figure 10.4.3. Polling box model for average weight of adult Americans.

do not know the true expected value (i.e., the population average). Thus, we do not know the center of the histogram. Second, we do not know the true SE because the SD of the population is unknown.

In the same way we estimated the population average with the sample average, we estimate the SD of the box with the SD of the sample. Given the hypothetical results in Figure 10.4.3 on the sample average and standard deviation, we would infer that the average weight in the population of U.S. adults is around 150 pounds give or take 1.5 pounds. We cannot give a definite answer because we know that our sample is subject to chance error from the sampling procedure. We know that our estimate is likely to be off from the truth because of chance error. A good estimate of the likely size of that chance error is 1.5 pounds.

Notice that we sampled without replacement yet ignored the correction factor. In the first example, with presidential heights, we had to use the correction factor. This is not an important issue in this example because the population is so large relative to the sample that no correction factor is needed. After all, 190 million minus 400 is almost 190 million, and when this is divided by 190 million and then we take the square root, we get almost 1.

Summary

This section has shown how statisticians work with a data generation process built on drawing a sample from an actual population. Although seemingly quite removed from coin flipping or dice, the underlying framework for the analysis remains the same. With a proper box model of the data generating process, we are able to organize the chance process and truly understand that sample statistics are random variables with their own probability histograms. The next section reviews how sample data can be used to test claims about population parameters.

10.5. Hypothesis Testing

Workbook: PValue.xla (Excel add-in)

This section reviews the structure and logic of a statistical procedure known as hypothesis testing or a test of significance. The two basic procedures of statistical inference are hypothesis tests and confidence intervals. Both are explained in greater detail in Chapter 16, but hypotheses tests are so misused and confusing that they deserve a little extra attention. We will introduce an Excel add-in called the P Value Calculator that allows a variety of statistical tests to be run and conclude by alerting you to common mistakes in interpreting the results of a hypothesis test.

We return to the Larry Bird basketball shooting example of Section 9.4. Suppose someone made a claim that Bird's true free-throw percentage is 80 percent. We take a sample of 200 free-throws and find that he makes 180 out of the 200 attempts. How do we use this evidence to evaluate the claim about Bird's true free-throw shooting prowess?

The basic question in inferential statistics is, Is the difference real or due to chance? In a hypothesis test, the difference referred to is the difference between the claimed value for a parameter (about the population) and the observed value (from the sample). From our work in this and the previous chapter we know that the observed value, whether it is a sample average or sum, is subject to chance error. If we can apply a box model to the data generation process, then we can approximate the likely size of the chance error. Once we know the likely size of the chance error, as summarized by the appropriate SE, we have a measuring stick to use to decide whether the difference is big enough that we can rule out the role of chance as an explanation for the observed difference.

Hypothesis tests contain one more element. In addition to the claimed value for a parameter called the *null hypothesis*, there is a second hypothesis, called the *alternative hypothesis*, which contradicts the null. Alternative hypotheses come in two varieties: the first says that null is false, and the second says in which direction it is false. In our case, the first type of alternative hypothesis would say that Bird's true shooting percentage is not 80 percent. This formulation allows evidence against the claim to come from either direction – much higher or lower observed sample percentages would be evidence against the claim. Therefore, this alternative hypothesis leads to a *two-tailed test*. The second type of alternative would say either that his true shooting percentage is greater than 80 percent or that it is less than 80 percent. This is called a *one-tailed test* because evidence against the null can come from only one direction.

In the free-throw prowess case, the claimed parameter value is a free-throw shooting percentage of 80 percent. A coin-flip box model can be used to describe the data generation process. The box contains four 1's and one 0 (reflecting the claimed shooting percentage). We take 200 draws with replacement and compute the sample average. We can multiply by 100 to get the sample percentage.

Once we have the box model, we need to figure out the shape of the probability histogram (or sampling distribution). Our Monte Carlo experiments and work with BoxModel.xls have shown that sums and averages of draws from a box converge toward the normal curve as the sample size increases regardless of the distribution of the box itself. This remarkable property of sample sums and averages is known as the *central limit theorem*. It allows us to substitute the normal curve as an approximation to the exact probability histogram.

The claim, or null hypothesis, fixes the center of the sampling distribution (in this case, at 80 percent), but we still need to figure out the variability in the sample percentage. There are two ways to determine the value of the SE of the sample percentage. The first is via Monte Carlo simulation as discussed for this example in Section 9.4. The second is to use analytical methods, which we describe here. The SE of the sample average is given by the formula:

$$\text{SE of the Sample Average} = \frac{SD(Box)}{\sqrt{n}}.$$

For our case, under the null hypothesis, the SD of the box works out to 0.4. With the SD of the box in hand we can compute the SE of the sample average to be about 0.0283 or about 2.8 percentage points.

We now have the shape of the probability histogram (obtained by relying on the central limit theorem), its center (as given by the null hypothesis), and its spread (which in this case we do not have to estimate because the null hypothesis implies a particularly configured box). We are ready to actually conduct the hypothesis test. We are trying to determine whether the difference between the claimed value and the observed value could be due to chance. We construct a test statistic, which in this case is called a *z-statistic*, as follows:

$$z\text{-statistic} = \frac{\text{Observed Value} - \text{Value Claimed under the Null}}{\text{SE (Sample Statistic)}}.$$

In our example, the test statistic works out to

$$z\text{-statistic} = \frac{0.90 - 0.80}{0.028}$$
$$= 3.57.$$

The point of the z-statistic is to standardize the measured difference between the observed and claimed values so that we can use the standard normal curve (with mean 0 and SD 1) to approximate the chances of obtaining a result as extreme or one more extreme than the observed result. The area under the normal curve corresponding to the more extreme results is known as the *probability value* or *P-value*. It is also called the *significance level*.

Conventional practice is to reject the null hypothesis if the computed *P*-value is less than 5 percent; sometimes researchers use a tighter 1-percent standard. In our example, the *P*-value works out to considerably less than 1 percent, and so we would reject the null hypothesis. In other words, on the basis of the evidence in the sample (180 free-throws made out of 200), we do not believe that the free-throw shooter is actually merely an 80-percent free-throw shooter and that this result was just bad luck on this sample.

Of course, the null could be true, but the chances of getting a result like 90 percent out of 200 free throws (or one even more extreme) from a four 1's and one 0 box are so low that we reject the claim that the box is configured that way. The z-statistic is said to be statistically significant because it is far enough away from 80 percent that we reject the null hypothesis.

We recommend installing and using our P Value Calculator add-in on this problem to generate a graph that will help you understand the logic of the hypothesis test. The add-in is available in the Basic Tools folder of the CD-ROM. Full installation instructions are available in the same folder.

Once the PValue.xla file is installed, execute Tools: PValues and select the Normal distribution. After clicking OK, fill in the Input tab so that it looks like Figure 10.5.1. Click the Next button to see the Results tab. Check the Show Picture box and click Finish. A picture, like Figure 10.5.2, is pasted on your Excel spreadsheet with the results of the test.

The results (shown in Figure 10.5.2) show that making 180 out 200 free throws, in standard units, is quite far from the center of the distribution on the assumption the null (80%) is true. We have strong evidence against the null, and therefore we do not believe it.

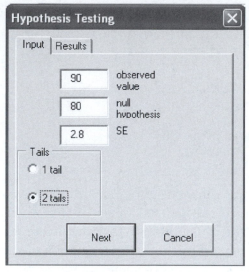

Figure 10.5.1. Using the P Value Calculator add-in.

Although this example looks simple, hypothesis testing is a fragile procedure. It is easy to make a variety of mistakes. Here are just a few.

Statistical inference, as exemplified by hypothesis testing, boils down to determining what the claim is about the data generating process, deciding on a box model that describes the data generating process, figuring out the shape of the sampling distribution, obtaining a measure of the likely size of chance error, deciding on a critical level of significance, and determining

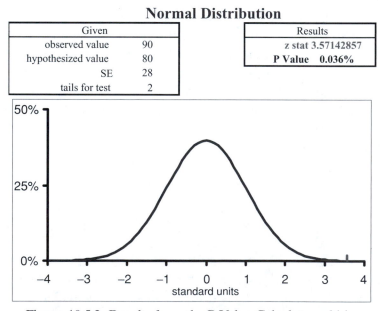

Figure 10.5.2. Results from the P Value Calculator add-in.

the probability of obtaining the observed result or one more extreme under the assumption that the null hypothesis is true. The process breaks down if the analogy between the data generating process and the box model is poor. In that case the machinery we have developed for determining the likely size of chance error does not work. A good example is the cluster sampling scheme for presidential heights in the previous section. There, the analogy between the data generation process and drawing rickets at random with replacement from a polling box simply does not apply (the problem is that the draws are not independent of each other) and the SE computed via the conventional formula is wrong. Even worse are samples of convenience. It is absolutely wrong to apply the sophisticated method of a hypothesis test to a nonrandom sample.

Another difficulty involves determining the shape of the probability histogram. We often rely on the central limit theorem. The bigger the sample size (the number of draws), the more the probability histogram of the sample sum or sample average converges to the normal curve. With the additional assumption that the box is normally distributed, then the distribution of the z-statistic is called *Student's t distribution*.[4] Other sample statistics (such as sums of squares) are known to have other distributions. You have to use the right distribution for the particular sample statistic you are working with in order to get the hypothesis test right.

The final obstacle to successful hypothesis testing involves the interpretation of the results. There are two common pitfalls. First, it is simply false that the P-value tells you the chances the null is true. In fact, the P-value is built on the assumption that the null is true. The P-value tells you the chances, if it is assumed the null is true, of getting a particular result or one more extreme. Second, even if the result is statistically significant, this says nothing about the practical importance of the result. Statistical significance is merely a statement that chance alone is not a good explanation for the observed difference. Because the SE and P-value depend on the sample size, even small observed differences can be "statistically significant" when the sample size is large. To test the practical importance of a result, apply it to the entire population and determine what that means.

Summary

The fundamental similarity between the coin-flip and polling box models means that the same basic hypothesis testing procedures can be used for problems involving polling box models as are used for problems involving

---

[4] The *t*-distribution is explained in detail in Chapter 16 . As n increases, the *t*-distribution converges rapidly to the normal distribution.

coin-flip box models. In fact, we will use the same procedures on other box models in this book.

The next section presents one final concept from the world of statistical theory. We point out that some sample statistics are not centered on their population analogues, but they get closer as the sample size increases. This is a desirable attribute.

10.6. Consistent Estimators

Workbook: Consistency.xls

In our discussions of the coin-flip and polling box models, the sample average was an *unbiased* estimator of the average of the box because the expected value of the sample average equaled the average of the box. "Unbiasedness" is a very desirable property for an estimator, but there are many situations in which it cannot be achieved. Thus, there may be no estimator that gives unbiased estimates of a given parameter. In that case the fallback is to search for a consistent estimator of the parameter in question. This section explains consistency via a simple example.

A *consistent* estimator of a parameter is one whose sampling distribution becomes ever more tightly concentrated around the true parameter value as the sample size increases.[5] Consistency is known as a *large-sample* or *asymptotic* property. It describes what happens as the sample size grows without limit. The opposite concept is an *exact finite-sample (small-sample)* property. For example, in the polling box model, the fact that the sample average is an unbiased estimator of the average of the box is an exact finite-sample result.

Our example of a biased but consistent estimator is the following. We use a box model in which the box contains an infinite number of tickets that are normally distributed and have a specified average and SD. A *Y* denotes the realized outcomes. The parameter we wish to estimate is the cube of the average of the box. Our estimator of this parameter will be the cube of the Sample Average (Sample Average[3]). It is very easy to demonstrate that the Sample Average[3] is a biased estimator of the cubed average of the box but that this bias disappears as the sample size increases.

Open the Consistency.xls file and go to the *Sample* sheet. Figure 10.6.1 displays a portion of that worksheet. The parameters of the data generation process are in the upper-left-hand corner. We have set both the average of the box and the SD to 5. Note that the values of the Cube of the Average

[5] This is a rough definition. For more rigorous treatment of this concept in terms of probability limits, see, for example, Amemiya (1994), p. 132, or Goldberger (1998), pp. 48–49, which contains a nice example.

Population Parameters	
Average of the box	**5.00**
SD of the box	**5.00**
Cube of the Average of the box	125.00
Reciprocal of the Average of the box	0.20

Sample Statistics	
Sample Average	0.69
Sample SD	5.67
Sample Average^3	0.34
1/Sample Average	1.44
Sample Size (n)	10

Observation	Y
1	8.43
2	4.50
3	4.16

Figure 10.6.1. Setup for example of blased but consistent estimators.
Source: [Consistency.xls]Sample.

of the box and the Reciprocal of the Average of the box are determined by the value you choose for the Average of the box. In column B, starting with cell B8, we draw a sample of normally distributed random variables obeying these parameters.

The sheet is set up so that you can draw samples of size 1 up to 200. You can control the sample size by changing the number in cell E6. The sheet opens with $n = 10$, and so only 10 observations are drawn in each sample. We compute the Sample Average in cell E2, the Sample SD in cell E3, and two statistics based on the Sample Average, its cube (Sample Average^3) and its reciprocal (1/Sample Average) in cells E4 and E5, respectively. Everything we say in this section about the consistency properties of the Sample Average^3 estimator pertains as well to the 1/Sample Average estimator of the Reciprocal of the Average of the box.

To demonstrate the consistency of the Sample Average^3 estimator, we used the Monte Carlo simulation add-in (described in Chapter 9) to run 3 Monte Carlo analyses of 10,000 repetitions each for sample sizes 10, 50, and 100. The results for each individual Monte Carlo simulation are in the *Ycubedn = 10*, *Ycubedn = 50*, and *Ycubedn = 200* sheets, respectively. We summarize the results in Figure 10.6.2.

The Monte Carlo results show that, as the sample size (n) increases, the center of the sampling distribution moves closer to the true parameter value, 125, and the spread of the sampling distribution becomes smaller and smaller. This is evidence that Sample Average^3 is a consistent estimator of the Average of the box.

Here is the intuition behind this result. When the sample size is small, there is considerable bounce in the sample average that is magnified when the sample average is cubed. You can see this by setting cell E6 to 10 and hitting

Comparison of Monte Carlo Results for Sample Average[3]			
n	10	50	200
Ave Estimate	161.7	131.8	127.6
SD Estimate	141.4	54.6	26.9
See *Ycubedn=10*, *Ycubedn=50*, and *Ycubedn=200* sheets.			

Figure 10.6.2. Demonstrating consistency via Monte Carlo simulation. *Source:* [Consistency.xls]Sample.

the F9 key repeatedly. Watch cell E4. It bounces wildly. A sample average of 7 becomes a Sample Average[3] of 343. That is very far away from 125. If you look at the Monte Carlo approximation to the sampling distribution in the *Ycubedn = 10* sheet, it will have a long right-hand tail. This is what is causing the small sample bias. The sampling distribution is not centered at 125.

As the sample size increases, however, the sample average estimates are concentrated ever more tightly around the true value of average of the box; in other words, the spread of the sampling distribution for both the sample average and the sample average cubed decreases with increasing sample size. Return to the *Sample* sheet, set cell E6 to 10, and hit the F9 key a few times. You will not obtain huge values of Sample Average[3] because the sample average remains fairly close to 5. The closer the Sample Average is to 5, the closer the Sample Average[3] is to 125; hence, the smaller the bias and the smaller the spread of the Sample Average[3] sampling distribution. See the *Ycubedn = 200* sheet to confirm that the expected value of Sample Average[3] (as approximated by the average of 10,000 repetitions of the data generation process) is much closer to 125. The bias is much smaller and the sampling distribution is much closer to the normal curve.

Summary

This section has demonstrated that a sample statistic may be biased but consistent. This means that the statistic is not centered on the true population parameter (a bad thing), but that the center of its sampling distribution gets closer to the true population parameter as the sample size increases and its spread gets smaller.

The final section in this chapter covers the same concepts we have reviewed in previous sections but in a more sophisticated language called the algebra of expectations. This language can be used to derive analytical formulas for expected values and SEs of sample statistics.

10.7. The Algebra of Expectations

Workbook: AlgebraofExpectations.xls

This section provides a more formal exposition of the fundamental concepts presented in this chapter. Previous sections relied, per our teaching philosophy, on Monte Carlo simulation to demonstrate properties of coin-flip and polling box models. We want you to be aware that there is another approach to determining the expected value or SE of a sample statistic. This alternative to Monte Carlo remains the conventional way students learn about the properties of chance processes. We proceed in two steps: First we define and apply the concept of the expectations (or expected value) operator $E()$ and then we demonstrate a few simple properties of this operator, which we call the algebra of expectations.

Introducing the Expectations Operator E( )

In mathematics, an operator is an action. You are familiar with the arithmetic operators: addition, subtraction, multiplication, and division. Like these operators, the *expectations operator* is applied to an expression (which goes between the brackets) and outputs a result called the expected value. Although the expectations operator can be applied to a constant (the result is then simply the constant), we are usually interested in taking the expected value of an expression that involves a random variable.

A *random variable* is a number determined by a chance process. You do not know the realized value of the random variable until you run the chance process. There are two kinds of random variables, discrete and continuous. We will work with *discrete random variables*, which are random variables that can take on a countable number of different values. A very simple example of a discrete random variable is a flip of a fair coin. In this case, there are only two possible outcomes, heads and tails. Let us assign a value of 0 to tails and 1 to heads.

To describe the coin flip process more formally, we can define a random variable we will call X. This random variable can take on the values:

$x_1 = 1$, which indicates that the coin flip turned up heads, and

$x_2 = 0$, which indicates that the coin flip turned up tails.

We use capital letters for random variables and corresponding small letters for possible values of the random variable.

Associated with a random variable is its *probability density function*, or *pdf*. The probability density function tells you the probability of a given outcome. In the case of a fair coin, the probability that the coin will turn up heads,

Figure 10.7.1. Probability density function for coin-flip random variable.
Source: [AlgebraofExpectations.xls]CoinFlip.

x_i	$P(X = x_i)$
0	0.50
1	0.50

denoted $P(X = x_1)$, is one-half; similarly $P(X = x_2)$ is also one-half. We will usually shorten such expressions to $P(x_1)$ and $P(x_2)$. The pdf for any random variable has two important properties: the probability of any outcome is greater than or equal to zero, and the sum of the probabilities of all possible outcomes is one.

The pdf for a discrete random variable can be represented in tabular form by listing the possible outcomes and their respective probabilities of occurring. Open the Excel workbook AlgebraOfExpectations.xls and go to the *CoinFlip* sheet to follow the exposition. The pdf of the coin flip random variable looks like Figure 10.7.1 copied from cells A3 to C5 in the *CoinFlip* sheet.

Figure 10.7.1 corresponds to the contents of the box in the coin-flip example of Section 10.3. The main difference is that, whereas the pdf specifies the probabilities of obtaining different outcomes, the box model represents the probabilities via the relative proportions of tickets in the box. A box with 64 total tickets, 32 1's and 32 0's, represents the coin-flip random variable equally well as the box with just two tickets, though the latter is preferred on the grounds of simplicity.

The pdf can also be represented graphically via a *probability histogram*, which shows the chances of particular events occurring. In the case of the coin flip, the probability histogram looks like Figure 10.7.2.

It is easy to confuse probability and empirical histograms. One way to understand the difference is to focus on what exactly is being displayed. Figure 10.7.2 is a probability histogram because it shows the chances of each outcome. Empirical histograms plot the frequencies of numbers in a list.

Probability Histogram

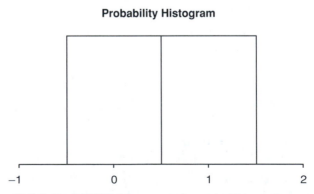

Figure 10.7.2. Probability histogram for coin-flip random variable.
Source: [AlgebraofExpectations.xls]CoinFlip.

Just about every random variable can be characterized by two numbers: its expected value and its standard deviation.[6] The *expected value* of a random variable is the average value that we expect to observe over the long run. The expected value of the coin-flip random variable is, fairly obviously, 0.5. Half the time we will get a 1, and half the time a 0 will result; the average of 0 and 1 is 0.5. In terms of the probability histogram, the expected value is the center of histogram.

More formally, the expected value is a probability-weighted sum of the outcomes for the random variable. The expectations operator is a shorthand way to represent this computation. In other words, when we apply the expectations operator $E()$, we find the expected value of a random variable by taking each outcome, multiplying it by the probability of that outcome's occurring, and summing up the result. Here is the algebra for the coin-flip random variable:

$$E(X) = P(x_1) \cdot x_1 + P(x_2) \cdot x_2$$
$$= \frac{1}{2} \cdot 0 + \frac{1}{2} \cdot 1$$
$$= \frac{1}{2}.$$

The expression $E(X) = \frac{1}{2}$ means that the expected value of X is $\frac{1}{2}$. Notice that the expected value in this case is equal to neither one of the two potential outcomes.

In general, when Y is a random variable having n possible outcomes, y_1 through y_n, we compute the expected value $E(Y)$ via the following formula:

$$E(Y) = \sum_{i=1}^{n} P(y_i) \cdot y_i.$$

The capital sigma summation symbol is a mathematical operator that you have seen before. It means that we sum up terms that all look like the expression to the symbol's right. The letter i is an index, which in this case runs from 1 to n. Each y_i is one of the possible values that the random variable Y can take on. The summation above means that

$$\sum_{i=1}^{n} P(y_i) \cdot y_i = P(y_1) \cdot y_1 + P(y_2) \cdot y_2 + \cdots + P(y_n) \cdot y_n.$$

In addition to the center of the pdf given by the expected value of X, we are often interested in the variability of X as measured by the SD or variance. Figure 10.7.3 (cells F2:J7 in the *CoinFlip* sheet) gives the details of the computation for the coin-flip example. By convention, $V(X)$ stands for

---

[6] Perhaps the most famous exception is the Cauchy distribution, which has neither an expected value nor an SD.

Variance and SD Computation		Deviation from Expected Value	Deviation Squared	Weighted Sum
x_i	$P(X=x_i)$	$x_i - E(X)$	$(x_i - E(X))^2$	$P(X=x_i) * (x_i - E(X))^2$
0	0.90	−0.10	0.01	0.009
1	0.10	0.90	0.81	0.081
$E(X)$	0.10		$V(X)$	0.09
			$SD(X)$	0.30

Figure 10.7.3. Computing of the variance and SD of the coin-flip random variable. *Source:* [AlgebraofExpectations.xls]CoinFlip

variance and $SD(X)$ for standard deviation. Click on the cells in the F2:J7 range to see the formulas used.

Once again, the expectations operator can be used as a shorthand way to represent the computations needed to determine the variance and SD. The *variance* of a random variable X (denoted $V(X)$) is defined as the expected value of the squared deviation from the expected value:

$$V(X) = E[(X - E(X))^2].$$

The *standard deviation (SD)* of a random variable X is the square root of its variance:

$$SD(X) = \sqrt{V(X)} = \sqrt{E[(X - E(X))^2]}.$$

More specifically, the variance of a discrete random variable is computed as a probability-weighted sum of the squared deviations:

$$V(X) = \sum_{i=1}^{n} (x_i - E(X))^2 \cdot P(x_i).$$

The standard deviation of a discrete random variable is simply the square root of the preceding sum:

$$SD(X) = \sqrt{\sum_{i=1}^{n} (x_i - E(X))^2 \cdot P(x_i)}. \tag{10.2.6}$$

The algebraic version of the variance computation in Figure 10.7.3 is

$$V(X) = \sum_{i=1}^{n} (x_i - E(X))^2 \cdot P(x_i)$$
$$= (0 - 0.5)^2 \cdot 0.5 + (1 - 0.5)^2 \cdot 0.5$$
$$= 0.25 \cdot 0.5 + 0.25 \cdot 0.5$$
$$= 0.25.$$

Simulation	X	Detailed Results for 1000-Repetition Monte Carlo		
		x_i	Empirical Frequency	Probability Histogram
Average Value	0.484	0	516	0.500
SD	0.500	1	484	0.500
Observation				

Figure 10.7.4. Results for 1,000-repetition Monte Carlo of coin-flip random variable. *Source:* [AlgebraofExpectations.xls]CoinFlip.

$$SD(X) = \sqrt{V(X)}$$
$$= \sqrt{0.25}$$
$$= 0.5.$$

Click on the Run Simulation button (in the *CoinFlip* sheet) to observe the result of a 1,000-repetition Monte Carlo experiment in which we simulate 1,000 realizations of the coin-flip random variable. You can change the pdf by altering the numbers in blue. We ran one such simulation and obtained the results given in Figure 10.7.4.

In this experiment, we figuratively flipped the coin 1,000 times. The first 100 repetitions of the Monte Carlo simulation are listed in the table on the left side of the shcct. Overall, we obtained 516 tails and 484 heads. The average value was 516 multiplied by 0 plus 484 multiplied by 1 divided by 1,000, or 0.484. The empirical SD of these 1,000 numbers was, to 3 decimal places, 0.500. The results are also depicted in an empirical histogram, which looks very much like the probability histogram. The Monte Carlo simulation thus provides intuitive support for the concepts of expected value and SD of a random variable. The expected value is the long-run average value for outcomes of the random variable, and the SD is the long-run spread of the outcomes. The empirical histogram generated by the Monte Carlo is not exactly the same as the probability histogram because we did not run an infinite number of repetitions. The probability histogram gives the exact long-run chances of particular outcomes, whereas the Monte Carlo simulation approximates the probability histogram.

Now go ahead and create a new random variable, a seriously unfair coin, by changing $P(X = x_1)$ to 0.90 (in cell B4). The worksheet immediately computes the expected value and SD of this new random variable: 0.1 and 0.3, respectively.[7] Notice that the probability histogram also reflects the new pdf. Click on the Run Simulation button. The empirical average and SD produced by the Monte Carlo simulation should be very close, though not exactly identical, to the computed expected value and SD of the random variable.

---

[7] If the sheet does not automatically recalculate, execute Tools: Options, click on the Calculation tab and make sure the Automatic Calculation choice is selected.

E(X)		
x_i	$P(x_i)$	$x_iP(x_i)$
1	1/6	0.17
2	1/6	0.33
3	1/6	0.50
4	1/6	0.67
5	1/6	0.83
6	1/6	1.00
$E(X)$		3.50

Figure 10.7.5. Computing the expected value of the fair die random variable.
Source: [AlgebraofExpectations.xls]Dice.

The Algebra of Expectations

The algebra of expectations largely consists of several convenient formulas for working with the expected value, variance, and standard deviation of random variables. The formulas depend on properties of the expectations operator. We will develop these formulas and demonstrate the properties of $E()$ in the context of a slightly more complicated example than the coin-flip box model.

Suppose you have been given the opportunity to roll a fair die and be paid $1 for every spot that comes up. Figure 10.7.5 (also available in the *Dice* sheet) lists the six possible outcomes from a roll of one die, the probability of each outcome, and multiplies each outcome by its corresponding probability.

Now suppose that, instead of making $1 per spot, you will make $10 per spot. Simply multiply every outcome by 10 to create a new random variable, which is $10X$. Rather than changing these cells, replacing 1 with 10, 2 with 20, and so on, examine cells EZ: G11, which reflect this new payoff. The new random variable and its expected value is displayed in Figure 10.7.6.

Note that each original x_i has been multiplied by the constant k, which in this case is 10. In the language of random variables, a *constant* is a value that is always the same in every realization of the chance process. The result is not unexpected: multiplying every outcome by 10 – in other words multiplying the original random variable by 10 – leads to a tenfold increase in the expected value. More generally, if we multiply the original random variable X by a

E(kX)		
k	10	
kx_i	$P(x_i)$	$(kx_i)P(x_i)$
10	1/6	1.67
20	1/6	3.33
30	1/6	5.00
40	1/6	6.67
50	1/6	8.33
60	1/6	10.00
$E(kX)$		35.00

Figure 10.7.6. $10-per-spot fair die random variable.
Source: [AlgebraofExpectations.xls]Dice.

E (a+kX)		
a	**−40**	
a + kx_i	P(x_i)	(a+kx_i)P(x_i)
−30	1/6	−5.00
−20	1/6	−3.33
−10	1/6	−1.67
0	1/6	0.00
10	1/6	1.67
20	1/6	3.33
E (a+kX)		−5.00

Figure 10.7.7. Paying to play the die game random variable.
Source: [AlgebraofExpectations.xls]Dice.

constant k, the expected value of the new random variable increases k-fold:

$$E(kX) = kE(X).$$

This is one of the basic properties of the expectations operator. You can demonstrate this property in the *Dice* sheet by choosing various values of k in cell F3.

As you doubtless know, most gambling games do not make money for the players. Let us make the game more realistic and charge you $40 per roll of the die. The new random variable would be $-40 + 10X$. The expected value computation is contained in Figure 10.7.7 (reproduced from cell range I2:K11 in the *Dice* sheet).

The expected value in the bottom right-hand corner of the figure tells you that the game has become a losing proposition on average. The results obtained in this example obviously generalize. If you add a constant to a random variable, the expected value of the result is the constant plus the expected value of the random variable. More formally, if a and k are constants, then

$$E(a + kX) = a + kE(X).$$

You can use the *Dice* sheet to demonstrate this fact by changing the values in cells F3 and J3 and noting the results.

We will now demonstrate similar rules for the Variance and SD of a random variable. First, let us review the computation of the variance as applied to the die random variable. The variance is computed as a weighted sum for which the weights are the probabilities of the different outcomes. In the case of the fair die, we have

$$V(X) = \sum_{i=1}^{n} (x_i - E(X))^2 \cdot P(X = x_i)$$

$$= \sum_{i=1}^{n} (x_i - 3.5)^2 \cdot \frac{1}{6}$$

$$= (1 - 3.5)^2 \cdot \frac{1}{6} + (2 - 3.5)^2 \cdot \frac{1}{6} + \cdots + (6 - 3.5)^2 \cdot \frac{1}{6}$$

$$= 2.92.$$

X			Deviation from EV	Deviation Squared	Weighted Sum
x_i	$P(x_i)$		$x_i - E(X)$	$(x_i - (EX))^2$	$P(x_i) *$ $(x_i - E(X))^2$
1	1/6		−2.50	6.25	1.04
2	1/6		−1.50	2.25	0.38
3	1/6		−0.50	0.25	0.04
4	1/6		0.50	0.25	0.04
5	1/6		1.50	2.25	0.38
6	1/6		2.50	6.25	1.04
$E(X)$	3 1/2			$V(X)$	2.92
				$SD(X)$	1.71

Figure 10.7.8. Computing the variance and SD of the fair die random variable. *Source:* [AlgebraofExpectations.xls]Dice.

This computation is done explicitly in the *Dice* worksheet. Figure 10.7.8 shows the calculations.

The rule for determining the variance and SD of a random variable equal to another random variable plus a constant is quite simple. If a is a constant,

$$V(a + X) = V(X); SD(a + X) = SD(X).$$

In words, if you add a constant to a random variable, its variance and SD do not change. This makes sense because, when a constant is added to a random variable, every outcome and the expected value are increased by the value of the constant. The deviations are therefore unchanged, and thus the SD and Variance are unaffected.

Next, consider multiplying a random variable by a constant. If k is a constant and X is a random variable:

$$V(kX) = k^2 V(X); SD(kX) = kSD(X).$$

In words, if you multiply a random variable by a constant, its Variance is multiplied by the square of that constant, whereas its SD is multiplied by the constant. The key to understanding this fact is to realize that the original deviations have been increased k-fold and the squared deviations have been magnified k^2-fold.

The *Dice* sheet has tables that can be used to demonstrate easily that adding a constant does not affect the variance or the SD of a random variable, but multiplying by a constant will change both the variance and SD.

We can use the tool of Monte Carlo simulation to provide experimental support for these simple rules for computing expected values, SDs, and Variances. Click on the View Simulation button in the *Dice* sheet. You will be taken to a table and a histogram that show the result of 1,000 repetitions of the composite random variables we have created.

Simulation	X	kX	$a + kX$
Average Value	$3.59	$35.90	−$4.10
SD	$1.71	$17.11	$17.11

Figure 10.7.9. Monte Carlo experiment results for die random variables. *Source:* [AlgebraofExpectations.xls]Dice.

Every time you click on the $\boxed{\text{Run 1,000 Repetition Simulation}}$ button, the computer simulates 1,000 rolls of a die and records the outcomes. Each experiment will produce slightly different results. The summary for the experiment we ran looks like Figure 10.7.9.

In our simulation of 1,000 plays, the average dollar value of the spots on one roll of the die was $3.59, the average value of 10 times the spots was $35.90, and the average value of our "winnings" in 1,000 plays of paying $40 for the privilege of receiving $10 times the number of spots on the die was negative $4.10. The respective expected values for X, kX, and $a + kX$ are $3.50, $35.00, and −$5.00. The average in the Monte Carlo experiment measures the center of the distribution of the random variable by brute force repetition of a finite number of plays and is, therefore, only an approximation to the expected value. One thousand repetitions is enough to obtain a good but not perfect approximation.

Similarly the SDs of the 1,000 outcomes are very close to the SDs we computed for the random variables X, kX, and $a + kX$. We computed the long-run spread of X to be 1.71, and the spread of the 1,000 simulated values of X was 1.71. Be clear on the difference between the two types of SDs mentioned in the previous sentence. The term $SD(X)$ is an expected value and thus is the exact value of the spread of the random variable, whereas the SD in the Monte Carlo experiment is the SD of a list of 1,000 numbers produced by simulating the random variable 1,000 times. The latter SD is an approximation of the former SD (the former SD is known as an SE when the random variable in question is a sample statistic). In our case, the approximation was very close (differing beyond two decimal places), but that is not always so.

The histogram of the Monte Carlo simulation results depicted in Figure 10.7.10 summarizes the outcome of the experiment in more detail. Figure 10.7.10 displays an empirical histogram corresponding to the random variable called X. The histogram for kX looks exactly like the one above except that the outcomes are multiplied by 10; the histogram for $a + kX$ (the outcomes of the more realistic gambling game) is then just shifted left by 40. In contrast, the probability histogram depicting the pdf for X (shown in Figure 10.7.11) is completely even.

Empirical Histogram

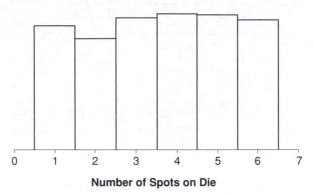

Number of Spots on Die

Figure 10.7.10. Empirical histogram of Monte Carlo simulation for die random variable.
Source: [AlgebraofExpectations.xls]Dice.

With a fair die, each outcome is equally likely to occur. As the number of repetitions in a Monte Carlo simulation of the die rolls rises, the empirical histogram comes to look increasingly like the probability histogram.

We conclude this section by applying the $E()$ operator and the properties of the expectations operator to more complicated random variables – namely, sums and averages of random variables. These general results are stated without proof.

Suppose that X and Y are two random variables and a and b two constants. Then,

$$E(X+Y) = E(X) + E(Y)$$
$$E(aX+bY) = aE(X) + bE(Y).$$

Probability Histogram

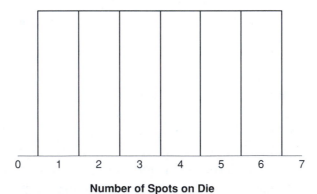

Number of Spots on Die

Figure 10.7.11. Probability histogram for die random variable.
Source: [AlgebraofExpectations.xls]Dice.

More generally, for random variables X_1, X_2, and so on up to X_n and constants w_1 up to w_n,

$$E\left[\sum_{i=1}^{n} w_i X_i\right] = \sum_{i=1}^{n} w_i E(X_i).$$

In words, the expected value of a weighted sum of random variables is the weighted sum of their respective expected values. Because of this property, $E()$ is said to be a *linear operator*. Loosely speaking, the expectations operator can be carried through the expression. The square and natural log are examples of nonlinear operators. After all, $(2 + 3)^2$ does not equal $2^2 + 3^2$ and $\ln(100+100)$ is not equivalent to $\ln(100) + \ln(100)$.

We now turn to formulas for the variance of sums of random variables. Although the formulas for the expected values listed above apply to all random variables, independent or not, the variance depends on whether the random variables are independent. If not, the formula for the variance is more complicated. Here are facts about the variance and SD for sums and weighted sums of independent random variables. We stress that these facts apply only to independent random variables.

$$V(X + Y) = V(X) + V(Y)$$

$$V(aX + bY) = a^2 V(X) + b^2 V(Y).$$

More generally, for mutually independent random variables X_1 to X_n and constants w_1 to w_n,

$$V\left[\sum_{i=1}^{n} w_i X_i\right] = \sum_{i=1}^{n} w_i^2 V(X_i).$$

and

$$SD\left[\sum_{i=1}^{n} w_i X_i\right] = \sqrt{\sum_{i=1}^{n} w_i^2 V(X_i)}.$$

We can apply these facts about the expected value of a weighted sum of random variables and the variance of a weighted sum of random variables to a situation we have already studied: repeated draws with replacement from a box. Each draw from the box is the realization of a random variable. Making the draws with replacement means that we are always drawing from the same box, and so the random variables have the same distribution (in the standard terminology, they are *identically distributed*). Because the draws are with replacement and each time a draw is made every ticket is equally likely to come out of the box, the draws are *independent*. In looking at the draws from the box, we are considering either a sum (with weights w_i all equal to 1) or an average (with weights w_i all equal to $1/n$) of random variables.

In this very important special case, the results (for the Sample Average) translate to

$$E(\text{Sample Average}) = E\left(\sum_{i=1}^{n} \frac{1}{n} X_i\right)$$

$$= \sum_{i=1}^{n} \frac{1}{n} E(X_i)$$

$$= \frac{n}{n} \text{Average of the Box}$$

$$= \text{Average of the Box}.$$

This result relies on the expected value of each and every draw from the box, or $E(X_i)$ for the ith draw from the box, being the average of the contents of the box. As for the SD of the average of independent draws from the same box,

$$V\left[\sum_{i=1}^{n} \frac{1}{n} X_i\right] = \sum_{i=1}^{n} \frac{1}{n^2} V(X_i)$$

$$= \frac{1}{n} V(Box)$$

$$= \frac{1}{n} SD(Box)^2.$$

The second line follows from the variances being all equal to each other because the draws are from the same box. Taking the square root, we arrive at

$$SD\left[\sum_{i=1}^{n} \frac{1}{n} X_i\right] = \frac{SD(Box)}{\sqrt{n}},$$

or, put in more familiar language, the SD of the Sample Average is the SD of the box divided by the square root of the number of draws.

Summary

This concludes our presentation of the expectations operator and the algebra of expectations. We will occasionally use $E()$ in the rest of this book, but our primary mode of exposition will be Monte Carlo simulation. The algebra of expectations is used to derive formulas or analytical expressions for the expected value and SD of a data generation process. The Monte Carlo method can demonstrate, but never prove, that a result is true.

10.8. Conclusion

This chapter has served as a quick review of statistical inference but also as an introduction to one of the basic metaphors of this book, the box model. We use box models to clarify our thinking about the data generation process. A great danger in econometrics is the failure to explicitly model the way in which the data were generated. Absent careful work at this initial, crucial stage, subsequent analyses, no matter how much time they take or sophisticated they appear, are worthless.

This chapter has also developed an algebraic framework usable for working out the expected values of sample statistics. This framework, called the algebra of expectations, can be extremely useful. You should think of the algebra of expectations as a complementary tool to the Monte Carlo simulation skills you will develop through the rest of this book. You can use the algebra of expectations to work out the expected value or SD of a statistic of interest and Monte Carlo simulation to check your work. Alternatively, you can use Monte Carlo simulation to clarify your view of the data generating process and to suggest results that should be provable via the algebra of expectations.

With Chapter 9's explanation of Monte Carlo simulation and this chapter's review of statistical inference, we are ready to embark on the study of regression for inference. We will develop a series of box models to firmly ground the DGP that underlies the probabilistic interpretation of regression.

10.9. Exercises

Use the BoxModel.xls workbook to analyze the properties of a five-sided die. Unlike a conventional six-sided die, the five-sided die has five faces, with 1, 2, 3, 4, and 5 dots. Suppose we throw it 25 times and average the 25 throws.

1. Draw the box model for this DGP.
2. Properly configure BoxModel.xls to represent this DGP. What does BoxModel.xls display as the average and SD of the box?
3. What are the exact chances of getting an average of 3.6 or more? Describe your procedure.
4. Does Monte Carlo simulation give similar results? Describe your procedure.
5. If the DGP changes so that we take 100 draws instead of 25 draws, what happens to the chances of getting an average of 3.6 or more? Describe your procedure. HINT: You can directly change the *Setup* sheet in BoxModel.xls.
6. Return to the *Setup* sheet and click the [Draw a Sample from the Box] button. Suppose you did not know the contents of the box. With your sample, test the claim that the average of the box is 3.6. Describe your procedure.
7. Open the Consistency.xls workbook. Is $e^{\text{SampleAverage}}$ an unbiased estimator of $e^{\text{AverageBox}}$? If not, is $e^{\text{SampleAverage}}$ a consistent estimator of $e^{\text{AverageBox}}$? Describe your procedure.
8. In a new workbook, we drew a standard normal random variable (average 0 and SD 1) in cells A1 and A2 and added them together in cell A3. Then we ran a 1,000-repetition Monte Carlo and got the results in Figure 10.9.1.

Sheet1!$A$1		Sheet1!$A$3		Notes
Average	−0.008	Average	0.021	
SD	1.0092	SD	1.3976	
Max	3.619	Max	4.225	
Min	−4.046	Min	−4.449	

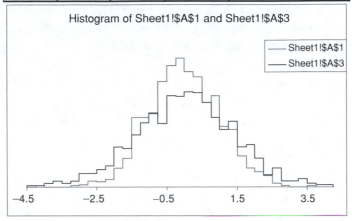

Figure 10.9.1. Monte Carlo simulation of adding two normal RVs.

Use the algebra of expectations to show that the Monte Carlo results for the average and SD for cell A3, the sum of the two standard normally distributed random variables, are reasonable.

References

As we have mentioned before, we borrowed the box model metaphor from an excellent statistics textbook and its corresponding instructor's manual:

Freedman, D., R. Pisani, and R. Purves (1998). Statistics, Third Edition. (New York: W.W. Norton & Company).

Freedman, D., R. Pisani, and R. Purves (1998). *Instructor's Manual for Statistics*, Third Edition. (New York: W.W. Norton & Company).

The following two econometrics textbooks do a good job of covering statistical inference:

Amemiya, T. (1994). *Introduction to Statistics and Econometrics*. Cambridge, MA: Harvard University Press.

Goldberger, A. S. (1998). *Introductory Econometrics*. Cambridge, MA: Harvard University.

Appendix: The Normal Approximation

The *normal approximation* is used to compute an estimate of a particular area under distributions which more or less resemble the normal curve. For example, many biological characteristics like height and weight have histograms for the general population which look a lot like the normal curve. The method can thus be used to find quick, roughly accurate answers to questions about how many people fall into certain height or weight categories.

Center (Average or EV)	202
Spread (SD or SE)	41
Upper Cutoff in actual units	160
Lower Cutoff in actual units	

Upper cutoff in SUs	−1.024
Lower cutoff in SUs	Minus Infinity
Area	**15.28%**

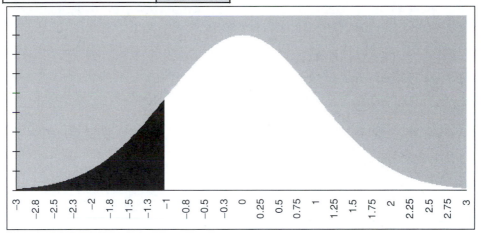

Figure 10.A.1. Applying the Normal Approximation.
Source: [BoxModel.xls]NormalApprox.

Consider the following example: one wishes to know the fraction of the adult male U.S. population which has a serum total cholesterol level below 160 milligrams per deciliter of blood. Cholesterol levels are pretty much normally distributed, so the normal approximation should be reasonably accurate.

Here is the procedure for using the normal approximation: First, one identifies the interval of interest. Second, one converts the interval in question into *standard units*. Standard units measure how far a particular value is from the average in terms of standard deviations. The mean total cholesterol level for adult males is 202 and the SD is 41.[8] Thus, a male with an actual level of 243 has a cholesterol level of 1 in terms of standard units while a male whose cholesterol level is −2 in standard units has an actual level of 120. Finally, one finds the area under the standard normal curve (with mean 0 and SD 1) for the interval in question. This is the approximate fraction of the population which falls into that interval.

Let us apply the normal approximation to this example. A serum total cholesterol level of 160 converts to about −1 in terms of standard units. The area beneath the normal curve from negative infinity to −1 is about 16 percent. The National Center for Health Statistics reports that a level of 160 was in fact the 15th percentile for the sample. The normal approximation works quite well in this particular case.

In this book, the normal approximation proves useful in answering questions about sampling distributions. The central limit theorem says that the sampling distribution (or probability histogram) for many sample statistics approaches the normal curve as the sample size increases. The normal approximation is used to

---

[8] These are figures derived from a survey conducted between 1988 and 1994 of 6587 males, ages 20 to 74 years old by the National Center for Health Statistics. The survey is the National Health and Nutrition Examination Survey. See www.cdc.gov/nchs/about/major/nhanes/datatblelink.htm.

estimate *P*-values for observed sample statistics. The *P*-value is the area under the sampling distribution for the null hypothesis corresponding to results as extreme as or more extreme than the one observed in the sample.

The *NormalApprox* sheet in BoxModel.xls can be used to implement the normal approximation. Figure 10.A.1 below shows how this sheet can be filled in to work the example in this appendix. The P Value Calculator add-In (introduced in Section 10.5) can also be used to apply the normal approximation.

11

The Measurement Box Model

It has generally been customary certainly to regard as an axiom the hypothesis that if any quantity has been determined by several direct observations, made under the same circumstances and with equal care, the arithmetical mean of the observed values affords the most probable value. . . .

Carl Friedrich Gauss[1]

11.1. Introduction

Regression is the dominant method of empirical analysis in economics. It has two basic applications: description and inference. The first eight chapters of this book use regression for description. Chapters 9 and 10 introduce and review tools for making statistical inference. We are now ready to see how regression is used when the data are a sample from a population.

The next few chapters prepare the ground for the study of regression as a tool for inference and forecasting. Inference in general means reasoning from factual knowledge or evidence. In statistics, we have a *sample* drawn from a *population* and use the sample to infer something about the population.

For example, suppose we have data on 1,178 people in the United States in 1989 selected at random from the adult working population. We have the level of experience and the wages of these people. Part 1 discusses the use of regression to provide a summary of the bivariate wage-experience data. Statistical inference aims at a much more ambitious goal. Instead of simply describing the relationship for those 1,178 people, we wish to discover the relationship between wage and experience for all of the adult workers in the United States. Our aim is to make educated guesses about the population based on information gathered from the sample.

Throughout our study of regression applied to inferential questions, we will emphasize the importance that chance and sampling error play in our educated guesses, which we will call *estimates*. Although the details require

---

[1] Gauss (1857, Article 177), cited by Lee (n.d., p. 96).

concentration and effort, the main idea – that an estimate based on a particular sample is likely to be off the true, unknown, population value – is not
difficult to grasp.

We stress the importance of understanding the role of chance in an inferential setting because regression for inference requires an explicit model of
the chance process. We do not want the student to memorize a list of rules
that must be met or, worse, assumed. Instead, our goal is true understanding
of different models of chance and their implications for regression analysis in
an inferential setting. Thus, much of the presentation in the rest of the book
is built on the idea of sampling and sampling error. Although proceeding
with caution over some difficult terrain, we do count on prior knowledge of
elementary statistical inference.

In this chapter we discuss a simple model for the data generation process
first used by astronomers as a way of using combining measurements of celestial bodies to estimate their true orbits. The problem these scientists faced
was that, despite strong theoretical evidence that planets ought to orbit along
smooth curves, their measurements did not all fit on a single curve. They realized that the data resulted from imperfect measurements of the exact location
of the planets. The scientists' task was somehow to reconcile the data to come
up with a single best estimate of the true orbit. In this endeavor astronomers
realized that, in general, it was a good practice to make use of all the observations. The question was how. The solution ultimately depended on arriving
at a satisfactory model of the data generation process.

We begin with this model in a book dedicated to econometrics because it
serves as an easily understandable bridge from the data generation processes
of basic statistics (what we have called the coin-flip and polling box models) to the classical econometric model of Chapter 13. Sections 11.2 through
11.5 discuss a univariate problem in which we measure a single quantity
repeatedly. We will show how the basic models of the data generating process reviewed in Chapter 10 can be modified to work out the properties of
the sample average in this measurement problem. In Section 11.6, a crucial
conceptual leap is made by extending the measurement box model to the
problem of the relationship between two variables estimated via a bivariate
regression.

Chapters 11 through 13 present three different descriptions of the data generation process. In Chapter 13, we point out that, mathematically speaking,
the measurement box model of this chapter and the classical econometric
model of Chapter 13 are identical. Why do we distinguish between them?
We do so because we wish to stress that one must have a coherent, plausible
explanation for the data generation process before one proceeds to statistical
inference. The measurement box model of this chapter assigns very different
roles to chance error than does the classical econometric model.

This chapter also demonstrates two complementary approaches applied throughout the rest of the book: the box model, which facilitates comprehension of the data generating process, and Monte Carlo simulation, which enables us to approximate the distribution of estimates obtained according to a specified data generating process.

11.2. Introducing the Problem

We will start with a hypothetical example designed to illustrate the problem of estimating a physical quantity using more than one measurement. Suppose you wanted to know the distance between two mountain peaks because such knowledge was extremely important to you. Each mountain reached a sharp point in the horizon. You took a picture of the two peaks and then ingeniously used geometry to calculate angles and so forth and eventually came up with an answer of 107.23 miles.

The answer seemed reasonable and everything was OK, but then a nagging doubt occurred: 107.23 miles seemed fairly precise (given the two decimal points), but that is equal to 566,174.4 feet, which, in turn, is equal to 6,794,092.8 inches. Thinking about the distance in millions of inches made you doubt your measurement. Surely, you thought, the measured distance could not have been that precise.

Figuring that there is only one way to find out, you measured again. You took another picture, carefully measured the distance on the photo with a fancy image scanner hooked to a computer, applied the same complicated geometric algorithm, and got . . . 106.41 miles.

"What will I do now?" you pondered. Having little else to do and a large quantity of film available, you decided to measure again and again and again! All told, you measured that distance 25 times. You did exactly the same thing every time, taking care to record each step accurately in a log book and double check your calculations. Not once did you obtain exactly the same measurement. Figure 11.2.2 contains the data you collected.

We are facing a problem of *statistical inference*. We do not know the true, exact distance between the mountain peaks. It exists, but our measuring

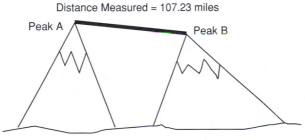

Figure 11.2.1. A distance measuring problem.

Observation	Distance Measured (miles)
1	107.23
2	106.41
3	105.97
4	106.13
5	108.35
6	105.60
7	105.55
8	105.64
9	106.80
10	105.57
11	108.77
12	108.56
13	108.65
14	105.99
15	105.48
16	106.83
17	107.12
18	105.51
19	106.19
20	106.71
21	106.59
22	107.71
23	106.82
24	106.18
25	105.95

Figure 11.2.2. Hypothetical distance measurements.

strategy is imperfect. The best we can do is use the data in the figure to *infer* an answer.

The first thing we have to do is figure out why the numbers are different. It is not that the mountains are moving. They may be on shifting, tectonic plates, but that could not possibly account for variation in the observed distances of a mile or so. Neither is it a case of mistake – like writing down the numbers incorrectly. The spread in the observed distances is being caused by the measuring strategy itself. Even when applied perfectly, there is randomness in the measurement process. This is a general property of measurement. The variation in observed measures has come to be called *measurement error*.

The Idea of Measurement Error

Sometimes, when you measure something, you can get an exact answer like the number of eggs in a carton or the number of days a person is out of work. Other times, however, you are measuring quantitative, continuous variables like your height or weight for which an exact answer is simply impossible. You cannot just say, "I am precisely 6 feet tall" because that is not *exactly* right. No one is exactly 6 feet tall as in

$$6.0000000000. \ldots$$

If we very, very carefully tried to measure height, say to five decimal places, by using special equipment, we would come up with a slightly different number for each measurement such as

$$6.00134, \ 6.00146, \ 6.00121, \ 6.00130, \ \text{and so on.}$$

Measurement error is pure chance error, which cannot be removed. The wind, air pressure, and dust generate extremely small random variations that give ever so slightly different answers. Clearly, more accurate devices can reduce measurement error, but it is impossible to eliminate measurement error entirely.

We must emphasize: in this context, measurement error does not mean there is a mistake in the measuring process. Measurement error does not refer to poor coding, a misreading, or various other "silly mistakes." In most situations, even if you measure as carefully as possible, you will still obtain different results each time the measurement is made. All of your measurements will still be different from the truly, perfectly, ideally exact answer.[2]

Summary

Once we realize that our measurements contain a component driven by pure chance, we are led to modeling the chance process generating the observed data. We are about to see that the situation just described has much in common with other chance processes such as coin flipping, free-throw shooting, games with dice, and polling voters. All of these situations are characterized by a common core idea of the role of chance in generating the observed outcome.

What we have to do to interpret the distance data as generated by a chance process is to model the chance process at work explicitly. For that, we need a box model. This is the topic of the next section.

11.3. The Measurement Box Model

Box models are visual analogies that help us understand the chance process at work. We must understand the way the data are generated before we

---

[2] In this chapter we discuss errors in measuring the dependent variable. Econometricians more commonly use the term "measurement error" when referring to errors in measuring independent variables. This situation, which is also called "errors-in-variables," results in complications that are beyond the scope of this book.

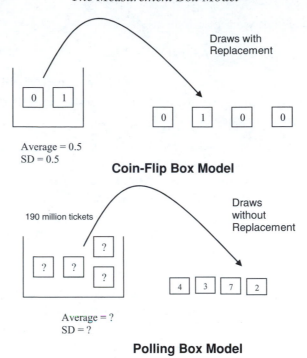

Coin-Flip Box Model

Polling Box Model

Figure 11.3.1. The coin-flip and polling box models.

can begin to apply the logic of statistical inference. Without a box model of the chance process that generated the data, you cannot use the methods of inference described in this chapter. Inferential analysis should always begin with an explicit statement of the chance process you assert generated your data.

Chapter 10 reviews two basic types of box models used to describe different data generation processes, which we summarize in Figure 11.3.1.[3] Both of the box models in Figure 11.3.1 assert that chance is at work in the observed results. Because chance is also at work via the idea of measurement error in our problem of measuring the distance between two peaks, we should be able to model the process – just like we have modeled other chance processes.

A Box Model for Measurement Error

The new box model is associated with Carl Friedrich Gauss (German, rhymes with "house," 1777–1855), who tackled the problem of how to combine astronomical measurements to obtain good estimates of the orbits of celestial

---

[3] We recommend a review of the issues underlying these box models because we are about to introduce a new box model. There are essential similarities we consider extremely helpful in understanding the material that follows.

bodies. We will describe the model in words and then draw a picture of what is going on before turning to a more mathematical presentation. Our idea is that the words and picture will help you develop intuition about the measurement box model that will enhance your understanding of the material.

Having decided that chance is at work in the observed measurements, what do we have to do to link this idea to a box model? We have to be able to say that the measurements are like draws from a certain kind of box. If it is possible to say this, then it is possible to perform statistical inference based on the specific box model to which we have made the analogy. Without a box model, this is not possible.

Here is how the measurement error model can be applied to this situation. Each observation (distance measured in miles in our example) is equal to the true distance plus a number written on a ticket that was drawn at random with replacement from the error box. Thus, the observed distance is actually a composite number because it is made up of two parts: the true distance plus the random draw. The data are interpreted as follows:

Measurement#1 = True Distance + 1st Draw from Error Box
Measurement#2 = True Distance + 2nd Draw from Error Box

· · ·

Measurement#25 = True Distance + 25th Draw from Error Box

The box, from which a random draw is being taken each time we measure, has the following characteristics:

- an unknown, possibly infinite number of tickets;
- the average of the tickets is zero; and
- the SD of the box is unknown.

Note that each measurement has exactly the same true distance component. Yet the observed measurements are different because each measurement has a different random draw value added to the same true distance value.

The sheet *Measuring* in the Measure.xls workbook enables you to disentangle the true distance and random draw values. Click on the | Take a Measurement | button a few times. Excel takes a random draw each time you measure and adds it to the true distance to generate the observed distance. This is the heart of the measurement box model. If necessary it is possible to click on the | Reset | button to clear out all the measurements and start again.

The Measurement Box Model in a Picture

Figure 11.3.2 captures the essential features of the measurement box model. Each measurement is like taking a draw from the box and adding it to the

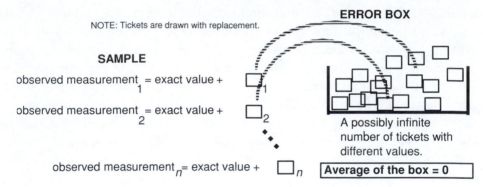

NOTE: Tickets are drawn with replacement.

Figure 11.3.2. The measurement box model.

true, exact value. We assume the average of the box is zero and that each draw is independent of every other draw. Violations of these assumptions are discussed in Chapters 18, 19, and 20. Finally, note that no assumption is made about the exact distribution of the errors. In other words, the histogram of the box contents could have many different shapes so long as the average of the box is zero.[4] More detailed comments about the assumptions can be found in the pages that follow.

Although the average of the box producing the errors is zero, the sample average of the errors actually drawn is almost certainly not zero. The smaller in absolute value the sample average of the errors, the closer our estimate is to the true parameter.

The Measurement Box Model in Equation Form

More formally, the measurement box model is represented like this:

$$y_i = \mu + \varepsilon_i, \quad i = 1, \ldots, n,$$
$$E(\varepsilon_i) = 0, \quad i = 1, \ldots, n$$
$$SD[\varepsilon_i] = \sigma, \quad i = 1, \ldots, n$$
$$\varepsilon_i \text{ is distributed independently of } \varepsilon_j, \forall i, j, i \neq j,$$

where

μ is the true, unknown, exact distance between two mountain peaks,

y_i is the ith observation (measurement),

ε_i is the ith measurement error, and

σ is some nonnegative constant.

---

[4] One technical point: We must also assume that the fourth moment of the error distribution is finite. The fourth moment of a random variable is the expected value of the fourth power of the random variable. In practice this means we are ruling out error term distributions like the Cauchy, which has no expected value and no variance.

We can see each y_i, but we do not know μ, σ, or each individual value of ε_i. The ε_i's are like tickets drawn from the box. There are n observations in total corresponding to the n draws from the box. The number of measurements (n) tells us the number of draws from the box. The first equation, $y_i = \mu + \varepsilon_i$, $i = 1, \ldots, n$, tells us that each observation is the sum of the true distance plus a random variable. The second equation, $E(\varepsilon_i) = 0, i = 1, \ldots, n$, tells us that the expected value of the random variable is zero. The third equation tells us that each and every error term has the same spread (SD, i.e., the errors are homoskedastic). The fourth equation (or rather statement) says that the error terms are independent of one another. Putting the first two equations together, recognizing that the true distance is a constant and taking expectations, we arrive at

$$E(y_i) = \mu, i = 1, \ldots, n,$$

or, in words, the expected value of each observation is the true distance. In plain English, the measuring device is on average right. The first equation plus the statement about independence of the error terms tell us that the measurements themselves are independent of one another.

Now, we do not presume to know the actual contents of the box containing the errors, and so we do not know how big the errors might be in absolute size. Obviously, the more precise the measuring device, the smaller in absolute value the numbers on the tickets will be (i.e., the smaller σ will be). When it is assumed, however, that the process that generated our observations is like drawing tickets from a measurement box, we are making some very important assumptions about the data generating process:

- We assume that the measurement process is *unbiased* when we say that the average of the box is zero. (In equation form, unbiased means $E(y_i) = \mu, i = 1, \ldots, n$.)
- We assume that each measurement is *independent* of every other measurement when we say that we are drawing with replacement from the box.
- We assume that all measurements are alike in the sense that each measurement faces the same array of possible errors when we say that we are drawing from the same box every time. (In statistical jargon, the errors are *identically distributed*; they all have the same expected value and the same SD.)

If these three assumptions do not hold, the statistical results that follow in the next two sections are wrong. Computer software may give you an SE, but it will not be valid. All is not lost, however. It may be possible to come up with a more complicated box model of the data generation process and to compute SEs based on the new model. In fact, violations of these assumptions are an important part of econometrics and are discussed in Chapters 18, 19, and 20.

Comparing the Measurement and Chapter 10 Box Models

We should take a moment to stress the differences between the measurement box model and the two standard box models of basic statistics. In the box models of Chapter 10, the tickets are observable once they are drawn. In the measurement box model, they are not.

We assume that the average of the box is zero for the measurement box. In the two earlier box models, the average of the box may be unknown and not necessarily zero. There may be an infinite number of tickets in the measurement box. In previous box models, the number of tickets in the box is simply the possible outcomes of a game (like two for coin flipping) or the size of the population from which the sample is drawn. In previous box models, we often want to estimate the average of the box. With the measurement box, it is assumed the average is zero and we instead want to estimate something else: a parameter such, as the distance between two objects.

Notice as well the philosophical difference between the measurement model and the polling model. In the latter we are interested in the population average, but we recognize that individuals differ from one another. Some people are taller, and some people shorter. In the measurement model, on the other hand, we believe that all observations measure the same value; the reason they differ is related to the measurement process.

Although it is important to distinguish the measurement box model from other box models, do not forget that all box models share a crucial common bond – chance is at work in generating the observed outcome. This common bond does not merely allow us to organize the world in a convenient fashion, but it facilitates the application of basic ideas of statistical inference to any data that are generated via a chance process.

Summary

Having established a box model for the observed distances, we are ready to make inferences about the true, exact distance between the two peaks. We will follow two routes to statistical inference, using Monte Carlo simulation in Section 11.4 and statistical theory in Section 11.5.

11.4. Monte Carlo Simulation

Workbook: Measure.xls

We are interested in the true, exact distance between the two mountain peaks, but we can only get an estimate from our sample. Because the data can be modeled as if they resulted from a simple random sample of measurement errors, we will be able to apply the methods of statistical inference. On the

assumption that our measurement of the distance between two peaks was unbiased (so that the errors in the box average to zero), the observed distances in our sample are a *composite number* of true distance plus draw from the error box:

$$\text{Individual Measurement} = \text{True Distance} + \text{Chance Error.}$$

The bad news is that we can not get rid of the chance error component of measurement error. In other words, it is not possible to solve for the true distance as follows:

$$\text{True Distance} = \text{Individual Measurement} - \text{Chance Error.}$$

The reason for this is that the chance error of any individual measurement is unknown. But what we can do is take many measurements and use the distribution of individual measurements to make a good guess about the true distance and the spread of observed sample average values. Thus although the components of an individual measurement cannot be disentangled, we can apply the box model to make inferences about the exact value of the unknown parameter and the variation in potential parameter estimates.

Monte Carlo Simulation

In this section Monte Carlo simulation is used to drive home the point that the sample average has a distribution (the probability histogram for the sample average) and to show how that distribution depends on the basic parameters of the model. The Excel workbook Measure.xls shows how. As you explore the sheet called *LiveSample*, click on the cells in the Measured Distance column to see the cell formulas.[5] Notice how the measurement box model is being applied. Hit F9 a few times to draw a new sample of 25 measurements.

Notice that the sample average changes every time you hit F9. Chance is involved in determining the sample average. The average bounces around the true, exact value. What we need is a measure of this variation in the sample average, which is called the SE of the sample average.

Click on the [Show Monte Carlo Simulation] button to take many samples, calculate their average, and get an approximation of the SE of the sample average by calculating the SD of the sample averages. It is an SD, not an SE, because it is based on a finite number of sample averages. The true SE of the sample average is based on an infinite number of samples. Figure 11.4.1 shows the output of one Monte Carlo experiment with 1,000 repetitions.

---

[5] In this workbook the errors are normally distributed. One of Gauss's contributions was to point out that the distribution of the tickets in the error box is immaterial so long as the mean was zero. Thus, we could have used the uniform distribution, for example, and nothing essential would change. More on this is presented in Chapter 14.

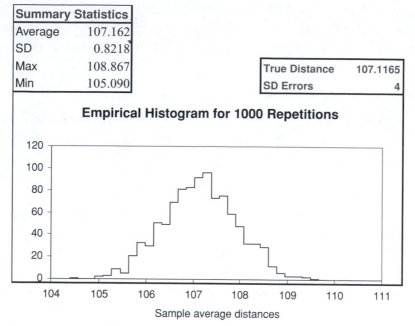

Summary Statistics	
Average	107.162
SD	0.8218
Max	108.867
Min	105.090

True Distance	107.1165
SD Errors	4

Figure 11.4.1. The Monte Carlo approximation to the probability histogram in the distance between two peaks measurement problem.
Source: [Measure.xls]LiveSample.

The True Distance and the precision of the measuring instrument, both of which would be unknown to our scientists, are given in the upper right in red on the Excel sheet. The Average is the average of the 1,000 separate estimates of the distance between the two peaks. Each estimate is the sample average of 25 individual measurements. The SD is the Monte Carlo approximation to the exact SE of the sample average.

As you work with the Monte Carlo simulation, keep in mind that it cannot be used to actually estimate the true distance between the two mountain peaks. Instead, Monte Carlo simulation is a kind of testing ground. Assuming you know the true distance, you can see the kinds of sample results obtained and, of utmost importance, the variability of the sample results.

You can run interesting experiments by changing the precision of the measuring instrument in cell D16 of the *LiveSample* sheet and then rerunning the Monte Carlo simulation. Qualitatively speaking, how does the spread of the empirical histogram pictured in Figure 11.4.1 depend on the precision of the measuring instrument?

Summary

By running Monte Carlo simulations, you should be able to convince yourself, first, that the sample average obtained from a single sample is likely to be a good estimate of the True Distance and, second, that the typical discrepancy between the sample average obtained and the True Distance depends directly on the spread of the tickets in the error box. In more precise statistical terms, the Expected Value of the sample average is the True Distance, and the SE of the sample average depends directly on the SD of the error box. It is to the SE of the sample average that we now turn.

11.5. Applying the Box Model

Workbook: Measure.xls

In the previous section we used Monte Carlo simulation to get a better feel for how the measurement box model works. We saw how Monte Carlo simulation, or drawing many, many samples from a known box, allows us to approximate the probability histogram for the sample averages. In practical applications, however, the key parameters employed to produce the Monte Carlo simulation are unknown – that is, the exact value of the thing we are trying to measure and the SD of the box representing the measurement errors. These parameters allow us to construct the probability histogram via statistical theory or to approximate it via Monte Carlo simulation. Without knowledge of the true parameter values, it would seem that statistical inference based on data from a single sample cannot accomplish very much.

Given the measurement box model for the data generation process, however, it turns out that a great deal can be said about the true value we are trying to measure. To appreciate why, we need to understand the three areas of this box model, as shown in Figure 11.5.1.

The Measure.xls workbook demonstrates these three areas. The *LiveSample* sheet shows both Area 1, the assumptions about the error box, and the data generating process, as captured in the Excel formulas that generate each observation, and Area 3, a single sample.[6] The *MCSim* sheet approximates the probability histogram for the sample average, that is, Area 2.

Statistical theory tells us that the Expected Value of the sample average, the center of the probability histogram, is the exact value (true distance) we are trying to measure. Statistical theory also says that

$$\text{SE(Sample Average)} = \frac{\text{SD(Box)}}{\sqrt{n}},$$

where n is the number of observations. Measure.xls can be used to obtain suggestive evidence in support of both propositions.

---

[6] The formula is "=ROUND(True_Distance+NORMALRANDOM(0,Error_SD),2)." This says that each observation is the sum of the true distance plus a normally distributed random variable that averages 0 and has a given SD. The resulting sum is rounded to two decimal places.

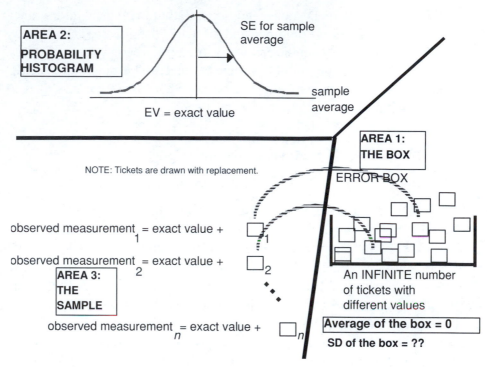

Figure 11.5.1. The three areas of the measurement box model.

This reasoning says that a plausible estimate of the True Distance is just the sample average. We still seem at a loss, however, in trying to determine how far away our sample average is likely to be from the exact value we are trying to measure. We need to know the spread of the error box in order to make this calculation, but the errors are not observed.

A crucial insight of statistical inference is that we can make do with using the SD of the measurements in the sample to estimate the SD of the errors in the box. Students often ask, "But how can one know the spread of the chance error when it cannot even be seen?" The answer is that the spread of the measurements is used to reveal the spread of the chance errors. The key is that we apply a property of the SD of a list of numbers: subtracting the same number from each number in the list, in this case an unknown exact value, leaves the SD unchanged. For a demonstration of this property in the context of this measurement problem, go to the *EstimatingSDBox* sheet of Measure.xls.

Let us apply this thinking to our concrete example of the distance between two mountain peaks. One simple random sample, if explicitly tied to a box model, can be used to make inferences about an unknown population parameter. In Figure 11.5.2, we estimate the true distance between the two peaks. It is important when applying this procedure to keep in mind that the point estimate itself is not the only important piece of information needed – we

Observation	Distance Measured (miles)
1	107.23
2	106.41
3	105.97
4	106.13
5	108.35
6	105.60
7	105.55
8	105.64
9	106.80
10	105.57
11	108.77
12	108.56
13	108.65
14	105.99
15	105.48
16	106.83
17	107.12
18	105.51
19	106.19
20	106.71
21	106.59
22	107.71
23	106.82
24	106.18
25	105.95

APPLYING THE BOX MODEL

106.652 sample average
1.043 sample SD

0.209 estimated SE of the sample average

The estimate for the true distance is the sample average, 106.652 miles.
The typical discrepancy between this estimate and the unobserved true distance is 0.209 miles.

Figure 11.5.2. Estimating the true distance and the SE based on a single sample. *Source:* [Measure.xls]DeadSample.

also need to know the spread in the estimate (i.e., the SE of the sample average). To find this SE we need to know the SD of the box (i.e., the precision of the measuring instrument). We do not observe the SD of the box, but it is possible to estimate it via the SD of the measurements. Armed with an estimated SD of the box, we can estimate the SE of the sample average via the standard formula. In the data described by Figure 11.5.2, the sample SD was 1.02. Therefore, the estimated SE of the sample average is $\frac{1.043}{\sqrt{25}} \cong 0.209$. This SE can be estimated only if the box model is specified and its conditions are met.

Summary

We conclude this section by discussing what could cause statistical inference to fail in the context of the measurement box model. Statistical inference can break down

- If the measurement process is *biased*. If did not notice that your ruler had the first inch snapped off so that when you read off $4\frac{1}{8}$ inches it was actually $3\frac{1}{8}$ inches, that would be bias.

- If the errors are not independent of one another. This is called *autocorrelation* or *serial correlation*. If you used a machine to read off the distance from the photo and it somehow kept the last measurement in memory, the next measurement would depend on the previous measurement.
- If the measurements are not all alike – that is, we were not always drawing from the same box and thus the errors are not identically distributed. This condition is known as *heteroskedasticity*.

Here is an example of heteroskedasticity: If you ran out of film on the tenth measurement and substituted a high-powered laser beam device to measure the peaks, you would not want simply to mix the observations together – the more precise laser beam observations should carry more weight.

We explore all of these problems in later chapters. In all three cases the box model does not apply, and inference using computed estimates and SEs gives incorrect answers.[7] The computer program used to analyze your data is unable to catch these violations of the measurement box model. The computer software assumes the data do not violate the requirements. Human judgment is required to determine how the data were generated before the data are submitted to the computer. This is worth remembering.

11.6. Hooke's Law

Workbook: HookesLaw.xls

In this section, we take an important step by extending the measurement model to cover the case of bivariate regression. Our fictional example comes from the world of physics. Robert Hooke (1653–1703, British) hypothesized that the "stretchiness" of a spring is proportional to the load placed on it. Expressed as an equation, Hooke's law relates the length of a spring to the load placed on it like this:

Length of spring (in cm) = Length with no load on it (in cm) $+ m \cdot$ Weight of the load (in kg), where m is a constant of proportionality measured in cm/kg known as the spring constant. Let us accept this as true – that is, it is absolutely true that the springiness of a spring is proportional to the weight placed on it.[8]

Every spring has an intrinsic value of m. Now, suppose you were asked to estimate the constant of proportionality for a particular spring. You enter the laboratory and are given a spring of some unknown springiness, some weights,

---

[7] There is one exception to this statement: heteroskedasticity in the univariate case (see Section 19.2). However, in the bivariate and multivariate cases, heteroskedasticity does impair inference.

[8] Actually, for you physics experts out there, Hooke's law is merely a linear approximation that works well within certain bounds. Physicists also point out that Hooke's law can be applied to any object. Hanging a board in the air and placing a weight at the bottom "stretches" the board (albeit not much!) and puts "stress" (vertical pressure) and "strain" (horizontal pressure) on the board.

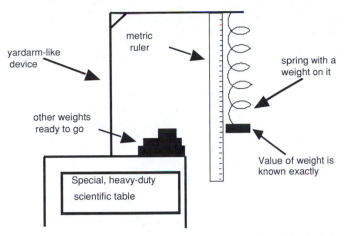

Figure 11.6.1. Experimental apparatus for testing Hooke's law.

and a ruler. Your job is to figure out the springiness of that particular spring. It has a constant of proportionality but its value is unknown. You proceed by hanging the spring from a small yardarm-type lab device and placing a weight on it, as in Figure 11.6.1.

You carefully measure and record the length of the spring with different weights (of known values) on the end of the spring. Obviously, when a weight is placed on the spring, it stretches. Thus, you end up with a measurement of the length of the spring for each given weight. When measuring the different lengths of the spring with the differing weights, you are careful to prevent one measurement from influencing another and ensure that the measuring process used is the same for every weight.

To analyze the data and arrive at an estimate of the springiness of our apparatus, we need a model of the data generation process. We will adapt the measurement box model to this new situation. The data generation process looks like Figure 11.6.2.

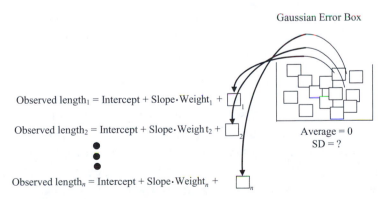

Figure 11.6.2. Box model for Hooke's law experiment.

As before, the errors are independent and identically distributed. They have an average of zero and an unknown SD. Their being identically distributed implies that the errors are independent of the weights. In plain English, this independence assumption says that a heavier than average weight does not mean, for example, that the measurement error is more likely to be positive, nor does a heavier than average weight mean that the spread of the measurement error increases. We highlight the independence of the error terms and the X variables because this turns out to be a very important assumption in models of data generation processes.

You can see a virtual version of the problem by exploring the sheet called *OneObs* in the HookesLaw.xls workbook. Do this now. Follow the instructions in the *OneObs* sheet to get a complete understanding of the concept that there is one, unchanging true length of the spring determined by the intercept and slope parameters.

By convention, econometricians represent the parameters with Greek letters:

$$\text{True Length of Spring}_i = \beta_0 + \beta_1 \text{Weight}_i, i = 1, \ldots, n.$$

The "i" subscript indexes observations. There are n observations. The *OneObs* sheet uses color as a guide. Red text means the number cannot be seen in real-world situations. But just because a variable cannot be directly observed does not mean it is unimportant or irrelevant. In fact, we know there is a true length built on the unknown intercept and slope we are trying to estimate.

The *OneObs* sheet also drives home the point that the observed length of the spring is different from the true length of the spring. The reason for this discrepancy is measurement error. Every time the spring is measured, an error resulting from that particular measurement is added to its true length. Thus, if we denote the error for the ith measurement by ε_i,

$$\text{Observed Length of Spring}_i = \text{True Length}_i + \varepsilon_i.$$

This formulation highlights the similarity between the more complicated bivariate model of this section and the univariate measurement error model considered in earlier sections of this chapter. Equivalently,

$$\text{Observed Length of Spring}_i = \beta_0 + \beta_1 \text{Weight}_i + \varepsilon_i.$$

Click the Get One Measurement button several times to build a data set. Each time you click the button, think about the data generation process. The crucial concept is that the observed length of the spring is composed of a fixed component (Intercept + Slope · Weight) plus an error term. Proceed to the *OneSample* sheet to see a data set with 100 observations. Each observation was generated as before. Figure 11.6.3 shows the generation of one sample.

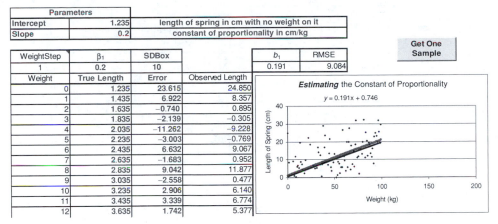

Figure 11.6.3. One sample.
Source: [HookesLaw.xls]OneSample.

Hitting F9 recalculates the entire workbook and draws 100 new observations in a flash. The fundamental idea demonstrated in this sheet is that the estimated slope is a random variable. Click the Get One Sample button (or simply hit the F9 key) and watch the dots, black line, and the m and b values in the $y = mx + b$ trend line display bounce around. The red line, however, stays perfectly still because it is based on the fixed parameters, not the estimated coefficients. The distinction between the bouncing behavior of the sample and the fixed red line is a crucial concept.

It is clear that the dots are dancing on the screen because they contain measurement error (via the data generation process explained in detail in the *OneObs* sheet). Because the fitted black line is based on the sample data, its intercept and slope will also be bouncing. The red line, however, contains no measurement error at all. It is a fixed, unchanging truth that we are trying to discern.

In inferential analysis, it is important to keep straight what is a parameter and what is an estimate. Econometricians use Greek letters to represent parameters and unobservable variables (in this chapter, we have seen μ, β, ε, and σ). We will use lowercase English alphabet letters to designate estimated parameters. For example, we use the symbol b_1 to designate our estimate of β_1. Many econometricians use hats ("circumflexes") to indicate an estimate of a parameter; thus, $\hat{\beta}_1$ would indicate the estimated value of β_1.

We present estimates of the regression slope, b_1, and the RMSE. It should be obvious that the slope estimate is fluctuating around the true value of the spring constant, which in this example is 0.2. The RMSE oscillates around the true value of the SD of the measurement box, which is 10 in this case.

The *MCSim* sheet drives home the notion that the estimated slope, b_1, is a random variable by running a Monte Carlo simulation. In each repetition,

Sample Slope Summary Statistics		Population Parameters	
Average	0.2019	Slope	0.2
SD	0.0336	Intercept	1.234567
Max	0.2983	SDBox	10
Min	0.1007	**Exact SE Slope**	**0.0346**

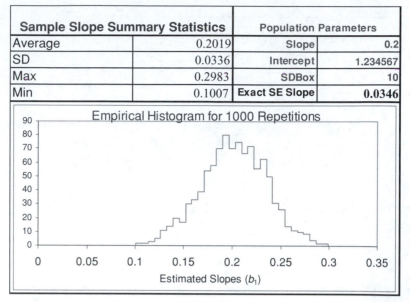

Figure 11.6.4. Monte Carlo simulation of the estimated slope.
Source: [HookesLaw.xls]MCSim.

100 observations are taken and a least squares line is fitted to the data. The estimated slope for each of the first 100 repetitions is recorded in column B. The sheet provides summary statistics and an empirical histogram of the 1,000 estimated slopes, as shown in Figure 11.6.4. The empirical histogram is an approximation to the probability histogram or sampling distribution of the slope estimate.

The Monte Carlo simulation makes clear that the estimated slope is a random variable. The good news is that it is apparently centered on the true, exact constant of proportionality, which suggests we have an unbiased estimator. The SD of the 1,000 estimated slopes, in this case .0336 is an approximation to the exact SE of the estimated slope, which is 0.0346 in this example. (The exact SE can be computed analytically, which is how the Exact SE Slope is being calculated in cell H7.) We explain the concepts of bias and the exact SE in detail in Chapter 14.

Summary

We used Hooke's law to show how the measurement box model can be applied in the context of a bivariate regression. The sample coefficients b_0 and b_1 from a regression of observed length of spring on weight are random variables with a probability histogram (or sampling distribution). The parameters β_0 and β_1 can be estimated from the sample data. The measurement error box model as applied to bivariate regression looks very similar to the box model as applied to univariate measurement. An important refinement arises from the presence of an independent variable: As noted, a crucial assumption is that the error terms are independent of the X variables.

11.7. Conclusion

The measurement box model described in this chapter was originally developed to handle the problem of modeling the data generating process for astronomical observations. Astronomy and economics may seem to be only distantly related fields. Nonetheless, the measurement box model is very closely related to the classical econometric model, which, as its name implies, has been the standard model for the data generating process for economic variables. The mathematical features of the measurement model – errors that are mean zero and are independently and identically distributed and observed values that are the sum of the error term and functions that are linear in the parameters of one or more independent variables – are shared by the classical econometric model. In Chapter 14 we will see that these common features imply that, for both models, the ordinary least squares estimator has certain optimal properties.

The difference between the measurement model and the classical econometric model has to do with the explanation of the data generating process. In the measurement model, the only reason univariate data differ from one another and the only reason bivariate data do not all lie on the same single regression line is the imperfection of the measurement process. In the classical econometric model there are other, more complicated, reasons for these discrepancies.

Although the measurement model provides concepts and intuition that will serve us well, we are not ready to jump into the classical econometric model. Chapter 12 considers an alternative means of describing the data generating process for economic variables. That chapter continues to use the basic box model metaphor, but the interpretation of the box contents is different.

11.8. Exercises

1. In this book we develop two different languages for describing data generation processes. The first uses the box model metaphor, whereas the second employs formal mathematical symbols. What box model concepts correspond to each of these formal mathematical symbols, statements, and equations?
   a. ε_i
   b. σ
   c. $E(\varepsilon_i) = 0, i = 1, \ldots, n$
   d. $SD(\varepsilon_i) = \sigma, i = 1, \ldots, n$
   e. ε_i is distributed independently of $\varepsilon_j, \forall i, j, i \neq j$.
   f. $y_i = \mu + \varepsilon_i, i = 1, \ldots, n$.

Summary Statistics	
Average	105.035
SD	0.8127
Max	107.630
Min	102.597

Figure 11.8.1. Results from Monte Carlo experiment.
Source: [Measure.xls]MCSim.

2. Suppose that the measuring device described in Sections 11.2 to 11.5 was systematically biased – in particular that the measurements on average were 0.5 km too big but all the other assumptions about the box model still held true. How would Figure 11.5.1, which shows the three areas of the measurement box model, change?

3. In the univariate measurement model described in Measure.xls, the residual is defined as the difference between the individual measurement and the sample average. No matter how many times you make 25 new measurements, in the *LiveSample* sheet you will notice that the residuals always average to zero (see cell E21). Why does this happen? The answer requires a little algebra.

4. Suppose you obtained the data in Figure 11.8.1 from the Measure.xls workbook. Note that the true distance is not revealed. You are told that in the Monte Carlo experiment there were 1,000 repetitions. In each repetition, 25 measurements were taken of the unknown distance. You are asked to give your best estimate of the true distance. What will it be and why?

5. Reconsider the hypothetical Galileo story of Section 6.2. Write down a measurement box model of the data generation process for Galileo's data on time and distance of a falling object.

References

Galileo actually plays a role in the development of the measurement model. According to Hald (1998, p. 33), the ideas that there is a true value to be estimated, that all observations suffer from error, and that errors are distributed symmetrically about zero were clearly put forth by Galileo in 1632:

Hald, Anders (1998). *A History of Mathematical Statistics from 1750 to 1930.* New York: John Wiley and Sons.

Two hundred years later, Gauss perfected the measurement model and worked out the properties of the ordinary least squares estimator when applied to data generated according to the model. The quotation from Gauss comes from

Gauss, Carl Friedrich (1857, 1963). *Theory of the Motion of the Heavenly Bodies Moving about the Sun in Conic Sections: A Translation of Gauss's "Theoria motus." With an appendix.* Boston, Little, Brown and Company, 1857. Reissued by Dover Publications, New York, 1963.

We found the quotation on page 96 of

Lee, Peter M. (n.d.) *Lectures on the History of Statistics.* Manuscript available from Peter Lee's History of Statistics page: <www.york.ac.uk/depts/maths/teaching/pml/hos/welcome.htm>.

This chapter owes a great deal to Freedman et al. (1998). All of the key ideas of this chapter, other than the use of Monte Carlo simulations, can be found in Chapters 6, 12, and 24 of their book.

12

Comparing Two Populations

Never will we know if the value of a statistic for a particular set of data is correct.

David Salsburg[1]

12.1. Introduction

In this brief chapter, we introduce yet another data generation process called the two box model. We will see how the sample average difference is distributed through Monte Carlo simulation and analytical methods.

The two box model is an extension of the polling box model (explained in detail in Chapter 10) and provides further practice with inferential methods. Although the rapidly expanding list of box models may seem daunting, do not despair. The same basic principles about variability of sample statistics and understanding the sampling distribution underlie all data generation processes.

Our approach in presenting the various box models is meant to illustrate the point that a properly configured box model can represent a wide variety of chance processes. We are also slowly building toward the box model that underlies regression analysis in an inferential setting.

Section 12.2 introduces the two box model, and Section 12.3 offers a Monte Carlo simulation to explore the sampling distribution of the same average difference. Section 12.4 presents a real-world application of the two box model.

12.2. Two Boxes

The two box model is essentially two polling box models combined. Instead of estimating a parameter or testing a hypothesis about a single population – for instance, the average wage of California residents – we are interested in

---

[1] Salsburg (2001, p. 66).

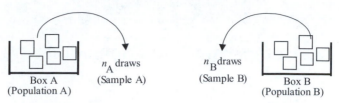

Figure 12.2.1. A picture of the two box model.

a comparison of two populations (e.g., the difference in the average wages of California and Nevada residents).

If we want to estimate the difference in average wages between men and women or test whether men have higher wages than women, the two box model might apply. Another example would be to estimate the difference in average SAT scores between the 1985 and 1995 test-taking cohorts[2] or determine whether students' scores on the SAT are statistically significantly different between 1985 and 1995 (on the assumption that the test has not changed in difficulty or scoring during that time).

Notice how these examples focus on estimating the difference in population averages or testing a hypothesis about the difference. In either case, the SE of the difference of the sample average will play a prominent role. We need a box model as well as data to obtain an estimate of the SE of the difference. Without a box model, we cannot obtain the SE.

A Two Box Model for Comparing Populations

Because we are comparing two different populations, we have two different boxes. Sample A is drawn from Box A, and Sample B is drawn from Box B. For the methods of this section to apply, the samples must be simple random samples that are independent of one another. They may be drawn without replacement, but we will assume that the number of tickets is large relative to the number of draws and thus that no correction factor is needed.

The two box model is depicted in Figure 12.2.1. Each box has a large, but finite, number of tickets representing each person in the population. There is a fixed, unknown average of each box and, therefore, a fixed, unknown difference of the population averages. This, of course, is what we are trying to estimate or infer. In addition, each box has a fixed, unknown standard deviation.

We will use Sample A to calculate the sample average of A and do the same for B. The difference between the two sample averages is our estimate of the difference between the two population averages. Chance or sampling

---

[2] In economics and demographics, a cohort is a group of people who all enter the scene at the same point in time.

error is in a realized sample average because not all of the tickets are drawn. Draw another sample and it will have a different set of tickets and thus a different sample average. Because the sample averages are random variables, the difference of the sample averages is also a random variable.

We need a new SE, the SE of the difference of the sample averages, to provide a give or take number on our estimate of the difference between the two population averages. To test a hypothesis about the difference between the population averages, this SE is also required to construct a z-statistic and get the P-value for a hypothesis test. The calculation of the SE is a little different than in the one-box case, but otherwise the process is the same.

Getting the SE of the Difference

We construct the SE of each sample average, SE_A for sample A and SE_B for sample B, as discussed in Section 10.4 (estimating the SD of each box, if necessary). Then, the SE of the difference of the sample averages is a function of SE_A and SE_B, following a square-root law, like this:

$$SEDifference = \sqrt{SE_A^2 + SE_B^2}.$$

This formula assumes that the samples are independent, simple random samples. If the samples are dependent or are not simple random samples, the SE will not be correct, and analyses that use the SE (such as hypothesis testing) will not be reliable.[3]

Once we have the SE of the difference of the sample averages, we can use it as the give or take number on our estimate, generate confidence intervals, and run hypothesis tests. We can find the z-statistic, in the usual way, like this:

$$z = \frac{\text{observed difference} - \text{hypothesized difference}}{\text{SE of the difference}}.$$

The P-value is the probability of drawing a sample that has this z-statistic, or one more extreme, if the null hypothesis is true. In large samples, the P-value can be computed using the normal distribution.

Summary

This section introduced the two box model and presented a formula for the SE of the difference of the sample average. The next section presents an example

---

[3] The formula for the SE of the difference of the sample averages can be derived via the algebra of expectations. Apply the rule for the variance and SD of a sum of independent random variables as shown in Section 10.7.

of the two box model in Excel that provides a concrete demonstration of how the samples are generated. It makes clear that the difference of the sample averages is a random variable with a sampling distribution.

12.3. Monte Carlo Simulation of a Two Box Model

Workbook: TwoBoxModel.xls

In this section we explore the sampling properties of the two box model. We focus on explicitly demonstrating the data generation process and empha-size the variability of the difference of the sample averages. When you draw two simple random samples from two separate populations and compare the sample averages, it is possible to create an *estimate* of the difference of the population averages.

Unfortunately, because you do not have the population averages them-selves, it is not possible to use the observed sample difference to make a definitive statement about the difference of the averages in the population. The difference of the sample averages is a good guess, but it has an inherent variability captured by the SE of the difference. This fundamental lesson is the heart of the TwoBoxModel.xls workbook.

Setting Up The Two Box Model

Go to the *HighSchool* sheet in the TwoBoxModel.xls workbook. Click the Make a Box Model button and provide the necessary information. The first time you create a box model, make the population small – for example, 100. Choose the default log normal distribution because wage distributions usually have long right-hand tails. Make the average wage in the population $10 per hour and the SD $5 per hour. A population histogram appears. Set the sample size at 25. The resulting parameters should look like Figure 12.3.1.

Clicking the Draw a Sample One Ticket at a Time button takes one draw, without replacement, from the population. The chosen observation is then reported, its cell is colored green in column A, and the value is written in column J. Scroll down (if

Parameters
Number Tickets
100
Average of the Box
$ 10.00
SD
$ 5.00
Number of Draws
25
Distribution of Box
Log Normal

Figure 12.3.1. Parameter settings for the two box model simulation.
Source: [TwoBoxModel.xls]HighSchool.

Parameters
Number Tickets
100
Average of the Box
$ 15.00
SD
$ 10.00
Number of Draws
25
Distribution of Box
Log Normal

Figure 12.3.2. Parameter settings for the two box model simulation.
Source: [TwoBoxModel.xls]College.

needed) until you spot the observation that was drawn. It is now out of the population and cannot be drawn again. Click the [Draw a Sample One Ticket at a Time] button a few times until you get the idea of how the sample is being generated. When you tire of drawing tickets one at a time, click the Cancel button on the message box.

Clicking the [Draw a Sample] button takes an entire sample, drawn without replacement, from the population and places it in column J (and column A of the *Difference* sheet). The sample average and SD are reported in cells G11 and G13. The correction factor (which is increasingly important as the number of draws approaches the total number of tickets in the population) is displayed in cell G23. The estimated (using the sample SD) and exact (using the population SD) standard errors of the sample average are reported in cells G25 and G26.

Click the [Draw a Sample] button several times. Note that the tickets in the population and parameters (in red) remain fixed, whereas the sample itself and all statistics based on the sample vary. The exact SE remains constant (because the SD of the box does not change), but the estimated SE bounces (because it is based on a bouncing sample SD).

Proceed to the *College* sheet and click on the [Make a Box Model] button. Create a box model with the parameters shown in Figure 12.3.2. As with the *High-School* sheet, you can create a sample one draw at a time or generate an entire sample by simply clicking the [Draw a Sample] button. The sample is displayed in column J and column B of the *Difference* sheet.

The *Difference* sheet shows the observed High School and College wages. Confirm that column A in the *Difference* sheet is identical to column J in the *HighSchool* sheet. Column B, of course, is a copy of the College sample. The *Difference* sheet displays the average and SD for each group and the difference of the sample averages. We obtained the results reported in Figure 12.3.3. Your results will be different because you have different samples.

The difference of the sample averages of $1.40 per hour is an estimate of the difference of the true or population average, which we know is $5 per hour. The estimate is off the true value because of sampling or chance error.

	Sample Average	Sample SD
High School	$ 12.10	$ 5.17
College	$ 13.50	$ 9.26
Difference (C-HS)	$ 1.40	

Figure 12.3.3. High school and college sample outcomes.
Source: [TwoBox.xls]Difference.

There are a few more high-wage high schoolers and a few more low-wage college grads in these two particular samples than one might have expected.

Of course, the presence of chance error in the sample flows into the sample averages and the difference of the sample averages. Thus, the difference of the sample average is a random variable with a sampling distribution.

Monte Carlo Simulation

Click the Draw a Sample from Each Box button in the *Difference* sheet to see the difference of the sample averages (in cell E4) bounce around. There is no doubt about it – each set of new samples pulled from the high school and college populations generates new sample averages and a new difference of the sample average. We could build up an approximation to the probability histogram of the difference of the sample average by tracking each cell E4 result after drawing new samples, but that would be slow and tedious.

Proceed to the *MCSim* sheet to see a much faster and easier approach. Each repetition consists of drawing a high school and college sample and then computing the difference of the averages of the two sample groups. With many repetitions, an approximation to the sampling distribution or probability histogram of the difference of the sample averages emerges.

Run your own Monte Carlo simulation by clicking on the Run Monte Carlo Simulation button and compare your results to those reported in Figure 12.3.4. Notice that the average of 10,000 differences of the sample averages, 4.994, is close to the difference of the population averages, 5.00. This suggests that the sampling distribution is unbiased – that is, it is centered on the true population difference. The SD of the 10,000 differences, 1.932, is also a good approximation of the exact SE of the difference of the sample averages, 1.946. The latter was computed using the square-root formula and the known population SDs. The Monte Carlo results support the formula for the exact SE of the difference of sample average.

That the sampling distribution is approximately normal even though the populations are log normally distributed demonstrates the central limit theorem. Finally, note that the minimum difference in 10,000 repetitions was −$1.64 per hour. For that particular realization of the chance process, the high school average wage was actually greater than the college average. The

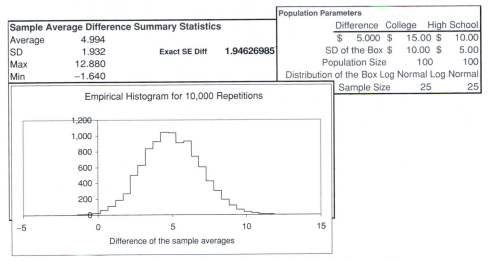

Population Parameters		
Difference	College	High School
$ 5.000	$ 15.00	$ 10.00
SD of the Box $ 10.00	$ 5.00	
Population Size	100	100
Distribution of the Box	Log Normal	Log Normal
Sample Size	25	25

Sample Average Difference Summary Statistics			
Average	4.994		
SD	1.932	**Exact SE Diff**	1.94626985
Max	12.880		
Min	−1.640		

Figure 12.3.4. Two box Monte Carlo simulation results.
Source: [TwoBoxModel.xls]MCSim.

empirical histogram shows that there were a few samples in which the difference of the sample averages was negative.

Summary

This section has demonstrated a two box model by using a fictional scenario in which we sampled from artificial high school and college populations. We showed that the difference of the sample averages is a random variable and verified the formula for calculating the SE (the square root of sum of the squared individual sample SEs).

The TwoBoxModel.xls workbook allows for experimentation. Explore how the SE of the difference changes as the number of draws increases or the underlying SDs of the boxes change. Try changing the population distributions to see how the sampling distribution is affected.

The next section uses a real-world example to illustrate the two box model. We will not know the true parameters, and thus they will need to be estimated. It will not be possible to take repeated samples, but we know the one sample we have is a single outcome from the random process that generated the data.

12.4. A Real Example: Education and Wages

Workbook: CPS90Workers.xls

This section explores an actual example of the two box model. We will use samples from two populations to make inferences about the difference between the two population averages. This example will be used to show the logical order involved in a hypothesis test. We present the research question and then proceed through a series of steps to answer the question.

The Research Question

Does education increase a person's wage? More precisely, if other factors that influence wages are held constant, do college-educated workers earn more than workers who have only a high school education? Human capital theory says that education increases the productive capacity of individuals. An individual obtaining an education is like a firm investing in physical capital: current outlays (tuition and foregone earnings) increase future returns (earnings from future jobs). If education increases productivity, it should increase wages.

Of course, we cannot simply compare the sample average wages of workers with college and high school degrees because we know the sample averages and sample difference are random variables. An average wage for college-educated workers might be obtained that is higher than the average wage of their high school counterparts just by pure chance. In other words, perhaps the population average wages are in fact the same and it was just luck that we drew a few more highly paid college workers and a few more lower paid high school workers. A hypothesis test will enable us to handle this issue.

The Null and Alternative Hypotheses

To conduct a hypothesis test, we need to define a null hypothesis and an alternative hypothesis.

Null Hypothesis: The average wage of workers with a college degree is equal to the average wage of workers with only a high school degree.

Alternative Hypothesis: The average wage of workers with a college degree is higher than the average wage of workers with only a high school degree.

Notice that the null represents the default answer that there really is no difference. Observed sample differences are caused by chance alone. We will test the null and decide to reject or not reject it.

The Data

The data that we will use to investigate this question come from the March 1990 Current Population Survey. They consist of two random samples of workers from the entire population of those people who had a job in

Data	Education		
	12	16	Grand Total
Average of Wage	$ 9.31	$ 14.06	$ 10.61
StdDev of Wage	$ 4.99	$ 7.14	$ 6.04
Max of Wage	$ 40.00	$ 44.23	$ 44.23
Min of Wage	$ 1.00	$ 1.38	$ 1.00
Count of Wage	819	308	1127

Figure 12.4.1. Summarizing wage data by high school and college. *Source*: [CPS90Workers.xls]PivotTable.

March 1990. For each observation (corresponding to an individual person), we have values for the following variables:

$$Education = \text{highest grade completed, in years}$$

$$Wage = \text{reported hourly wage, in \$ per hour}$$

The first sample, which has 819 observations, is a random sample of all those working in March 1990 who had 12 years of education (i.e., a high school degree). The second sample, which has 308 observations, is a random sample of all those working in March 1990 who had 16 years of education (i.e., a college degree).

A PivotTable in the CPS90Workers.xls workbook, shown in Figure 12.4.1, summarizes the data from the two groups.

Is the Difference Real or Due to Chance?

The college grad sample has a higher average wage than the high school sample. Have we found the answer to our question? Should we conclude that the population of people with 16 years of education has a higher average wage than the population of people with 12 years of education? Not yet. Although the sample averages support an affirmative answer, there is still the possibility that the population averages are actually equal and the difference observed is simply due to the luck of the draw. To determine if this difference is real or due to chance, we need to use a test of significance. To do this, we need to construct a box model that represents the data generation process.

Setting Up the Box Model

The first box contains individual wages of workers who have 12 years of education. The second box contains the wages of workers who have 16 years of education. Figure 12.4.2 depicts the two box model and actual samples in this case. We will argue that the data were generated according to Figure 12.4.2. In fact, the CPS uses a cluster sampling scheme, not the pure

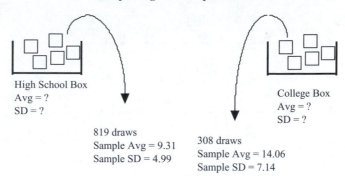

High School Box
Avg = ?
SD = ?

College Box
Avg = ?
SD = ?

819 draws
Sample Avg = 9.31
Sample SD = 4.99

308 draws
Sample Avg = 14.06
Sample SD = 7.14

Figure 12.4.2. The box model for comparing high school and college wages.

simple random sampling design required by the two box model. The cluster sampling means our computation of the SE of the difference in the sample average is a little off. We can legitimately argue, however, that the data were generated by a random process. For the purposes of illustrating the two box model, we will proceed as if the two box model applies.

We believe it is of utmost importance to tie the data to a box model. You cannot use the sophisticated methods explained in this book to determine the variability of a sample statistic unless the data generation process is explicitly connected to a box model. Often, the tie will not be exact. In this case, it is best to state the lack of agreement in the actual DGP from the ideal box model being used to justify the application of statistical methods.

Figure 12.4.2 allows us to recast our null and alternative hypotheses in the language of the box model.

Null Hypothesis: Both boxes have the same average, or, the difference between the averages is equal to zero.

Alternative Hypothesis: The college box has a higher average than the high school box, or, the difference between the average for the college box and the average of the high school box is positive.

Constructing the Test Statistic and Interpreting the Results

With a box model that reflects the data generating process, explicit statements of the null and alternative hypotheses, and sample data, we are ready to construct the test statistic. We will use the z-statistic because the sample sizes are large enough that we know, from the central limit theorem, the sampling distribution of the difference of the sample averages is approximately normal. We know the observed difference: it is 4.75 (=14.06 − 9.31). The null hypothesis gives us the hypothesized difference, which is zero. To find the z-statistic, we still need the SE of the difference.

The sample of 819 workers with 12 years of education has an SD of 4.99. Using this SD as the SD of the high school population, we get an estimated

SE of the sample average equal to

$$\frac{4.99}{\sqrt{819}} = \frac{4.99}{28.62} \approx 0.17.$$

The sample of 308 workers with 16 years of education has an SD of 7.139. Using this SD as the SD of the college box, we obtain an estimated SE of the sample average equal to

$$\frac{7.14}{\sqrt{308}} = \frac{7.14}{17.55} \approx 0.41.$$

The SE of the difference between these two sample averages is

$$\sqrt{SE_A^2 + SE_B^2} = \sqrt{0.17^2 + 0.41^2}$$

$$= \sqrt{0.0289 + 0.1681}$$

$$= 0.44.$$

The z-statistic, then, is

$$\frac{4.75}{0.44} \approx 10.7.$$

The z-statistic tells us that, if the null is true, the observed difference is 10.7 standard errors away from the hypothesized difference of zero.

The P-value for this z-statistic is tiny. We reject the null that there is no difference in the average wage of high school and college-educated people in the United States in March 1990 because our sample result (or one more extreme) is ridiculously unlikely to have been observed if there really were no difference.

A Brief Note on Confounding

The data confirm that college-educated workers earn more than workers with only a high school education. Suppose, however, we want to know whether getting a college education will increase your wage if everything else is held constant. If we take someone who currently has a high school education and send that person to college, will that person's hourly wage increase by 5 dollars? This is a more difficult question to answer, and we may not be able to answer it if there is confounding. If the two populations are not alike in every way except for their level of education, then we may have confounding. The test of our null hypothesis does not tell us whether there is confounding and may lead us to the wrong conclusion if confounding exists.

Virtually every study shows that better educated workers have higher wages. Much controversy, however, remains over the interpretation of this result. Do better educated workers have higher wages because the schooling improves their productivity or because they were more talented in the first place? Perhaps people who are less talented get less schooling because they do not like education. In other words, another factor, innate ability, may be confounding the comparison between the wages of the two groups. Econometricians also use the term omitted variable bias to describe this situation. We discuss this issue in more detail in Chapter 18.

Summary

This section has been devoted to a real-world application of the two box model with an emphasis on the logic of hypothesis testing. We estimated the difference in the average wage between college and high school educated workers with the sample difference. Given a concern that the observed difference might be due to chance alone, we ran a test of significance.

We began the hypothesis test by explicitly tying the data from the CPS sample to the two box model. The tie was not perfect, but it was close enough. The important lesson is that we made an argument for using the two box model. Without this argument, we cannot justify the use of the formula for the SE of the difference in the sample averages. The rest of the testing procedure was fairly mechanical. We constructed a test statistic, computed the corresponding *P*-value, and made a decision to reject the null.

12.5. Conclusion

This brief chapter serves as a stepping stone to our eventual goal, the classical econometric model. By examining a data generation process in which two groups are being compared (for example, wages of high school versus college educated people), we are taking a small step toward a regression that explores the effect of education on earnings.

This chapter especially emphasizes the idea that a sample difference between two groups is a random variable that changes with each new sample. Although the sample difference is important, remember that the SE of the sample difference is also crucial. Without this give or take number, we have no way of knowing whether the observed sample difference reflects an actual difference between the two population averages. Every statistic derived from a data generation process has a sampling distribution, and much effort is focused on determining the center, spread, and shape of the statistic's probability histogram. Of course, if the sample was not generated by a random process, you have no business applying the methods demonstrated here.

These lessons remain in force as we turn to the next chapter, which introduces the classical econometric model.

12.6. Exercises

Workbook: CPS90ExpWorkers.xls

These exercises are organized around the research question: Does experience increase a person's wage in the United States?

Open the Excel workbook, CPS90ExpWorkers.xls. The *Intro* sheet explains the variables.

1. Report the average wage for Experienced and Inexperienced workers.
2. The difference between the average wage of the Experienced workers and the average wage of the Inexperienced workers is $3.10 per hour. Why can we not conclude that experience raises a person's wage based on this fact?
3. Draw a two box model that represents the data generation process.
4. State the null and alternative hypotheses.
5. Find the SE of the difference of the sample averages. Show your work.
6. On the assumption that the null is true, draw a rough sketch of the sampling distribution of the difference of the sample averages. Mark the location of the $3.10 per hour difference we observed in our sample.
7. Would you reject the null hypothesis? Explain.

References

We drew on Freedman et al. (1998), Chapter 27 for our discussion of the two box model. The two box model is nonstandard terminology describing a test of differences between means. Hypothesis testing has long been a source of confusion. For a well written account of the logic behind hypothesis testing and a fun introduction to the history of statistics, we recommend

Salsburg, D. (2001). *The Lady Tasting Tea: How Statistics Revolutionized Science in the Twentieth Century*. New York: Henry Holt and Company.

Salzburg's explanation of the source of the term *significant* is worth quoting as follows:

Somewhere early in the development of this general idea, the word significant came to be used to indicate that the probability was low enough for rejection. Data became significant if they could be used to reject a proposed distribution. The word was used in its late-nineteenth-century English meaning, which is simply that the computation signified or showed something. As the English language entered the twentieth century, the word significant began to take on other meanings, until it developed its current meaning, implying something very important. Statistical analysis still uses the word significant to indicate a very low probability computed under the hypothesis being tested. In that context, the word has an exact mathematical meaning. Unfortunately, those who use statistical analysis often treat a significant test statistic as implying something much closer to the modern meaning of the word (p. 98).

13

The Classical Econometric Model

... the class of populations we are dealing with does *not* consist of an infinity of different individuals, it consists of an infinity of possible *decisions* which might be taken with respect to the value of *y*.

Trygve Haavelmo[1]

13.1. Introduction

This chapter will introduce and discuss the classical econometric box model. We will use CEM as our acronym for this fundamental model. In other books and articles, you might see this model referred to as the classical linear model or the classical regression model. The name is not as important as the content.

The CEM has been by far the most commonly used description of the data generation process in econometrics. Understanding the requirements, functioning, and characteristics of the CEM is extremely important because modeling the data generation process is a crucial step in econometric analysis. Without a model of how the data were generated, inference is impossible. Subsequent chapters present more complicated box models designed to handle some of the situations in which this basic model deals inadequately with the data generation process.

Sections 13.2 and 13.3 present a hypothetical example designed to provide an intuitive understanding of the CEM, and Sections 13.4 and 13.5 describe the CEM in a more formal way.

13.2. Introducing the CEM via a Skiing Example

Workbook: Skiing.xls

The heart of this chapter, and a crucial idea in econometrics, is the data generation process (DGP) specified by the CEM. This section uses an extended

---

[1] Haavelmo (1944) in Hendry and Morgan (1995, p. 488).

Women Super Giant Slalom Medal Results in the 1998 Winter Olympics				
Medal	Athlete	Country	Time (min:s.00)	Time (s)
Gold	Picabo Street	USA	01:18.02	78.02
Silver	Michaela Dorfmeister	AUT	01:18.03	78.03
Bronze	Alexandra Meissnitzer	AUT	01:18.09	78.09

Figure 13.2.1. Women super giant slalom results, 1998 Winter Olympics. *Source:* [Skiing.xls]Picabo.

hypothetical example to illustrate the DGP embedded in the model. We could instead have launched into a dry, abstract description of the model and its requirements, but we think you will have more fun and learn more by beginning with an example that makes intuitive sense.

Super G at the 1998 Nagano Olympics

Olympic skier Picabo (pronounced PEEK-a-boo) Street is poised to come shooting out of the gate. She will reach speeds in excess of 70 mph as she completes her Super G run. Her competitors will try to beat her time. One after the other they come rocketing down the mountain. In the 1998 Winter Olympic Games in Nagano, Japan, the final standings for the Super G medals are presented in Figure 13.2.1.

We are going to consider ways to model the outcome of this and other imaginary races from an econometric perspective. Our goal is to give an informative example of the CEM. We will work toward that model by starting one we have already encountered. How can the measurement box model be used to interpret each individual time?

The Measurement Box Model

A simplistic application of the measurement error DGP would give a cynical and clearly false explanation of what happened at Nagano as follows. Each skier actually had the exact same time on her run in the Super G, but the official clock sometimes registered a faster time, sometimes a slower time. Picabo Street happened to have been the luckiest skier, and so she got the gold medal!

Now this story is nonsense, but let us write down the model anyway for purposes of comparison to more realistic models:

Model 1: *Observed Time$_i$* = *True Time* + ε_i for $i = 1, \ldots, n$.

Subscript i indexes skiers, and thus, for example, *Observed Time$_9$* would be the time for the ninth skier. There are n skiers in all. The observed time for skier i is the true time, which is the same for all skiers (you can tell

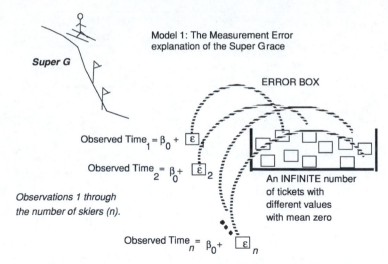

Figure 13.2.2. A measurement box model for observed ski times.

because there is no subscript on *True Time*) plus ε_i, a draw from a measurement box. All the draws are independent, meaning, for example that a clock that was too slow for one skier tells us nothing about the likely amount of the timing error for any other skier. The SD of the error box depends on the precision of the timing system and that precision did not vary during the competition (e.g., a better timing device was not installed after the second skier's run).

Model 1 applies the univariate measurement box model not to the distance between two mountains, but to the time taken by world-class skiers hurtling down a mountain. The observed time is composed of two unobservables: (1) a true, unchanging value, plus (2) a random, chance error term generated by the measuring device itself. Figure 13.2.2 is a picture of Model 1.

Notice that the measurement box model, as currently implemented, is based on no information about each skier. It is assumed that the skiers are identical and that, owing to the vagaries of the timing system, some pick positively numbered tickets from the box on their way down the mountain (which is bad because they want to get down there fast!), whereas others draw negatively numbered tickets. The parameter β_0 indicates the true, unknown time for each skier.

One way to estimate the fixed, unknown True Time would be to take the sample average of all 11 skiers' times. Furthermore, if we wanted to predict any individual skier's time, we would guess the sample average, give or take the SD of the sample (which would be our estimate of the SD of the box). We repeat that Model 1 is just the univariate measurement box model.

But we ought to reject Model 1. Why is Model 1 unsatisfactory? There are three good reasons. First, owing to modern technology and the scrutiny of the entire skiing world, the Olympic timing system is actually quite precise. Measurement errors for the clock in the Super G are considerably less than a hundredth of a second (Picabo Street's winning margin over Michaela Dorfmeister at Nagano). Second, it seems likely that, even among the very best skiers in the world, some are better than others, and so the assumption that the true time was the same for all skiers is silly. Third, even if all the skiers were equally talented, there is no way they would take the same time coming down the mountain. Snow, wind, and the path left by other skiers must have an impact on each skier's time. Our conclusion is that the measurement box model, as implemented in Model 1, does not describe this data generation process.

Notice that we do not blindly assume a data generation process. In this case, we have rejected Model 1 because it does not accurately depict the way the observed times were generated. Similarly, we would reject a model of the data generation process based on the polling box model because the way observed ski times are generated is not from a box with a fixed average and a finite number of tickets each representing a single skier.

A New DGP to Describe Observed Ski Times

To represent the data generation process in the skiing example correctly, we are going to need a new box model. We will call it the classical econometric box model or CEM for short. Before we begin, let us think more realistically about what causes differences in skiing times. Athletic performance clearly depends on raw talent, the time spent practicing the sport, and luck. Now there is no way to influence raw talent and luck, but it is possible to adjust time spent practicing. Skiers know that the more you train, the lower your time, but no one knows how much you can improve by increasing training. Furthermore, it is possible to measure how much time an athlete spends training, but it is very hard to measure either talent or luck.

The box model for skiing must correct the three flaws in the simple measurement error model. First, we will eliminate measurement error as an important explanation for differences in observed times. There is undoubtedly some measurement error in the observed ski time, but it is so small in this case (compared with the other sources of variation in times of skiers) that measurement error can be safely ignored. Second, we explicitly model training time as a variable that helps to explain differences in the true time of each skier – more training, we think, yields a lower true time ceteris paribus. Third, we will allow observed time to be influenced by two other factors as well: luck and pure talent.

In this more realistic model, each skier has a true, exact, but unknown time on a given hill on a given day. That time is determined by his or her training and talent. What each observed time represents is a composite number formed according to Model 2:

$$\text{Model 2: } Time_i = \beta_0 + \beta_1 \cdot Training_i + \beta_2 \cdot Talent_i + v_i, i = 1, \ldots, n.$$

In Model 2, the error term, v_i, represents luck: good luck is a negative error term, reducing the observed time, whereas bad luck is a positive error term. The observed time is different from the true time because of luck.

Although Model 2 is a much more satisfactory description of the data generating process, it cannot be estimated. The problem is that Talent is unobserved: medical science is incapable of measuring raw skiing talent.[2] For purposes of estimating the model, talent must be dumped into the error box. A model we actually could estimate is Model 3:

$$\text{Model 3: } Time_i = \beta_0 + \beta_1 \cdot Training_i + \varepsilon_i, i = 1, \ldots, n.$$

The source of the chance error (ε_i) in Model 3 can be found in two places. First, each error term in part represents the impact of omitted variables. An omitted variable is an independent variable that influences the dependent variable, but is not included in the regression model. Although we have high-lighted natural ability (talent) as an obvious determinant of performance, there are potentially many more omitted variables such as the motivation and health of each skier. The second component of the error in each obser-vation reflects the inherent randomness in the world (slight wind shifts while flying down the mountain, bumps, etc.) or, in other words, just plain luck. Thus, Model 3's error term ε_i is really the sum of all omitted variables (like talent), measurement error (which is small compared to the other two sources of error), and just plain luck (the v term in Model 2). The i subscript reminds us that the value of the error term varies from one skier to the next.

Figure 13.2.3 is a graphical representation of the CEM treatment of Model 3. Each ticket drawn from the box is a composite error term rep-resenting the effect of talent, luck, measurement error, and other factors. Because each draw from the error box is made at random and with replace-ment, the chance errors are independent of the included X variables. In this case, that means the amount of training a skier has tells us nothing about his or her talent. Because the draws are with replacement, the box is the same for all of the skiers. That rules out situations in which, for example, skiers

---

[2] Researchers, however, do try to measure the relationship between exercise and how well the body performs using regression techniques. For example, see Winter, Eston, and Lamb (2001).

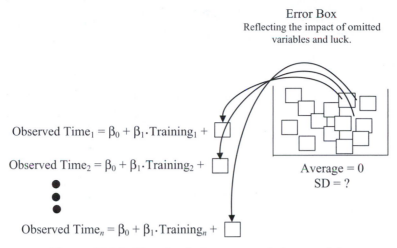

Figure 13.2.3. The classical econometric box model.

with more training have more consistent times, which would imply that there is a smaller spread in better trained skiers' error terms.

Comparing Box Models

Suppose we knew the values of the four unknown parameters in Model 2: the intercept, two slopes, and SD of the error box. Then for each individual skier we could predict the amount of time he or she would take coming down the mountain given the number of hours that skier trained and his or her talent level. Mathematically speaking, this situation would be just like the Hooke's law example. If we knew the exact physical characteristics of the spring (the intercept and slope parameter values), we could compute the exact length of the spring for different weights. The skier's true time (with a zero draw from the box) and the exact length of the spring are deterministic functions of the parameters and independent variables. In both cases, the observed values of the dependent variables are different from the true, deterministic values. This is due to the presence of the error terms in the models.

Despite the formal similarity, there is a big philosophical difference between the two models. That difference lies in the explanation for the presence of the error terms. In the CEM, the error term no longer reflects an imperfect measurement instrument. Instead it summarizes the impact of all the factors not explicitly included in the model: motivation, quality of training, equipment, and plain old luck. For economists, this idea that the error term reflects factors influencing the outcome that they cannot measure is an appealing concept. Because it is usually impossible for economists to collect information on all the relevant variables, we attribute variation in observed dependent variables to factors that have not been measured.

Summary

This section introduced our hypothetical shing example. It forms the backbone of our presentation of the CEM. This discussion may seem overly abstract; therefore, let us implement these notions in a concrete, visual presentation to explain more clearly what is going on. The next section shows how Excel can be used to simulate the ideas presented here and gives you a chance to see the data generation process of the CEM in action literally.

13.3. Implementing the CEM via a Skiing Example

Workbook: Skiing.xls

To demonstrate the operation of the classical econometric box model, let us imagine an experimental setup that could generate the data. Suppose the Austrian Ski Federation, stung from their defeat at Nagano, is determined to figure out the effect of training on performance. Therefore, the federation has decided to perform a series of tests designed to determine the effect of training on ski times. They will take groups of 25 skiers and apply a training regimen to each skier. One will train 8 hours per day, whereas another might train only 2 hours per day. After 6 months, the 25 skiers will race and their times will be recorded.

Open the Excel file Skiing.xls. Go to the sheet called *EstimatingBeta1*, which implements the DGP of the classical econometric model. The purpose of this workbook is to clarify the roles played by the observed and unobserved variables in the data generating process of the CEM.

Let us take a tour through the *EstimatingBeta1* sheet, as depicted in Figure 13.3.1. As you work on understanding the information presented on this sheet, we suggest clicking on cells to reveal formulas and noting which cells bounce and which remain constant as we simulate the data generation process. As usual, all of the parameters and variables that would be unknown to the econometrician are in red text. Training and Observed Time are in black text because they are observed.

The key parameter of interest is β_1, the coefficient on Training Time, which has been set at -0.5 and is in units of seconds/hours per day. This means that, for every additional hour of training per day, the skier's time falls by 0.5 seconds. Although this may not seem like much, when you consider that races are won by hundredths of a second, maybe training that extra hour every day really is worth it. Of course, we have cooked all of these data and really do not know how much training affects skiing performance; however, we do think training, whether for skiing or in the classroom, really matters.

Population Parameters		
β_0	100	(s)
β_1	−0.5	(s/hr per day)
β_2	−0.2	(s/index points)
SD of Nus	0.5	(s)
r(Training, Talent)	0.29	Sample Correlation between Training and Talent

Model 3: Time = $\beta_0 + \beta_1$Training + ε			
b_1	−0.637	100.612	b_0
est. SE(b_1)	0.088	0.472	est. SE(b_0)
R^2	0.695	1.270	RMSE
F	52.309	23	df
RegSS	84.400	37.110	SSR

Average	4.52	−0.436	97.827	−0.091	−0.004	97.7348
Max	9	11.884	101.462	0.916	2.623	102.12
Min	0	−12.867	93.123	−0.593	−2.286	93.21
SD of Nus	2.95	6.45	2.22	0.39	1.31	2.25

Skier	Training (hr per day)	Talent$_i$	True Time$_i$ (s)	v_i(s)	β_2Talent$_i$ + v_i(s)	Observed Time (s)
A	7	1.503	96.199	−0.146	−0.447	96.05
B	8	−8.895	97.779	−0.431	1.348	97.35
C	9	11.884	93.123	0.916	−1.460	94.04
D	4	10.655	95.869	0.103	−2.028	95.97
E	2	0.683	98.863	0.519	0.383	99.38
F	7	3.936	95.713	−0.187	−0.974	95.53
G	2	−8.303	100.661	0.258	1.919	100.92
H	7	−0.585	96.617	0.054	0.171	96.67
I	0	2.491	99.502	−0.237	−0.735	99.26
J	3	−6.514	99.803	−0.569	0.734	99.23
K	2	−2.287	99.457	−0.528	−0.071	98.93
L	5	−3.637	98.227	−0.593	0.134	97.63
M	9	4.229	94.654	−0.251	−1.097	94.40
N	1	−0.248	99.550	0.067	0.117	99.62
O	6	−2.237	97.447	−0.070	0.378	97.38
P	4	3.851	97.230	−0.450	−1.220	96.78
Q	4	0.802	97.840	−0.510	−0.670	97.33
R	1	0.959	99.308	−0.244	−0.436	99.06
S	3	3.405	97.819	−0.016	−0.697	97.80
T	8	−12.867	98.573	−0.045	2.528	98.53
U	3	−5.192	99.538	−0.216	0.823	99.32
V	1	−7.177	100.935	0.276	1.711	101.21
W	1	−9.810	101.462	0.661	2.623	102.12
X	7	1.471	96.206	−0.559	−0.853	95.65
Y	9	10.991	93.302	−0.088	−2.286	93.21

Race		
Winner	Y	93.21	s

Observed Time as a function of Training

[Add Regression Line] [Remove Regression Line]

Figure 13.3.1. The skiing example.
Source: [Skiing.xls]EstimatingBeta1.

Click on one of the Observed Time cells in column G. We clicked on cell G18 to reveal the following formula:

$$= \text{ROUND}(\text{Beta0} + \text{Beta1}^*\text{Training} + \text{Beta2}^*\text{Talent} + \text{Nu}, 2)$$

The formula puts Model 3 of the previous section into play. Nu is an error term reflecting luck and measurement error. Because we do not observe talent, our error term is actually Beta2*Talent+Nu. The values of this composite error term are given in column F. The ROUND function is used to force the computed result to be rounded to the second decimal place.

A key assumption of the CEM is that the omitted X's that help make up the tickets in the error box must be independent of the included X's. For this to be true when we implement the skiing example, the correlation between Talent and Training must be zero on average. Cell B6, which reports the sample correlation between Talent and Training, shows that in each individual sample the correlation will not be exactly zero. As you repeatedly draw samples, however, you will observe that this correlation bounces around zero, as claimed by the CEM. Use the Monte Carlo simulation add in to demonstrate that the correlation between Training and Talent is indeed zero on average.

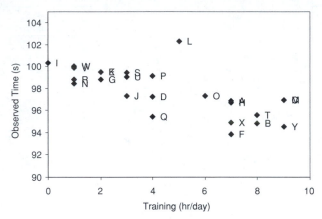

Figure 13.3.2. Results of one race.
Source: [Skiing.xls]EstimatingBeta1.

In Chapter 18, we will see how a nonzero long-run correlation between the error term and the *X* variable affects the sampling distributions of regression slopes causing biased estimates of the slopes.

Another condition required by the CEM is that the composite error terms shown in column F, consisting of Talent and luck, vary with every new sample of 25 skiers. Thus, we cannot describe the DGP as taking the same 25 people with the same talents and racing them over and over. If, for example, the first skier always had more talent than the second skier, then the two skiers would not be drawing from the same error box. To meet the requirements of the CEM, we must imagine that each time, the experiment is run, the Austrian Ski Federation gets a set of 25 new skiers and forces the training protocol upon them (in column B), and thus we are getting 25 new Talents in every sample.[3]

Having seen how the observed times are generated, let us race. Click on the Race button. A typical outcome of a race from a set of 25 skiers might look like Figure 13.3.2.

There are several things to notice about this chart. First, there seems to be a negative relationship between time in the race and training time. This is not an accident because the value of β_1 has been set to -0.5, meaning that, if everything else is held constant, an increase of 1 hour per day in training time results in a decrease in time on the course of -0.5 seconds. Second, even though several skiers have the same amount of training time, they do not have the same race time.

---

[3] Data sets in which the same individuals are observed more than once are called panel data. Models for the DGP appropriate to panel data are beyond the scope of this book. See Wooldridge (2003).

Model 3: Time = $\beta_0 + \beta_1$ Training + ε			
b_1	−0.471	99.778	b_0
est. SE(b_1)	0.084	0.450	est. SE(b_0)
R^2	0.578	1.211	RMSE
F	31.481	23	df
RegSS	46.171	33.733	SSR

Figure 13.3.3. Regression results.
Source: [Skiing.xls]EstimatingBeta1.

Click the Race button a few times more. The winner, the skier with the lowest time, is reported in cell J13. The Observed Time as a function of Training chart also shows the winner. Skiers C, M, and Y seem to win more often than the others. Race repeatedly by clicking the button and watch poor skier I. This skier will almost never win. Do you understand why? Is it talent? No, I is as likely to be a talented skier (as shown in the Talent column) as the others.

Skier I's problem is training. The Austrian Ski Federation always assigns zero training to skier I, whereas C, M, and Y always get, on the other hand, the maximum amount of training – a grueling 9 hours per day. The others sometimes overcome less training by sheer talent or a lucky draw. Click the Race button repeatedly and keep an eye on the winner. There is no doubt about it – the higher-training-time skiers usually do better.

Now that we have explored the sheet and understand the data generation process, let us turn our attention to estimating the crucial training parameter β_1. Click the Add Regression Line button (below the chart) and then click the Race button repeatedly. Each new set of 25 skiers is like a new realization of the chance process. We can fit an OLS regression line to each new sample of 25 observed times and associated training values.

We use LINEST to report regression results in the table above the chart. Of course, every new race will have new regression results, but Figure 13.3.3 displays a typical output.

Notice that the intercept and slope coefficients are the same as those reported by the Trendline in the chart. Everything in the table except df (the degrees of freedom, the number of observations minus the number of coefficients) changes with every click of the Race button. This means that all of these statistics are random variables.

If you did not know the parameter on training, β_1, but had a sample of 25 observations, it would seem natural to use the fitted slope coefficient as an estimate. Notice, however, that the sample slope coefficient is almost never exactly equal to −0.5. Fortunately, you can also see by repeatedly clicking the Race button that the coefficient does seem to be bouncing around −0.5.

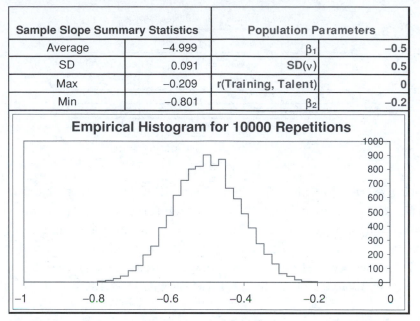

Sample Slope Summary Statistics		Population Parameters	
Average	−4.999	β_1	−0.5
SD	0.091	SD(v)	0.5
Max	−0.209	r(Training, Talent)	0
Min	−0.801	β_2	−0.2

Figure 13.3.4. Monte Carlo simulation of the sample slope.
Source: [Skiing.xls]MCSim.

Exactly how much bounce is there in the sample slope coefficient (i.e., what is the SE of b_1, the OLS estimator of β_1)? This question lies at the very heart of inferential regression analysis.

To answer it, we must do more than observe the regression results as each new race is run. Although it is possible to use analytical techniques to work out the SE of b_1 – see Chapter 15 – for now we will attack the question via the brute force approach of Monte Carlo simulation.

Monte Carlo Simulation

Go to the *MCSim* sheet in Skiing.xls and click on the [Run a Monte Carlo Simulation] button. Running the default 10,000 repetitions will produce results like those in Figure 13.3.4.

We have taken 25 skiers and assigned their training times per the A to Y protocol in the *EstimatingBeta1* sheet and then raced them and fitted a line to the resulting observed-time as a function of training-time scatter plot. We have done this 10,000 times. Figure 13.3.4 displays summary statistics of the 10,000 sample slopes on the training time independent variable.

The average of the 10,000 sample slopes is −0.499, which is very close to the true, but unknown, slope parameter β_1. This suggests (though it does not conclusively prove) that our strategy of using the sample slope to estimate the unknown slope parameter will, on average, be right. In fact, the sample slope estimator we are using is indeed unbiased.

Of crucial importance is the SD of the 10,000 sample slopes, which equals 0.091 in our Monte Carlo experiment. This is an approximation to the true, exact SE (which we would see if we ran an infinite number of repetitions). We do not have anything to compare this number to because we do not yet know how to compute the exact SE. You certainly do not want to compare it with $SD(v)$, although this quantity does influence the SE of the sample slope.

Notice that the regression output is producing an estimated SE for each sample but not the true, exact SE (which is a fixed, unchanging constant). The regression is estimating the SD of the errors using the SD of the residuals. Return to the *EstimatingBeta1* sheet and run a few races, keeping an eye on cell J4. Notice how this number is bouncing around – sometimes higher and sometimes lower than 0.10. This will be explained in more detail in Chapter 15.

Why Can We Assume That the Average of the Error Box Is Zero?

The careful student might wonder why it makes sense to assume that the average of the error box is zero when the errors reflect the influence of omitted variables. Why should the impact of the omitted variables average out to zero? The answer that they need not average to zero, but the average impact of the error terms will be absorbed by the intercept term. To see this, go to the *NonZeroMeanTalent* sheet. To follow the discussion, make sure that the parameter values in cells B2, B3, and B4 are $\beta_0 = 100$, $\beta_1 = -0.5$, and $\beta_2 = -0.2$, respectively. In cell B7, you can set the average value of Talent. Note, by hitting F9 repeatedly (or using the MCSim add-in) that, when the average value of Talent is set to 0, the estimate of the intercept term, b_0 (reported in cell J3) is on average 100, which is the same as the value of the parameter β_0. Why is this the case? The answer is that, when the average level of Talent is zero, the average influence of Talent on skiing time is zero.

Suppose, however, that the average value of Talent increases – for instance, to 10. Now people will on average ski faster because they are on average more talented. How much faster? The value of the Talent parameter, β_2, is -0.2. Therefore, the average time will fall by -0.2×10, or 2 seconds. The key points are (1) that the average value of b_0, the intercept term, will also fall by 2 seconds, but (2) the sampling distribution (center and spread) of the slope, b_1, is unaffected by a change in the average value of Talent. You can verify this with before and after simulations using the MCSim add-in. In general, the expected value of the intercept term will differ from the intercept parameter by the average impact of the omitted variable or variables. The average value of the omitted variables, however, does not affect the sampling distribution of the OLS estimates of the slope parameters, as long as the error term is independent of the X variables.

Summary

This section has introduced the classical econometric model by implementing in Excel the data generation process described in our make-believe skiing example. It may not seem like much, but we have made great progress in understanding the fundamental box model used in economics. The next section will present the model in more general terms and highlight important requirements for it.

13.4. CEM Requirements

In the previous sections, we tried to provide a motivation for the classical econometric model. In this section we give a more formal statement of the model. This box model is the one most commonly used by econometricians in empirical analysis.

   This section has two parts: a description of the CEM and the requirements of the model. In any given application, these requirements cannot simply be assumed; rather, the data must actually be generated according to the rules of the CEM. If not, then the CEM does not apply and the regression results generated are wrong.

The CEM in Words and Pictures

For every observation, the observed Y variable equals a linear function of the observed X variable(s) plus a draw from a box. The draws from the box reflect the influence of variables other than those included in the regression equation on the dependent variable. The tickets in the box usually are infinite in number and have mean zero. The draws are made with replacement. The X's are fixed in repeated sampling. There is no exact linear relationship between the X variables.

   Usually, the draws from the box are called *error terms*[4] (not residuals!) and are said to reflect the influence of *omitted variables* as well as just plain luck. The statement that that the X's are fixed in repeated sampling means that every sample that could have been drawn would have had the same values for the independent variables (the X's stay fixed) but different values of the error terms. In the Monte Carlo simulations of this book, we almost always hold the X's constant when drawing another sample. A consequence of our statements about the draws and the X's is the following: The draws from the

---

[4] Some authors call the error terms disturbances.

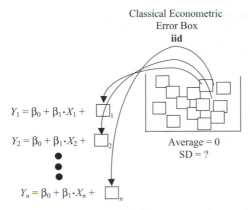

Figure 13.4.1. The classical econometric model.

box (error terms) are *independent* of the X's. This means that knowing the value of X tells us nothing about the value of the error that will be drawn.

This assumption is critical for inference because it implies that there is no confounding of the linear relationship between the Y variable and the X variable(s). Often, careful examination of the data will show that this assumption is unwarranted.

Figure 13.4.1 shows what the model looks like in a picture for the bivariate case. In this picture the subscripts index the observation number; there are a total of n observations. In the bivariate case there is only one independent variable.

The case of more than one independent variable is easily accommodated in the model by simply adding X variable terms onto the deterministic part of the equation as follows:

$$Y_i = \beta_0 + \beta_1 X_{1i} + \beta_2 X_{2i} + \dots \beta_K X_{Ki} + \varepsilon_i.$$

The i subscript runs from 1 to the total number of observations, whereas K signifies the number of independent regressors (or X variables) in the multivariate equation. Be careful to observe that, in this notation, the first subscript after X_{35}, for instance, refers to the X variable (in this case the third) whereas the second subscript refers to the observation (in this case the fifth).

In both bivariate and multivariate specifications, the average of the box is zero. This box is often called a Gaussian error box[5] because, although the tickets do not represent measurement error, in statistical terms they behave just like measurement error.

---

[5] To be more accurate, the error term is often called a Gaussian error term. The word "box" is much less commonly used. We think it helps students to visualize the model.

There are two philosophical interpretations of the role played by errors and omitted variables in the CEM. The first view is that, if absolutely everything were known about an observation (i.e., the values of all possible relevant X variables were observed), then the value of the Y variable for that observation could be predicted perfectly. The second view is that there is always some inherent randomness contributing to the outcome (the Y variable), which can never be eliminated. Under the first, deterministic view, the error term in principle could be removed if all relevant X variables were included. (Notice that we are talking about adding more explanatory variables, not more observations.) Under the second view, the error term will always be necessary – if only to account for the role played by mere chance. The first view implies that the box contains an extremely large number of tickets because there are many X variables that influence the outcome and there are many possible values for each X variable. The second view suggests that the box may contain an infinite number of tickets.

The philosophical debate over whether we have a great many or an infinite number of tickets in the box has little bearing on the application of the CEM. In practice, economists typically posit that the error term reflect not only the influence of omitted variables but also the effect of measurement error on the Y variable.

Requirements of the CEM

Let us restate the mathematical features of the classical econometric model in more formal terms. We will use words and equations.

1. The model must be linear in the parameters, and it contains an additive error term:

$$Y_i = \beta_0 + \beta_1 X_{1i} + \beta_2 X_{2i} + \ldots \beta_K X_{Ki} + \varepsilon_i.$$

   Various transformations of the Y and X variables are, of course, permitted.
2. The Xs are fixed in repeated sampling.
   This is often an unrealistic assumption, but it makes demonstrations of the basic results of statistical inference much easier. Almost all of the results we will present are also true if one makes the more realistic assumption that the data (Xs and Ys) are a random sample from a population generated according to the equation given in the first requirement above.
3. The error terms have mean zero:

$$E(\varepsilon_i) = 0, \quad i = 1, \ldots, n.$$

This assumption may seem unrealistic in light of the claim that the errors reflect the influence of omitted variables, which presumably have on net a nonzero effect. However, if one includes an intercept term in the model, the mean influence of omitted variables will be absorbed into the intercept.

4. The error terms are independent of one another:

$$\varepsilon_i \text{ is distributed independently of } \varepsilon_j, \text{ for all } i \neq j.$$

If on the other hand, a previous draw affects the current or a future draw, this is called autocorrelation. This is a problem often encountered in time series analysis and is discussed in Chapter 20 on autocorrelation. (We actually could make the weaker assumption that the errors are merely uncorrelated with one another.)

5. Each error term draw comes from the same box with the same SD:

$$SD(\varepsilon_i) = \sigma, \quad i = 1, \ldots, n$$

This is known as homoskedasticity. A separate chapter on heteroskedasticity (Chapter 19) discusses the effects of not having the same spread in the errors for each draw from the box.

6. The error terms are independent of the X's.
The fixed-in-repeated-samples requirement together with the mean-zero error term requirement already guarantees that the error terms are uncorrelated with the X's. We include the independence condition in the list of requirements to emphasize that the errors should not be related to the included X's. The situation in which omitted variables (which are summarized in the error term) are correlated with the included X's is also known as confounding. The resulting coefficient estimates are biased. This violation is explored in Chapter 18.

7. A technical requirement is that the X's, including the intercept term, cannot have an exact linear relationship. This avoids the problem of perfect multicollinearity.

Notice that, in this presentation of the classical econometric model, we have not specified the exact distribution of the error terms. Although for convenience our Excel workbooks typically draw errors from the normal distribution, most of the results we will obtain in later chapters do not depend on the errors coming from a normal distribution.

In the next few chapters, we will use Monte Carlo simulation to demonstrate the properties of OLS regression as applied to the classical econometric model. The Monte Carlo simulations faithfully implement the CEM. For example, in our Monte Carlo experiments we almost always keep the same set of X's from one repetition to the next.[6] This automatically enforces the assumption of fixed X's in repeated sampling. We implement the box model metaphor of repeatedly drawing with replacement from the same error box by drawing repeatedly from a pseudorandom number generator designed to produce numbers randomly with the specified distribution for the errors (including specified mean and SD).

Summary

This section has presented the classical econometric box model and listed its requirements. If the requirements are violated, the model does not apply,

---

[6] For exceptions, see Chapters 18, 19, and 21.

and the usual regression results may be wrong and cannot be trusted. Three important categories of violations are omitted variable bias, autocorrelation, and heteroskedasticity. These issues are reviewed in more detail in Chapters 18, 19, 20.

It is important to remember that the mere existence of omitted variables does not automatically cause omitted variable bias. In fact, econometricians assume that part of the error term is composed of omitted independent variables (e.g., Talent in the skiing example). It is when the omitted variable is correlated with an included X variable that confounding emerges.

13.5. Conclusion

The classical econometric model is just one of many ways to conceptualize the process by which the data were generated. Its popularity arises from the way in which it encapsulates economists' views about how their observational data are produced, from the fact that it can be used to motivate the use of a multiple linear regression, and from the relative ease of working out the properties of the OLS estimator when the data are generated according to the assumptions of the model.

Mathematically speaking, the CEM is very similar to the measurement box model of Chapter 11. In fact the mathematical summary given in Section 13.5 for the CEM could apply equally well to the measurement box model. The difference between the measurement box model and the classical econometric model lies in the story told about the data generation process.

The CEM is a very powerful tool in part because of the flexibility of multiple regression. The techniques introduced in Chapters 6 and 8 concerning functional form and dummy variables can be used to generate an extremely wide variety of data generating processes that fit this model. The CEM can therefore provide a compact yet flexible summary of the data generating process that relates dependent and independent variables.

The next two chapters, Chapter 14, "The Gauss–Markov Theorem," and Chapter 15, "Understanding the Standard Error" go on to explore the properties of the CEM. These two chapters will cover three important points, which we highlight now to emphasize their importance and indicate the path of future work:

1. The OLS Estimator is just one of many recipes to estimate population parameters. It turns out that, when the CEM applies, the OLS Estimator is in a certain sense the best estimator to use. The Gauss–Markov theorem states this formally.
2. Software reports standard errors for each coefficient in the regression equation. If the CEM requirements are met, reported SEs can be used to measure the spread of the sampling distribution of the OLS estimator.

3. In general, the SE of the OLS estimator depends on the sample size, the SD of the box, and the SD of the X's.

13.6. Exercises

1. In Section 5.7 we discussed a regression of Hourly Wages on Education.
   a. Write down a model for the data regression process that conform to the CEM, and could be used to support this regression.
   b. What evidence did we present in Section 5.7 that suggests the data do not in fact conform to the CEM?
2. In Section 12.4 we proposed a two box model for the data generation process in an example in which Hourly Wages was the dependent variable and educational attainment (as measured by whether the worker had a college degree) was the independent variable. Instead of comparing the sample averages directly, as we did in Section 12.4, we could have run a regression of Hourly Wage on a dummy variable, College (equal to 1 if the worker had a college education 0 and otherwise). The results would be

$$\text{Predicted Hourly Wage} = 9.31 + 4.75\,\text{College}$$
$$\text{RMSE} = 5.66.$$

   a. Write down a model for the data-regression process that conforms to the CEM.
   b. The RMSE is a measure of something about the box in the CEM. What exactly?
   c. In estimating the two box model, there is no RMSE. What is there instead? In what ways, therefore, is the CEM more restrictive than the Two Box model in this particular application?
3. Suppose that Training in fact has nothing to do with skiing time, in other words suppose that $\beta_1 = 0$. What would happen? To answer the question, set $\beta_1 = 0$ and $\beta_2 = -0.2$ in the *EstimatingBeta1* sheet. Then go to the *Winners* sheet and run a Monte Carlo experiment. Explain the results, copying and pasting graphs into your answer sheet as necessary.
4. In the text we claim that we have set things up so that the long-run correlation between the observed variable Training and the unobserved variable Talent is zero.
   a. Verify this by using the Monte Carlo add-in to find the distribution of the correlation between Training and Talent recorded in cell B6 of the EstimatingBeta1 sheet of Skiing.xls. Set $\beta_1 = -0.5$ and $\beta_2 = -0.2$ and SDnu = 0.5 in the *EstimatingBeta1* sheet. Copy and paste your results into the answer sheet.
   b. Next run a Monte Carlo simulation in which you compare the computed correlation coefficient (recorded in cell B6) and the estimate of the regression slope (recorded in cell I3). The MCSim add-in will spit out the first 100 values of each random variable. Draw a scatter graph with the regression slope on the y-axis and the correlation coefficient on the x-axis. Interpret the graph and explain the relationship shown between the two random variables.
5. Independence between two random variables X and Y means that $E(XY) = E(X) \cdot E(Y)$, the expected value of the product of two random variables, equals the product of their expected values. Suppose that, as assumed in the CEM, an error term ε with mean zero is independent of the variable X. Then the expected value of the product εX is 0. Check that the composite error term in the skiing example obeys the rule that the product of two random variables equals the product of their expected values by using the Monte Carlo add-in to approximate the distributions of the products $(\beta_2 Talent_A + v_A)\,Training_A$ and $(\beta_2 Talent_B + v_B)\,Training_B$ in 1,000 repetitions. Use the *EstimatingBeta1*

worksheet, on which we have set the mean of the error terms equal to zero by making both Talent and v zero-mean random variables. The composite error terms are in Column F. Sort the skiers alphabetically with the [Race and Sort by Ski Order] button.

6. Go to the *NonZeroMeanTalent* sheet. Make sure that the parameter values in cells B2, B3, and B4 are $\beta_0 = 100$, $\beta_1 = -0.5$, and $\beta_2 = -0.2$, respectively. Use the MCSim add-in to verifty that, when the average value of Talent is set to 0 (in cell B7), the estimate of the intercept term b_0 (reported in cell J3) is on average 100, the same as the value of the parameter β_0, and that the average value of b_1 is -0.5. Next set the average value of Talent to 10. Use the MCSim add-in to show (1) that the average value of b_0, the intercept term, will also fall by 2 seconds, but (2) the sampling distribution (center and spread) of the slope b_1 is unaffected by a change in the average value of Talent.

References

Useful (though difficult) readings on the origins of the classical econometric box model are contained in *The Foundations of Econometric Analysis*, edited by D. Hendry and M. S. Morgan (Cambridge, UK: Cambridge University Press, 1995). See especially papers by Koopmans (Chapter 24, especially pp. 278–279, on repeated sampling) and T. Haavelmo (Chapter 42, especially pp. 487–489) and the commentary by the editors on these papers in their introduction. The original citation for the Haalvemo article is

Haavelmo, T. (1944). "The Probability Approach to Econometrics," Supplement to *Econometrica* **12**: iii–vi+1–115.

Arthur Goldberger, in *A Course in Econometrics* (Cambridge, MA: Harvard University Press, 1990), provides a clear and careful discussion of the assumptions of the standard model. His approach differs in that it places much less emphasis on the error term.

Our skiing regression model is entirely fictional, but there are regression analyses of the relationship between exercise and how well the body performs. A discussion of such studies is in

Winter, E. M., R. G. Eston, and K. L. Lamb (2001). "Statistical Analyses in the Physiology of Exercise and Kinanthropometry.(Statistical Data Included)" *Journal of Sports Sciences* **19**: 761–775.

The abstract says in part that

research into the physiology of exercise and kinanthropometry is intended to improve our understanding of how the body responds and adapts to exercise. . . . The aim of this review is to examine the use of four techniques that are especially relevant to physiological studies: (1) bivariate correlation and linear and non-linear regression, (2) multiple regression, (3) repeated-measures analysis of variance and (4) multi-level modelling. The importance of adhering to underlying statistical assumptions is emphasized and ways to accommodate violations of these assumptions are identified.[7]

---

[7] The abstract is available at <static.highbeam.com/j/journalofsportsssciences/october012001/ statisticalanalysesinthephysiologyofexerciseandkin/>.

14

The Gauss–Markov Theorem

[J]ust a year after getting his degree, Mansfield Merriman, Ph.D. Yale 1876, wrote of Gauss's elegant demonstration of the "Gauss-Markov" theorem that "The proof is entirely untenable." In charity to Merriman it might be added that no less a mathematician than Poincaré also misconstrued the nature of Gauss's result.

Stephen M. Stigler[1]

14.1. Introduction

This chapter brings together all the key ideas in this book:

- In order to do inference one must have a model of the data generating process.
- There are many possible estimators of the population parameters.
- Estimators can be classified according to whether they are unbiased – that is, on average correct.
- Many, but by no means all, estimators are linear estimators.
- One of the main criteria for comparing estimators is the variance of the estimator.
- When the data are generated according to the classical econometric box model, ordinary least squares is the best estimator in the class of linear, unbiased estimators – best, that is, according to the criterion of finding the estimator with the minimum variance for a given sample size.

This last statement is often stated in shorthand as "OLS is BLUE" (best linear unbiased estimator) and is known as the Gauss–Markov theorem from which the title of this chapter is derived. This theorem explains the preeminence of the OLS estimator in econometrics.

The Gauss–Markov theorem also works in reverse: when the data generating process does not follow the classical econometric model, ordinary least squares is typically no longer the preferred estimator. Much of econometrics concerns pointing out the deficiencies of OLS and finding better estimators under particular violations of requirements of the CEM.

---

[1] Stigler (1978, p. 260).

Throughout this chapter, we work with the classical econometric model. To make matters as clear as possible, we begin with a simple problem: estimating the population average for a single variable. This case, considered in Section 14.2, allows us to introduce the notion of linear estimators and to demonstrate that there are many possible estimators for a given population parameter. Section 14.3 races various estimators to show how we decide the winner. Section 14.4 presents a formal proof of the Gauss–Markov theorem for the univariate case. Sections 14.5 and 14.6 consider the more complicated bivariate case. Once again, we will show that there are many possible estimators of the parameters, that some of them are linear (i.e., weighted sums of the dependent variable), and that the OLS estimator is in fact the best estimator in the bivariate case. Finally, Section 14.7 uses the algebra of expectations to present the ideas in this chapter in a more formal way.

The Gauss–Markov theorem is a crowning achievement in statistics. The time and effort spent in understanding this material are well worth it.

14.2. Linear Estimators

Workbook: GaussMarkovUnivariate.xls

This section examines linear estimators in the context of the simplest version of the classical econometric model. An *estimator* is a recipe for obtaining an *estimate* of a population parameter. A simple analogy explains the core idea: An estimator is like a recipe in a cook book; an estimate is like a cake baked according to the recipe. The first major goal of this section is to show that, for any given model of the data generation process, there is always more than one way to estimate a population parameter. Thus, we have a decision to make: From the set of estimators, which one should we use? In other words, which one is best?

We proceed by dividing the entire set of possible estimators into subsets. Estimators can be classified according to whether they are *linear*. The second major goal of this section is to explain what linear means in the context of estimators and to demonstrate that there are many linear estimators (including the OLS estimator).

Estimating the Population Average

Suppose we want to estimate a single parameter, the population average, and we have a sample of 10 observations. Suppose that a reasonable mathematical model for the data generation process is

$$Y_i = \beta + \varepsilon_i, \quad i = 1, \ldots, 10.$$

Here β is the population average we want to estimate, and the ε_i's represent draws from a box with an infinite number of tickets whose mean is zero and with an unknown standard deviation. The 10 draws are independent of each other.

The last two sentences sound like standard boilerplate language that the reader will have skipped to avoid falling into a coma. Be warned, however: If the box model does not apply, then the claims we make about the sample average are false. In fact, much of the rest of this book is about what happens when the conditions of the classical econometric box model do not apply. We worry that some readers will miss this key point. That is why we write the Excel workbooks. We hope that you are sufficiently interested in the way that the cells are created that you learn about the data generation process there.

This DGP works well with a measurement error story (like the distance between two mountain peaks), but it could apply to a situation in which the errors represent random luck plus the influence of omitted variables that combine to make the individual value bigger or smaller than the population average. Thus, this DGP is an example of the classical econometric model applied to univariate data.

If you want to get technical, think of the independent variable as a series of 1's hidden inside the intercept term. That is, the DGP can be written

$$Y_i = \beta \cdot 1 + \varepsilon_i, \quad i = 1, \ldots, 10.$$

Every observation contains the number 1 as the single independent variable. By extension, note that in a bivariate or multiple regression equation the intercept parameter can be interpreted as being multiplied by an X variable that has a 1 for every value.

Open the Excel workbook GaussMarkovUnivariate.xls now and go to the *UnivariateSample* sheet to see the display shown in Figure 14.2.1 (drawn with the true population average β set to 200 and SD(ε) set to 5).

On the screen, everything in red text means that we would not actually observe that cell; black text cells are observable. For example, neither the population average β, nor the SD of the ε_i's, nor the ε_i's themselves can be seen. We can see the Y_i's, which are composed of the constant β plus a random component, ε_i.

β	ε_i	Y_i
200	−5.63	194.37
200	−1.28	198.72
200	−5.76	194.24
200	4.42	204.42
200	−7.78	192.22
200	−1.88	198.12
200	2.25	202.25
200	12.84	212.84
200	−0.23	199.77
200	−4.20	195.80

Figure 14.2.1. A univariate sample.
Source: [GaussMarkovUnivariate.xls] Univariate Sample.

β	ε_i	Y_i	Sample Average Estimator			
			w_i	$w_i\beta$	$w_i\varepsilon_i$	w_iY_i
200	−2.02	197.98	0.1	20	−0.202	19.798
200	−7.46	192.54	0.1	20	−0.746	19.254
200	7.44	207.44	0.1	20	0.744	20.744
200	2.37	202.37	0.1	20	0.237	20.237
200	7.99	207.99	0.1	20	0.799	20.799
200	6.32	206.32	0.1	20	0.632	20.632
200	−0.31	199.69	0.1	20	−0.031	19.969
200	−0.78	199.22	0.1	20	−0.078	19.922
200	5.12	205.12	0.1	20	0.512	20.512
200	−0.74	199.26	0.1	20	−0.074	19.926
Sum	17.93	2017.93	1.0	200	1.793	**201.793**

Figure 14.2.2. Illustration of the sample average estimator.
Source: [GaussMarkovUnivariate.xls]UnivariateSample.

You can draw a new sample by hitting the F9 key. Click on one of the ε_i cells such as cell B8. The formula is, "= normalrandom(0,SDepsilon)." Every time you recalculate the workbook by hitting F9, Excel recalculates the formula and draws a new epsilon value from a box that is normally distributed with mean zero and SD = 5. Each of the draws (represented by the 10 cells from B6:B15) comes from the same, unchanging box, and they are independent. Click on one of the Y cells to see that its formula is simply β plus ε. The population average, β, remains constant, but the Y values bounce because the ε's bounce. The *UnivariateSample* sheet is a faithful implementation of the DGP, $Y_i = \beta + \varepsilon_i, i = 1, \ldots, 10$.

To see the Sample Average estimator in action, click on the [Show Estimator] button. Several new columns appear, as depicted in Figure 14.2.2. The information to focus on first in Figure 14.2.2 is the columns displayed in black on the computer screen: the Y_i, w_i, and $w_i Y_i$ columns. As noted above, the Y_i column displays the 10 observed values in the sample. The sum of the 10 observations is, in this specific case, 2017.93. With 10 observations, the sample average estimate is 201.793, the number in bold in the lower right-hand corner.

Think of the Sample Average as a weighted sum: take each observation (Y_i), multiply it by a weight (w_i), and sum up the products (the $w_i Y_i$'s). In the specific case at hand,

$$\text{Sample Average} = 0.1 \cdot 197.98 + 0.1 \cdot 192.54 + \cdots + 0.1 \cdot 199.26$$
$$= 19.798 + 19.254 + \cdots + 19.926$$
$$= 201.793.$$

More generally, the Sample Average can be represented as follows:

$$\text{Sample Average} = w_1 \cdot Y_1 + w_2 \cdot Y_2 + \cdots + w_n \cdot Y_n,$$

where the w_i's are all equal to $\frac{1}{n}$.

β	ε_i	Y_i	w_i	$w_i\beta$	$w_i\varepsilon_i$	w_iY_i
				Diminishing Weights Estimator		
200	−2.02	197.98	0.5	100	−1.011	98.989
200	−7.46	192.54	0.25	50	−1.864	48.136
200	7.44	207.44	0.125	25	0.930	25.930
200	2.37	202.37	0.0625	12.5	0.148	12.648
200	7.99	207.99	0.03125	6.25	0.250	6.500
200	6.32	206.32	0.01563	3.125	0.099	3.224
200	−0.31	199.69	0.00781	1.5625	−0.002	1.560
200	−0.78	199.22	0.00391	0.78125	−0.003	0.778
200	5.12	205.12	0.00195	0.39063	0.010	0.401
200	−0.74	199.26	0.00195	0.39063	−0.001	0.389
Sum	17.93	2017.93	1.0	200	−1.446	**198.554**

Figure 14.2.3. The diminishing weights estimator.
Source: [GaussMarkovUnivariate]UnivariateSample.

There are many other (in fact an infinite number) weighted-sum estimators of the population average. To see another one, click on the Change Estimators button. This button cycles through a series of estimators. Keep clicking it until you see the Diminishing Weights Estimator similar to the display in Figure 14.2.3.

This estimator is a different recipe for producing an estimate of the population average β. Yet it has the exact same form as the sample average. Thus, the calculation of the Diminishing Weights estimator proceeds in exactly the same fashion as the computation of the Sample Average estimator.

The Diminishing Weights estimate can be obtained as follows. Take each observation (Y_i), multiply it by a weight (w_i), and sum up the products (the $w_i Y_i$'s). In the specific case at hand,

$$Diminishing\ Weights\ Estimate = 0.5 \cdot 197.98 + 0.25 \cdot 192.54$$
$$+ \cdots + 0.00195 \cdot 199.26$$
$$= 98.989 + 48.136 + \cdots + 0.389$$
$$= 198.554.$$

More generally, the Diminishing Weights estimate can be represented as follows:

$$Diminishing\ Weights\ Estimate = w_1 \cdot Y_1 + w_2 \cdot Y_2 + \cdots + w_n \cdot Y_n,$$

where the w_i's are equal to 1/2, 1/4, 1/8, and so on. Each weight equals a power of $\frac{1}{2}$. The very last weight breaks the pattern in that it is not half as big as the previous weight but rather equal to the previous weight.[2]

Two other estimators are still available. Click the Change Estimators button again, and you will see the 0.9 Estimator; one more click and you will see the Random Linear Estimator. Like the other two, both these estimators are weighted sums of the Y values. The title of the 0.9 Estimator matches the sum

[2] More precisely, $w_i = \frac{1}{2^i}$ for $i = 1, \ldots, n-1$, and $w_n = \frac{1}{2^{n-1}}$.

of its weights. The Random Linear Estimator produces a random set of nine weights, and the last weight is chosen so the sum of the weights equals 1.

Note the essential similarity between the formulas for these four estimators: each involves weights multiplied into the Y's. Thus, all are linear functions of the Y's. All four are therefore *linear estimators*.

Digression on Linearity

Because this is the third time in this book the word linear has been used in a different sense, let us try to be clear about the various definitions of the term.

- Linear in the independent variables. A linear functional form is one in which the dependent variable is a linear *function of the independent variable(s)*. For example, in the equation

$$Y = a + bX,$$

with a and b constants, Y is a linear function of X. The X appears raised only to the first power. There are no terms involving X raised to a power other than one or zero (e.g., no X^2, X^3 or X^{-1} terms).
- Linear in the regression coefficients. In linear least squares, the equation for the regression line is a linear *function of the coefficients*. In nonlinear least squares, the coefficients enter into the regression in a nonlinear way. Here are two examples:

$$\text{Linear in } b_0 \text{ and } b_1 : Y = b_0 + b_1 X^2$$
$$\text{Nonlinear in } b_0 \text{ and } b_1 : Y = \frac{1}{b_0} + b_1^{-0.5} X.$$

Notice that, in the first equation, X enters nonlinearly, whereas in the second equation X enters linearly. However the adjective linear in linear least squares has to do with the coefficients. Each of the parameters enters into the equation raised to the first power.
- Linear in the dependent variables. The third (and thankfully, last) way we will use the word linear has to do with what the recipe for estimating the population parameters does with the dependent variable. The four estimators we have introduced are linear estimators because they are linear *functions of the Y's*. Each Y_i appears raised to the first power in the formulas for these estimators.

This last definition of linear is important because estimators are recipes in which the ingredients are the data, the values of the independent and dependent variables. We classify estimators by how they handle the ingredients – in particular how the values of the dependent variable enter into the formula for estimating the population parameters.

We have introduced four linear estimators for the population average. What is an example of a nonlinear estimator? The Sample Median is a good answer. It is impossible to write the Sample Median as a weighted sum of the Y's without first sorting the Y's in order to find the middle observation (or middle two observations if the number of observations is even). Because we do not know which observation will be the middle in advance, we cannot write down a weighted sum The Sample Median is therefore not a linear estimator.

The Sample Average Is the Least Squares Estimator

Before closing this section, we will tie up a loose end. In Section 5.4 we showed that the sample average is the least squares estimator for describing the central tendency of a univariate data set. Now we restate that result: The sample average is the least squares estimator of the population average. Notice the difference in language. In Part 1 of this book, no model is presented for the data generating process. We could only speak about describing the data at hand. In Part 2, we typically regard the data as representing a sample from a larger (quite possibly infinite) population. Rather than merely describing data, we are attempting to infer the value of an unknown parameter that in a sense lies behind the data.

To remind you that the sample average is the least squares estimator, go to the *SampleAveIsOLS* sheet. You will see an augmented version of the table you first encountered in the OLSFormula.xls workbook discussed in Section 5.4. The difference between the two tables is that, in Section 5.4, we just gave you the Y values and said nothing about the population average β and the error terms, the ε_i's. In other words there was no model for the data generation process.

The *SampleAveIsOLS* sheet is depicted in Figure 14.2.4. Because you have seen this demonstration before, we will highlight the new elements. The true population average is 200. Observed Y is the unobserved population average plus an unobserved error. The sample average is a weighted sum of the observed Y's. Now turn to the Sample Average Residuals column. Each residual is the actual observed Y less the sample average. Students often confuse residuals and errors. To avoid falling into this trap, note the following well:

- The residuals are not the same concept as the errors, nor are they equal to the errors.
- The residuals sum to zero (and therefore average zero). This is always true for residuals produced by least squares estimates, when an intercept term is included.
- The errors in the sample do not sum to zero.

We will leave the rest to you. Use Solver to find the estimate of the population average that minimizes the sum of squared residuals. In every sample, Solver's solution will be the same as the estimate produced by the Sample Average estimator. As you repeatedly draw samples, you will remind yourself

Population Parameters	
β	200
SD(ε)	5

	Sample Average		
Sample Average	202.375	OLS SSR	264.80
Solver Estimate	202.375	Solver SSR	264.80

β	ε_i	Y_i	Sample Average w_i	Sample Average $w_i Y_i$	Sample Average Residuals	Sample Average Residuals Squared
200	−3.13	196.87	0.1	19.687	−5.506	30.318
200	−3.00	197.00	0.1	19.700	−5.375	28.888
200	3.63	203.63	0.1	20.363	1.254	1.572
200	9.62	209.62	0.1	20.962	7.245	52.494
200	8.53	208.53	0.1	20.853	6.151	37.841
200	−4.50	195.50	0.1	19.550	−6.879	47.325
200	−2.67	197.33	0.1	19.733	−5.044	25.437
200	8.57	208.57	0.1	20.857	6.196	38.389
200	2.80	202.80	0.1	20.280	0.423	0.179
200	3.91	203.91	0.1	20.391	1.534	2.353
Sum	23.75	2023.75	1	**202.375**	0.000	264.796

Figure 14.2.4. Showing that the Sample Average is the OLS estimator. *Source:* [GaussMarkovUnivariate.xls]SampleAveIsOLS.

of an obvious but important point. An estimator is a recipe for obtaining an estimate. Each time we draw a new sample from the same population, we are liable to get a new, quite possibly unique, estimate of the same underlying population parameter.

Summary

This section has accomplished two major goals. First, we have seen that there are many estimators, or recipes, that can be applied to a sample of 10 data points to estimate the population average. We are going to work with just four of them, but it is clear that there are many, many other recipes that could be applied to the data. Second, we have explained what makes an estimator a linear estimator. Our four candidates are linear estimators because they can be written as a linear function of the dependent variable.

We are well positioned to ask the obvious question: From all of the estimators available, how do we pick the best one? Read on to find out.

14.3. Choosing an Estimator

Workbook: GaussMarkovUnivariate.xls

The previous section showed that we divide estimators according to whether or not they are linear estimators. Another way that we group estimators is

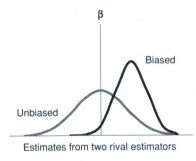

Estimates from two rival estimators

Figure 14.3.1. Biased and unbiased estimators of a population parameter.

by their expected values. *Unbiased* means that the estimator on average gets the right answer. Put differently, the estimator is accurate. Of course, any particular sample estimate of a population parameter is very likely to be different from the true value of that parameter because chance plays a role in generating the sample. An unbiased estimator, however, does not produce estimates that are systematically wrong. In this section, we show that one of our four linear estimators is biased and, therefore, out of the running.

We then turn to the three remaining candidates. Monte Carlo simulation allows us to race the estimators in head-to-head to competition. We will see that the choice of the best estimator is grounded in the idea of precision. When choosing among unbiased estimators, we pick the one with the least variability.

Eliminating Biased Estimators from Contention

An unbiased estimator is one that is, on average, accurate. Another way of putting this is that the probability histogram for the estimator (also known as the sampling distribution) is centered on the true population parameter. Figure 14.3.1 offers a visual definition of bias.

Biased estimators are systematically wrong, and so they are out of the hunt.[3] After all, you could get lucky and get a tasty cake from a flawed recipe, but most of the time bad recipes produce bad cakes.

So, which one is the biased estimator in our group of four linear estimators? To find out, open the GaussMarkovUnivariate.xls workbook and proceed to the *MonteCarlo* sheet. This sheet enables you to race three alternative linear estimators, one at a time, against the Sample Average.

First up is the Diminishing Weights Estimator. We drew 10,000 samples, obtained the sample average and diminishing weights estimates from each sample, and kept track of the results. The output shows the averages and SDs

---

[3] You might be thinking that a slightly biased but spiked sampling distribution would be preferred to an unbiased but spread out probability histogram. That is an interesting idea but is beyond the scope of this book. The concept of Mean Squared Error addresses this issue.

Population Parameters		Sample Average Estimates		Diminishing Weights Estimator Estimates	
β	200	Average	200.01	Average	200.02
SD(ε)	5	SD	1.60	SD	2.90

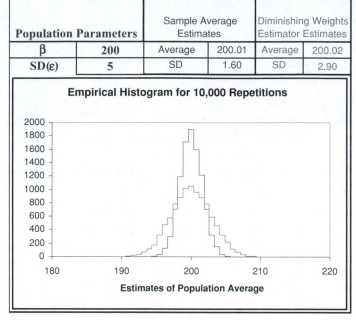

Figure 14.3.2. Sample Average versus Diminishing Weights.
Source: [GaussMarkovUnivariate.xls]MonteCarlo.

of the estimates produced by the two estimators. Figure 14.3.2 displays our results; yours will be slightly different.

The empirical histograms generated by the Monte Carlo simulation are approximations to the respective probability histograms for the Sample Average and Diminishing Weights estimators. It seems clear that the sampling distributions for both estimators are centered on the true population average. The display shows the average of the 10,000 estimates to two decimal places. They are both quite close to 200.

Next, race the Random Linear estimator against the Sample Average. You should see that the Random Linear estimator is also centered on the value of the population parameter. If you are nervous about your average of 10,000 repetitions not being close enough to 200, run another Monte Carlo with more repetitions – 100,000, for instance. The more repetitions you run, the closer the approximation of the Monte Carlo's empirical histogram to the true probability histogram. Increasing the number of repetitions is always an option when using the Monte Carlo method.

Finally, let us consider the 0.9 estimator. The results are striking. Figure 14.3.3 shows that the 0.9 estimator is shifted off of the true value of β. Instead of being centered around 200, it is centered around 180. This means that our estimate will usually be around 180, but the truth is actually 200. The 0.9 estimator is systematically wrong. It is inaccurate. This is bias.

Population Parameters		Sample Average Estimates		0.9 Estimator Estimates	
β	200	Average	200.02	Average	180.02
SD(ε)	5	SD	1.59	SD	1.43

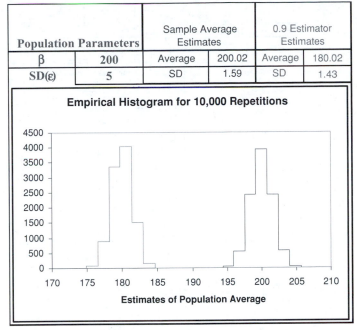

Figure 14.3.3. Sample Average versus 0.9 Estimator.
Source: [GaussMarkovUnivariate.xls]MonteCarlo.

In 10,000 repetitions, the 0.9 estimator never gave us an estimate close to β. This is a bad recipe. We exclude the 0.9 estimator and all biased estimators from the race.

Choosing a Winner

We have eliminated the 0.9 estimator (and all other biased estimators) from contention, but we still have many candidates to choose from in the set of linear, unbiased estimators. We are using the Sample Average, Diminishing Weights, and Random Linear estimators as examples of linear, unbiased estimators. Which one is the best from this group?

The criterion for best estimator first stated by statisticians in the nineteenth century is that the best estimator has the smallest standard error (SE) of all linear, unbiased estimators. The SE is a measure of the expected size of the deviation between the estimate and the expected value of the estimate. Many other possible criteria could be used and, in fact, occasionally are used to rank estimators. The minimum SE criterion has two main advantages: first, the SE is a good measure of the precision of an estimator; second, the SE has nice mathematical properties that make it easy to work with.

Let us apply this criterion to the example at hand. From the Monte Carlo sheet, we can easily judge the three estimators. Figure 14.3.4 shows the results

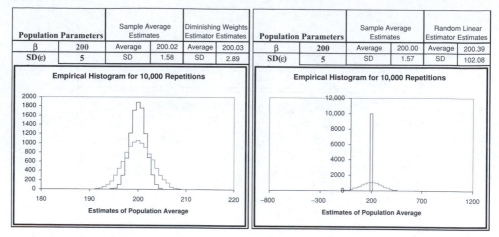

Population Parameters		Sample Average Estimates		Diminishing Weights Estimator Estimates	
β	200	Average	200.02	Average	200.03
SD(ε)	5	SD	1.58	SD	2.89

Population Parameters		Sample Average Estimates		Random Linear Estimator Estimates	
β	200	Average	200.00	Average	200.39
SD(ε)	5	SD	1.57	SD	102.08

Figure 14.3.4. Choosing the best linear unbiased estimator.
Source: [GaussMarkovUnivariate.xls]MonteCarlo.

of a comparison of the Sample Average with the other two linear, unbiased estimators.

In the Monte Carlo results, the SD of the 10,000 sample estimates approximates the exact SE of the estimator. We can readily see that the Sample Average has the lowest SE of the three. This fact can also be visually appreciated. The Sample Average has the most concentrated histogram of the three. The Random Linear estimator is unbiased, but its spread is huge relative to that of the Sample Average estimator. On average, the Random Linear estimator gets the right answer, but it also gives estimates quite far from the truth. The Diminishing Weights estimator is better than the Random Linear estimator but not as good as the Sample Average.

Thus, of these three linear, unbiased estimators, we would select the Sample Average as the best linear, unbiased estimator. The phrase "best linear, unbiased estimator" is used so often that we refer to it by its acronym, BLUE. We say, "If the DGP follows the classical econometric model, then the Sample Average is BLUE." The Sample Average wins the race because it has the smallest SE. In other words, it is both accurate (unbiased) and the most precise (smallest SE) of these three linear estimators.

Unfortunately, our comparison of three linear, unbiased estimators does not come close to a much more powerful statement that the Sample Average estimator has the smallest SE of *all* of the linear, unbiased estimators of the population average. This remarkable claim is known as the Gauss–Markov theorem. To prove the theorem, we need to show that the Sample Average estimator has a smaller SE than any other linear, unbiased estimator. Because there are an infinite number of such estimators, we will not be able to use Monte Carlo techniques to prove the result we are after. We can confidently assert that careful Monte Carlo experiments will always declare the Sample Average the winner against any alternative linear, unbiased estimator for the population average, but the reason we know that is because of the analytical proof.

Summary

This section has used Monte Carlo methods to demonstrate the notion of bias and to show that the Sample Average has the lowest SE of three linear, unbiased estimators. Biased estimators are systematically wrong. In other words, the sampling distribution of a biased estimator is not centered on the population value we are trying to estimate. When we take a random sample and compute a sample estimate, it is like drawing the estimate from the estimator's sampling distribution. If it is not centered on the truth, the estimator is said to be biased and, therefore, inaccurate.

Even after we eliminate all of the biased, linear estimators, we are still left with an infinite number of potential candidates. The winner is chosen based on which one has the least variability. This makes common sense. If they are all unbiased, they are all centered on the population value we are trying to estimate. But the ones with large SEs (like the Random Linear estimator) can produce wild results. Very high estimates do indeed cancel out with very low estimates, and so on average all is well, but we prefer estimates that are unbiased and tightly clustered around the truth. Our Monte Carlo results showed that the Sample Average was indeed the winner because it had the smallest SE of the three unbiased estimators.

The Gauss–Markov theorem goes one step farther. It guarantees that the Sample Average will have the lowest possible SE of *any* linear, unbiased estimator. The next section proves this remarkable result.

14.4. Proving the Gauss–Markov Theorem in the Univariate Case

Workbook: GaussMarkovUnivariate.xls

This section presents a formal proof of the Gauss–Markov theorem in the univariate case and also tries to explain exactly what is going on in the proof by using Excel. We approach the proof by working with our 10-observation example. We then consider the more general case of *n* observations.

Gauss–Markov with 10 Observations

Open the GaussMarkovUnivariate.xls workbook and go to the *ComputingSEs* sheet. The table in the *ComputingSEs* sheet, reproduced in

| SD(ε) | 5 | | | | |
| Variance(ε) | 25 | | | | |

	Weights (w_i)			$w_i^2 SD(\varepsilon)^2$	
Observation	Sample Average	Diminishing Weights Estimator	Sample Average	Diminishing Weights Estimator
1	0.1	0.5	0.2500	6.2500
2	0.1	0.25	0.2500	1.5625
3	0.1	0.125	0.2500	0.3906
4	0.1	0.0625	0.2500	0.0977
5	0.1	0.03125	0.2500	0.0244
6	0.1	0.015625	0.2500	0.0061
7	0.1	0.0078125	0.2500	0.0015
8	0.1	0.0039063	0.2500	0.0004
9	0.1	0.0019531	0.2500	0.0001
10	0.1	0.0019531	0.2500	0.0001
Sum	1	1	2.500	8.333
		SquareRoot	1.581	2.887

Figure 14.4.1. Computing the SEs of the OLS and diminishing weights estimators. *Source:* [GaussMarkovUnivariate.xls]ComputingSEs.

Figure 14.4.1, computes the exact SEs of different estimators of the population average. Each and every *linear* estimator of the population average can be analyzed in the table – just put the weights into the appropriate cells – and the table will compute the SE. If an estimator is to be unbiased, it must meet an additional condition: The weights must sum to one. The Change Estimators button cycles through different competing estimators.

The left half of the table simply reports the weights for the OLS estimator and a competing estimator. The right half of the table computes the exact SE for the two estimators. Recall that the general formula for the exact SE is

$$SD\left(\sum_{i=1}^{n} w_i Y_i\right) = \sqrt{\sum_{i=1}^{n} w_i^2 Var(\varepsilon_i)}$$

$$= \sqrt{\sum_{i=1}^{n} w_i^2 SD^2(\varepsilon_i)}.$$

Each cell in the right half of the table computes one of the terms in the sum. We have set up the workbook so that the SD of the errors is controlled by the *UnivariateSample* sheet. In Figure 14.4.1, the SD of the error terms has been set to equal 1 and the Diminishing Weights estimator (in addition to the OLS estimator) has been selected. The very first entry in the last column reads 6.25. The computation behind this number is straightforward:

$$w_1^2 SD^2\left(\varepsilon_1\right) = (0.5)^2 \cdot 5^2$$
$$= 6.25.$$

The table sums up all the individual $w_i^2 SD^2\left(\varepsilon_i\right)$ entries and then takes the square root of the sum to obtain the SE of the estimator. As you can see, the OLS estimator has a smaller SE than the Diminishing Weights estimator. If you run a Monte Carlo simulation (as we did in Figure 14.3.4), you will find that the Monte Carlo approximations to the SEs are very close to the exact SEs computed in the table.

Are there linear estimators with smaller SEs than the OLS estimator? The answer is yes: Change the estimators until you reach the 0.9 Estimator. Its SE is guaranteed to be 90 percent as large as the SE of the OLS estimator. Unfortunately, the 0.9 Estimator is biased. As we explained in the previous section, this removes it from contention.

Thus, the problem is to find that set of weights for a linear, unbiased estimator that has the smallest possible SE. This can be viewed as a constrained optimization problem that Excel's Solver can easily handle. The objective function to be minimized is the SE, and the constraint is that the weights must sum to 1. To see the Solver setup, click on the Show Solver button. Execute Tools: Solver, and a display like that of Figure 14.4.2 will appear. Click the Solve button to get the optimal solution.

The solution – the set of weights in column F – is guaranteed to be identical to the weights used by the Sample Average estimator. In other words, in this specific case of 10 observations, the Sample Average estimator is BLUE.

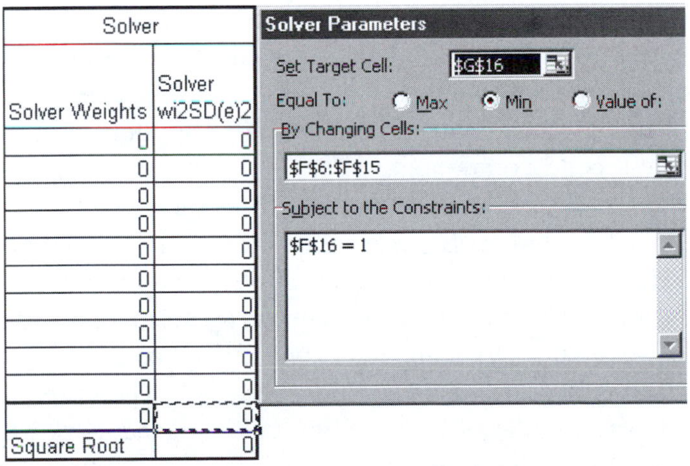

Figure 14.4.2. Using Solver to find minimum SE weights subject to the constraint of unbiasedness.
Source: [GaussMarkovUnivariate.xls]ComputingSEs.

SD(ε)	1
Variance	1

	Weights (w_i)			w_i^2SD(ε)^2		
Observation	Sample Average	Alternative Estimator	Difference	Sample Average	Alternative Estimator	Difference
1	0.1	0.0675	0.0325	0.01	0.0046	0.001058
2	0.1	0.0379	0.0621	0.01	0.0014	0.003857
3	0.1	0.1606	−0.0606	0.01	0.0258	0.003667
4	0.1	0.0992	0.0008	0.01	0.0098	6.01E-07
5	0.1	0.1666	−0.0666	0.01	0.0278	0.004438
6	0.1	0.1402	−0.0402	0.01	0.0197	0.001614
7	0.1	0.0433	0.0567	0.01	0.0019	0.003211
8	0.1	0.1875	−0.0875	0.01	0.0351	0.007651
9	0.1	0.1012	−0.0012	0.01	0.0102	1.42E-06
10	0.1	−0.0040	0.1040	0.01	0.0000	0.010806
Sum	1	1	0.0000	0.100	0.136	0.036	Variance
			SquareRoot	0.316	0.369	0.191	SE

Figure 14.4.3. Demonstration of Gauss–Markov proof.
Source: [GaussMarkovUnivariate.xls]GaussMarkovThm.

The key to understanding why the Sample Average is guaranteed to be the best linear, unbiased estimator is to realize that it weights the data optimally. Linear estimators are weighted sums that contain two components:

$$\sum_{i=1}^{n} w_i Y_i = \sum_{i=1}^{n} w_i \beta + \sum_{i=1}^{n} w_i \varepsilon_i.$$

Because β is a constant, the first component, $\sum_{i=1}^{n} w_i \beta$, can be written as $\beta \sum_{i=1}^{n} w_i$. In as much as the weights (the w_i's) sum to 1, the first component equals the true population average β. The second component, $\sum_{i=1}^{n} w_i \varepsilon_i$, has an expected value of 0 because the DGP follows the CEM. Because the expected value of the estimates is β, linear estimators whose weights sum to one are unbiased. Figure 14.4.3 shows the Sample Average and an Alternative Estimator that is linear and unbiased.

All linear, unbiased estimators, however, are not equivalent. It is the difference in the second component, $\sum_{i=1}^{n} w_i \varepsilon_i$, that causes the difference in the behavior of linear, unbiased estimators. The equal weighting of the Sample Average means that its SE is smallest in the class of linear, unbiased estimators. The intuition is that the Sample Average does not allow any individual observation, which might have a large error term, to outvote the other observations. Estimators like the Diminishing Weights estimator, which give much weight to the first observation, do a great job when the first observation is close to the population average but are far off the mark when the first observation contains a large positive or negative error term. The SE of the Diminishing Weights estimator reflects the resulting increased variability of the estimator.

Gauss–Markov with n Observations

The formal algebraic proof goes beyond Excel's Solver in that it works for any number of observations. We begin by pointing out that any alternative linear, unbiased estimator to the Sample Average has this basic form:

$$Alternative\ Estimator = \sum_{i=1}^{n} w_i Y_i.$$

These weights are presumably different from the least squares weights, which are all $1/n$. Label the difference between the weights d_i. That is $d_i = w_i - \frac{1}{n}$. The *GaussMarkovThm* sheet, reproduced by Figure 14.4.3, gives an example for our 10-observation case. The column labeled "Difference" contains the d_i's. The differences must sum to zero to guarantee unbiasedness. Verify that cell D16 is, in fact, zero. Hit the F9 key to recalculate the workbook and get a new Alternative Estimator. Cell D16 continues to evaluate to zero, which maintains the constraint that the Alternative Estimator is unbiased.

The variance of the linear, unbiased Alternative Estimator is then given by this equation:

$$Var(Alternative\ Estimator)$$
$$= \sum_{i=1}^{n} w_i^2 SD(\varepsilon)^2$$
$$= SD(\varepsilon)^2 \sum_{i=1}^{n} \left(\frac{1}{n} + d_i\right)^2$$
$$= SD(\varepsilon)^2 \left[\sum_{i=1}^{n} \left(\frac{1}{n}\right)^2 + \sum_{i=1}^{n} (d_i)^2 + 2\sum_{i=1}^{n} \left(\frac{1}{n} \cdot d_i\right)\right]$$
$$= SD(\varepsilon)^2 \left[\sum_{i=1}^{n} \left(\frac{1}{n}\right)^2 + \sum_{i=1}^{n} (d_i)^2 + \frac{2}{n}\sum_{i=1}^{n} (d_i)\right]$$
$$= SD(\varepsilon)^2 \left[\sum_{i=1}^{n} \left(\frac{1}{n}\right)^2 + \sum_{i=1}^{n} (d_i)^2 + \frac{2}{n} 0\right]$$
$$= SD(\varepsilon)^2 \left[\sum_{i=1}^{n} \left(\frac{1}{n}\right)^2 + \sum_{i=1}^{n} (d_i)^2\right]$$
$$= SD(\varepsilon)^2 \sum_{i=1}^{n} \left(\frac{1}{n}\right)^2 + SD(\varepsilon)^2 \sum_{i=1}^{n} (d_i)^2$$
$$= Var(Sample\ Average) + SD(\varepsilon)^2 \sum_{i=1}^{n} (d_i)^2.$$

In other words, the variance of the alternative estimator is the sum of the variance of the Sample Average plus a quantity guaranteed to be nonnegative because it is a sum of squares. Thus, *any* alternative linear, unbiased estimator has a greater variance than the Sample Average estimator. We conclude that the Sample Average estimator has the smallest variance and therefore the smallest SE of all linear, unbiased estimators of the population average.

The *GaussMarkovThm* sheet shows the decomposition of the variance of alternative estimators (we use random numbers to generate different alternatives) into a sum of the variance of the Sample Average and the sum of the squared differences multiplied by the square of the SD of the error terms on the right. Recalculate the *GaussMarkovThm* sheet repeatedly (by hitting F9) and you will see that cell G16 is always positive. Use the Monte Carlo simulation add-in on cell G16 for a more convincing demonstration. The Alternative Estimator is unbiased, but it is always less precise than the Sample Average (which is the OLS Estimator).

Summary

This section proved what the Monte Carlo results from Section 14.3 suggested: If the DGP follows the classical econometric model, the Sample Average estimator is BLUE. This statement, known as the Gauss–Markov theorem, is what justifies the use of the sample average to estimate the population average.

The next section shows that the Gauss–Markov theorem carries over to regression analysis. Just as in the univariate case, we will see that OLS is BLUE when fitting a line to a cloud of bivariate data.

14.5. Linear Estimators in Regression Analysis

Workbook: GaussMarkovBivariate.xls

In this section and the next we discuss linear, unbiased estimators in the bivariate case. We assume that the classical econometric model applies. The approach closely mirrors our work in the previous sections in this chapter. We characterize linear estimators as weighted sums of the data. We show that the weights for the OLS estimator in the bivariate case are different from those in the univariate case – they are a complicated function of the X's, and they sum to 0, not 1. As in the univariate case, however, the weights reveal whether the estimator is biased. All linear, unbiased estimators in the bi- and multivariate cases have weights that sum to zero. As before, we will race the OLS estimator against alternative linear, unbiased estimators. We will use Monte Carlo experiments to demonstrate that the OLS estimator of the bivariate slope is the best (i.e., the minimum-variance linear, unbiased estimator).

The DGP Follows the CEM

The model for the data generation process is the following:

$$Y_i = \beta_0 + \beta_1 \cdot X_i + \varepsilon_i, \quad i = 1, \ldots, n.$$

Here β_0 and β_1 are, respectively, the intercept and slope parameters we want to estimate, and the ε_i's are assumed to be repeated draws from an error box (always the same one) with an infinite number of tickets whose mean is zero and with an unknown standard deviation. The n draws are independent of each other. The X's are fixed in repeated sampling. These assumptions, taken together, guarantee that the ε_i's are independent of the X's. Thus the value of the draw from the box, ε_i, has nothing to do with the value of X_i.

To better understand the data generation process of the CEM in the bivariate case, go to the *BivariateSample* sheet in the GaussMarkovBivariate.xls workbook. As shown in Figure 14.5.1, the first four columns display the data generation process.

Population Parameters			
β_0	10		
β_1	5		
SD(ε)	50		
β_1	ε_i	X_i	Y_i
5	22.11	10	82.11
5	−39.84	15	45.16
5	115.87	22	235.87
5	−12.86	30	147.14
5	−15.18	45	219.82
5	85.03	50	345.03
5	5.50	65	340.50
5	46.04	75	431.04
5	−24.84	89	430.16
5	−5.78	100	504.22
Sum	176.06	501.000	2781.06

Figure 14.5.1. Implementing the data generation process in Excel.
Source: [GaussMarkovBivariate.xls]BivariateSample.

The true, unknown population parameters are given in the upper, left-hand corner. As usual, all values that would not be observed by the econometrician are in red. The formula for each ε_i (in column B) is "=normalrandom(0,SDepsilon)." This fulfills the requirement that the average of the box be zero and that each draw come from the same box. As required, the X values remain fixed in repeated sampling. Finally, the Y values in each row are faithful to the classical econometric model requirements because the formula for each Y_i is "=beta0+beta1*Xi + epsilon."

The OLS Estimator of the Slope Is a Linear Estimator

We turn now to the OLS estimator of the slope parameter, β_1. We initially concentrate on the weights that go into the estimator. The relevant computations are displayed in Figure 14.5.2.

In Section 5.4 we discussed the formulas for the OLS Slope and Intercept (b_0 and b_1, respectively) and pointed out that the Slope coefficient is a weighted sum of the Y values. In the next few paragraphs, we will remind you of those formulas and point to how they are implemented in GaussMarkov-Bivariate.xls.

The OLS estimator for the Slope is obtained via the following formula:

$$Slope = \sum_{i=1}^{n} w_i \cdot Y_i,$$

where

$$w_i = \frac{(X_i - \bar{X})}{\sum_{i=1}^{n}(X_i - \bar{X})^2}, \quad i = 1, \ldots, n,$$

n is the number of observations and $\bar{X}$ is the average value of the X_i's in the data set. Since the variance of X is defined as

$$Variance(X) = \frac{\sum_{i=1}^{n}(X_i - \bar{X})^2}{n},$$

the weights for the OLS estimator can be written as

$$w_i = \frac{(X_i - \bar{X})}{n \cdot Variance(X)}, \quad i = 1, \ldots, n.$$

The first and second columns from the left in Figure 14.5.2 break the computation of the weights into two parts. The first column simply gives the deviations of each individual X_i from the average value of X. The Excel equation for each cell in this column is "=Xi-Xmean," and each cell in the column is named Xdeviationi. The cell labeled Variance X is used in the computation

OLS Estimate	4.794
Mean X	55
Variance X	825

$X_i - \text{Avg}(X)$	OLS w_i	$w_i X_i$
−45	−0.00545	−0.0545
−35	−0.00424	−0.0848
−25	−0.00303	−0.0909
−15	−0.00182	−0.0727
−5	−0.00061	−0.0303
5	0.00061	0.0364
15	0.00182	0.1273
25	0.00303	0.2424
35	0.00424	0.3818
45	0.0055	0.5455
0.000	0.000	1.000

Figure 14.5.2. Computing the OLS estimator in the bivariate case.
Source: [GaussMarkovBivariate.xls] BivariateSample.

of each weight.[4] The formula for w_i just above tells us that the weights themselves are the deviations of the X's from the mean X divided by the product of the number of observations and the variance of the X's. The Excel formula for each weight is "= XDeviationi/(10*VarX)."

Before moving on, we should note one instance in which the weights and the OLS estimator are undefined. This is the case of perfect multicollinearity between the X's and the intercept term. Multicollinearity arises in the bivariate setting when the X's are all the same. That makes the variance of X equal to zero, causing the weights to be undefined. As shown in Chapter 7, with perfect multicollinearity there are an infinite number of different estimates of the slope that minimize the sum of squared residuals, meaning that there is no single, unique least squares estimate.

The upshot of all this is that the OLS slope estimator is a linear estimator, that is, b_1 is a linear function of the Y's. The weight multiplying each Y value is a complicated function of the X's, but the Y's themselves enter linearly into the formula.

In Section 14.2 we showed that a key property of the Sample Average estimator weights – namely that they summed to 1 – guaranteed that the Sample Average estimator of the population average was unbiased. Furthermore, we showed that any linear estimator whose weights sum to 1 is unbiased. We are about to demonstrate that the OLS estimator for the bivariate case has not one but two crucial properties, which, taken together, imply that it produces unbiased estimates of the slope. As before, any estimator sharing

---

[4] Notice that the formula for the variance in cell F3 is =SUMPRODUCT(XDeviationi,XDeviationi)/10. This SUMPRODUCT function sums up the 10 squared deviations of each X value from the mean of the X's. The variance is the average of the squared deviations of the X's from their mean. The variance of X is also the square of the population SD of the X's.

these properties will be an unbiased estimator of the slope in the bivariate case.

The table in the *BivariateSample* sheet, which is reproduced in Figure 14.5.2, reveals the two important, general (i.e., true for any values of the X's) properties about the OLS weights.

1. The sum of the weights is 0 (not 1 as in the univariate case).
   This fact follows directly from the definition of the weights. Each numerator is the deviation of each individual X_i from the mean of the X's. The sum of these deviations must be 0. Because the sum of the weights is the sum of the deviations divided by n multiplied by the Sample Variance, the sum of the weights must be 0. Here is the algebra:

$$\sum_{i=1}^{n} w_i = \sum_{i=1}^{n} \frac{(X_i - \bar{X})}{\sum_{i=1}^{n}(X_i - \bar{X})^2}$$

$$= \frac{1}{\sum_{i=1}^{n}(X_i - \bar{X})^2} \sum_{i=1}^{n}(X_i - \bar{X})$$

$$= \frac{1}{\sum_{i=1}^{n}(X_i - \bar{X})^2} \cdot 0$$

$$= 0.$$

2. The sum of the products of the weights with the X's is 1.
   This property of the OLS estimator is harder to show algebraically. It relies on the following somewhat surprising fact:

$$\sum_{i=1}^{n}(X_i - \bar{X}) \cdot X_i = \sum_{i=1}^{n}(X_i - \bar{X})^2.$$

To demonstrate that $\sum_{i=1}^{n} w_i X_i = 1$, we plug this fact into the computation below:

$$\sum_{i=1}^{n} w_i X_i = \sum_{i=1}^{n} \frac{(X_i - \bar{X}) \cdot X_i}{\sum_{i=1}^{n}(X_i - \bar{X})^2}$$

$$= \frac{1}{\sum_{i=1}^{n}(X_i - \bar{X})^2} \sum_{i=1}^{n}(X_i - \bar{X}) \cdot X_i$$

$$= \frac{\sum_{i=1}^{n}(X_i - \bar{X})^2}{\sum_{i=1}^{n}(X_i - \bar{X})^2}$$

$$= 1.$$

You can use the *BivariateSample* worksheet to verify that these two properties are indeed general. Click on the `Change the X's` button several times to appreciate that the sum of the weights in cell F16 is always 0, whereas the sum of the product of the weights with the X values in cell G16 is always 1. Of course this is not a proof but just a demonstration.

At this point you may have a question. The least squares weights sum to 1 in the univariate case, but now we are telling you they sum to 0 in the bivariate case. How can that be? The answer is that the two sets of weights are elements of two separate recipes designed to handle two different situations. We are about to see how the bivariate least squares weights produce unbiased estimates of the slope, which is a trickier proposition than obtaining unbiased estimates of the population average.

The OLS Estimator of the Slope Is an Unbiased Estimator

Showing that OLS is an unbiased estimator in the bivariate case is a more complicated proposition algebraically than it was in the univariate case. Our method of decomposing the sum of the $w_i Y_i$ terms into columns should help you understand what is going on.

We begin by substituting the equation for the DGP into the formula for the OLS estimator for the Slope:

$$\text{Slope} = \sum_{i=1}^{n} w_i (\beta_0 + \beta_1 X_i + \varepsilon_i)$$

$$= \sum_{i=1}^{n} w_i \beta_0 + w_i \beta_1 X_i + w_i \varepsilon_i.$$

Each Y_i term is the sum of a weight times the sum of the intercept parameter β_0, the product $\beta_1 \cdot X_i$, and an error term ε_i. The table shown in Figure 14.5.3 decomposes the weighted sum of the OLS estimator of the Slope into three separate components.

None of the three components is directly observed, and so they show up in red on the computer screen. All that we can observe are the $w_i Y_i$'s (the right-most column).

The decomposition reveals some surprising facts. The first component, $\sum_{i=1}^{n} w_i \beta_0$, sums to 0. Why? The reason is that the sum can be rewritten

$w_i\beta_0$	$w_i\beta_1 X_i$	$w_i\varepsilon_i$	$w_i Y_i$
−0.045	−0.225	−0.100	−0.370
−0.039	−0.296	0.157	−0.178
−0.032	−0.347	−0.366	−0.744
−0.023	−0.339	0.029	−0.332
−0.006	−0.129	0.009	−0.126
0.000	−0.003	−0.001	−0.004
0.017	0.544	0.009	0.570
0.028	1.049	0.129	1.205
0.044	1.944	−0.109	1.879
0.056	2.802	−0.032	2.825
0.000	5.000	−0.274	**4.726**

Figure 14.5.3. Decomposing the sum of the products $w_i Y_i$ into its three components. *Source:* [GaussMarkovBivariate.xls] BivariateSample.

as $\beta_0 \sum_{i=1}^{n} w_i$ and we know that the sum of the weights is 0. Thus, the influence of β_0 on the slope estimate is removed. Try this: Change the value of β_0 in cell B2 and observe that the slope estimate is unchanged even though all the Y_i values change. Second, the product of the weights with the $\beta_1 X_i$ terms sums to β_1 (i.e., the sum of the $w_i X_i \beta_1$ column is β_1). Again this follows from the special properties of the OLS weights and can be verified from the sheet: Change the value of β_1 and observe that the value of the sum of the $w_i X_i \beta_1$ column is always β_1. This has nothing to do with the specific X values in the example. Hit the Change the X's button and observe that the sum of the $w_i X_i \beta_1$ column does not change.

The last component is a weighted sum of the error terms, which will bounce around zero whenever you draw a new sample. Notice that, in keeping with the fixed-X's-in-repeated-sampling assumption, recalculating the sheet by hitting the F9 key repeatedly takes another 10 draws from the error box but does not change the X's.

Let us sum up what has been learned via this decomposition of the sum of the products of the weights and the Y's. The first component, the $w_i \beta_0$ terms, is guaranteed to sum to 0. The second component, the $w_i X_i \beta_1$ terms, is guaranteed to sum to β_1. The third component, the $w_i \varepsilon_i$ terms, sums to a number that bounces around 0. Thus, the overall sum of the three components bounces around β_1.

Hit F9 repeatedly. It appears that the OLS slope estimator is unbiased. A simple Monte Carlo simulation with the MCSim add-in confirms this. Figure 14.5.4 was created by tracking cell F1 in the *BivariateSample* sheet. The average is close to 5, the value of β_1. This is strong evidence that the OLS slope estimator is indeed unbiased. To prove that the OLS slope estimator is unbiased, we must employ the algebra of expectations by computing the expected value of the slope estimator and showing that it equals β_1. That is done in Section 14.7.

Other Linear, Unbiased Estimators

The OLS estimator is not the only linear, unbiased estimator of the slope in the bivariate version of the classical econometric model. It is possible to come up with other linear unbiased estimators on the basis of straightforward intuition. We will discuss two alternative linear, unbiased estimators: the Extreme Points estimator and the Average Slopes estimator.

The Extreme Points estimator simply takes the slope of the first and last points in the bivariate data set. Figure 14.5.4 displays a graph of this estimator. The other points are ignored. Figure 14.5.5 shows how the Extreme Points Line simply connects the first and last observations.

The Extreme Points Estimator is just one of many two-point estimators; related two-point estimators would connect other points. The slope estimate

Summary Statistics		Notes
Average	5.026	
SD	0.5668	
Max	6.503	
Min	3.418	

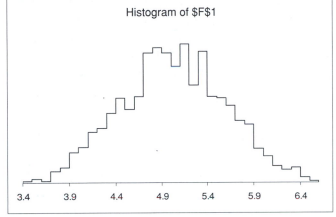

Figure 14.5.4. 1,000 OLS estimates.
Source: [GaussMarkovBivariate.xls]BivariateSample and MCSim add-in.

for the Extreme Points estimator can be computed as follows:

$$Slope = \frac{Y_{10} - Y_1}{X_{10} - X_1}.$$

This means that the Extreme Points estimator can be written as a linear function of the Y's:

$$\text{Extreme Points Estimate} = \sum_{i=1}^{n} w_i \cdot Y_i,$$

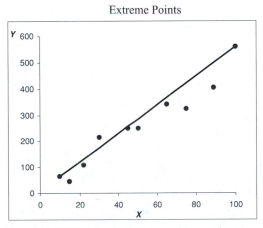

Figure 14.5.5. The extreme points estimator.

where the weights are

$$w_1 = -\frac{1}{X_{10} - X_1}$$

$$w_i = 0, \quad i = 2, \ldots 9$$

$$w_{10} = \frac{1}{X_{10} - X_1}.$$

Thus, the Extreme Points estimator is linear. It is straightforward to show that the weights of the Extreme Points estimator share the two properties we highlighted for the OLS estimator and therefore that the Extreme Points estimator is unbiased:

1. The sum of the weights is 0.

$$w_1 + w_2 + \cdots + w_9 + w_{10} = -\frac{1}{X_{10} - X_1} + 0 + \cdots + 0 + \frac{1}{X_{10} - X_1}$$
$$= 0.$$

2. The sum of the products of the weights and the X's is 1.

$$w_1 X_1 + w_2 X_2 + \cdots + w_9 X_9 + w_{10} X_{10} = -\frac{1}{X_{10} - X_1} X_1 + 0 \cdot X_2$$
$$+ \cdots + 0 \cdot X_9 + \frac{1}{X_{10} - X_1} X_{10}$$
$$= \frac{-X_1}{X_{10} - X_1} + \frac{X_{10}}{X_{10} - X_1}$$
$$= \frac{X_{10} - X_1}{X_{10} - X_1}$$
$$= 1.$$

The *BivariateEstimators* sheet contrasts the OLS estimator with either the Extreme Points or the Average Slopes estimator (which we are about to discuss). Click on the [Change the Alternative Estimator] button to select which estimator you want to compare with the OLS estimator. For now, make sure that the Alternative Estimator is the Extreme Points estimator and observe that the same three-way decomposition of the weighted sum applies to the Extreme Points estimator as to the OLS estimator. The columnar decomposition is visible in columns I through L of the *BivariateEstimators* sheet. Once again the results do not depend on the particular X's employed (so long as the X's do not all have the same value). The [Change the X's] button cycles through various possibilities.

Another possible estimator of the slope is the average of the slopes of the lines formed by connecting adjacent points together. It takes a little work to find the weights for the Average Slopes Estimator. The slope of the first line is $\frac{Y_2 - Y_1}{X_2 - X_1}$, the slope of the second line is $\frac{Y_3 - Y_2}{X_3 - X_2}$, and so on. This means that Y_1

is multiplied by $\frac{-1}{X_2 - X_1}$, whereas Y_2 is multiplied by $\frac{1}{X_2 - X_1}$ and $\frac{-1}{X_3 - X_2}$. Carrying this logic further, we find that the weights are as follows:

$$w_1 = \frac{1}{9} \cdot \left(-\frac{1}{X_2 - X_1} \right)$$

$$w_i = \frac{1}{9} \cdot \left(\frac{1}{X_i - X_{i-1}} - \frac{1}{X_{i+1} - X_i} \right), \quad i = 2, \ldots 9$$

$$w_{10} = \frac{1}{9} \cdot \left(\frac{1}{X_{10} - X_9} \right).$$

The 1/9 terms show up because we are taking the average of the slopes. Again, it can be shown that the weights sum to 0, the product of the weights with the X's is 1, and thus that the expected value of the estimator of the slope is β_1. The *BivariateEstimators* sheet demonstrates these facts.

It is interesting to note that the Average Slopes Estimator and Extreme Points Estimator result in exactly the same recipe when the X's are equally spaced. This occurs for one of the sets of X values in the *BivariateEstimators* sheet – namely, the one in which the X's are 10, 20, . . . , 100.

Summary

In this section, we have emphasized that the OLS estimator is a weighted sum of the values of the dependent variable and therefore a linear estimator. Monte Carlo results suggest that the OLS slope estimator is unbiased when the classical econometric model applies.

The fact that OLS is a linear, unbiased estimator is not particularly distinctive. There are an infinite number of other linear, unbiased estimators. Two of them are the Extreme Points and Average Slopes Estimators, which we chose because they are relatively easy to describe.

From this sea of linear, unbiased estimators, why is OLS the best choice? The next section shows that, despite the infinite number of competitors, when the CEM applies, the OLS estimator is guaranteed to be the minimum-variance estimator in the class of linear, unbiased estimators.

14.6. OLS is BLUE: The Gauss–Markov Theorem for the Bivariate Case

Workbook: GaussMarkovBivariate.xls

In this section we return to the Gauss–Markov theorem – this time for the bivariate case. The theorem says that, when the classical econometric model (CEM) of the data generation process applies, the OLS estimator is the Best Linear Unbiased Estimator. Our approach is straightforward: We

Set 1	Set 2	Set 3
X_i	X_i	X_i
10	10	8.219
15	20	12.993
22	30	31.121
30	40	41.735
45	50	43.073
50	60	62.422
65	70	70.127
75	80	78.052
89	90	88.427
100	100	101.159
		(random)
		slightly different each time

Figure 14.6.1. Three sets of X values.
Source: [GaussMarkovBivariate.xls]Q&A.

perform Monte Carlo experiments to find approximate SEs for the OLS estimator and two competing estimators. You will not be surprised to hear that OLS decisively wins these Monte Carlo races. This is suggestive but by no means conclusive evidence that OLS is in fact the minimum-variance linear, unbiased, estimator under the CEM.

The GaussMarkovBivariate.xls workbook enables you to approximate the SE of three estimators of the sample slope: the OLS estimator, the Extreme Points estimator, and the Average Slopes estimator. We will walk you through a few races. We invite you to run other races in exercises at the end of this chapter and in the *Q&A* sheet.

To set up a Monte Carlo experiment, first go to the *BivariateEstimators* sheet and choose the set of X's you want to use by clicking on the Change the X's button. The three sets of X's you can choose from are given in Figure 14.6.1. Set 3 is actually a collection of random X's that changes slightly each time you toggle through. Finally, you can set the values of the parameters of the CEM. We chose the values given in Figure 14.6.2.

We selected Set 2 of the X's, returned to the Monte Carlo sheet, and ran a 10,000-repetition Monte Carlo experiment that raced OLS versus Extreme Points (by clicking on the Extreme Points option in the *MonteCarlo* sheet). Figure 14.6.3 shows our results.

In this Monte Carlo experiment the approximate SE of the OLS estimator is 0.528, whereas the approximate SE of the Extreme Points estimator is

Population Parameters	
β_0	10
β_1	5
SD(ε)	50

Figure 14.6.2. Population parameters for the Monte Carlo experiment.
Source: [GaussMarkovBivariate.xls]BivariateEstimators.

Population Parameters		OLS Estimates		Extreme Points Estimates	
β_1	5	Average	5.00	Average	4.99
SD(ε)	50	SD	0.551	SD	0.786

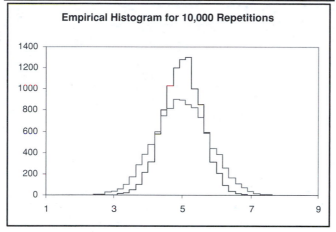

Empirical Histogram for 10,000 Repetitions

Figure 14.6.3. OLS versus extreme points estimator.
Source: [GaussMarkovBivariate.xls]MonteCarlo.

0.787. This is strong evidence that the OLS estimator has a smaller SE than the Extreme Points estimator.

The OLS estimator has defeated Extreme Points for this particular DGP, but what if the spread of the errors was different? Would OLS win again? Change cell B4 in the *BivariateEstimators* sheet and then race the estimators again. What happens? The result is the same: OLS wins.

Let us try a more sophisticated experiment. This one caused some controversy when the properties of OLS were being discovered. The question is this: Does the status of OLS as BLUE depend on the distribution of the errors? In other words, suppose the errors came from another distribution such as a uniform distribution. Would OLS still win?

You can answer this question with Monte Carlo simulation. The first step is to change the distribution of the errors. Return to the *BivariateEstimators* sheet and set cell B4 to 50. Next, change the formula for the epsilons in the *BivariateEstimators* sheet from "= normalrandom(0, SDepsilon)" to "= uniform(0, SDepsilon)." You can change the first cell, A6, then, fill down the formula. Another approach is to select all of the epsilons (in cell range A6:A15) and execute Edit: Replace in order to replace "normalrandom" with "uniform." The new formula makes the errors come from a box that is uniformly distributed in the interval −86.6 to 86.6.[5] The average of this box

---

[5] See the Random.xls workbook in the Basic Tools/Random Number folder if you are interested in how this interval is determined.

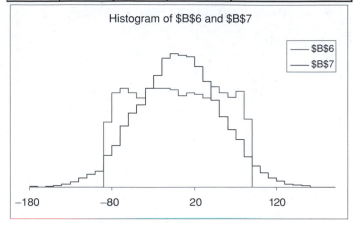

$B$6		$B$7		Notes
Average	−0.183	Average	0.808	
SD	50.1283	SD	49.4003	
Max	86.590	Max	187.808	
Min	−86.545	Min	−173.936	

Figure 14.6.4. Normal versus uniform error distributions.

remains 0 and the SD is still 50. Hit F9 to see that the error draws are equally likely to come from anywhere in the interval (unlike the normalrandom formula that concentrates the draws around zero).

To see the difference between the normal and uniform error distributions, we used the Monte Carlo simulation add-in to track two cells. One cell used the uniform formula and the other the normalrandom formula. Both cells had mean 0 and SD of 50. Figure 14.6.4 shows the results.

As you can see, the uniform distribution has a rectangular shape. That means any of the numbers within the interval are equally likely to be chosen. You are more likely to get a draw from the center of the normal distribution and the tails are much longer (in theory, infinitely long).

To make a fair comparison with the normal error distribution used to create Figure 14.6.3, we need to make sure that everything else is the same. Make sure the SD of the errors is 50 and that the *BivariateEstimators* sheet is based on Set 2 of the X's.

With the *BivariateEstimators* sheet prepared, you are ready to run the Monte Carlo. You cannot, however, use the *MonteCarlo* sheet because it is hard-wired to use a normal distribution for the errors. Fortunately, you have the Monte Carlo simulation add-in at your disposal. Use it to track cells E1 and G1. We did and got the results displayed in Figure 14.6.5.

In our 10,000-repetition Monte Carlo with uniformly distributed errors, OLS beats Extreme Points handily once again. Figure 14.6.5 shows that both are centered on the population parameter value, but the OLS estimator is

OLS Estimates (E1)		Extreme Points (G1)		Notes
Average	5.000	Average	4.968	*n*=10
SD	0.5553	SD	0.7744	SD=50
Max	6.724	Max	6.868	Set 2 *X*'s
Min	3.487	Min	3.151	Uniform(0, 50) Errors

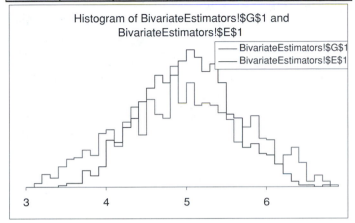

Figure 14.6.5. OLS versus extreme points estimators with a uniform error box. *Source:* [GaussMarkovBivariate.xls]BivariateEstimators and MCSim add-in.

more concentrated around that value than the Extreme Points estimator. Whether the distribution of the errors is normal or uniform does not affect the outcome – OLS wins in the either case.

Figure 14.6.6 collects the results from the Monte Carlo simulations in Figures 14.6.3 and 14.6.5. If you compare the Monte Carlo results from the normally and uniformly distributed errors, you can see that neither the expected value nor the SE of the two estimators is affected by the distribution of the errors. As long as the distribution of the errors is centered on zero, both remain unbiased. Because the SD is 50 for both the uniform and normal error distributions, the standard errors of the two estimators are also unaffected.

This result may seem counterintuitive. After all, surely the distribution of the errors must have some effect. In fact, it does. If you compare the histograms of the OLS estimator in Figures 14.6.3 and 14.6.5, the normally distributed errors produce a more normal looking sampling distribution than

	OLS Estimator		Extreme Points Estimator	
Error	Average	SD	Average	SD
Distribution	(Approximate EV)	(Approximate SE)	(Approximate EV)	(Approximate SE)
Normal	5.00	0.551	4.99	0.786
Uniform	5.00	0.555	4.97	0.774

Figure 14.6.6. No effect of error distribution on EV and SE of sampling distribution.

the uniformly distributed errors. Thus, we can conclude that, although the expected values and SEs are unaffected by the distribution of the errors, the shape of the sampling distribution does depend on the distribution of the errors.[6]

We close this section by turning to a comparison of the OLS and Average Slopes estimators. It is straightforward to run a Monte Carlo that shows that the OLS estimator wins. For the Set 2 X's, Average Slopes is even worse than Extreme Points. It is unbiased, but its SE (as approximated by the empirical SD) is almost three times as large as that of the Extreme Points estimator.

No matter what comparison you make (and we encourage you to try various combinations of X's and parameter values with the Extreme Points and Average Slopes estimators), you will find that the Monte Carlo approximation of the SE of the OLS estimator is always lower than those of its two competitors. In this set of three linear, unbiased estimators, OLS is BLUE. If we posit other linear, unbiased candidates, OLS will beat them too.

Summary

We already know, however, that Monte Carlo cannot be used to prove the Gauss–Markov theorem because you can not possibly race every linear, unbiased estimator in the infinite set of this category. We used the method of Monte Carlo in this section to demonstrate that there are other linear estimators available and that the winner, OLS, is chosen on the basis of being unbiased and having the smallest SE.

The next section presents an approach that can unequivocally establish the dominance of the OLS estimator. By computing the exact expected value and SE, the algebra of expectations can be used to prove the Gauss–Markov theorem.

14.7. Using the Algebra of Expectations

Workbooks: GaussMarkovUnivariate.xls; GaussMarkovBivariate.xls

The material in this section provides a window to a more mathematical presentation of ideas that have already been covered. This section will use the algebra of expectations (reviewed in Chapter 10) to derive analytical formulas for random variables. We follow the organizational scheme of the chapter. First, we work on the univariate case of estimating the population average, and then we analyze the slope estimator in a bivariate regression.

---

[6] We discuss the shape of the sampling distribution of the OLS slope estimator in more detail when we present the z- and t-statistics in Chapter 16.

Estimating the Population Average

Section 14.3 uses Monte Carlo simulation to approximate the sampling distribution of four estimators of the population average. We use the empirical histogram generated by repeated sampling as a stand-in for the true probability histogram. We compute the average and SD of 10,000 estimates as approximations to the exact expected value and SE, respectively. This section takes a more conventional approach to finding the expected value and SE of a sample statistic: derivation of a formula. The formula will tell us the expected value and SE that would result from a Monte Carlo using an infinite number of repetitions.

It is convenient to recapitulate the most important rules about the algebra of expectations before we apply them to derive formulas. We use the symbol k to indicate a constant and X and Y to indicate random variables.

Rule 1: The expected value of a constant is the constant itself. In particular, the expected value of a population parameter is simply the population parameter itself,

$$E(\beta) = \beta.$$

Rule 2: The expected value of the sum of two or more random variables is the sum of the expected values,

$$E(X + Y) = E(X) + E(Y).$$

Rule 3: The expected value of the product of a constant and any other term is the product of the constant and the expected value of the other term,

$$E(k\beta) = kE(\beta). \text{ and } E(kX) = kE(X)$$

Return to the *UnivariateSample* sheet in GaussMarkovUnivariate.xls, click the ⸢Hide Estimator⸥ button, and reexamine the resulting table, which will look like Figure 14.7.1.

β	ε_i	Y_i
200	−2.39	197.61
200	2.95	202.95
200	0.55	200.55
200	−2.59	197.41
200	1.60	201.60
200	1.59	201.59
200	4.01	204.01
200	−0.98	199.02
200	−5.37	194.63
200	−1.25	198.75

Figure 14.7.1. A univariate sample.
Source: [GaussMarkovUnivariate.xls] UnivariateSample.

Each row represents an observation. Each Y_i is made up of two components: the population average β (the population parameter) and the draw from the error box ε_i. Applying the rules stated above, we have

$$
\begin{aligned}
E(Y_i) &= E(\beta + \varepsilon_i) \\
&= E(\beta) + E(\varepsilon_i) \ [\text{Applying Rule 2}] \\
&= \beta + 0 [\text{Applying Rule 1 and the fact that } E(\varepsilon_i) = 0] \\
&= \beta.
\end{aligned}
$$

In essence we are saying that, on average, we expect the value of each Y_i to be the true population parameter β. A quick inspection of Figure 14.7.1 should convince you that this is a reasonable statement about the sample. You can repeatedly draw samples (by hitting the F9 key) and find that the values of each Y bounce around the true population average (in this case, 200).

Let us use the algebra of expectations to find the expected value of the Sample Average estimator. The data generating process is the classical econometric model for the univariate case, $Y_i = \beta + \varepsilon_i, i = 1, \ldots, n$:

$$
\begin{aligned}
E\left[\sum_{i=1}^{n} \frac{1}{n} Y_i\right] &= E\left[\sum_{i=1}^{n} \frac{1}{n} (\beta + \varepsilon_i)_i\right] [\text{Using the CEM}] \\
&= E\left[\sum_{i=1}^{n} \frac{1}{n}\beta\right] + E\left[\sum_{i=1}^{n} \frac{1}{n}\varepsilon_i\right] [\text{Applying Rule 2}] \\
&= \beta + \sum_{i=1}^{n} \frac{1}{n} E(\varepsilon_i) [\text{Applying Rules 1 and 2}] \\
&= \beta + \sum_{i=1}^{n} \frac{1}{n} \cdot 0 [\text{Using the fact that } E(\varepsilon_i) = 0] \\
&= \beta.
\end{aligned}
$$

In any given sample, the Sample Average estimate will not equal β, but its long run average will be β. Therefore, the Sample Average estimator is unbiased.

What about the spread of the Sample Average estimator? To compute the SE of an estimator, analytically one must recognize that the estimator is a random variable. The SE is actually the SD of a random variable. The general strategy in bringing the algebra of expectations to bear on such a problem is to compute the Variance of the estimator and at the end take its square root to get the SD of the estimator. Here are the usual steps:

- Find the components of the estimator that are random variables (you can ignore the constants because they do not change the variance).
- Use standard formulas for computing the variances of sums.
- Hope that the random variables are independent of one another because that simplifies the formulas a great deal.

To make progress in computing the SE of linear estimators, we need a few rules for computing variances and SDs. The following rules are similar to rules one can apply for computing empirical variances and SDs. You must understand, however, that the variances we are talking about in this section are expected values of random variables. We use the symbols a and k to indicate constants and X and Y to indicate random variables.

Rule 1: The variance of a constant multiplied by a random variable is the product of the square of the constant and the variance of the random variable. In equation form, this is expressed as

$$Var(kX) = k^2 Var(X).$$

Rule 2: The variance of a constant is zero:

$$Var(a) = 0.$$

Rule 3: The variance of the sum of a constant and a random variable is just the variance of the random variable:

$$Var(a + X) = Var(X).$$

Rule 4: The variance of a sum of independent random variables is the sum of the variances:

$$Var(X + Y) = Var(X) + Var(Y)$$

when X and Y are independent random variables.

An implication of Rule 1 is that the SD of a random variable multiplied by a constant is just the product of the constant and the SD of the random variable. It is easier to understand this in equation form:

$$SD(kX) = k \cdot SD(X).$$

Our goal is to compute the variance (and then the SD) of a weighted sum of random variables, which is the way we are thinking about the linear estimators of the population average. Combining Rules 1 and 4, we obtain the following result. If X and Y are independent random variables and a and b are two constants, then

$$Var(aX + bY) = a^2 Var(X) + b^2 Var(Y).$$

In the case of linear estimators for 10 observations generated according to the CEM, the random variables are the Y_i's and the constants are the w_i's. The individual Y_i's are sums of a constant β, the population average, and individual error terms, the ε_i's. Applying Rule 3, we obtain

$$Var(Y_i) = Var(\beta + \varepsilon_i) = Var(\varepsilon_i),$$

for every i (every observation).

Then the variance of a linear estimator of the population average is

$$Var\left(\sum_{i=1}^{n} w_i Y_i\right) = \sum_{i=1}^{n} Var\left(w_i Y_i\right)$$

$$= \sum_{i=1}^{n} w_i^2 Var\left(Y_i\right)$$

$$= \sum_{i=1}^{n} w_i^2 Var\left(\varepsilon_i\right).$$

The spread of a linear estimator of the population average is

$$SD\left(\sum_{i=1}^{n} w_i Y_i\right) = \sqrt{\sum_{i=1}^{n} w_i^2 Var\left(\varepsilon_i\right)}$$

$$= \sqrt{\sum_{i=1}^{n} w_i^2 SD^2\left(\varepsilon_i\right)}.$$

These formulas are more general mathematical versions of the rules previously stated (in Chapter 10) for computing the SE of sample sums and averages. Applying these formulas to the example in GaussMarkov-Univariate.xls, we obtain the following values for the exact SE of the Sample Average and Diminishing Weights estimators in the 10-observation case:

$$SE(\text{Sample Average Estimator}) = 0.316\,SD(\varepsilon)$$
$$SE(\text{Diminishing Weights Estimator}) = 0.577\,SD(\varepsilon).$$

See the sheet *ComputingSEs* in GaussMarkovUnivariate.xls for details of the computation.

Estimating β_1

To compute the exact expected value and SE of a linear slope estimator, we apply the expected value and variance rules to the weighted sum that implements the recipe for the estimator. The algebra begins like this:

$$E\left[\sum_{i=1}^{n} w_i Y_i\right] = E\left[\sum_{i=1}^{n} w_i\left(\beta_0 + \beta_1 X_i + \varepsilon_i\right)\right]$$

$$= E\left[\sum_{i=1}^{n} w_i \beta_0\right] + E\left[\sum_{i=1}^{n} w_i \beta_1 X_i\right] + E\left[\sum_{i=1}^{n} w_i \varepsilon_i\right].$$

The first term on the right-hand-side, $E\left[\sum_{i=1}^{n} w_i \beta_0\right]$, is the expected value of a constant – it does not change when a new sample is drawn. We showed in Section 14.5 that the term inside the expectation sign sums to zero.

The second term can be rewritten

$$E\left[\sum_{i=1}^{n} w_i \beta_1 X_i\right] = E\left[\beta_1 \sum_{i=1}^{n} w_i X_i\right]$$

$$= \beta_1 \sum_{i=1}^{n} w_i X_i$$

$$= \beta_1 \cdot 1$$

$$= \beta_1.$$

The final term, $E\left[\sum_{i=1}^{n} w_i \varepsilon_i\right]$, is a weighted sum of constants multiplied by the error terms, but each error term has expected value 0; thus, the weighted sum has expected value 0. Let us be more specific because we wish to highlight a point that will be important in the discussion of omitted variable bias. Here is the algebra:

$$E\left[\sum_{i=1}^{n} w_i \varepsilon_i\right] = \sum_{i=1}^{n} E(w_i \varepsilon_i)$$

$$= \sum_{i=1}^{n} w_i E(\varepsilon_i)$$

$$= \sum_{i=1}^{n} w_i \cdot 0$$

$$= 0.$$

The legitimacy of the move from the first line to the second depends on the fact that the X's, and therefore functions of the X's like the weights, are fixed in repeated sampling. Because the w_i's do not change from one sample to the next, they can be treated as constants in taking expectations. If, on the other hand, the X's were to change from one sample to the next, we would need to make additional assumptions to get the desired result.

Putting the three terms back together, we get

$$E\left[\sum_{i=1}^{n} w_i Y_i\right] = E\left[\sum_{i=1}^{n} w_i (\beta_0 + \beta_1 X_i + \varepsilon_i)\right]$$

$$= E\left[\sum_{i=1}^{n} w_i \beta_0\right] + E\left[\sum_{i=1}^{n} w_i \beta_1 X_i\right] + E\left[\sum_{i=1}^{n} w_i \varepsilon_i\right]$$

$$= 0 + \beta_1 + 0$$

$$= \beta_1.$$

The conclusion of our calculations is that the expected value of the sum of the three terms is β_1. Thus, the OLS estimator for the Bivariate CEM is unbiased. Similar computations would show that the OLS estimator of the intercept is unbiased. More complicated but similar computations can be used to prove the unbiasedness of the OLS estimators of all the parameters in multiple regression versions of the CEM.

We turn now to computing the exact SE of the OLS estimator via the algebra of expectations. The basic building block in the formula for the variance of a linear estimator based on the Y's is Variance(Y_i), the variance of each individual observation on Y. The assumptions of the classical econometric model make it easy to compute this variance, as follows

$$Var(Y_i) = Var(\beta_0 + \beta_1 X_i + \varepsilon_i)$$
$$= Var(\varepsilon_i).$$

This derivation works because $\beta_0 + \beta_1 X_i$ is a constant which does not vary from one sample to the next, and Rule 3 says that the variance of a constant plus a random variable is just the variance of the random variable. Armed with this fact, we can work out the variance of any linear estimator for the classical econometric model.

$$Var\left(\sum_{i=1}^{n} w_i Y_i\right) = \sum_{i=1}^{n} Var(w_i Y_i)$$
$$= \sum_{i=1}^{n} w_i^2 Var(Y_i)$$
$$= \sum_{i=1}^{n} w_i^2 Var(\varepsilon_i).$$

This implies that the SE of a linear estimator is:

$$SD\left(\sum_{i=1}^{n} w_i Y_i\right) = \sqrt{\sum_{i=1}^{n} w_i^2 Var(\varepsilon_i)}$$
$$= \sqrt{\sum_{i=1}^{n} w_i^2 SD^2(\varepsilon_i)}.$$

Note that these formulas apply no matter how many X variables there are in the model, though the weights get much more complicated once one goes beyond the bivariate model.

We can use the *ComputingSEs* sheet in GaussMarkovBivariate.xls to do the tedious work of computing the variances and SEs for the different estimators we have considered. The *ComputingSEs* sheet looks Figure 14.7.2.

SD(ε)		5						
Variance		25						
			Weights (w_i)			$w_i^2 SD(\varepsilon)^2$		
Observation	X's	OLS	Extreme Points	Average Slopes	OLS	Extreme Points	Average Slopes
1	10.00	−0.005	−0.011	−0.022	0.001	0.003	0.012
2	15.00	−0.004	0.000	0.006	0.000	0.000	0.001
3	22.00	−0.003	0.000	0.002	0.000	0.000	0.000
4	30.00	−0.002	0.000	0.006	0.000	0.000	0.001
5	45.00	−0.001	0.000	−0.015	0.000	0.000	0.005
6	50.00	0.000	0.000	0.015	0.000	0.000	0.005
7	65.00	0.002	0.000	−0.004	0.000	0.000	0.000
8	75.00	0.003	0.000	0.003	0.000	0.000	0.000
9	89.00	0.004	0.000	−0.002	0.000	0.000	0.000
10	100.00	0.006	0.011	0.010	0.001	0.003	0.003
Sum	501.00	0	0	0	0.003	0.006	0.029
Mean	50.10			Square Root	**0.053**	**0.079**	**0.170**
Variance	890.49						

Figure 14.7.2. Computing the SEs of different estimators of the bivariate slope. *Source:* [GaussMarkovBivariate.xls]ComputingSEs.

The X's are in the second column from the left. The weights for the three estimators are computed in the third through fifth columns, and the individual $w_i^2 SD^2 (\varepsilon_i)$ terms for each estimator are calculated in the last three columns. The SEs are displayed in the bottom row in bold – they are the square roots of the variances. For this particular choice of the X's, and given that the SD of the error terms is 5, the exact SE of the OLS estimator is 0.053, the exact SE for the Extreme Points estimator is 0.079, and the exact SE for the Average Slopes Estimator is 0.170. The approximate SEs from the Monte Carlo experiments will be quite close to the exact SEs in the ComputingSEs table. Try it! You will find that both the exact computation using the algebra of expectations and the Monte Carlo approximation tell the same story: OLS is always better – has a lower variance (SE) than the Extreme Points and the Average Slopes estimators.

This is of course not a proof of the Gauss–Markov theorem, nor will we give a formal proof for the bivariate case – the algebra is just too messy. We can, however, offer some further insight into the problem by using Excel's Solver.

Just as was the case for in the univariate setting, the problem of obtaining the minimum-variance, linear, unbiased estimator of the bivariate slope can be thought of as a constrained optimization problem. To solve this optimization problem, we want to find the estimator that has the minimum variance subject to the constraints that the weights sum to 0 and the product of the weights with the X's sum to 1. More formally, we want to choose a set of $w_i, i = 1, \ldots, n$ to minimize the quantity $\sum_{i=1}^{n} w_i^2 Var(\varepsilon_i)$ subject to the constraints that $\sum_{i=1}^{n} w_i = 0$ and $\sum_{i=1}^{n} w_i X_i = 1$. The constraints guarantee that the estimator will be unbiased.

In the last three columns of the table in the *ComputingSEs* sheet, we have set up Solver to handle this problem for the specific 10-observation case. When you execute Tools: Solver, you will see that it is set up to minimize the value in cell K16 (the sum $\sum_{i=1}^{n} w_i^2 Var(\varepsilon_i)$, where the weights are those in column I) subject to two constraints: that the sum of column I (the weights) is 0 and the sum of column J (the weights multiplied by the X's) is 1. Click Solve, and Solver will obtain the least squares weights. Now click the Change the X's button and the Solver solution will no longer meet the constraints. Use Solver again, and once again Solver will obtain the least squares weights.

The Solver demonstration shows that, for the specific 10-observation cases available in the GaussMarkovBivariate.xls workbook, the OLS estimator is the Best Linear Unbiased Estimator.

Summary

This section has demonstrated, though it does not prove, the Gauss–Markov theorem for the bivariate version of the classical econometric model. The proofs for the bivariate and multiple regression cases can be succinctly presented with matrix algebra, but we will not give them here. You should, however, continue to use the concepts we have developed to think about the OLS estimator. The OLS estimator is a weighted sum of the dependent variable; given a model of the data generating process, those weights, together with the SD of the error box, determine the spread of the OLS estimator's sampling distribution. The OLS estimator is preferred by econometricians because, when the classical econometric model applies, its SE is smallest among the class of linear, unbiased estimators. Finally, the Gauss–Markov theorem does not depend on any assumption about the distribution of the error terms other than the two assumptions that the SD of the errors is a finite number and their expected value is 0. The tickets in the error box might be normally distributed, uniformly distributed, or come from other distribution which meets the two basic requirements about their expected value and SD. This can be seen in the formulas for the exact SE, which depend on just the SD of the errors, not their distribution.

14.8. Conclusion

This chapter spells out several crucial ideas in inferential econometrics:

- When a chance process is at work generating the observed Y's, a sample is a realization of the chance process.
- There are many estimators, or recipes, that can be used to obtain an estimate of a population parameter.

- The resulting estimates are random variables whose value depends on the sample, which is merely one possible outcome of the chance process. Drawing a new sample and applying the same estimator will produce a new estimate.
- Econometricians prefer unbiased estimators because they are accurate – that is, on average, correct.
- In addition, the smaller the SE of the estimator's sampling distribution the better. The SE signals the precision of the estimator.
- Provided that the data were generated according to the classical econometric model, the Gauss–Markov theorem says that the OLS estimator is the best linear unbiased estimator available. "Best" refers directly to having the lowest SE.
- The Gauss–Markov theorem does not require that the error terms follow any particular distribution. All that is required of the distribution is that the expected value of the errors be zero and the errors have a finite SD.

Because the OLS estimator is based on minimizing the sum of squared residuals, beginning students often mistakenly believe that solving this minimization problem is the source of the desirability of the OLS estimator. In fact, minimizing the SSR is simply the recipe that defines OLS. The Gauss–Markov theorem addresses a different optimization problem – that is, to find the most precise (smallest SE) linear unbiased estimator.

In this chapter, we introduced three crucial concepts: linear, unbiased, and estimator. We stressed that the properties of an estimator depend on the data generating process. We used the algebra of expectations and the notions of random variables and constants to work out the expected value of the estimators we considered. A key to understanding this extremely important chapter is mastering the vocabulary, which means being able to make crucial distinctions. You should be able to tell what the difference is between an estimator and an estimate, a linear and a nonlinear estimator, a biased and an unbiased estimator, and a residual and an error.

14.9. Exercises

1. Here is an estimator for the population average that might be applied when you know the data generating process produces only nonnegative numbers. Take each number in the sample, square it, find the average of the squared values, and take its square root. In equation form, the formula for this Weird estimator is

$$\sqrt{\frac{\sum_{i=1}^{n} Y_i^2}{n}}.$$

Is this Weird estimator linear? Why or why not? Is it unbiased? A simple example that supposes there are only two possible, equally likely values for Y_i will suffice to answer the question about bias.

Questions 2–6 use the GaussMarkovUnivariate.xls workbook.

2. The Odd estimator of the population average gives each odd-numbered observation a weight of $2/n$. Apply this estimator in the *UnivariateSample* sheet. What do the weights in column D look like?

3. Use the Monte Carlo simulation add-in to analyze the sampling distribution of the Odd estimator. Is it biased? What part of the Monte Carlo results did you use to answer this question?

4. Would you prefer the Odd estimator or the Sample Average estimator? Explain your choice.

5. Explore the consequences of changing the error distribution from normal to uniform in the *UnivariateSample* sheet. (Section 14.6 compares the normal and uniform distributions.) Replace the normalrandom formula in column B with the uniform function. What effect does this have on the sampling distribution of the Sample Average? In your answer, comment on the expected value, SE, and shape of the sampling distribution.

6. From the *UnivariateSample* sheet, use Excel's MEDIAN function to compute the sample median of the observed Y values. Use the Monte Carlo simulation add-in to race the Median against the Sample Average. Who wins? Why? Questions 7–10 use the GaussMarkovBivariate.xls workbook.

7. In the *BivariateSample* sheet, create the Missing Last Value estimator. This silly estimator uses the same weights as the OLS slope estimator but makes the weight of the tenth observation equal to 0. Without running a Monte Carlo, can you tell if this estimator is biased? Explain.

8. Use the algebra of expectations to compute the exact expected value and SE of the Missing Last Value estimator by means of Set 2 of the X's (see the *Q&A* sheet for the values of the X's in Set 2).

9. Run a Monte Carlo simulation of the Missing Last Value estimator. Evaluate the results, commenting on the approximate expected value and SE.

10. Compare the Monte Carlo results in the previous question with the exact solutions obtained in Question 8. Do you find substantial agreement? Explain.

References

Because Johann Carl Friedrich Gauss died in 1855 and Andrei Andreyevich Markov was born a year later, they obviously did not collaborate on the famous theorem that bears their names. It is difficult to pinpoint when the term *Gauss–Markov* became commonplace. Jerzy Neyman undoubtedly played an important role. He explicitly pointed to A. A. Markoff as an overlooked contributor to the case for the least squares estimator, "The method is not a new one, but as it was published in Russian, it is not generally known" (Neyman 1934, p. 564). Neyman introduces his treatment of least squares by crediting Markoff, "I proceed now to the Markoff method of finding the best linear estimates" (p. 565). Neyman's title to a section makes his position clear, "Note II: The Markoff Method and Markoff Theorem on Least Squares" (p. 593). The discussion of Neyman's paper reports that Professor Fisher said that "Dr. Neyman advocated, wisely, in his opinion, the system which he ascribed to Markoff, though this was in essence the system of Gauss" (p. 616). Perhaps Neyman's paper and Fisher's reaction led to combining Gauss and Markov to describe the theorem guaranteeing that, if the CEM applies, then OLS is BLUE.

For further reading, we recommend the history of econometrics sources cited in previous chapters, including Stigler (1986) and Hendry and Morgan (1995).

A useful Web site is <members.aol.com/jeff570/mathword.html>. It contains a listing of the earliest known uses of mathematical words and terms.

Neyman, Jerzy (1934). "On the Two Different Aspects of the Representative Method: The Method of Stratified Sampling and the Method of Purposive Selection," *Journal of the Royal Statistical Society* **97**(4): 558–625.

Stigler, Stephen M. (1978). "Mathematical Statistics in the Early States," *The Annals of Statistics* **6**(2): 239–265.

15

Understanding the Standard Error

But to know how to compute the standard error of a function, it is first necessary to know how to compute the probable values of the parameters, their weights, and their standard errors, by the method of least squares.

Henry Schultz[1]

15.1. Introduction

The previous chapter made clear that a single OLS estimate from one realized sample is like a draw from the probability histogram of the OLS sample estimates. The Gauss–Markov theorem says that, if the requirements of the classical econometric model are met, then the OLS estimator is BLUE – that is, of the class of linear and unbiased estimators, the OLS estimator has the smallest standard error.

This chapter is devoted to more practical concerns about the SE of the OLS estimator. In the next section, we restate the formulas for the SE in the univariate and bivariate cases in much simpler language that will allow for an intuitive understanding of the SE. Section 15.3 shows how to compute the estimated SE reported by OLS routines such as Excel's LINEST function. Section 15.4 illustrates the properties of the SE of the OLS estimator by a simple discovery exercise. Section 15.5 discusses the concept of consistency and applies it to a discussion of the estimated RMSE. The final section introduces another standard error, the SE of forecasted Y. Throughout this chapter, we work with the classical econometric model of the data generation process.

15.2. SE Intuition

Workbook: SEb1OLS.xls

In the previous chapter, we were able to derive, via the algebra of expectations, the exact SE of the OLS estimator for univariate and bivariate CEM

[1] Schultz (1930, p. 12).

applications. This section shows how these formulas can be restated in much more intuitive terms.

Univariate CEM: Estimating the Population Average

We begin by considering the univariate version of the classical econometric model (CEM):

$$\text{Univariate CEM: } Y_i = \beta + \varepsilon_i, \quad i = 1, \ldots, n.$$

Here β is the population average we want to estimate. The ε's are assumed to be repeated draws from a classical econometric error box (always the same one) with tickets whose mean is zero and with an unknown standard deviation. The n draws are independent of each other.

Section 14.7 showed that the SE of a linear estimator of the population average using weights w_1 through w_n is given by the formula:

$$SD\left(\sum_{i=1}^{n} w_i Y_i\right) = \sqrt{\sum_{i=1}^{n} w_i^2 Var\left(\varepsilon_i\right)}$$

$$= \sqrt{\sum_{i=1}^{n} w_i^2 SD^2\left(\varepsilon_i\right)}.$$

We know from work in the last chapter that the OLS estimator of the population average is the sample average that uses weights equal to $1/n$ for every observation. We can substitute in $1/n$ for w_i:

$$SE\left(Sample\ Average\right) = \sqrt{\sum_{i=1}^{n} \left(\frac{1}{n^2}\right) SD^2\left(\varepsilon_i\right)}$$

Now the sum from 1 to n of any constant is simply n times the constant. Thus, the sum from 1 to n of $(1/n)^2$ is $1/n$. This means we can rewrite the formula for SE of the sample average in a more intuitive way as

$$SE\left(Sample\ Average\right) = \sqrt{\frac{1}{n} SD^2\left(\varepsilon\right)} = \frac{SD(\varepsilon)}{\sqrt{n}} = \frac{SD(Box)}{\sqrt{\#\ of\ draws}}.$$

When written in words, the formula for the SE of the sample average is much easier to understand. It says, quite simply, that the spread of the sample average estimates depends directly on the spread of the tickets in the box and inversely on the square root of the number of draws.

Bivariate CEM: Estimating the Slope (β_1)

A similar, but more algebraically complicated, approach can be used to simplify the formula for the SE of the OLS slope estimator in a bivariate regression equation. The DGP is described by

$$\text{Bivariate CEM: } Y_i = \beta_0 + \beta_1 \cdot X_i + \varepsilon_i, \quad i = 1, \ldots, n.$$

Here β_0 and β_1 are, respectively, the intercept and slope parameters that we want to estimate. The ε_i's are assumed to be repeated draws from a classical econometric error box (always the same one) with tickets whose mean is zero and with an unknown standard deviation. The n draws are independent of each other. The ε_i's are assumed to be independent of the X's. Thus, the value of the draw from the box, ε_i, has nothing to do with the value of X_i.

Although the intercept has a formula for the SE just like the slope, we will not derive an intuitive formula for the SE of the OLS sample intercept in order to concentrate our efforts on the much more important SE of the OLS sample slope.

As in the univariate case, we start from the fundamental result that the SE of a linear estimator of a population parameter can be written as a weighted sum of a random variable:

$$SD\left(\sum_{i=1}^{n} w_i Y_i\right) = \sqrt{\sum_{i=1}^{n} w_i^2 \, Var\left(\varepsilon_i\right)}$$

$$= \sqrt{\sum_{i=1}^{n} w_i^2 SD^2(\varepsilon_i)}.$$

Unlike the univariate case, however, in which the weights were a convenient and easy $1/n$, the weights for the OLS estimator of β_1 are given by a more complicated formula (derived in Section 14.5):

$$w_i = \frac{\left(X_i - \bar{X}\right)}{n \cdot Variance(X)}, i = 1, \ldots, n$$

By substituting the expression for the weights into the formula for the SE of a linear estimator, we obtain:

$$SE(OLS\,Sample\,Slope) = \sqrt{\sum_{i=1}^{n} \left[\frac{\left(X_i - \bar{X}\right)}{n \cdot Variance(X)}\right]^2 SD^2(\varepsilon_i)}$$

We can simplify this expression by squaring the numerator and denominator, noting that the sum of the squared deviations from the average X (in the numerator) is equal to n times the variance of the X's, and canceling terms,

$$SE(OLSSampleSlope) = \sqrt{\sum_{i=1}^{n} \frac{(X_i - \bar{X})^2}{n^2 \cdot Variance^2(X)} SD^2(\varepsilon_i)}$$

$$= \sqrt{\frac{n \cdot Variance(X)}{n^2 \cdot Variance^2(X)} SD^2(\varepsilon)}$$

$$= \sqrt{\frac{SD^2(\varepsilon)}{n \cdot Variance(X)}}$$

$$= \frac{SD(\varepsilon)}{\sqrt{n} \cdot SD(X)}$$

Note that because the errors all come from the same box, they all have the same SD. Thus it is possible to replace $SD^2(\varepsilon_i)$ with $SD^2(\varepsilon)$, as we did in moving from the second line to the third line above. Thus the analytical formula for the SE of the OLS estimator of the slope in a bivariate regression can be reduced to something quite simple and intuitively appealing:

$$SE(OLSSampleSlope) = \frac{SD(\varepsilon)}{\sqrt{n} \cdot SD_X} = \frac{SD\,(Box)}{\sqrt{\#\,\text{of draws}} \cdot SD\,\text{of the}\,X\text{'s}}.$$

Notice the close similarity between the formula for the SE of the OLS sample slope and its univariate analogue, the SE of the sample average. Both have the SD of the error box in the numerator and both have a square root of the number of draws from the box in the denominator. The SE of the OLS sample slope has an extra term, the SD of the X's, that is not present in the univariate case. Note that since X is fixed, the SD of the X's is computed using n, the number of observations, not $n-1$.

Implementing the SE of the OLS Sample Slope Formula

Open the Excel workbook SEb1OLS.xls and go to the *ExactSEb1* sheet to see the formula for the SE of the OLS sample slope in action. Figure 15.2.1 shows the information on the screen. Cell range A1:B4 contains the β_0, β_1, and SD(ε) parameter values.

In red text on your computer screen, cell F4 contains the exact SE of the sample slope. Figure 15.2.2 shows, via Excel's Auditing feature, that the exact SE cell depends on three other cells.

Click the Draw Another Sample (F9) button repeatedly. The Y's and the OLS Fitted Line bounce (both in the table and on the chart). Notice that n, the SD of X, and all cells (and the line) in red stay fixed. Especially pay attention to the fact that the exact SE(b1), the SE of the OLS sample slope, is constant.

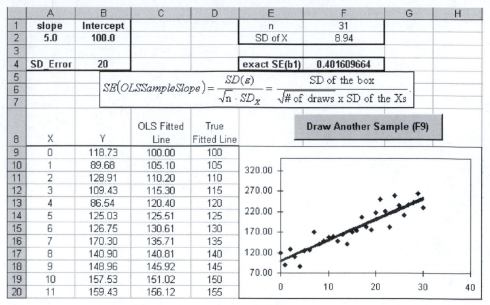

Figure 15.2.1. The exact SE stays fixed.
Source: [SEb1OLS.xls]ExactSEb1

This demonstrates, visually and concretely, that the SE of the OLS sample slope is a fixed number that exists for a particular characterization of the DGP described by the classical econometric model. Its value depends on the three elements in its formula: SD of the errors, n, and SD of X.

With the classical econometric model, we will always know the number of draws and the SD of the X values. If we know the SD of the errors, we can compute the SE of the OLS sample slope exactly, which is a value that is fixed and unchanging. Unfortunately, this is rarely the case. The next section reveals the obvious solution to this predicament, but first we will provide a formula for the SE of one of several slope estimators in the multivariate case.

The SEs in the Multivariate CEM

The formula for the SE in the multivariate case is one notch more complicated than in the bivariate case. Suppose we are interested in the kth slope term

slope	Intercept			n	31
5.0	100.0			SD of X	8.94
SD_Error	20			exact SE(b_1)	0.401609664

Figure 15.2.2. Tracing precedents of the exact SE.
Source: [SEb1OLS.xls]ExactSEb1

b_k. Its SE is given by the formula

$$SE(b_k) = \frac{SD(\text{Box})}{\sqrt{\text{\# of draws}} \cdot SD(X_k) \cdot \sqrt{1 - R_k^2}}.$$

In this expression, the symbol R_k^2 means the R^2 from a regression of X_k (the X variable corresponding to b_k) on all the other independent variables, including an intercept term. Notice that the $\frac{1}{\sqrt{1-R_k^2}}$ term is the only difference between the formula for the SE of a slope estimator in the multivariate case and the formula for the SE of the slope estimator in the bivariate case. This last term has the effect of increasing the SE of coefficients whose corresponding X variables are highly correlated with other X's. In the case of perfect multicollinearity between X_k and other X variables, $R_k^2 = 1$ and $SE(b_k)$ is undefined. The typical practical remedy is to drop one of the X variables from the regression.

Summary

This section presented formulas for the SE of the sample average and OLS sample slope in bivariate and multivariate settings. Much of the work for these formulas was presented in Section 14.7. Our goal in this section was to derive an intuitive version of the formulas that we can use to explain the behavior of the SE under different conditions.

The formulas derived in this section are exact SEs because they do not rely on Monte Carlo simulations to approximate the SE and they are based on knowing the SD of the error distribution. The next section relaxes this unrealistic assumption and explains how we estimate the SE when the SD of the box is unknown.

15.3. The Estimated SE

Workbook: SEb1OLS.xls

The previous section showed that the exact SE of the OLS sample slope is

$$SE(OLSSampleSlope) = \frac{SD(\varepsilon)}{\sqrt{n} \cdot SD_X} = \frac{SD(\text{Box})}{\sqrt{\text{\# of draws}} \cdot SD \text{ of the } X\text{'s}}.$$

In practice we are generally unable to compute this formula because we do not know the SD of the box. We must therefore estimate it. This section will show that, if the CEM applies, the natural estimator for the unknown $SD(\varepsilon)$ value is the RMSE, the spread of the residuals from the regression. We will also demonstrate that this is exactly what LINEST (and other standard regression software packages) do in computing an estimated SE of the OLS sample slope.

RMSE Estimates SD(ε)

Begin by going to the *EstSEb1* sheet in SEb1OLS.xls. This sheet is based on the *ExactSEb1* sheet. However, we have added two variables, Residuals and Errors, in columns E and F. To reveal how the two series are computed, click on cells in these two columns. The Residuals are the observed Y values minus the predicted Y from the OLS Fitted Line. Errors, on the other hand, are the observed Y values minus the points on the True Fitted Line. By subtracting the True Fitted Line, we are in essence removing the deterministic component of Y, leaving only the error component.

To see that the residuals closely follow the errors, scroll over to the Errors and Residuals as a function of X chart and click on the [Draw Another Sample (F9)] button a few times. You should see that residuals and errors track each other. Figure 15.3.1 shows an example. The values are not perfectly aligned because the residuals are not the errors. The residuals are based on the estimated intercept and slope coefficients from a particular sample, whereas the errors use the true parameter values for the intercept and slope.

Another, perhaps more instructive, graph (top left corner on cell H60) shows the Errors and Residuals as a scatter plot (with the Residuals on the X-axis). Again, repeatedly draw new samples and watch the graph, which is

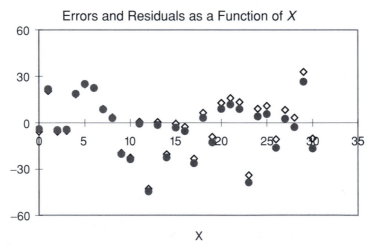

Figure 15.3.1. One view of errors and residuals.
Source: [SEb1OLS.xls]EstSEb1.

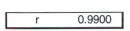

Errors and Residuals: Scatter Plot

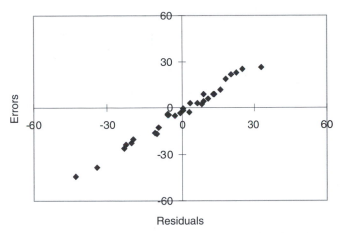

Figure 15.3.2. Another view of errors and residuals.
Source: [SEb1OLS.xls]EstSEb1.

shown in Figure 15.3.2. This is strong visual evidence that the residuals do a
good job of tracking the errors.

As noted in Chapter 5, the RMSE is essentially the SD of the residuals, the only difference being that the RMSE as conventionally calculated
uses the number of degrees of freedom in place of the number of observations in the formula. (We discuss the reasons for this – generally minor –
adjustment in Section 15.5.) Because the residuals are good estimates of
the errors, the RMSE ought to be a good estimator of the SD of the error
box. We will demonstrate that the RMSE is at least adequate in this task,
though far from perfect, via a Monte Carlo simulation for the bivariate
case.

The Monte Carlo simulation is based on the parameters in the *EstSEb1*
sheet. Make sure that the SD_Error parameter is set to 20 and then go to
the *MCSim* sheet to run your own Monte Carlo simulation. Compare your
results to those given in Figure 15.3.3.

The key result is the average of the 10,000 RMSEs: 19.7999. This is just
slightly less than 20 but far enough away to suggest something is awry. It is
an unfortunate fact that the RMSE is a biased estimator of the true value
of the spread of the errors, $SD(\varepsilon)$. This bias gets smaller as the number of
observations in the sample increases. Because the bias is in practice negligible
and no better estimator available is, we use the RMSE to estimate $SD(\varepsilon)$. We
discuss this issue in greater detail in Section 15.5.

RMSE Summary Statistics		Population Parameter	
Average	19.7999	**SDErrors**	20
SD	2.61012		
Max	29.7099		
Min	10.2707		

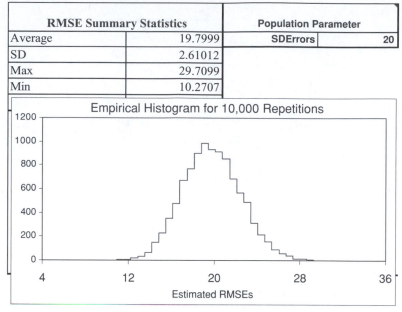

Figure 15.3.3. RMSE Monte Carlo simulation.
Source: [SEb1OLS.xls]MCSim.

The SE of the OLS Sample Slope in Practice

Now that we have an estimator for the unknown SD of the box, the RMSE, we can simply substitute this into the formula for the SE of the OLS sample slope:

$$SE\ (OLS\ Sample\ Slope) = \frac{SD(\varepsilon)}{\sqrt{n} \cdot SD(X)}$$

$$= \frac{\text{SD(Box)}}{\sqrt{\text{\# of draws}} \cdot \text{SD of the}\,X\text{'s}}$$

$$\text{Estimated SE}\ (OLS\ Sample\ Slope) = \frac{\text{Estimated SD (Box)}}{\sqrt{\text{\# of draws}} \cdot \text{SD of the}\ X\text{'s}}$$

$$\text{Estimated SE}\ (OLS\ Sample\ Slope) = \frac{RMSE}{\sqrt{n} \cdot SD_X}$$

Scroll over to cell O8 in the *EstSEb1* sheet to see a demonstration of the fact that LINEST is performing exactly the substitution given above, as shown in Figure 15.3.4. As you can see by comparing the cells with yellow backgrounds while repeatedly clicking the replace [Draw Another Sample (F9)] button, LINEST's estimate of the SE of the slope coefficient always equals the value derived from our formula.

SHOWING HOW LINEST USES RMSE TO ESTIMATE THE SD(ε)

	slope	Intercept	
estimate	4.531	108.188	estimate
estimated SE(b_1)	0.42576	7.43566	estimated SE(b_0)
R^2	0.80	21.20	RMSE
F test	113.26	29	df
Reg SS	50917.71	13037.35	SSR

estimated SE(b_1)   0.42576   using the formula

Figure 15.3.4. LINEST uses RMSE.
Source: [SEb1OLS.xls]EstSEb1.

Summary

This section introduced the estimated SE of the OLS sample slope. We now have three different types of SEs to consider:

- Exact SE: a formula that uses the SD of the errors when it is known;
- Estimated SE: using the RMSE to estimate the unknown SD of the errors in the formula; and
- Approximate SE: obtained from a Monte Carlo simulation that uses the SD of the sample slopes from many repetitions of the DGP.

In practice, it is the estimated SE on which we must rely. The exact SE is unknown, and we typically only have one sample to work with; thus we cannot use Monte Carlo methods to approximate the SE.[2]

15.4. Determinants of the SE of the OLS Sample Slope

Workbook: SEb1OLS.xls

The intuitive reformulation of the SE of the OLS sample slope estimator in Section 15.2 led to the following formula:

$$SE(OLSSampleSlope) = \frac{SD(\varepsilon)}{\sqrt{n} \cdot SD_X} = \frac{SD(\text{Box})}{\sqrt{\text{\# of draws}} \cdot SD \text{ of the } X\text{'s}}.$$

This section points out the obvious relationships between the SE of the OLS sample slope and its three influences. It does so by asking the reader to walk through the *DeterminantsofSEb1* sheet in the SEb1OLS.xls workbook. The sheet is organized in horizontal fashion with text boxes across the top that contain instructions. Read the text box at the beginning of the sheet to familiarize

---

[2] This statement is not strictly accurate. It is possible to use bootstrapping techniques, which are similar to Monte Carlo simulations, to estimate SEs. This book introduces bootstrap methods in Chapter 23.

yourself with the layout of the sheet. Click on cells to read the formulas. Scroll right to perform the first of three discovery exercises. Each discovery exercise has a "Thinking" button that will help you understand the point.

We offer three figures generated by following the instructions in the *DeterminantsofSEb1* sheet that demonstrate three lessons. Each figure compares two histograms. The same base case (SD_Error $= 1$, SD of $X = 8.66$, and $n = 90$) is used in the left panel of each figure. As you work through the *DeterminantsofSEb1* sheet, compare your results to ours. Your exact SEs should be the same, but your estimated SEs will probably be different from ours.

Figure 15.4.1 shows what happens to the SE of the sample slope when the SD of the errors increases ceteris paribus. We changed the SD of the errors from 1 to 3. The exact SE rises threefold from 0.012 (with some of the rounding error in the displayed result).

Figure 15.4.2 demonstrates the effect on the SE of the sample slope given changes in the sample size. When n falls from 90 to 30, the denominator in the SE of the sample slope formula is cut – but not by a third – because the formula shows that the SE varies inversely with the square root of n. In fact, the square root of 90 is around 9.5, and so its reciprocal is about 0.1. The square root of 30 is approximately 5.5, and 1/SQRT(30) is roughly 0.18. Thus, the SE rises by about 80 percent, as confirmed by Figure 15.4.2.

Finally, Figure 15.4.3 explores changes in the spread of the X variable. As the SD of X falls, the SE rises. In Figure 15.4.3, we changed the step size of the X variable from 1 to 0.1, dramatically reducing the variation in X. This tenfold decrease in the SD of X directly caused a tenfold increase in the SE of the sample slope.

As you work through the *DeterminantsofSEb1* sheet, we hope that you not only see the three lessons in the three figures in this section but also explore the Thinking buttons. By hitting F9 and watching the effect of changing these three crucial parameters, you cement your understanding of the relationship between the SE and its determinants. You also develop intuition about the variability in the sample slope coefficient.

Summary

This section demonstrated that the SE of the OLS slope estimator in the bivariate case depends directly on the SD of the error distribution and inversely on the number of observations and the spread of the X's. We realize that the formula for the SE of b_1 makes this obvious, but by changing the spreadsheet and directly observing the results, we hope you will understand better the factors that drive the SE of the slope in a bivariate regression.

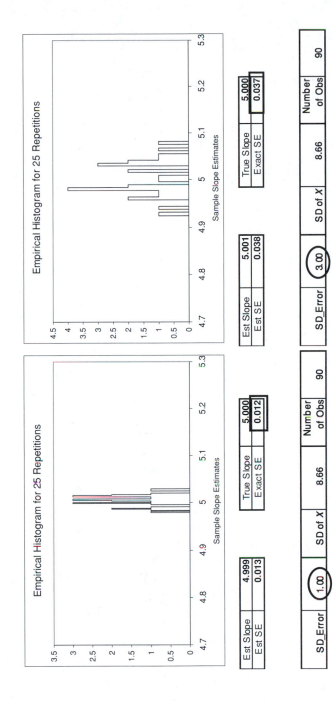

Figure 15.4.1. As the SD of the errors rises, the SE rises.
Source: [SEb1OLS.xls]SampDist.

389

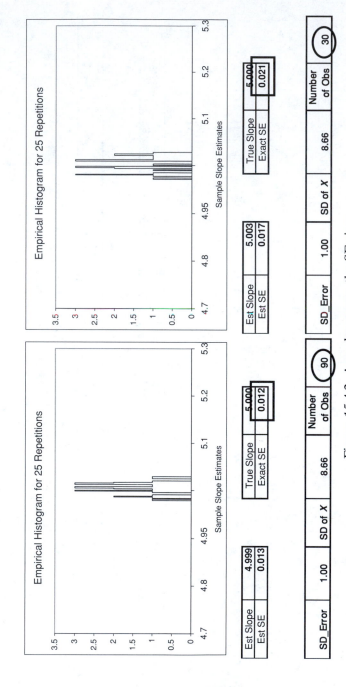

Figure 15.4.2. As *n* decreases, the SE rises.
Source: [SEb1OLS.xls]SampDist.

390

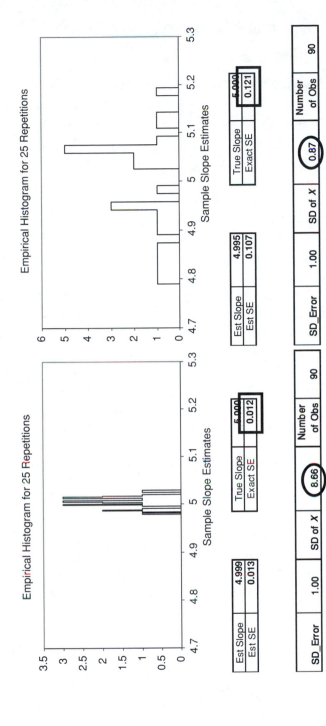

Figure 15.4.3. As SD of *X* decreases, the SE rises.
Source: [SEb1OLS.xls]SampDist.

391

15.5. Estimating the SD of the Errors

Workbook: EstimatingSDErrors.xls

The crucial step in estimating the SE of the sample slope is estimating the SD of the error distribution. After all, in the formula for the SE of the sample slope, the square root of n and the SD of the X's are known.

$$SE\,(OLSSampleSlope) = \frac{SD(Box)}{\sqrt{\text{\# of draws}} \cdot \text{SD of the}\,X\text{'s}}.^3$$

It is the term in the numerator, the SD of the box, which is abbreviated as $SD(\varepsilon)$, that poses a problem. As earlier sections of this chapter demonstrated, when this parameter is known, we can compute the exact SE. Computer regression software (including Excel's LINEST function) reports an estimated SE (not an exact SE) because it substitutes an estimate for the unknown $SD(\varepsilon)$. Standard practice is to use the RMSE (also known as the Standard Error of the Regression) as the estimator of the SD of the errors. Section 15.3 demonstrated that Excel's LINEST function plugs in the RMSE to compute the estimated SE of the sample slope.

This section addresses three issues: first, the reason the RMSE is not simply the SD of the residuals but instead is adjusted for the number of degrees of freedom; second, why even after the adjustment the RMSE is biased; third, the fact that nevertheless the RMSE is a consistent estimator, meaning that its sampling distribution becomes ever more tightly concentrated around the true value of the SD of the error box as the number of observations increases.[4]

How can we estimate the spread of the errors? Because the residuals can be thought of as estimates of the error terms, the obvious candidate is the spread of the residuals. From the *Data* sheet of the EstimatingSDErrors.xls workbook, run a Monte Carlo simulation of cell J8, the SD of the residuals, with $n = 10$. In a few seconds, you have an approximation to the sampling distribution of this statistic. Your results should be similar to ours, which are displayed in Figure 15.5.1.

Notice that the average of the SD of the Residuals, an approximation to the expected value of the random variable SD of the Residuals, is about 4.4 – quite far from 5 (the value of the SD of the errors in cell B5 of the *Data* sheet). This is strong evidence that the SD of the Residuals is biased.

We can improve on the SD of the Residuals as an estimator of the SD of the Errors by adjusting it based on the number of observations in the sample and

---

[3] Recall that in this formula we are using the SD as computed with the number of observations n, not $n-1$.

[4] Section 10.6 offers a brief review of the concept of consistency.

Summary Statistics		Notes
Average	4.423	*n=10*
SD	1.0691	
Max	8.702	
Min	1.572	

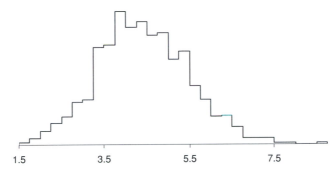

Histogram of $J$8

1.5   3.5   5.5   7.5

Figure 15.5.1. Monte Carlo simulation of the SD of the residuals.
Source: MCSim add-in run on [EstimatingSDErrors.xls]Data.

the number of parameters being estimated. This is similar to the adjustment made to the sample SD. By multiplying the SD of the Residuals by $\sqrt{\frac{n}{n-k}}$, where n is the sample size and k is the number of parameters being estimated, we obtain a better estimator of the SD of the Errors.[5] Statisticians refer to the number of observations minus the number of parameters being estimated, $n-k$, as the number of degrees of freedom. LINEST, like most regression software, reports this number. Of course, the adjusted SD of the Residuals is exactly the RMSE. Compare cells J7 and G12 in the *Data* sheet to confirm this.

You could simply take our word for the fact that the RMSE is a better estimator of SD(ε) than the SD of the Residuals or you could run your own Monte Carlo simulation. Because the latter approach takes a few seconds, why not give it a spin? In the MCSim add-in input box, track both G12, the RMSE reported by LINEST, and J8, the unadjusted SD of the Residuals. Figure 15.5.2 reports our results. How did you do?

Because the true SD of the Errors parameter is 5, we have convincing evidence that the RMSE, the adjusted SD of the Residuals, outperforms the simple, unadjusted SD of the Residuals. The average of 1,000 RMSEs,

---

[5] Note that we use the population SD of the Residuals in cell J8. If the sample SD is used, then the adjustment factor would use $n-1$.

$G$12		Data!$J$8		Notes
Average	4.839	Average	4.328	
SD	1.2143	SD	1.0861	
Max	9.152	Max	8.186	
Min	1.710	Min	4.529	

Histogram of $G$12 and Data!$J$8

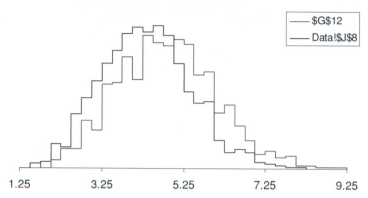

Figure 15.5.2. Comparing RMSE and SD of the residuals.
Source: MCSim add-in run on [EstimatingSDErrors.xls]Data.

4.839, is much closer to 5 than the average of 1,000 SD of the Residuals, 4.328.[6]

The RMSE's superiority over the SD of the Residuals explains why we do not use the SD of the Residuals to estimate the SD of the errors, but Figure 15.5.2 brings some negative news as well. The RMSE is biased (i.e., its sampling distribution is not centered on the true parameter value, 5). This is not an artifact of too few repetitions of the Monte Carlo simulation. You can run a 10,000-repetition (or more) Monte Carlo and the empirical histogram will get ever closer to the true probability histogram for the RMSE; however, the center of that probability histogram will not get closer to 5.

The fact that the RMSE is biased leads to an obvious question: Why do we use it? There are two reasons. First, the RMSE, though biased, is consistent. This means that, as we increase the sample size, the sampling distribution converges on the true parameter value. Second, in Chapter 16 we will see that, when the sample size is small but the error terms are normally distributed, the bias does not matter.

We can demonstrate the consistency result fairly easily. Simply return to the *Data* sheet, click the ⎡Set N⎤ button, and change the number of observations

---

[6] The average value of the RMSE is exactly $\sqrt{\frac{n}{n-k}}$ times as big as the average value of the SD of the Residuals (in our example the adjustment factor is $\sqrt{\frac{10}{10-2}} \approx 1.12$). The spread of the RMSE is affected by exactly the same multiplicative factor.

$G$12		Data!$J$8		Notes
Average	4.984	Average	4.883	$n=50$
SD	0.5151	SD	0.5047	
Max	6.515	Max	6.384	
Min	3.383	Min	3.314	

Histogram of $G$12 and Data!$J$8

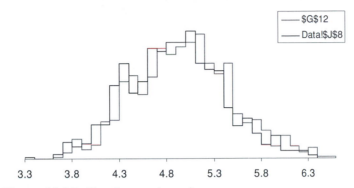

Figure 15.5.3. Consistency in action.
Source: MCSim add-in run on [EstimatingSDErrors.xls]Data.

to 50. Next, run the same Monte Carlo simulation as used previously, tracking the RMSE and the SD of the Residuals. In the Notes box, include the number of observations for easy reference. Figure 15.5.3 displays our results. Yours should be similar.

Notice how much better the RMSE is doing when $n = 50$ (in Figure 15.5.3) compared with $n = 10$ (in Figure 15.5.2). You might point out that the SD of the Residuals is doing better also. This is true. Both of these estimators provide consistent estimates of SD(ε), but we prefer the RMSE over the SD of the Residuals because it is closer to the SD of the Errors parameter.[7]

The *Q&A* sheet asks you to run a 100-observation Monte Carlo simulation. Not surprisingly, the average of the RMSEs is almost 5. With $n = 100$, the SD of the Residuals also does a great job of estimating the SD(ε). The adjustment factor, $\sqrt{\frac{n}{n-k}}$, works out to be $\sqrt{\frac{100}{100-2}}$, which is about 1.01. With n so high, the two are essentially the same statistic.

You might wonder whether it would be possible to somehow adjust the RMSE to take the bias into account. A major problem with this approach is that the distribution of the error terms is not necessarily known. On the *Data* sheet you can experiment with a nonnormal distribution for the errors

---

[7] The conventional criterion for comparing biased estimators is Mean Squared Error, which is defined as $E\left[(Estimator - Parameter)^2\right]$ – that is, the expected value of the square of the deviation of the estimate from the true parameter value. It can be shown that the RMSE outperforms the SD of the Residuals on this measure. We leave a demonstration of this fact to the reader as an exercise.

by choosing the $\boxed{\begin{smallmatrix} \text{Set N} \\ \text{Exponential Dist} \end{smallmatrix}}$ button.[8] A question on the *Q&A* sheet asks you to see how changing the error distribution affects the bias in the RMSE. In Chapter 16 we will see that it is possible to nullify the biased-in-small-samples problem of the RMSE if one assumes that the errors are normally distributed.

Why Is the RMSE a Biased Estimator of the SD of the Errors?

Let us take a moment to see why the RMSE is a biased estimator of the SD of the errors. The reason, ironically, is that the RMSE is the square root of an unbiased estimator of the variance of the errors. That is, the sum of squared residuals divided by the number of degrees of freedom is an unbiased estimate of the variance (the square of the SD) of the error terms. We ask you to check that this is the case in the *Q&A* sheet of EstimatingSDErrors.xls. Now in general, the expected value of the square root of an unbiased estimator is not equal to the square root of the expected value of that estimator. That means that the expected value of the RMSE is not equal to the square root of the variance of the errors.

Here is a simpler example of the same phenomenon: Suppose that half of a population has the value 9 and half of the population has the value 16. The population average is, therefore, 12.5. Draw a random sample of size 1 from the population. The expected value of the sample average (which is just the value of the single observation you picked) is $\frac{1}{2} \cdot 9 + \frac{1}{2} \cdot 16 = 12.5$, the population average. Thus this crude estimator is unbiased. Now the square root of the population average is $\sqrt{12.5} \approx 3.54$. The expected value of the square root of the however sample average is, however, $\frac{1}{2} \cdot \sqrt{9} + \frac{1}{2} \cdot \sqrt{16} = \frac{1}{2} \cdot 3 + \frac{1}{2} \cdot 4 = 3.5$. Therefore, the square root of the sample average (sample size one) is a biased estimator of the square root of the population average. Increasing the sample size will reduce the bias in the square root of the sample average.

The Estimated SE Is a Biased, But Consistent Estimator of the Exact SE

We close this section by making sure we connect the dots. We have noted that the estimated SE uses the RMSE as an estimate of the SD of the error distribution and have shown that the RMSE is a biased, but consistent estimator. Thus, it stands to reason that the estimated SE is a biased, but consistent estimator of the exact SE.

Monte Carlo simulation can be used to demonstrate this point. From the *Data* sheet, use the button to set *n* to 3 observations and enter the formula

---

[8] See the workbook ExponentialDist.xls in the \ Basic Tools \ RandomNumber folder to learn about the error distribution we use in this example.

Data!$F$10		Data!$F$11		Notes
Average	5.004	Average	0.796	
SD	1.0089	SD	0.6018	
Max	9.129	Max	3.918	
Min	0.962	Min	0.000	

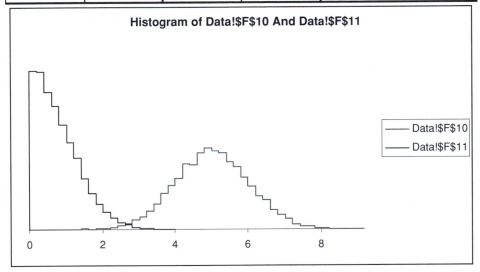

Histogram of Data!$F$10 And Data!$F$11

——— Data!$F$10
——— Data!$F$11

Figure 15.5.4. The Estimated SE is biased.
Source: MCSim add-in run on [EstimatingSDErrors.xls]Data.

"=SQRT(3)" in cell B5 to make the SD of the errors equal to the square root of 3. Because the SD of the X's is 1 and we set the SD of the errors equal to the square root of n, the exact SE is therefore 1. Use the Monte Carlo simulation add-in to track the sample slope (cell F10) and its estimated SE (F11) with 10,000 repetitions. Figure 15.5.4 shows our results. The SD of the 10,000 sample slopes is very close to 1, the exact SE. The average of the 10,000 estimated SEs, however, is 0.796 – quite far from 1. This is strong evidence that the estimated SE is indeed a biased estimator of the exact SE. The source of the bias can be traced directly to the RMSE.

You can run a Monte Carlo simulation with $n = 30$, ceteris paribus, to see that the estimated SE does a much better job of estimating the exact SE. As n increases, the bias of the estimated SE gets smaller and smaller. The consistency of the estimated SE is directly tied to the consistency of the RMSE.

Summary

The bottom line of this section is the following: When you run a regression, the software will almost certainly report the RMSE and the estimated SE of the sample coefficients. The estimated SE of the sample coefficients uses the RMSE as an estimate for the unknown SD of the box. The RMSE is a biased estimator of the SD of the errors, but the bias becomes negligible as the sample size increases.

15.6. The Standard Error of the Forecast and the Standard Error of the Forecast Error

Workbook: SEForecast.xls

Previous sections in this chapter have emphasized the SE of the sample slope. By hitting the F9 key and recalculating the sheet, we have made it clear that the sample slope is a random variable with a sampling distribution.

This section explores two other commonly used SEs associated with the problem of forecasting the SE of the Forecast and the SE of the Forecast Error. We show how these SEs are computed and explore their properties. As usual, our emphasis will be on the basics, emphasizing the visual presentation and making heavy use of Monte Carlo simulation.

We begin with an important distinction between Forecasted Y and Predicted Y. In this book, Predicted Y means the value of Y predicted for an observation in the sample based on its X value. Forecasted Y, on the other hand, means the value of Y forecasted for a new observation not already in the sample based on the value of X, which we assign for that new observation. When we forecast, we assume that the same data generating process applies to the new observation as applied to the data in the sample. Forecasted Y is often used in the context of trying to guess the future value of some variable of interest or the value of a dependent variable if a change occurs in the value of one or more independent variables. For example, a state may wish to forecast next year's tax revenues, or a car manufacturer may want to forecast demand for an SUV if it lowers its price.

Very closely related to Forecasted Y is the Forecast Error, which is defined simply as

$$\text{Forecast Error} = \text{Actual } Y - \text{Forecasted } Y.$$

Both Forecasted Y and the Forecast Error are random variables. In this section we explore the determinants of the spread in these two random variables and explain how to construct simple forecasts. We speak of *point forecasts* and *interval forecasts*. The point forecast is simply the value of Forecasted Y obtained from the regression estimates. The interval forecast is a point forecast plus an associated give or take number that gives a confidence interval for the forecast. In practical applications, one must decide whether to use the SE of Forecasted Y or the SE of the Forecast Error to construct the confidence interval. The latter is usually the right choice.

Forecasting can be an extremely complicated business. We will keep things simple by supposing that a model for the data generating process conforming to the CEM has already been correctly specified and that the model using an OLS regression on sample data has already been estimated. Furthermore, we assume that the value of the independent variable(s) for which we are forecasting are already known. Thus, we will not consider two important sources of errors in forecasts: having an incorrect model for the data generating process and not knowing the values of the independent variables that will generate Forecasted Y.

We begin our discussion with a bivariate example of the classical econometric model:

$$Y_i = \beta_0 + \beta_1 X_i + \varepsilon_i, \quad i = 1, \ldots, n.$$

The standard assumptions of the CEM apply. We are interested in forecasting the value of Y given a new value of X, call it X_F (for future X), not in the sample. We would like to know how far off our forecast of Y (Forecasted Y) is likely to be from the actual, not yet observed, future value of Y, which we will call Actual Y or Y_F. The model is implemented in SEForecast.xls on the *Two Components* sheet, which you should open now.

Figure 15.6.1 displays the set up. True parameter values, including the spread of the error terms, are located in the upper-left-hand corner. Cells A12 through B41 (not in the figure) contain the sample data. Note that we use the normal distribution to generate the error terms; however, the distribution of the error terms does not affect the results presented in this section. Estimates of the intercept and slope parameters (b_0 and b_1, respectively) based on the sample are reported at the top of the sheet in cells D2 and D3.

True Parameters		Estimates	
β_0	100	b_0	66.01
β_1	1	b_1	1.68
SD Error	50	RMSE	49.18
Three Forecasts			
X_F	Actual Y (Y_F)	Forecasted Y	Forecasted Y from True	Forecast Error
120	181.8	267.4	220	−85.6
200	236.8	401.6	300	−164.8
300	445.0	569.4	400	−124.5

Figure 15.6.1. Variability in forecasting.
Source: [SEForecast.xls]TwoComponents.

Cells C7, C8, and C9, the three cells in the Forecasted Y column of Figure 15.6.1, contain forecasts of Y for three different values of X_F (120, 200, and 300). The three forecasts are each computed via the following formula:

$$\text{Forecasted } Y = b_0 + b_1 X_F.$$

Hitting the F9 key draws a new set of errors and therefore a new sample. The values of b_0 and b_1 and the Forecasted Y's all bounce, which is incontrovertible evidence that Forecasted Y is a random variable.

The values of Actual Y, reported in cells B7, B8, and B9 are determined according to the data generating process:

$$Y_F = \beta_0 + \beta_1 X_F + \varepsilon_F,$$

where ε_F is a new draw from the same distribution of errors that produced the sample data. We report three separate values of Actual Y, corresponding to the three different values of X_F.

The values in the Forecasted Y from True column (cells D7, D8, and D9) do not bounce. These are forecasts based on the true parameter values:

$$\text{Forecasted } Y \text{ from True} = \beta_0 + \beta_1 X_F.$$

The difference between Actual Y and Forecasted Y from True is just the error term ε_F. The point of including Forecasted Y from True in the table is to show that, even if we knew the true parameter values, we would still not forecast perfectly because of chance error (the influence of luck and omitted variables).

The final column in the table is the Forecast Error, which is the difference between Actual Y and Forecasted Y. Hit F9 and the Forecast Errors change, indicating that it, too, is a random variable. Where does the Forecast Error come from? To answer this question, compare the equation for Actual Y,

$$Y_F = \beta_0 + \beta_1 X_F + \varepsilon_F,$$

with the equation for Forecasted Y,

$$\text{Forecasted } Y = b_0 + b_1 X_F.$$

One part of the Forecast Error is due to using the estimated intercept (b_0) and slope (b_1) instead of the true intercept (β_0) and True Slope (β_1); we call this Estimation Error. The second part of the Forecast Error comes from the error term ε_F; we call this Chance Error. Note that the Estimation Error component of the Forecast Error is also the source of the bounce in Forecasted Y, whereas the Chance Error component is not present in Forecasted Y.

Figure 15.6.2, based on the chart displayed in the cell range F1:I12, provides intuition on the two components of the Forecast Error. The numerical values

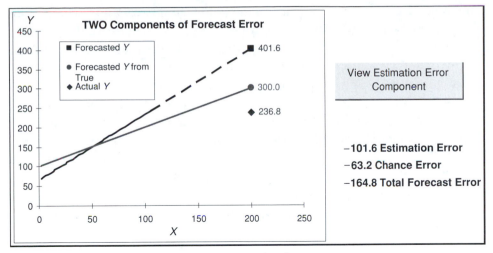

Figure 15.6.2. Decomposing forecast error.
Source: [SEForecastedY.xls]TwoComponents.

in the chart correspond to those in Figure 15.6.1. The estimated intercept and slope are 66.01 and 1.68, respectively. Forecasted Y when $X_F = 200$ is, therefore, $66.01 + 1.68 \cdot 200 = 401.6$.

Two lines are displayed in the chart in Figure 15.6.2. The line with the steeper slope is the sample regression line (in black on the computer screen). The dashed portion of this line indicates we are extrapolating from the in-sample data (contained in the range roughly 0 to 100) out to an X value of 200, at which, as noted, our forecast is that Y will take on the value 401.6. The less steep (red) line in Figure 15.6.2 reflects the true parameter values. According to the true parameter values, we expect that Y will equal 300 when X is 200. The diamond shaped point is Actual Y when X is 200; in this case, Y_F is 236.8. To the right of the chart, Figure 15.6.2 displays the numerical values of the two components of the Forecast Error and their sum, the Total Forecast Error.

To more clearly distinguish the Estimation and Chance Error components, click on the View Estimation Error Component button, which is a toggle whose text changes. You will see only the estimated regression line and the true regression line. The numerical value of the Estimation Error is -101.6 in our example. This component of the Forecast Error results from the slope and intercept of the estimated line not being equal to the true parameter values. Click once again and you will see just the true regression line and Actual Y. The Chance Error component of Forecast Error is the deviation of Actual Y from the true regression line. This is just the error term ε_F, whose value in this case is -63.2. Click on the button again to return the display to its original form.

The total Forecast Error is the sum of the Estimation Error and Chance Error components – namely −164.8. You will see a different estimated regression line and Actual Y on your screen. Experiment with the toggle button and use the F9 key to view the two different sources of the Forecast Error.

The forecast in our example, in Figure 15.6.2, is quite poor. However Forecasted Y is on average right. This follows from the fact that Forecasted $Y = b_0 + b_1 X_F$. Since both b_0 and b_1 are random variables, Forecasted Y is a random variable. We know that both b_0 and b_1 are unbiased estimators of their respective parameters and we can treat X_F as a constant. Thus the expected value of Forecasted Y is $\beta_0 + \beta_1 X_F$. Since Actual $Y = \beta_0 + \beta_1 X_F + \varepsilon_F$, and the expected value of the error term is zero, the expected value of Actual Y is also $\beta_0 + \beta_1 X_F$. Therefore Forecasted Y is an unbiased estimator of Actual Y.

The SE of Forecasted Y

Now we know that Forecasted Y is a random variable bouncing around $\beta_0 + \beta_1 X_F$. But what is its SE and what does that SE depend on? In a moment we will give you the analytical formula for the exact SE of Forecasted Y, but first we want to build some intuition to help you better understand that formula. Figure 15.6.3, the middle chart in the *TwoComponents* sheet, provides an important clue about the SE of Forecasted Y. The chart allows you to compare the Forecast Error for two values of X_F, 300 and a number between 0 and 750 that you select with the scroll bar. The chart demonstrates that, the farther away from the center of the data X_F, is the bigger in general the vertical distance between the estimated regression line and the true regression line. Therefore, Forecasted Y bounces more the farther X_F is from the center of the X's. Verify this fact by hitting the F9 key several times.

Careful examination of either chart in the *TwoComponents* sheet as you repeatedly hit F9 suggests a related fact: the regression line tends to intersect the true regression line somewhere near the center of the X's. This means that forecasts involving an X_F closer to the center of the sample data have the smallest spread.

The formula for the exact SE of Forecasted Y in the bivariate case with n observations is

$$SE(\text{Forecasted} Y) = SD(\text{Errors}) \cdot \sqrt{\frac{1}{n} + \left[\frac{(X_F - \bar{X})}{\sqrt{n} \cdot SD(X)} \right]^2}.$$

The symbol $\bar{X}$ stands for the average value of the X's in the sample.

This somewhat daunting formula is easier to understand if we consider two extreme cases: the situation in which we are forecasting for a value of X_F

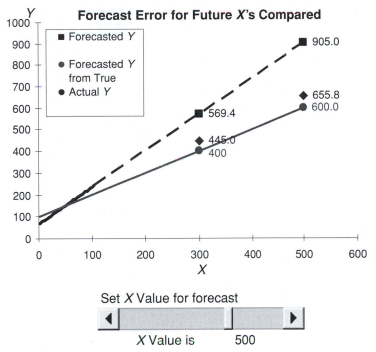

Figure 15.6.3. Demonstrating increasing SE of forecasted Y as X moves farther from the center of the sample.
Source: [SEForecastedY.xls]TwoComponents.

equal to the average of the X's in the sample, and when we are forecasting for an X very far from the average of the X's in the sample.

1. In the first case the squared term equals zero and the SE of Forecasted Y reaches its minimum value, $\frac{SD\,(\text{Errors})}{\sqrt{n}}$. This is just what we noted above: the spread of Forecasted Y is smallest at the center of the data set.
2. In the second extreme case in which we are forecasting far from the center of the sample, the $\frac{1}{n}$ inside the square root becomes relatively unimportant, and the formula for SE of Forecasted Y approximately reduces to

$$SE(\text{Forecasted}\,Y) \approx SD\,(\text{Errors}) \cdot \frac{\left|X_F - \bar{X}\right|}{\sqrt{n} \cdot SD\,(X)}$$

$$= \left|X_F - \bar{X}\right| \cdot \frac{SD\,(\text{Errors})}{\sqrt{n} \cdot SD\,(X)}$$

$$= \left|X_F - \bar{X}\right| \cdot SE\,(b_1).$$

In other words, in this case the spread of Forecasted Y is approximately the product of the spread in the slope coefficient and the absolute value of the distance of the value of X for which we are forecasting from the center of the X's in the sample.

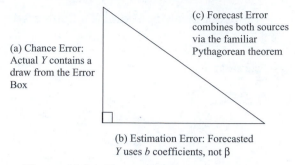

Figure 15.6.4. Two sources of forecast error.

The SE of the Forecast Error

As noted, the Forecast Error contains not only the Estimation Error present in Forecasted Y but also Chance Error that goes into the determination of Actual Y. We depict the two sources of error in the forecast in Figure 15.6.4.

The right triangle of Figure 15.6.4 is an accurate metaphor for the determination of the Forecast Error. We drew the two sources of error as the sides of a right triangle because the sum of the square of the SE of the Chance Error and the square of the SE of the Estimation Error is equal to the square of the SE of the Forecast Error. In other words, the variance of the Forecast Error equals the sums of the variances of its two components. This follows because, under our assumptions, the two components are independent of one another. All this implies that the SE of the Forecast Error obeys a square-root law:

$$\text{SE of Forecast Error} = \sqrt{SD\left(\text{Errors}\right)^2 + SE\left(\text{Forecasted Y}\right)^2}.$$

The implication of this square-root formula is that the spread of the Forecast Error is not simply the sum of the spreads in Chance Error and Estimation Error components. Figure 15.6.5 captures an outcome that helps explain why we do not simply add the spread in the two sources of error. Notice how the negative Estimation Error gets canceled out to some degree by the fact that the Chance Error in observed Y happens to be positive. The resulting total Forecast Error is not that bad.

The analytical formula for the SE of the Forecast Error in the bivariate case is

$$SE(\text{Forecast Error}) = SD(\text{Errors}) \cdot \sqrt{1 + \frac{1}{n} + \left(\frac{(X_F - \bar{X})}{\sqrt{n} \cdot SD(X)}\right)^2}.$$

Figure 15.6.6 depicts how the exact SE of Forecasted Y and the exact SE of the Forecast Error depend on the value of X_F. The figure replicates the third chart in the *TwoComponents* sheet.

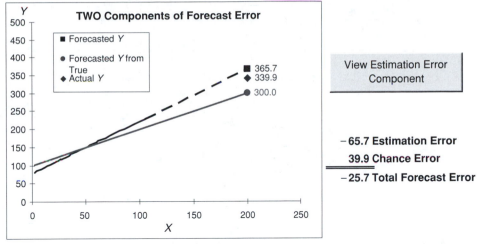

Figure 15.6.5. Decomposing forecast error.
Source: [SEForecast.xls]TwoComponents.

Multivariate Forecasting

The basic ideas about forecasting outlined for the bivariate case carry over to the multivariate setting. We demonstrate these facts using the *Trivariate* sheet. Once again, the data in the sample are generated according to the classical econometric model. The values of Actual *Y* are determined by the equation

$$Y_F = \beta_0 + \beta_1 X_{1F} + \beta_2 X_{2F} + \varepsilon_F,$$

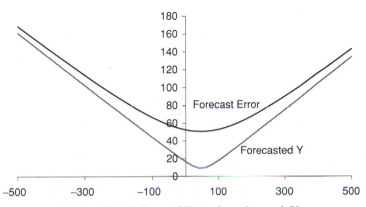

Figure 15.6.6. Exact SEs as functions of X_F.
Source: [SEForecast.xls]Bivariate.

True Parameters			Estimates	
β_0	100		b_0	108.21
β_1	1		b_1	0.77
β_2	-2		b_2	-1.67
SD Error	50		RMSE	48.63

Three Forecasts					
X_{1F}	X_{2F}	Actual Y	Forecasted Y	Forecasted Y from True	Forecast Error
120	100	25.5	32.9	20	-7.4
200	100	205.0	94.2	100	110.8
300	100	247.8	170.8	200	77.0

Figure 15.6.7. Setup for the Trivariate sheet.
Source: [SEForecast.xls]Trivariate.

where ε_F is a new draw from the same distribution of errors that produced the sample data. We report three separate values of Actual Y corresponding to the three different combinations of X_{1F} and X_{2F}: The three forecasts are each computed via the following formula:

$$\text{Forecasted } Y = b_0 + b_1 X_{1F} + b_2 X_{2F}.$$

Figure 15.6.7 shows the basic setup for the trivariate example. It is no longer possible to draw two-dimensional graphs of the regression plane and Forecasted and Actual values of Y.

Estimating the SEs of Forecasted Y and the Forecast Error

In the Basic Tools \ HowTo folder we outline a straightforward procedure for estimating the SE of the Forecasted Y in the bivariate and multivariate cases. With this procedure you need not bother to work with the formulas, which are very unwieldy in the multivariate case.

Monte Carlo Simulation

Monte Carlo simulation can be used to verify the analytical formulas for the SEs. Go to the *MCSim* sheet to see a Monte Carlo simulation for the bivariate case. The Monte Carlo experiment uses the parameters on the *MCSim* sheet to generate a sample and then computes the Forecasted and Actual Y's, along with the Forecast Error.

Forecasted Y is computed by first fitting a line to a sample (using the X values in the *TwoComponents* sheet) and then using that sample-fitted line to predict Y given $X = 200$. Forecasted Y bounces because each sample generates a different fitted line. The outcome we are most interested in is the Forecast Error. This is calculated by subtracting the Forecasted Y from the Actual Y.

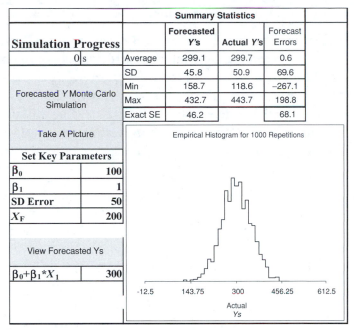

Simulation Progress		Summary Statistics		
		Forecasted Y's	Actual Y's	Forecast Errors
0 s	Average	299.1	299.7	0.6
	SD	45.8	50.9	69.6
	Min	158.7	118.6	−267.1
Forecasted Y Monte Carlo Simulation	Max	432.7	443.7	198.8
	Exact SE	46.2		68.1

Figure 15.6.8. Monte Carlo simulation of forecast outcomes.
Source: [SEForecast.xls] MCSim.

Click the [Forecasted Y Monte Carlo Simulation] button to run your own Monte Carlo simulation. Compare your results to those reported in Figure 15.6.8. The Monte Carlo experiment makes it clear that the error from a forecast of Y is a random variable with a sampling distribution. At $X_F = 200$, the center of Forecasted Y is located at about 300. This demonstrates that the forecast is unbiased because Actual Y is also centered at 300 (when $X = 200$ and given that the true intercept is 100 and the true slope is 1). Another way of making the same point is to see that the center of the Forecast Errors is zero (actually 0.6 in this experiment). The SD of the 1,000 Forecasted Y values, 45.8, approximates the exact Standard Error of Forecasted Y, 46.2. Similarly, the SD of 1,000 forecast errors, 69.6, is very close to the exact SE of the forecast error, 68.1. The [View Forecasted Ys] button is a toggle that allows you to display three separate histograms from the Monte Carlo experiment for the Forecast Errors, Forecasted Y's, and Actual Y's.

The *MCSim Trivariate* sheet performs the same kinds of Monte Carlo experiments for the trivariate example using the X values in the *Trivariate* sheet. We have set the values of X_{1F} and X_{2F} to approximately their respective sample averages. This is the situation in which both the SE of Forecasted Y and the SE of the Forecast Error are minimized. You should experiment with other values for X_{1F} and X_{2F} to verify that the spread increases as the forecast values of the independent variables move away from the sample averages.

Summary

In this section we have explored the basics of forecasting. We have assumed that the researcher has sample data and the correct model of the data generating process. He or she wishes to forecast the future value of the dependent variable based on assumed values of the independent variables. We called this future value Actual Y, and emphasized that its value will depend on a draw from the error distribution. Applying the estimated sample coefficients to the assumed X values produces a point forecast called Forecasted Y:

$$\text{Forecasted } Y = b_0 + b_1 X_{1F} + \cdots + b_K X_{KF}.$$

Forecasted Y is a random variable, which is an unbiased estimator because its expected value is the expected value of the Actual Y we are trying to forecast. Forecasted Y has its own SE, which depends in turn on the SEs of the slope coefficients. In forecasting we usually are interested in a different SE – namely the SE of the Forecast Error. This SE takes into account not only the variability in the regression line that determines Forecasted Y, but also the spread of the error term, which is an integral part of Actual Y.

In many forecasting applications, the basic CEM assumption that the error terms are independent of one another is likely to be wrong. Chapter 20 discusses what happens when this is the case and how econometricians deal with the problem.

We end this section on a practical note. You may be using software that reports the SE of the forecast error and facilitates easy calculation of forecast confidence intervals. If not, please see the file HowToFindSEForecast.doc in the Basic Tools \ HowTo folder for a simple recipe.

15.7. Conclusion

This chapter has presented the following two formulas for standard errors in a bivariate OLS regression:

$$SE\,(SampleSlope) = \frac{SD(\varepsilon)}{\sqrt{n} \cdot SD_X} = \frac{SD(\text{Box})}{\sqrt{\text{\# of draws}} \times SD \text{ of the } X\text{'s}}$$

$$SE\,(ForecastError) = SD_{\text{Errors}} \cdot \sqrt{1 + \frac{1}{n} + \left(\frac{(X_{\text{value}} - \bar{X})}{\sqrt{n} \cdot SD_X}\right)^2}.$$

Both SEs provide similar information about their respective sampling distributions. They tell you the size of the typical deviation from the expected value for the statistic. Both can be used to create confidence intervals or to conduct tests of significance (as the next chapter explains). Both rely on the spread of the error distribution. Usually, this parameter is unknown and must be estimated. The RMSE is the estimator of choice for this task. Although it is biased, it is a consistent estimator of the SD of the errors.

In the case of the SE of the sample slope, you can immediately see that the SE varies according to the spread of the errors, the number of observations, and the spread of the X values. The formula for the SE of the Forecast Error is somewhat more complicated, but it reveals that there are two sources of error in operation: Chance and Estimation error. An important lesson embedded in the formula is that the farther away you are forecasting from the center of the sample, the greater the variability in the forecast.

The lessons of this chapter apply to multiple regression as well: In every case the SE is smaller the greater the spread in the X values, the greater the sample size, and the smaller the spread in the errors. All estimates of SEs depend on the RMSE. The formula for the SE of the slope in a multiple regression is similar to that for a bivariate regression, the one difference being that the SE of the slope in the multiple regression depends on the size of the correlation between a particular independent variable and the other independent variables in the model. Standard statistical software computes SEs for slope coefficients. A How To document demonstrates how to compute SEs for forecasts.

15.8. Exercises

1. What is the difference between the exact SE of the sample slope and the estimated SE of the sample slope? Which one is reported by regression software?
2. In the *ExactSEb1* sheet in SEb1OLS.xls, the exact SE in cell F4 is about 0.4. If someone wanted the SE to be cut in half, how could you change the setup to make this so?
3. Run a Monte Carlo simulation that compares the performance of the RMSE to the SD of the Residuals using the Mean Squared Error criterion with $n = 10$.

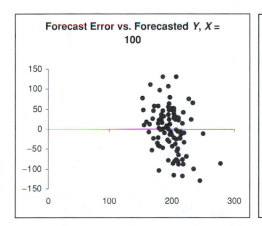
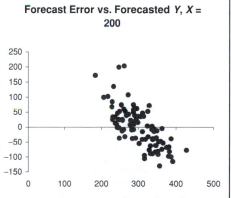

Figure 15.8.1. Forecast errors forecasted Y's, $X = 100$ and $X = 200$.
Source: [SEForecast.xls]MCSim.

You will have to create a new formula in a cell in the *Data* sheet of EstimatingS-DErrors.xls that computes the squared deviation of each sample's RMSE from the SD Errors parameter. Create another cell that does the same thing for the SD of the Residuals. Find the average of the squared deviations of the estimates from the true parameter value. The empirical average is a good approximation to the expected value with a large number of repetitions. Take a picture of your results and paste it in a Word document. What do you conclude?

4. Explain why we do not use the RMSE as the SE of the Forecast Error. Take pictures from the SEForecast.xls workbook to support your argument.

5. In the *MCSim* sheet of SEForecast.xls, we chose $\beta_0 = 100$, $\beta_1 = 1$, and SD (Error) = 50. We then ran two Monte Carlo simulations of forecasts, one with X set to 100 and the second with X set to 200. We graphed the Forecast Errors against Forecasted Y for the first 100 repetitions in both experiments. The two graphs in Figure 15.8.1 show our results. Explain the different patterns that you see in the two graphs.

References

A seminal paper on the SE of a forecast and the one that provided the epigraph to this chapter is

Schultz, Henry (1930). "The Standard Error of a Forecast from a Curve." *Journal of the American Statistical Association* 25(170): 139–185.

The procedure for estimating the SE of Forecasted Y is discussed on page 203 of

Wooldridge, Jeffrey M. (2003). *Introductory Econometrics: A Modern Approach*, Second Edition. Mason, Ohio: Thomson South-Western.

16

Confidence Intervals and Hypothesis Testing

We would not assert that every economist misunderstands statistical significance, only that most do, and these some of the best economic scientists.... Simulation, new data sets, and quantitative thinking about the conversation of the science offer a way forward. The first step anyway is plain: stop searching for economic findings under the lamppost of statistical significance.

Deirdre N. McCloskey and Stephen T. Ziliak[1]

16.1. Introduction

This chapter shows how a single sample can be used to construct confidence intervals and test hypotheses about population parameters. Hypothesis testing, also known as testing for significance, is a fundamental part of inferential econometrics.

Statistical significance should not, however, be confused with practical importance. Just because we can reject a null hypothesis and claim a statistically significant result, does not mean that the result matters. In economics, many data sets are large n, which means it is easy to find statistically significant results that are not of practical importance. Tests of significance have a place in econometrics but are not the be all and end all of inference.

Hypothesis testing can be confusing, but it has a coherent, stable framework that should help you organize the complicated details. The next section demonstrates that there is a sampling distribution for each sample statistic that is a random variable. Section 16.3 will explain how confidence intervals are constructed and interpreted. We then turn to the logic of hypothesis testing (Section 16.4) and explain why the t distribution is so often used (Section 16.5). The chapter's last section puts the ideas into practice by working on a real-world example.

---

[1] McCloskey and Ziliak (1996, pp. 111–112).

16.2. Distributions of OLS Regression Statistics

Workbook: LinestRandomVariables.xls

This section focuses on the basic regression statistics reported by Excel's LINEST function to make a simple, but crucial point: Each statistic, because it is derived from a sample with chance error, is a random variable with its own particular type of distribution. In addition, we show that the sampling distribution of a statistic depends on several crucial factors, including (1) the distribution of the errors, (2) the recipe used to create the statistic, (3) the values of the X's, and (4) the number of observations in the sample.

Open the LinestRandomVariables.xls workbook and go to the *Data* sheet. We have implemented the bivariate version of the classical econometric model: the X's are fixed in repeated samples, and, of course, the parameters are constant across samples. The error terms are like tickets drawn with replacement from a box. Because the Y's are composed of the deterministic component ($\beta_0 + \beta_1 X$) and chance error (ε), they vary from one sample to the next. The *Data* sheet (see Figure 16.2.1) demonstrates the fact that Excel's LINEST function reports nine separate, sample-based random variables.

From the *Data* sheet, hit F9 to recalculate the workbook. The errors change, which leads to changes in the observed Y values. When the realized chance errors change (which is what happens when you hit the F9 key and draw a new sample), so does the observed Y.

Previous chapters have shown that changing the observed Y's changes the sample intercept and slope of the fitted line. But notice how 9 of the 10 values in the 5×2 LINEST output bounce every time F9 is hit. Only the degrees of freedom for the regression stay constant at 8 (this is computed by subtracting the number of parameters being estimated, 2, from the number of observations, 10).

The fact that the numbers in the LINEST output bounce is a clear demonstration that they are random variables. This means each sample statistic reported by LINEST has a sampling distribution (also known as a probability histogram). But what might the sampling distribution of each sample statistic look like? What determines its expected value, SE, and shape?

Several fundamental factors determine the distribution of a sample statistic. First, the distribution of the errors affects the distribution of the regression sample statistics. In addition, the computations applied to a statistic (averaging, squaring, etc.) influence the resulting sampling distribution. Finally, the values of the X's and the number of observations in the sample also affect the sampling distribution. In the next part of this section, we focus on the distribution of the errors and then turn to the computation of a particular statistic.

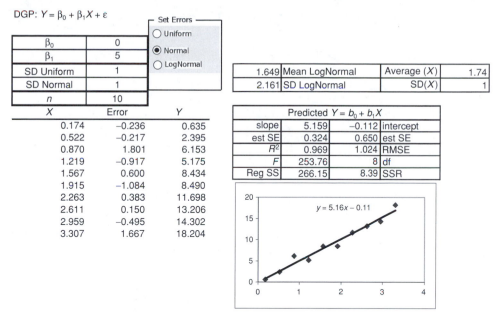

DGP: $Y = \beta_0 + \beta_1 X + \varepsilon$

β_0	0
β_1	5
SD Uniform	1
SD Normal	1
n	10

Set Errors
- ○ Uniform
- ● Normal
- ○ LogNormal

1.649	Mean LogNormal	Average (X)	1.74
2.161	SD LogNormal	SD(X)	1

X	Error	Y
0.174	−0.236	0.635
0.522	−0.217	2.395
0.870	1.801	6.153
1.219	−0.917	5.175
1.567	0.600	8.434
1.915	−1.084	8.490
2.263	0.383	11.698
2.611	0.150	13.206
2.959	−0.495	14.302
3.307	1.667	18.204

Predicted $Y = b_0 + b_1 X$			
slope	5.159	−0.112	intercept
est SE	0.324	0.650	est SE
R^2	0.969	1.024	RMSE
F	253.76	8	df
Reg SS	266.15	8.39	SSR

$y = 5.16x - 0.11$

Figure 16.2.1. Random variables reported by LINEST.
Source: [LinestRandomVariables.xls]Data.

The Distribution of the Errors

The *Data* sheet allows you to choose three different error distributions – uniform, normal, or log-normal – in order to see the effect that the error distribution has on the sampling distribution of a particular statistic.[2]

Because we are dealing with an error distribution and a sampling distribution, things can become pretty confusing. It is important to keep track of where you are in the problem. Figure 16.2.2 depicts the data generating process of the bivariate case of the classical econometric box model. It is a map to help keep things clear and organized.

The box model graphic in Figure 16.2.2 shows the logical order of the data generation process and the road to the sampling distribution. The error distribution is the source of the variation in the observed Y's, which in turn is used in the calculation of sample-based statistics reported by LINEST. Thus, the distribution of the errors plays an important role in the distribution of the sample-based statistics.

The *ErrorDist* sheet in the LinestRandomVariables.xls workbook shows how we can use Excel to generate uniformly, normally, and log-normally distributed random variables. Column A uses the formula RANDOM(), which

---

[2] The `Advanced Topic: Another Error Dist` button allows you to experiment with a fourth type of error distribution based on Student's t. This enables sampling from a distribution with "fat tails."

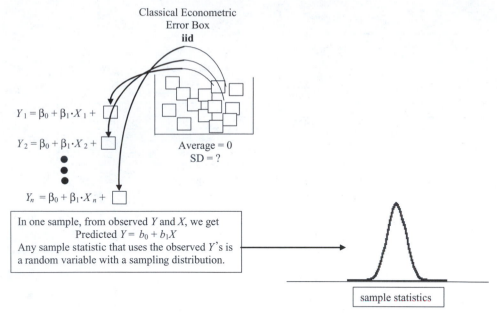

Figure 16.2.2. The bivariate CEM.

generates a uniformly distributed random variable from the interval (0,1). In Column B, we use the function NORMALRANDOM(mean, SD). The two arguments of the NORMALRANDOM function are the mean and SD, respectively, of the normal distribution we wish to draw from. (Note that cells F4 and F5 contain these two parameter values that describe the normal distribution.) Column C takes e (the base of the natural log, the transcendental number 2.71828...) raised to the power of the value in column B. This creates a log-normally distributed random variable. The values in column C are all positive because the negative numbers in the exponent simply trigger the reciprocal (2 raised to the −2 is 1/4 or 0.25).

Click on the Draw Histogram button and click OK to draw a histogram of 1,000 values from a uniform distribution. Select the cell range B2:B1001 to draw a histogram of the normal values. Repeat the procedure to see the log-normal distribution. Figure 16.2.3 displays empirical histograms of 1,000 draws each from the three distributions.

In the uniform distribution, the 1,000 values are roughly evenly distributed across the interval from 0 to 1 in the histogram, whereas the normal values are more bunched up in the center and gradually fade away in the tails and the log-normal has a long right-hand tail (due to exponentiation). The empirical histograms displayed in Figure 16.2.3 are just approximations to the actual probability density functions.

What effect would drawing from a uniform, normal, or log-normal distribution have on the sample-based statistics generated by LINEST? Intuitively, you would expect the distribution of the errors to matter because the observed

1,000 Draws from a Uniform Distribution

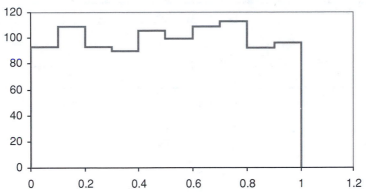

1,000 Draws from a Normal Distribution

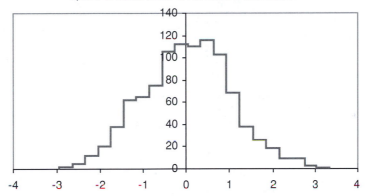

1,000 Draws from a Log Normal Distribution

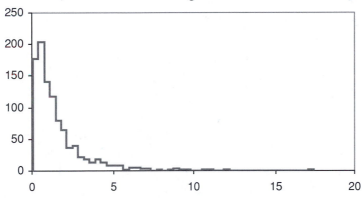

Figure 16.2.3. Three distributions.
Source: [LinestRandomVariables.xls]ErrorDist.

Summary Statistics		Statistic	Slope
Average	5.007	Error Box	Normal
SD	0.319	SD	1.00
Max	6.168		
Min	3.695	n	10

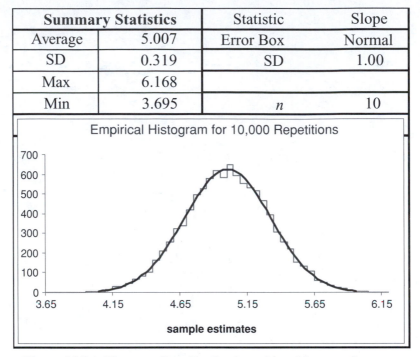

Figure 16.2.4. The sampling distribution of b_1 with normal errors.
Source: [LinestRandomVariables.xls]MCSim.

Y's depend on the errors, which in turn affect the sample statistics reported by LINEST. But what exactly is the effect?

Let us focus on the sample slope. Suppose, for example, that the errors are normally distributed. Go to the *Data* sheet and make sure the Normal option in the Set Errors box is chosen. If the number of observations is not already set to 10, click on the Set N button to make the number of observations equal to 10. Then go to the *MCSim* sheet. Select the slope option and run a Monte Carlo simulation. Click the Show Normal Distribution button to superimpose a normal curve on the histogram. Figure 16.2.4 shows our results.

These results provide fairly convincing evidence that the sample slope is normally distributed when the errors are normally distributed. Note also that the OLS sample slope is apparently unbiased and the approximate SE from this Monte Carlo experiment (0.319) is close to the exact SE (see the formula in cell H1 of the *MCSim* sheet) of about 0.3162.

In contrast, Figure 16.2.5 shows what happens to the sampling distribution when we use log-normally distributed errors. The normal curve does not fit as well, indicating that in this case the sampling distribution is not that close to normal.

At this point we must make a very important distinction between small-sample and large-sample results for sampling distributions. Small sample

Summary Statistics		Statistic	Slope
Average	4.989	Error Box	LogNormal
SD	0.670	SD	2.16
Max	11.135		
Min	−1.468	n	10

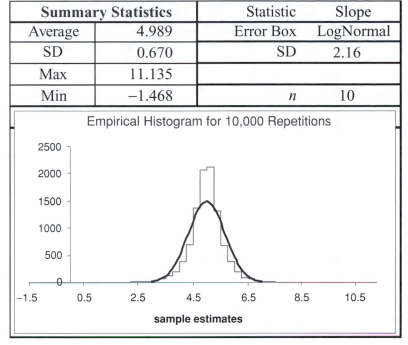

Figure 16.2.5. The sampling distribution of b_1 with log-normal errors.
Source: [LinestRandomVariables.xls]MCSim.

results pertain to small sample sizes. We have demonstrated that, in small samples (such as $n = 10$), normally distributed error terms lead to sample slopes that are normally distributed; log-normally distributed error terms lead to sample slopes that are not close to being normally distributed. The term large-sample result, sometimes called an asymptotic result, refers to what happens as the sample size increases and becomes large. The central limit theorem plays a crucial role in asymptotic analysis of sample statistics. It says that in many cases the sampling distribution of sums of random variables converges toward the normal curve.

Fortunately for inferential econometrics, the central limit theorem applies in this case: we can demonstrate that, as the number of observations, n, increases, for almost all error distributions, the sampling distributions of b_0 and b_1 converge to normal even if the errors were not initially normally distributed.

To do so, we continue working with a log-normal error distribution, steadily increasing the number of observations. Figure 16.2.6 shows the progression. We held the SD of the X's and the error distribution constant while varying n in the *Data* sheet. The sampling distribution, far from normal in Figure 16.2.5, with $n = 10$, gets closer and closer to the normal curve as n rises. Even for $n = 90$, in the right panel of Figure 16.2.6, the sampling distribution is not

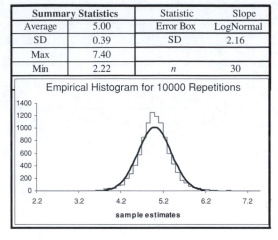

Summary Statistics		Statistic	Slope
Average	5.00	Error Box	LogNormal
SD	0.39	SD	2.16
Max	7.40		
Min	2.22	n	30

Empirical Histogram for 10000 Repetitions

sample estimates

Summary Statistics		Statistic	Slope
Average	5.00	Error Box	LogNormal
SD	0.27	SD	2.16
Max	7.21		
Min	3.48	n	60

Empirical Histogram for 10000 Repetitions

sample estimates

Summary Statistics		Statistic	Slope
Average	5.00	Error Box	LogNormal
SD	0.23	SD	2.16
Max	6.22		
Min	3.82	n	90

Empirical Histogram for 10000 Repetitions

sample estimates

Figure 16.2.6. The central limit theorem in action.
Source: [LinestRandomVariables.xls]MCSim.

exactly normal. It keeps getting closer and closer to normal as the sample size increases but never quite reaches true normality.

Convergence of the probability histogram of b_1 to the normal curve is quite quick for the uniform distribution and for log-normal distributions in which the SD of the underlying normal distribution is small (e.g., 0.5). Convergence to the normal curve, however, is much slower when errors are log-normally distributed if the SD of the underlying normal distribution is large (say 2).

The convergence of the sampling distribution of the OLS slope estimator to the normal curve is a powerful result. It tells us that the sampling distribution of the OLS estimator will be approximately normal if n is large even if the distribution of the errors is not normal. For many applications, normally distributed errors may be reasonable, but the convergence result says we do not have to worry if the errors are nonnormally distributed as long as the sample size is large. In other words, the convergence of the sampling distribution to the normal curve when the errors are nonnormally distributed frees us from having to make a restrictive assumption about the distribution of the errors.

In practice, when the sample size is large, econometricians know they do not have to worry about the effect of the distribution of the errors on the sampling distribution of the OLS estimator. For small samples, however, all bets are off. Unfortunately, there is no magic cutoff between small and large samples. All we can say is that the bigger the sample, the closer the convergence to the normal curve.

The Distribution of LINEST Random Variables

Should you conclude that all sample statistics converge to the normal curve as the sample size increases? Absolutely not. Would the additional assumption of a normally distributed error box guarantee that all sampling distributions converge to the normal curve? The answer is still no. The intuition behind this is rather obvious: For statistics such as RMSE and sum of squared residuals (SSR), the squaring involved in the computation of these statistics leads to long tails.

We can approximate the sampling distribution of these statistics easily by simply clicking on the appropriate button in the *MCSim* sheet. Figure 16.2.7 shows the Monte Carlo approximation to the sampling distribution of the SSR when the distribution of the error terms is normal.

Clearly, the SSR for this DGP is not normally distributed.[3] You can approximate the sampling distributions of other statistics by running your own Monte

---

[3] In fact, SSR with Normal errors is distributed chi-squared with $n-k$ degrees of freedom.

Summary Statistics		Statistic	SSR
Average	7.960	Error Box	Normal
SD	3.978	SD	1.00
Max	34.545		
Min	0.446	n	10

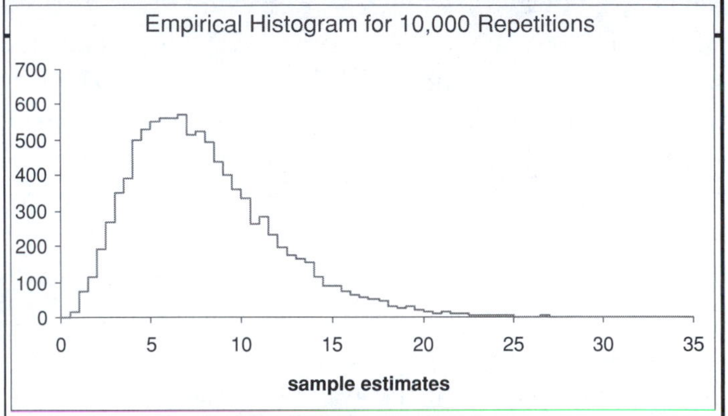

Figure 16.2.7. The sampling distribution of SSR with normal errors. *Source:* [LinestRandomVariables.xls]MCsim.

Carlo simulations. Many sampling distributions do not have names. This does not change the fact that the sampling distributions exist.

Summary

This section has shown that, within the context of the classical econometric model, statistics based on bouncing sample data are random variables. The distributions of these random variables depend on the recipe used to calculate the statistic and the distribution of the errors. If the errors are normally distributed, then the OLS slope estimator's sampling distribution is also normally distributed.

If the errors are not normally distributed, we invoke the extremely helpful central limit theorem: The sampling distribution of the sample slopes converges to the normal curve as the number of observations increases. Thus, a large sample size protects us against having to determine the shape of the sampling distribution when the distribution of the errors is not normal. This is true in the multivariate case as well as the bivariate case, and it holds for almost every possible distribution of the error terms.

Our discussion of convergence to the normal curve used the sampling distribution of the sample slope. There are other sample statistics that converge to the normal, but we cannot say that all sample statistics behave this way.

16.3. Understanding Confidence Intervals

Workbook: ConfidenceIntervals.xls

The previous section showed that the distribution of the errors affects the sampling distribution of b_1. We showed that, if the errors are normally distributed, then the sample slope will also be normally distributed. If the errors are not normally distributed but the sample size is large, then we can rely on the central limit theorem to rescue us – the sampling distribution of b_1, though not normal, will approach the normal curve as n increases.

This section is devoted to explaining the confidence interval. This is a difficult idea to grasp, and so we will resort to our usual combination of live graphics and Monte Carlo simulation. Before we dive in, however, let us set the stage by providing a brief introduction to the use of confidence intervals and tests of significance.

Consider two examples: the rate of return to an additional year of education and the male–female wage gap in the labor market. Economic theory may lead you to believe that more education leads to higher income, but it does not say by how much. Thus, you may be interested in estimating the unknown true parameter value of the return from an additional year of education. With the male–female wage gap, on the other hand, we may want to test a claim that there is no wage gap after controlling for factors other than gender that determine the wage. Of course, we may also want to test someone's claim about the rate of return to education or estimate the size of the wage gap.

To make matters more concrete, suppose we had data from the CPS on some measure of pay, educational attainment, gender, and other control variables (such as race, union status, and so on). We posit a semilog model for the data generating process and assume the classical econometric model applies as follows:

$$\text{Ln}\,(\text{Wage}_i) = \beta_0 + \beta_1 \,\text{Education in Years}_i + \beta_2 \,\text{Female}_i + \text{Other Terms} + \varepsilon_i.$$

We estimate the following equation:

$$\text{Predicted Ln}\,(\text{Wage}_i)$$
$$= b_0 + b_1 \,\text{Education in Years}_i + b_2 \,\text{Female}_i + \text{Other Terms}.$$
$$\text{(SE)(SE)} \qquad\qquad\qquad \text{(SE)}$$

We can use these results in two ways: to estimate an unknown parameter and to test a hypothesized value for an unknown parameter. If we are interested in the former, we will want to use confidence intervals; if the latter, we will turn to a hypothesis test.

In the earnings function regression, b_1 can be interpreted as a rate of return on education because it is approximately the percentage change in wage given one more year of education. Suppose $b_1 = 0.07$. This would be an estimate of the unknown true parameter (β_1). Because b_1 is a random variable with a sampling distribution, econometricians report the point estimate along with a confidence interval. The confidence level (typically 95 percent) reports the chances that the interval covers the true, but unknown β_1. This section explains how this rather amazing feat can be accomplished. Notice, however, that we could also use the sample results to test a claim about β_1. Someone might say that the true parameter is 10 percent and that the observed value of 7 percent is due to chance error. The way to test such a claim is to use a hypothesis test. Section 16.4 discusses hypothesis tests.

In fact, the same two approaches can be used with any coefficient from an estimated regression. We might be interested in the size of the male–female wage gap, in which case we would report the b_2 estimate along with its associated confidence interval, or we might want to test the claim that there is no wage gap, which implies that $\beta_2 = 0$ and that an observed value of b_2 less than zero is due solely to chance variation.

This section assumes that the sampling distribution of the OLS slope estimator is normal (either because the errors are normal or because the number of observations is large) and focuses on how econometricians use a single sample to estimate an unknown parameter. In such cases, creating an interval by putting upper and lower bounds on the estimate is a way to communicate the level of confidence in the estimate.

Confidence Intervals in Action

The workbook ConfidenceIntervals.xls demonstrates the logic behind confidence intervals. Go to the *UniformCI* sheet. You will see a plot of the probability density function for the uniform distribution on the interval 0 to 1 drawn in blue. Superimposed on the same graph is a pink point, representing a single draw from the uniform distribution. Figure 16.3.1 is an example of the display.

The expected value (EV) of a single draw from the uniform distribution on the (0,1) interval is 0.5. Hit the F9 key several times and watch the point bounce around. Notice that you almost never hit the expected value.

Let us play a game. Here are the rules:

1. Take a draw from a distribution. We can play with any distribution, but we will use just two, the uniform and the normal.
2. Next, create an interval by going from your realized draw, plus or minus a number that you choose.
3. Determine if your interval covers the EV of the distribution. The interval covers the EV if the interval contains the value of the expected value.

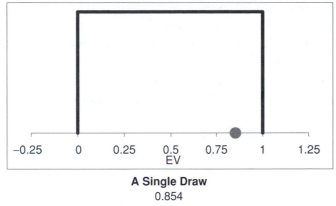

A Single Draw
0.854

Figure 16.3.1. A single draw from a uniform distribution.
Source: [ConfidenceIntervals.xls]UniformCI.

You win the game if the interval covers the EV, but you lose if it does not. If you draw a new value and construct a new confidence interval repeatedly, what fraction of the time will you cover the EV and win? Put another way, what is the chance that on a single draw your confidence interval will cover the EV?

The answer to this question is our confidence level in the interval. The question can be answered analytically or via Monte Carlo simulation.

You can play this game and gain some intuition about confidence intervals by clicking on the | Show Confidence Interval Calculations | button in the *UniformCI* sheet. This adds a confidence interval of width 0.2 on either side of the point and draws another value from the uniform distribution. Figure 16.3.2 is an example.

Hit F9 repeatedly and watch the interval bounce around. Sometimes it covers the expected value, 0.5; sometimes it does not.

How can we figure out what fraction of the time it covers? There is an analytical answer to this question. Because the distribution is uniform, for

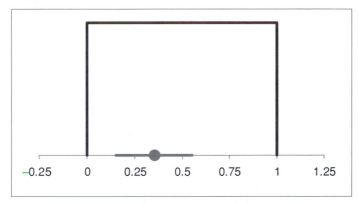

Figure 16.3.2. A single confidence interval from a uniform distribution.
Source: [ConfidenceIntervals.xls]UniformCI.

the interval to cover the EV, the drawn value must be between 0.3 and 0.7. What are the chances of drawing a value in this range? 40 percent.

We can also obtain an answer via Monte Carlo simulation. Click on the Monte Carlo button to take 10,000 draws from which 10,000 intervals are created. The percentage of intervals that cover the EV is reported in cell K13. As usual, the Monte Carlo approach provides a reasonable approximation to the exact answer.

Change the interval width to 0.45 (in cell B12) and hit the F9 key a few times. The interval is longer, and you cover more often. How often will you cover? The exact answer is 90 percent. Running a Monte Carlo simulation confirms this result.

Intervals that cover a given percentage of the time are named accordingly. When cell B12 is 0.2, we have a 40-percent confidence interval, and when it is 0.45 we have a 90-percent confidence interval. Notice that we are expressing our confidence in the interval, which is what is bouncing around.

We can also "back out" a confidence level. In other words, if you desire a given percentage of times that you want the interval to cover, you can then compute the required length of the interval. Click the Set Confidence Level button and enter a 95-percent confidence level. The necessary plus and minus number, called the critical value, is 0.475, and it is placed in cell B12.

Uniform distributions are rarely, if ever, used for confidence intervals. We used the uniform distribution because it is easy to work with and see what is going on. A much more common distribution from which to create confidence intervals is the normal distribution. Go to the *NormalCI* sheet to see how confidence intervals based on this distribution can be created.

The game is the same: Take a draw, create an interval, and then determine if you covered the EV. The question is the same: What are the chances that I cover the EV? The idea behind the confidence interval is the same: A 95-percent confidence interval says that 95 percent of the intervals constructed this way will cover the EV. The only difference lies in the distribution – the normal is not evenly distributed like the uniform and it has tails that actually never touch the horizontal axis.

Begin by clicking on the Reset button in the *NormalCI* sheet. This will ensure that the sheet starts out with a small +/− Value of 0.2 applied to a draw from a standard normal distribution (i.e., a distribution with EV equal to 0 and SD equal to 1). Hit F9 to see the confidence interval bounce. Every so often, it covers the EV. How often? We will forego the explanation of the analytical approach and go straight to Monte Carlo simulation. Click the Monte Carlo button to get an approximate answer to the question. If roughly 16 percent from such a small interval seems high, consider the advantage offered by the normal distribution – many draws will come from close to the EV (unlike the uniform where the draws are evenly spread out) so even such a tiny interval has a decent chance of covering the EV.

Change the +/− Value in cell B12 to 1.0. Run a Monte Carlo simulation to see that you have created a 68-percent confidence interval (because intervals constructed this way cover the EV roughly 68 percent of the time). Finally, click the Set Confidence Level button and create a 95-percent confidence interval. Notice that the interval runs 1.96 units above and below the drawn value.

Let us summarize: we take a draw from a given distribution and build an interval around that draw by going a certain distance above and below the draw. The confidence level conveys the chances that an interval of a given length will cover the expected value of that distribution. If we know the shape of the distribution, its EV and SD, we can compute the interval length needed to achieve a desired confidence level. Similarly, with sufficient knowledge, given the length of the interval, we can compute the confidence level. With this understood, we are ready to proceed to constructing confidence intervals for the sample slope.

Confidence Intervals for b_1 – Known Box

Suppose we draw a sample from a data generating process that obeys the classical econometric box model, and run a regression to get a single estimate of β_1. Where is this b_1 value relative to the expected value of the sampling distribution?

We will reduce the problem to a more manageable size by noticing that we can treat the realized b_1 as a draw from its sampling distribution. Figure 16.3.3 is a picture of the CEM, which we will use in our examples. The process of generating observed Y's and running a regression on the sample data to get b_1 can be distilled simply to drawing a b_1 from its probability histogram. When the CEM applies, the expected value of b_1 is β_1. Notice also that, if we know the SD of the errors, we can compute the SE of b_1 exactly using the formula derived in Sections 14.7 and 15.5.

Because we have reduced the problem to drawing a value from a distribution, we can apply the same approach that we used with the uniform and normal distributions. We will compute the chances that an interval of a particular length covers the expected value (β_1 because our OLS estimator is unbiased). The probability histogram for the sample slopes will be exactly normally distributed when the error terms are normally distributed or approximately normally distributed when n is large. Thus, the confidence interval will be based on the normal distribution.

The *Data* sheet provides an example of the procedure for constructing a 95-percent confidence interval, which is reproduced in Figure 16.3.4.

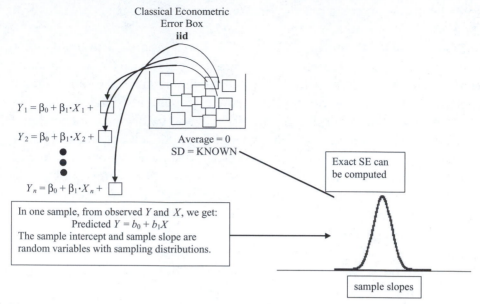

Figure 16.3.3. The classical econometric model with known SD of the error box.

The exact SE in this case is 0.316 based on the known SD of the normally distributed box in cell B6 (and the SD of the X's and n). The center of the confidence interval is the sample slope b_1 to which we add and subtract $1.96 \cdot$ Exact SE.

To see how this creates a 95-percent confidence interval, return to the *NormalCI* sheet and enter 0.316 in cell G20. Hit F9, and the normal curve will compress (because the spread is much smaller), but the interval in cells B14:C15 has not been corrected to reflect the new SE. Click the $\boxed{\text{Set Confidence Level}}$ button and click OK to create a 95-percent confidence interval. Hit F9 a few times to see that the interval bounces and covers EV quite often. To verify that we have indeed created a 95-percent confidence interval, run a Monte Carlo simulation.

Confidence Interval for b_1 – Unknown Box

In practice, we do not know the SD of the error box. That means we cannot determine the exact SE of b_1, the slope estimate. Our recourse is to use

Predicted $Y = b_0 + b_1 X$			
slope	5.359	−0.264	intercept
est SE	0.259	0.519	est SE
R^2	0.982	0.818	RMSE
F	429	8	tdf
Reg SS	287	5	SSR

Constructing the Confidence Interval–Exact SE			
$b_1 + 1.96$ ExactSE	$b_1 - 1.96$ ExactSE	b_1	Covered?
5.979	4.739	5.359	1
Exact SE	0.316		

Figure 16.3.4. Constructing a confidence interval for the sample slope.
Source: [ConfidenceIntervals.xls]Data.

Predicted $Y = b_0 + b_1 X$			
slope	5.373	−0.257	intercept
est SE	0.389	0.780	est SE
R^2	0.960	1.229	RMSE
F	191	8	df
Reg SS	289	12	SSR

Constructing the Confidence Interval–Exact SE

$b_1 + 1.96$ ExactSE	$b_1 - 1.96$ ExactSE	b_1	Covered?
5.993	4.753	5.373	1
Exact SE	0.316		

Constructing the Confidence Interval–Estimated SE

$b_1 + 1.96$ EstSE	$b_1 - 1.96$ EstSE	b_1	Covered?
6.135	4.611	5.373	1
Estimated SE	0.389		

Reporting the Estimated Equation

Predicted $Y =$	−0.257	+	$5.373X$
	(0.78)		(0.389)

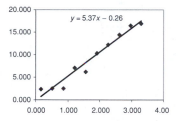

$y = 5.37x - 0.26$

Figure 16.3.5. Different confidence intervals for the same data set.
Source: [ConfidenceIntervals.xls]Data.

the RMSE to estimate the SD of the error box. We can then plug this estimate of the box's SD into the formula for the SE of b_1. The result is the
estimated SE. What are the consequences for confidence intervals of using
the estimated SE instead of the exact SE in setting upper and lower bounds
on the confidence intervals? The bottom line is that, when the sample size
is large (let us say n greater than 30), the estimated SE is a good substitute for the exact SE and the resulting confidence intervals behave quite
well. When the sample size is small, confidence intervals are less reliable and
inference may be severely compromised because the estimated SE is biased.
In Section 16.5, we will talk about what can be done to rescue matters when
one must use a small sample for inference but the error terms are normally
distributed.

The first consequence of using the estimated SE is that the length of the
confidence interval will vary from one sample to the next. We contrast estimated SEs and exact SEs on the *Data* sheet. Figure 16.3.5 is an example with
10 observations.

We computed the exact SE (with our knowledge of the SD of the error
box, the square root of the number of observations, and the SD of the X's).
In this case it turns out to be 0.316. This value for the exact SE stays fixed for
every sample we might draw. The estimated SE, on the other hand, uses the
RMSE to estimate the SD of the error box. The RMSE bounces around (hit
F9 and note how cell G12 changes) and, therefore, so does the estimated SE
(cell K20) and the width of the confidence intervals.

The second consequence of using the estimated SE instead of the exact SE is
that, for small samples, confidence intervals based on the normal curve may be
unreliable. This is true no matter the distribution of the errors. To demonstrate
the poor performance of confidence intervals for small samples, go to the
Data sheet and use the ⬜Set N button to set n to 3. We use this absurdly small

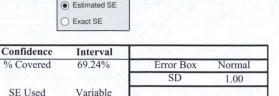

Choose SE	
● Estimated SE	
○ Exact SE	

Confidence	Interval			
% Covered	69.24%		Error Box	Normal
			SD	1.00
SE Used	Variable			
			n	3

Figure 16.3.6. Performance of 95-percent confidence interval when $n = 3$ using estimated SE.
Source: [ConfidenceIntervals.xls]MCSim.

sample size so we can clearly demonstrate the unreliability of the confidence intervals when the SD has to be estimated. Make the distribution of the errors Normal. Go to the *CIMCSim* sheet and run a 10,000-repetition Monte Carlo experiment. You will obtain results similar to those given in Figure 16.3.6.

The 95-percent confidence intervals did very poorly, covering the true parameter value only 69 percent of the time. Pause to look at the graph of the first 100 confidence intervals and verify that they have varying lengths, reflecting different estimates of the SE in different samples. Now use the radio button option for the exact SE (0.577 in this case) and run a second 10,000-repetition experiment. You should obtain results like those presented in Figure 16.3.7.

The confidence intervals are now performing as advertised: Very close to 95 percent of the intervals covered the true parameter value. Take a look at the graph of the first 100 confidence intervals to see that they all have the same length.

Similar experiments with small n can be performed for the two other error distributions that can be specified on the *Data* sheet. You will find that the confidence intervals do not do the job (cover the true parameter 95 percent of the time) when the estimated SE is employed, but that they perform remarkably

Choose SE	
○ Estimated SE	
● Exact SE	

Confidence	Interval			
% Covered	94.88%		Error Box	Normal
			SD	1.00
SE Used	0.5774			
			n	3

Figure 16.3.7. Performance of 95-percent confidence interval when $n = 3$ using exact SE.
Source: ConfidenceIntervals.xls!MCSim.

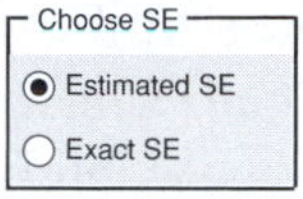

Choose SE
⦿ Estimated SE
○ Exact SE

Confidence	Interval			
% Covered	94.69%		Error Box	Log Normal
			SD	2.16
SE Used	Variable			
			n	30

Figure 16.3.8. Performance of 95-percent confidence interval for $n = 30$, LogNormal Errors.
Source: [ConfidenceIntervals.xls]MCSim.

well when the exact SE is used (covering the true parameter close to 95 percent of the time).

Unfortunately, in practice one must use estimated SEs. In general that means that inference may be severely compromised for *small* samples. This is true for both confidence intervals and hypothesis testing (which is covered in the next section). If the errors are normally distributed, the situation can be rescued by basing the confidence interval bounds on the *t*-distribution. This procedure is explained in Section 16.5.

The good news is that as *n* increases, confidence intervals using the estimated SE with the normal curve work better and better. You can verify this via Monte Carlo experiments. As one example, we set the error distribution to be lognormal, set *n* to 30, chose estimated SEs for computing the confidence interval, and ran a Monte Carlo simulation. Figure 16.3.8 displays the results.

The confidence intervals based on the normal curve covered the true parameter just about 95 percent of the time. You ought to perform similar experiments for the normal and uniform error distributions with varying sample sizes. Even with a sample size as small as 10 observations and log normal errors, over 90-percent coverage from a 95-percent confidence interval results.

Summary

This section has discussed one main branch of inference – creating confidence intervals when estimating a parameter. Confidence intervals are constructed by adding and subtracting a value to a draw from a distribution. The level of confidence is the probability that the interval covers the expected value of the distribution.

Applied to the sample slope, we use the result that the sampling distribution of b_1 is either exactly normal (when the errors are normally distributed) or approximately normal (when the errors are not normally distributed but the sample size is large). In practice, a complication is that the SD of the errors must be estimated. The larger the sample size, the better the confidence interval based on the normal curve works. When using the estimated SE, extremely small sample sizes can cripple the confidence interval method. In economics, we rarely deal with such small sample sizes and, thus, confidence intervals based on the normal curve are an accepted, common way of expressing the variability in an estimate.

The next section discusses a second way to use the SE of an estimator. Instead of using the SE as a give or take number to signal the precision of the estimate, we can test a claim about the true parameter value by constructing an appropriate test statistic.

16.4. The Logic of Hypothesis Testing

Workbook: HypothesisTest.xls

The previous section explored how confidence intervals are used when estimating a parameter; this section is devoted to the second main branch of inference, hypothesis testing. Hypothesis tests are used when some claim has been made about the parameters governing the data generation process. Instead of reporting the parameter estimate along with a confidence interval, we use the parameter estimate and its estimated SE to test the claim about the value of the parameter.

This section ignores complicated calculations and subtle details in order to focus on the essential logic of hypothesis testing. Because it is easy to get confused when doing tests of significance, keeping the fundamental strategy clear should be helpful.

Suppose a particular value is proposed for a population parameter. A hypothesis test simply asks whether the proposed population parameter is so implausible that it cannot be believed. Notice that it is the proposed population parameter that is being tested. The claim that the population parameter is a given value is called the null hypothesis. We will have to decide to reject or not reject the claimed value of the population parameter. According to the null hypothesis, any deviation from the claimed value in a single sample is due to mere chance. Often, the null hypothesis is a "straw man" we hope to reject.

Unlike the null, the alternative hypothesis is not tested. We reject or do not reject the null, not the alternative. Strictly speaking, we never accept the alternative; instead, we reject the null.

We reject the proposed parameter value if there is strong enough evidence against the claimed value. Evidence comes from the sample data and is based on the idea of implausibility. If, given the proposed parameter value, the sample estimate or one more extreme is highly unlikely to be observed, we will reject the claimed value. If on the other hand, given the proposed parameter value, it is quite possible we could have observed the sample estimate or one more extreme, then we do not reject the claimed value. We say there is not enough evidence to reject the null.

Implausibility is, by definition, vague. How many heads in a sample of 100 coin flips would you have to see before you rejected the notion that the coin was fair? By convention, two standards have been developed: statistically significant and highly statistically significant.

We will apply the two standards to the coin-flip example. You expect to see 50 heads in 100 coin flips, give or take 5 heads. The sampling distribution of the number of heads in 100 coin flips is approximately normal. Thus, if the coin was fair, you would expect the number of heads in 100 coin flips to vary between 45 and 55 heads about 68 percent of the time, whereas about 95 percent of 100 coin flips will yield between 40 and 60 heads. If you saw, say, 80 heads in 100 coin flips, you would certainly be dubious about the fairness of the coin. Such an outcome is certainly possible but extremely unlikely because it is 6 standard units away from the expected outcome under the null hypothesis that the coin is fair. Thus, you would reject the null hypothesis that the coin is fair.

The chances of getting a particular value or one more extreme, given that the null hypothesis is true, is called the probability, or P, value or the observed level of significance. A test of significance computes the P-value and then rejects the null if the P-value is small. P-values less than 5 percent are said to be statistically significant, whereas those below 1 percent, are highly statistically significant.

In the coin-flip example, 80 heads would be a highly statistically significant result because it has a P-value less than 1 percent – in other words, such a result, or one more extreme, on the assumption the null is true, occurs less than 1 percent of the time that 100 coins are flipped.

To compute a P-value, the sampling distribution, or probability histogram, must be known. Although many statistics are normally distributed, there are many other nonnormal sampling distributions. Irrespective of the distribution, the P-value is always interpreted the same way – it is the chance of getting a particular value or one more extreme given that the null hypothesis is true. The smaller the P value, the stronger the evidence against the null.

Warning: Many students incorrectly believe that the P-value represents the chance that the null is true. Because the P-value is computed on the basis that the null hypothesis is true, the P-value is not the chance that the null is true.

The Excel workbook HypothesisTest.xls puts these ideas to work with uniform and normal distributions. As with confidence intervals, the uniform distribution (on the interval 0 to 1) is used here because it is easy to work with, whereas the normal is, in practice, a commonly used sampling distribution for hypothesis testing.

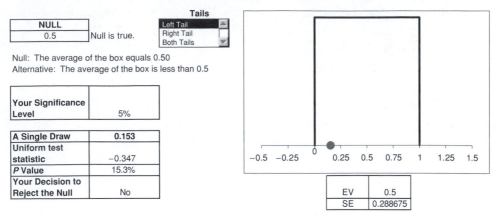

Figure 16.4.1. Playing the hypothesis test game with the uniform distribution. *Source:* [HypothesisTest.xls]Uniform.

As with confidence intervals, hypothesis testing has a set of rules. Here are the rules for the procedure:

1. Take a draw from a distribution – we can play with any distribution, but we will use just two: the Uniform and the Normal.
2. Center the distribution on the value indicated by the null hypothesis (i.e., make the expected value of the distribution the value under the null).
3. Determine the chances of obtaining a draw like the one you got (in step 1) or one more extreme. This is the *P*-value. Step 3 requires that you decide if it is a one- or a two-tailed test.
4. Decide if there is enough evidence (if the *P*-Value is small enough) to reject the null.

Let us put the rules into play with the uniform distribution. Follow along on the *Uniform* sheet of HypothesisTest.xls.

In Figure 16.4.1, the null is set at 0.5 and it is true (because the expected value of the distribution is, in fact, 0.5). We select a one-tailed test: Only values that are much lower than 0.5 will be evidence against the null. We drew a value of 0.153. What are the chances of obtaining this draw or one more extreme? Because we have selected a one-tailed (left-tail) test, more extreme values are only smaller (more negative) values. The chance of getting 0.153 or smaller from a uniform $(0, 1)$ distribution is 15.3 percent. This is weak evidence against the null: after all, if the null is true, getting 0.153 or less is reasonably common.

Hit the F9 key. Notice that, when the drawn value is above 0.5, you get *P*-values over 50 percent. You reject the null and conclude that the draw is "statistically significant" when the draw is below 0.05 (which happens about 1 in 20 clicks of the F9 key). "Highly statistically significant," by convention, is reserved for *P*-values below 1 percent. When testing hypothesis, you

should report the *P*-value and let the reader decide what is enough evidence against the null to reject it.

The one- versus two-tailed test is a tricky concept that is easy to confuse. Consider the following example as a means of grasping that the way the research question is framed drives the type of test.

Suppose a light bulb box says that bulbs will last for 1,000 hours. Unbeknownst to them, two separate people do the same experiment. One works for *Consumer Reports* and the other for GE (who makes the bulbs). They each get 100 light bulbs and turn them on. Then each person records how long each bulb lasted.

The GE person will run a two-sided test. He or she wants to know from a quality control point of view if the bulbs are lasting 1,000 hours. A bulb that lasts too long is costly for GE. There can be evidence against the null from either side – too short or too long. If that person gets a sample average of 1005.23 hours with an SE of the sample average of 1, he or she will reject the null that the bulbs last an average of 1,000 hours.

The *Consumer Reports* person, on the other hand, will run a one-sided, left-tailed test. He or she only cares if GE is falsely advertising the bulbs as lasting too long. If that person gets the same average of 1005.23, the null is not rejected and the case is closed.

The *Normal* sheet applies the same rules for hypothesis testing using a normal distribution. This is called a *z*-test. Go to the *Normal* sheet and hit F9 a few times. Notice that the *P*-value is computed by finding the area under the normal curve.

There is nothing new here. You set the null, which may be false or true. The null is a statement about where the sampling distribution is centered. You then take a draw from the true, unknown sampling distribution. This draw is used to test the null. Given the draw and the sampling distribution under the null, we can compute the chances of getting the realized value (or one more extreme – including whether more extreme evidence can come from either direction). This is called the *P*-value. The *P*-value is used to decide if there is enough evidence to reject the null.

If the null is true, then you will reject the null about as often as the level of significance you choose. You may think that in order to better guard against rejecting a true null you should set the significance level for rejection quite low, say 0.1 percent. But consider the following example: Set the expected value under the null (in cell B7) to 1 (and hit the F9 key). The entire distribution has shifted and it is now, incorrectly, centered at 1. The draws are still coming from a normal distribution with an expected value of 0, so the null is now false.

Notice that the value of the null hypothesis is a claim about the position of the distribution. The null claims that the distribution is such that the expected value is 1, but the draws continue to come from a normal distribution centered

The truth: draws come from a Normal(0,1) distribution.
Maintained assumption: The draws come from a box with tickets that are normally distributed.

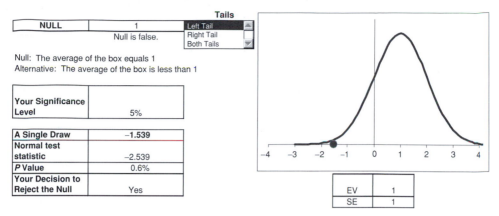

		Tails
NULL	1	Left Tail
	Null is false.	Right Tail
		Both Tails

Null: The average of the box equals 1
Alternative: The average of the box is less than 1

Your Significance Level	5%

A Single Draw	−1.539
Normal test statistic	−2.539
P Value	0.6%
Your Decision to Reject the Null	Yes

EV	1
SE	1

Figure 16.4.2. Testing the null hypothesis of a uniform distribution with EV = 0.75. *Source:* [HypothesisTest.xls]Uniform.

on 0. Hypothesis testing reduces to the following simple idea: assuming the null is true, what are the chances of getting a draw like the one obtained or one more extreme?

Hit the F9 key a few times. Figure 16.4.2 is a picture of one possibility. In the case depicted in Figure 16.4.2, the realized draw, −1.539, yields a *P*-value of 0.6 percent. Let us review what this means. Assuming that the null of a normal distribution centered on 1 is true, we would expect to get a draw like −1.539 or smaller, 0.6 percent of the time. That means that we have strong evidence against the null and, therefore, if we were using the typical criteria of either 5-percent or 1-percent significance levels, we would reject the claim that the center of the distribution is 1. But because we are employing the extremely conservative significance level of 0.1 percent, we would not reject this false null. In order to guard against rejecting a true null, we have rendered the test less capable of detecting false nulls.

Summary

While this section has focused on the logic and mechanics of hypothesis testing, the next section shows that, if the errors are normally distributed, then the sampling distribution of the test statistic, $(b_1 - \text{null})/\text{estSE}$, will be *t*-distributed. This is why many papers in the econometrics literature use *t*-tests (instead of the *z*-test based on the normal curve).

16.5. Z- and T-Tests

Workbooks: ZandTTests.xls; ConfidenceIntervals.xls

Read almost any empirical paper in economics that uses regression and you will probably see the *t*-statistic. The *t*-statistic has almost completely

superseded the z-statistic even for data sets with extremely large sample sizes. This section explains why. In all that follows, we continue to suppose that the classical econometric model applies for a bivariate model. We will work with the Excel workbook ZandTTests.xls.

Section 16.2 demonstrated the central limit theorem at work in the sampling distribution of the OLS slope estimator. As applied to sample slope estimates, we remind you that the CLT says that, no matter the distribution of the error terms (the tickets in the error box), the probability histogram for the OLS slope estimate b_1 approaches a normal distribution as the number of observations rises. The spread of the probability histogram is the exact SE, and its center is the true parameter value β_1. We used Figure 16.2.6 to show that, with a log-normal error distribution, as the number of observations increases the superimposed normal curve more closely matches the approximate sampling distribution of the sample slope generated by the Monte Carlo simulation. This is the central limit theorem in action.

This section is concerned with the sampling distribution of yet another sample-based statistic: a slope hypothesis test statistic. This statistic is formed by subtracting the value claimed by the null hypothesis from the observed sample slope value and then dividing this entire quantity by an SE. The SE can be either exact or estimated depending on whether the SD of error distribution is known or has to be estimated. Once we have the value of the test statistic itself, we compute a P-value. It is here that things get messy. Different distributions will give different P-values. We have to find the appropriate distribution to get the P-value exactly right.

The material is difficult to follow because there are several forks in the road. We add structure to the section by following the flowchart depicted in Figure 16.5.1. There are three crucial questions. The first question is at the center of Figure 16.5.1: How big is the sample? A large sample size makes life much easier. As n increases, the central limit theorem works in our favor to make the sampling distribution of the slope hypothesis test statistic increasingly normal. We use 30 observations as a rough rule of thumb to denote a large sample size, but the bigger the sample, the closer the sampling distribution gets to the normal curve. If we have a large sample, we use the normal curve to compute the P-value and call the test statistic a z-statistic.

For small sample sizes, things get complicated. In this case, Figure 16.5.1 shows that we are faced with a second question: Are the errors normally distributed? If not, we may be in danger. Regression software will proceed as if the errors are normal and the SD has to be estimated. The software will use the t-distribution to compute the P-value. If the sample size is small and the errors are not normally distributed, the reported P-value may not be reliable.

If we know the errors are normally distributed (or can argue that they are reasonably close to normally distributed), then we consider our third and final question: Is the SD of the errors known? This question is a bit unrealistic

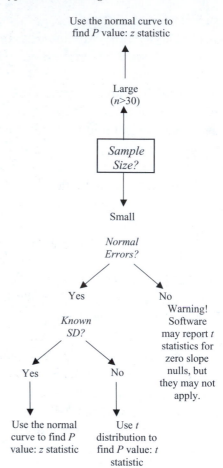

Figure 16.5.1. To z or to t – that is the question.

because it is highly unlikely that the SD of the errors is known. In practically all real-world applications, we do not know the SD of the error box and we estimate this parameter with the RMSE. In this case, the appropriate distribution to use to compute the P-value is the t-distribution and the test statistic is called a t-statistic.

It is time to put these abstract ideas into practice. Open the ZandTTests.xls workbook and proceed to the *Data* sheet. We have implemented the classical econometric model on this sheet. Let us apply the flow chart in Figure 16.5.1. Is the sample size small? Most definitely, for a sample of five observations is quite small. We use such a ridiculously small n to show the difference between normal and t-distributions.

Cell F18 has the test statistic which is based on the true null that $\beta_1 = 5$. We will take evidence against the null from above and below the null so that it is a two-tailed test. Note that the errors are drawn from a normal distribution. Hit F9 to recalculate the sheet and confirm that the test statistic is a random

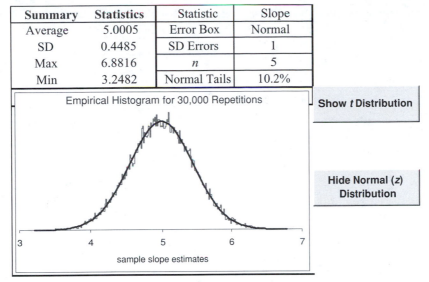

Summary	Statistics	Statistic	Slope
Average	5.0005	Error Box	Normal
SD	0.4485	SD Errors	1
Max	6.8816	n	5
Min	3.2482	Normal Tails	10.2%

Empirical Histogram for 30,000 Repetitions

sample slope estimates

Show *t* Distribution

Hide Normal (*z*)
Distribution

Figure 16.5.2. The OLS slope estimator is normally distributed.
Source: [ZandTTests.xls]MCSim.

variable. The big question concerns the shape of the sampling distribution of the test statistic. Proceed to the *MCSim* sheet to answer this question.

As a first pass, Monte Carlo the sample slope itself. The default number of repetitions is set quite high at 30,000 to obtain close approximations to the true probability histograms. Figure 16.5.2 shows the results. Click the Show Normal (z) Distribution button to superimpose the normal distribution over the Monte Carlo histogram. It matches up quite nicely. Click the Show *t* Distribution button on your Monte Carlo results to see that the *t*-distribution, however, poorly fits the empirical histogram. Normal Tails reports the fraction of sample slopes that fell outside +/− 1.645 SEs of the expected value. This number should be close to 10 percent if the distribution is really normal. Both the visual display and the Normal Tails measure agree; if the errors are normal, the OLS slope estimator is normally distributed.

But what about the test statistic, (sample slope − null)/estimated SE? Is it also normally distributed when the errors are normal? We have reason to be doubtful because the test statistic is a random variable (the sample slope) divided by another random variable (the estimated SE). The estimated SE is a random variable because we are using the RMSE to estimate the SD of the errors. Hence, unlike the case of the sample slope, in which we had one random variable, in the usual case when the SD of the errors is unknown, the test statistic we are dealing with has two sources of variability. We would expect this to affect the sampling distribution. But does it, and, if so, how?

The *MCSim* sheet enables a quick answer to this question. Figure 16.5.3 has our results. Yours should be similar. This time the *t*-distribution fits

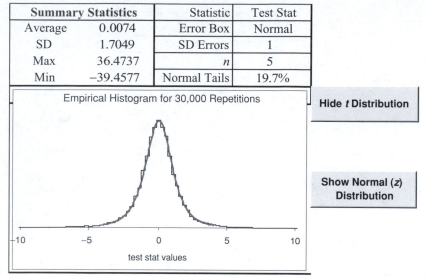

Figure 16.5.3. Test statistic is *t*-distributed.
Source: [ZandTTests.xls]MCSim.

the empirical histogram almost perfectly. The test statistic is definitely
t-distributed and not normally distributed.

It is instructive to compare Figures 16.5.2 and 16.5.3. The Error Boxes, SD
Errors, and *n* are the same, but the statistic being analyzed is different. In Figure 16.5.2, it is simply the sample slope and it is clearly normally distributed.
Figure 16.5.3 shows the sampling distribution of the test statistic (not the
sample slope) and this time it is the *t*-distribution that fits well.

The Normal Tails measure confirms that the distribution of the test statistic
is not normal. Instead of a 10-percent chance of getting a value +/− 1.645
or more SEs away from the expected value as the normal curve would predict, almost 20 percent of the samples are in this interval. With $n = 5$, the
t-distribution has fatter tails and is less spiked than the normal. If we used
the normal curve to compute a *P*-value, we would get it wrong.

Perhaps a little intellectual history will help explain what is going on. In
1908, an author who called himself "Student" published the first paper that
obtained an exact small-sample result. Student was actually William Sealy
Gosset.

The reason for the pseudonym was a policy by Gosset's employer, the brewery Arthur
Guinness Sons and Co., against work done for the firm being made public. Allowing
Gosset to publish under a pseudonym was a concession that resulted in the birth of
the statistician "Student," the creator of Student's t-test.   Lehmann (1999, p. 418)

Gossett discovered that, if the classical econometric model applied, if
the errors were normally distributed, and if the SD of the errors was

estimated using the RMSE, then the exact probability histogram of the test statistic, (sample slope − null)/estimated SE, followed the *t*-distribution. Gosset pointed out that the normal curve does a poor job of approximating the distribution of this test statistic when *n* is small.

The problem lies in the fact that the estimated SE is a random variable because the SD of the box is being estimated by the RMSE and the RMSE is a random variable. Gosset showed that adding more structure to the problem by specifying the distribution of the errors enabled derivation of the exact sampling distribution of the test statistic.

He also made a more contentious claim: the *t*-distribution applies even if the errors are only roughly normal. "This [normality] assumption is accordingly made in the present paper, so that its conclusions are not strictly applicable to populations known not to be normally distributed; yet it appears probable that the deviation from normality must be very extreme to lead to serious error." (Student, 1908, p. 1). In other words, although the *t*-distribution is exactly correct only if the errors are normally distributed, it will continue to do a good job of approximating the distribution of the test statistic, (sample slope − null)/estimated SE, for many nonnormal error distributions.

The *t*-distribution looks very much like the standard normal distribution, but its shape depends on the number of "degrees of freedom." The number of degrees of freedom equals the number of observations minus the number of parameters being estimated. In the bivariate case, two parameters are being estimated, and so the number of degrees of freedom is $n − 2$. When *n* is small, the *t*-distribution deviates substantially from the standard normal curve. Figure 16.5.4 presents three comparisons of normal and *t*-distributions. On the top, with only 3 degrees of freedom, the *t*-distribution deviates considerably from the normal. The deviation is quite small for DF = 10 and is almost nonexistent in the bottom graph, where DF = 30.

You can compare the standard normal and *t*-distributions for any value of the degrees of freedom parameter in the *tDist* sheet. Notice how the standard normal stays fixed because it does not depend on the degrees-of-freedom parameter. Notice also how the *t*-distribution gets closer and closer to the normal as the number of degrees of freedom rises.

Figure 16.5.4 shows that using the *t*-distribution only matters when *n* is small. In economics, this is rarely the case. Regression software, however, will almost always report *t*-statistics for the null hypothesis that the true parameter value is 0 and a *P*-value based on the *t* distribution. For practical purposes, when you read about a *t*-statistic in an article, if the sample size is greater than 30, you may safely substitute in your mind the normal curve and the *z*-statistic. That is, the *P*-value might as well be based on a normal curve.

To cement this point, return to the *Data* sheet and set the sample size to 20 observations (using the Normal error distribution). This is a very small

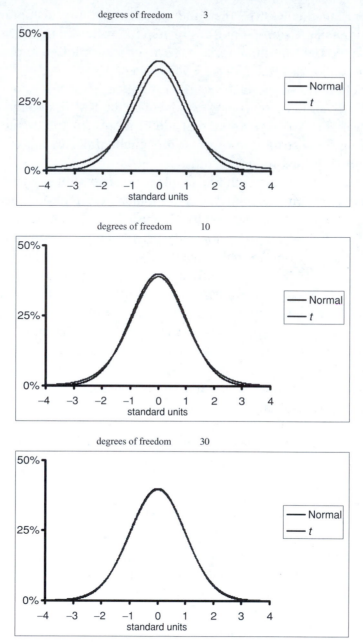

Figure 16.5.4. Normal and *t*-distributions with varying df.
Source: [ZandTTests.xls]tDist.

sample size for work in economics. Proceed to the *MCSim* sheet and run a Monte Carlo simulation of the test statistic. Our results are presented in Figure 16.5.5. We superimposed the normal curve to show that it does a reasonably good job, but it is not perfect because it is too high in the center. We know that the sampling distribution in Figure 16.5.5 is actually *t*-distributed

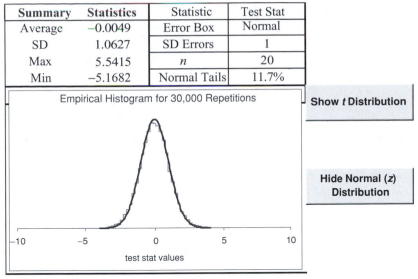

Summary	Statistics	Statistic	Test Stat
Average	−0.0049	Error Box	Normal
SD	1.0627	SD Errors	1
Max	5.5415	n	20
Min	−5.1682	Normal Tails	11.7%

Show *t* Distribution

Hide Normal (*z*) Distribution

Figure 16.5.5. *t*-distribution with $n = 20$.
Source: [ZandTTests.xls]tDist.

with 18 degrees of freedom. The Normal Tails measure, 11.7 percent, shows we are a little off from the expected 10 percent. As n increases, the test statistic will always be exactly *t*-distributed, but the normal curve will be an increasingly good approximation.

The t-Distribution and Confidence Intervals

We conclude this section by tying up a loose end. Section 16.3 showed that a confidence interval for the sample slope built with the estimated SE and using the normal curve performed poorly with a sample size of 5 observations. Although the sample slope is normally distributed (assuming the errors are normally distributed), the fact that we have to use the RMSE to estimate the SD of the errors causes the confidence interval to be too short and, therefore, fewer than 95 percent of the confidence intervals constructed using 1.96 times the estimated SE will cover the parameter.

Now that we understand the *t*-distribution, we can revisit this problem and show how the *t*-distribution can be used to construct a confidence interval that performs as advertised. Open the ConfidenceInterval.xls workbook and proceed to the *CIMCSim* sheet. Click on the CI with the *t* Distribution button (to the right of the histogram). Two new sheets appear in the workbook, *tCI* and *CItM-CSim*. The *tCI* sheet is similar to the *UniformCI* and *NormalCI* sheets. You set the confidence level and an interval of appropriate width, based on the *t*-distribution, is constructed. You can hit F9 to see the interval bounce around

Confidence Interval			
%Covered	94.93%	Error Box	Normal
		SD	1.00
SE Used	Variable		
		n	5

Figure 16.5.6. Confidence intervals with the *t*-distribution. *Source:* [ConfidenceIntervals.xls]CItMCSim.

and run a Monte Carlo simulation to confirm that the interval covers with the given confidence level.

With 3 degrees of freedom, compare the length of the 95-percent confidence interval in the *tCI* sheet to the *Normal* sheet. The confidence interval in the *tCI* sheet is longer, using a give or take number of 3.182 SEs, than the CI in the *NormalCI* sheet, which adds and subtracts 1.96 SEs around the drawn value to get a 95-percent confidence interval. This is due to the fact that the *t*-distribution has fatter tails than the normal distribution.

Set $n = 5$ in the *Data* sheet with Normal errors, then go to the *CItM-CSim* sheet and run a Monte Carlo simulation of the confidence interval. Figure 16.5.6 shows the results. Unlike the *CIMCSim* sheet, which computed the interval length based on the normal curve and, therefore, performed poorly, the *CItMCSim* sheet computes intervals based on the *t*-distribution and, therefore, gets it right: About 95 percent of the intervals cover the true parameter value.

Just as we saw with hypothesis testing, if the errors are normally distributed and their spread must be estimated (by the RMSE), then small samples require that the *t*-distribution be used to construct confidence intervals correctly. As the sample size increases, the *t*-distribution gets closer and closer to the normal curve. Thus, for large samples, it hardly matters if the confidence interval is constructed with the normal or *t*-distribution. Software and most empirical papers will report confidence intervals based on the *t*-distribution.

Summary

This section has explained the reason behind the commonplace use of the *t*-distribution. Gosset discovered that the test statistic, (slope − null)/estimatedSE, is not normally distributed. The fact that the estimated SE is a random variable affects the sampling distribution of the test statistic. Regression software and articles in journals use the *t*-distribution to compute a *P*-value because, if the errors are normally distributed, then the *t*-distribution is the correct distribution. If the sample size is small, using the *t*-distribution instead of the normal is the right thing to do. If the sample size is large, the *t*-distribution remains the exactly correct distribution, but it becomes almost identical to the normal curve.

16.6. A Practical Example

Workbook: CigDataInference.xls

To make the ideas in this chapter clearer, we relate the abstract points made in the previous sections to the example introduced in Chapter 1 studying the demand for cigarettes. We have cross-sectional data from 1960 at the state level on per capita cigarette sales, average price of cigarettes, and per capita income. We focus on hypothesis testing and show how to display regression results.

In Chapter 1, two models were developed to describe the data, but we had not yet introduced the classical econometric model. We restate the models, this time adding an error term and assuming that the classical econometric model applies. The two models are as follows:

$$\text{Model 1: } Quantity\ Demanded_i = \beta_0 + \beta_1 \cdot Price_i + \varepsilon_i, \quad i = 1, \dots, 47$$

$$\text{Model 2: } Quantity\ Demanded_i = \beta_0 + \beta_1 \cdot Price_i + \beta_2\ Income_i + v_i,$$
$$i = 1, \dots, 47,$$

where Quantity Demanded is measured by per capita sales of cigarettes in a given state in a given year, Price is the average price per pack of cigarettes in that state, Income is per capita income in that state, i indexes the 47 states (including the District of Columbia) with nonmissing data, and the error terms ε_i and v_i, respectively, reflect the influence of omitted variables (e.g., tastes and preferences formed by religion and education), measurement error, and the inherent randomness in the world. Let us suppose that the classical econometric model applies: The errors are all drawn from the same error box, they are independent of one another, and they are uncorrelated with Price (in Model 1) and Price and Income (in Model 2). (Note that the error terms of Model 1 come from different boxes and will have a different SD than those of Model 2.) We also assume that the independent variables are fixed in repeated sampling. The unit of observation is, obviously, states. In Chapter 1 we demonstrated that in the bivariate analysis of Model 1 the relationship between Quantity Demanded and Price is confounded by the fact that omitted variables (such as Income) are correlated with price. A demand curve cannot be estimated by simply fitting a line to a cloud of price and quantity points. We therefore focus our attention on Model 2. Later in this section a third model for the data generation process using a logarithmic functional form is introduced.

It is easy to criticize the application of the CEM in this case. When we introduced this example in the first chapter, we pointed out several complicating factors. There are problems with measuring the variables, aggregation, and simultaneous equations bias (discussed in Chapter 24). Good econometric practice recognizes and explicitly states the difficulties in the empirical application of a theoretical model.

The fact that perfection cannot be attained does not mean we should give up and announce that all applied work is flawed. Instead, we do our best and realize that there are quality differences in empirical analysis. Model 2 is undoubtedly superior to Model 1. Are there even better models? Yes. Chapters 18, 19, 20, and 24 present methods that can be applied when various violations of the CEM are present. For now, we will use Model 2 as an example of how to create a confidence interval and conduct tests of significance. The remainder of this section briefly indicates the hypotheses suggested by economic theory for Model 2. We actually test the hypotheses and discuss how to present the results. Finally, we compare the results obtained to those for a third model, using a different functional form.

There are two crucial parts to the statement of a hypothesis:

1. A definite statement about a parameter or parameters of the model dictated by the economic theory, called the *null hypothesis*. (The parameter is the true, exact, unknown value.) Usually, though not always, this is a statement the theory asserts is not true.

The two null hypotheses relevant to Model 2, expressed in English, are that, with income held constant, price has no effect on the quantity demanded of cigarettes, and, with price held constant, income has no effect on the quantity demanded of cigarettes. The two null hypotheses, expressed in terms of parameters of the model, are

$$\text{Null Hypothesis on Price: } \beta_1 = 0$$
$$\text{Null Hypothesis on Income: } \beta_2 = 0.$$

2. An alternative statement about a parameter of the model, which contradicts the null. This is called the *alternative hypothesis*. This alternative statement can take two forms: one- and two-tailed tests, respectively.

Economists generally think that, as price rises, quantity demanded falls. On the other hand, there is no strong presumption about whether cigarettes are normal goods or inferior goods (i.e., about the effect of income on quantity demanded). This means that the alternative hypothesis in English with regard to price is that, with income held constant, quantity demanded falls as price rises; the alternative hypothesis in English with regard to income is that, with price held constant, quantity demanded changes as income rises. In terms of Model 2, the two alternative hypotheses, expressed in compact mathematical notation, are

$$\text{Alternative Hypothesis on Price: } \beta_1 < 0$$
$$\text{Alternative Hypothesis on Income: } \beta_2 \neq 0.$$

The first is a one-tailed test; the second a two-tailed test.

Model (2): Multiple Regression Analysis				
	Price	Per Capita Income	Intercept	
Estimate	−5.808	0.0351	198.9	Estimate
Estimated SE	1.756	0.0067	52.444	Estimated SE
R^2	0.561	18.769	#N/A	RMSE
F-stat	28.16	44	#N/A	df
Reg SS	19,837	15,500	#N/A	SSR

Figure 16.6.1. LINEST presentation of OLS results for Model 2. *Source:* [CigDataInference.xls]1960Analysis.

The essential prerequisite for being able to conduct a test of significance on a particular claim about the population is that the stipulated box model is a good analogy to the data generating process for the data at hand. If so, the estimated slope in a regression can be related to the probability histogram of all the possible estimates that could have been obtained. That probability histogram for the sample estimates is centered on the true value of the population parameter. The typical estimate will be within one SE of the true population parameter. The area under the probability histogram above a given interval gives the probability that the sample estimate will fall in that interval. We can compute such areas by stating the interval endpoints in terms of standard units and using the normal approximation.

We now show how to test the hypotheses above using Model 2 and the 1960 data set. Open the CigDataInference.xls workbook and go to the *1960Analysis* sheet. Excel's LINEST function displays the results given in Figure 16.6.1. These results are conventionally reported in one of two ways: either as an equation with SEs written below coefficient estimates,

$$\text{PredictedQpercapita} = 199 - 5.81 \text{ Price} + 0.035 \text{ Income},$$
$$(52.4) \quad (1.76) \quad \quad (0.0067)$$

or, more commonly (especially with many independent variables), in a table, which might look like Figure 16.6.2.

Before we demonstrate the hypothesis testing procedure, we show you how to construct a confidence interval. The coefficient on Price, −5.8, tells us that a one-cent increase in the price of a pack of a cigarettes leads to a decrease of 5.8 packs per person per year. Of course, we know that the estimated coefficient is a random variable with an estimated SE of 1.8 (rounding up from 1.756 reported in Figures 16.6.1 and 16.6.2). We can indicate the variability in our estimate by reporting the estimate as "−5.8 +/− 1.8" or by constructing a confidence interval.

We will follow convention and create a 95-percent confidence interval. We have to add and subtract a value from the coefficient estimate to create the interval. The value depends on the distribution of the estimated coefficient. If we use the normal curve, then we multiply the estimated SE by 1.96. (Since the normal curve is an approximation anyway, we often multiply by 2, but

Typical Display of Results	
Dependent Variable: Quantity per capita	
Independent Variable	Estimate
Intercept	198.939
	(52.444)
Price	−5.808
	(1.756)
Per Capita Income	0.0351
	(0.007)
R^2	0.56
n	47
Note: SEs in parentheses.	

Figure 16.6.2. Tabular presentation of OLS results for Model 2.
Source: [CigDataInference.xls]1960Analysis.

we are going to compare the normal to the t-distribution in a moment, so we will use the exact value needed to create a 95-percent confidence interval with the normal curve.) The resulting 95-percent confidence interval, based on the normal curve, is from −9.25 to −2.37. You can examine the formulas for these bounds in cells G39 and H39.

Since we are using the estimated SE, we know (from Section 16.3) that the confidence interval based on the normal curve is incorrect. If we assume that the errors are normally distributed, then the correct distribution to use for the confidence interval computation is the t-distribution. We can find the value to add and subtract from the estimated coefficient with Excel's TINV function. Cell F48 uses this function to find the critical value of 2.015. In cells G44 and H44, we use this value to compute the 95-percent confidence interval based on the t-distribution, −9.35 to −2.27.

The 95-percent confidence intervals from the normal and t-distributions are so close because the sample size, 47, is large enough that the two distributions are almost identical. Reporting a coefficient estimate along with a give or take number (the estimated SE) or providing a confidence interval are two good ways to convey the variability in the coefficient estimate.

We can also use the estimates to conduct the two hypothesis tests outlined above. The test statistic for the null hypothesis – that the price does not affect per capita quantity demanded, that is, $\beta_1 = 0$ – is computed as follows:

$$\text{test statistic} = \frac{-5.808 - 0}{1.756}$$
$$= -3.31.$$

Using the normal approximation for the sampling distribution of b_1 under the null, we find that the P-value for a one-tailed test is about 0.05 percent. If we make the assumption that the errors are normally distributed, that gives us license to use the *t*-distribution, and the *P*-value would be computed as about 0.09 percent.[4] In either case, at standard levels of significance, we decisively reject the null hypothesis and conclude that, as the price of cigarettes rises, quantity demanded falls.

The test statistic for the null hypothesis that the per capita income does not affect per capita quantity demanded (i.e., $\beta_2 = 0$) is computed as follows:

$$\text{test statistic} = \frac{0.0351 - 0}{0.0067}$$
$$= 5.24.$$

The *P*-value for this two-tailed hypothesis test is extremely small – less than 0.000 percent – no matter whether one uses the normal approximation or the *t*-distribution.

We thus have strong evidence that, in 1960 at least, quantity demanded falls as price increases and rises as income increases. This knowledge that there is an effect and the direction it takes is nice, but economists generally want to know how big the effect is. In other words, economists ought to be less interested in claiming statistical significance and more concerned with measuring the magnitude, and practical importance, of the effect.

The slope estimates are our best estimates of the magnitude of the effects of price and income on quantity demanded. It is good practice to couch these estimates in the form of confidence intervals, which tell us something about how much variability there is in each estimate. An approximate 95-percent confidence interval for the price slope (b_1) is (-9.25, -2.37); for the income slope (b_2) the approximate 95-percent confidence interval is (0.22, 0.48). Confidence intervals based on the *t*-distribution are slightly wider. See the *1960Analysis* sheet for details on these computations.

Another useful way to quantify the impact of price and income is to compute the price and income elasticities of demand. These work out to -1.26 and 0.613, respectively. Thus a 1-percent increase in price, with income held constant, is associated with a 1.26-percent decrease in quantity demanded, whereas a 1-percent increase in per capita income, with price held constant, is associated with a 0.613-percent increase in quantity demanded. Of course we really ought to put give-or-take numbers on these elasticities. Computing the estimated SE of an elasticity is an advanced topic. See the HowToUseDeltaMethod.xls workbook in the Basic Tools\How To folder for more information.

---

[4] Details on these calculations are available in the *1960Analysis* sheet. LINEST does not output *P*-values, but the sheet shows how the Excel function TDIST can be used. Excel's Data Analysis: Regression tool reports the *P*-value for a two-tailed test. The P Value Calculator add-in packaged with this book computes *P*-values for a variety of distributions and is more flexible because the user can select one- or two-tailed tests.

Model (3): Logarithmic Functional Form			
	ln Price	ln Per Capita Income	Intercept	
Estimate	−1.24	0.563	4.5	Estimate
Estimated SE	0.382	0.113	1.732	Estimated SE
R^2	0.539	0.156	#N/A	RMSE
F-stat	25.75	44	#N/A	df
Reg SS	1.25	1.07	#N/A	SSR

Figure 16.6.3. LINEST presentation of OLS results for Model 3. *Source:* [CigDataInference.xls]1960Analysis.

An Alternative Functional Form

Economic theory does not dictate that demand curves are straight lines (i.e., linear functions of price and income). Therefore, it is appropriate to investigate other nonlinear functional forms. A popular alternative to the linear functional forms of Models 1 and 2 is the double-log functional form we incorporate in Model 3:

Model 3: $\ln Quantity\ Demanded_i = \beta_0 + \beta_1 \cdot \ln Price_i + \beta_2 \ln Income_i + \eta_i,$
$$i = 1, \ldots, 47,$$

where ln indicates we are taking natural logs of each of the variables, and we rename the error term η to stress that this is a different model from the first two. As before, we will suppose that the requirements of the classical econometric model are met. Chapter 6 discusses nonlinear functional forms; refer back to this chapter to refresh your memory. In particular, Section 6.5 points out that the coefficients in a double-log model directly measure (in this case) the constant price and income elasticities of demand.

The *1960 Analysis* sheet presents the LINEST results for Model 3 reported here in Figure 16.6.3.

We have now estimated three different models of the demand for cigarettes. A convenient, space-saving way to present the results is to put them all into one table, as shown in Figure 16.6.4.

The table in Figure 16.6.4 facilitates comparisons between the three models. For example, the table makes clear that including income in the regression substantially improves the fit of the linear functional form. Econometricians are in the habit of using a rule of thumb: If the absolute value of a coefficient is more than twice its SE, then the difference between 0 and the coefficient estimate is statistically significant. A glance at the table will verify that all the null hypotheses that each of the parameters is equal to zero will be rejected. The table also shows that there is pretty good agreement between the

Summary of Results for the Three Models			
Independent Variable	Q_{pc}	Q_{pc}	ln Q_{pc}
Price	−8.856 (2.094)	−5.808 (1.756)	
Income		0.351 (.0067)	
ln Price			−1.24 (0.382)
ln Income			0.563 (0.113)
Price Elasticity	−1.93	−1.26	
Income Elasticity		0.613	
R^2	0.284	0.561	0.539
n	47	47	47
Standard errors are in parentheses. Elasticities in Models 1 and 2 are evaluated at sample means			

Figure 16.6.4. Tabular presentation of OLS results for Models 1, 2, and 3.
Source: [CigDataInference.xls]1960Analysis.

linear and double-log models (2 and 3) on the value of the price and income elasticities. The notes to the table help the reader to interpret it; you will see some tables in which it is the *t*-statistics, not the SEs, which are placed beneath the coefficient estimates. We have followed conventional practice in choosing not to report the intercept estimates for the models because these results are not especially interesting.

Summary

This section has illustrated a practical application of statistical inference and the manner in which economists typically report their results. Our example is the one we used in the first chapter of this book; you now are able to appreciate the inferential side of the story.

We used this example to demonstrate how to perform a test of significance and display regression results. But you should be aware that a hypothesis test is often much less interesting than the actual estimate itself and its practical importance. Remember that the hypothesis test merely serves to rule out the argument that chance alone could have caused the observed result. Statistical significance can never be substituted for practical importance. Economists use elasticity as a way to measure practical importance, but there are other approaches as dictated by the context of the problem.

16.7. Conclusion

This chapter has presented the logic and implementation of confidence intervals and hypothesis testing. Although confusing to students and often incorrectly used by researchers, the fundamentals should be clear: Every sample-based statistic has its own sampling distribution, and if we can determine its SE we can create a confidence interval or test a claim about the true value of the parameter.

We prefer a simple approach to reporting the variability of an estimate and suggest that you routinely provide the estimated SE along with the statistic in your own work. When you are reading tables or regression output, remember to take the observed statistic and wrap ±1 SE around it to get a sense of the variability in the statistic.

If you are working with confidence intervals, do not forget that the true parameter value is fixed and it is the interval itself that is bouncing. Thus, "95 percent of the intervals constructed this way would cover" is right, whereas "95 percent of the time the parameter falls in the interval" is wrong.

With regard to hypothesis testing, you should understand the special situations in which they are appropriate. If you do a test of significance, do not adopt the "significant" and "highly significant" convention. Report the observed P-value and let the reader decide what that means. Of course, always keep in mind that statistical significance has nothing to do with practical or economic importance.

Finally, there is little need to worry about the details and fine points of the t-distribution. As n rises, the t and normal distributions become increasingly indistinguishable. Thus, although software and empirical papers will use the t-distribution, when n is large, the t-distribution can safely be interpreted as the normal curve.

16.8. Exercises

Workbook: SemiLogEarningsFn.xls

In Chapter 6, we used the data in the *EducWageData* sheet in the SemiLogEarningsFn.xls workbook to regress education on wages. At that time, we did not have a model of the data generation process. Therefore, regression analysis was used strictly as a description of the data.

These exercise questions return to that data set, but this time we will use the estimated standard errors to create confidence intervals and perform tests of significance. For the purposes of these questions, we simply assert that the data generation process follows the classical econometric model. We consider two models:

$$\text{Linear Model}: Wage_i = \beta_0 + \beta_1\, Education_i + \varepsilon_i$$
$$\text{Semilog Model}: \ln Wage_i = \beta_0 + \beta_1\, Education_i + \varepsilon_i$$

1. Open SemiLogEarningsFn.xls (in the Chapter 6 folder on the CD-ROM) and proceed to the *EducWageData* sheet. Use the Regression option in Excel's Data Analysis add-in to run regressions on the two models. Use the Confidence Level option to create a 90-percent confidence interval for the Education variable. Report your results in a nicely formatted table with SEs in parentheses under the parameter estimates.
2. In Chapter 6, we interpreted the coefficients on Education in the two models. For the Linear Model, one more year of education is associated with an additional $1.65 per hour in the wage. The interpretation of the Semi-Log Model is different: each additional year of education is associated with a wage increase of approximately 10 percent. But now we are treating the data as a sample and the coefficients are viewed as random variables. For each model, interpret the coefficient on Education, including information that expresses the variability in the estimate.
3. In your work for Question 1, the Data Analysis: Regression output generated 95-percent and 90-percent confidence intervals. Explain why the 90-percent intervals are smaller.
4. For the Linear Model, conduct a two-tailed test of the claim that education has no effect on wage. Your answer should include clearly stated null and alternative hypotheses, a test statistic, a *P*-value, and a decision on rejecting or not rejecting the null.
5. Trying to convince her son to go to college, mom (who happens to be an econometrician) argues that the rate of return to education is incredibly statistically significant, and this proves that college is worth it. What do you think of this logic?
6. For the Semilog Model, we want to conduct a two-tailed test of the claim that the true rate of return for one more year of education (i.e., β_1) is 8 percent. Why is it not possible to use the reported *P*-value from Excel's Data Analysis: Regression output to answer this question?
7. Use the P Value Calculator add-in (see Section 10.5 for instructions) to conduct a two-tailed test of the claim that the true rate of return for one more year of education (i.e., β_1) is 8 percent. Show all of your work. What do you conclude?

References

As explained in the chapter, W. S. Gosset's original paper on the *t*-distribution was published under a fake name: Student (1908), "The Probable Error of a Mean," *Biometrika* **6**(1): 1–25. The paper is remarkable in several respects, including Gosset's description of a Monte Carlo simulation:

Before I had succeeded in solving my problem analytically, I had endeavoured to do so empirically. The material used was a correlation table containing the height and left middle finger measurements of 3000 criminals, from a paper by W. R. Macdonnell (*Biometrika*, Vol. I. p. 219). The measurements were written out on 3000 pieces of cardboard, which were then very thoroughly shuffled and drawn at random. As each card was drawn its numbers were written down in a book which thus contains the measurements of 3000 criminals in a random order. Finally, each consecutive set of 4 was taken as a sample – 750 in all – and the mean, standard deviation, and correlation of each sample determined. The difference between the mean of each sample and the mean of the population was then divided by the standard deviation of the sample, giving us the z of Section III. (p. 3)

For more on the history of Gosset and the t-distribution, see Eric L. Lehmann (1999), "'Student' and Small-Sample Theory," *Statistical Science* **14**(4): 418–426.

On the present state of hypothesis testing in econometrics, we recommend Deirdre N. McCloskey and Stephen T. Ziliak (1996), "The Standard Error of Regressions," *Journal of Economic Literature* **34**(1): 97–114. They present a reasonable list of best-practice techniques and test the extent to which empirical economics conforms. We agree with their critique of hypothesis testing and emphasis on interpreting the practical importance of an estimate. We also strongly support their views on simulation:

Most scientists (and historians) use simulation, which in explicit, quantitative form is becoming cheaper in economics, too. It will probably become the main empirical technique, following other observational sciences. Econometrics will survive, but it will come at last to emphasize economic rather than statistical significance. We should of course worry some about the precision of the estimates, but as Leamer has pointed out the imprecision usually comes from sources other than too small a sample. (p. 114)

17

Joint Hypothesis Testing

"Well", [Pearson] said "I do not know how old I was, but I was sitting in a high chair and I was sucking my thumb. Someone told me to stop sucking it and said that unless I did so the thumb would wither away. I put my two thumbs together and looked at them for a long time. 'They look alike to me,' I said to myself. 'I can't see that the thumb I suck is any smaller than the other. I wonder if she could be lying to me.'"

Walker (1958, p. 13)

17.1. Introduction

Chapter 16 shows how to test a hypothesis about a single slope parameter in a regression equation. This chapter explains how to test hypotheses about more than one of the parameters in a multiple regression model. Simultaneous multiple parameter hypothesis testing generally requires constructing a test statistic that measures the difference in fit between two versions of the same model.

An Example of a Test Involving More than One Parameter

One of the central tasks in economics is explaining savings behavior. National savings rates vary considerably across countries, and the United States has been at the low end in recent decades. Most studies of savings behavior by economists look at strictly economic determinants of savings. Differences in national savings rates, however, seem to reflect more than just differences in the economic environment. In a study of individual savings behavior, Carroll et al. (1999) examined the hypothesis that cultural factors play a role. Specifically, they asked the question, Does national origin help to explain differences in savings rate across a group of immigrants to the United States? Using 1980 and 1990 U.S. Census data with data on immigrants from 16 countries and on native-born Americans, Carroll et al. estimated

453

a model similar to the following:[1]

$$Savings\ Rate_h = \beta_0 + \beta_1 \cdot Age_h + \beta_2 \cdot Education_h + \beta_3 \cdot Argentina_h$$
$$+\beta_4 \cdot China_h + \cdots + \varepsilon_h.$$

For reasons that will become obvious, we call this the *unrestricted model*. The dependent variable is the household savings rate. Age and education measure, respectively, the age and education of the household head (both in years). The error term reflects omitted variables that affect savings rates as well as the influence of luck. The subscript h indexes households. A series of 16 dummy variables indicate the national origin of the immigrants; for example, $China_h = 1$ if both husband and wife in household h were Chinese immigrants.[2] Suppose that the value for the coefficient multiplying China is 0.12. This would indicate that, with other factors controlled, immigrants of Chinese origin have a savings rate 12 percentage points higher than the base case (which in this regression consists of people who were born in the United States).

If there are no cultural effects on savings, then all the coefficients multiplying the dummy variables for national origin ought to be equal to each other. In other words, if culture does not matter, national origin ought not to affect savings rates ceteris paribus. This is a null hypothesis involving 16 parameters and 16 equal signs:

$$\text{Null hypothesis:}\ \beta_3 = \beta_4 = \cdots = \beta_{18} = 0.$$

The alternative hypothesis simply negates the null hypothesis, meaning that immigrants from at least one country have different savings rates than immigrants from other countries:

$$\text{Alternative hypothesis: Not}\ \beta_3 = \beta_4 = \cdots = \beta_{18} = 0.$$

Now, if the null hypothesis is true, then an alternative, simpler model describes the data generation process:

$$Savings\ Rate_h = \beta_0 + \beta_1 \cdot Age_h + \beta_2 \cdot Education_h + \varepsilon_h.$$

Relative to the original model, the one above is a *restricted model*. We can test the null hypothesis with a new test statistic, the *F*-statistic, which essentially measures the difference between the fit of the original and restricted models above. The test is known as an *F*-test. The *F*-statistic will not have a normal distribution. Under the often-made assumption that the error terms

---

[1] Their actual model is, not surprisingly, substantially more complicated.

[2] There were 17 countries of origin in the study, including 900 households selected at random from the United States. Only married couples from the same country of origin were included in the sample. Other restrictions were that the household head must have been older than 35 and younger than 50 in 1980.

are normally distributed, when the null is true, the test statistic follows an *F*-distribution, which accounts for the name of the statistic. We will need to learn about the *F*- and the related chi-square distributions in order to calculate the *P*-value for the *F*-test.

F-Test Basics

The *F*-distribution is named after Ronald A. Fisher, a leading statistician of the first half of the twentieth century. This chapter demonstrates that the *F*-distribution is a ratio of two chi-square random variables and that, as the number of observations increases, the *F*-distribution comes to resemble the chi-square distribution. Karl Pearson popularized the chi-square distribution beginning in 1900.

The Whole Model *F*-Test (discussed in Section 17.2) is commonly used as a test of the overall significance of the included independent variables in a regression model. In fact, it is so often used that Excel's LINEST function and most other statistical software report this statistic. We will show that there are many other *F*-tests that facilitate tests of a variety of competing models.

The idea that there are competing models opens the door to a difficult question: How do we decide which model is the right one? One way to answer this question is with an *F*-test. At first glance, one might consider measures of fit such as R^2 or the sum of squared residuals (SSR) as a guide. But these statistics have a serious weakness – as you include additional independent variables, the R^2 and SSR are guaranteed (practically speaking) to improve. Thus, naive reliance on these measures of fit leads to kitchen sink regression – that is, we throw in as many variables as we can find (the proverbial kitchen sink) in an effort to optimize the fit.

The problem with kitchen sink regression is that, for a particular sample, it will yield a higher R^2 or lower SSR than a regression with fewer X variables, but the true model may be the one with the smaller number of X variables. This will be shown via a concrete example in Section 17.5.

The *F*-test provides a way to discriminate between alternative models. It recognizes that there will be differences in measures of fit when one model is compared with another, but it requires that the loss of fit be substantial enough to reject the reduced model.

Organization

In general, the *F*-test can be used to test any restriction on the parameters in the equation. The idea of a restricted regression is fundamental to the logic of the *F*-test, and thus it is discussed in detail in the next section. Because the *F*-distribution is actually the ratio of two chi-square (χ^2) distributed random variables (divided by their respective degrees of freedom), Section 17.3 explains the chi-square distribution and points out that, when the errors are normally distributed, the sum of squared residuals is a random variable with a chi-square distribution. Section 17.4 demonstrates that the ratio of two chi-square distributed random variables is an F-distributed random variable. The remaining sections of this chapter put the F-statistic into practice. Section 17.5 does so in the context of Galileo's model of acceleration, whereas Section 17.6 considers an example involving food stamps. We use the food stamp example to show that, when the restriction involves a single equals sign, one can rewrite the original model to make it possible to employ a t-test instead of an F-test. The t- and F-tests yield equivalent results in such cases. We apply the F-test to a real-world example in Section 17.7. Finally, Section 17.8 discusses multicollinearity and the distinction between confidence intervals for a single parameter and confidence regions for multiple parameters.

17.2. Restricted Regression

Workbook: NoInterceptBug.xls

The first step in understanding the F-test is appreciating the idea of a restricted regression. After describing exactly what is being restricted, we offer several types of restrictions as examples. The word *restricted* in this context is synonymous with constrained or limited. What is being restricted is the values of the coefficients that can be used to minimize the SSR (in order to fit the least squares line). In an unrestricted regression, we are free to choose any values of the coefficients (intercept and slope terms) from negative to positive infinity. Anything that does not allow the coefficients to be freely chosen can be considered a type of restriction.

Three Examples

There are many kinds of restrictions that can be imposed on a linear regression equation. Let us examine three examples. Consider the following regression model:

$$Y_i = \beta_0 + \beta_1 X_{1i} + \beta_2 X_{2i} + \varepsilon_i.$$

If apply the restriction or constraint that $\beta_2 = 0$, then we can write the restricted regression version as

$$Y_i = \beta_0 + \beta_1 X_{1i} + \varepsilon_i.$$

Not surprisingly, when comparing these two regressions, the unrestricted regression is often called the *long regression*, and the restricted specification is dubbed the *short regression*. Of course, the unrestricted regression in this comparison becomes a restricted or short regression if we include another X variable in the model. Thus, the labels, short and long, describing regression are used to compare two regression equations and not as absolute terms.

Another kind of restriction often applied is called regression through the origin. This restriction forces the intercept to be zero:

$$Y_i = \beta_1 X_{1i} + \beta_2 X_{2i} + \varepsilon_i.$$

Unfortunately, in versions prior to Excel 2003, Excel suffers from a bug that incorrectly computes the regression SSR, R^2, and F-statistic (for the whole model F-test that is explained below in this section) when there is no intercept. The Excel workbook NoInterceptBug.xls offers an example of the bug when regression without a constant term is done with Trendline, LINEST, and Data Analysis: Regression. Although the problem with the reported results is obvious in the example provided in the workbook, this will not always be the case.[3]

A third type of restriction is to zero out all of the explanatory models, leaving a severely stripped-down regression equation:

$$Y_i = \beta_0 + \varepsilon_i.$$

This regression equation says, in effect, that none of the explanatory (or X) variables matter at all (i.e., that the true parameters multiplying the X's all equal 0). The test of the original model against the intercept model is the whole-model F-test that most software (including Excel's LINEST) prominently reports. In this case, the number of constraints is the number of slope parameters in the model.

There are many other restrictions that can be applied to regression equations. Forcing one slope parameter to equal another is a form of restricted regression. In fact, the single-parameter hypothesis (z- or t)-test covered in the previous chapter is a special case of restricted regression because it amounts to imposing the restriction that a single-slope parameter be equal to a particular value (be it zero or any other constant).

---

[3] In regression through the origin, it is possible for the R^2 as we have defined it to be negative. Intuitively, this can happen because the line of average Y may do a better job than the constrained regression in explaining the overall variation in Y. Many statistical packages and Excel 2003 redefine R^2 as follows when there is no intercept:

$$R^2 = 1 - \frac{SSR}{\sum_{i=1}^{n} Y_i^2}.$$

Summary

The idea of restrictions in regression equations is a powerful, ubiquitous concept. In every case, it means that some kind of constraint or limitation has been placed on the coefficient values in fitting an equation to a set of data. The next section is a first step toward understanding how the F-distribution is used in joint hypothesis testing.

17.3. The Chi-Square Distribution

Workbook: ChiSquareDist.xls

Because the F-distribution is the ratio of two chi-square distributed random variables, understanding the chi-square distribution is a prerequisite for understanding the F-distribution.

If the realized values of a normally distributed variable are squared and then summed, the sums are not normally distributed. In 1900, Karl Pearson worked out the distribution of the sum of squared normally distributed random variables and named it the chi-square (χ^2) distribution.[4] (The normally distributed random variables must have mean zero and SD one.) If you take the ratio of two independent random variables each having a chi-square distribution, you get a variable with an F-distribution.

The explanation above is fairly abstract. It might help to think about this more concretely: If we take a simple random sample from a box with normally distributed tickets and sum the draws, and then repeat the procedure for many more samples, the resulting distribution of the sum of the draws is normal. The sample average will also have a normal distribution because it is the sum of the draws divided by the number of draws.

But if we multiplied the draws, the resulting distribution of the product of the draws would not be normal. The key idea here is that there are various numerical recipes that can be applied to the sample data. For any recipe, the resulting outcome will have a particular distribution that may not necessarily be normally distributed. We presented this idea in the previous chapter when we showed that the LINEST statistics are random variables and have sampling distributions, but they are not necessarily normally distributed (such as the RMSE and R^2).

If we apply a more complicated recipe than the sum to a normally distributed random variable (with mean 0 and SD 1), first squaring the values and then summing them, the resulting distribution is not normal but

---

[4] Pearson also gave modern statistics many other terms and concepts including normal curve, kurtosis, skedasticity (and its two primary types, homoskedasticity and heteroskedasticity), standard deviation, and the Greek letter sigma (σ) as a symbol for the SD. See Walker (1958).

chi-square. The number of random variables squared and summed is called the "degrees of freedom" of the chi-square distribution.

Open the Excel workbook ChiSquareDist.xls to see an implementation of the chi-square recipe. Each sheet has a number for its name that indicates the degrees of freedom (or number of random variables being squared and summed). Look in several of the numbered sheets. Click on the cells in columns B and C and note the formulas being used. Column B reports the total, or sum, of the realized normally distributed random variables. Notice how each value in column C is simply the square of the value in column B. Summing the squared values in column C generates a realization of a single draw from a chi-square distribution. Hit F9 to recalculate the sheet and draw another single value from the chi-square distribution.

From the *1* sheet, click the [Draw Empirical Histograms] button to create your own Monte Carlo approximation to the chi-square distribution with one degree of freedom. Enter the number of repetitions and click OK. Excel will then draw as many normally distributed random numbers as indicated by the sheet name and sum them. The pink histogram and summary statistics text show the empirical distribution of the sum of the normal draws for as many repetitions as you selected. At the same time, Excel squares each normally distributed value and sums the squares. The resulting blue histogram is a Monte Carlo approximation to the probability density function of the chi-square distribution. The more repetitions you request, the closer the pink and blue histograms will get to the exact normal and chi-square distributions, respectively.

The chi-square distribution is skewed right for small values of the degrees-of-freedom parameter that controls the chi-square distribution. The sheets of the workbook make this clear. Figure 17.3.1 displays an approximation

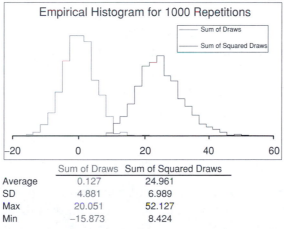

Empirical Histogram for 1000 Repetitions

— Sum of Draws
— Sum of Squared Draws

	Sum of Draws	Sum of Squared Draws
Average	0.127	24.961
SD	4.881	6.989
Max	20.051	52.127
Min	−15.873	8.424

Figure 17.3.1. A chi-square random variable with 25 degrees of freedom versus a normally distributed random variable.
Source: [ChiSquareDist.xls]25.

(based on 10,000 draws) of the chi-square distribution resulting from the summation of 25 squared normal random draws.

Squaring the draws gives a distribution that is everywhere positive and skewed to the right. It is clearly not normal. In fact, it is chi-square.

As the number of degrees of freedom increases, the chi-square distribution approaches the normal distribution. Click on the *50* sheet to convince yourself of this fact. Create chi-square distributions with greater degrees of freedom to demonstrate this convergence. The expected value of the chi-square distribution is the number of degrees of freedom, whereas the SD of the chi-square distribution is the square root of twice the number of degrees of freedom.

With Normally Distributed Errors, the SSR is Chi-Square Distributed

The chi-square distribution finds its most direct application in regression with the sum of squared residuals. Assume that the classical econometric model applies. Then if, in addition, the error terms are normally distributed, the sum of squared residuals will be exactly chi-square distributed with the number of degrees of freedom equal to the number of observations minus the number of parameters being estimated.

This fact makes sense when you consider the recipe being applied to generate the SSR. The residuals are simply realizations of the observed Y's minus the deterministic component ($b_0 + b_1X$ in a bivariate regression). The residuals are good estimates of the errors. When the errors are normally distributed with mean zero and we square and sum them, per the SSR recipe, we are essentially creating a chi-square realization! There are two additional details we must mention. First, there is the nasty fact that the number of degrees of freedom seems wrong – it is not the number of squared residuals but rather that number less the number of parameters being estimated. Second, when the SD of the underlying normally distributed errors is not 1, the distribution of the SSR is scaled up by the variance of the error terms. Thus, it is the SSR divided by the variance of the errors that is distributed chi-square.

Summary

This section has shown that if a given number of realizations from a standard normally distributed random variable are squared and then summed, the resulting distribution is chi-square. The next section demonstrates that the ratio of two chi-square-distributed random variables is F-distributed.

17.4. The *F*-Distribution

Workbook: FDist.xls

The Excel workbook FDist.xls demonstrates that, if a random variable that is chi-square distributed is divided by its number of degrees of freedom and then a second random variable that is distributed chi-square is divided by its number of degrees of freedom, and then finally the ratio of these variables is formed, an *F*-distributed random variable will result.

The FDist.xls workbook works just like the ChiSquareDist.xls workbook from the previous section. Each sheet name reveals the degrees of freedom for the numerator and denominator in the *F*-distribution.

The *F*-distribution requires two degrees-of-freedom parameters – one for the chi-square in the numerator and another for the chi-square in the denominator. They need not be the same. For example, you can click the | Create My Own | button and create an *F*-distribution with 10 degrees of freedom in the numerator and 5 in the denominator. Figure 17.4.1 displays a histogram of a Monte Carlo approximation to the probability density function of the $F(5,5)$ random variable. Because the *F*-distribution has a very long right-hand tail when the number of degrees of freedom is small, we have cut off the display, collapsing all of the top 2 percent of the values into the last bin on the right. For example, in Figure 17.4.1 every outcome with a value of 7.7 or above is collapsed into the bin running from 7.7 to 7.95.

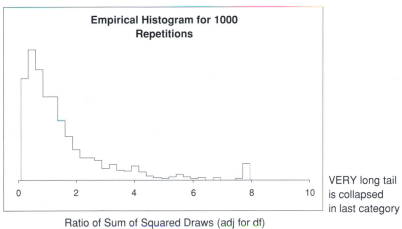

Ratio of Sum of Squared Draws (adj for df)	
Average	1.818
SD	5.726
Max	146.633
Min	0.071

Figure 17.4.1. An empirical approximation to the *F*-distribution with degrees of freedom (5,5).
Source: [FDist.xls]5.5.

Summary

This section and the previous one are simply building blocks. They are designed to acquaint you with two basic distributions, the chi-square and *F*. The next sections in this chapter provide examples of how the *F*-distribution can be used with a restricted regression to test a variety of hypotheses.

17.5. An *F*-Test: The Galileo Example

Workbook: FDistGalileo.xls

The previous sections have defined the *F*-distribution as the ratio of two chi-square random variables and have shown the *F*-distribution for a variety of degrees-of-freedom values. This section offers our first application of an *F*-test. We begin with a general description of the test and then apply it to the Galileo functional form example introduced in Section 6.2.

The General Idea Behind the F-Test

The basic idea behind the *F*-test is the following: We compare the fit of a restricted model to that of an unrestricted model using the sum of squared residuals (SSR) as our guide. Because, practically speaking, a restriction will increase the SSR, we must determine if the restriction is large enough to warrant rejecting the restricted model. If the difference in fit between the two models is not very big and could have resulted from chance alone, then we decide in favor of the restricted model. If the difference is big, and chance alone is an unlikely explanation, we reject the restricted model.

To implement the test, we need a way to measure fit and a way to decide if the difference in fit is big or small. We measure fit by working with the SSR. The percentage loss in fit is the difference between the SSR of the restricted model and the SSR of the unrestricted model divided by the SSR of the unrestricted model:

$$\text{Percentage Loss of Fit} = \frac{\text{Restricted Sum of Squared Residuals} - \text{Unrestricted Sum of Squared Residuals}}{\text{Unrestricted Sum of Squared Residuals}}.$$

For technical reasons, to ensure the statistic follows the *F*-distribution under the null hypothesis, we must adjust the numerator and denominator; thus, the actual *F*-statistic looks like this:

$$F\text{-statistic} = \frac{\dfrac{\text{Restricted SSR} - \text{Unrestricted SSR}}{\text{Number of Constraints}}}{\dfrac{\text{Unrestricted SSR}}{\text{Number of Observations} - \text{Number of Parameters Estimated}}},$$

Degrees of freedom in the numerator $=$ Number of Constraints

Degrees of freedom in the denominator $=$ Number of Observations

$-$ Number of Parameters Estimated.

The *F*-test procedure strongly resembles other tests of significance. We locate the resulting ratio on a graph of the appropriate *F*-distribution (i.e., the one with correct numerator and denominator degrees of freedom). This allows us to find a *P*-value, and then we use that value in the customary way. The *P*-value tells us, given that the null hypothesis is true, the probability of obtaining a result like the observed result or one that is even more extreme. If the *P*-value is large (above 5 percent is the typical standard, though sometimes 1 percent is used), we do not reject the null hypothesis. That is, we decide for the restricted version of the model. If the *P*-value is small (below 5 percent, sometimes below 1 percent), then we reject the restricted version in favor of the unrestricted version.

There is one subtle point about the construction of the *F*-statistic in this case. When the errors are normally distributed, the actual distribution of the Unrestricted SSR is chi-square $(n - k)$, where n is the number of observations and k is the number of parameters multiplied by the variance of the error terms. The difference in SSRs, the Restricted SSR less the Unrestricted SSR, however, also follows a chi-square distribution that has been scaled up by the variance of the error terms. The variance of the error terms present in both the numerator and the denominator cancels out, and the resulting statistic is distributed according to the *F*-distribution under the null hypothesis.

Applying the F-Test to the Galileo Example

Let us look at an example that has been considered before: the data on the distance traveled by a falling object that was analyzed by our fictional Galileo. You will recall that Galileo had strong theoretical reasons for preferring a parsimonious model of the relationship between distance and time. He believed that objects accelerate as they fall toward earth. Thus, distance should increase in proportion to the square of the amount of time that the object had fallen. Furthermore, Galileo thought the rate of acceleration to be constant. That would require that distance not depend on time in addition to the square of time. Finally, Galileo knew that the distance traveled cannot be anything but zero at time zero. These considerations suggested that the restricted model, $Distance = \beta_2 Time^2 + \varepsilon$, is a good description of the behavior of falling objects. The unrestricted model, $Distance = \beta_0 + \beta_1 Time + \beta_2 Time^2 + \varepsilon$, is more flexible, but Galileo thought his version to be correct.

Note that we are describing a hypothesis test in which the null hypothesis says that the restricted version is true, whereas the alternative says it is not. Interestingly, the traditional roles of null as a straw man and the alternative as the thing we really believe in are frequently reversed in this application of testing methodology. With *F*-tests, economists often have a sharper version of the theory that they think may well be true – this is the null hypothesis; the straw man may instead be the weak version of the theory – the alternative hypothesis.

The workbook FDistGalileo.xls contains several sheets. The *Solver* sheet demonstrates how the restricted version of the model can be viewed as a constrained optimization problem (using Solver). The *Solver* sheet makes clear that the restricted regression has a larger SSR because the constrained optimization problem is not free to choose values of b_0 and b_1. To run Solver on the unrestricted problem, execute Tools: Solver; then click on the Options button. Click the Load Model button and select the cell range (in yellow) from R9:R13. After asking whether you wish to reset previous Solver cell selections (you should click OK), Solver incorporates this Solver Model into the Solver Dialog box. You are asking Solver to minimize the value in cell Q13 (the SSR) by changing cells Q9 through Q11 (the intercept and slope parameters). Click Solve to have Solver compute the unrestricted regression solution.

To add the constraints that the intercept and slope on time (b_0 and b_1) must be equal to 0, use the Load Model approach again by loading the Solver Model in cells Z9:Z13. This time Solver will minimize the SSR but will impose the restriction. You should be able to reproduce, with Solver, exactly the same b_2 and SSR values provided by LINEST. Solver's solutions to the restricted and unrestricted optimization problems of minimizing the SSR are shown in Figure 17.5.1.

The *Example* sheet is live. Every time the sheet is recalculated, a new sample based on 50 draws from a normally distributed error box is created.

Unrestricted Optimization		Restricted Optimization	
b_0	4.728	b_0	0
b_1	−6.438	b_1	0
b_2	11.885	b_2	9.91966
min SSR	745.762	min SSR	889.236

Figure 17.5.1. Solver solutions to unrestricted and restricted problems of minimizing the SSR.
Source: [FDistGalileo.xls]Solver.

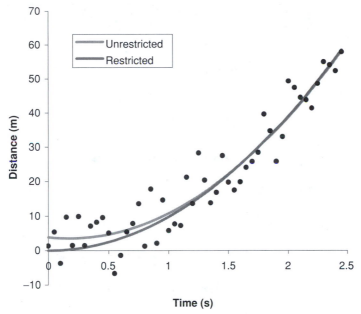

Figure 17.5.2(a). Unrestricted versus restricted model.

Unrestricted Regression			Restricted Regression	
b_2	b_1	b_0	Slope	Intercept
8.15	0.31	2.73	9.05	0.00
1.37	3.47	1.84	0.25	#N/A
0.92	4.50	#N/A		4.82
281.34	47	#N/A		49.00
11,414	**953**	#N/A		**1,139**

Figure 17.5.2(b). Regression results for unrestricted and restricted models. The SSRs are emphasized.
Source: [FDistGalileo.xls]Example.

The *X* values are held fixed. Hit F9 a few times and keep your eye on the F7 and I7 cells. The minimum SSR of the restricted regression is always greater than its unrestricted counterpart.

In Figure 17.5.2 we deliberately picked an example in which there is apparently a big difference between the two models. The unrestricted regression is the higher curve through most of the range.

The *FTestProc* sheet enables repeated testing of samples from the *Example* sheet to be done. Figure 17.5.3 shows the procedure for implementing the *F*-test using the data in our example.

The *F*-Test

SSR for null (Galileo is right)
Restricted Model   1139

SSR for alternative hypothesis
Unrestricted Model   953

Intuition:

If the deviation of the Restricted from the Unrestricted Model is large,
we reject the null that β_0 and β_1 are zero

Getting the *F*-Test Exactly Right:

$$\text{Fstatistic} = \cfrac{\cfrac{\text{Residuals Sum of Squared Residuals} - \text{Unrestricted Sum of Squared Restricted}}{\text{Number of Constraints}}}{\cfrac{\text{Unrestricted Sum of Squared Residuals}}{\text{Number of Observations} - \text{Number of Parameters Estimated}}}$$

Additional Information for the *F*-Statistic

Number of Constraints	2
Number of Observations	50
Number of Parameters Estimated	3

F-Statistic	*P*-Value
4.58657	1.51%

Significance Level
5%

Reject Restricted Regression?
Yes

Figure 17.5.3. A single-sample implementation of the F-test.
Source: [FDistGalileo.xls]FTestProc.

In the example of Figure 17.5.3, we have implemented the procedure for an *F*-test. At conventional levels of significance, we would incorrectly reject the restricted model because its loss of fit is large enough to conclude that something other than chance alone is responsible for the difference in the fit of the two models.

The [Run SSR MC] and [Run F Stat MC] buttons in the *Example* sheet take you to the *MCSSR* and *MCF* sheets, where you can run Monte Carlo simulations of the Unrestricted SSR and the *F*-statistic. For now, we assume that the error terms are normally distributed. The Monte Carlo approximation of the *F*-statistic's sampling distribution when the null is true for the Galileo example looks like Figure 17.5.4.

The superimposed curve is the actual $F(2, 47)$ distribution. It fits the Monte Carlo–generated empirical histogram quite well because, when the null is

Sample F Summary Statistics		# Constraints	2
Average	1.041	# Observations	50
SD	1.098	# Parameters	3
Max	13.117	Error Box	Normal
Min	0.000	% Rejected at 5%	4.86%

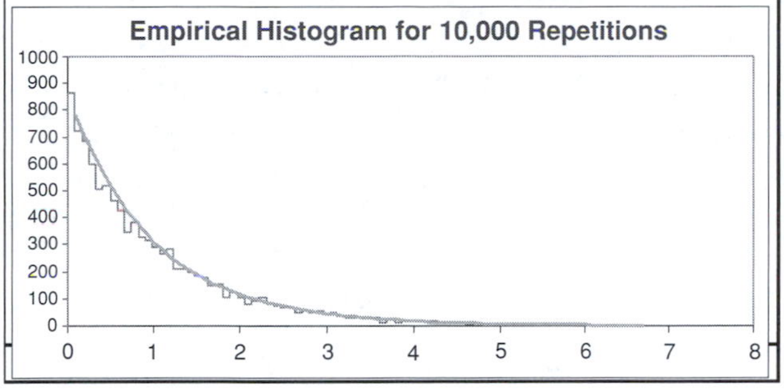

Empirical Histogram for 10,000 Repetitions

Figure 17.5.4. The approximate F-distribution for the Galileo example. *Source:* [FDistGalileo.xls]MCF.

true, the *F*-statistic really is *F*-distributed. The "% Rejected at 5%" box reports the fraction of repetitions that produced an *F*-statistic greater than the value associated with a 5-percent level of significance. If all is well, this should read about 5 percent. In this case, the *F*-statistic is working very well.

Nonnormal Errors

What happens when the error terms are not normally distributed? We have given you the option of running Monte Carlo experiments using uniformly and exponentially distributed errors and also the ability to adjust the sample size.[5] You will find that the probability histogram for the SSR deviates quite considerably from the chi-square distribution when the errors are nonnormal and the sample size is small. Surprisingly, however, the *F*-statistic, which depends on the SSR, is much more resilient. The probability histograms for the *F*-statistics look fairly close to being *F*-distributed even when the errors are exponentially distributed and the sample size is small. The tail is a little "too fat" in such cases: We tend to reject the true null too often.

Summary

We conclude this section with a list of the steps for performing an *F*-test:

1. Identify the restricted and unrestricted models.
2. Run each model and find the SSR for each model.
3. Calculate the *F*-statistic.

---

[5] The file ExponentialDist.xls in the\Basic Tools\RandomNumber folder discusses the exponential distribution.

4. Find the *P*-value using the *F*-distribution with the correct degrees of freedom for the numerator and denominator.
5. Reach a conclusion about the null.

The *F*-test can be used to test a large variety of possible hypotheses in a regression model. Strictly speaking, the *F*-test requires the additional assumption not contained in the CEM that the error terms are normally distributed. Monte Carlo evidence, however, shows that it can be fairly resilient to non-normal errors. In the sections that follow, we consider a few of the possibilities.

17.6. *F*- and *T*-Tests for Equality of Two Parameters

Workbook: FDistFoodStamps.xls

In this section we show how to test a restriction stating that two parameters in the model are equal. We will demonstrate use of the *F*-statistic and the *t*-statistic to test such single-constraint restrictions. We will use a fictional example based on a real question to illustrate our discussion.

Suppose we want to know whether an additional dollar of food stamps has the same impact on the demand for food as does an additional dollar of cash income. Economic theory says that, if people would ordinarily spend more on food than they receive in food stamps, then the receipt of food stamps should have the same effect on people as cash income. But whether people treat food stamps the same as cash remains an open question that requires empirical analysis.[6]

The following model could be used to examine this question:

$$\text{Food Purchases} = \beta_0 + \beta_1 \text{ Number of adults in family}$$
$$+ \beta_2 \text{ Number of children in family}$$
$$+ \beta_3 \text{ Cash Income}$$
$$+ \beta_4 \text{ Value of Food Stamps} + \varepsilon.$$

We assume that the classical econometric model applies. In more compact notation, the unrestricted model reads like this:

$$Y_i = \beta_0 + \beta_1 X_{1i} + \beta_2 X_{2i} + \beta_3 X_{3i} + \beta_4 X_{4i} + \varepsilon_i, \quad i = 1, \ldots, n.$$

The null hypothesis we want to test involves more than one parameter. In terms of the parameters, the null and alternative hypotheses read as follows:

$$\text{Null Hypothesis: } \beta_3 = \beta_4.$$
$$\text{Alternative Hypothesis: } \beta_3 \neq \beta_4.$$

---

[6] See Whitmore (2002) for recent evidence on the cash-equivalent value families place on food stamps.

β_0	200
β_1	600
β_2	400
β_3	0.3
β_4	0.3
SD(Errors)	100

Figure 17.6.1. Parameter values for food stamps example.
Source: [FDistFoodStamps.xls]Example.

To test this hypothesis, let us write the restricted model as follows:

$$Y_i = \beta_0 + \beta_1 X_{1i} + \beta_2 X_{2i} + \gamma (X_{3i} + X_{4i}) + \varepsilon_i, \quad i = 1, \ldots, n.$$

Here γ stands for the common parameter that multiplies both Cash Income and Value of Food Stamps. To use the *F*-test, we employ a trick: We define a new variable that is just the sum of Cash Income and Value of Food Stamps and run the restricted regression using that new variable.

Open the Excel workbook FDistFoodStamps.xls and go to the *Example* sheet. You will see a fictional data set with 50 observations and four independent variables (cell range A9:E59, labels included). Notice that we have set up the sheet so that the null hypothesis is true – β_3 really does equal β_4. The values of the parameters in our example are shown in Figure 17.6.1. If your workbook has different values, click on the ⌐Reset⌐ button to restore them to those in our example.

Using LINEST, we estimate the restricted (D1:H7) and unrestricted (I1:L7) regression models. This sheet is live, and thus a new sample is drawn every time it is recalculated. Figure 17.6.2 is an example of the results.

On the *Example* sheet, hit F9 a few times while watching the SSR reported by LINEST for the two models. As in the preceding results, the restricted regression always has a higher SSR than the unrestricted regression. Is the performance loss severe enough, however, to lead us to reject the restricted model?

Unrestricted: $Y = \beta_0 + \beta_1 X_1 + \beta_2 X_2 + \beta_3 X_3 + \beta_4 X_4 + \varepsilon$					Restricted: $Y = \beta_0 + \beta_1 X_1 + \beta_2 X_2 + \gamma(X_3 + X_4) + \varepsilon$			
b_4	b_3	b_2	b_1	b_0	g	b_2	b_1	b_0
0.26	0.30	398.73	584.09	266.80	0.30	398.10	584.18	248.87
0.04	0.01	26.83	9.18	53.55	0.00	26.72	9.14	48.67
1.00	99.58				1.00	99.22		
3574.13	45				4800.02	46.00		
1.42E+08	446,223				1.42E+08	452,838		

Figure 17.6.2. Unrestricted and restricted regression results.
Source: [FDistFoodStamps.xls]Example.

The question is answered via an *F*-test. The *F*-statistic for our example would be computed as follows:

$$F\text{-statistic} = \frac{(SSR_{\text{Restricted}} - SSR_{\text{Unrestricted}})/\#Constraints}{SSR_{\text{Unrestricted}}/(n-k)}$$

$$= \frac{(452{,}838 - 446{,}223)/1}{446{,}223/(50-5)}$$

$$= 0.67.$$

The intuition behind the construction of this test statistic is as follows: If food stamps are treated the same as cash, then the restricted model should do almost as well as the unrestricted one. We need some measure of how big a difference exists between the two models. That is supplied by taking into account the number of restrictions (in this case only 1) and the fit supplied by the unrestricted model (its SSR adjusted by the number of degrees of freedom). Both numerator and denominator in the *F*-statistic are scaled by the variance of the error terms; this factor cancels.

Notice that there is just one constraint in this hypothesis. The *P*-value is reported in cell J9. The cell formula reveals that we simply asked for the area under the *F*-distribution (with numerator degrees of freedom 1 and denominator degrees of freedom $n-k$, or 45) that is to the right of the *F*-statistic. Because the *P*-value in our example is 42 percent, we do not reject the null that the restricted model is correct. This is good news because the null is true.

Another way to gain some intuition on what is going on with this *F*-test is to explore the Raw Loss of Fit Measures area of the *Example* sheet (beginning in cell G13). Hit F9 and watch the *P*-value (J9), Percentage Difference (H19), and b_3, b_4 coefficients (H24:I25). The coefficients in cells I24 and I25 bounce but are restricted to be equal, whereas they are unrestricted in the H24 and H25 cells. Notice that only when the gap between the coefficients is large do we reject the null that the restricted model is correct. Figure 17.6.3 gives an example in which the (true) null is rejected.

In this sample, the null is rejected (incorrectly) because we happened to get a sample in which the unrestricted regression minimized the SSR with a large deviation between the coefficients on food stamps and cash income. When you choose a 5-percent level of significance, this will happen only about 1 in 20 times in situations in which the null is true and either the errors are normally distributed or there are a large number of observations.

The *FTestProc* sheet shows the recipe for conducting the *F*-test as reproduced in Figure 17.6.4. Notice that the procedure is identical to that used for the FDistGalileo.xls *F*-test. In fact, no matter the form of the restriction, the

F-Stat	9.992	P-value	0.3%

Raw Loss-of-Fit Measures		
Difference		
(Restricted SSR – Unrestricted SSR)		
110679		
Percentage Difference		
(Restricted SSR – Unrestricted SSR)/Unrestricted SSR		
22.2%		

	Unrestricted	Restricted
b_0	124.70	198.03
b_1	606.62	606.24
b_2	345.08	347.66
b_3	0.29	0.31
b_4	0.45	0.31

Figure 17.6.3. A sample in which we would reject the true null at the 5-percent level of significance.
Source: [FDistFoodStamps.xls]Example.

The *F*-Test

SSR for null (Cash and Food Stamps are the same)
Restricted Model   429442

SSR for Alternative Hypothesis
Unrestricted Model   413148
Intuition:
If the deviation of the Restricted from the Unrestricted Model is large,
we reject the null that β_3 equals β_4

Getting the *F*-Test Exactly Right:

$$F\text{-statistic} = \frac{\dfrac{\text{Restricted Sum of Squared Residuals} - \text{Unrestricted Sum of Squared Residuals}}{\text{Number of Constraints}}}{\dfrac{\text{Unrestricted Sum of Squared Residuals}}{\text{Number of Observations} - \text{Number of Parameters Estimated}}}$$

Additional Information for the *F*-Statistic

Number of Constraints	1
Number of Observations	50
Number of Parameters Estimated	5

	F-statistic	*P*-value
	1.77474	18.95%
Significance Level		5%
Reject Restricted Regression?		No

Figure 17.6.4. Running an *F*-test.
Source: [FDistFoodStamps.xls]FTestProc.

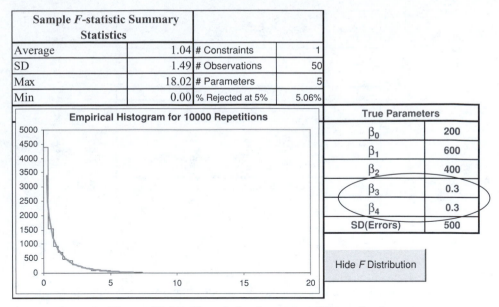

Sample *F*-statistic Summary Statistics			
Average	1.04	# Constraints	1
SD	1.49	# Observations	50
Max	18.02	# Parameters	5
Min	0.00	% Rejected at 5%	5.06%

True Parameters	
β_0	200
β_1	600
β_2	400
β_3	0.3
β_4	0.3
SD(Errors)	500

Hide *F* Distribution

Figure 17.6.5. *F*-statistics for true null hypothesis.
Source: [FDistFoodStamps.xls]MCF.

same procedure is used to conduct the *F*-test. You can use *FTestProc* sheet as a template to conduct your own *F*-tests.

Monte Carlo Evidence

Because the value of the true parameters can be controlled, we can investigate how the *F*-statistic behaves across samples when the null hypothesis is true. To perform this investigation, go to the *MCF* sheet. Figure 17.6.5 shows results from a Monte Carlo experiment with 10,000 repetitions.

In our example, the number of constraints is 1 and the number of observations minus the number of parameters is 45. If the null hypothesis is true, the fraction of repetitions producing *F*-statistics above 4.06 ought to be about 5 percent (for an F(1,45) distribution), and the empirical histogram for the Monte Carlo repetitions ought to closely follow the entire *F* (1,45) distribution. Both these conditions were met in our experiment. The "% Rejected at 5%" box shows what fraction of the repetitions produced an *F*-statistic greater than 4.06. The green line in the graph (on your computer screen) is a superimposed F(1,45) distribution.

To see how the *F*-test performs when the null is *not* true, go back to the *Example* sheet and change the value of β_3 to 0.6, holding the other parameter values constant. We did this and obtained the results depicted in Figure 17.6.6.

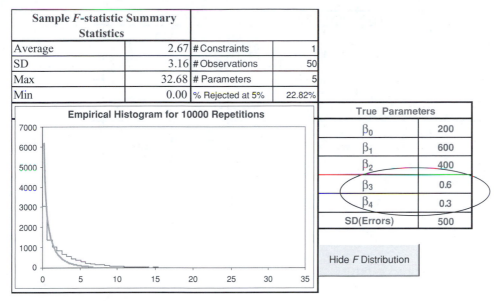

Sample *F*-statistic Summary Statistics			
Average	2.67	# Constraints	1
SD	3.16	# Observations	50
Max	32.68	# Parameters	5
Min	0.00	% Rejected at 5%	22.82%

True Parameters	
β_0	200
β_1	600
β_2	400
β_3	0.6
β_4	0.3
SD(Errors)	500

Hide *F* Distribution

Figure 17.6.6. *F*-statistics for false null hypothesis.
Source: [FDistFoodStamps.xls]MCF.

The F-statistic is large enough to reject the null hypothesis about 23 per-cent of the time using the 5-percent level of significance (once again that is the 4.06 cutoff). The good news is that we are about four times more likely to reject this false null hypothesis than the true null hypothesis. The bad news is that in these circumstances there is still about a 77-percent chance that we will draw the incorrect inference – namely that the propensities to consume food out of income and food stamps are the same. You can experiment to show that the greater the difference between the true food stamp and income parameters, the more likely you are to reject the false null.

The Relationship between F- and T-Statistics

The attentive reader might wish to ask the following question: Is it possi-ble to test restrictions with just one constraint like the one in this section using the *t*-statistic instead of the *F*-statistic? The answer is yes. Very for-tunately, the *F*-statistic and the *t*-statistic give exactly the same answer. The *t*-statistic has the advantage that it can be used to test single-tailed alternative hypotheses, whereas the *F*-statistic cannot be used to perform such one-tailed tests.

In our food-stamp example, although the restriction involves two parame-ters, there is just one equals sign in the restriction, meaning just one constraint. This makes it possible to run a *t*-test by cleverly rewriting the model. Recall

Unrestricted: $Y = \beta_0 + \beta_1 X_1 + \beta_2 X_2 + \beta_3 X_3 + \beta_4 X_4 + \varepsilon$				
b_4	b_3	b_2	b_1	b_0
0.28	0.30	396.00	602.10	244.47
0.05	0.01	27.78	9.50	55.45
1.00	103.11			
3406.36	45			
1.45E+08	**478,430**			

Restricted: $Y = \beta_0 + \beta_1 X_1 + \beta_2 X_2 + \gamma(X_3 + X_4) + \varepsilon$			
g	b_2	b_1	b_0
0.30	395.74	602.13	237.06
0.00	27.50	9.41	50.09
1.00	102.10		
4631.77	46		
1.45E+08	**479,559**		

Unrestricted: $Y = \beta_0 + \beta_1 X_1 + \beta_2 X_2 + \beta_3(X_3 + X_4) + \delta(X_4) + \varepsilon$				
d	b_3	b_2	b_1	b_0
−0.02	0.30	396.00	602.10	244.47
0.05	0.01	27.78	9.50	55.45
1.00	103.11			
3406.36	45			
1.45E+08	**478,430**			

Test Statistics	Statistic	P-value
F-stat	0.106	75%
t-stat	−0.326	75%
t-stat²	0.106	n/a

Figure 17.6.7. Two unrestricted and one restricted regressions.
Source: [FDistFoodStamps.xls]tStat.

that the original, unrestricted model reads as follows:

$$Y_i = \beta_0 + \beta_1 X_{1i} + \beta_2 X_{2i} + \beta_3 X_{3i} + \beta_4 X_{4i} + \varepsilon_i, \quad i = 1, \dots, n.$$

The restriction says that $\beta_3 = \beta_4$. We can incorporate the restriction into the original model in this fashion: Create a new variable that is the sum of X_3 and X_4 but also include X_4 separately in the regression:

$$Y_i = \beta_0 + \beta_1 X_{1i} + \beta_2 X_{2i} + \beta_3 (X_{3i} + X_{4i}) + \delta X_{4i} + \varepsilon_i, \quad i = 1, \dots, n.$$

When OLS is run on this model, exactly the same results are obtained as with OLS on the unrestricted model: All the coefficient estimates are the same as are the other regression statistics. The one exception proves the rule. The new coefficient is an estimate of δ, but the sum of the coefficient estimates for δ and β_3 is equal to the value of the coefficient estimate of β_4 in the unrestricted model. To see that this is indeed the case, go to the *tStat* sheet in FDistFoodStamps.xls. As Figure 17.6.7 shows, we report three closely related regressions in this sheet.

The two regressions at the top of Figure 17.6.7 are the unrestricted and restricted models we have already seen in the *Example* sheet. The third regression at the bottom on the left is the rewritten, unrestricted model. As claimed above, all of the estimates for the two unrestricted regressions are exactly the same with the one exception being the coefficient estimate for δ, which is not a parameter in the original version of the unrestricted model. We see that the two unrestricted models are essentially the same. The main difference is that the original unrestricted model gives us the estimated SE of b_4, whereas the rewritten unrestricted model gives us the estimated SE of $d = (b_4 - b_3)$. We can therefore use the rewritten model to test the null hypothesis that $\beta_3 = \beta_4$ against the alternative hypothesis $\beta_3 \neq \beta_4$.

The lower right-hand corner of Figure 17.6.7 displays the F-statistic (cell K10 in the *tStat* sheet) obtainable from the comparison of the restricted and unrestricted regressions. The comparable t-statistic (in cell K11) is computed as follows:

$$t\text{-statistic} = \frac{d - 0}{\text{Estimated SE}\,(d)}.$$

We compute the P-values for the two test statistics (in cells L10 and L11) and find that they are exactly the same. Note that we use the two-tailed P-value for the t-test. Finally, we note that the square of the t-statistic (cell K13) is exactly equal to that of the F-statistic. If you hit F9, a new sample will be drawn and new estimates and new values of the test statistics will be generated, but the equivalencies just pointed out will still hold true.

Summary

To review, we have shown that, when there is just one restriction, it is possible to rewrite the original model in order to use the t-statistic in place of the F-statistic. There is one advantage to this procedure: it is possible to test one-sided hypotheses with the t-statistic but impossible to do so with the F-statistic. The next section explains how to test a claim that more than one coefficient in the model is equal to zero.

17.7. *F*-Test for Multiple Parameters

Workbook: FDistEarningsFn.xls

In this section we show how to test a restriction that says that multiple (but not all) parameters in the model are all equal to zero. We use a real example based on a model of earnings. We gathered data on 15,756 individuals from the March 2002 CPS on total personal income, sex, race, and education. We are especially interested in whether or not males earn more than females and whether the gains to income from increases in education vary between males and females. The basic, unrestricted model we start from looks like this:

$$Total\ Personal\ Income_i = \beta_0 + \beta_1 Education_i + \beta_2 Black_i + \beta_3 Male_i$$
$$+ \beta_4\ Male \cdot Education_i + \varepsilon_i, \quad i = 1, \ldots, n.$$

If β_3 is nonzero, then males receive an income boost or penalty versus females. If β_4 is nonzero, then the slope of the relationship between income and education is not the same for men and women.

One possible restricted version of this model says that being male does not matter, and thus both the intercept-shifter β_3 and the slope-shifter β_4 are zero. The restricted version thus reads like this:

$$Total\ Personal\ Income_i = \beta_0 + \beta_1 Education_i + \beta_2 Black_i$$
$$+ \nu_i, \quad i = 1, \ldots n.$$

We make the standard CEM assumptions about the data generating process.[7] In this case, with a very large sample, there is no need to assume that the errors are normally distributed. In English, the null and alternative hypotheses are as follows:

Null: Being male does not affect earnings.
Alternative: Being male does affect earnings.

In terms of mathematical symbols, the null and alternative hypotheses read as follows:

$$\text{Null Hypothesis: } \beta_3 = \beta_4 = 0.$$

$$\text{Alternative Hypothesis: Not the null.}$$

Open the Excel workbook FDistEarningsFn.xls and go to the *Data1* sheet. You will see a real-world data set with 15,756 observations, which we can use to estimate these two models and run an *F*-test to decide if we should reject the Restricted model. As Figure 17.7.1 shows, we decisively reject the null hypothesis that being male does not affect one's earnings. The *F*-statistic is huge and the *P*-value is nearly zero.

You should always pay attention to the practical importance of a result that has been deemed statistically significant. Statistical significance means that chance alone is a poor explanation of the observed difference. Statistical significance says nothing about the practical importance of the observed difference. In this case, the impact of being a male is quite big, though at first the results seem somewhat contradictory. From the coefficient estimate b_3, it appears that males make \$26,700 less than women. However, the coefficient estimate on the interaction term, b_4, tells us that every additional year of education boosts male's personal income by \$3,562 more than females' income. Thus, males catch up to females as education increases. Figure 17.7.2 contrasts predicted values for nonblack males and females.

The null hypothesis says that the two predicted income functions coincide. As we saw, the *F*-test provides very strong evidence against the null. The *Q&A* sheet asks you to perform a similar analysis involving the variables Black and Education.

---

[7] The fact that in real-world applications like this one the *X*'s are not fixed in repeated samples is a problem. More realistic descriptions of the data generating process, however, do not change the story in material ways.

$$Total\ Personal\ Income_i = \beta_0 + \beta_1 Education_i + \beta_2 Black_i + \beta_3 Male_i$$
$$+ \beta_4 Male \cdot Education_i + \varepsilon_i, i = 1, ..., n.$$

Unrestricted regression				
maleeduc	male	black	educ	intercept
3562	−26700	−4454	3065	−17744
209	2753	974	149	1970
0.179	39413	#N/A	#N/A	#N/A
860.44	15751	#N/A	#N/A	#N/A
5.3464E+12	2.447E+13	#N/A	#N/A	#N/A

$$Total\ Personal\ Income_i = \beta_0 + \beta_1 Education_i + \beta_2 Black_i + v_i, i = 1, ..., n.$$

Restricted Regresssion			F-stat	597.77
black	educ	intercept	P-value	0%
−5282	4880	−31859		
1010	109	1446		
0.117	40879	#N/A		
1044.01	15753	#N/A		
3.4892E+12	2.632E+13	#N/A		

Figure 17.7.1. *F*-test of hypothesis that being male does not affect personal income. *Source:* [FDistEarnngsFn.xls]Data1.

One feature of Figure 17.7.2 requires comment. The regression estimates make little sense for people with very low levels of education: negative predicted incomes just are not plausible. The assumption that the relationship between income and education is linear is not reasonable for low levels of education.

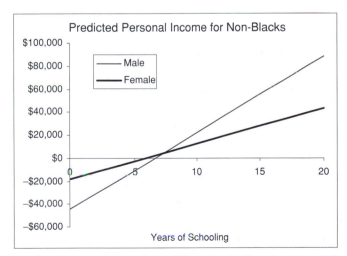

Figure 17.7.2. Comparing male and female predicted personal income. *Source:* [FDistEarnngsFn.xls]Data1.

Summary

LINEST, like most regression software, reports a whole model F-test that the coefficients of all of the included X variables are zero. This section showed how to test the claim that a subset of the coefficients equal zero. By running two regressions, one unrestricted and the other restricted (by dropping the variables that supposedly do not matter), the resulting SSRs and degrees of freedom can be incorporated in an F-test. In our example, we rejected the claim that being male does not affect personal income. The next section discusses situations in which hypotheses tests give conflicting answers.

17.8. The Consequences of Multicollinearity

Workbook: CorrelatedEstimates.xls

Our aim in this section is to highlight a seeming paradox that often occurs in empirical hypothesis testing: It is entirely possible that two estimated coefficients can be found to be statistically insignificant separately (the two null hypotheses that each parameter is equal to zero are not rejected), whereas the joint hypothesis that both are equal to zero is soundly rejected. Our explanation of this apparent contradiction will show that estimates of different parameters are correlated random variables and will replace the notion of a confidence interval for a single parameter with that of a *confidence region* for multiple parameters.

To make these points, we will work with an artificial trivariate example in which the data are generated according to the classical econometric model. We have

$$Y_i = \beta_0 + \beta_1 \cdot X_{1i} + \beta_2 \cdot X_{2i} + \varepsilon_i, \quad i = 1, \ldots, n.$$

Here β_0 is the intercept parameter and β_1 and β_2 are the slope parameters we want to estimate. The ε_i's are assumed to be repeated draws from an error box (always the same one) with tickets whose mean is zero with an unknown standard deviation. The n draws are independent of each other. The X's are fixed in repeated sampling. Therefore the ε_i's are independent of the X's.

The *Example* sheet in the CorrelatedEstimates.xls workbook contains a data set with 10 observations that conforms to this model. We will contrast the results of the following hypothesis tests:

Separate Null Hypotheses:

Individual Null Hypothesis 1: $\beta_1 = 0$

Individual Null Hypothesis 2: $\beta_2 = 0$

Joint Null Hypothesis: $\beta_1 = 0$ and $\beta_2 = 0$.

	Estimate	SE	*t*-stat	*P*-value
b_1	1.01	0.92	1.10	31%
b_2	1.02	0.92	1.11	30%
RMSE	11.76	*F*-stat	121.94	0%

Figure 17.8.1. Individual nulls not rejected while joint null is rejected.
Source: [CorrelatedEstimates.xls]Example.

The separate null hypotheses look at only one parameter, whereas the joint null hypothesis says that both slope coefficients are equal to zero. It would seem that if the joint null hypothesis is rejected, then there will be evidence that at least one of the slope parameters is not equal to zero. We shall see, however, that this logic is flawed.

In the *Example* sheet click on the [Make Alternative Hypothesis True] button. This button sets the values of the (hidden) true parameters in the model so that strange things will happen. In particular, the type of outcome displayed in Figure 17.8.1 is very common.

In the sample results depicted in Figure 17.8.1, the *t*-statistics tell us that we cannot reject the individual null hypotheses that $\beta_1 = 0$ and $\beta_2 = 0$, and yet the *F*-statistic says that we can decisively reject the null hypothesis that β_1 and β_2 are jointly equal to zero. (An *F*-statistic of 121.94 with $n = 10$ is huge, and although the *P*-value is not exactly zero, it is really close!)

If you do not see an outcome like this, just hit the F9 key a few times. Very shortly, a qualitatively similar outcome will show up. Write down the results you obtain for later use.

A result like the one in Figure 17.8.1 should seem contradictory to you. The (*t*- or *z*-) statistics corresponding to the separate null hypotheses seem to be telling us that it is quite possible that both β_1 and β_2 are equal to zero, whereas the *F*-statistic says that it is not true that both are equal to zero.

To understand what is going on, go to the *Setup* sheet. Do not make any changes yet. There is much information in this sheet, and so you should take a few moments to absorb it. The true parameter values are given in the upper-left-hand corner as shown in Figure 17.8.2.

We do not worry about β_0. The key point here is that all three null hypotheses, the separate individual nulls that $\beta_1 = 0$ and that $\beta_2 = 0$ and the joint null that both β_1 and β_2 are equal to 0, are indeed false. (When you clicked on

Population Parameters	
β_0	10
β_1	1
β_2	1
SD(ε)	10

Figure 17.8.2. True population parameters for our example.
Source: [CorrelatedEstimates.xls]Setup.

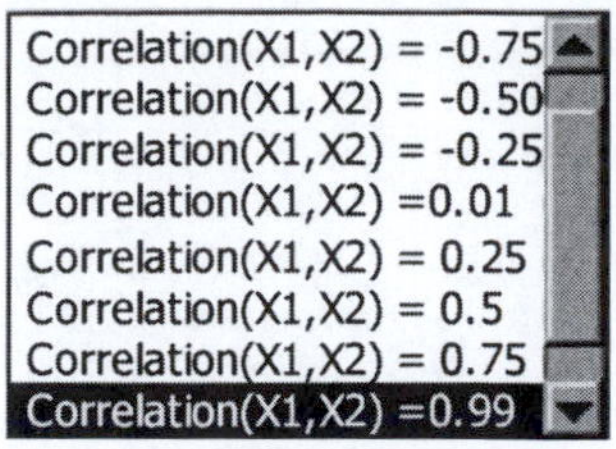

Correlation(X1,X2) = -0.75
Correlation(X1,X2) = -0.50
Correlation(X1,X2) = -0.25
Correlation(X1,X2) =0.01
Correlation(X1,X2) = 0.25
Correlation(X1,X2) = 0.5
Correlation(X1,X2) = 0.75
Correlation(X1,X2) =0.99

Figure 17.8.3. Setting the correlation between X_1 and X_2.
Source: [CorrelatedEstimates.xls]Setup.

the | Make Alternative Hypothesis True | button, both values of the slope parameters were set equal to 1.) The data in cells B7:G16 faithfully conform to the classical econometric model. Finally, note that you can control the correlation between X_1 and X_2. As Figure 17.8.3 shows, we have deliberately selected the case in which there is almost perfect positive correlation between the X's. You will shortly see why this near-perfect multicollinearity makes the paradoxical situation we have encountered quite likely.

Think about the paradox in this way: In many samples produced by this data generation process, we do not have enough evidence to reject either separate null hypothesis; yet, in almost all samples there is more than enough evidence to refute the joint null.

The *joint sampling distribution* under the joint null hypothesis will reveal the cause of the paradox. In the *Setup* sheet, set both β_1 and β_2 to 0. This choice makes the joint null hypothesis (and, of course, both individual null hypotheses) true. Be sure that the correlation between the X's stays equal to 0.99 and that you keep the SD of the errors equal to 10. Now click on the | Go to Monte Carlo | button. Once you have run a Monte Carlo simulation, summary statistics for the slope estimates much like those in Figure 17.8.4 will result.

Also displayed on the *MonteCarlo* sheet (and in Figure 17.8.5) is a scatter diagram for the slope estimates. Each dot on the graph reflects the result from one of the first 400 repetitions in the Monte Carlo simulation. The x-coordinate of each point gives the value for b_1, and the y-coordinate gives the value for b_2 for a particular repetition.

	b_1		b_2	
Average estimate		0.00	Average estimate	0.00
SD estimates		0.765	SD estimates	0.766
Max estimate		2.54	Max estimate	2.23
Min estimate		−226	Min estimate	−2.47

Figure 17.8.4. Summary of Monte Carlo results for b_1 and b_2.
Source: [CorrelatedEstimates.xls]MonteCarlo.

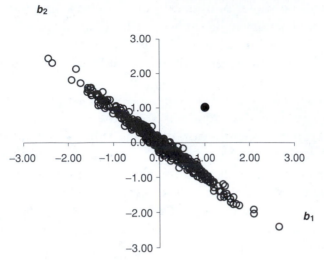

Figure 17.8.5. Scatter diagram of Monte Carlo results for b_1 and b_2 (X's highly correlated) when both slope parameters equal zero.
Source: [CorrelatedEstimates.xls]MonteCarlo.

Figure 17.8.5 is the footprint of an approximate joint sampling distribution of b_1 and b_2 for our data generation process under the null hypothesis that both slope parameters equal zero. The exact joint sampling distribution, or probability histogram, for b_1 and b_2 would have to be graphed in three dimensions with the frequency axis coming out of the page. If you could see this three-dimensional histogram, it would be tallest around the origin – (0,0), the assumed values of β_1 and β_2 – with its height falling gently as it goes either southeast or northwest and quite steeply as one heads northeast or southwest. You can get some sense of this by trying to pick out the density of the points – the denser the points, the taller the three-dimensional histogram.

Because of the very strong positive correlation between the X's, the joint sampling distribution under the null hypothesis has an unusual shape – it is cloud shaped like a thin ellipse with a main axis (a line running through the middle of the ellipse the "long way") that has a slope of about -1. This ellipse tells us that when the joint null hypothesis (that both slope parameters are zero) is true, the estimates b_1 and b_2 are typically *not* zero, but when b_1 is positive, b_2 is extremely likely to be negative. Conversely, when b_1 is negative, it is very likely that b_2 is positive. In other words, the slope estimates are strongly negatively correlated.

We have superimposed the observed value of $b_1 = 1.01$ and $b_2 = 1.02$ that we obtained earlier (see Figure 17.8.1) on the graph in Figure 17.8.5. The reason for the decisive rejection of the joint null hypothesis is now

clear. The realized values of b_1 and b_2 are far away from the cloud of estimates we would obtain if the null hypothesis were true. In other words, the actual sample estimates lie well outside any plausible realization from the joint sampling distribution of the sample estimates under the null hypothesis.

On the other hand, we can also understand why each *individual* null hypothesis was not rejected. The estimated SE of the estimates in each case was around 0.9. From the point of view of an individual estimate, we should not be surprised to find values for the slope parameters within two SEs of the true value. Therefore, anything in the range of -1.8 to 1.8 for either slope estimate is quite compatible with the individual null hypothesis that the true slope is zero for either parameter. Considered all by itself, a value of 1.01 for b_1 is not at all remarkable even if the true value of β_1 is 0, nor, taken in isolation, is a value of 1.02 for b_2 anything special.

It is the fact that *both* slope estimates are positive that would be very unusual were the joint null to be true. The F-statistic of 121.94 with $n = 10$ implies an incredibly small P-value, which means that, assuming the null is true, a result like $(1.01, 1.02)$ is almost (though not quite) impossible.

We have noted that it is the unusually high correlation between the X's that makes likely the paradoxical outcome of not rejecting individual null hypotheses but rejecting the seemingly identical joint null hypothesis. Let us now see what happens when we go to the opposite extreme: near-zero correlation between the X's. Return to the *Setup* sheet, choose a correlation coefficient of 0.01, and set the values of the two slope parameters both equal to 1. Next run a Monte Carlo simulation. The results will be similar to those displayed in Figure 17.8.6.

The first thing to note in Figure 17.8.6 is that, when there is very little correlation between the X's, there is next to no correlation between the slope estimates; this is obvious from the scatter diagram. Next, observe that the paradox we very often encountered when there was extremely high correlation between the X's is now incredibly rare. The histograms for the t-statistics and the F-statistics in the lower part of Figure 17.8.6 both show that few if any repetitions produced statistics consistent with the null hypothesis at standard significance levels. Finally, note that the SEs of the slope estimates are now much smaller than they were when the correlation between the X's was 0.99 (on the assumption the SD of the errors was not changed in the mean time).

What is going on behind the scenes? In the trivariate case, the SEs of the slope estimates depend on the correlation between the X's as well as on the SD of the X's. Furthermore, the correlation between the slope estimates depends negatively on the correlation between the X's.

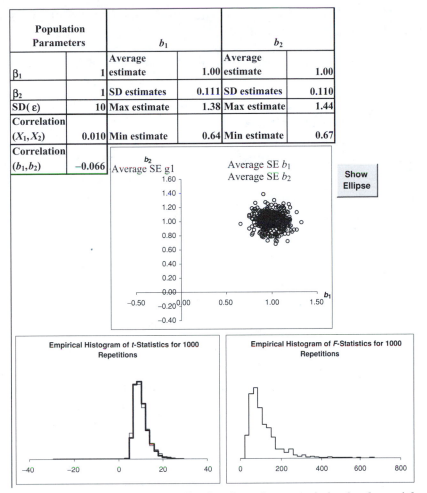

Population Parameters		b_1		b_2	
β_1	1	Average estimate	1.00	Average estimate	1.00
β_2	1	SD estimates	0.111	SD estimates	0.110
SD(ε)	10	Max estimate	1.38	Max estimate	1.44
Correlation (X_1,X_2)	0.010	Min estimate	0.64	Min estimate	0.67
Correlation (b_1,b_2)	−0.066				

Figure 17.8.6. Scatter diagram and distribution of test statistics for b_1 and b_2 (X's uncorrelated) when both slope parameters equal one.
Source: [CorrelatedEstimates.xls]MonteCarlo.

Section 15.2 showed that the intuitive version of the formula for the SE of a slope coefficient, b_k, in a regression with multiple X variables is

$$SE(b_k) = \frac{SD(\varepsilon)}{\sqrt{n} \cdot SD(X_k) \cdot \sqrt{1 - R_k^2}}.$$

R_k^2 is the R^2 from a regression of X_k on the other X variables. In the special case of two X variables, the square root of R_k^2 is simply the correlation coefficient between X_1 and X_2, $r(X_1, X_2)$. Go to cell A20 in the *Setup* sheet to see a demonstration that the square root of R^2 from the bivariate regression of X_2 on X_1 is exactly equal to $r(X_1, X_2)$. By substituting $r(X_1, X_2)$ for R_k^2, we get the formulas for the SEs of the two estimated slope coefficients in the case of the regression of Y on X_1 and X_2:

$$SE(b_1) = \frac{SD(\varepsilon)}{\sqrt{n} \cdot SD(X_1) \sqrt{1 - r(X_1, X_2)^2}}$$

$$SE(b_2) = \frac{SD(\varepsilon)}{\sqrt{n} \cdot SD(X_2) \sqrt{1 - r(X_1, X_2)^2}}.$$

Notice that the larger r is in absolute value, the greater the SE of the slope estimate.[8] With $r(X_1, X_2) = 0.99$, the SE increases by a factor of 7 (the inverse of the square root of the quantity 1 minus 0.99 squared) compared to the case of no correlation in the X's. The SDs of the estimates in the Monte Carlo simulations in Figures 17.8.4 and 17.8.6 confirm this result (using $r(X_1, X_2) = 0.01$ instead of exactly zero).

The Joint Confidence Region

The scatter charts of (b_1, b_2) pairs in Figures 17.8.5 and 17.8.6 suggest that the sample estimates will be scattered around the true parameter values in particular patterns that depend on the correlation between the X's. In general the sample estimates will lie in an ellipse centered on the true parameter values. This is the footprint of the sampling distribution. The shape of the ellipse depends on the correlation between the X's and on their SDs. The shape is close to a circle when the X's have the same SD and when the correlation between the X's is close to zero. The footprint becomes a tilted, elongated ellipse as the correlation between the X's increases in absolute value.

Using statistical theory, one can draw ellipses that will in the long run contain a certain percentage of all sample outcomes. To see such an ellipse, set the values of the true slope parameters to zero in the *Setup* sheet and set the correlation between the X's to −0.5. Go to the *MonteCarlo* sheet and run a Monte Carlo experiment. Click on the Show Ellipse toggle button and you will see a graph like that of Figure 17.8.7. The ellipse encloses approximately 95 percent of the 400 points in the scatter diagram.[9]

---

[8] Here are a few notes about how we constructed the example. In the workbook we set up the two X variables so that they have the same SD. This guarantees that both the estimated and exact SEs will be equal for b_1 and b_2; that of course would generally not be the case in a real example. Also, given the way we have set up the workbook, the exact long-run correlation between the slope estimates is equal to −1 multiplied by the correlation between the X's. In general, although this exact correspondence will not occur, it is the case that the degree of correlation between the X's will negatively affect the correlation between the slope estimates.

[9] This button always draws an ellipse based on a true null hypothesis of zero slope values. Thus, the "center" of this ellipse is always the point (0,0).

b₂

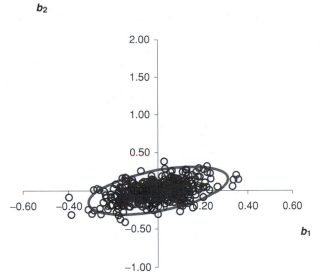

Figure 17.8.7. Scatter diagram of Monte Carlo results for b_1 and b_2 with 95-percent ellipse (Correlation between X's $= -0.5$; true slope parameters both zero). *Source:* [CorrelatedEstimates.xls]MonteCarlo.

Now suppose that we obtain sample estimates but do not know the true parameter values. What is the 95-percent joint confidence region for our estimates? Recall that confidence intervals in the individual-parameter case are centered on the parameter estimate. On the basis of confidence interval, logic the 95-percent joint confidence region is just the 95-percent ellipse centered around our parameter estimates rather than around the true (unknown) parameter values. To see such a confidence region, scroll over to cells Q2 through U14 in the MonteCarlo sheet.

Figure 17.8.8 displays an example. We centered the 95-percent confidence ellipse around the sample estimates from the first repetition in the Monte Carlo experiment. In this case, the (true) null hypothesis that both slope parameters are zero is covered: the point (0,0) lies within the 95-percent confidence region. Suppose, however, that the joint null hypothesis was that the true parameter values were $\beta_1 = 0.6$, $\beta_2 = 0$, respectively. In that case, the confidence region built on our sample estimates would not cover that point and we would reject the joint null hypothesis. The exact shape and size of the confidence ellipse depends on the correlation between the X's and on the size of the RMSE.[10]

It is rather difficult to construct confidence regions without specialized software. Nonetheless, it is important you realize that the joint confidence region

---

[10] For computational convenience we cheated just a bit by using the true spread of the error terms in constructing the confidence region.

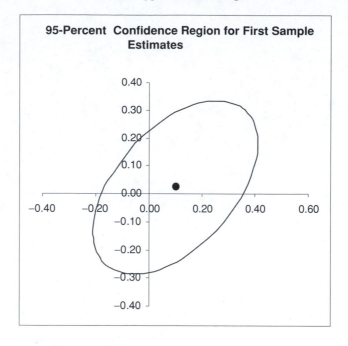

| Coefficient Estimates | |
Estimated b_1	Estimated b_2
0.10	0.02

Figure 17.8.8. 95-percent confidence region for estimates from first repetition in Monte Carlo simulation (Correlation between X's $= -0.5$).
Source: [CorrelatedEstimates.xls]MonteCarlo.

is not a rectangle built on the individual coefficient confidence intervals; rather it is an ellipse whose shape reflects the correlation between the X's.

Summary

We can draw the following lessons from this discussion:

- Joint null hypotheses are different from single, separate null hypotheses.
- Slope estimates are correlated random variables for which the correlation depends on the correlation of the X's.
- A strong correlation between the X variables makes it hard to figure out which independent variable is causing the dependent variable to vary – sometimes the best we can do is to talk about the joint range that parameters could fall in.
- The greater the (multi-)collinearity between included X's, the higher the SEs of the individual coefficients.

- Joint confidence regions are the multivariate analogue to univariate confidence intervals.

17.9. Conclusion

In Chapter 6 on functional form of the regression and Chapter 8 on dummy variables, we emphasized the flexibility of regression analysis. This chapter has extended the idea of flexibility of regression to hypothesis testing. Before reading this chapter, you were aware that an SE of the sample slope can be used to test a claim about the true parameter value of the slope, but that is really just the tip of the iceberg. In this chapter we have reviewed just a few of the many restrictions that can be imposed and tested via linear regression.

Although each particular application is different, the fundamental procedure stays constant. In the case of imposing restrictions in a regression model, the basic idea is to compare the (properly adjusted) SSR from restricted and unrestricted regressions. Because imposing a restriction is practically guaranteed to increase the SSR, we need a decision rule to determine if the gain in SSR is high enough to convince us to reject the restricted model. We use the usual hypothesis-testing logic to compute the P-value (from the F-distribution) and decide on rejecting or not rejecting the null hypothesis.

Strictly speaking, use of the F-statistic requires adding an assumption to the classical econometric model that the errors are normally distributed. If one is working with a small sample, this assumption matters. The P-value from the F-statistic is not to be trusted if errors are nonnormal and the sample is small. When the sample size is large, the normality assumption is not needed and, in general, the F-statistic works well.

This concludes our examination of well-behaved classical econometric models. Beginning with the next chapter on omitted variable bias, we will turn to a variety of complications in the data generation process.

17.10. Exercises

Workbook: MyMonteCarlo.xls

1. The *Dead* sheet in FDistFoodStamps.xls contains data that does not bounce. The data were generated according to the following DGP:

$$\text{Food Purchases} = \beta_0 + \beta_1 \text{ Number of adults in family}$$
$$+ \beta_2 \text{ Number of children in family}$$
$$+ \beta_3 \text{ Cash Income}$$
$$+ \beta_4 \text{ Value of Food Stamps} + \varepsilon.$$

a. Test the following null hypothesis:

$$\text{Null Hypothesis}: \beta_1 = \beta_2.$$
$$\text{Alternative Hypothesis}: \beta_1 \neq \beta_2.$$

Use both the F- and t-statistic procedures and show that they produce equivalent results. The P-value Calculator Add-In may prove helpful.

b. Perform this hypothesis test:

$$\text{Null Hypothesis}: \beta_1 = \beta_2.$$
$$\text{Alternative Hypothesis}: \beta_1 > \beta_2.$$

2. In the food stamps example (FDistFoodStamps.xls), check to see whether the SD of the errors (and therefore the variance of the errors) affects the distribution of the F-statistic. Use 10,000 repetitions. The SD of the errors is controlled by cell B7 of the *Example* sheet.

3. In the *Setup* sheet of the CorrelatedEstimates.xls, set both β_1 and β_2 to 1 and set the SD of the errors equal to 10. Set the correlation of the X's to 0.99. Using the Monte Carlo add-in, run a Monte Carlo experiment that approximates the sampling distribution of the sum $b_1 + b_2$. Take a picture of the results. Change the correlation of the X's to -0.99 and repeat the experiment. Compare the results and give an intuitive explanation for the difference in the sampling distributions.

4. Create your own Monte Carlo study. The workbook MyMonteCarlo.xls contains the functions NormalRandom(), Uniform(), and Expo() in a Visual Basic module. Use this file and these functions to see how well the Whole Model F-Test performs under alternative assumptions about the error terms – that they are normally, uniformly, or exponentially distributed. Use the sample with three X variables (fixed in repeated sampling) that we have helpfully placed in the *Data* sheet. Set the SD of the errors equal to 10. Make the true values of the parameters β_1, β_2, and β_3 all equal to zero so that the null hypothesis of the Whole Model F-test is true. Approximate the distribution of the F-statistics for the three error distributions using the LINEST function to obtain the Whole Model F-statistic and the MCSim Add-in. Compare the three distributions and write up your conclusions.

5. In a hypothetical data set with 400 adults in the New York metropolitan area, 250 own their homes and 150 do not. Of the home owners, 245 own a car. Of the 150 non-home-owners, only 25 own a car. A researcher runs a regression of expenditures on movie entertainment on the dummy variable OwnHome and OwnCar. She finds that at the 5 percent significance level she cannot reject the two individual null hypotheses that the parameters multiplying these coefficients are zero, but that she can decisively reject the null hypothesis that both parameters are jointly equal to zero (P-value $= 0.2\%$). Can you explain why she might have obtained such a result?

References

Our savings example from the introduction is derived from

Carroll, C. D., B.-K. Rhee and C. Rhee (1999). "Does Cultural Origin Affect Saving Behavior? Evidence from Immigrants." *Economic Development and Cultural Change* **48**(1): 33–50.

This paper contains interesting results on food stamps:

Whitmore, D. (2002). "What Are Food Stamps Worth?" *Princeton University Industrial Relations Section Working Papers*. Princeton, New Jersey.

For more on Karl Pearson, with biographical details and an overview of the intellectual history of statistics, we recommend

Walker, H. M. (1958). "The Contributions of Karl Pearson." *Journal of the American Statistical Association* **53**(281): 11–22.

18

Omitted Variable Bias

...if the more educated workers tend to be more intelligent, motivated, or blessed with advantageous family backgrounds, ... then the more educated workers typically would have received higher wages even without their additional schooling. It therefore is difficult to ascertain how much of the empirical association between wages and schooling is due to the causal effect of schooling and how much is due to unobserved factors that influence both wages and schooling.

John Bound and Gary Solon[1]

18.1. Introduction

In this chapter we discuss the consequences of not including an independent variable that actually does belong in the model. We revisit our discussion in Chapter 13 about the role of the error term in the classical econometric model. There we argue that the error term typically accounts for, among other things, the influence of omitted variables on the dependent variable. The term *omitted variable* refers to any variable not included as an independent variable in the regression that might influence the dependent variable. In Chapter 13 we point out that, so long as the omitted variables are uncorrelated with the included independent variables, OLS regression will produce unbiased estimates. In this chapter we focus on the issue of omitted variables and highlight the very real danger that omitted variables are in fact correlated with the included independent variables. When that happens, OLS regression generally produces biased and inconsistent estimates, which accounts for the name omitted variable bias.

The chapter begins, in the next section, by emphasizing the importance of the issue of omitted variable bias and tying the problem directly to the fact that economists generally have data from an observational study rather than a controlled experiment. We then split the work into three parts.

---

[1] Bound and Solon (1999).

First, Section 18.3 uses cooked data from the skiing example to develop an intuitive understanding of omitted variable bias. Next, in Section 18.4 we work with real data. In this case, the true parameter values are unknown. By seeing how parameter estimates change when additional X variables are included in the regression, however, we will be able to detect strong evidence of omitted variable bias. The fixed X's assumption of the classical econometric model is hard to reconcile with a view of omitted X's that vary from one sample to the next. Therefore, in Section 18.5 we consider a new data generation process, the random X's model, which does away with the assumption of fixed X's in favor of random X's. This new DGP is used to investigate omitted variable bias in samples of varying sizes from a given population. We show that the bias stays constant as the sample size increases.

18.2. Why Omitted Variable Bias Is Important

Omitted variable bias is a crucial topic because almost every study in econometrics is an observational study as opposed to a controlled experiment. Very often, economists would like to be able to interpret the comparisons they make as if they were the outcomes of controlled experiments. In a properly conducted controlled experiment, the only systematic difference between groups results from the treatment under investigation; all other variations stem from chance. In an observational study, because the participants self-select into groups, it is always possible that varying average outcomes between groups result from systematic differences between groups other than the treatment. We can attempt to control for those systematic differences by explicitly incorporating variables in a regression. Unfortunately, if not all of those differences have been controlled for in the analysis, we are vulnerable to the devastating effects of omitted variable bias.

The epigraph to this chapter highlights one major area in which omitted variable bias has been very commonly suspected to play a role: the returns to schooling. (Here the "treatment" is how many years of schooling a person gets.) The suspicion is that people with more education may differ from people with less education in many ways that are difficult to measure. For example, one's wage may depend on factors such as motivation or parental upbringing that cannot easily be quantified, or factors like intelligence, which are usually not reported in surveys used by economists. We see that more education is correlated with higher wages but do not know whether to attribute the higher wages to education or to the omitted variables that cannot be included in our regression analysis.

Another example of omitted variable bias is the issue of discrimination in home mortgages, which will be discussed in Chapter 22. In that case we are interested in an important question: Are blacks discriminated against in mortgage applications? This question cannot be answered via a simple comparison in an observational study of loan denial rates. It is, in fact, true that blacks are denied loans more often than whites, but this raw, unadjusted comparison of loan denial rates is inadequate to answer the question. The problem is that discrimination occurs when otherwise similar applicants are treated differently solely on the basis of a personal characteristic like race. In the raw comparison, however, we are not taking into account the fact that there may be systematic differences between black and white applicants that might be the cause of the different outcomes. The simple comparison omits these factors (income, other debts, etc.) from the analysis. As a measure of discrimination, the raw difference is almost certainly biased owing to this omission.

One way to overcome the problem of omitted variable bias in observational studies is to conduct controlled experiments. Researchers have in fact conducted experiments that attempt to determine whether there is racial discrimination in home mortgages. The traditional remedy to the omitted variable bias problem in an observational study, however, is to include other variables in the model in an attempt to control statistically for systematic differences other than race between black and white applicants.

Note, however, that although the analysis can be improved, we can never really slay the omitted variable dragon in the context of an observational study. Every additional control may improve our study, but we are never immune to the charge that yet another subtle, hidden variable has not been accounted for. This is a frustrating reality when working with data from observational studies.

Summary

Another name for omitted variable bias is confounding. The bottom line is that we want to measure the effect that an X variable has on the dependent variable correctly – that is, accurately and precisely for the given question. If variables that matter are omitted or ignored, we will mistakenly attribute too much or too little to the included X variable. We often worry that the relationship between the Y and X variables is confounded by other variables our analysis has not taken into account.

The next section uses a previously presented hypothetical example to explain the conditions under which omitted variable bias affects regression analysis. It also makes clear the devastating effects of omitted variable bias.

18.3. Omitted Variable Bias Defined and Demonstrated

Workbook: SkiingOVB.xls

Chapter 13 introduced the classical econometric model. Here are the essential requirements:

$$Y_i = \beta_0 + \beta_1 X_{1i} + \beta_1 X_{2i} + \dots \beta_1 X_{Ki} + \varepsilon_i.$$

$$E(\varepsilon_i) = 0, i = 1, \dots, n.$$

$$SD(\varepsilon_i) = \sigma, i = 1, \dots, n.$$

ε_i is distributed independently of ε_j, for all $i \neq j$.

The errors are independent of the X's.

The X's are fixed in repeated sampling.

The X's, including the intercept term,

cannot have an exact linear relationship.

These statements describe a model that is linear in the parameters, with an additive error term. The three conditions on the error term, ε_i, ensure that it is well-behaved, meaning that the distribution of each individual error term is centered on zero with the same spread (also known as homoskedasticity) and one error draw has no effect on another error draw (i.e., there is no auto-correlation). The next requirement is examined in detail in this section, which focuses on the implications of violating the condition that the errors be independent of the X's. The final requirement rules out perfect multicollinearity, thereby ensuring that there is a unique OLS solution.

As we will see, the requirement that the X's are fixed in repeated sampling is decidedly unrealistic when we are considering the impact of the omitted X variables, whose values we think will change from one sample to the next. However, almost all of the results we have presented are also true if one makes the more realistic assumption that the data (X's and Y's) are a random sample from a population which is generated according to the equation given above. (See Sections 18.5 and 19.7 and associated Excel files where we discuss and demonstrate an alternative, more realistic DGP called the Random X's Model.)

Chapter 14 demonstrates that, if the requirements of the classical econometric model are met, the OLS estimator of the sample slope is BLUE – the Best Linear Unbiased Estimator. This means that the sampling distribution of b_1^{OLS}, the OLS estimator of the first slope parameter, has two desirable properties. First, the OLS estimator is unbiased (i.e., the expected value of b_1^{OLS} is β_1). Second, the spread of the OLS probability histogram (or sampling distribution) for b_1^{OLS} is less than the spread of any other linear, unbiased estimator of β_1.

Notice how the evaluation of an estimator focuses on the center and spread of its sampling distribution. To be centered off the true parameter value is

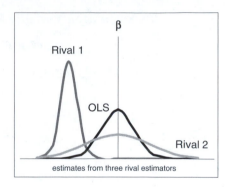

Figure 18.3.1. OLS beats rivals.

called bias; this means the estimator is inaccurate. Rival 1 in Figure 18.3.1 is biased. The estimates it produces are systematically, on average, wrong. The spread of the estimator speaks to its precision. The smaller the SE, the better the estimator because it is more precise. Rival 2 is unbiased, but OLS is also unbiased and more precise; thus, we prefer OLS.

Unfortunately, we cannot simply obtain unbiased estimates automatically with maximum precision. The best linear unbiased property of the OLS estimator depends on the chance process that generated the data. If any of the conditions of the box model are not satisfied, the OLS results are less than ideal. A violation of the requirements can affect the OLS estimator by changing the center, the spread of its sampling distribution, or both.

If the violation changes the center so that the expected value of the sampling distribution is no longer equal to the true parameter value, this is called bias. There are different kinds of bias, and we use a descriptive word or phrase to indicate the cause of the bias. In the case of omitting a relevant X variable that is correlated with an included X variable, the bias is caused by the omitted variable; hence, the name omitted variable bias is used.[2]

Omitted variable bias results from violating the requirement that the draws from the Error Box are independent of the X's. If this assumption does not hold, then the OLS estimates are quite possibly biased. This means that the sampling distribution of the OLS estimates is not centered on the true parameter value. Our estimates are on average wrong.

A Fictional Example

A fictional, concrete example will help you master this difficult concept. Let us return to the Picabo Street skiing example of Chapter 13 to see what omitting a relevant variable means and what effect this has on the regression results. Open the SkiingOVB.xls workbook in this chapter's Excel Files folder. This

---

[2] Chapter 24 discusses simultaneity bias. In future work in econometrics you may see terms such as self-selection bias or specification bias. In each case, the idea is that something has shifted the sampling distribution of the estimator so that it is no longer centered on the true parameter value.

file is very similar to the Skiing.xls workbook of Chapter 13. (You may want to look over Sections 13.2 and 13.3 quickly to refresh your memory.)

Go to the *EstimatingBeta1* sheet and click the Race button a few times. Cell I3 reports the OLS estimate of β_1 (which is equal to -0.5 in cell B3) from a regression that omits Talent as an explanatory variable. There should be clear evidence that b_1 (in cell I3) is bouncing around -0.5. This means that, even though Talent is omitted, the OLS estimator of the slope on Training is unbiased. In other words, there is no omitted variable bias here even though we have an omitted variable! How can this be?

The answer lies in cell B6, which sets the correlation between Talent and Training. Because this correlation is set at zero, the omitted variable is functioning simply as another source of random error in the DGP. Remember that the errors in the classical econometric model have three sources:

1. Omitted variables independent of the included X's,
2. measurement error, and
3. inherent randomness.

As long as cell B6 is set at zero, the omitted variable will not bias the estimate of the Training slope coefficient. Talent is simply part of the well-behaved error box. What happens if Talent and Training are correlated? To answer this question, click the Exploring Omitted Variable Bias button.

You are now in the same workbook, but we have hidden the *Estimating-Beta1* sheet and replaced it with a new sheet, *TrueModel*. The *TrueModel* sheet is basically the same as the *EstimatingBeta1* sheet, except it has an extra button, Redraw Talent (with Exact Rho) and displays different information. To follow this discussion, make sure that the value of the correlation between Training and Talent is set to zero in cell B6, and for good measure hit the Redraw Talent (with Exact Rho) button. Also, check that the true parameter values for the two slope coefficients for Training and Talent are -0.5 and -0.2, respectively (in cells B3 and B4).

Figure 18.3.2 displays the results of two regressions (you will see slightly different numbers because you will have a different sample) for which we have set the value of the correlation between Talent and Training to be exactly 0

Predicted Time = $g_0 + g_1$ Training			
	g_1	g_0	
	−0.551	79.337	
est. SE	0.085	0.457	est. SE
R^2	0.645	1.230	RMSE
F	41.834	23	df
Total SS	63.323	34.815	SSR

Predicted Time = $b_0 + b_1$ Training + b_2 Talent			
	b_2	b_1	b_0
	−0.185	**−0.551**	80.079
est. SE	0.014	0.029	0.165	est. SE
R^2	0.961	0.418		RMSE
F	269.182	22		df
Total SS	94.285	3.853		SSR

Figure 18.3.2. Short and long regressions in *TrueModel* sheet; Talent uncorrelated with Training.
Source: [Skiing.xls]TrueModel.

(not on average zero across samples but exactly zero in this sample). The first (the *short regression*) regresses Time on Training only. The model is

$$\text{Short Regression: } Time_i = \gamma_0 + \gamma_1 \cdot Training_i + \varepsilon_i, \quad i = 1, \ldots, n.$$

This is the regression that the Austrian Ski Federation analysts actually run. The second (*long regression*) regresses Time on Training and Talent. The model is

$$\text{Long Regression: } Time_i = \beta_0 + \beta_1 \cdot Training_i$$
$$+ \beta_2 \cdot Talent_i + v_i, \quad i = 1, \ldots, n.$$

This is the regression that the Austrians would like to run but cannot because they have no way of measuring Talent objectively. The Austrians, like most econometricians, must settle with estimating a regression that has at least one important omitted variable.

When Training and Talent are uncorrelated, however, the fact that the Austrians are stuck with the short regression does not hurt them. Hit F9 a few times and notice how the slope coefficients on Training are exactly the same in both regressions (we have emphasized these coefficients in the display).[3] That is because, as currently constructed, the DGP follows the requirements of the CEM. There is a relevant variable, Talent, omitted from the short regression, but Talent is completely uncorrelated with Training and thus does not affect the OLS estimator of the slope.[4] We could run a Monte Carlo to demonstrate this, but it seems clear from resampling a few times that all is well.

Now, change cell B6 to 0.9 and click the $\boxed{\substack{\text{Redraw Talent}\\ \text{(with Exact Rho)}}}$ button. The results, as shown in Figure 18.3.3 and in the various displays on your computer screen, are dramatic. Your numbers will be slightly different, but the change will be equally striking.

Suddenly, the slope on Training is poorly estimated by g_1, the OLS estimator from the short model. Repeated resampling (hitting F9 over and over again) shows that the g_1 estimates in cell H3 are not centered on -0.5, the true parameter value. (Note that, as the sheet is set up, the omitted Talent values do not change when a new sample of error terms is drawn. In these simulations, it is as if we are sending the same skiers down the mountain repeatedly.)

The reason for the bias is clear: When the correlation of Training and Talent is set to 0.9, you have violated the independence-of-omitted-X's-requirement

---

[3] The estimates of the intercept coefficient differ because we have made the mean of Talent nonzero. See Section 13.3 to recall that a nonzero value of the omitted variable affects the expected value of the intercept term but not the slope.

[4] More generally, if Talent is on average uncorrelated with Training (rather than being exactly uncorrelated as in this example), the short- and long-slope estimates for Training will differ in individual samples, but their expected values will be the same.

Predicted Time = $g_0 + g_1$Training			
	g_1	g_0	
	−0.928	81.093	
est. SE	0.058	0.309	est. SEe
R_2	0.919	0.830	RMSE
F	259.971	23	df
Total SS	179.274	15.861	SSRT

Predicted Time = $b_0 + b_1$Training + b_2Talent			
	b_2	b_1	b_0
	−0.219	**−0.518**	80.117
st. SE	0.045	0.094	0.298e
R^2	0.961	0.590	
F	69.220	22	
Total SS1	87.474	7.660	

			st. SE
			RMSE
			df
			SSR

Figure 18.3.3. Omitted-variable bias demonstrated.
Source: [Skiing.xls]TrueModel.

of the classical econometric model. This has directly caused the poor performance in the OLS estimator.

What is the story behind the nonzero correlation? Suppose that instead of randomly assigning Training to 25 skiers (a point we stressed in Chapter 13), the Austrian Ski Federation merely allowed 25 skiers to train whatever time they wanted to train. The Federation analysts would merely watch and record Training time and then observed ski times in a race. This is the quintessential observational study. It is also a big problem for the short regression if Talent and Training are not independent.

For example, it could be that more talented skiers tend to train considerably more than less talented skiers. This would lead to a high positive correlation between Training and Talent. In the short regression, what would happen is that Training would get too much credit because it is strongly, positively correlated with Talent. In this version of events, highly trained skiers do well because they trained more and are more talented. The short regression sees and accounts for only the variation in Training, not the variation in Talent.

By setting the correlation between Training and Talent to 0.9, we have enforced this idea that better skiers train more with a vengeance. When the omitted variable effect is so pronounced, it is easy to see by resampling a few times on the sheet that the short regression slope coefficient on Training is biased.

Summary

We close this section with some additional notes about omitted variable bias. First, omitted variable bias is not a problem even when the omitted variable is correlated with the included variable in the special case that the true value of the slope of the dependent variable on the omitted variable (β_2) is zero. This of course means that the omitted variable does not belong in the regression. The reason the bias disappears is that bias depends on the true value of the parameter multiplying the omitted variable. When that parameter is zero, the expected value of the OLS slope on the included variable is unaffected by inclusion or exclusion of the omitted variable. Second, although we have stressed that bias shows up when the omitted variable is correlated with the included variable, it should be emphasized that the size of the bias depends not on that correlation directly but rather on the slope of the auxiliary regression of the omitted variable on the included variable (see the next section for more discussion of this point).

Finally, we have described the short regression slope coefficient as a biased estimator of the effect of Talent on Time. We need, however, to be very careful with our language and logic. The short and long regressions address two different questions. The short regression answers the question, How much faster will skiers go who have trained 1 hour more per day? The long regression answers the question, How much faster will a given skier go if we increase his or her training by an hour a day? The first question does not presume that skiers who have trained 1 more hour are otherwise identical to skiers who have not. The second question does presume that the skiers who have trained more are otherwise the same as those who have not.

As determined by the circumstances, we may wish to answer one or the other of these questions. If the objective is to predict skiing performance based on your knowledge of how much someone has trained, you would want the answer to the first question. The Austrian Ski Federation wants to know how training affects skiing performance, and thus it wants an answer to the second question.

We next turn to a real example of omitted variable bias, in which once again we need to pay careful attention to the question being asked.

18.4. A Real Example of Omitted Variable Bias

Workbook: ComputerUse1997.xls

In this section we explore omitted variable bias using an actual data set. The inspiration for this example is a 1993 paper by Alan Krueger that asks whether people who use computers at work earn higher wages than otherwise similar workers who do not use computers.[5] Krueger performs numerous analyses in the paper. We will replicate just one small portion of his work, using more recent data than Krueger had at his disposal.

Krueger writes that his paper "focuses on the issue of whether employees who use computers at work earn more as a result of applying their computer skills" (p. 34). The simplest way to address this issue is to make a direct comparison of the wages of those who do and do not use computers at work.

---

[5] Krueger (1993).

Summary Statistics				
	All Workers		Computer	Noncomputer
Variable	Average	SD	Average	Average
ln Hourly Wage	2.41	0.56	2.60	2.21
Comp At Work	0.51	0.50	1	0
Education	13.31	2.56	14.29	12.29
Comp At Home	0.35	0.48	0.49	0.21
White	0.85	0.35	0.88	0.83
Male	0.51	0.50	0.46	0.57
Age	38.47	12.49	39.03	37.89

Figure 18.4.1. Summary statistics for computer use data set.
Source: [ComputerUse1997.xls]Data.

Computer-using workers and other workers, however, may differ systematically in other ways, and it may be those other characteristics that explain why computer-using workers earn more than others. Therefore, Krueger attempts to control for other factors besides computer use that may influence wages.

The Current Population Survey has a special supplement asking people about their use of computers (and in more recent years, Internet use). Krueger used the October 1984 and October 1989 CPS supplements. We employ the October 1997 supplement. Two of Krueger's models look like this:

Short Regression:

$$\ln Wage_i = \gamma_0 + \gamma_1 CompAtWork_i + \varepsilon_i.$$

Long Regression:

$$\ln Wage_i = \beta_0 + \beta_1 CompAtWork_i + \beta_2 Education_i + \nu_i.$$

The dependent variable, $\ln Wage_i$, is the natural logarithm of individual i's hourly wage. The variable $CompAtWork_i$ is a dummy variable equal to 1 if individual i uses a computer at work, and this variable is 0 if he or she does not. The variable $Education_i$ measures years of schooling completed. The error term in the short regression, ε_i, comprises both the error term in the long regression, ν_i, and the impact of Education, $\beta_2 Education_i$. In the actual paper, Krueger's long regression included a host of other control variables such as sex, race, marital status, and potential labor force experience. To keep things simple, we will focus only on Education as a variable omitted from the short regression.

The file ComputerUse1997.xls contains 12,699 observations on adult workers. The data are presented in the *Data* sheet.[6] Summary statistics for the data set are in Figure 18.4.1. We present the average and SD of several variables for

---

[6] Raw data with recoding formulas are in the *RawData* sheet. See the *Notes* sheet for information on the data set.

Table 18.4.1. *Results from Regression Analyses of ln Wages*

OLS Regression Estimates of the Effect of Computer Use on ln Wages

Independent Variable	Short Regression	Long Regression
Intercept	2.207	1.138
	(0.007)	(0.023)
CompAtWork	0.393	0.219
	(0.009)	(0.009)
Education	–	0.087
		(0.002)

Source: [ComputerUse1997.xls]Data. Estimated SEs are in parentheses.

all workers and the averages within the two categories of computer users and nonusers. The summary statistics reveal some large differences between the two categories of workers: Computer users at work on average earn higher hourly wages, are better educated, and are much more likely to own a computer at home. They are also more likely to be white and female and are on average a little older than nonusers.

We ran both the short and long regression using these data and obtained the results shown in Table 18.4.1. This table provides strong evidence that omitted variable bias may contaminate the results of the short regression. The estimate for the dummy variable *CompAtWork* in the short regression says that people who use a computer at work have a log of hourly wage 0.393 higher than people who do not use a computer at work. In terms of hourly wage this translates into a huge 48 percent premium for workers who use computers at work versus those who do not. The long regression, in which we control for years of education, tells a different story. Now the log differential is only 0.219, which translates into a 25 percent premium for computer-using workers.

Here is the explanation for the difference between the two regressions: People who used computers at work in 1997 were on the average better educated than those who did not; as Figure 18.4.1 shows, computer users had on average 2.0 years more education than nonusers. The long regression attributes part of the higher wages of computer users to their higher education and part to their use of computers. The short regression attributes the entire wage gap to the use of computers. The precise difference between the short-regression and long-regression estimated coefficients can be explained by the omitted variable rule discussed in Section 7.7.

The auxiliary regression of *Education* on *CompAtWork* gives an intercept of 12.3 and a slope of 2.0 (see the cell range L17:M20 in the *Data* sheet). This regression simply verifies what we already saw in Figure 18.4.1: Workers who use a computer at work on average have 2.0 more years of education than nonusers. The average education level of nonusers, 12.3 years, is the same as the intercept in the auxiliary regression.

The omitted variable rule says that the slope in the short regression of ln *Wages* on *CompAtWork* is equal to

1. The corresponding slope in the long regression, plus
2. The product of the auxiliary regression slope of *Education* on *CompAtWork* and the slope of *Ln Wage* on *Education* in the long regression.

Denote the short-regression slope as g_1 and the long-regression slopes as b_1 (for *CompAtWork*) and b_2 (for *Education*). Denote the auxiliary regression slope of *Education* on *CompAtWork* by d_1. Then, in equation form,

$$g_1 = b_1 + d_1 \cdot b_2$$
$$= 0.219 + 2.0 \cdot 0.087$$
$$= 0.393.$$

Let us try to say this in English. In the long regression each additional year of *Education* increases the *Ln Wage* by 0.087. We know that computer users have 2 more years of *Education* than nonusers. Thus, the *Ln Wage* advantage for computer users due to *Education* is $2.0 \cdot 0.087 = 0.174$. This means that in the short regression in which we leave out *Education*, the effect of computer use on ln *Wage* is 0.174 higher than it is in the long regression.

Our results are comparable to Krueger's. In his analyses of the October 1984 and 1989 supplements, Krueger found log wage gaps of 0.276 and 0.325, respectively, between those who used a computer at work and those who did not. In a long regression with several control variables, including *Education*, potential labor force experience, urban location, union membership, marital status, urban residence, and race, Krueger found that the wage gap fell to 0.170 and 0.188 in 1984 and 1989, respectively. We used only one control variable to keep our example simple, whereas Krueger wanted to hunt down as many potential sources of omitted variable bias as he could.

Summary

This section presented a real example of omitted variable bias. The measured computer-use wage premium is about 18 percent greater in the simple raw comparison than it is when education is included as a control variable. The difference arises from the positive association between computer use, the included variable, and education, the omitted variable. The omitted variable rule gives an exact formula for the difference, but the magnitude of the bias in this case can be easily appreciated as the result of the two-year advantage in schooling that computer users have over nonusers. In the long regression each year of schooling is associated with about 9 percent higher wages; a two-year advantage translates into an 18 percent wage premium, and this is the size of the omitted variable bias.

Krueger's argument that the computer-use wage premium exists because workers able to use computers are more valuable to their employers is controversial. This claim is itself subject to the criticism that important variables have been omitted from the analysis. Critics of Krueger's paper point out that people who use pencils on the job also earn substantially higher wages than those who do not with factors like education controlled. One way of interpreting the critics' findings is to say that there are other, unmeasured skills that are positively correlated with both computer (or pencil) use and the value of a worker to his or her employer. Because these skills are not measured in surveys used by econometricians, they are omitted from the wage regression. As a result, higher wages are attributed to on-the-job computer use rather than the variables that are really causing higher wages – these unmeasured skills.[7]

18.5. Random *X*'s: A More Realistic Data Generation Process

Workbook: ComputerUse1997.xls

In this section we introduce and demonstrate a more realistic model of the data generating process than the classical econometric model. We call it the random *X*'s model. To illustrate this model, we pretend that the very large sample in the ComputerUse1997.xls data set is a "population." In this demonstration of the new DGP, each observation is like a draw at random from a box containing the entire population of 12,699 tickets. Each ticket holds information on three variables for a single individual: *Ln Wage*, *CompAtWork*, and *Education*. Unlike the classical econometric model, we are not working with *X*'s which are unchanged from one sample to the next.

This DGP bears a strong resemblance to the polling box model described in Section 10.4. The two differences between the random *X*'s model and the polling model are, first, that each ticket contains values for more than one variable describing an individual, and second, that we posit a linear functional relationship (called the *population regression function*) between the dependent and independent variables. What about the error term? Although we could avoid any mention of an error term in this model, the notion of an error term is a very convenient way to talk about the joint distribution of the independent and dependent variables. Thus, for our purposes, in this model the error term is, as before, the difference

---

[7] See DiNardo and Pischke (1997), who carefully discuss possible interpretations of the evidence.

between a population regression function of the independent variables (e.g., $\beta_0 + \beta_1 CompAtWork_i + \beta_1 Education_i$) and the observed value of the dependent variable (e.g., $LnWage_i$). We assume that the average value of the error terms is zero for every combination of X variables in the data set.[8] We also assume that the spread of the error terms is constant across all combinations of X variables in the data.

In our example, the true values of the parameters are those given in the Long Regression box of the Data sheet of ComputerUse1997.xls. Thus, the errors can be computed as follows:

$$Error_i = LnWage_i - (1.138 + 0.219 \cdot CompAtWork_i + 0.087 \cdot Education_i),$$
$$i = 1, \ldots, 12{,}699.$$

The reason we introduce this DGP now is it that makes little sense to pretend that included X's are fixed in random sampling when the omitted X's are varying from one sample to the next. Furthermore, many data sets can be well described by this model. For example, in the Current Population Survey, we can think of the individuals in the sample as random draws from the larger population of all people in the United States. Imagine a box containing one ticket for each person in the United States. On each ticket is written the person's age, sex, race, and a whole host of other values of variables measured by the survey. The CPS consists of about 160,000 random draws from this box each month.[9] The X's we include in regressions using the CPS are clearly not fixed but random.

Note that the assumptions just made are not quite satisfied in our example. The average value of the error terms is not exactly zero for every combination of values of the two X variables, nor is the SD of the error terms constant across X-variable combinations. These violations of the random X's model assumptions, however, are slight enough not to make a noticeable difference in this example.

A key assumption is that the tickets are drawn at random from the box containing the population. A more formal way of putting this is to say that the (X, Y) observations in the sample are independent and identically distributed. We can easily implement this assumption on an Excel sheet. Go to the *SampleCompAtWork* sheet. This sheet displays a random sample of size 100 from the "population" in the *Data* sheet. Figure 18.5.1 is a representative example. Using the auxiliary regression, the Formula box (cell G19)

---

[8] By combination we mean {Education = 12, CompAtWork = 1}, {Education = 12, CompAtWork = 0}, and so on. You might think of these combinations as defining cells in a two-dimensional PivotTable.

[9] In actual fact the sampling scheme of the Current Population Survey is much more complicated than just drawing at random from a box. See CPS.doc in the Basic Tools\InternetData\CPS folder for more information.

Long Regression			Auxiliary Regression	
Education	CompAtWork	Intercept	CompAtWork	Intercept
0.127	**0.051**	0.742	2.561	12.356
0.023	0.110	0.290		
0.328	0.464	#N/A		
23.70	97	#N/A		
10.19	20.85	#N/A		

Auxiliary Regression of Education on CompAtWork

Short Regression	
CompAtWork	Intercept
0.377	2.314
0.106	0.073
0.114	0.530
12.626	98.00
3.542	27.492

Difference	Formula
0.326	0.326

0.326 = 2.561 x 0.051

Sample	Avg	SD
ln Wage	2.50	0.56
CompAtWork	0.48	0.50
Education	13.59	2.41

Figure 18.5.1. Long and short regressions for CompAtWork in a 100-observation sample.
Source: [ComputerUse1997]SampleCompAtWork.

applies the omitted variable rule to compute the difference in coefficient estimates for the sample slope of ln *Wage* on *CompAtWork* in the short and long regressions. The Difference box (cell F19) verifies the accuracy of the omitted variable rule. The *SampleEducation* sheet performs exactly the same analysis when the focus is on the sample slope of ln *Wage* on *Education*. Notice that you can choose to draw the samples with or without replacement. Almost all surveys of individuals use samples drawn without replacement.

We can apply the random X's model to study how the expected value of the omitted variable bias varies as we change the sample size. You can use the *MCSim* sheet to draw repeated samples of any size between 4 and 2,000 observations. Figure 18.5.2 shows the Monte Carlo approximation to the sampling distributions for the short and long regressions in which we focus on the slope coefficient for *CompAtWork*. The average estimates for the two regressions are very close to the corresponding parameters of the population regression functions reported in Section 18.4 and on the *Data* sheet. In this experiment, the expected value of the bias is approximated as 0.177 (the difference between the long regression and short regression average slopes), in the population, the bias is 0.174. We leave it as an exercise for you to verify that the expected value of the bias appears to remain constant as the sample

Short Regression		Long Regression		Repetitions	Sample size
Average estimate	0.393	Average estimate	0.216	100,000	10
SD estimates	0.354	SD estimates	0.394		

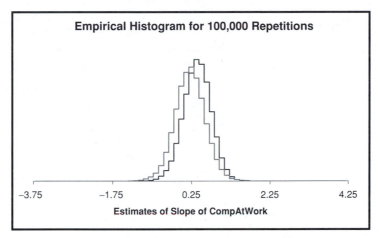

Figure 18.5.2. Monte Carlo simulation results comparing short-regression to long-regression estimates of slope of ln wage on CompAtWork.
Source: [ComputerUse1997.xls]MCSim.

size increases. The lesson is clear: When relevant variables correlated with included variables are omitted from a regression, the resulting estimates will be biased. This bias does not go away as the sample size increases.

The primary focus of the *MCSim* sheet is to investigate bias in samples of different size when relevant variables are omitted. This sheet, however, can also be used to demonstrate that OLS behaves the same way under the random X's model as it does when the classical econometric model correctly describes the data generation process. In both models, OLS is unbiased (when the long regression is studied) and the distribution of the sample slope approaches the normal curve as the sample size increases. Consequently, statistical inference with the random X's model proceeds almost exactly as discussed for the CEM in Chapters 15 through 17.

Summary

This section introduced a new, more realistic model of the data generation process in which the X's (the independent variables) are themselves changing from sample to sample. Throughout this book we have maintained the fixed-X's-in-repeated-sampling assumption of the classical econometric model for reasons of convenience. The model is easier to describe and the algebra of expectations needed to prove the unbiasedness of the OLS estimator and to compute its exact SE is considerably simplified with the fixed-X's assumption. Fortunately, almost all results we obtained with the fixed-X's assumption carry over to the random X's model of the data generation process.

18.6. Conclusion

Omitted variables are a part of the general background noise that forms the classical econometric error box. Along with measurement error and inherent randomness in the world, they are an assumed part of inferential regression analysis. Why, then, do we *sometimes* worry about omitted variables?

This chapter has focused on a special kind of omitted variable – not only is it not included in the model, but it belongs there and is correlated with the included X variables. This is devastating to the regression because the estimated coefficients are no longer centered on their true parameter values. In fact, omitted variable bias is another name for a common term in statistics: confounding. It is difficult to spot, and all observational studies have it potentially lurking in the background. Omitted variable bias is a big problem for anyone wanting to estimate a parameter with observational data accurately.

The basic lesson about confounding in this chapter is also presented in Chapter 7, which introduces multiple regression. As noted in Chapter 7, the primary motivation for multiple regression is to avoid confounding. The difference between Chapter 7 and this chapter is that we now have ways to talk about the data generating process and can make statements about the expected value of the OLS estimates.

In this chapter we have introduced a new model for the data generation process: the random X's model. Fortunately, the claims made about the classical econometric model (the Gauss–Markov theorem and hypothesis testing) also hold true in the random X's model. The next chapter makes use of the random X's model in another application with real data. Chapter 21 presents other models for the data generation process that also dispense with the requirement that X's be fixed in repeated samples.

18.7. Exercises

1. Explain why it is important to include control variables like *Age* and *Education* in the model of savings behavior discussed in Section 17.1.
2. Use the *MCSim* sheet in the ComputerUse1997.xls data set to demonstrate that the bias of the short regression does not change as the sample size increases. Do this for both the sample slope of ln *Wage* on *Education* and for the sample slope on ln *Wage* on *CompAtWork*.
3. Suppose you obtain a data set that includes a measure of IQ in addition to standard data on wages and education. You run a short regression of wages on education and then a long regression of wages on both education and IQ. How do you think

the slope of wage on education will differ between the two regressions? Explain your reasoning.

4. Set the correlation between *Training* and *Talent* (cell B6) in the *TrueModel* sheet of SkiingOVB.xls equal to 0.9 but make the value of β_2 equal to 0. Hit F9 a few times. You should find that the two slope coefficients in cells I3 and O3 are not equal. However, as stated in Section 18.3, omitted-variable bias is no longer present.

   a. Verify that this is true in our example by running a Monte Carlo simulation to approximate the distribution of g_1 (the short regression slope on Training) for this case.

   b. The omitted variable rule says that $g_1 = b_1 + d_1 \cdot b_2$, where g_1 is the short regression slope on the included variable, b_1 is the corresponding long-regression slope, b_2 is the long-regression slope on the omitted variable, and d_1 is the slope of the auxiliary regression of the omitted variable on the included variable. Now in the set-up of SkiingOVB.xls, d_1 is a constant because the X's do not change from one sample to the next (this is not true in the samples we create in ComputerUse1997.xls). The other terms are random variables. Take expected values of both sides of the omitted-variable rule to show that g_1 is unbiased when $\beta_2 = 0$.

5. Consider the case in which *Education* is included but *CompAtWork* is omitted in the short regression explaining the log of wages. Using the information in the *Data* sheet of ComputerUse1997.xls, carefully explain the computation of the difference in coefficient estimates for the sample slope of ln *Wage on Education* in the short and long regressions. Do so with equations, and in English.

References

The epigraph to the chapter is from

Bound J., and G. Solon (1999). "Double Trouble: On the Value of Twins-Based Estimation of the Return to Schooling," *Economics of Education Review* **18**: 169–182.

The noted economist Zvi Griliches (1930–1999) popularized the omitted variable rule and wrote fundamental papers about different types of bias in estimates of the return to education as well as in many other areas of economics and econometrics. A fascinating interview with Griliches is

Krueger, A. and T. Taylor (2000). "An Interview with Zvi Griliches," *Journal of Economic Perspectives* **14**(2): 171–189.

The example in Section 18.4 is based on

Krueger, A. (1993). "How Computers Have Changed the Wage Structure: Evidence from Microdata, 1984–1989," *Quarterly Journal of Economics* **108**(1): 33–60.

This paper is eminently readable, and we highly recommend it to students who have studied introductory econometrics. Krueger's thesis is controversial. One paper that criticizes his work is

DiNardo, J. and J-S. Pischke (1997). "The Returns to Computer Use Revisited: Have Pencils Changed the Wage Structure Too?" *Quarterly Journal of Economics* **112**(1): 291–303.

The random X's model introduced in Section 18.4 is more carefully described in Goldberger (1998, Chapters 6 and 13; see especially pp. 134–135). Another book that presents a very similar version of the data generating process is James H. Stock and Mark W. Watson (2003). *Introduction to Econometrics* Boston: (Pearson Education). See their Chapter 4.

19

Heteroskedasticity

Our word is a modern coinage, derived from the two Greek roots hetero (ἕτερο), meaning "other" or "different," and skedannumi (σκεδάννυμι), meaning to "scatter."

J. Huston McCulloch[1]

19.1. Introduction

In this part of the book, we are systematically investigating failures to conform to the requirements of the classical econometric model. We focus in this chapter on the requirement that the tickets in the box for each draw are identically distributed across every X variable. When this condition holds, the error terms are *homoskedastic*, which means the errors have the same scatter regardless of the value of X. When the scatter of the errors is different, varying depending on the value of one or more of the independent variables, the error terms are *heteroskedastic*.

Heteroskedasticity has serious consequences for the OLS estimator. Although the OLS estimator remains unbiased, the estimated SE is wrong. Because of this, confidence intervals and hypotheses tests cannot be relied on. In addition, the OLS estimator is no longer BLUE. If the form of the heteroskedasticity is known, it can be corrected (via appropriate transformation of the data) and the resulting estimator, generalized least squares (GLS), can be shown to be BLUE. This chapter is devoted to explaining these points.

Heteroskedasticity can best be understood visually. Figure 19.1.1 depicts a classic picture of a homoskedastic situation. We have drawn a regression line estimated via OLS in a simple, bivariate model. The vertical spread of the data around the predicted line appears to be fairly constant as X changes. In contrast, Figure 19.1.2 shows the same model with heteroskedasticity. The vertical spread of the data around the predicted line is clearly increasing as X increases.

---

[1] McCulloch (1985, p. 483).

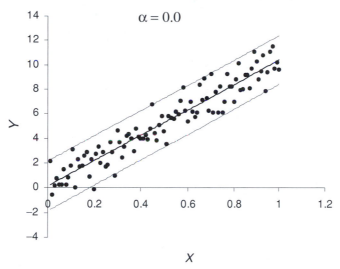

Figure 19.1.1. Homoskedasticity in a simple, bivariate model.
Source: [Het.xls]GenBiVar with $\alpha = 0$.

One of the most difficult parts of handling heteroskedasticity is that it can take many different forms. Figure 19.1.3 shows another example of heteroskedasticity. In this case, the spread of the errors is large for small values of X and then gets smaller as X rises. If the spread of the errors is not constant across the X values, heteroskedasticity is present.

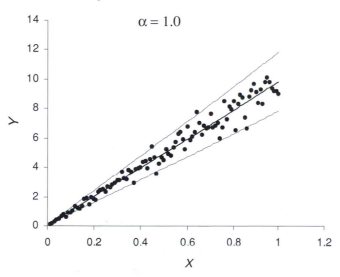

Figure 19.1.2. Heteroskedasticity in a simple, bivariate model.
Source: [Het.xls]GenBiVar with $\alpha = 1$.

Regression Line with 2 SE Bands

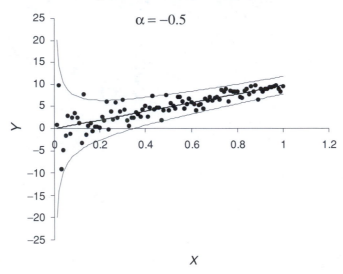

Figure 19.1.3. Another form of heteroskedasticity.
Source: [Het.xls]GenBiVar with $\alpha = -0.5$.

This chapter is organized around four basic issues:

- Understanding the violation itself
- Appreciating the consequences of the violation
- Diagnosing the presence of the violation
- Correcting the problem.

The next two sections (19.2 and 19.3) describe heteroskedasticity and its consequences in two simple, contrived examples. Although heteroskedasticity can sometimes be identified by eye, Section 19.4 presents a formal hypothesis test to detect heteroskedasticity. Section 19.5 describes the most common way in which econometricians handle the problem of heteroskedasticity – using a modified computation of the estimated SE that yields correct reported SEs. Section 19.6 discusses a more aggressive method for dealing with heteroskedasticity comparable to the approaches commonly employed in dealing with autocorrelation in which data transformation is applied to obtain the best linear unbiased estimator. Finally, Section 19.7 offers an extended discussion of heteroskedasticity in an actual data set.

19.2. A Univariate Example of Heteroskedasticity

Workbook: Het.xls

To better understand what heteroskedasticity is as well as its consequences, in this section and the next we examine three contrived examples. The first two examples are based on the notion of measurement error in which two

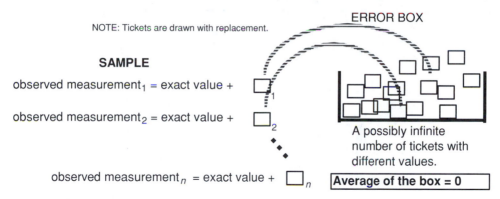

Figure 19.2.1. The DGP for a homoskedastic measuring instrument.

different devices with different levels of precision are used to generate the data. The third example is a more complicated model that allows a variety of forms of heteroskedasticity. In each of the three cases, we discuss the box model for the data generating process, display the heteroskedasticity visually, and show its impact via Monte Carlo simulation.

In this section, we examine heteroskedasticity in the context of a univariate data generation process. We build on the simple example used to discuss measurement error in Chapter 11. We are interested in measuring the distance between two mountain peaks. We have a measuring instrument that is subject to measurement error but is unbiased. Furthermore, every individual measurement is independent of every other. The model for the data generating process is depicted in Figure 19.2.1. Because the error term for each observation comes from the same box, this model is homoskedastic.

The best (most precise) estimate of the distance between the two points from the sample we collect is simply the sample average. The level of precision is measured by the standard error. As observed in Chapter 11, estimates based on averages of individual measurements are subject to a square-root law – that is, the standard error of the sample average estimator is given by the following formula:

$$SE \text{ of the Sample Average} = \frac{SD(Box)}{\sqrt{Number\ of\ Measurements}}.$$

This formula works so long as the spread of the measurement errors is constant across measurements. When this condition – that the measurement errors are *identically distributed* – fails to hold, we are dealing with heteroskedasticity.

How might heteroskedasticity arise? In the case of measurement error, heteroskedasticity could occur if the precision of the measuring instrument were to change between observations. In this artificial example, we suppose that there are two instruments with different levels of precision.

What is Heteroskedasticity?–Univariate Example

True Distance	25	Overall Average	24.73
Precision Ratio	4	OverallSD	3.86
		Estimated SE	0.61

Instrument 1

Precision of Instrument 1	1.0

Obs.No.	Error	Measurement
1	-0.96	24.04
2	-0.03	24.97
3	1.50	26.50
4	1.06	26.06
5	1.19	26.19
6	-0.48	24.52
7	-0.74	24.26
8	0.05	25.05
9	1.07	26.07
10	-1.42	23.58
Average	0.12	25.12
SD	1.03	1.03
SE	0.23	

Instrument 2

Precision of Instrument 2	4.0

Obs. No.	Error	Measurement
11	0.89	25.89
12	-0.62	24.38
13	-12.00	13.00
14	-0.48	24.52
15	-5.68	19.32
16	4.68	29.68
17	1.90	26.90
18	4.88	29.88
19	5.55	30.55
20	-5.72	19.28
Average	-0.66	24.34
SD	5.64	5.64
SE		1.26

View Residuals | Go to Monte Carlo Simulation

Draw Another Sample

Distance Measurements from Two Instruments

- Instrument 1
- Instrument 2
- Overall Average

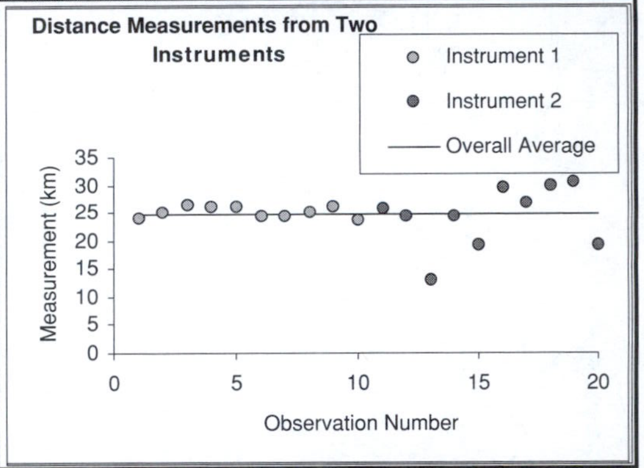

Avg1 = 25.12	SD1 = 1.03
Avg2 = 24.34	SD2 = 5.64
OverallAvg = 24.73	OverallSD = 3.86

Figure 19.2.2. The univariate measurement example.
Source: [Het.xls]Univariate.

Open the workbook Het.xls and go to the *Univariate* sheet. Measurements from Instrument 1, which is more precise, and Instrument 2, which is less precise, are displayed in a table and accompanying chart. The first 10 observations come from Instrument 1, and the second 10 come from Instrument 2. The overall average distance is indicated by a horizontal line. As usual, red lines and red text pertain to values that would be unknown to the observer.

Figure 19.2.2 displays the *Univariate* sheet. The key parameters (located in cells in the upper left portion of the sheet, where you can alter their values) governing the simulation are True_Distance, Precision_Ratio, and SDInstrument1. True_Distance gives the exact distance we are trying to measure, SDInstrument1 gives the precision of Instrument 1, and Precision_Ratio tells us how much less precise Instrument 2 is than Instrument 1. The spread of the measurements for Instrument 1 is given by SDInstrument1, which is initially set at 1 kilometer. Because the Precision_Ratio is set initially at 4, SDInstrument2 is 4 kilometers.

The measurements are simulated using techniques we have employed several times before. For example, the formula in cell B9 reads "=NORMALRANDOM(0,SDInstrument1)." This says that the first error term is a normally distributed random variable with mean zero and a spread equal to SDInstrument1 (given in cell B6). The formula in cell C9 is "=True_Distance+Error1." Thus, the actual measurement is equal to the true distance plus the error. The name "Error1" refers to a draw from the first error box. The formula in cell F9 is "=True_Distance+Error2"; here, "Error2" refers to a draw from the second error box. More formally, we have the following model:

$$\text{Observed Distance}_i = \text{True Distance} + \varepsilon_i,$$

where ε_i is a draw from a normally distributed error box with mean 0 and SD of SDInstrument1 when $i \leq 10$ and SDInstrument2 when $i > 10$. Pictorially, the model looks like Figure 19.2.3.

We now consider three different estimates of the true distance based on three different sample averages:

1. Avg1 is the average of the 10 measurements with Instrument 1.
2. Avg2 is the average of the 10 measurements with Instrument 2.
3. OverallAvg is the average of all 20 measurements.

Figure 19.2.4 displays the 20 measurements along with average and SD information. Click the Draw Another Sample button a few times. It is clear from the chart that observations 11 through 20 are less precise; the empirical SDs confirm that impression. In the sample in Figure 19.2.4, the overall average of 24.64 is exactly midway between the two averages from the two instruments; this is because we took the same number of measurements from both. The

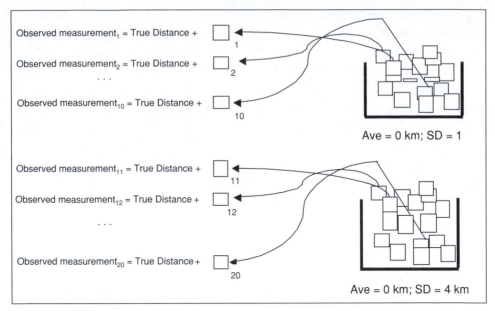

Figure 19.2.3. Box model for heteroskedastic, univariate measurements.

empirical SDs (0.76 and 4.93) are rather different from the SD of the respective boxes (1 and 4), but this is not unusual when we deal with only 10 draws from each box. In the case of an equal number of measurements from both devices, the overall SD will typically be about halfway between the SDs of the two subsamples, though not exactly halfway.

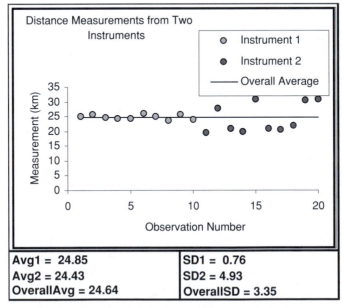

Avg1 = 24.85	SD1 = 0.76
Avg2 = 24.43	SD2 = 4.93
OverallAvg = 24.64	OverallSD = 3.35

Figure 19.2.4. Heteroskedastic, univariate data.
Source: [Het.xls]Univariate.

The View Residuals button is a three-way toggle. Click on the button and a display of the residuals appears in place of the original graph. Click again, and a graph of the errors appears. Observe how closely the residuals track the errors in this model. Because they are estimates of the errors, residuals can be a good diagnostic tool for observing heteroskedasticity in the errors. Click once more, and the original graph of the measured distances will appear.

Comparing the Precision of the Three Sample Averages

Next we wish to compare the SEs of the three different sample averages that have just been introduced. Without too much difficulty, you can compute the exact SE for each of the three sample averages being considered: the sample average for measurements from Instrument 1 alone, the sample average for Instrument 2, and the overall sample average; however, we will instead use a Monte Carlo simulation to obtain approximate SEs for the different sample averages. To do so, click on the third button, Go to Monte Carlo Simulation , which takes you to the Monte Carlo simulation sheet. Each repetition of the simulation takes another 20 measurements and reports the averages and estimated SEs for each instrument and their overall counterparts. We compute the estimated SEs by using the sample SDs in place of the unknown true SDs. Figure 19.2.5 shows the result from a typical simulation with 10,000 repetitions.

We display numerical results for Instruments 1 and 2 and the combination of the two instruments (called Overall). The chart display in Figure 19.2.5 contains histograms of Instrument 1 and Overall sample averages. In the Excel workbook, the displays are color coordinated. A toggle button, View Instrument 1 versus Instrument 2 , changes the histogram to contrast Instrument 1 and 2. The toggle button alters the chart displayed but uses the same numerical results.

The Monte Carlo simulation tells an interesting story. First, all three averages are quite close to the True Distance of 25, and so, not surprisingly, we have evidence that the averages are unbiased estimators. Second, the spread of the sampling distribution, as approximated by the SD of the 10,000 samples, is about four times bigger for the estimate derived from Instrument 2 than it is for Instrument 1. This is because the SEs of the sample averages are directly proportional to the SDs of the respective error boxes.

Third, it is somewhat surprising that the overall average, based on all 20 measurements, has a greater spread than the average from Instrument 1, which is based on only 10 measurements. On the one hand, it is not difficult to see why this is happening: the precision of the estimates based on all 20 measurements is being dragged down by the 10 relatively imprecise measurements from Instrument 2. On the other hand, it would seem that those 10 measurements are additional measurements and therefore must add some additional information. This is in fact true, and when corrections

True Distance	25	Average	SD	Average Estimated SE	Exact SE
Univariate Monte Carlo Simulation					
	Instr. 1	25.002	0.317	0.325	0.316
	Instr. 2	24.971	1.264	1.299	1.265
	Overall	24.986	0.650	0.655	0.652

View Instrument 1 versus Instrument 2

Take a Picture

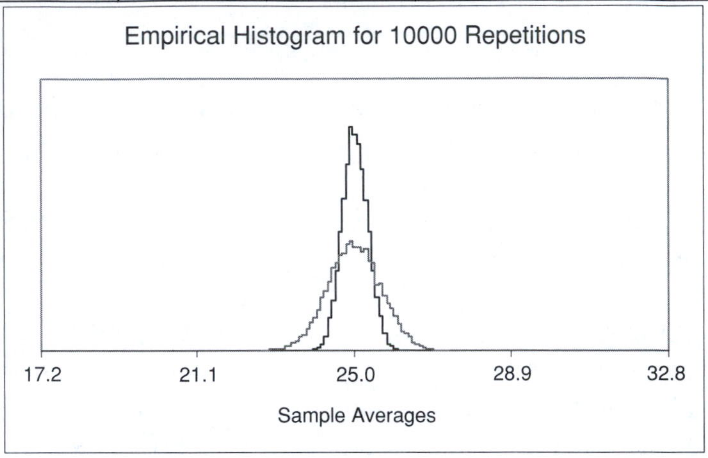

Empirical Histogram for 10000 Repetitions

17.2   21.1   25.0   28.9   32.8

Sample Averages

Precision of Instrument 1 = 1.0
Precision of Instrument 2 = 4.0

Figure 19.2.5. Comparing sample averages from two instruments.
Source: [Het.xls]UniMCSim.

for heteroskedasticity are discussed, it will be seen that there is an unbiased estimator (called the GLS estimator) that makes use of all 20 measurements and has a smaller SE than the estimate based on Instrument 1 measurements alone.

Analytic Computation of the SEs of the Sample Averages

It is a relatively simple matter to compute analytically the exact SEs of the three sample averages we have considered. Let us introduce some notation. Each estimator has the following form:

$$\text{Sample Average} = \sum_{i=1}^{n} w_i Y_i.$$

Here the w_i's are weights, each equal to $\frac{1}{n}$, where n is the number of observations being averaged, and the Y_i's are the measurements. Each measurement is the sum of the true distance and a draw from the error box.

In our model of the data generation process, the error terms are independent of one another. That means that each one of the measurements (the true distance plus a draw from the error box) is independent of every other measurement. The sample averages are therefore sums of independent random variables. We have already computed the SE of such sample averages in Section 14.4 in which it is shown that the spread of a linear estimator of the population average is

$$SD\left(\sum_{i=1}^{n} w_i Y_i\right) = \sqrt{\sum_{i=1}^{n} w_i^2 Var(\varepsilon_i)}$$

$$= \sqrt{\sum_{i=1}^{n} w_i^2 SD^2(\varepsilon_i)}.$$

Notice that this expression allows for the SD of the error term to vary across observations. Now apply the formula to obtain the SEs for each of our three estimators. We assume that the Precision Ratio remains 4 and the SD of the measurements from Instrument 1 is 1. For the Sample Average based on Instrument 1 alone, we have

$$ExactSE(\text{Sample Average for Instrument1}) = \sqrt{\sum_{i=1}^{n} w_i^2 Var(\varepsilon_i)}$$

$$= \sqrt{\sum_{i=1}^{10} \left(\frac{1}{10}\right)^2 1}$$

$$= \sqrt{10 \cdot \frac{1}{100}}$$

$$= 0.316.$$

Note that the $Var(\varepsilon_i)$ term is constant across the first 10 observations and equal to the square of the SD of the measurements from instrument 1 (in this case 1).

The SE of the Sample Average based on Instrument 2 is four times as big because the error terms from the second instrument have an SD four times greater:

$$ExactSE(\text{Sample Average for Instrument 2}) = \sqrt{\sum_{i=11}^{20} w_i^2 Var(\varepsilon_i)}$$

$$= \sqrt{\sum_{i=11}^{20} \left(\frac{1}{10}\right)^2 4^2}$$

$$= 4 \cdot \sqrt{10 \cdot \frac{1}{100}}$$

$$= 1.264.$$

Finally, the SE of the Overall Average is a slightly more complicated sum:

$$ExactSE(\text{OverallAverage}) = \sqrt{\sum_{i=1}^{20} w_i^2 Var(\varepsilon_i)}$$

$$= \sqrt{\sum_{i=1}^{10} \left(\frac{1}{20}\right)^2 1^2 + \sum_{i=11}^{20} \left(\frac{1}{20}\right)^2 4^2}$$

$$= \sqrt{10 \cdot \frac{1}{400} + 10 \cdot \frac{1}{400} \cdot 16}$$

$$= \sqrt{\frac{170}{400}}$$

$$= 0.652.$$

Because the weights sum to one for each of the three estimators, it is easy to show that they are all unbiased. Thus, in this case the OLS estimator, the Overall Sample Average, is not BLUE because there is another linear unbiased estimator, the Instrument 1 Average, which has a smaller SE than the OLS estimator. In Section 19.6 we identify yet another estimator (the GLS estimator), which is termed Best for this data generation process (i.e., this estimator has the smallest SE in the class of linear, unbiased estimators).

Summary

In this section we have demonstrated the nature of heteroskedasticity in a simple, univariate context. This example illustrates one of the important consequences of heteroskedasticity – the OLS estimator is no longer BLUE (i.e., there are other linear, unbiased estimators that have smaller SEs than the OLS estimator). In Section 19.6, we see how, given enough information about the nature of the heteroskedasticity, one can obtain the BLUE estimators. The next section goes on to consider heteroskedasticity in the bivariate setting.

19.3. A Bivariate Example of Heteroskedasticity

Workbook: Het.xls

In this section, we turn to bivariate data generation processes to study the nature and consequences of heteroskedasticity. In these examples we highlight the second major consequence of heteroskedasticity – biased estimated

SEs. In other words, the OLS-reported SEs for the coefficients are wrong and cannot be trusted.

A Measurement Error Example: Hooke's Law Revisited

Like the case we studied in Section 19.2, the first example of this section employs the measurement error paradigm. It is the Hooke's law example revisited. This time there are two apparatuses for measuring the length of a spring when a weight is attached to it. The first is set up for weights from 10 to 39 kg. The second is used for the heaviest weights ranging from 50 to 95 kg. Heteroskedasticity occurs because the second instrument is less precise than the first. We take 30 measurements from the first instrument and then move the spring to the second instrument for another 10 measurements. The model for the data generating process is

$$ObservedLength_i = \beta_0 + \beta_1 Weight_i + \varepsilon_i,$$

where the spread of the ε's is SDBox1 for $i \leq 30$ and SDBox2 for $i > 30$.

Go to the *SimpleBiVar* sheet in Het.xls now. Because this is a bivariate model, there is one more parameter than there was before. We have set the true intercept at 11.235 cm and the constant of proportionality at 0.4. The first instrument has an SD of 0.2 cm; the second, 0.8 cm. Click on cells in columns B, C, and D to see how this model is implemented in Excel. You can see that we continue to simulate normally distributed errors. The three buttons on the *SimpleBiVar* sheet work in the same way as the buttons on the *Univariate* sheet. A fourth button, View B-P Test, will be used when we discuss the diagnosis of heteroskedasticity.

This setup will give us a fairly precise estimate of the constant of proportionality for our spring, as Figure 19.3.1 makes clear. That figure and the displays of residuals and errors in the *SimpleBiVar* sheet all show abundant evidence of heteroskedasticity, however. Click on the Go to Monte Carlo Simulation button to see why we need to worry about heteroskedasticity in this case. Run your own Monte Carlo simulation for 10,000 repetitions by clicking on the Run Monte Carlo Simulation button. You should obtain results like those shown in Figure 19.3.2.

We present results for the slope estimate only and focus on two comparisons. Compare the average of the b_1 estimates to the true value of β_1: It appears that the OLS estimator is unbiased. This supports the first claim about the effects of heteroskedasticity: The OLS estimator remains unbiased.

The crucial comparison, however, is between the average of the estimated SEs and the empirical SD of the slope estimates (the b_1's). The former is the typical value of the estimated spread of the sampling distribution. The latter is a good approximation to the true spread of the sampling distribution (the

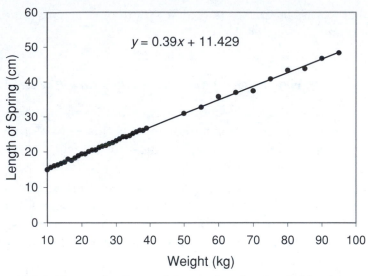

Figure 19.3.1. Regression line and data points for simple bivariate model.
Source: [Het.xls]SimpleBiVar.

Sample b_1 Summary Statistics			Population Parameters	
Average	0.400		β_1	0.4
Min	0.385		SD1	0.2
Max	0.415		SD2	0.8
			Average	
SD	0.0046		**Estimated SE**	0.0028

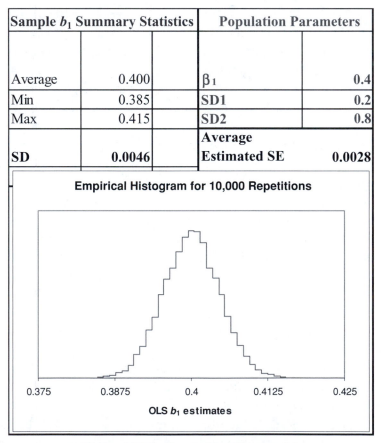

Figure 19.3.2. Simple bivariate model.
Source: [Het.xls]SimpleBiVarMC.

Sample Number	Sample b_1	OLS Estimated SE	P-Value for True Null
1	0.3969	0.0023	19%

Figure 19.3.3. Results from a single repetition in the Monte Carlo experiment.
Source: [Het.xls] SimpleBivarMC.

exact SE). The point is that, on average, the estimated SE is too small. The empirical SD for our slope estimates was 0.0046, but the average estimated SE was only 0.0028. In this case, using OLS misleads us into believing that we have a more precise estimate of the constant of proportionality than is actually the case. The bias in the estimated SE is the second major consequence induced by heteroskedasticity.

Why should we care about biased SEs? Because they seriously hamper statistical inference. Let us demonstrate this in the context of hypothesis testing. We will test the true null hypothesis that $\beta_1 = 0.4$ against the two-sided alternative that $\beta_1 \neq 0.4$ in each of the 10,000 samples that we drew. For example, take a look at results from the first repetition in our Monte Carlo experiment, as shown in Figure 19.3.3.

The test statistic in this case is

$$\text{test statistic} = \frac{b_1 - \text{hypothesized value of } \beta_1}{\text{SE}(b_1)}$$
$$= \frac{0.3969 - 0.4}{0.0023}$$
$$= 1.304.$$

The *P*-value is about 19 percent.[2] You can use the P value Calculator add-in to confirm this. Choose the *t*-distribution with 38 degrees of freedom.

Let us look at the distribution of all 10,000 *P*-values in the simulation. Click on the View Histogram of P-Values button to see something similar to the display in Figure 19.3.4.

Figure 19.3.4 tells us that, for the particular heteroskedastic data generation process chosen, if we were testing the true null hypothesis that the slope is 0.4 and used a 5-percent level of significance, we would falsely reject the null about 22 percent of the time. In other words, we chose a significance that leads us to believe we will reject the true null hypothesis only 5-percent of the time, however, there is in fact roughly a 22-percent chance that we will reject the true null.

A much less obvious problem with the OLS estimator in the simple bivariate case is that OLS is no longer BLUE. Just as the estimator derived from the overall average in the univariate measurement case was clearly not the

---

[2] When the errors are normally distributed, a *t*-statistic is appropriate, and in fact we used the *t*-distribution to compute *P*-values in our Monte Carlo routine.

Sample *P*-Value Summary Statistics			Population Parameters	
Average	0.349		beta1	0.4
SD	0.307		SD1	0.2
Max	0.994		SD2	0.8
Min	0.000		%*P* Val<5%	22.40%

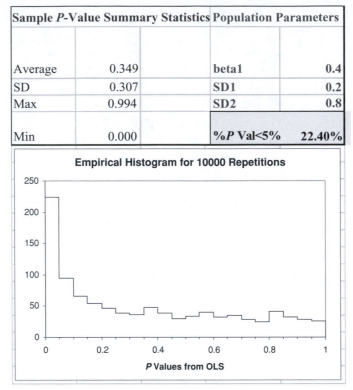

Figure 19.3.4. *P*-values in a simple bivariate model.
Source: [Het.xls]SimpleBivarMC.

best estimator, our OLS estimator is also inferior to estimators that take the heteroskedasticity into account. We return to this issue in Section 19.6.

More General Heteroskedasticity in the Bivariate Setting

So far the errors in our models in this section have been generated by two boxes. Heteroskedasticity is usually more complicated and can take a variety of forms. To illustrate the possibilities, consider a model in which every single error is drawn from a different box. The data generating process is harder to describe than it was for our first two examples. As in the first example of this section, we have a simple bivariate model:

$$Y_i = \beta_0 + \beta_1 \cdot X_i + \varepsilon_i.$$

The complication is in the error term. Let us suppose that there are 100 observations and X varies from 0.01 to 1.00 in steps of 0.01. In this example, the error terms are determined by the following equation:

$$\varepsilon_i = X_i^\alpha \cdot v_i,$$

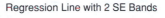
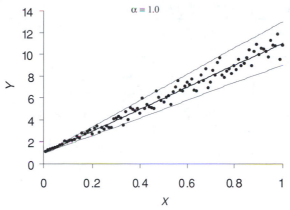

Figure 19.3.5. Heteroskedasticity in the general bivariate model with evenly spaced X's.
Source: [Het.xls]GenBiVar.

where v_i is a normally distributed random variable whose SD is initially set at 1. Thus, the spread of each error term is a function of its associated X value and a parameter called α :

$$SD(\varepsilon_i) = X_i^{\alpha}.$$

These formulas look intimidating, but the *GenBivar* sheet in Het.xls will clarify the model. Open that sheet now. The parameters governing this model are contained in cells B3 through B6. The initial values of β_0 and β_1 are 0 and 10, respectively. Thus, the equation for the true model is

$$Y_i = 0 + 10 \cdot X_i + \varepsilon_i.$$

The value of α should be set at 1. If it is not, change it to 1 and hit F9 to recalculate the sheet. The SD of the error terms is therefore equal to the value of X_i. The chart of the regression line includes two bands drawn two SEs vertically above and below the regression line. Thus, in Figure 19.3.5, at $X_{100} = 1$ (the one-hundredth observation), the upper band is 2 units above the regression line and the lower band is 2 units below the regression line. As you can see, about 95 percent of all the points fit between the two bands.

Now change α to 2 and hit F9. The error terms associated with smaller values of X are extremely small but spread out more rapidly than they did before as X increases. Click on the View X$^{\alpha}$ Chart button to see how the spread of the errors changes as X increases. Change α to -0.5 to see another possible pattern of heteroskedasticity.

In this model, each error term comes from its own individual box. The consequences for estimation, however, are similar to those for the two-box,

Sample b_1 Summary Statistics			Population Parameters	
Average	10.000		β_1	10
Min	9.244		α	2.0
Max	10.682		SD $_V$	1.0
SD	0.1966		Average Estimated SE	0.1554

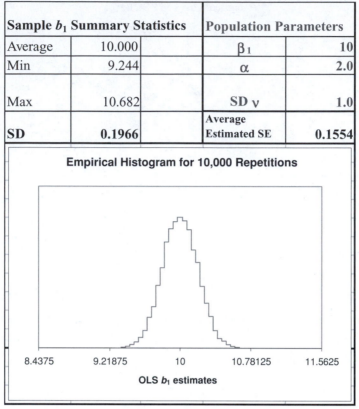

Empirical Histogram for 10,000 Repetitions

8.4375   9.21875   10   10.78125   11.5625

OLS b_1 estimates

Figure 19.3.6. Heteroskedasticity with $\alpha = 2$ and X's evenly spaced and
varying from 0.01 to 1.
Source: [Het.xls]GenBiVarMC.

Hooke's law case we just considered: The OLS estimates are unbiased, but
the estimated SEs are wrong. These assertions can be demonstrated with
Monte Carlo experiments. To run the Monte Carlo experiments, first confirm
that $\alpha = 2$ and then click the [Go to the Monte Carlo Simulation] button. Click the [Run Monte Carlo Simulation] button
and choose the number of repetitions desired. The Monte Carlo simulation
should produce something like the results shown in Figure 19.3.6.

   With $\alpha = 2$, the heteroskedasticity would best be characterized as moder-
ately damaging. As before, the two numbers to be compared are the average
of the estimated SEs (0.1554), the typical estimated measure of the spread
of the sampling distribution of b_1, and the SD of the estimates (0.1966),
which is a good approximation of the true spread of the sampling distribution (i.e., the exact SE of b_1). This comparison shows that the OLS estimates of the SE are typically about 21 percent lower than the true SE. Click
on the [View Histogram of P-Values] button to see the effect the biased estimates of the SE
have on hypothesis testing. As in the previous example, we test the true
null in each repetition. We find that at the 5-percent significance level, we

Sample *P*-Value Summary Statistics			Population Parameters	
Average	0.425		β_1	10
SD	0.302		α	2
Max	1.000			
Min	0.000		%*P* Val<5 %	11.74%

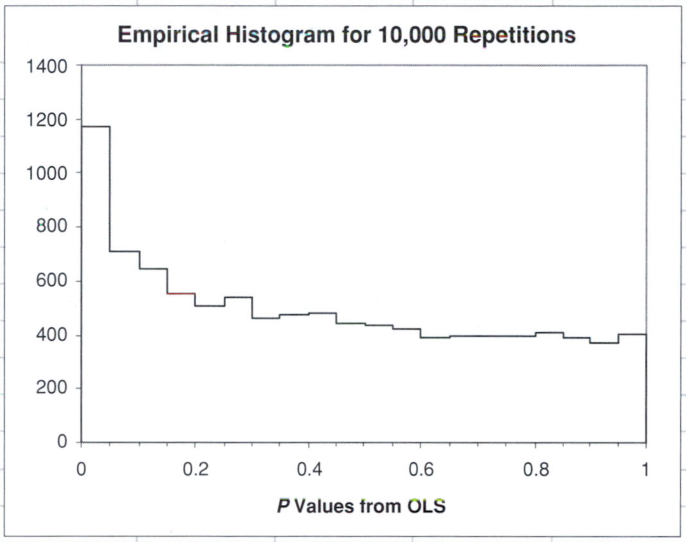

Figure 19.3.7. *P*-values with $\alpha = 2$ and *X*'s varying from 0.01 to 1. *Source:* [Het.xls]GenBiVarMC.

would reject the true null about twice as often as we should, as shown in Figure 19.3.7.

With $\alpha = 1$, you will find that the heteroskedasticity makes very little difference in terms of the estimated SEs. You should not conclude, however, on the basis of these Monte Carlo experiments, that heteroskedasticity is an unimportant issue in the general bivariate case.

To drive this point home, go back to the *GenBiVar* sheet and click on the Change the Xs button. This button replaces the 100, evenly spaced *X*'s we've been dealing with so far with a set graphed in Figure 19.3.8.

Now the *X*'s vary from 0 to about 15 and are concentrated in the beginning of this range. Next, set α to 2 and go the *GenBiVarMC* sheet to run a Monte Carlo simulation. You should obtain results similar to those shown in Figure 19.3.9.

Now the heteroskedasticity is very noticeable: The typical estimated SE vastly underestimates the true SE. Click on the View Histogram of *P*-Values button to see how hypothesis testing might be affected. This example shows that the

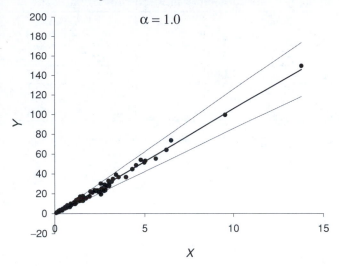

Figure 19.3.8. Heteroskedasticity with unevenly spaced X's.
Source: [Het.xls]GenBiVar.

Sample b_1 Summary Statistics For Unevenly Spaced X's			Population Parameters	
Average	9.994		β_1	10
Min	8.511		α	1.0
Max	11.605		SD_ν	1.0
SD	0.4774		Average Estimated SE	0.1277

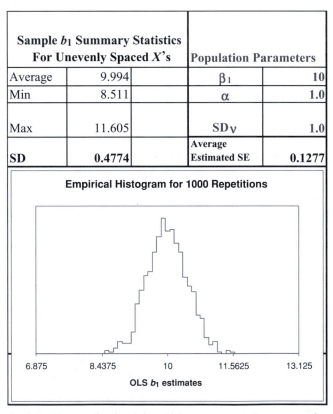

Figure 19.3.9. Heteroskedasticity with $\alpha = 2$ and X's unevenly spaced.
Source: [Het.xls]GenBiVarMC.

distribution of the X's interacts with the type of heteroskedasticity to determine how much damage heteroskedasticity causes.

Summary

In Sections 19.2 and 19.3 we have presented some basic, contrived models of heteroskedasticity. The purpose of these examples was to demonstrate what heteroskedasticity is and to show its consequences. The two problems caused by heteroskedasticity are that standard OLS estimates of the SEs of slope parameters are incorrect and that the OLS estimator is no longer Best in the class of linear, unbiased estimators. We have used Monte Carlo simulation to demonstrate that the reported SEs are wrong. Before we show that OLS is not BLUE, we discuss how one can diagnose heteroskedasticity.

19.4. Diagnosing Heteroskedasticity with the B–P Test

Workbooks: Het.xls; BPSampDist.xls

~~... section we discuss ways~~ to determine whether the error terms in a model are heteroskedastic. This is an important topic for two reasons: First, as we have noted, heteroskedasticity causes problems for inference; second, heteroskedasticity is extremely common. Heteroskedasticity is so prevalent that many econometricians routinely avoid using the standard OLS estimated SEs. What they do instead is explained in the next section of this chapter.

A standard theme of this book is that one should act both on the basis of theory and data. Diagnosis ought to begin with theory. In the case of heteroskedasticity, there are occasionally precise theoretical reasons for worrying that the errors have varying SDs for different values of the independent variables; very often there are less well-defined arguments for the presence of heteroskedasticity; and sometimes there is just a vague suspicion that the assumption of homoskedasticity is too strong.

Theoretical Reasons to Worry about Heteroskedasticity

An example of a compelling theoretical case for heteroskedasticity is that of grouped data (e.g., a situation in which each observation represents the average behavior of the inhabitants of a single state). When the groups are of different sizes, the error terms are almost guaranteed to have different spreads for different observations. A typical, looser argument for heteroskedastic errors is the one made for consumption regressions. The error term in most accounts reflects unobserved tastes and preferences. A plausible case can be made that the variation in the impact of tastes and preferences increases as consumers' income rises. For example, spending by poor people on automobiles probably varies less than that of rich people. Most people below the poverty line buy used cars; some millionaires drive old Honda Civics, whereas others own fleets of Bentleys.

Diagnosing Heteroskedasticity in the Data

If you have a theoretical reason for worrying about heteroskedasticity, how can you test for its presence in your data set? There are many different tests for heteroskedasticity. In this book, we focus on a relatively simple test that is fairly intuitive. We call it the Breusch–Pagan test (B–P for short), though Breusch and Pagan originally proposed a slightly different procedure.

The intuition for the B–P test is straightforward. If the errors have different spreads for different X's, then the residuals ought to as well. Why? The reason is that the residuals are good estimators of the errors. One way to measure the spread of the residuals is to square them. Then if heteroskedasticity is present there ought to be some type of relationship between the squared residuals and the corresponding X's. In other words, knowledge of the value of the X variables ought to help us to predict the size of the residuals. On the other hand, if there is no heteroskedasticity, there ought to be no relationship between the squared residuals and the corresponding X's.

How can one test for that relationship? Run an *auxiliary regression* of the squared residuals on all the X's:

$$\text{Residuals}_i^2 = \gamma_0 + \gamma_1 X_{1i} + \gamma_2 X_{2i} + \cdots + \gamma_k X_{ki} + \eta_i,$$

where i indexes observations. Then test the null hypothesis that

$$\gamma_1 = \gamma_2 = \cdots = \gamma_k = 0,$$

(i.e., that none of the X's are related to the squared residuals). This is the F-statistic for overall significance of the regression (also called the whole-model F-statistic), which is discussed in Chapter 17. The whole-model F-statistic is reported by almost all regression packages, including Excel's Data Analysis and LINEST.

You can see examples of the B–P test procedure for particular samples by clicking on the View B–P Test buttons in the *SimpleBiVar* and *GenBiVar* sheets of Het.xls. For the simple bivariate case (the one based on Hooke's law), the scatter plot associated with the auxiliary regression makes it very clear that there is some relationship between the residuals and the X's. Recall that the story in this case is that we switched measuring instruments when we started using heavier weights. The second instrument is much less precise than the first. In this example, the B–P test procedure requires that we run an original

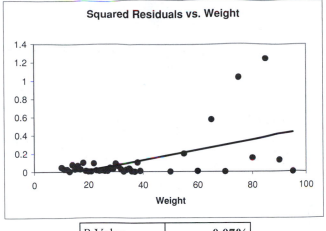

P-Value	0.07%
Regression of Res² on Weight	

Slope	Intercept
0.006	−0.098
0.002	0.066
0.262	0.225
13.457	38
0.682	1.926

Figure 19.4.1. Artificial regression behind the Breusch–Pagan test. *Source:* [Het.xls]SimpleBivar.

regression of length of the spring on the weight, obtain the residuals, and then square them. Then we run an auxiliary regression of the squared residuals on the original X variable – in this case the Weight. The scatter plot and regression results for a typical sample resemble those of Figure 19.4.1.

From the scatter plot shown in Figure 19.4.1, it is obvious that something happens to the residuals when we switch to the scale designed for heavier weights. The OLS regression line picks up on this, for the positive slope tells us that the squared residuals appear to increase in size as the weights get bigger. The test statistic is in bold: It is the F-statistic for the overall significance of the regression (13.457 in this case). The null hypothesis says that all the regression slopes (in this case just one) are jointly equal to zero; there is no relationship between the size of the squared residuals and the X's. If the null hypothesis is true, the F-statistic is distributed $F(1,38)$ because there is just one independent variable in our auxiliary regression, which determines the numerator degrees of freedom, whereas the denominator degrees of freedom equals the number of observations, 40, less the number of parameters in the regression, 2 (slope and intercept).

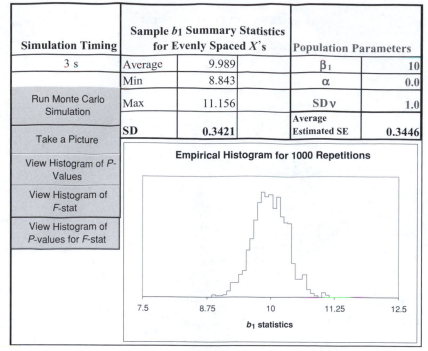

Simulation Timing	Sample b_1 Summary Statistics for Evenly Spaced X's		Population Parameters	
3 s	Average	9.989	β_1	10
	Min	8.843	α	0.0
Run Monte Carlo Simulation	Max	11.156	SD v	1.0
Take a Picture	SD	0.3421	Average Estimated SE	0.3446
View Histogram of *P*-Values				
View Histogram of *F*-stat				
View Histogram of *P*-values for *F*-stat				

Figure 19.4.2. Approximate sampling distribution of b_1 with homoskedasticity ($\alpha = 0$).
Source: [BPSampDist.xls]GenBiVarMCSim.

The B–P Sampling Distribution

To see the behavior of the B–P statistic for the general bivariate model, open the BPSampDist.xls workbook. Set α (the parameter governing the degree of heteroskedasticity) equal to 0 in the *GenBiVar* sheet. When $\alpha = 0$, there is no heteroskedasticity in the error terms. Click the Draw Another Sample button and note the *P*-values for the whole-model *F*-test from the auxiliary regression in cell H13.

To see the performance of the B–P statistic (i.e., the auxiliary regression's *F*-statistic), with $\alpha = 0$, click the Go to the Monte Carlo Simulation button and run a Monte Carlo experiment. You should find the average estimated SE of b_1 to be very close to the spread of the empirical histogram (the SD of the slope estimates), which is the Monte Carlo approximation to the true SE of b_1. Figure 19.4.2 displays the Monte Carlo results.

Click on the View Histogram of F stats button to see the Monte Carlo approximation to the B–P statistic's sampling distribution, as shown in Figure 19.4.3.

The histogram depicted in Figure 19.4.3 is close to the histogram of the exact F(1, 38) distribution we expect to see when the null that there is no heteroskedasticity is true. To obtain further evidence about the performance of the B–P statistic when the null is true, click the Go Back to Histogram of Betas button and

Sample B–P Summary Statistics		Population Parameters	
Average	1.01	β_1	10
Min	0.00	α	0.0
Max	14.04	SD(v)	1.0
SD	1.36		

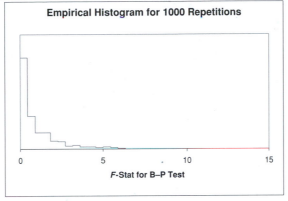

Empirical Histogram for 1000 Repetitions

F-Stat for B–P Test

Figure 19.4.3. Approximate sampling distribution of B–P statistics when the null is true.
Source: [BPSampDist.xls]GenBiVarMCSim.

click on the ⧉View Histogram of *P*-values for *F*-statistics button. Something resembling Figure 19.4.4 will appear.

What happens to the test statistic when there is heteroskedasticity? Change α to 1 in the *GenBiVar* sheet and run another Monte Carlo simulation. Results similar to those shown in Figure 19.4.5 will be obtained.

There is a huge difference between Figures 19.4.3 and 19.4.5. The *F*-statistics are now much bigger. In fact, in this example the B–P test turns out to be extremely good at sniffing out heteroskedasticity.

Under the null hypothesis of no heteroskedasticity, we expect to find B–P statistics (whole-model *F*-statistics from the auxiliary regression) greater than 4 about 5 percent of the time. With $\alpha = 1$, however, the center of the sampling distribution is about 23, and the minimum in our 1,000 samples was 5.74. In this (admittedly contrived) example, the B–P test succeeds every time in its task of detecting heteroskedasticity.

To drive the point home, click on the ⧉View Histogram of *P*-values for *F*-statistics button. Something like Figure 19.4.6 will appear. In 1,000 repetitions, the B–P test rejected the false null every time at the 5-percent significance level. It is interesting to note that, when $\alpha = 1$, although our diagnostic test has no trouble finding heteroskedasticity, the heteroskedasticity itself does relatively small damage to inference. To verify that statistical inference is not badly harmed,

Sample P-Value Summary Statistics		Population Parameters	
Average	0.486	β_1	10
SD	0.290	α	0
Max	0.998		
Min	0.000	%P Val<5%	5.90%

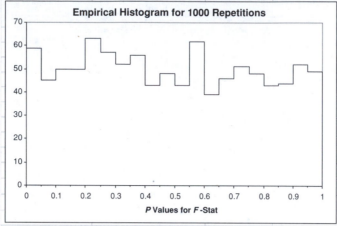

Empirical Histogram for 1000 Repetitions
70
60
50
40
30
20
10
0
0
0.1
0.2
0.3
0.4
0.5
0.6
0.7
0.8
0.9
1
P Values for F-Stat

Figure 19.4.4. P-values for B–P test when the null is true.
Source: [BPSampDist.xls] GenBiVarMCSim.

Sample F-stat Summary Statistics		Population Parameters	
Average	23.07	β_1	10
Min	5.74	α	1.0
Max	63.46	SD(ν)	1.0
SD	7.38		

Empirical Histogram for 1000 Repetitions
0
10
20
30
40
50
60
70
F-Stat for B–P Test

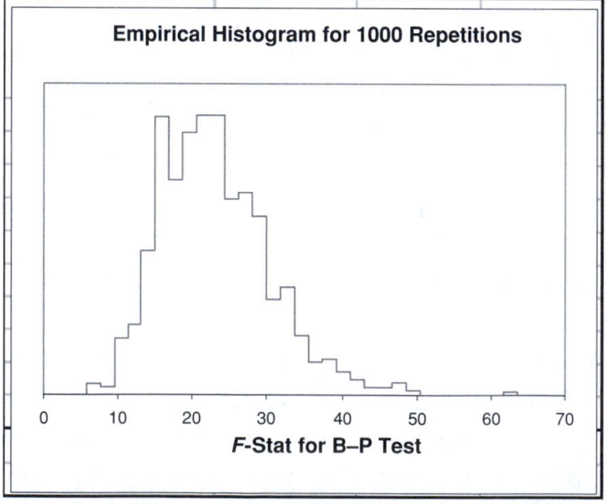

Figure 19.4.5. B–P statistics when the null is false ($\alpha = 1$).
Source: [BPSampDist.xls]GenBiVarMCSim.

Sample *P*-Value Summary Statistics for B–P Test		Population Parameters	
Average	0.000	β_1	10
SD	0.002	α	1
Max	0.045		
		%*P* Val<5%	
Min	0.000		100.00%

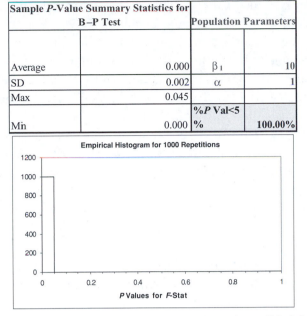

Figure 19.4.6. *P*-values for B–P test when the null is false.
Source: [BPSampDist.xls]GenBiVarMCSim.

make the same comparisons we did for the $\alpha = 2$ case at the end of Section 19.3. You will find the average value of the estimated SEs to be about 10 percent greater than the SD of the empirical distribution of the slope estimates, and a hypothesis test based on a true null hypothesis about the slope β_1 rejects just a little more often than it should.

Summary

The B–P test is based on the fact that the residuals typically are good estimates of the errors. If the spread of the errors varies as the X values change, then that ought to show up when the (squared) residuals are regressed on the X's. The whole-model F-statistic on the appropriate auxiliary regression is a useful diagnostic tool for finding a dependence of the squared residuals on the X's. If the B–P test tells you that there is heteroskedasticity in your data, what can you do about it? The next two sections outline two different approaches to dealing with heteroskedasticity.

19.5. Dealing with Heteroskedasticity: Robust Standard Errors

Workbooks: HetRobustSE.xls; OLSRegression.xla (Excel add-in in the Basic Tools folder)

This section and Section 19.6 describe two different approaches to tackling the problem of heteroskedasticity. The first avenue of attack, discussed in this section, is to use OLS but to replace the conventional estimate of the SE – which, as we have seen, can be severely biased – with something called robust standard errors. One need not know the exact form of the heteroskedasticity to implement robust standard errors. We will explain how robust standard errors are obtained and present evidence that they indeed are much less biased than the standard estimate of the SE. The second approach, called generalized least squares or GLS (discussed in Section 19.6), is to transform the data so that the heteroskedasticity is removed. The advantage of robust standard errors over the GLS approach is that one need not know the form of the heteroskedasticity to deal with the problem. In addition to explaining the logic behind robust standard errors, this section introduces an Excel add-in that facilitates easy computation of robust SEs (and offers additional OLS output beyond LINEST's capabilities).

Robust standard errors are estimates of the standard errors of the estimated coefficients that take into account the heteroskedasticity revealed by the data. The way in which this is done is explained below for the bivariate case. The multivariate case is more complicated, but the basic idea is the same. The word *robust* is used in this context to mean "impervious to the heteroskedasticity." In other words, although conventional OLS estimated SEs break down if the DGP is not homoskedastic, robust SEs keep working well.

The explanation of exactly how robust standard errors work is somewhat complicated, but in the bivariate case, at least, it is fairly easy to gain an intuitive grasp of what is going on. Here are formulas for the conventionally reported OLS estimated SE and the robust estimated SE:

$$OLS\ Estimated\ SE\ (b_1) = \sqrt{\sum_{i=1}^{n} w_i^2 RMSE^2}$$

$$Robust\ Estimated\ SE\ (b_1) = \sqrt{\sum_{i=1}^{n} w_i^2 e_i^2}.$$

In the above expressions, n is the number of observations, the w_i's are weights which depend on the X's and the e_i's are the residuals corresponding to each observation. In the above sums RMSE is a constant which is the same across all n observations, while the value of the squared residual, e_i^2, varies across observations. The difference between the OLS and robust estimated SE's is that the OLS SE uses just one measure of the spread of the error terms, the RMSE, while the robust SE uses n different estimates of the spread of the error terms, the n squared residuals. The intuition behind the robust SE is that the changing squared residuals better estimate the varying spread of the errors than the unchanging RMSE.

A more formal explanation of the robust SE goes as follows. We begin with the classical econometric model in the bivariate case,

$$Y_i = \beta_0 + \beta_1 X_i + \varepsilon_i, \quad i = 1, \dots, n,$$

where each ε_i is a draw from a single error box with a standard deviation $SD(\varepsilon_i)$. All the ε_i's are independent of one another and are uncorrelated with the X's, which are fixed in repeated sampling.

We know how to compute the SE of the OLS estimator of the slope b_1. Recall that the OLS estimator of b_1 is a weighted sum of the Y's,

$$b_1 = \sum_{i=1}^{n} w_i Y_i,$$

where each of the OLS weights is given by the formula

$$w_i = \frac{(X_i - \bar{X})}{\sum_{i=1}^{n}(X_i - \bar{X})^2}.$$

In words, this formula says that each observation's weight (w_i) is the deviation of that observation's X value from the average of the X values (i.e., the numerator) divided by the variance of the X's multiplied by the number of observations (i.e., the denominator).

Our assumptions that the ε_i's are independent and that the X's are fixed in repeated samples make the variance (the square of the SE) of b_1 easy to compute, as follows:

$$Var(b_1) = \sum_{i=1}^{n} w_i^2 SD(\varepsilon_i)^2.$$

The formula for the exact SE is simply the square root of this expression:

$$Exact\,SE(b_1) = \sqrt{\sum_{i=1}^{n} w_i^2 SD(\varepsilon_i)^2}.$$

Homoskedasticity means that each of the error terms comes from the same box. When each error term is drawn from the same box, the $SD(\varepsilon_i)$ is the same value for every observation; thus, the formula can be simplified to

$$Var(b_1) = \sum_{i=1}^{n} w_i^2 SD(\varepsilon)^2$$

where $SD(\varepsilon)$ is just the SD of the error box.

The conventional OLS estimate of the SE uses the RMSE as an estimate of SD(ε):

$$OLS \; Estimated \; SE(b_1) = \sqrt{\sum_{i=1}^{n} w_i^2 RMSE^2}.$$

Now suppose that the requirement that the errors come from the same box is violated. In other words, we have,

$$Y_i = \beta_0 + \beta_1 X_i + \varepsilon_i, \quad i = 1, \ldots, n,$$

where each ε_i is a draw from a separate error box with its own standard deviation $SD(\varepsilon_i)$. All the ε_i's are independent of one another and are uncorrelated with the X's, which are fixed in repeated sampling. This is no longer the classical econometric model because the errors are not identically distributed for each observation. For one observation, the SD of the error box may be small but for another observation it may be quite large.

What effect will the heteroskedasticity have on the formula for the exact SE of the OLS slope estimator? Well, the formula is the same as before:

$$Exact \; SE(b_1) = \sqrt{\sum_{i=1}^{n} w_i^2 SD(\varepsilon_i)^2},$$

where ε_i is the ith observation's error term. We cannot, however, treat all of the $SD(\varepsilon_i)$ as being equal to each other because the whole point of heteroskedasticity is that each error term comes from a different box. We can emphasize the fundamental difference between the homoskedastic and heteroskedastic DGPs by simply comparing the formulas for the exact SEs side by side as follows:

$$Homoskedastic \; Exact \; SE(b_1) = \sqrt{\sum_{i=1}^{n} w_i^2 SD\,(\varepsilon)^2} \; versus$$

$$Heteroskedastic \; Exact \; SE(b_1) = \sqrt{\sum_{i=1}^{n} w_i^2 SD(\varepsilon_i)^2}.$$

The two formulas look identical, but there is one difference between them: The formula for the heteroskedastic DGP has an epsilon with a subscript. The homoskedastic formula is missing the subscript. This seemingly minute difference is actually critical. The exact SE for the homoskedastic case uses one single number to represent the SD of the error box for all of the observations because it is assumed in the classical econometric model that the error distributions is the same for all of the observations. In contrast, the exact SE for the heteroskedastic DGP employs a different SD of the error box for each observation. This difference carries over into the estimated versions of the formulas:

$$OLS \ Estimated \ SE \ (b_1) = \sqrt{\sum_{i=1}^{n} w_i^2 RMSE^2} \ \text{versus}$$

$$Robust \ Estimated \ SE \ (b_1) = \sqrt{\sum_{i=1}^{n} w_i^2 e_i^2}.$$

Notice that the formulas use the weights in the same way and the only difference is in how the spread of the errors is treated. The problem with the conventional OLS estimated SE in the presence of heteroskedasticity is the underlying assumption that every error term has the same spread. The OLS SE uses the RMSE as an overall single estimate of the spread of the error terms. This is a mistake, however, because, in fact, there is no overall single, constant SD of the box.

The robust standard error, however, is faithful to the true heteroskedastic DGP because it uses the square of each individual residual as an estimate of the spread of the associated error term. Because the robust SE pays attention to the varying spread of the error terms, it does a better job than the conventional OLS estimate of the SE.

Now because the error terms and therefore the residuals bounce around a great deal and can be close to zero even when the error terms have a high SD, it would seem that the robust SE procedure should not work that well. We will see, however, that the robust SE generally does a better job than the OLS estimated SE when heteroskedasticity is present. In fact, it does an adequate job even when there is no heteroskedasticity.

It's time to put these ideas into practice. The *ComputingSE* sheet of Het-RobustSE.xls compares the computation of the conventional OLS SE with that of the robust SE in the general bivariate case considered in Section 19.3:

$$Y_i = \beta_0 + \beta_1 \cdot X_i + \varepsilon_i.$$

We have 100 observations, and X varies from 0.01 to 1.00 in steps of 0.01. The error terms are determined by the following equation:

$$\varepsilon_i = X_i^{\alpha} \cdot v_i.$$

Parameters	
β_0	0
β_1	10
α	2.0
SD_V	1

Figure 19.5.1. Parameter values for Monte Carlo simulation. *Source:* [HetRobustSE.xls]ComputingSE.

Although you can change the value of α, we set it to 2 to make the comparisons more dramatic. We set the value of the parameters that govern the example (and the associated Monte Carlo simulation) as shown in Figure 19.5.1.

The *ComputingSE* sheet is set up to show how each of the three SEs (exact, conventional OLS estimated, robust) of the OLS slope are computed. Columns G and H compute the weights (the w_i's), column L computes the squared residuals, and columns I, J, and K compute the individual terms in the three sums that produce the three SEs. The sums, which are the exact variance and the two estimated variances, are reported in cells I10, J10, and K10. The exact and estimated SEs are in cells I9, J9, and K9, as shown in Figure 19.5.2.

Click on the Draw Another Sample button or simply hit F9 to draw a new sample. You will see the OLS-reported SE and robust SE bounce around to reflect new residuals (that go into the RMSE and squared residuals used in computing the two estimates), but the exact SE does not change. Note that, usually, the OLS SE is too low, whereas the robust SE is closer to the exact, true SE. A Monte Carlo simulation will confirm this first impression.

To graphically compare the three weighted sums that are used to compute the exact variance, the conventional OLS variance, and the robust SE variance, click on the View Graph of Contributions to Variance button. It graphs the values in columns I, J, and K. Figure 19.5.3 is an example.

As you can see, the robust SE contributions are widely scattered, but they actually track the exact SE contributions better than the OLS estimated SE – particularly for low values of X for which the exact SE and robust SE contributions essentially coincide.

The *MCSim* sheet uses a Monte Carlo simulation to confirm that robust SEs do a better job than OLS estimated SEs of estimating the true SE of the OLS slope. Figure 19.5.4 displays output from one simulation.

	Exact	Estimated OLS	Robust
SE	0.196	0.177	0.201
Variance	0.039	0.031	0.040

Figure 19.5.2. Exact and estimated variances and SEs. *Source:* [HetRobustSE.xls]ComputingSE.

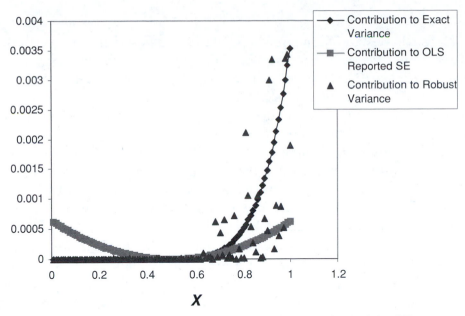

Figure 19.5.3. Comparing elements of three versions of the SE.
Source: [HetRobust.xls]ComputingSE.

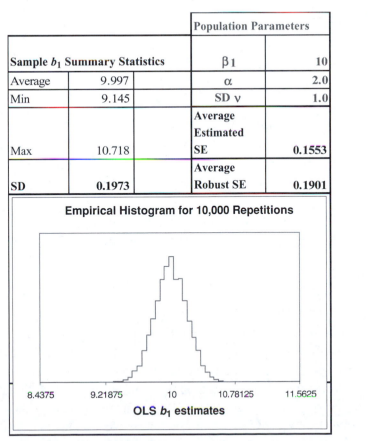

	Population Parameters	
Sample b_1 Summary Statistics	β_1	10
Average	9.997	α	2.0
Min	9.145	SD ν	1.0
Max	10.718	Average Estimated SE	0.1553
SD	0.1973	Average Robust SE	0.1901

Empirical Histogram for 10,000 Repetitions

8.4375   9.21875   10   10.78125   11.5625

OLS b_1 estimates

Figure 19.5.4. Comparing robust and OLS estimated SEs.
Source: [HetRobustSE.xls]MCSim.

As usual, we start our interpretation of the results with the average of the 10,000 sample slopes. The closeness of this average to the true parameter value is evidence that the OLS sample slope estimator is an unbiased estimator of β_1 even in the presence of heteroskedasticity. Next, notice that, as advertised, the empirical SD of the 10,000 estimates of b_1 in the Monte Carlo experiment (0.1973 in Figure 19.5.4) is very close to the computed, exact, analytic SE it is approximating, 0.196 as reported in Figure 19.5.2.

We now turn our attention to the Average Estimated SE and Average Robust SE. In Figure 19.5.4, the average value of the robust SE (0.1901) is much closer to the exact SE (0.196) than the average value of the OLS estimated SE (0.1553). Like the OLS estimated SE, the robust SE is a biased estimator of the exact SE, but the bias is much smaller than that for the OLS estimated SE. The reason the robust SE is almost unbiased is that it is a consistent estimator of the exact SE. Thus, as the sample size increases, the center of the sampling distribution of the robust SE gets closer to the exact SE. This is not true for the OLS estimated SE. It is not only biased but inconsistent. A larger sample size will not improve the performance of the OLS estimated SE. We encourage you to run similar Monte Carlo experiments for different degrees of heteroskedasticity by changing α.

The OLS Regression Add-In

Robust SEs are not available in the core Excel application; however, an Excel add-in, called OLSRegression.xla, is included with this book in the Basic Tools \ ExcelAddIns \ OLSRegression folder. This add-in computes and reports robust SEs (along with a few other OLS regression statistics). Full documentation on installation and use is available in the OLSRegression.doc file in the Basic Tools folder of the CD-ROM that accompanies this book.

Use the Add-In Manager to install the OLS Regression add-in. After successful installation, a new item, OLS Regression ..., will appear in the Tools menu. Click on this option, and a dialog box will pop up, as seen in Figure 19.5.5.

To test drive the OLS Regression add-in, go to the *ComputingSE* sheet and click on the `Draw A Dead Sample` button. The program will create a new worksheet called *DeadSample* as well as computations of OLS parameter estimates, the exact SE, the OLS estimated SE, and the robust SE for the slope b_1. With the OLS Regression add-in installed, execute Tools: OLS Regression ... Click on the "X Variable(s) Range" dialog box and enter the X data, being sure to include the label that identifies the data by simply selecting the appropriate cells on the *DeadSample* sheet. Do the same for the Y data. You can safely ignore the other options at this time. Click OK when you are ready. The

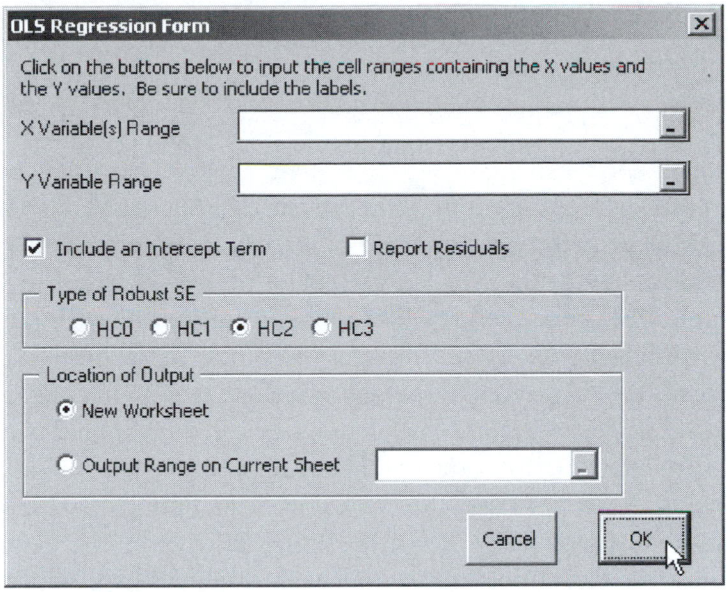

Figure 19.5.5. OLS regression add-in dialog box.
Source: OLSRegression.xla add-in

computer spends a little time making the computations, and the result appears in a new worksheet. Figure 19.5.6 is an example. Your results will be a little different because you will have a different sample.

You can confirm that the results in the first two columns are the same as those generated by LINEST (or Excel's Data Analysis: Regression add-in). What the OLS Regression add-in gives you that is unavailable in Excel is the robust SE, which, if you have reason to believe there is heteroskedasticity in the data, is preferred to the OLS estimated SE. Our default implementation of the robust SE makes a correction (the HC2 choice in the OLS Regression add-in) that has been found to work well in small samples. If you wish to obtain exactly the same result as the *DeadSample* sheet, use the HC0 option in the OLS Regression add-in. For more on this issue, please see the documentation

Regression Statistics for Y(i)			
No. of obs.	100	SSR	15.4524381
No. of missing obs.	0	TSS	872.624106
Mean of Dep Var	5.071845	R^2	0.98229199
RMSE	0.397087	F-stat	5436.21808
Variable	Estimate	SE	Robust SE (HC2)
Intercept	−0.05013	0.080017	0.04210152
X(i)	10.14253	0.137562	0.14371302

Figure 19.5.6. Sample output from OLS regression add-in.

in the OLSRegression.doc file in the Basic Tools folder of this book's CD-ROM.

Summary

Previous sections have shown that the presence of heteroskedasticity means that the OLS estimated SE reported is wrong. This section has used the analytical formulas for the SE to explain the reason for the breakdown in the SE computed via conventional methods. By substituting a single number, the RMSE, when in fact each observation has its own SD of the error box, the conventional method generates a biased and inconsistent estimator of the true SE. The inconsistency is the real killer. It means that no matter the sample size, the poor performance of the OLS estimated SE will not improve. Irrespective of the sample size, the center of the sampling distribution of the OLS estimated SE will differ from the exact SE of the OLS estimator of the sample slope. The conventional approach, using a single number to represent the SD of the error box, works if the errors all come from the same box. This is why homoskedasticity is a requirement for the classical econometric model. In the presence of heteroskedasticity, the OLS estimated SE cannot be trusted.

This section has demonstrated the first of two strategies for dealing with heteroskedasticity: Use OLS but get the SE right. We have shown that by using each observation's residual as an estimate of each observation's own SD of the errors, we can obtain a consistent estimate of the true SE of the OLS sampling distribution. The OLSRegression.xla add-in offers a convenient, easy way to estimate robust SEs from sample data.

Although robust SEs are a marked improvement over conventional OLS SEs, they do not end the story of heteroskedasticity. Unfortunately, the third consequence of violating the requirement of homoskedasticity – OLS is not BLUE – remains. The next section explains how, if the form of the heteroskedasticity is known, GLS can be used to get Best Linear Unbiased Estimates.

19.6. Correcting for Heteroskedasticity: Generalized Least Squares

Workbook: HetGLS.xls

In this section we discuss how to obtain a better estimator than OLS given enough information on the nature of the heteroskedasticity. The correction for heteroskedasticity involves a transformation of the regression equation. When we transform the equation to improve the estimation, we are using generalized least squares (GLS). The basic idea behind GLS is to give more weight to observations that enjoy more compact error-term distributions because these observations will have less bounce from the true regression line.

The ordinary least squares approach is not sophisticated enough to use the fact that the observations with the smaller spread in the error box should be given more weight. The ordinary least squares method is ordinary because it gives every observation equal weight. This means that the OLS estimator is not BLUE – that is, there are other linear, unbiased estimators that have sampling distributions with smaller SEs. If we know enough about the differing spreads to be able to weight the observations via the GLS estimator correctly, OLS can be improved upon. We will demonstrate this point by first returning to the univariate example of Section 19.2 and then addressing the regression examples covered in Section 19.3. We will also show that the estimated SEs from the GLS estimator are consistent.

The Univariate Case: Finding the Optimal Estimator

Recall that Section 19.2 discusses an artificial example of distance measurements in which the first measuring instrument is more precise than the second measuring instrument. For this example, 10 measurements from each instrument were obtained and the Instrument 1 Average distance, the Instrument 2 Average, and the Overall Average were compared. When Instrument 1 was 4 times more precise than Instrument 2, both Monte Carlo evidence and analytical methods showed, somewhat surprisingly, that the Instrument 1 Average was better than the Overall Average in the sense that it had a smaller SE. In other words, the OLS estimator, which used all the data, was inferior to an estimator that used only part of the data. We hinted that there, is in fact, an estimator that is superior to both the Overall and Instrument 1 Averages.

That estimator is the GLS estimator in the univariate case. The GLS estimator applies the basic idea that estimates that are more precise should get more weight. The solution will involve including all 20 measurements in the estimator but giving more weight to the Instrument 1 measurements and less to the Instrument 2 measurements. The result will have a smaller SE than the Instrument 1 Average. The problem regards, what the weights ought to be.

One way to determine the proper weights is to use Excel's Solver. The *UniComputingSE* sheet in HetGLS.xls is set up to compute the SE, using the general formula

$$SD\left(\sum_{i=1}^{n} w_i Y_i\right) = \sqrt{\sum_{i=1}^{n} w_i^2 Var(\varepsilon_i)}$$

$$= \sqrt{\sum_{i=1}^{n} w_i^2 SD^2(\varepsilon_i)}.$$

Set the Precision Ratio parameter in cell B3 to 2. This means that Instrument 1 is twice as precise as Instrument 2 (as you can see in cells B5 and B6). Run Solver to solve the constrained optimization problem as follows:

$$\min_{w_i} \sqrt{\sum_{i=1}^{n} w_i^2 SD^2 \left(\varepsilon_i \right)} \text{ subject to } \sum_{i=1}^{n} w_i = 1.$$

The constraint is necessary to ensure that the estimator is unbiased. We make Solver's job easier by noting that, in the optimal solution, there are only two values for the weights – one for the observations from 1 to 10 and another for observations 11 to 20.

With the Precision Ratio at 2, the optimal weights are 0.08 and 0.02. The problem can also be solved via calculus using the Lagrangian multiplier method. The general, calculus solution reveals that the ratio of the weights is the square of the Precision Ratio.

The $\boxed{\text{Go to Monte Carlo Simulation}}$ button takes you to the *UniMCSim* sheet presenting Monte Carlo evidence showing that the GLS estimator indeed outperforms the Instrument1 estimator, which is demonstrated in Section 19.2 to be preferable to the OLS estimator.

The *UniMCSim* sheet (see Figure 19.6.1) enables comparison of GLS to OLS and GLS to just Instrument 1. Generalized least squares beats both competitors. Of course, this is hardly a proof that GLS is BLUE, but it is suggestive evidence in favor of GLS. That GLS using the optimal weighting scheme is the best possible linear, unbiased estimator can be rigorously proved, but we leave that for more advanced treatments.

The Transformation for Regression Models

In this discussion, we tackle the problem of finding the best, linear, unbiased, estimator in the presence of known heteroskedasticity for the bivariate case. Heteroskedasticity can be corrected via GLS – a technique that relies on transforming the original equation, the errors, of which do not meet the classical requirements, into something new whose errors do meet the conditions demanded by the classical econometric model. When the form of heteroskedasticity is known, we can follow a procedure to return the DGP to one that faithfully meets the requirements of the CEM – and, thus, OLS applied to the transformed model is, once again, BLUE.

For ease of presentation, let us consider a simple bivariate model:

$$Y_i = \beta_0 + \beta_i X_i + \varepsilon_i.$$

	Average	SD	Estimated SE	Exact SE
Instr. 1	25.00	0.32	0.33	0.32
OLS	25.00	0.35	0.36	0.35
GLS	25.00	0.28	0.37	0.28

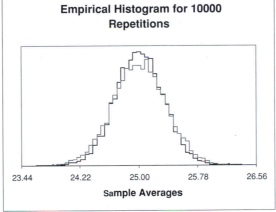

Empirical Histogram for 10000 Repetitions

Sample Averages

Precision of Instrument 1 = 1.00
Precision of Instrument 2 = 2.00
GLS Weight1 = 0.08
GLS Weight2 = 0.02

Figure 19.6.1. GLS versus OLS in the univariate case.
Source: [HetGLS.xls]UniMCSim.

We will model heteroskedasticity as follows:

$$\varepsilon_i = k_i v_i,$$

where ε_i is the heteroskedastic error term, v_i is an independent and identically distributed error term, and i indexes the individual observations. The homoskedastic error term (v_i) is multiplied by a factor k_i that varies across observations. The larger in absolute value k_i is, the larger the SD of ε_i will be. In fact, the relationship is

$$SD(\varepsilon_i) = |k_i| \, SD(v_i).$$

Note that all the v_i terms have the same SD; what makes the SD of the ε_i's vary is the differing values of the k_i's. Our basic equation can be rewritten in terms of the homoskedastic error term as follows:

$$Y_i = \beta_0 + \beta_i X_i + k_i v_i.$$

Here is the key to GLS: To transform the equation so that the error term is simply v_i, all we have to do is divide the entire equation by k_i as follows:

$$\frac{1}{k_i}Y_i = \frac{1}{k_i}\beta_0 + \frac{1}{k_i}\beta_1 X_i + \frac{1}{k_i}\varepsilon_i$$

$$\frac{Y_i}{k_i} = \frac{1}{k_i}\beta_0 + \beta_1\frac{X_i}{k_i} + v_i.$$

The transformed equation now has a homoskedastic error term. Note that the intercept term has been replaced by $\frac{1}{k_i}$. This means that you need to be very careful when implementing GLS to specify in LINEST (or whatever software you are using) that there is no intercept and to include a column of data containing $\frac{1}{k_i}$ as an X variable. Of course, to do this we need to know what k_i is. Understanding the process that generated Y may help us ascertain how k_i is determined. .

We have implemented the GLS correction for the general bivariate model studied in Section 19.3. Recall that in the general bivariate model, the spread of the error terms was given by this equation:

$$SD(\varepsilon_i) = X_i^{\alpha}.$$

The GLS transformation in this case is

$$\frac{1}{X_i^{\alpha}}Y_i = \frac{1}{X_i^{\alpha}}\beta_0 + \frac{1}{X_i^{\alpha}}\beta_1 X_i + \frac{1}{X_i^{\alpha}}\varepsilon_i$$

$$\frac{Y_i}{X_i^{\alpha}} = \frac{1}{X_i^{\alpha}}\beta_0 + \beta_1 X_i^{1-\alpha} + v_i.$$

Note once again, that this regression must be estimated without an intercept term and with an X variable containing the values of $\frac{1}{X_i^{\alpha}}$.

Go to the *GenBivariate* sheet in HetGLS.xls to see this transformation put into practice. You can change the values of each of the parameters given in red in the upper left-hand corner of the sheet. Of most interest is the parameter α. The *GenBivariate* sheet computes the GLS estimate and its estimated SE. There are two possible sets of X values that can be used in these simulations. For now, choose the X values which start at 0.01 and go up to 1 in increments of 0.01. Click on the <button>Go to the Monte Carlo Simulation</button> button to obtain Monte Carlo evidence showing the superiority of the GLS procedure when heteroskedasticity is present (i.e., when α is not 0).

One special feature of the Monte Carlo simulation is that it asks you to specify the value of α to include in the GLS correction. Thus, if a is the number chosen as our estimate of α, the GLS estimator we actually report uses $\frac{1}{X_i^{a}}Y_i$ for the dependent variable and $\frac{1}{X_i^{a}}$ and X_i^{1-a} for the independent variables.

b_1	OLS	GLS (a = 1)	Population Parameters	
Average	9.970	10.007	β 1	10
SD	**1.066**	**0.543**	α	1.0
Average Estimated SE	0.999	0.545	SD $_v$	5.0

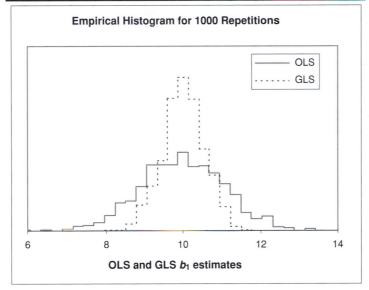

Figure 19.6.2. Comparison of OLS and GLS estimators with $\alpha = 1$; $a = 1$.
Source: [HetGLS.xls]GenBivarMCSim.

We set $\alpha = 1$, chose $a = 1$, and found that GLS does much better than OLS. See Figure 19.6.2. Compare the SDs of the two sets of estimates, 1.066 and 0.543, in this figure. These are Monte Carlo approximations to the SEs of the OLS and GLS estimators, respectively. You would much rather use the GLS estimator than the OLS estimator because you are more likely to draw a b_1 near the true parameter value β_1. Notice that not only does GLS have a smaller SE than OLS, but it appears that the GLS-estimated SE is close to being unbiased (this is in fact the case: the GLS-estimated SE is consistent, meaning that, as the sample size increases, the bias of the GLS-estimated SE vanishes).

However, when we again set $\alpha = 1$, but choose a value of -0.5 for a, so that we are using the wrong value to make the transformation, the GLS estimator with an incorrect adjustment for heteroskedasticity does not outperform

b_1	OLS	GLS (a = 0.5)	Population Parameters	
Average	9.999	9.984	$\beta 1$	10
SD	1.045	1.660	α	1.0
Average Estimated SE	0.998	1.478	SD v	5.0

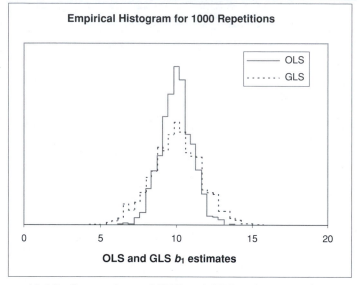

Figure 19.6.3. Comparison of OLS and GLS estimators with $\alpha = 1, a = -0.5$. *Source:* [HetGLS.xls]GenBivarMCSim.

OLS. See Figure 19.6.3. Note that, even though we have put in the wrong correction, the incorrect GLS estimator is still unbiased.

At this level of exposition, we are unable to prove that GLS is in fact BLUE. We can, however, offer some suggestive evidence via Monte Carlo simulations. If the GLS estimator (i.e., the one obtained by multiplying the equation by $\frac{1}{X_i^\alpha}$) is indeed the minimum-variance estimator, then a different transformation must produce an estimator inferior to the GLS estimator. That is, multiplying the equation by $\frac{1}{X_i^a}$, where a is a number different than α, must produce an estimator with a higher variance (and therefore SE). In fact you will find that the estimator with the smallest SE (as approximated by the Monte Carlo simulation) is the one in which we transform by the $\frac{1}{X_i^\alpha}$ factor. Any choice for the exponent other than α produces an approximate SE which is greater than the GLS approximate SE (even though it may have a smaller approximate SE than the OLS approximate SE).

Summary

This section is another one of those good news and bad news stories. First, we consider the good news. If you know the form of the heterskedasticity, it is possible to transform the data and access an estimator called GLS that is BLUE. This is a best-case scenario because you would have the most precise estimator from the class of linear, unbiased estimators.

The bad news is that work with $\alpha = 1$ and $a = -0.5$ reveals a serious complication with GLS: You have to know the exact form of the heteroskedasticity to gain the full benefits of GLS. This has proven to be a major obstacle to the widespread acceptance of GLS-based methods. Heteroskedasticity is not a simple yes or no condition. It comes in many varieties. If the type is unknown, then the cure (i.e., the transformation you implement to carry out GLS) may be worse than the disease, simple OLS. In the last few years, econometricians have increasingly relied on OLS with robust SEs (to avoid the problem of the incorrect OLS estimated SEs) instead of the more aggressive GLS approach.

19.7. A Real Example of Heteroskedasticity: The Earnings Function

Workbook: WagesOct97.xls

The purpose of this section is to show how heteroskedasticity affects inference in real data sets. Because it is usually impossible to observe an entire population, we need to pretend that we have such information. Because our example comes from real data, however, it does shed light on the practical consequences of heteroskedasticity in a way that artificial examples of previous sections cannot. Our example will provide more evidence on how well robust SEs deal with heteroskedasticity and will also highlight a common way in which econometricians handle heteroskedasticity: by changing the functional form of the regression. Finally, the example in this section provides another example of the more realistic Random X's data generation process introduced in Section 18.5.

The WagesOct97.xls file contains data which come from the Outgoing Rotation Groups of the October 1997 Current Population Survey. There are 12,699 observations. Only individuals whose hourly wage could be computed are retained in the data set. Besides Hourly Wage, the variables included are Male and College. The Male variable is self-explanatory. College is a dummy variable that equals 1 if the individual has a 4 year college degree and 0 otherwise.[3]

In this section we will pretend that the 12,699 people in the data set are an entire population. This allows us to know the "true" population regression

---

[3] Details on how the variables were created are contained in the *Codebook* sheet of WagesOct97.xls.

StdDevp of Linear Error		
College	▼	Total
	0	$6.28
	1	$9.77
Grand Total		$7.39

Figure 19.7.1. Standard deviations of Error terms by Education.
Source: [WagesOct97.xls]PivotTable.

functions for the relationships to be investigated. We are interested in the relationship between Hourly Wage, treated as the dependent variable, and College and Male, treated as independent variables (later in this section we make the log of the hourly wage the dependent variable). The population regression function is

$$\text{Hourly Wage} = 9.420 + 2.971 \text{ Male} + 7.963 \text{ College}.$$

Each person's actual hourly wage contains an error term:

$$\text{Observed Hourly Wage}_i = 9.420 + 2.971 \times \text{Male}_i + 7.963 \text{ College}_i + \text{Error}_i,$$
$$i = 1, \ldots, 12{,}699.$$

As usual, i indexes individuals. We assume that the error term reflects luck and the influence of omitted variables. In the population, obtaining a college degree, if the variable Male is held constant, is associated with an increase in Hourly Wage of $7.96 per hour. Furthermore, males make on average of $2.97 more than females with the same level of education. The errors are heteroskedastic as the PivotTable in Figure 19.7.1 makes clear. The errors are also heteroskedastic when considered relative to Male, as Figure 19.7.2 shows.

We will draw samples from the population and use them to estimate the population regression functions. The *Sample* sheet allows you to do so. You have the option of choosing whether the dependent variable should be Hourly Wage or ln Hourly Wage; for now we will examine results for the regression of Hourly Wage on Male and College.

This example simulates the random X's data generation process introduced in Section 18.5. There it is asserted that each observation is like a draw from a box containing the entire population of 12,699 tickets.[4] Each ticket holds information on three variables for a single individual, Hourly Wage, Education, and Male. Unlike the classical econometric model, we are not working with X's that are unchanged from one sample to the next.

Click on the Draw Sample With Replacement **Hourly Wage** button to draw a sample. A dialog box allows you to determine how many observations to include in the sample. You must include at least four in order to have enough to obtain regression

---

[4] As in the simulations from the ComputerUse1997.xls data set in Chapter 18, the draws are made with replacement, meaning that the same observation could appear more than once in any given sample.

StdDevp of Linear Error	
Male ▾	Total
0	$ 6.50
1	$ 7.93
Grand Total	$ 7.26

Figure 19.7.2. Standard deviations of error terms by Gender.
Source: [WagesOct97.xls]PivotTable.

estimates. If you choose the default value of 100, you will obtain results similar to those shown in Figure 19.7.3. The values of the dependent variable (in this case Hourly Wages), College, and Male are displayed in columns A through C. Column D holds the squared residuals. For each sample, we run a B–P test in which the squared residuals are regressed on Education and Male.

Every time a new sample is drawn, you will obtain an entirely (or almost entirely) new set of observations. The sample average values of Education and Male will therefore vary from one sample to another. This is not the fixed-*X*-in-repeated-samples scheme that characterizes the classical econometric model.

To study the issue of heteroskedasticity more carefully, click on the Go to Monte Carlo Simulation button. This sheet allows you to choose which independent

Sample	Avg	SD
Hourly Wage	12.71	6.62
Male	0.48	0.50
College	0.27	0.45
n	100	

Sample Regression		
College	Male	Intercept
6.316	3.676	9.240
1.289	1.145	0.856
0.270	5.716	#N/A
17.93	97	#N/A
1171.75	3169.11	#N/A

Breusch-Pagan Test		
Education	Male	Intercept
19.266	11.774	20.837
13.488	11.986	8.954
0.031	59.818	#N/A
1.572	97	#N/A
11,248	347,080	#N/A
P-value		
21.30%		

Figure 19.7.3. Results for typical sample of 100 observations.
Source: [WagesOct97.xls]Sample.

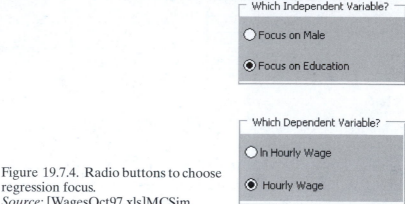

Figure 19.7.4. Radio buttons to choose regression focus.
Source: [WagesOct97.xls]MCSim.

variable to focus on and which dependent variable to include in the regression (as shown in Figure 19.7.4). With the Hourly Wage as the dependent variable and focus on Education as the independent variable, you are ready to go. The Monte Carlo will therefore run many repetitions of this regression model:

$$HourlyWage_i = \beta_0 + \beta_1 College_i + \beta_2 Male_i + \varepsilon_i.$$

This means that the histogram and other summary statistics will pertain to b_1, the slope on education. Click on the button, choose a sample size (make it 25 for this first analysis), and wait a while. The computer has much work to do. In every repetition, the computer first draws a new sample of size 25 on the 3 variables (*HourlyWage*, *Male*, and *College*), then runs an OLS regression, and finally calculates the robust SE of b_1. Figure 19.7.5 displays a typical result of such a simulation.

Three conclusions can be drawn from different comparisons we can make using the results of this Monte Carlo experiment. First, there is clear evidence of heteroskedasticity: The average conventional OLS estimate of the SE of b_1 is 3.363, whereas the Monte Carlo approximation to the SE (the SD of the b_1 estimates) is 4.444. Second, the robust SEs definitely perform better than the OLS SE's, because their average value is 3.862. Third, the robust SEs are apparently still biased downward.

It turns out that robust SEs can perform poorly for small samples but do better and better as the sample size increases. To demonstrate this fact, we ran three additional Monte Carlo simulations, each with 10,000 repetitions. Figure 19.7.6 is a table with the pertinent results. This figure presents evidence that the robust SEs are consistent estimators of the SE of the slope, whereas the regular OLS estimated SEs appear to be biased even in

Slope Estimates			
Average estimate of b_1	7.940	Number of Repetitions	1000
SD estimates	4.444	n	25
Mean OLS SE	3.363		
Mean Robust SE	3.862		

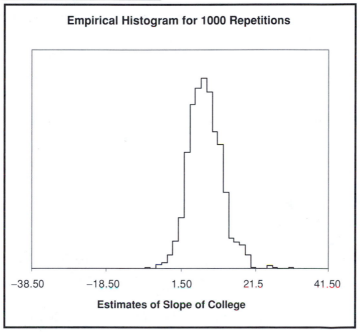

Empirical Histogram for 1000 Repetitions

−38.50   −18.50   1.50   21.5   41.50

Estimates of Slope of College

Figure 19.7.5. Estimating the effect of Education on Hourly Wage with 25 observations.
Source: [WagesOct97.xls]MCSim.

Results for 10,000-Repetition Monte Carlo Experiments						
Dependent Variable: Hourly Wages; Slope of College						
Number of Obs	SD of OLS Estimates	Average OLS SE	Average Robust SE	Average Slope Estimate	Ratio OLS SE/SD of OLS	Ratio Robust SE/SD of OLS
25	4.394	3.325	3.792	7.930	76%	86%
100	2.052	1.648	1.982	7.949	80%	97%
400	1.018	0.830	1.001	7.960	82%	98%
		True Slope		7.963		

Figure 19.7.6. Testing the performance of robust and OLS SEs.
Source: [WagesOct97.xls]MCSim.

large samples. Notice that, as we would expect from the square-root law, the SE of the slope for *College* falls roughly by half for every quadrupling of the sample size.

Robust SEs do not always perform better than OLS estimated SEs. You can demonstrate this fact by choosing Hourly Wage as the dependent variable and focusing on the results for the slope on Male. In this case, the average of the OLS estimated SEs will be closer to the empirical SD than the average of the robust SEs for sample sizes of 100 or less. The discrepancy between robust SEs and OLS estimated SEs gets smaller as the sample size increases. It turns out just through luck that though heteroscedasticity is present, the OLS estimated SE is not far off from exact SE in this case.

Using a Different Functional Form to Handle Heteroskedasticity

Robust SEs are one way to deal with heteroskedasticity. Another approach is to specify a different functional form. A very common procedure in analyses of wages is to take the log of the dependent variable. Although we will not present the evidence here, you can use the WagesOct97.xls workbook to demonstrate that, when the log of the hourly wage is the dependent variable, heteroskedasticity is a much smaller problem than it is when hourly wage is the dependent variable and that robust SEs do not perform any better than regular OLS SEs. There is, however, not much harm in using robust SEs either.

As demonstrated in Chapter 6, we also have strong theoretical reasons for believing that the semilog functional form applies to earnings functions. In other words, when we are trying to explain differences in pay, it is percentage changes that vary linearly with education and experience. Nevertheless, the fact that heteroskedasticity is reduced when we use the log of hourly wages instead of the raw hourly wage data itself partly accounts for the common use of the log of hourly wages in earnings functions.

Summary

This section has investigated the performance of robust SEs in a situation more closely approximating actual conditions than contrived data sets. We find that the robust SE approach performs fairly well.

We have also taken the opportunity to work with the random X's data generation process. Although in this book we have emphasized the classical econometric model, it is important to be aware that econometrics utilizes other DGPs as well. One of our central messages is that valid statistical inference depends on careful modeling of the data generation process.

19.8. Conclusion

This chapter has given extensive coverage to a violation of one of the assumptions of the classical econometric model – namely that the error terms have the same spread, or in box model terms, are drawn from the same box. We outlined four steps for thinking about the problem: understanding the violation itself, appreciating the consequences of the violation, diagnosing the presence of the violation, and finally, correcting the problem. Our discussion has underlined a point made in Chapter 10: When the analogy between the data generating process and the box model is imperfect, statistical inference breaks down. With the B–P test we have extended our repertoire of test statistics, this time using the test statistic as a diagnostic tool. Finally, we have highlighted one approach to dealing with violations of the classical econometric model: the construction of statistics that are robust to the violation. In the next chapter, on autocorrelation, we will see a different violation, the same four steps for thinking about the problem, and a different featured approach to dealing with the violation.

We conclude this chapter with a strong visual message. Figure 19.8.1 illustrates that there are three consequences when a DGP fails to meet the classical econometric model's requirement that errors be homoskedastic.

1. The OLS estimator remains unbiased. The sampling distribution of the OLS estimator remains centered on the true parameter value even in the presence of heteroskedasticity. This is good news.
2. The OLS estimated SE is wrong. This is bad news. In Figure 19.8.1, we show this consequence as an imaginary sampling distribution (which accounts for the dashed line) that is exceptionally spiked. In other words, we get OLS estimated SEs that appear to be exceptionally small, but that is because the formula for the OLS estimated SE breaks down when there is heteroskedasticity. The precision

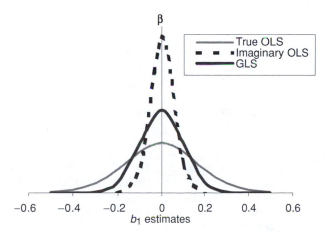

Figure 19.8.1. Three consequences from heteroskedasticity illustrated.

promised by the estimated SE is a mirage, and the true sampling distribution of the OLS estimator has more variability than that indicated by the OLS estimated SE. Furthermore, this problem will not go away as the sample size increases. This is the primary reason you should never trust the OLS estimated SE in the presence of heteroskedasticity. Any procedure that uses the OLS estimated SE, such as confidence intervals and tests of significance, is also contaminated.

3. The OLS estimator is no longer BLUE; but the GLS estimator is BLUE. Figure 19.8.1 shows that GLS is more tightly clustered around the true parameter value than the true OLS sampling distribution. There is no doubt about it: If you know the form of the heteroskedasticity, then you can improve on OLS. In practice, this turns out to be a big "if," which explains the rise of robust SEs as the primary method of dealing with heteroskedasticity. Unlike the conventional OLS estimated SE, the robust SE consistently estimates the exact SE of the OLS estimator, thereby more accurately signaling the true precision of the OLS coefficient estimate.

19.9. Exercises

In Chapter 6, we use the data in the *EducWageData* sheet in the SemiLogEarnings.xls workbook to regress education on wages, for no model of the DGP is introduced before Chapter 6. Therefore, the regression analysis is used strictly as a description of the data.

Chapter 16 returns to that data set, and the estimated standard errors are obtained to create confidence intervals and perform tests of significance. We simply assert that the DGP follows the classical econometric model. The following two models are presented:

$$\text{Linear Model: } Wage_i = \beta_0 + \beta_1 Education_i + \varepsilon_i$$

$$\text{Semilog Model: } \ln Wage_i = \beta_0 + \beta_1 Education_i + \varepsilon_i.$$

We return to this data set once again, this time with an eye toward examining the issue of heteroskedasticity.

1. Open SemiLogEarnings.xls (in the Chapter 6 folder on the CD-ROM) and proceed to the *EducWageData* sheet. Use the Regression option in Excel's Data Analysis add-in to run regressions on the two models. Report your results in a nicely formatted table with SEs in parentheses under the parameter estimates.
2. We are worried, however, that there is heteroskedasticity. Run a B–P test on each model. Describe your procedure. Your answer should include clearly stated null and alternative hypotheses, a test statistic, a *P*-value, and a decision on rejecting or not rejecting the null.
3. In answering the previous question, you reject the null for the linear model, but not for the semilog model. Suppose that for the linear model someone asks for a two-tailed test of the claim that education has no effect on wage. They use the results from your answer to Question 1. What is the problem?
4. Use the OLSRegression.xla add-in to find robust SEs for the linear model. Report your regression results in a nicely formatted table with SEs in parentheses under the parameter estimates.

5. In addition to the theoretical argument for the semilog functional form presented in Chapter 6, your work in Question 2 on the semilog model is an example of why we routinely take the natural log of the dependent variable (a measure of remuneration) in earnings function regressions. What part of your answer to Question 2 helps explain the popularity of the semilog functional form?

References

Our opening quotation comes from McCulloch, J. Huston (1985). "Miscellanea: On Heteros*edasticity," *Econometrica* **53**(2): 483. McCulloch makes a strong case for the "k" spelling and concludes by arguing that

if heteros*edasticity were spelled with a c, it would thus have had to have entered the English language either in 1066 with the Norman invaders or else in the middle ages from Latin, neither of which was the case. Furthermore, it would have to be pronounced "heterossedasticity," which it is not. Heteroskedasticity is therefore the proper English spelling.

A quick look at the econometrics texts on our bookshelves was not conclusive. We resorted to a Google search for both versions and "k" had more hits: 161,000 to 114,000. Convinced by McCulloch, we went with "heteroskedasticity" in this book.

The citation for the B–P Test is Breusch, T. S. and A. R. Pagan (1979). "A Simple Test for Heteroskedasticity and Random Coefficient Variation," *Econometrica* **50**: 987–1007. See Wooldridge (2003), p. 257, for more information.

The shift from attempts to correct OLS in the presence of heteroskedasticity to accepting OLS but computing the estimated SEs via robust SEs started in the 1980s. In *Estimation and Inference in Econometrics* (New York: Oxford University Press, 1993), Davidson and MacKinnon credit "an extremely influential paper by White (1980)" (p. 552). That paper is

White, Halbert (1980), "A Heteroskedasticity-Consistent Covariance Matrix Estimator and a Direct Test for Heteroskedasticity," *Econometrica* **48**(4).

There are a variety of approaches to compute robust SEs. See the documentation for the OLS Regression add-in for more information.

20

Autocorrelation

A great deal of use has undoubtedly been made of least squares regression methods in circumstances in which they are known to be inapplicable. In particular, they have often been employed for the analysis of time series and similar data in which successive observations are serially correlated.

James Durbin and Geoffrey S. Watson[1]

20.1. Introduction

In this part of the book (Chapters 20 and 21), we discuss issues especially related to the study of economic time series. A time series is a sequence of observations on a variable over time. Macroeconomists generally work with time series (e.g., quarterly observations on GDP and monthly observations on the unemployment rate). Time series econometrics is a huge and complicated subject. Our goal is to introduce you to some of the main issues.

We concentrate in this book on static models. A static model deals with the contemporaneous relationship between a dependent variable and one or more independent variables. A simple example would be a model that relates average cigarette consumption in a given year for a given state to the average real price of cigarettes in that year:

$$Q_t = \beta_0 + \beta_1 \cdot RealPrice_t + \varepsilon_t, \quad t = 1960, \dots, 1989.$$

In this model we assume that the price of cigarettes in a given year affects quantity demanded in that year.[2] In many cases, a static model does not adequately capture the relationship between the variables of interest. For example, cigarettes are addictive, and so quantity demanded this year might

---

[1] Durbin and Watson (1950, p. 409).
[2] We are implicitly assuming that changes in quantity demanded are due entirely to shifts in the supply curve. If this is not the case, a single equation model is inappropriate.

depend on prices last year. Capturing this idea in a model requires some additional notation and terminology. If we denote year t's real price by $RealPrice_t$, then the previous year's price is $RealPrice_{t-1}$. The latter quantity is called a one-period *lag* of *RealPrice*. We could then write down a *distributed lag* model:

$$Q_t = \beta_0 + \beta_1 \cdot RealPrice_t + \beta_2 \cdot RealPrice_{t-1} + \varepsilon_t, \quad t = 1960, \ldots, 1989.$$

Although highly relevant to time series applications, distributed lag models are an advanced topic that is not covered in this book.[3]

Let us return to the static model:

$$Q_t = \beta_0 + \beta_1 \cdot RealPrice_t + \varepsilon_t, \quad t = 1960, \ldots, 1989.$$

As always, before we can proceed to draw inferences from regressions from sample data, we need a model of the data generating process. We will attempt to stick as close as possible to the classical econometric model. Thus, to keep things simple, in our discussion of static models we continue to assume that the X's, the independent variables, are fixed in repeated samples. Although this assumption is pretty clearly false for most time series, for static models it does not do too much harm to pretend it is true. Chapter 21 points out how things change when one considers more realistic models for the data generating process.

Unfortunately, we cannot be so cavalier with another key assumption of the classical econometric model: the assertion that the error terms for each observation are independent of one another. In the case we are considering, the error term reflects omitted variables that influence the demand for cigarettes. For example, social attitudes toward cigarette smoking and the amount of cigarette advertising both probably affect the demand for cigarettes. Now social attitudes are fairly similar from one year to the next, though they may vary considerably over longer time periods. Thus, social attitudes in 1961 were probably similar to those in 1960, and those in 1989 were probably similar to those in 1988. If that is true and if social attitudes are an important component of the error term in our model of cigarette demand, the assumption of independent error terms across observations is violated.

These considerations apply quite generally. In most time series, it is plausible that the omitted variables change slowly over time. Thus, the influence of the omitted variable is similar from one time period to the next. Therefore,

---

[3] For a good treatment of distributed lag models, see Wooldridge (2003), pp. 326–329 and 601–607.

the error terms are correlated with one another. This violation of the classical econometric model is generally known as autocorrelation of the errors. As is the case with heteroskedasticity, OLS estimates remain unbiased, but the estimated SEs are biased.

For both heteroskedasticity and autocorrelation there are two approaches to dealing with the problem. You can either attempt to correct the bias in the estimated SE, by constructing a heteroskedasticity- or autocorrelation-robust estimated SE, or you can transform the original data and use generalized least squares (GLS) or feasible generalized least squares (FGLS). The advantage of the former method is that it is not necessary to know the exact nature of the heteroskedasticity or autocorrelation to come up with consistent estimates of the SE. The advantage of the latter method is that, if you know enough about the form of the heteroskedasticity or autocorrelation, the GLS or FGLS estimator has a smaller SE than OLS. In our discussion of heteroskedasticity we have chosen to emphasize the first method of dealing with the problem; this chapter emphasizes the latter method. These choices reflect the actual practice of empirical economists who have spent much more time trying to model the exact nature of the autocorrelation in their data sets than the heteroskedasticity.

In this chapter, we analyze autocorrelation in the errors and apply the results to the study of static time series models. In many ways our discussion of autocorrelation parallels that of heteroskedasticity. The chapter is organized in four main parts:

- Understanding autocorrelation
- Consequences of autocorrelation for the OLS estimator
- Diagnosing the presence of autocorrelation
- Correcting for autocorrelation

Chapter 21 goes on to consider several topics that stem from the discussion of autocorrelation in static models: trends and seasonal adjustment, issues surrounding the data generation process (stationarity and weak dependence), forecasting, and lagged dependent variable models.

20.2. Understanding Autocorrelation

Workbook: AutoCorr.xls

Chapter 9 uses free-throw shooting as a vehicle to explain Monte Carlo simulation. The model assumed independence in free-throw shooting. This means that making or missing the previous free throw has no effect on the current free throw. Independence means that the shooter does not get hot – the probability of making the next free throw does not increase after making the

t	Z	Lagged Z
1	−4.49	.
2	0.55	−4.49
3	17.08	0.55
4	−7.05	17.08
5	6.13	−7.05
r(Z, Lagged Z)	−0.55	

Figure 20.2.1. Lagging a variable.

first free throw or after making six in a row.[4] Flipping coins is also an example of an independent chance process. It does not matter if five heads have been flipped in a row; the chances that the next flip will be heads remains 50 percent. The coin does not remember previous results.

Of course, not all processes are independent. In other words, past results sometimes *do* influence the current outcome. If missing five shots in a row makes the shooter hesitate or alters his or her mechanics, thereby lowering the chances of making the next shot, that is autocorrelation at work. The weather is clearly dependent on previous results. The position of the hurricane on today's weather map depends on where it was yesterday. Today's temperature depends on yesterday's temperature. You would do a decent job of predicting the temperature tomorrow just by guessing today's 85°F because weather tends to persist.

This section describes the terminology used in discussing autocorrelation and then presents a detailed explanation of a particular type of autocorrelation called the AR(1) model. The AutoCorr.xls file will enable you to walk through the process that generates observed Y in an AR(1) model.

The Naming Scheme

We begin with some basic terminology. Autocorrelation is sometimes called serial correlation. These terms used to have slightly different meanings, but now they are essentially synonyms. *Auto*, which means *self*, signifies that a series is correlated with itself.

Subscripts are generally used to specify the time period in which a variable is observed. Thus, Z_1 means the value of Z in period 1, whereas Z_6 is its value in period 6. *Lagging* a variable means reading its previous value. In general, Z_t lagged one period is equal to Z_{t-1}. The numbers in Figure 20.2.1 illustrate the concept of lagging. The third value is 17.08. At $t = 4$, Z's lagged value is 17.08, or Z's previous value. At $t = 1$, there is no value for Z lagged one

---

[4] This may not describe the typical playground player, but it does seem to hold for professionals (see Gilovich and Tversky, [1985]).

period because there is no previous data for Z.[5] A period is often used to indicate a missing value.[6]

The correlation coefficient r of the four pairs of Z and Lagged Z (from $t = 2$ to $t = 5$) equals -0.55. Because this correlation coefficient is found by correlating Z with one-period lags of itself, it is an estimate of the *first-order autocorrelation coefficient*. If you found the correlation coefficient between Z_t and Z_{t-2}, you would have an estimate of the second-order autocorrelation coefficient.[7]

Autoregression, and its adjective *autoregressive*, means that a variable is expressed in an equation in terms of itself. The DGP for such a variable is called an autoregressive process. The parameters of the process can be estimated by regressing current values of the variable on previous, or lagged, values of itself, which accounts for the name autoregression.

The *order* of an autoregressive process is given by the highest lag length involved:

$$\text{AR(1) (First-order autoregression)}: \quad Z_t = \beta_0 + \beta_1 Z_{t-1} + \varepsilon_t$$
$$\text{AR(2)(Second-order autoregression)}: \quad Z_t = \beta_0 + \beta_1 Z_{t-1} + \beta_2 Z_{t-2} + \varepsilon_t$$

Autocorrelation and autoregression are confusing terms. You can keep things straight by noting that, from a single variable, Z_t, its ith lagged counterpart, Z_{t-i}, can be created. The ith order autocorrelation can be estimated by calculating the correlation coefficient between the original series (the Z_t's) and the ith lag of that series (the Z_{t-i}'s). The ith order autoregression is found by regressing Z_t on Z_{t-1}, Z_{t-2}, ..., and Z_{t-i}.

The AR(1) Model of Autocorrelation

The idea of autocorrelation is applicable to any series of numbers. With regard to the errors in a regression equation, autocorrelation refers to a situation in which the errors, as they are sequentially drawn from the box, are related to each other systematically.

This book focuses on first-order autocorrelation. A first-order autoregressive, or AR(1), process is often the starting point of analysis.

The AR(1) model can be written in the form of two equations as follows:

$$Y_t = \beta_0 + \beta_1 X_t + \varepsilon_t, \tag{1}$$

---

[5] Similarly, if the data were quarterly, a four-period lag would read the value four periods ago. At $t = 5$ (the first quarter of the second year), Z is 6.13 and Z lagged four periods is -4.49. *Leading* a variable reads values ahead.

[6] Do not use blanks to indicate missing values because many software packages and spreadsheets (including Excel) will interpret a blank as a zero.

[7] The estimates of the autocorrelation coefficients are well-behaved provided that the underlying series are stationary, which is a concept discussed in Chapter 21.

where the error terms are generated by a first-order autoregressive process:

$$\varepsilon_t = \rho\varepsilon_{t-1} + v_t. \tag{2}$$

Note that this AR(1) process has no intercept term. With no intercept term in the AR(1) process, we are considering the simplest possible AR(1) model.

The symbol v_t represents the tth draw from a classical econometric error box. When ρ is less than one in absolute value, it can be interpreted as the correlation coefficient between the errors and their values lagged one period. Because the sample correlation coefficient is usually denoted by an r, it makes sense for the analogous population parameter to be ρ, the Greek letter for r.

When ρ is positive, one speaks of positive autocorrelation; when ρ is negative, negative autocorrelation. This book concentrates on positive autocorrelation, which is more common in economic time-series models. In this chapter we restrict our discussion to cases in which ρ is less than one in absolute value. As usual, most of what we have to say about the bivariate case will carry over immediately to the multivariate case of more than one independent variable.

The AR(1) Process in Action

Having described the two equations and the new variables v and ρ, we are ready to begin learning how an AR(1) process actually works.

The second equation in the model,

$$\varepsilon_t = \rho\varepsilon_{t-1} + v_t,$$

says that each error term is composed of ρ times the previous ε error term (ε_{t-1}) plus a draw from the error box (v_t). When ρ is positive and close to 1, the current error term will closely resemble the previous error term. When ρ is 0, there is no autocorrelation (i.e., the error terms are independent of each other). This is exactly what the classical econometric model requires. Any ρ not equal to zero generates autocorrelation because the errors terms are not independent of each other.

You can put these ideas into practice and better learn the concept of autocorrelation by exploring the *AR1Process* sheet in AutoCorr.xls. Read and scroll down the sheet. The example itself starts with the initial values of the table in row 34. Click the [Reset] and [New Starting Values] buttons as needed. The [Generate Another Observation] button walks you through how each observation is generated. The key idea is that the previous ε error term influences the current ε error term – this is autocorrelation. Note that, although we observe the data starting in 1985, it is assumed the process that generates the data started

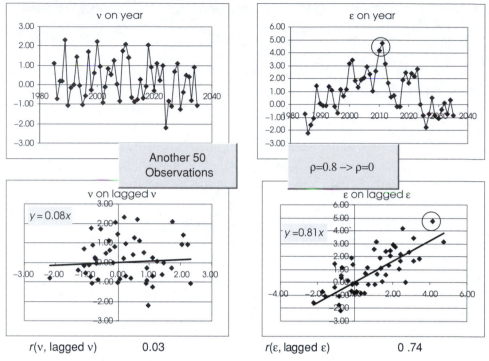

$r(v, \text{lagged } v)$ 0.03 $r(\varepsilon, \text{lagged } \varepsilon)$ 0 .74

Figure 20.2.2. Views of autocorrelation.
Source: [AutoCorr.xls]AR(1)Process.

sometime in the past; thus, we need a previous value for ε, which the computer furnishes.

As you click the button to build up an Observed *Y* value, the button caption changes and message boxes pop up to report on each step of the process. The crucial step occurs when ρ is multiplied by the previous value of ε. The arrows we use to focus attention on how $\rho\varepsilon_{\text{previous}}$ is calculated are part of Excel's auditing feature. You can remove the arrows by executing Tools: Formula Auditing: Remove All Arrows or by clicking on the Reset button.

To see how an autocorrelated process propagates itself, click on the Generate 50 Observations button and then scroll down to see a set of four graphs, as in Figure 20.2.2. The graphs on the left focus on v, the uncorrelated, clean random component, whereas on the right we have ε, the autocorrelated, total error in the model. Compare the top graphs to each other. The v graph is random; over time, the values of v are dispersed all over. Low values are equally likely to be followed by low or high values. The ε graph exhibits a more up and down pattern. There are periods of persistent lows and then switches to persistent highs. Click on the Another 50 Observations button a few times to refresh the graphs. The up and down pattern in the ε's is a telltale sign of autocorrelation. What happens is that a negative ε value tends to generate

Year	ε
2010	4.15
2011	4.74

Figure 20.2.3. The highlighted pair of observations.
Source: [AutoCorr.xls]AR(1)Process.

another negative value, but this is only a tendency. A positive ε value can follow a negative one if there is an exceptionally high v drawn from the error box. The series then jumps from negative to positive and stays positive for a while until it switches back to negative.[8] This description does not fit the v-on-year graph at all.

Another way to see autocorrelation is through the errors themselves. Graphing v or ε against either one's lagged value reveals an obvious difference. The v-on-lagged-v graph is a formless blob, whereas the ε on lagged ε chart exhibits an upward-sloping orientation.

Note how the same data are used in creating the ε-on-year and ε-on-lagged-ε graphs. The circle in Figure 20.2.2 draws attention to the particular pair of values for ε listed in Figure 20.2.3. In the ε-on-year graph, these observations are side by side, whereas in the ε on lagged ε graph, they are x, y coordinates 4.15, 4.74.

Click on the Another 50 Observations button to refresh the graphs. The positive orientation you repeatedly see in the ε-on-lagged-ε graph is a direct manifestation of the AR(1) process. The v-on-lagged-v graph shows no persistent orientation. On occasion, as you repeatedly refresh the graphs, a sample that does not produce a formless blob for the v-on-lagged-v-graph may arise, but this is sampling error at work. The ε-on-lagged-ε graph, you must admit, is persistently positively oriented with a decidedly nonzero slope.[9] These graphs show that the ε random terms are autocorrelated but the v's are not. This will prove to be important when we turn our attention to correcting the autocorrelation.

Another way to understand autocorrelation is to compare autocorrelated and unautocorrelated processes. The $\rho=0.8 \rightarrow \rho=0$ button enables you to toggle back and forth from $\rho = 0.8$ to $\rho = 0$. The button tells you the current value of rho. Click on this button a few times and focus on the ε graphs (because the v graphs are not autocorrelated no matter the value of ρ).

Use the buttons to convince yourself that, as ρ approaches 1, the stronger the autocorrelation becomes. Click on the $\rho=0.1 \rightarrow \rho=0.95$ button to toggle back

---

[8] With $|\rho| < 1$ and a 0 intercept, the process will stay centered on 0, rising and falling but never exploding away. You are free to experiment and ponder the effects of $\rho = +1$ and $\rho > 1$ (or the negative counterparts of these values) by changing ρ in cell C34 and clicking on the appropriate buttons. Before you try large values of ρ, try values close to 1, such as 1.1 or −1.2.

[9] Note that, because we know the process has no intercept, regression is employed through the origin.

and forth between $\rho = 0.1$ (low autocorrelation) and $\rho = 0.95$ (high auto-correlation). Clearly, autocorrelation is present whenever ρ is not zero, but it intensifies in strength as ρ nears one.

Summary

This section has focused on explaining the concept of autocorrelation. The basic idea is that, unlike flipping a coin, an autocorrelated chance process "remembers" the previous results. A common starting point of analysis is the AR(1) Model. In addition to the usual regression equation, a second, autoregressive equation says that the current error is equal to a parameter ρ multiplied by the previous error plus a "clean," unautocorrelated error. The *AR1Process* sheet in the AutoCorr.xls file makes clear that autocorrelation generates patterns in the errors (whether viewed over time or as a function of their lagged values).

20.3. Consequences of Autocorrelation

Workbook: AutoCorr.xls

Autocorrelation means that current values are influenced by past values. If there is autocorrelation in the errors of a regression model, draws from the error box are no longer independent of one another. This section explores the consequences of an AR(1) positively autocorrelated error model for the OLS estimator.

The Data Generation Process

We assume the following static model of the DGP applies:

$$(1) \quad Y_t = \beta_0 + \beta_1 X_t + \varepsilon_t, \quad t = 1, \ldots, T,$$

where the error terms are generated by a first-order autoregressive process:

$$(2) \quad \varepsilon_t = \rho \varepsilon_{t-1} + v_t, \quad t = 1, \ldots, T.$$

The v_t error terms are assumed to be draws from a normally distributed error box in which the draws are independent and identically distributed. We assume the absolute value of the autoregressive parameter ρ is less than 1. (If ρ equals 1, we are dealing with a random walk, which it turns out makes a big difference in the DGP.) Our argument can easily be extended to the case with multiple X's in Eq. (1). We assume the X's are fixed in repeated sampling. This assumption is discussed in more detail at the end of this section.

Three Econometric Consequences of Autocorrelation

When the AR(1) description of the data generating process applies, there are three consequences for the OLS estimator of the parameters in Eq. (1).

(1) OLS Estimates Remain Unbiased

Autocorrelation in the error terms does *not* cause the OLS coefficient estimates to be biased. In other words, the coefficient estimates will still on average be equal to the true parameter value.

(2) OLS Estimated SEs are Inconsistent

If there is autocorrelation in the error terms, then the estimated standard errors from OLS regression will be biased and this bias does not go away as the sample size increases. In the case of positive autocorrelation, the estimated standard errors will typically be too small.[10] The resulting test statistics produced from OLS regressions will be too big and the confidence intervals too narrow. In other words, OLS estimates will appear to be more precise than they actually are. Inference based on the OLS estimated SE is flawed. This is a serious problem.

(3) OLS is not BLUE; GLS is BLUE

Autocorrelated errors destroy a primary virtue of OLS because the OLS estimator is no longer the best linear unbiased estimator. A better estimator (in theory at least) than the OLS estimator is available. The best linear unbiased estimator in the presence of autocorrelation is called the generalized least squares, or GLS, estimator. GLS works by first transforming the original autocorrelated model into the classical econometric model. GLS is better than OLS because GLS has a smaller SE.

These three fundamental points can be made clearer by working with a Monte Carlo simulation of a model in which there is first-order autocorrelation. This section will illustrate via our example that OLS coefficient estimates are unbiased but the estimated SEs are systematically wrong. The section on correcting the AR(1) error model will demonstrate that GLS is superior to OLS in the presence of autocorrelated errors.

---

[10] Even if there is positive autocorrelation in the errors, the OLS reported SEs are not absolutely guaranteed to be too small because the values of the X variable(s) affect the SE. Usually, the X's themselves are positively autocorrelated, which does ensure that the OLS reported SEs are smaller than their true values. A problem using Monte Carlo simulation to demonstrate this point is included in the *Q&A* sheet of the AutoCorr.xls file.

A Monte Carlo Simulation of the Consequences of Positive, First-Order Autocorrelation

A simple model of positive, first-order autocorrelation can be represented by the following two equations:

$$Y_t = \beta_0 + \beta_1 X_t + \varepsilon_t$$

$$\varepsilon_t = \rho \varepsilon_{t-1} + \nu_t,$$

where $0 < \rho < 1$ and ν is drawn from a normal distribution.

Claim #1: The OLS estimates, b_0 and b_1, are *unbiased* even if ρ is not equal to zero.

Claim #2: The estimated SEs of the OLS coefficient estimates are systematically biased if ρ is not equal to zero.

How do we test these two claims?

The sheet *AR1Model* in the AutoCorr.xls workbook is ready to implement a Monte Carlo simulation that illustrates the performance of the OLS estimator in an autocorrelated model.

Begin by noting that there are 60 observations and the X variable ranges from 8 to 125 (as reported in the Summary Statistics table in range A69:F76). The X values are fixed and will remain so throughout the Monte Carlo simulation. Unlike the *AR1Process* sheet example of the previous section, the X variable is not the year. The X variable has a time dimension, but time is captured by the t variable in range A9:A68.

The dependent variable, Y_t, is generated in the range E9:E68. Cell E10, for example, like the other Y cells, contains a formula describing the chance process that generates the data: =beta0+beta1*X+Error (note that we haved named cells containing parameters and variables on the Excel worksheet). The Error term is especially important. The Error value is coming from the cell right next to it, D10, with formula: =rho*D9+C10. Click on cell D10; then click on the formula itself, in the formula bar, to activate Excel's auditing feature. The error term in this model, ε, depends on ρ, the previous ε drawn, and a random error draw ν. Figure 20.3.1 shows these computations in cells B3 through D10 of the *AR1Model* sheet.

For any nonzero ρ, the errors will be autocorrelated. Note that cell C10 has a formula stating that ν =NORMALRANDOM(0,SDnu). Regardless of the value of ρ, the ν's are not autocorrelated.

Hit F9 a few times to get a sense of what is going on. The X variable is fixed, but the other columns are bouncing around. As you hit F9 and recalculate, Excel draws a new value of ν for each observation, which leads to a new ε error term and a new Y. Predicted Y changes because the sample OLS intercept and slope coefficients (in cells H2 and G2 are changing) change as each new sample of 60 observed Y's are drawn.

Parameters	
beta0	10
beta1	0
ρ	0
SD ν	10

X(t)	ν(t)	ε(t) (Error)
8	15.74	0.71
13	9.59	=rho*D9+C10

Figure 20.3.1. Understanding autocorrelation.
Source: [AutoCorr.xls] AR1Model.

The parameter values and OLS regression results are also provided on the chart (cell E20). Figure 20.3.2 displays the results from one particular sample. Although all appears well, severe problems lurk in the background. Concentrate on the sample slope (cell G2), the estimated SE (cell G3), and cell G4, which reports the P-value for the null that β_1 (beta1) is zero. Note that β_1 is, in fact, zero. This means that we should correctly fail to reject the null, at the 5-percent level of significance, 95 percent of the time. Now, hit F9 many times in a row. Something is wrong. As you hit F9, look at how often the result is statistically significantly different from zero. In other words, the P-value is less than 5 percent much too often and we are rejecting the true null too many times. What is going on?

To answer this question, we move away from hitting F9 and turn to its more systematic counterpart, Monte Carlo simulation. Click on the

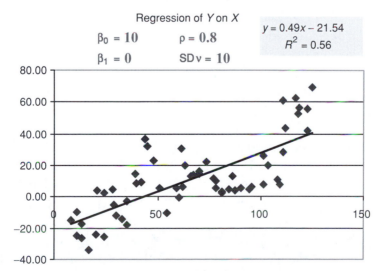

Figure 20.3.2. OLS regression from AR(1)Model.
Source: [AutoCorr.xls] AR1Model.

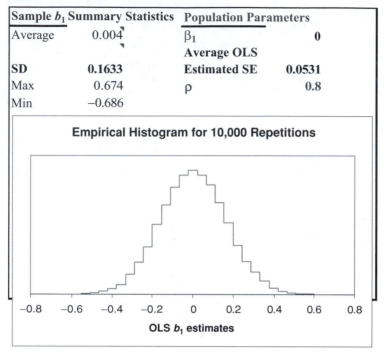

Sample b_1 Summary Statistics		Population Parameters	
Average	0.004	β_1	0
		Average OLS	
SD	0.1633	**Estimated SE**	0.0531
Max	0.674	ρ	0.8
Min	−0.686		

Figure 20.3.3. OLS b_1 Monte Carlo simulation.
Source: [AutoCorr.xls] b1MCSim.

b_1 Monte Carlo Simulation Show button. Ten thousand repetitions of "hitting F9" are displayed in the *b1MCSim* sheet. Figure 20.3.3 shows our results.

The 10,000 OLS sample slopes are used to create the empirical histogram in Figure 20.3.3. It approximates the probability histogram (or sampling distribution) of the OLS b_1 estimator. Because we have so many repetitions, the approximation is quite close. The *y*-axis in the histogram is suppressed to lessen clutter and focus attention on the shape of the histogram. Either a frequency (number of samples from 0 to 10,000) or relative frequency (percentage of samples) *y*-axis interpretation is valid. Thus, very few samples, either as a number or a percentage, had b_1 estimates above 0.5.

The evidence in Figure 20.3.3 supports the two claims about the consequences of autocorrelation in the error terms. First, note that the average sample slope of the 10,000 repetitions is very close to zero, which is the true value of the slope parameter we are estimating. This suggests that the OLS estimator is unbiased.

The OLS estimated SEs, however, are wrong. The Monte Carlo approximation to the true SE of the sample slope is 0.1633. The average of the OLS estimated SEs is a very low 0.0531. This demonstrates the second claim that autocorrelation can produce a misleading OLS estimated SE.

The average of the OLS estimated SEs is an important, but confusing, piece of evidence. Let us focus on how the results of the Monte Carlo are being generated. By repeated sampling, we obtain not only OLS b_1 estimates from each sample but also OLS estimated SEs from each sample. Because the OLS b_1 estimate is a random variable, we can use the average and SD of the 10,000 b_1 estimates to approximate the center and spread of the probability histogram of the b_1 estimator.

Similarly, the OLS estimated SE is a random variable. Given a sample, the spread of the residuals is used to estimate the unobserved SD of the error box. Each sample generates its own estimated SD of the errors and, therefore, the OLS estimated SE varies from sample to sample. By taking the average of the 10,000 OLS estimated SEs, we are finding the center (i.e., expected value) of the OLS estimated SE probability histogram. That it is far away (0.0531) from the SD of the 10,000 b_1 estimates (0.1633) shows that, in general, OLS poorly estimates the spread of the b_1 estimator.

The OLS estimated SE is typically too low because its formula applies to an independent error process. Ordinary least squares uses a formula (in the bivariate case) to calculate the estimated SE of b_1 that relies on the RMSE.

$$\text{OLS Estimated SE}(b_1) = \frac{RMSE}{\sqrt{n} \cdot SD_X}.$$

With AR(1) errors, the true SE of the OLS b_1 estimator is given by a much more complicated formula. The evidence in Figure 20.3.3 tells us that the true SE of the OLS b_1 estimator is around 0.1633.[11] Using the usual OLS formula instead of the correct formula for an AR(1) error process will generate estimates of the SE of the OLS b_1 estimator that are around 0.0532. Thus, OLS estimated SEs are misleading.

Run your own Monte Carlo simulation by clicking on the b_1 Monte Carlo Simulation button in the *b1MCSim* sheet. Do you get similar results? Use the Take A Picture button to keep track of your simulations. Each time you take a picture, the graphic is pasted below the previous picture. As determined by the speed of your computer, 10,000 repetitions may take a long time. The Monte Carlo simulation can be accelerated by clicking on the Speed Up Simulation option. Because it does not have to update the Simulation Progress cell, Excel runs much faster. The drawback is that no feedback on the progress of the simulation is provided.

Your results will be similar but not exactly the same as ours. When running your own Monte Carlo simulation, new error terms, observed Y's, and

---

[11] In fact, the exact OLS SE can be calculated for this process. Given the initial X's, $\rho = 0.8$, and $SD\nu = 10$, the OLS true SE of b_1 is 0.1635. The matrix algebra behind the correct formula is shown beginning in cell A100 of the AR1Model sheet.

OLS sample slopes and estimated SEs will be drawn over and over again. Although your Monte Carlo numbers will not be exactly the same as ours, your conclusion will be: The average OLS slope is close to zero, and the average OLS estimated SE is much smaller than the SD of sample slopes in the simulation. This suggests that OLS produces unbiased estimates of β_1 but that the estimated SE is wrong.

You should be aware that the expected value of the OLS estimated SE is less than the true OLS SE result depends on the particular conditions of this chance process. In the *AR1Model* sheet, $0 < \rho < 1$ and the correlation between X and lagged X is positive (cell AR1Model!B76 shows that the sample correlation $r(X_t, X_{t-1}) = 0.992$). In general, autocorrelation of the error terms causes the OLS estimated SE to be wrong, but the OLS estimated SE is not necessarily too small. If the X's were negatively autocorrelated, the OLS estimated SEs would be too large.[12] Question 5 in the *Q&A* sheet of AutoCorr.xls asks you to explore this issue of the relationship between correlation in the X's and the bias in the estimated SE for b_1.

Getting the wrong SE is no minor drawback. Confidence intervals and hypotheses tests based on the wrong SE must, naturally, also be wrong. To see this, scroll over to the *P*-value results starting in cell R4 of the *b1MCSim* sheet.

The histogram in Figure 20.3.4 makes an important point about the consequences of autocorrelation in the errors. Focusing on the *P*-values is another way of illustrating the claim that OLS in the presence of autocorrelation yields misleading results. The problem is that the *P*-values generated by the OLS estimator, because they are based on the wrong SEs, are all bunched up at low values. Suppose we choose a *P*-value of 5 percent as our significance level cutoff. We should then reject the true null only 5 percent of the time, but at the 5-percent significance level the null was rejected in more than half of the 10,000 samples in this simulation. Put another way, given the population parameters in this example, if you were testing the null that $\beta_1 = 0$ and using the standard 5-percent significance level, OLS gives you a better than even chance of drawing the wrong conclusion that β_1 is not zero. That is a severe flaw.

To describe the situation further, in Figure 20.3.5 we compare the true sampling distribution of the OLS slope estimator under the null hypothesis that $\beta_1 = 0$, with an SE of 0.165 (as approximated by Monte Carlo simulation in Figure 20.3.3) with the incorrect probability histogram, which we would draw using the typical OLS estimated SE of 0.053.

The arrows indicate the 5-percent critical values for the spiked normal curve. If the null is true and if the SE is 0.053 (as reported by OLS),

---

[12] And, as mentioned in a previous footnote of this chapter, if the X's were not at all autocorrelated (highly unlikely in a time series setting), the autocorrelation in the errors would have no effect on the OLS estimator.

Sample *P* Value Summary Statistics		Population Parameters	
Average	0.204	β_1	0
SD	0.283	ρ	0.8
Max	0.999		
Min	0.000	**%*P* Val<5%**	**51.30%**

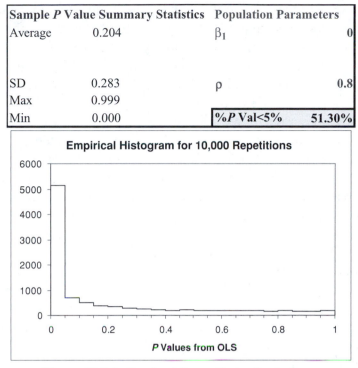

Figure 20.3.4. *P*-value Monte Carlo simulation.
Source: [AutoCorr.xls]b1MCSim.

then only 5 percent of the samples should produce slope estimates out-side the arrows. The broader-shaped normal curve shows the actual sampling distribution. About 50 percent of the b_1 estimates fall outside the arrows.

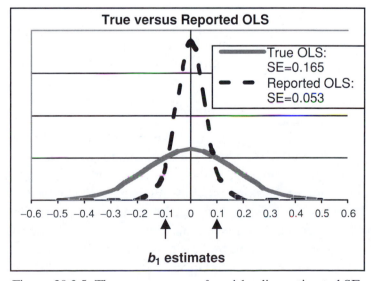

Figure 20.3.5. The consequence of a misleading estimated SE.

Suppose you drew a sample that generated an OLS sample slope coefficient of 0.2. Along with the 0.2 parameter estimate, OLS would report an estimated SE – for instance, 0.05. Suppose you relied on the OLS estimated SE to reconstruct the probability histogram under the null. Because the OLS estimated SE is wrong, the reconstructed probability histogram would be as well. You would reject the zero null because it would seem that the sample estimate would be way out in the tail of the b_1 probability histogram under the null. Chance alone is highly unlikely to have generated such a result. You would *think* that the true probability histogram under the null would be a histogram centered on 0 with an SE of 0.05. In fact, the true SE is much larger, which means the true probability histogram is much less spiked. The true OLS probability histogram shows that a sample slope of 0.2 when $\beta_1 = 0$ is not all that rare.

To further reinforce the lessons that OLS coefficient estimates are unbiased but the estimated SEs are wrong, return to the *AR1Model* sheet and change ρ to 0 (in cell C6). This kills the autocorrelation and removes the violation of the classical econometric model requirements. Run another Monte Carlo simulation from the *b1MCSim* sheet and compare the b_1 and *P*-value histograms under $\rho = 0.8$ and $\rho = 0$. Use the Take A Picture button as needed. What effect does removing the autocorrelation have on the Monte Carlo simulation results? Our results look like those shown in Figure 20.3.6.

With $\rho = 0$, the discrepancy between the Monte Carlo approximation of the true SE and the average OLS estimated SE has disappeared. In other words, the OLS estimated SE is accurately estimating the true SE of the probability histogram of the sample slope. The simple formula used by OLS to estimate the SE of b_1 once again applies because $\rho = 0$. The estimated SE gives us a probability histogram under the null that is, on average, correct.

The *P*-value histogram also behaves as advertised. The true null is rejected at the 5-percent significance level about one in twenty times (unlike the over 50-percent rejection rate that resulted when $\rho = 0.8$).

Summary

This section has shown that first-order autocorrelation in the errors leads to biased OLS estimated SEs but unbiased estimates of the true parameters. The misleading OLS estimated SE is a serious problem that taints conclusions about the precision of the slope estimate and can cause hypothesis testing to go awry. These conclusions apply in much more general situations than the simple model addressed in this section. Thus, we have a strong incentive to determine if autocorrelation in the errors is present. In the next section, we explain how to diagnose autocorrelation.

Sample b_1 Summary Statistics		Population Parameters	
Average	0.000	β_1	0
		Average Reported SE	0.0368
SD	0.0371	ρ	0
Max	0.145		
Min	−0.137		

Sample P Value Summary Statistics		Population Parameters	
Average	0.498	β_1	0
SD	0.287	ρ	0
Max	1.000		
Min	0.000		
		%P Val<5%	5.11%

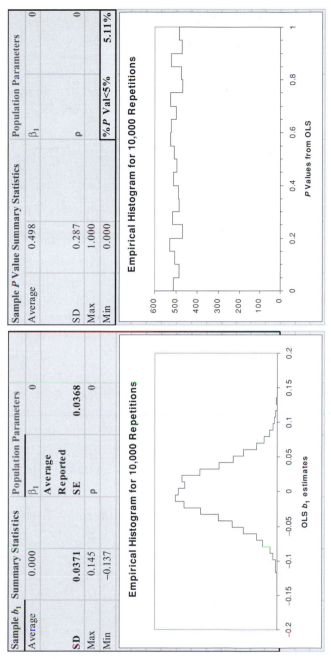

Figure 20.3.6. $\rho = 0$ Monte Carlo simulation.
Source: [AutoCorr.xls]b1MCSim.

20.4. Diagnosing Autocorrelation

Workbook: AutoCorr.xls

In previous sections we have explained the concept of autocorrelation and
the consequences of using the OLS estimator. Autocorrelation in the errors
leads to misleading OLS estimated SEs and OLS is no longer BLUE (a claim
demonstrated in the next section). Thus, we have a compelling interest in
determining if autocorrelation is present in the data we work with. This section describes how to go about figuring out if autocorrelation is present in
a sample. Because time series models often exhibit autocorrelated errors,
econometricians routinely use the methods described herein to test time
series regressions for autocorrelation.

Detecting autocorrelation in the errors of a regression model is not a simple matter. Recall that we cannot observe the error terms, because the values
of the true parameters are unknown. We do, however, have a sample from
which we can estimate the true parameters and calculate residuals. Because
patterns in the residuals tend to reflect patterns in the error terms, diagnosing autocorrelation amounts to examining the residuals and deciding if the
evidence is strong enough to conclude that autocorrelation is present.

This section will explore three ways of using the residuals to detect autocorrelation. The first two approaches are based on a scatter plot of the residuals
and provide support for understanding the most common – but rather complicated – method, the Durbin–Watson test. We continue to work with the
AR(1) Model for the process that generates the error terms,

$$\varepsilon_t = \rho \varepsilon_{t-1} + v_t, \quad t = 1, \ldots, T,$$

with the v_t's independent and identically distributed draws from a classical
econometric error box. At the end of the section we caution you that our
detection procedures are flawed when the AR(1) model does not apply.

Eyeballing the Residuals

The first step in diagnosing autocorrelation is to draw a scatter plot of residuals
as a function of their lagged values. This gives you a rough idea if the residuals
are correlated with each other.

Open the *Graphs* sheet in the AutoCorr.xls workbook to see how the
eyeball method works. Although the graphs in this sheet are based on data
in the *AR1Model* sheet, you can choose between two values of ρ, 0 and 0.8.
Click the toggle button (located below the graphs) a few times to see this.
Make sure that ρ is set equal to 0.8. Autocorrelation will then be apparent in
the ε and residuals graphs. Figure 20.4.1 displays a typical example.

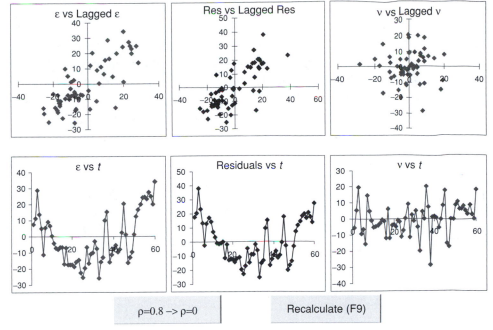

Figure 20.4.1. Examining the residuals.
Source: [AutoCorr.xls]Graphs.

Figure 20.4.1 contains three sets of graphs: on the left are the ε_t's, in the middle the residuals, and on the right are the v_t's that underlie the ε_t's. The top row of charts shows the variables graphed against their own lagged values; the bottom row shows the variables graphed against time. Both the ε_t's and v_t's are unobserved and therefore are depicted in red in the Autocorr.xls workbook (and show up as a lighter shade than the residuals in the black-and-white Figure 20.4.1).

The six graphs reveal some important facts about the AR(1) process. First, observe the difference between the overall pattern in the time series graph of the ε_t's (bottom middle) and the time series graph of the v_t's (bottom right). The autocorrelated ε_t's change in a relatively smooth fashion, whereas the independent v_t's bounce around a great deal.

Second, note that in the time series graphs the residuals do a very good job of tracking the ε_t's. Though the relationship is not exact because of sampling error, the pattern of the residuals pretty faithfully reflects the pattern of the errors. Hit F9 a few times to see that this phenomenon is not a fluke of a single sample.

Next, switch your attention to the top row. The positive relationship between the ε_t's and their lagged counterparts is obvious in the scatter diagram on the left. We don't observe the ε_t's, but the close similarity between the ε_t's and the residuals means that the autocorrelation also shows up quite clearly in the scatter diagram of the residuals against lagged residuals. The eyeball test for first-order autocorrelation is thus very simple: Compute the residuals and the one-period lag of the residuals. Then draw a scatter diagram with the lagged residuals on the x-axis and the residuals on the y-axis. Positive autocorrelation will then manifest itself as a positively sloped cloud on the scatter diagram.

Notice that the scatter graph of the v_t's against their lagged counterparts shows a much weaker positive relationship in this case, which is no surprise because in fact these error terms are unrelated to their own lagged values. Similarly, if you set the value of ρ to zero and then repeatedly resample (by hitting the F9 key), you should in general see no obvious pattern in any of the graphs in the first row. Occasionally, however, you will see a graph of the residuals against lagged residuals in which it appears there might be some evidence of either positive or negative autocorrelation with $\rho = 0$, this is due to chance error.

Testing for Autocorrelation via the Sample Estimate of ρ

The residuals-versus-lagged-residuals scatter plot suggests a formal hypothesis test for autocorrelation: Under the null, the slope of the regression of errors on lagged errors should be zero. Of course, we must use the residuals as a proxy for the errors, and thus the null hypothesis will refer to the slope of the residuals regressed against lagged residuals. If the sample slope is far enough away from zero in standard units, we will reject the null that ρ is zero. In the AutoCorr.xls workbook, the data are being generated by an AR(1) process with no intercept in the equation for the error terms:

$$\varepsilon_t = \rho \varepsilon_{t-1} + v_t.$$

Thus, a good estimate of ρ is the slope of the regression through the origin of residuals against lagged residuals.[13] We call this test for first-order autocorrelation the estimated ρ test. Scroll down to row 40 of the *Graphs* sheet to see this test in action. Click the ρ toggle button a few times and set $\rho = 0.8$. Hit F9 repeatedly. The test is performing well. Cell E44 shows that we are rejecting the false null that there is no autocorrelation.

To calculate the observed difference from zero of the estimate of ρ in standard units, we will use the SE of the slope of the regression through the

---

[13] In fact, there are a variety of ways to get an estimate of ρ. A slightly different estimate of ρ can be obtained by the sample correlation coefficient between the residuals and lagged residuals. This estimate of ρ is extremely close to the slope of the regression of residuals on lagged residuals *with* an intercept included – the only difference being the treatment of the first and last observations. This point is explained in more detail at [AutoCorr.xls] Graphs!Q30. In addition, given that most econometric software packages report the Durbin–Watson d statistic (which will be explained in detail later in this section), another estimate of ρ is $1 - d/2$. Further explanation of the different estimators of ρ is available in [AutoCorr.xls]Graphs!Q1.

origin and apply the z-statistic under the presumption that the probability histogram is approximately normally distributed. There is one problem with this procedure: The data generating process clearly does not conform to the classical econometric model. The difficulty is that the X's in the regression, being the lagged residuals, are obviously not fixed in repeated samples; therefore, we cannot be sure that standard results apply.

It turns out that the unusual data generating process does indeed cause problems, though they go away as the sample size gets large. To show exactly what is going on requires much messy algebra, which we will forgo here. The main results are that the sample slope is a biased estimator of ρ, that there is no known unbiased estimator, and that the bias goes away in large samples (i.e., the sample slope is a consistent estimator of ρ). Furthermore, the probability histogram converges toward the normal curve as the sample size increases.

We demonstrate these facts via a Monte Carlo simulation. First, use the ρ toggle button to make sure ρ is set equal to 0.8. We draw a sample of 60 observations with every repetition, and then calculate the OLS regression of Y on X. The residuals are obtained from this regression. Next we run a regression through the origin of residuals on lagged residuals to obtain a slope that is our estimated ρ. This is done 10,000 times to obtain an empirical distribution of estimated ρ that approximates its long-run frequency distribution (or probability histogram). To run this Monte Carlo simulation, click on the $\boxed{\text{Show Estimated } \rho \text{ Monte Carlo}}$ button at Graphs!C50. You are sent to the *rhoMCSim* sheet, make sure that you choose 60 observations in the Number Obs option box. Click on the $\boxed{\text{Estimated } \rho \text{ Monte Carlo}}$ button. Our results are shown in Figure 20.4.2. This Monte Carlo simulation reveals good and bad news about the estimated ρ test. First we present the good news. When $\rho = 0.8$, the distribution of estimated ρ is centered far from zero. We will reject the false null the vast majority of the time. The test really does detect autocorrelation in our constructed example – 60 observations generated according to the AR(1) model with a ρ of 0.8 and the given values of X.

Here is the bad news. The distribution of estimated ρ is not normal, and it is not centered on 0.8. The average of the 10,000 estimated ρ's in this run was 0.700, and the distribution has a long tail toward zero.

These results signify that the probability histogram for estimated ρ (the slope of the regression through the origin of residuals on lagged residuals) is not centered on the true value of ρ and is not normally distributed. Fortunately, as the sample size increases, the distribution of estimated ρ will converge to the normal distribution and the expected value of estimated ρ will converge to ρ. In other words, we are working with a consistent estimator for ρ.

Sample rho Summary Statistics		Population Parameters	
Average	0.700	ρ	**0.8**
SD	0.1034	Average Reported SE	0.0919
Max	0.960	Number Obs	60
Min	0.129		

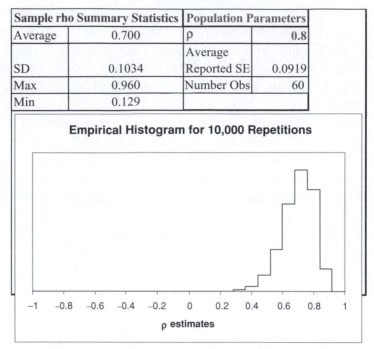

Empirical Histogram for 10,000 Repetitions

ρ **estimates**

Figure 20.4.2. Estimated ρ Monte Carlo simulation.
Source: [AutoCorr.xls]rhoMCSim.

That the bias of estimated ρ is inversely related to the sample size can be illustrated by the method of Monte Carlo simulation. By setting the number of observations in the Monte Carlo simulation in the *rhoMCSim* sheet (click on the desired radio button in the Number Obs option controller), you can verify that our estimator of ρ improves as the sample size increases. Figure 20.4.3 gives our results for 10 and 20 observations. The Monte Carlo results in Figure 20.4.3 clearly demonstrate that estimated ρ's small sample probability histogram depends on the sample size (and, it turns out, on the particular values of X in the sample). With 10 observations, estimated ρ is centered around 0.1 (that is very far from the true value of 0.8), and, consequently, we will mistakenly fail to reject the null of no autocorrelation quite frequently. As the sample size increases to 20, estimated ρ's expected value is around 0.4; as has already been seen, its expected value rises to around 0.7 with 60 observations. As the number of observations rises, estimated ρ's expected value approaches ρ.

Thus, for large sample sizes, the estimated ρ test for detecting autocorrelation in the errors is a good solution. For small samples, however, the bias in estimated ρ is crippling. Because of this, James Durbin and Geoffrey S. Watson created a statistic that applies even in small samples.

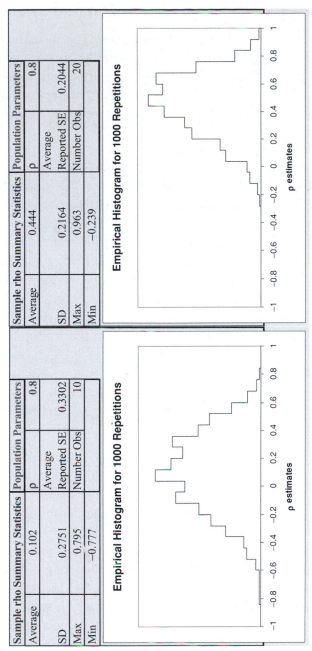

Sample rho Summary Statistics		Population Parameters	
Average	0.102	ρ	0.8
SD	0.2751	Average Reported SE	0.3302
Max	0.795	Number Obs	10
Min	−0.777		

Empirical Histogram for 1000 Repetitions

ρ estimates

Sample rho Summary Statistics		Population Parameters	
Average	0.444	ρ	0.8
SD	0.2164	Average Reported SE	0.2044
Max	0.963	Number Obs	20
Min	−0.239		

Empirical Histogram for 1000 Repetitions

ρ estimates

Figure 20.4.3. Estimated ρ with varying sample size.
Source: [AutoCorr.xls]rhoMCSim.

Testing for Autocorrelation via the Durbin–Watson **d** statistic

Durbin and Watson wanted to detect autocorrelation (because the OLS estimated SEs are wrong and OLS is not BLUE) no matter the sample size. They
knew that directly testing estimated ρ from the residuals works only for large
samples. In 1950 and 1951, they published two important papers that showed
how to test for first-order autocorrelated errors even if the sample size is
small.

Durbin and Watson's statistic (originally called the d statistic and also
known as the DW statistic) is rather complicated. Furthermore, it applies
only if the chance process that generates the data follows an AR(1) process, the errors are normally distributed, and the model is correctly specified.
Since the 1950s, a great deal of effort has been spent on generalizing the
Durbin–Watson strategy (e.g., dealing with the case in which lagged Y variables are included as regressors). The problem of detecting autocorrelation
in the errors generated by a variety of autoregressive processes (including
higher order autoregressive and moving average schemes) in small samples
remains unsolved, however. As a practical matter, the Durbin–Watson test
is routinely run as a general diagnostic even though the strict requirements
of the test are not met.

In this section, we set up an AR(1) chance error process with the correctly
specified model. We can then explain and demonstrate how the Durbin–
Watson d statistic can be used to detect autocorrelation. We begin with the d
statistic itself:

$$d = \frac{\sum_{t=2}^{T} \left(residuals_t - residuals_{t-1} \right)^2}{\sum_{t=1}^{T} residuals_t^2}.$$

Notice how the formula uses the residuals (not the errors, for the errors
cannot be observed) and forms a ratio. The observed d value in any given
sample is a random variable because the residuals contain chance error.

Go to [AutoCorr.xls] AR1Model!R2 to see the formula applied and to
verify that d is a random variable. Set $\rho = 0.8$ in cell AR1Model!C6 if needed.
Clearly, recalculating the sheet by hitting F9 draws a new sample with new
realized chance errors and observed Y's. This results in new OLS b_0 and b_1
coefficient estimates. The new observed and new predicted Y's generate new
residuals and thus a new value of d.

Note that, with $\rho = 0.8$, d seems to be bouncing around 0.5 or so. Pay close
attention as you hit F9 and convince yourself that d is never negative. Now
remove the autocorrelation by changing the value of ρ in cell C6 to zero. Now
d is bouncing around 2. This is the key to the Durbin–Watson test: If there
is no first-order autocorrelation, d will be close to 2; if there is first-order
autocorrelation, d will be far away from 2.

As with the estimated ρ test, the null hypothesis is that there is no first-order autocorrelation (i.e., ρ is equal to 0). That would mean that the errors are really independent of each other and that you can go ahead and use the OLS estimated SEs because the classical econometric model applies. If the null is true, then the expected value of d is equal to 2 and we would expect to see a value of d near 2.

The alternative hypothesis is that there is first-order autocorrelation, (i.e., ρ is not equal to 0). If the alternative is true, then the expected value of d is not equal to 2. If the observed value of d from a given sample is really far away from 2, then we would conclude that autocorrelation is present.

Suppose you obtain a $d = 1.62$. Is this value "around 2" or "really far away from 2"? To answer that, you would need to know the sampling distribution of the Durbin–Watson d statistic. Then you would know how far away from 2 would be far enough to be statistically significantly different from 2 so that you would reject the null that there is no autocorrelation.

Life would be much easier if the Durbin–Watson d statistic were normally distributed. We'd just find the SE of the Durbin–Watson statistic, compute a z-statistic, and be done. Unfortunately, the Durbin–Watson statistic is neither normally distributed nor easily described by two parameters (center and spread) like the normal distribution. The Durbin–Watson d statistic has its own sampling distribution that depends on the process generating observed Y and the values of the independent variables (the X's). We can approximate the Durbin–Watson d distribution using Monte Carlo simulation.

Click on the DW Monte Carlo Simulation Show button to continue learning about the Durbin–Watson d test. Figure 20.4.4 displays Monte Carlo simulations of 10,000 repetitions with $\rho = 0.8$ and $\rho = 0$.

Clearly, when $\rho = 0.8$, the average d is far from 2 (the expected value under the null of no autocorrelation), whereas $\rho = 0$ generates a probability histogram centered on 2. The histogram on the right implies that we would reject the null of no autocorrelation if we observed a d statistic less than 1.5 (or greater than 2.5) or so. After all, under the null of no autocorrelation, we would expect to see values near 2. The histogram shows that values below 1.5 and above 2.5 are unlikely.

Although Monte Carlo simulation can be used to illustrate the sampling distribution of the d statistic under alternative values of ρ, it makes little sense to actually compute a d statistic P-value with Monte Carlo simulation. What is needed is the exact probability histogram of the Durbin–Watson d statistic.

Unfortunately, the distribution of the d statistic depends not only on ρ but also on the particular values of the X variable(s) in the regression! Durbin and Watson were stumped by this complication because it means the d statistic cannot be tabulated – a different table would be needed for every different data set. As a workaround, they created an ingenious solution involving upper

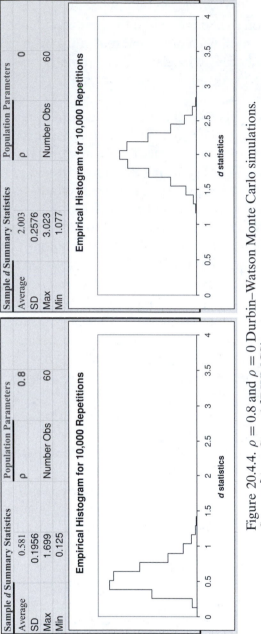

Figure 20.4.4. $\rho = 0.8$ and $\rho = 0$ Durbin–Watson Monte Carlo simulations.
Source: [AutoCorr.xls]DWMCSim.

and lower bounds for the *d* statistic. Many statistics and econometrics texts still provide printed tables based on this method. Fortunately, improvements in numerical algorithms and ever faster computers have made these tables unnecessary. High-quality econometric software should report not only the Durbin–Watson *d* statistic but also its associated exact *P*-value. Once the *P*-value is obtained, significance testing proceeds as usual – low *P*-values are evidence against the null of no autocorrelation.

This book comes with an Excel add-in called the P Value Calculator that will compute and report the Durbin–Watson *d* statistic and *P*-value. To access the P Value Calculator add-in, you must load and install the Excel add-in file, *PValue.xla*. The Basic Tools/Excel Add-Ins folder contains a Word file called PValue.doc with complete instructions. Once the P Value add-in is available, it can be used to calculate the Durbin–Watson *d* statistic and *P*-value as described below.

You can practice the Durbin–Watson test by clicking the `Create One Sample` button (near cell Y3 of the *AR1Model* sheet). A new sheet is inserted into the workbook with a dead sample. Use this sample to find the residuals from the OLS regression of *Y* on *X*. You can use LINEST and then manually compute the residuals or the Regression option in Excel's *Data Analysis ToolPak* add-in (Tools: Data Analysis: Regression), making sure to check the Residuals box.

Now that the residuals have been obtained, click on the Tools menu and select the P Values... item to display the P Value Calculator form. Select the Durbin–Watson *d* choice and click the Next button to get the Durbin–Watson Analysis dialog box shown in Figure 20.4.5. Next, click on the Input X Data

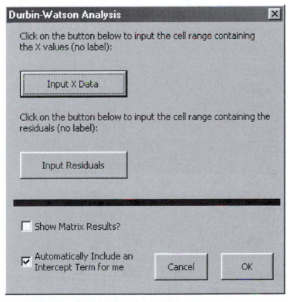

Figure 20.4.5. Dialog box for Durbin–Watson analysis in *P*-values add-in.

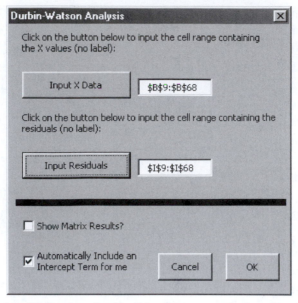

Figure 20.4.6. Dialog box for Durbin–Watson analysis in *P*-value add-in with data ranges selected.

and Input Residuals buttons. You will be prompted to select cell ranges. The *X* data are contained in column A (range A2:A61), whereas the location of the residuals depends on how you computed them. It does not matter if the *X* variables are on one sheet and the residuals on another. Simply select the appropriate ranges when prompted.

After you have provided the *X* data and residuals information, the Durbin–Watson Analysis dialog box might look like Figure 20.4.6.

Click OK, and Excel will go to work. The time needed to make the complicated calculations depends on the number of observations, number of *X* variables, and, of course, the speed of your computer. Upon completion, the results are reported to you via a message box, which looks like Figure 20.4.7. Your result will be different from that shown in Figure 20.4.7 because you are working with a different sample. Of course, with $\rho = 0.8$, you probably will also obtain a very small *P*-value and reject the null of no autocorrelation.

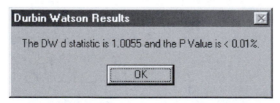

Figure 20.4.7. Results from Durbin–Watson analysis, where $\rho = 0.8$, using *P*-value add-in.

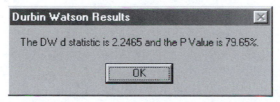

Figure 20.4.8. Results from Durbin–Watson analysis, where $\rho = 0$, using *P*-value add-in.

You can practice some more by setting $\rho = 0$, clicking the Create One Sample button, and finding the *P*-value for the Durbin–Watson *d* statistic. In this case, we could not reject the null of no autocorrelation, as shown in Figure 20.4.8.

Summary

This section has demonstrated how to detect an AR(1) process autocorrelation in the errors via visual inspection of the residuals on lagged residuals scatter plot, the estimated ρ hypothesis test, and the Durbin–Watson *d* statistic test of significance. Sample evidence can be used to reach a decision concerning the presence of autocorrelation.

Unfortunately, there are serious complications involved in diagnosing autocorrelation in practice. Rejection of the null hypothesis of no autocorrelation by either the estimated ρ or Durbin–Watson test does not mean that an AR(1) process with a nonzero ρ is present in a particular application.

This depressing result must be emphasized. This section has focused exclusively on a first-order autocorrelated error-process associated with a bivariate regression equation. The model contains two equations:

$$Y_t = \beta_0 + \beta_1 X_t + \varepsilon_t$$

$$\varepsilon_t = \rho \varepsilon_{t-1} + v_t.$$

Higher order autocorrelated or more complicated error-generating processes might produce a residuals pattern detected by the estimated ρ and Durbin–Watson tests as first-order autocorrelation. In other words, these tests are incapable of distinguishing between *types* of error processes, of which there are infinitely many.

Thus, it is important to remember that the tests discussed in this section presume proper specification of the regression equation (and included *X* variables) and a first-order autocorrelated error process. Deviations from the AR(1) model, whether in the observed *Y* or error-generating equations, may be picked up as first-order autocorrelation.

20.5. Correcting Autocorrelation

Workbook: AutoCorr.xls

Suppose that you conclude that you have first-order positive autocorrelation. What can you do about it?

If the AR(1) model applies, the autocorrelation can be removed. The data can be *transformed*, and thus, once again, the process that generated the data meets the requirements of the classical econometric model. We then run OLS on the transformed data. Applying OLS on appropriately transformed data is called the GLS estimator, and it is BLUE.

In this section we will first show the algebraic rationale behind the transformation and then demonstrate GLS using the data in the *AR1 Model* sheet in AutoCorr.xls. A Monte Carlo simulation will compare the OLS and GLS estimators to support the claim that GLS is BLUE (and OLS is not) under an AR(1) error process.

In practice, ρ is unknown. Nevertheless, on the assumption that the errors follow the AR(1) process, it is possible to estimate ρ, transform the data using the estimated ρ, and run OLS on the transformed data. This procedure, called feasible generalized least squares (FGLS) usually improves on OLS.

The Algebra behind GLS

Our AR(1) autocorrelated error model contains the following two equations:

$$Y_t = \beta_0 + \beta_1 X_t + \varepsilon_t$$
$$\varepsilon_t = \rho \varepsilon_{t-1} + v_t,$$

where $-1 < \rho < 1$ and the v's are draws from a normal error distribution.[14]

The idea behind correcting this first-order autocorrelated error process is not difficult. We simply *transform* the model so that we get rid of the ε errors that are systematically related to the previous errors, leaving only the v errors that represent independent, identically distributed draws from a normally distributed error box. The *Graphs* sheet shows that no matter the value of ρ, v remains well behaved. Replacing ε with v is the key to the correction.

Starting with the AR(1) model, we can do some simple algebra that will remove the ε errors and, thus, the autocorrelation. If the regression equation is misspecified[15] or the error process does not follow the AR(1) model, the transformation presented below will not work.

---

[14] In Autocorr.xls, the v's are normally distributed, but normality is not an essential assumption for this discussion.

[15] See the exercises for an example in which misspecification induces apparent autocorrelation.

Begin by substituting the error-generating equation into the equation that generates the observed Y:

$$Y_t = \beta_0 + \beta_1 X_t + \rho \varepsilon_{t-1} + \nu_t.$$

Our goal is to remove $\rho \varepsilon_{t-1}$, leaving only ν_t as a pure error term with all the properties of the classical econometrics model.

Because each individual Y is generated the same way, the equation for the previous Y, Y_{t-1}, is

$$Y_{t-1} = \beta_0 + \beta_1 X_{t-1} + \varepsilon_{t-1}.$$

Multiply the equation above by ρ to get

$$\rho Y_{t-1} = \rho \beta_0 + \rho \beta_1 X_{t-1} + \rho \varepsilon_{t-1}.$$

Subtract this equation from the first one to obtain

$$Y_t - \rho Y_{t-1} = \beta_0 - \rho \beta_0 + \beta_1 X_t - \rho \beta_1 X_{t-1} + \rho \varepsilon_{t-1} + \nu_t - \rho \varepsilon_{t-1}.$$

This equation can be rewritten (simply by collecting terms) as a model whose error term is a pure, independently and identically distributed error, ν_t:

$$Y_t - \rho Y_{t-1} = \beta_0 (1 - \rho) + \beta_1 X_t - \rho \beta_1 X_{t-1} + \nu_t.$$

If we define new variables $Y_t^* = Y_t - \rho Y_{t-1}$ and $X_t^* = X_t - \rho X_{t-1}$, then we have

$$Y_t^* = \beta_0 (1 - \rho) + \beta_1 X_t^* + \nu_t.$$

This model no longer contains X and Y but rather *transformations* X^* and Y^* of the independent and dependent variables that involve ρ. Note that β_0 and β_1 are the original parameter values of the model. Running OLS on the transformed model is called generalized least squares. Notice as well that when $\rho = 0$, the transformation reduces to the familiar OLS model. Our new model is called generalized least squares because the transformation applied here is one of many possible transformations, which includes OLS as a particular case.[16]

The intercept term in the transformed model deserves special mention. As we know, OLS implicitly treats the X value for the intercept term as a 1 for each observation. Mathematically,

$$Y_t = \beta_0 + \beta_1 X_t + \varepsilon_t$$

---

[16] Heteroskedastic error models can also be algebraically manipulated to meet the homoskedasticity requirement (see Chapter 19) when the form of the heteroskedasticity is known.

is identical to

$$Y_t = \beta_0 \times 1 + \beta_1 X_t + \varepsilon_t.$$

The transformed model, however, has changed the intercept term from 1 to $(1-\rho)$:

$$Y_t^* = \beta_0(1-\rho) + \beta_1 X_t^* + v_t.$$

We will have to pay close attention when estimating this model. Either we need to interpret the reported intercept coefficient as an estimate of $\beta_0(1-\rho)$, or we can tell the computer software to suppress the usual intercept in favor of the transformed intercept. In Excel, this is done by including a new X variable – a column of $(1-\rho)$'s – and running the regression without an intercept.

There is an additional sticky detail to consider. How do we transform the first observation? No previous observed value of the independent or dependent variables is available, and thus we cannot apply the formula for the transformed model on the first observation.

In early work on autocorrelated models, the first observation was simply thrown out.[17] Intuitively, if the number of observations is large, this procedure might not be too harmful. With small samples, however, removing observations can cause parameter estimates to be noticeably less precise. It turns out that the following formula is the correct transformation to apply to the first observation:

$$Y_1^* = \sqrt{(1-\rho^2)}\,Y_1$$

$$X_1^* = \sqrt{(1-\rho^2)}\,X_1$$

$$\text{Intercept}_1^* = \sqrt{(1-\rho^2)}.$$

The explanation for why this is the appropriate transformation is beyond the scope of this book. Intuitively, what this transformation accomplishes is to ensure that the error term in the transformed equation for the first observation has the same spread as the other error terms (i.e., the spread of the v's).[18]

In summary, if you run OLS on the AR(1) model,

$$Y_t = \beta_0 + \beta_1 X_t + \varepsilon_t$$

$$\varepsilon_t = \rho\varepsilon_{t-1} + v_t,$$

---

[17] See, for example, Cochrane and Orcutt (1949).
[18] That is, $SD(\sqrt{1-\rho^2}\varepsilon_1) = SD(v_1)$. For more details, see Greene (2000), p. 543, or Goldberger (1991), pp. 302–3.

there are three consequences: (1) although the OLS coefficient estimates are unbiased, (2) the reported SEs are wrong and (3) OLS is not BLUE.

Algebraic manipulation shows that the model can be transformed into one with a well-behaved error term:

$$Y_t^* = \beta_0 (1 - \rho) + \beta_1 X_t^* + v_t.$$

Running OLS on this model is called GLS. It generates the right SEs and it is BLUE.

Ordinary least squares and GLS use the same coefficient-fitting algorithm (minimize the sum of the squared residuals), but the algorithm is applied to different values of Y and the X (including the intercept term). For OLS, the original values are used, whereas transformed data are utilized with GLS.

An Example of GLS Estimation

In cells AE9:AH68 of the *AR1Model* sheet, the original intercept, X, and the Y data have been appropriately transformed. Click the View Formula button to see how the algebra of the previous section has been applied. Note how the first observation has a different transformation than the rest. Click the View Formula Results button to return the display to its original setting.[19]

With the data transformed, we can now use OLS to estimate the coefficients. We apply LINEST to the transformed data, taking care to specify that LINEST does not include an intercept term. The formula reads "=LINEST(AG9:AG68,AE9:AF68,0,1)": the transformed Y values are in column AG, the values of the transformed intercept term are in column AE, the transformed X values are in column AF, and finally, the 0 indicates that LINEST is not to add an intercept term. The sample coefficients in cells AF2 and AG2, labeled b_1GLS and b_0GLS, are the GLS estimates of the slope and intercept parameters.

Figure 20.5.1 is an example of Excel's output. In equation form, these results could be reported like this:

$$\text{Predicted } Y = \underset{(10.74)}{8.54} + \underset{(0.14)}{0.02} \ X.$$

Note that Y and X are the original, untransformed values. Interpretations of slope, elasticities, predictions, and forecasts proceed as usual using untransformed Y and X values.

It is important to realize that the GLS transformation is applied simply to get the best (minimum SE) coefficient estimates. Once the parameter

---

[19] The button merely changes a display option in Excel. You can control this display setting, and others, by executing Tools: Options (or Preferences) and clicking on the View tab.

GLS	b_1 GLS	b_0 GLS
estimate	0.02	8.54
SE(estimate)	0.14	10.74
P Value	64%	

Figure 20.5.1. Output for the GLS estimator,
bivariate example.
Source: [Autocorr.xls]AR1Model.

ρ	0.8

estimates are obtained, focus shifts back to the original data. Because the parameter estimates do not need to be transformed, this is completely straightforward. Predicted Y is computed by multiplying the parameter estimates into the original data. See cells AP9 to AP69 in the *AR1Model* sheet for the computation. As always, residuals are computed as observed Y less predicted Y.

Evaluating the GLS Estimator

Having shown how the GLS transformation is applied, we now explore its properties. We compare the OLS and GLS estimators and use Monte Carlo simulation to demonstrate the superiority of GLS.

Begin by returning to the beginning of the *AR1Model* sheet. Make sure ρ is set at 0.8; then go back to the GLS results. Hit F9 to draw a new sample. Figure 20.5.2, with top-left corner on cell AQ9, compares the predicted Y's

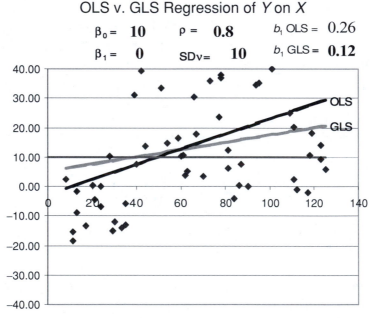

Figure 20.5.2. Fitting lines with OLS and GLS.
Source: [Autocorr.xls]AR1Model.

generated by OLS and GLS. In Figure 20.5.2, GLS gives us a slope estimate closer to the truth than OLS. Of course, this is only one sample. Hitting F9 repeatedly as you watch the chart should show you that the GLS predicted Y line bounces around much less than the OLS-predicted Y line. Because $\beta_0 = 10$ and $\beta_1 = 0$, the closer the predicted Y is to the horizontal (red) line $Y = 10$, the better.

As was pointed out in the section on consequences of OLS estimation of an AR(1) error model, the failure of OLS is apparent in cell G4. Instead of incorrectly rejecting the true null of $\beta_1 = 0$ only 5 percent of the time, OLS is reporting P-values less than 5 percent more than half of the time. Go to cell AF4 and repeatedly recalculate the sheet. Notice that, with GLS, the P-values appear to be much more evenly distributed.

Of course, a more systematic approach than repeatedly recalculating is to draw many samples and display the parameter estimates. Click the

GLS b_1 Monte Carlo Simulation Show button to go to the *b1GLSMCSim* sheet. Run your own Monte Carlo simulation and compare it to our results in Figure 20.5.3.

The Monte Carlo results suggest that the GLS estimator is unbiased (with $\beta_1 = 0$, the average of our 10,000 sample slopes was 0.001) and the reported SE is right: The Monte Carlo approximation to the exact SE is 0.1398, which is very close to the average of the reported SEs of 0.1403. Unlike the OLS estimator, the GLS estimator does not suffer from reporting the wrong SEs. Furthermore, the distribution of the P-values is correct. For example, in our simulation, in 5.19 percent of the repetitions we found a P-value below 5 percent.

The fact that GLS does not mislead us about the precision of the estimator is appealing, but that alone does not drive our decision to use GLS over OLS. After all, we could find and use the correct formula to determine the true SE of the OLS estimator to eliminate the misleading nature of the OLS-estimated SE.[20]

The superiority of GLS over OLS – although both are unbiased linear estimators – is the result of GLS having a smaller SE. In fact, though it is not proved here, in this case, GLS is indeed the best linear unbiased estimator. That is, the GLS estimator has the smallest spread in its sampling distribution of *all* unbiased linear estimators.

To see a head-to-head competition between OLS and GLS, click on the OLS v. GLS Monte Carlo Simulation Show button (in the *AR1Model* or *b1GLSMCSim* sheets). With $\rho = 0.8$, a Monte Carlo simulation with 10,000 samples shows that GLS beats OLS, as shown in Figure 20.5.4. Although the victory does not appear to be overwhelming, the ratio of the OLS to the GLS SE is 1.168, which means that

---

[20] The true OLS SE is derived using matrix algebra beginning in cell A100 of the *AR1Model* sheet in AutoCorr.xls.

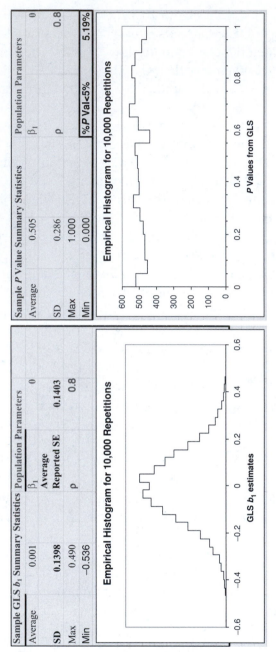

Sample GLS b_1 Summary Statistics		Population Parameters	
		β_1	0
Average	0.001	Average Reported SE	0.1403
SD	0.1398	ρ	0.8
Max	0.490		
Min	−0.536		

Sample P Value Summary Statistics		Population Parameters	
		β_1	0
Average	0.505	ρ	0.8
SD	0.286		
Max	1.000		
Min	0.000	%P Val<5%	5.19%

Figure 20.5.3. GLS Monte Carlo simulation for $\rho = 0.8$.
Source: [Autocorr.xls]b1GLSMCSim.

	OLS b_1		GLS b_1	Population Parameters	
Average	−0.001	Average	0.000	β_1	0
SD	0.1624	SD	0.1391	ρ	0.8
Max	0.665	Max	0.573		
Min	−0.593	Min	−0.585		

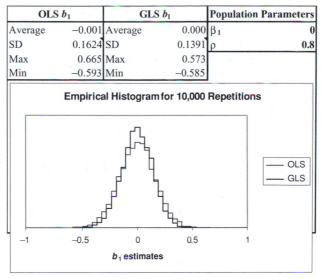

Figure 20.5.4. OLS versus GLS Monte Carlo simulation with $p = 0.8$. *Source:* [Autocorr.xls]OLSGLSMCSim.

the OLS SE is about 17 percent bigger than its GLS competitor. If you want a more visually compelling example, increase the value of ρ in cell C6 of the *AR1Model* sheet. With $\rho = 0.95$, GLS is almost twice as precise as OLS, as seen in Figure 20.5.5. Clearly, as ρ approaches 1, the gains from using GLS increase.

	OLS b_1		GLS b_1	Population Parameters	
Average	0.004	Average	0.004	β_1	0
SD	0.4163	SD	0.2376	ρ	0.95
Max	1.515	Max	0.891		
Min	−1.542	Min	−0.849		

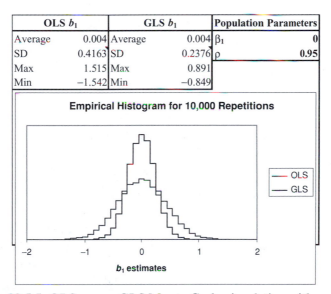

Figure 20.5.5. OLS versus GLS Monte Carlo simulation with $\rho = 0.95$. *Source:* [Autocorr.xls]OLSGLSMCSim.

Feasible Generalized Least Squares

Although the superiority of GLS over OLS is quite clear, there is a very important practical problem with the GLS procedure. Typically, we do not know the value of ρ. This crucial piece of information is needed to transform the data.

Faced with an unknown population parameter, we proceed as usual – we estimate it. In this case, we use the residuals of the original autocorrelated regression equation to obtain an estimate of ρ. As described in Section 20.4, Diagnosing Autocorrelation, there are many alternatives to choose from in estimating ρ.[21] No matter what estimator is used, whenever an estimate of ρ – instead of ρ itself – is used to transform the data, the procedure is called feasible generalized least squares (FGLS). It is called feasible GLS because, if ρ is unknown, GLS is unattainable. By estimating ρ, we substitute a feasible estimator in place of its unworkable ideal.

Beginning in cell AZ1 of the *AR1Model* sheet of AutoCorr.xls, we apply the FGLS procedure. Click on the View Formula button to see the formulas we use. Notice how exactly the same algebra is applied as in the GLS procedure. The only difference is that we use our estimate of ρ, not ρ itself. In this FGLS implementation, the estimate (named rho_estimated) is given in cell BD6, which reports the slope of the regression through the origin of the residuals on lagged residuals. Click the View Formula Results button to return Excel to its default display cell results view.

It turns out that there are many ways to implement FGLS. We have chosen one named for Prais and Winsten. The special feature of their estimator is that they use the first observation, whereas competing versions of FGLS throw it out. Monte Carlo evidence shows that the Prais–Winsten estimator generally performs better than an alternative procedure called Cochrane–Orcutt, which uses the identical transformation except for discarding the first observation.[22]

Unfortunately, FGLS is not as good an estimator as GLS. What is the source of the problem with FGLS? The answer is the need to estimate ρ. After explaining why estimated ρ is to blame, we run head-to-head competitions of FGLS against GLS and FGLS against OLS. The results show that all are unbiased estimators of β_1 but differ in precision. As would be expected, FGLS ranks between OLS and GLS.

To understand why having to estimate ρ hampers FGLS, first set $\rho = 0.8$ in cell C6 of the *AR1Model* sheet, then hit F9 repeatedly. As you do so, focus on the estimated ρ values in cell BD6. There is a problem there. Estimated ρ is biased downward – it is persistently too low. You will get values greater than

[21] Further explanation of the variety of estimators of ρ is available in [AutoCorr.xls]Graphs!Q1.
[22] See Rao and Griliches (1969).

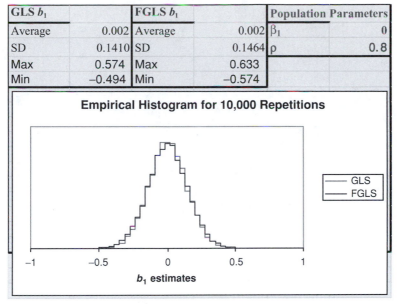

GLS b_1		FGLS b_1		Population Parameters	
Average	0.002	Average	0.002	β_1	0
SD	0.1410	SD	0.1464	ρ	0.8
Max	0.574	Max	0.633		
Min	−0.494	Min	−0.574		

Figure 20.5.6. GLS versus FGLS Monte Carlo simulation.
Source: [Autocorr.xls]GLSFGLSMCSim.

0.8 on occasion, but most values of estimated ρ are less than 0.8. The previous section ran Monte Carlo simulations of estimated ρ (see also the *rhoMCSim* sheet in AutoCorr.xls). We found the average of 10,000 estimated ρ's to be 0.700, when $\rho = 0.8$. If we get estimated ρ wrong and then use this wrong value to transform the data, it stands to reason that FGLS will not do as well as GLS.

There are many FGLS estimators. All are biased in small samples, but some are better than others in certain situations (discussion of which is beyond the scope of this book).[23]

Using our estimated ρ as the slope of regression through the origin of residuals on lagged residuals with $\rho = 0.8$ and 60 observations, let us test drive and compare FGLS to GLS and OLS.

We begin with the obvious – FGLS is not as good as GLS. Near cell BH1 of the *AR1Model* sheet, you will find the GLS v. FGLS Monte Carlo Simulation Show button. Click on it and then run your own Monte Carlo simulation that calculates b_1 estimates using GLS and FGLS. For 10,000 samples, given the initial fixed values of X, 60 observations, and $\rho = 0.8$, our results, reproduced in Figure 20.5.6, show GLS is slightly superior to FGLS.

Of course, this result depends on a set of particular parameter (and X) values. For example, when we change ρ to 0.95, GLS performs much better than FGLS, as can be seen in Figure 20.5.7.

---

[23] See Rao and Griliches (1969) and Taylor, (1981). Rao and Griliches consider autocorrelated X's, and Taylor demonstrates that the values of the X variables influence which estimator of ρ is best.

GLS b_1		FGLS b_1		Population Parameters	
Average	−0.002	Average	−0.002	β_1	0
SD	0.2380	SD	0.3175	ρ	0.95
Max	0.872	Max	1.317		
Min	−0.834	Min	−1.373		

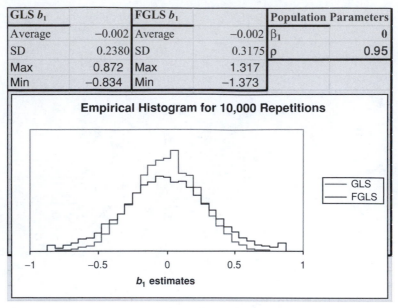

Figure 20.5.7. GLS versus FGLS, $\rho = 0.95$, Monte Carlo simulation.
Source: [Autocorr.xls] GLSFGLSMCSim.

OLS b_1		FGLS b_1		Population Parameters	
Average	0.002	Average	0.001	β_1	0
SD	0.1631	SD	0.1457	ρ	0.8
Max	0.607	Max	0.541		
Min	−0.572	Min	−0.507		

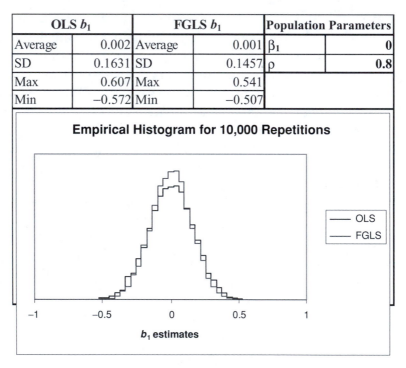

Figure 20.5.8. OLS versus FGLS Monte Carlo simulation.
Source: [Autocorr.xls]OLSFGLSMCSim.

In practice, comparing FGLS with GLS is not especially relevant. After all, if a crucial parameter value is unknown, it is not especially helpful to note that you would be able to do better if you knew it. Of much greater importance is comparing OLS and FGLS – two viable, real-world alternatives.

Click on the ⌜OLS v. FGLS Monte Carlo / Simulation Show⌝ button in the *AR1Model* sheet and run your own Monte Carlo simulation that compares OLS and FGLS. Our results are given in Figure 20.5.8. The evidence is clear: FGLS beats OLS. They are both unbiased, but FGLS has a smaller SE, which means it is more precise. As was the case with GLS versus OLS, as ρ approaches 1, the victory margin of FGLS over OLS will increase. You can demonstrate this by changing ρ to 0.95 and running your own Monte Carlo simulation.

The superiority of FGLS over OLS makes sense if you remember that GLS contains OLS as a special case. Ordinary least squares is equal to FGLS with estimated ρ set at 0. Thus, even though FGLS is hampered by a downward biased estimate of ρ, this is far better than treating ρ as if it were zero, which is the implicit assumption made by OLS.

Summary

An AR(1) error process can be converted into an independent error process via an appropriate algebraic transformation of the data. When ρ is known, running OLS on the transformed data is called GLS. Advanced statistical theory can be used to show that GLS is BLUE. This means that OLS (or any other linear unbiased estimator) is less precise than GLS. This is the primary reason GLS is preferred over OLS in the estimation of AR(1) autocorrelated error models. Although this section does not prove that GLS is BLUE, it has demonstrated through Monte Carlo simulation that GLS beats OLS, the third claim posited in Section 20.3.

Once AR(1) autocorrelation in the errors is detected, OLS should be abandoned in favor of its more precise competitor GLS. In practice, however, ρ is not known and must be estimated. The process of estimating ρ, transforming the data, and running OLS on the transformed data is called FGLS. Because there are many ways to estimate ρ, there are many FGLS estimators. We chose one that tested well in Monte Carlo simulations. Although not as good as its ideal counterpart, GLS, the primary virtue of the FGLS procedure is that, in terms of precision, it beats OLS.

An alternative method for dealing with autocorrelation is to use OLS in conjunction with a serial correlation–robust estimate of the SE. The advantage of this procedure is that it works for more general types of serial correlation than the AR(1) process discussed in this chapter.[24] In contrast, the

---

[24] For details on this approach, see Wooldridge (2003), pp. 410–414.

FGLS procedure outlined in this chapter applies only to the AR(1) process. Procedures for transforming data in the presence of other autocorrelation processes are beyond the scope of this book.

20.6. Conclusion

Workbooks: CPIMZM.xls; Luteinizing.xls

This chapter has used computer-generated data to illustrate important concepts about autocorrelation. This section summarizes the critical points and then offers two examples with real-world data.

The Highlights of Autocorrelation

With a first-order autoregressive (AR1) autocorrelated error model,

$$Y_t = \beta_0 + \beta_1 X_t + \varepsilon_t$$
$$\varepsilon_t = \rho \varepsilon_{t-1} + v_t,$$

the errors, ε_t, are not independently distributed because the previous error, ε_{t-1}, influences the current error whenever ρ is not zero. We say that the errors are autocorrelated.

There are three important consequences when OLS is used to estimate β_0 and β_1 in the presence of an autocorrelated data generation process:

1. The estimates of β_0 and β_1 are unbiased.
2. The OLS estimated SEs of the estimated coefficients are wrong and usually too low. Inference is flawed. This problem does not go away as the sample size increases.
3. Ordinary least squares is not BLUE; GLS is the best (smallest SE) linear unbiased estimator.

Because OLS estimated SEs are misleading and the OLS estimator is not BLUE if autocorrelation exists, we need to know if the errors are autocorrelated. We have discussed three diagnostic procedures:

1. Examine the scatter diagram of residuals plotted against lagged residuals.
2. Apply the estimated ρ test in which estimated ρ is the slope of the regression of residuals on lagged residuals.
3. The Durbin–Watson test is often used because, unlike the estimated ρ test, it does not suffer from small sample bias. This test is not, however, a perfect solution because strict requirements must be met for it to be strictly applicable. In fact, the next chapter demonstrates that the estimated ρ test is more resilient in the face of violations of the classical econometric model than the Durbin–Watson test.

Once first-order autocorrelated errors are detected, it is possible to correct the autocorrelation. BLUE estimates of β_0 and β_1 in an AR1 model can be obtained via GLS. By appropriately transforming the original data (and applying a special formula to the first observation) and then running OLS on the transformed data, linear unbiased estimates with the minimum SE are found. The GLS coefficient estimates and SEs are then reported with the original data in the usual way:

$$\text{Predicted } Y = \begin{array}{cc} b_0^{\text{GLS}} & + \quad b_1^{\text{GLS}} \quad X \\ (\text{SE}_{b_0}^{\text{GLS}}) & (\text{SE}_{b_1}^{\text{GLS}}) \end{array}$$

The transformed data are merely a means to an end – best linear unbiased estimation – and are discarded once the parameter estimates, and SEs are obtained.

When ρ is unknown, it must be estimated, and the same transformation procedure is applied with the estimated value of ρ. Using an estimate of ρ in the data transformation and then applying OLS is called feasible GLS. Although GLS is better than FGLS, if ρ is unknown, GLS is not within our reach. Of the attainable choices, FGLS is better than OLS.

If the autocorrelation in the errors is not AR(1) or of unknown form, more advanced methods beyond the scope of this book are needed.

Two Real-World Examples

You can apply the diagnosis and correction of an AR1 error model to real-world data in the CPIMZM.xls workbook. Follow the steps in the *Analysis* sheet to see how the ideas presented in this chapter are put into practice. The *BusCycleData*, *MoneyData*, and *CPIData* sheets contain important and interesting documentation.[25]

The example illustrates textbook lessons.[26] Note how the autocorrelation in the original model is picked up by the diagnostics, how OLS and FGLS differ, and how the transformation greatly lowers estimated ρ. The end result, however, is far from perfect. The last step shows that the transformed model still suffers from autocorrelation. Much more work is needed because the AR(1) model probably does not adequately describe the way in which the errors were generated.

A second example can be found in the Luteinizing.xls workbook. Luteinizing hormone levels (which are involved in the menstrual cycle) are measured on a healthy woman in 10-minute intervals over an 8-hour

---

[25] The example is completely worked out in the CPIMZMAnswers.xls workbook. The *DWOrig* and *DWTran* sheets were created by using the Durbin–Watson d option in the P Values Calculator and selecting the Show Matrix Results option.

[26] The example is used as a teaching device giving the student an opportunity to put in practice the procedures described in the text. Handling trend and other complications implicit in this example requires methods beyond the scope of this book.

time period. This example shows how FGLS can be used to correct the
autocorrelation in the data and the AR(1) model appears to be a good description
of the process generating the errors in this case.

The world beyond the carefully controlled environment under which we
run Monte Carlo simulations is messy and unclear. You will rarely run the perfect
regression or ideal test in the real world. The FGLS estimator provides
better analysis than OLS, but we may not have exactly the right answer. Furthermore,
the analysis of time series data is an advanced, complicated topic
in econometrics. The discussion of autocorrelation in this chapter introduces
an important issue, but you should know that there is much more to the study
of autocorrelation than the Durbin–Watson statistic applied to an AR(1)
process.

20.7. Exercises

Workbooks: Misspecification.xls; FreeThrowAutoCorr.xls

1. Recall the fable about Galileo (see Chapter 6) in which he estimated the model

$$\text{Predicted Distance} = -124.82 + 96.83 \times \text{Time}$$
$$\text{(ft)} \qquad\qquad \text{(ft)} \quad \text{(ft/s)} \quad \text{(s)}.$$

This is a good example of a model in which the functional form is incorrect. Recall
that the true model includes neither an intercept nor a Time term (just Time^2).
Open the file Misspecification.xls and perform the estimated ρ test on the model
above. Your answer should include clearly stated null and alternative hypotheses,
a test statistic, a P-value, and a decision on rejecting or not rejecting the null.
2. Now run a Durbin–Watson test. Your answer should include clearly stated null
and alternative hypotheses, a test statistic, a P-value, and a decision on rejecting
or not rejecting the null.
3. We actually know that autocorrelation is not really present in these data. Why,
then, is it showing up in our tests?
4. Simply for practice, go ahead and run an FGLS estimation of the model. Describe
your procedure in transforming the data and report your results.

Open the FreeThrowAutoCorr.xls workbook and use it to answer the questions
below. Read the *Intro* sheet and explore the workbook to get a sense of what is
going on.
5. Click on cell B11 in the *Model* sheet. The heart of the formula is "B10+IF
(C10=1,zeta,-zeta)." Explain how this formula is inducing autocorrelation.
6. What effect does increasing autocorrelation have on the sampling distribution of
the percentage of made free throws? Describe your procedure in answering this
question.
7. Does autocorrelation have the same effect on the sampling distribution of the
percentage of made free throws if $\mu=0.8$? Describe your procedure in answering
this question.
8. If autocorrelation is present, what is wrong with using the conventional estimated
SE formula (in cell K27)? How do you know?
HINT: Use the MCSim.xla add-in to run a Monte Carlo simulation on cell K27.

References

Durbin and Watson's original papers are as follows:

Durbin, J. and G. S. Watson (1950). "Testing for Serial Correlation in Least Squares Regression: I," *Biometrika* **37**(3/4):409–428.

Durbin, J. and G. S. Watson (1951). "Testing for Serial Correlation in Least Squares Regression: II," *Biometrika* **38**(1/2):159–177.

Original papers that introduced FGLS estimators are as follows:

Cochrane, D. and G. Orcutt (1949). "Application of Least Squares Regression to Relationships Containing Autocorrelated Error Terms," *Journal of the American Statistical Association* **44**(1):32–61.

Prais, S. J. and C. B. Winsten (1954). "Trend Estimators and Serial Correlation." Unpublished Cowles Commission discussion paper Statistical No. 383. Chicago.

Monte Carlo studies of FGLS estimators are contained in the following:

Rao, P. and Z. Griliches (1969). "Small-Sample Properties of Several Two-Stage Regression Methods in the Context of Auto-Correlated Errors," *Journal of the American Statistical Association* **64**(325):253–272.

Taylor, William E. (1981). "On the Efficiency of the Cochrane–Orcutt Estimator" *Journal of Econometrics* **17**:67–82.

The following are econometrics textbooks that cover autocorrelation in more depth, in addition to Wooldridge (2003):

Goldberger, A. S. (1991). *A Course in Econometrics*. Cambridge, MA: Harvard University.

Greene, W. H. (2000). *Econometric Analysis*. New York: Prentice Hall.

We cited the following article on streaks in basketball in Chapter 9:

Gilovich, T., R. Vallone, and A. Tversky (1985).

21

Topics in Time Series

It seems necessary, then, that all commercial fluctuations should be investigated according to the same scientific methods with which we are familiar in other complicated sciences, such especially as meteorology and terrestrial magnetism. Every kind of periodic fluctuation, whether daily, weekly, monthly, quarterly, or yearly, must be detected and exhibited, not only as a study in itself, but because we must ascertain and eliminate such periodic variations before we can correctly exhibit those which are irregular and non-periodic, and probably of more interest and importance.

W. S. Jevons[1]

21.1. Introduction

In this chapter we discuss further topics relating to time series analysis. Time series econometrics is a vast field. Our aim in this chapter is to expose you to some of the main techniques for modeling time series and to call attention to important issues pertaining to the data generation process for variables that change over time. Sections 21.2 through 21.4 demonstrate basic techniques for dealing with time series using a trend term and dummy variables and making seasonal adjustments. Sections 21.5 and 21.6 examine important issues pertaining to the data generation process. For OLS to produce consistent estimates of parameters, time series must be stationary and cannot be strongly dependent. Section 21.5 examines the issue of stationarity, while Section 21.6 tackles the subject of weak dependence. In time series, lagged dependent variables are very often included as regressors. Section 21.7 discusses lagged dependent variables in general and Section 21.8 contains a practical example of the use of lagged dependent variables in the estimation of money demand. Section 21.9 provides an introduction to forecasting using time series methods.

---

[1] Jevons (1862) in Hendry and Morgan (1995, pp. 113–114).

21.2. Trends in Time Series Models

Workbooks: IndiaPopulation.xls; ExpGrowthModel.xls; AnnualGDP.xls; Spurious.xls

This section covers the use of trends in time series models. Trends are a simple and effective means for incorporating a steady upward or downward movement over time into the behavior of a time series. There are two important uses of trends in modeling economic time series. First, a trend can provide a succinct, summary description of how a variable has changed over time. As such, a trend can be useful for forecasting purposes, provided that there is reason to believe that the variable will continue to change in the same way in the future. (Section 21.9 covers forecasting of time series.) Second, including a trend in a time series can guard against incorrect inferences. The first part of this section illustrates two functional forms for trends via simple examples. The second part of this section demonstrates that time series models which do not account for trends are potentially subject to significant problems.

Two major functional forms for trends in economic variables are the linear and exponential. We apply these functional forms initially to the problem of modeling the time path of the population of India, the world's second most populous country. We obtained data on India's population from the U.S. Census Bureau. According to Census Bureau estimates, India's population increased from 368 million people in 1950 to 998 million in 1999. (By way of comparison, the U.S. population was about 273 million in 1999.) The data and sources are in the Excel workbook IndiaPopulation.xls.

Linear Trend

A simple approach to modeling how an economic variable changes over time is to treat it as following a linear trend. This means estimating the following equation:

$$y_t = \beta_0 + \beta_1 t + \varepsilon_t.$$

The time trend term (usually abbreviated "t" as in the equation above) is typically chosen equal to 0 in the first period (that is, the first observation) and to increase by 1 during each successive period. As we ask you to demonstrate in an exercise, this choice is arbitrary; any starting point can be used so long as the trend term increases by 1 when the time of the observation increases by 1 unit. (The time period need not be 1 year; it could be quarters of a year, months, weeks, etc.) We assume for now that the errors obey the classical econometric model (later we allow the error terms to be autocorrelated).

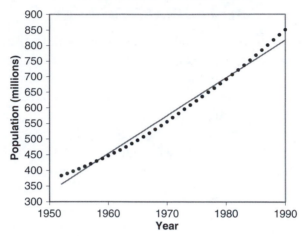

Figure 21.2.1. Linear trend model of India's population.
Source: [IndiaPopulation.xls]Data.

Adopting a linear trend assumes the following model for India's population:

$$Population_t = \beta_0 + \beta_1 t + \varepsilon_t,$$

for $t = 0$ to 40, corresponding to the years 1950 to 1990, with population measured in millions. We obtain the following results:

$$\text{Predicted Population in millions} = 331.74 + 12.13t$$

$$(5.47) \quad (0.24)$$

The estimated SEs are given in parentheses.[2] Figure 21.2.1 shows the data and the fitted line.

The linear trend model assumes that the value of the dependent variable (the one you are forecasting) goes up or down by a constant amount every year. Thus, this model says that the population of India rose by about 12.1 million people every year.

You should be skeptical of using a linear trend to model India's population, for both empirical and theoretical reasons. The empirical case against the linear extrapolation model is very easy to make. A quick look at Figure 21.2.1 shows that the rate of population growth was not constant over time. The 12.1-million-people-per-year rate is the predicted constant increase in units

---

[2] Note that we computed the estimated SEs under the standard assumption that the errors are homoskedastic and independent, which is highly questionable in the case of population.

of millions of people per year, but the change in the number of people per year was obviously lower in the early 1950s and clearly much higher in the 1980s.

The theoretical case against linear extrapolation for forecasting population requires a model of population growth. We present a simple model in the workbook ExpGrowthModel.xls. This model suggests that constant percentage growth rates for population are plausible.

Log-Linear (Exponential) Trend

A commonly used alternative to a linear trend is the log-linear or exponential trend in which the series grows or declines by a constant percentage instead of a constant absolute number. In other words, this is a semi-log model (see Chapter 6.4) with the dependent variable transformed by the natural log function and the X variable unchanged. The regression model is written as follows:

$$\ln y_t = \beta_0 + \beta_1 \cdot t + \varepsilon_t.$$

We assume for now that the errors obey the classical econometric model (later we allow the error terms to be autocorrelated). This model for the logarithm of y implies that the equation for the level of y is

$$y_t = \exp(\beta_0 + \beta_1 \cdot t + \varepsilon_t)$$
$$= \exp(\beta_0) \cdot \exp(\beta_1 \cdot t) \cdot \exp(\varepsilon_t).$$

As pointed out in Section 6.4, in this model $100 \cdot \beta_1$ is approximately equal to the percentage change in y_t corresponding to a one unit change in t.

In Excel, the log-linear specification can be estimated by taking the natural log of the dependent variable and then running OLS (via the Data Analysis add-in or LINEST) or, because it is a bivariate model, charting the data and using the Trend line approach.

Using our population data for India, we obtain the following fit for the log-linear model:[3]

$$\text{Predicted } \ln(\text{Population}) = 5.895 + 0.0213t.$$
$$(.0001) \quad (.002)$$

Figure 21.2.2 shows the results.

---

[3] The R^2 from this regression is 0.9994. Very high R^2's are not unusual in regressions in which the dependent variable follows a strong trend. When the regression includes another independent variable other than the trend, an adjusted R^2, which takes into account the trend, can give a better picture of the explanatory power of the model. For details, see Wooldridge (2003), pp. 351–353.

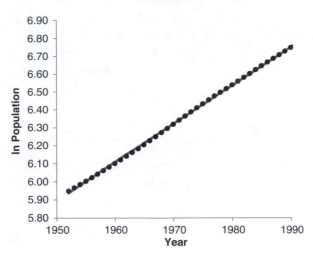

In Population and Trend Line, Estimation Period, 1950-1990

Figure 21.2.2. Logarithmic trend line for India's population.
Source: [IndiaPopulation.xls]Data.

The dependent variable in the log-linear model is in terms of logarithms of population in millions. To get back to population in millions, we need to exponentiate, or take the antilog as follows:

$$y_t = \exp(\ln y_t)$$

$$Population_t = \exp(5.895 + 0.0213 \cdot t)$$

$$= \exp(5.895) \cdot \exp(0.0213 \cdot t)$$

$$= 363.2 \cdot 1.0215^t.$$

In fact for technical reasons, this is almost, but not quite, the correct procedure. It turns out that there is an additional multiplicative factor we need to append to the expression above. In this case the correction makes very little difference (assuming the error terms are normally distributed, we need to multiply this expression by 1.0003), but it can make an important difference in other applications. For further details, see the How To file called How-ToPredictYfromLnY.doc in the Basic Tools \ HowTo folder. Notice that the preceding calculation tells us the percentage growth rate is 2.15 percent – just a little more than the slope coefficient in the log-linear regression.

Figure 21.2.3, a graphical comparison of the linear and exponential trend models with predicted values expressed in levels, shows the clear superiority of the latter method of fitting a trend to Indian population. The actual population series (the dots) is almost indistinguishable from the exponential trend.

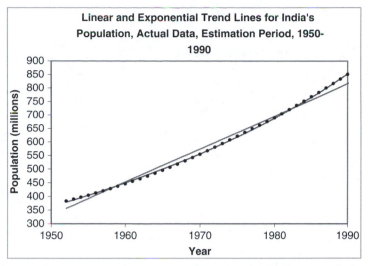

Figure 21.2.3. Comparing two trend models for India's population. *Source:* [IndiaPopulation.xls]Data.

Example: U.S. Real GDP, 1947–2003

As a second example, we present linear and log-linear trend results for annual gross domestic product (GDP) between 1947 and 2003. In these models the trend term might reflect the combined impact of labor-force growth, capital accumulation, and technological progress over time. The models implicitly assume that, taken together, these factors lead to a constant (linear or exponential) rate of growth in GDP. The error term might capture the influence of other variables, e.g., economic policy.[4] The purpose of the trend model may be strictly descriptive, summarizing the rate of economic growth over time. The data and analysis are contained in the file AnnualGDP.xls. All figures are billions of real dollars with 2000 as the base year. (Comparing economic variables over time often requires taking into account the effect of inflation by converting nominal figures into real figures.)

We ran both linear and log-linear trend models. The linear trend is clearly inappropriate, as Figure 21.2.4 demonstrates. The linear trend underpredicts GDP initially, overpredicts in the intermediate years, and underpredicts at the end of the time series: The level of GDP is rising at an increasing rate. On the other hand, a model in which GDP rises at a constant percentage rate, the log-linear trend, does a much better job, as seen in Figure 21.2.5.

---

[4] It is possible to measure labor-force growth and capital accumulation and thus include these variables in the regression. However, it is very hard to measure technological progress. Thus a trend term is often included to proxy for technological progress.

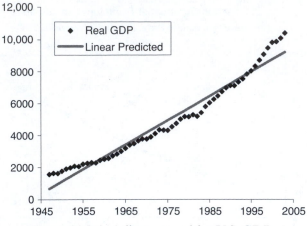

Figure 21.2.4. A linear trend for U.S. GDP.
Source: AnnualGDP.xls[Data].

The equation for the log-linear trend is

$$\text{Predicted Log GDP}_t = 7.3921 + 0.0334t.$$

As noted for the first example, in moving from an equation involving logs to one involving levels, we need to take into account an additional multiplicative factor. Although the resulting correction was trivial in the case of predicting India's population, it is fairly important in the case of predicting U.S. GDP. To produce Figure 21.2.5 we used the general correction procedure described in the HowToPredictYfromLnY.doc file in the Basic Tools \ HowTo folder. We began by regressing $\exp(7.3921 + 0.0334t)$ on actual GDP without an

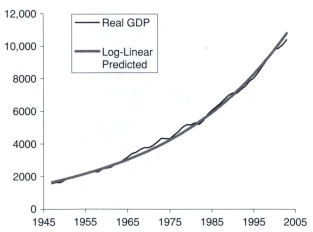

Figure 21.2.5. A log-linear trend for U.S. GDP.
Source: [AnnualGDP.xls]Data.

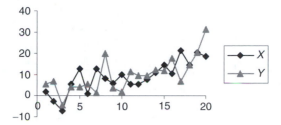

Figure 21.2.6. Time series plot for two trending variables.
Source: [Spurious.xls]Trends.

intercept. This gave a slope coefficient of 0.99.[5] We then computed Log-Linear Predicted GDP as follows:

$$\text{Log-Linear Predicted GDP}_t = 0.99 \cdot \exp(7.3921 + 0.0334t).$$

Our regression tells us that the trend rate of growth in real GDP was about 3.4 percent per year.

Trends and Spurious Regression

It is important to be aware of trends in analyzing the relationship between two variables that are changing over time. One reason is that it is easy for investigators to be fooled into believing that there is a real relationship between two variables when in fact the two variables are unrelated. For example, if both variables are following an upward trend over time, it will appear that the "dependent" variable is increasing because the "independent" variable is increasing. We will show this with an example.

Open the file Spurious.xls and go to the *Trends* sheet. Figure 21.2.6 shows two variables, X and Y, graphed against time. The data generating process for the two variables is the following:

$$X_t = \gamma_1 \cdot t + \eta_t$$
$$Y_t = \beta_0 + \beta_1 \cdot X_t + \beta_2 \cdot t + \varepsilon_t.$$

The error terms in both equations are draws from an error box (i.e., independent and identically distributed). Also, the error terms are independent of one another: Knowing the value of η_t tells us nothing about the value of ε_t. Notice that this DGP is *not* the classical econometric model because X is not fixed in repeated samples.

---

[5] If we had assumed that the errors were normally distributed, our correction factor would instead have been 1.000826. The resulting series is computed in Column R of the *Data* sheet, starting in cell R4.

Short Regression		Long Regression			Omitted Variable Rule
$X(g_1)$	Intercept	$X(b_1)$	$t(b_2)$	Intercept	Auxiliary Regression
0.61	4.24	**−0.03**	1.01	−0.635	Regress t on X
0.22	2.49	0.32	0.39	2.892	X (d_1) | Intercept
0.30	7.02	0.50	6.13	#N/A	0.64 | 4.83
7.86	18	8.45	17	#N/A	Bias in g_1:
387.8	887.7	635.7	639.8	#N/A	**0.65** $=b_2{}^*d_1$

Figure 21.2.7. Short and long regressions of trending Y on trending X.
Source: [Spurious.xls]Trends.

Let us look at what happens when $\beta_1 = 0$ – that is when there is no relationship between Y and X. The *Trends* sheet should be set up for this case, with β_1 set to zero in cell B3.

In general, *spurious regression* means that we believe X and Y are related when in fact, they are not. In this example, a regression of Y on X that does not include a trend term typically gives biased estimates of the slope of Y on X. This is essentially an omitted variable problem, as is demonstrated at the conclusion of this section. Another spurious regression problem is presented later in this chapter.

Consider two regressions that can be estimated with these data. The short regression just includes X, whereas the long regression includes X and t. Figure 21.2.7 displays representative results.

The key parameter estimates are highlighted in bold. The OLS estimator, g_1, short regression (on the left of Figure 21.2.7) is biased, as you can see by hitting the F9 key several times: The estimate of the slope of Y on X is not centered on 0, the true value. In contrast, the long regression estimates (displayed in the center of the figure) are unbiased, as can be demonstrated with a Monte Carlo analysis (see the *Q&A* sheet). The omitted variable rule says that the size of the difference between the short- and long-regression coefficients for X depends on the slope of the omitted variable on the included variable (this is d_1 in our example). Specifically,

$$\text{Difference in Regression Slopes of } Y \text{ on } X$$
$$= \text{Slope of } t \text{ on } X \times \text{Slope of } Y \text{ on } t$$
$$= 0.64 \times 1.01$$
$$= 0.65.$$

In the example of Figure 21.2.7 an increase of one unit in X predicts an increase of 0.64 units in t. Because it omits t but includes X, the short regression of Y on X attributes changes in Y that stem from changes in t to changes in X. Because the slope of Y on t changes from one sample to the next, the size of the difference in estimated regression slopes will change even if we hold the values of X constant while drawing a new sample of Y values. Observe that the estimated SE of the slope of Y on X in the short regression is generally considerably smaller than the slope estimate itself. Thus, the short regression is likely to lead to a statistically significant but false finding that changes in X are associated with changes in Y, ceteris paribus.

Summary

This section has served as an introduction to the use of trends in time series. A trend term serves as a convenient way to summarize the change in a variable over time. We introduced two popular functional forms for trends, linear and log-linear, but there are many others. Trends also play an important role in statistical inference. When both dependent and independent variables contain trends, neglecting to include a trend can lead to biased estimates of the regression parameters. This is called spurious regression. In the next section, we turn to a useful device for modeling changes in a dependent variable over time: dummy variables.

21.3. Dummy Variables in Time Series Models

Workbooks: TimeSeriesDummyVariables.xls; CoalMining.xls

In addition to incorporating trends, dummy variables are a second common strategy for modeling the way in which economic variables change over time. Dummy variables are a way to shift the predicted series up or down for a portion of the sample period.

Dummy Variables in Time Series

Dummy variables can be used to track innovations that affect the value of a variable at particular points in time but not throughout the entire period under study. Here is a simple example. A dairy food manufacturer might be interested in the impact of retail price and coupons on sales of its premium ice cream. During some weeks the manufacturer issues a coupon for the ice cream; at other times it does not offer any coupons. A way to model the relationship between Sales, Price, and coupon policies is to define a dummy variable, *Coupon*, which is an indicator of whether there was a limited-time coupon for the ice cream in the Sunday papers for a given week. Specifically,

$$Coupon_t = 1 \text{ when there is a coupon in week } t$$
$$Coupon_t = 0 \text{ when there is no coupon in week } t$$

The file TimeSeriesDummyVariables.xls works out this example. Go to the *Sales* sheet. Figure 21.3.1 shows the path of sales over time. The data were

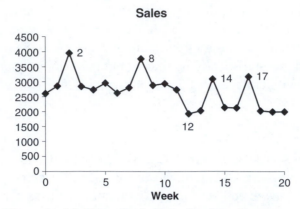

Figure 21.3.1. Hypothetical retail sales of ice cream.
Source: [TimeSeriesDummyVariables.xls]Sales.

generated according to the following simple model:

$$IceCreamSales_t = \beta_0 + \beta_1\ RetailPrice_t + \beta_2\ Coupon_t + \varepsilon_t, \quad t = 0, \dots, 20.$$

The error term accounts for the influence of weather and other factors. In weeks 2, 8, 14, and 17, the firm issued coupons good for those weeks, and this is clearly reflected in upward hikes in sales for those weeks. In week 12, the firm raised the price of the ice cream by $1.00; this shows up in Figure 21.3.1 as a downward shift to a permanently lower level (if you think of the last 9 weeks as permanent) of sales. Of course, there is some bounce in sales, reflecting the influence of the error term. (Hit F9 to see this.)

   An OLS regression of Sales on Retail Price and Coupon easily picks out the impact of coupons on sales, as the LINEST output in Figure 21.3.2 demonstrates. This shows how a dummy variable can be used in a time series model to capture time-specific effects.

Example: Coal Mine Safety

We turn now to an actual example of the use of dummy variable in a time series study provided by Andrews and Christenson's analysis of the impact of federal regulations on coal mining safety during the period 1940 to

Regression of Sales on ...		
Coupon	Retail Price	Intercept
1079.2	−757.2	5817.1
56.6	44.9	199.7
1.0	101.6	#N/A
302.8	18	#N/A
6253084	185838	#N/A

Figure 21.3.2. Regression of sales on price and a dummy variable, Coupon.
Source: [TimeSeriesDummyVariables.xls]Sales.

Variables:	
T%m	percent of coal mechanically loaded
Sm/m	average number of men working per mine
St/m	average output per mine (tons)
R	dummy variable: government regulation in place
W	dummy variable: war currently taking place
F	fatal injury rates per million man hours worked (in underground bituminous coal mines)
NF	nonfatal injury rates per million man hours worked
NFP	nonfatal, permanent disability, injury rates per million man-hours.

Figure 21.3.3. Variables in Andrews and Christenson's (1974) study of coal mine safety.

1965.[6] In their model, the fatality rate in the U.S. underground coal mining industry depends on the level of technology, the average size of mines, and federal regulation. All of these are measured on an annual basis, and so there are 26 observations in the data set – a relatively short time series. Andrews and Christenson argue that the use of more modern technology (measured by the percent of coal mechanically loaded) might reduce the fatality rate. They assert that safety in small mines is worse than safety in large mines, implying that as the average number of workers per mine falls, safety should decline. Unfortunately, decreases in the number of workers per mine might also reflect improvements in technology, clouding the interpretation of this variable.

Andrews and Christenson's main research question is, Did the Coal Mine Safety Act of 1952 improve coal mine safety? The 1952 Act gave the Bureau of Mine Safety increased powers, including the ability to shut down mines that failed to correct violations of safety regulations. The authors use two dummy variables in their regression: one for observations during World War II (during which changes in the labor force might have pushed up accident rates) and one for years in which government regulation was in place (1953 and after).

We reproduce just one part of Andrews and Christenson's study: their model labeled F4, which analyzes fatal accident rates. The variables are defined as shown in Figure 21.3.3. The *ModelF4* sheet in CoalMining.xls presents the data. Columns B and C contain the dummy variables for Regulation and War.

Andrews and Christenson's Model F4 is as follows:

$$F_t = \beta_0 + \beta_1 R_t + \beta_2 W_t + \beta_3 T\%m_t + \beta_4 Sm/m_t + \varepsilon_t.$$

---

[6] Andrews, W. H. and C. L. Christenson (1974).

Variable	Estimate	SE
Intercept	3.482	0.501
R	0.028	0.105
W	0.076	0.105
T%m	−0.023	0.005
Sm/m	−0.017	0.004

Figure 21.3.4. OLS results for Andrews and
Christenson Model F4.
Source: [CoalMining.xls]ModelF4.

As the authors mention, there are many other factors besides the included
independent variables that influence the fatality rate, the most prominent
of which might be luck. Thus, there is ample reason for the presence of an
error term. We assume that the error term follows the classical econometric
model. (In the *Q&A* sheet, we ask you to test for first-order autocorrelation
in the errors.) As Figure 21.3.4 shows, the regression results do not support
the contention that federal regulation has improved mine safety.

The coefficient estimate for W, taken literally, says that fatal accident rates
were 0.076 fatalities per million man hours higher during World War II than
after the war; the coefficient estimate for R indicates that accident rates during
the years when the Coal Mine Safety Act was in effect were also slightly
higher than during the previous, less-regulated period. However, both null
hypotheses that the true parameters relating to W and R are zero cannot be
rejected. Thus, we cannot say that either war or regulation affected coal mine
safety.[7]

On the other hand, the estimates for the variables reflecting technology
and mine size are statistically significant, and the estimates indicate that
these variables have very large impacts on the fatality rate. This is not so
obvious given the seemingly small coefficient estimates of −.023 and −0.17,
respectively. The elasticity of the fatality rate with respect to the technology
measure, however, is −1.28, whereas the elasticity of the fatality rate with
respect to the size measure is −0.55 (both elasticities are evaluated at sample
means – see the *Model F4* sheet for more detail on these computations).
Furthermore, the technology measure increased from 35.4 to 89.2 between
1940 and 1965. According to the regression estimates, this alone would have
caused a decrease in the fatality rate of 1.36 fatalities per million man hours
ceteris paribus; similarly, the decrease in mine size over the same period
would have led to an increase ceteris paribus of 0.78 fatalities per million
man hours. The actual observed rate fell from 1.70 in 1940 to 1.23 fatalities
per million man hours in 1965.

We would argue that this study provides suggestive but not conclusive evidence that technology and mine size have affected mine safety. There are

---

[7] Nor can we reject that joint null hypothesis that both dummy-variable parameters are equal to zero.
The *F*-statistic was 0.51 and the *P*-value 61 percent.

only 26 observations in the data set, and the authors admit that "all too often the available data do not correspond very closely to the variables in the models – and that is the case with our model" (Andrews and Christenson, 1974, p. 366). Nevertheless the impact of technological improvement on safety is an important issue. At least one other study has found that technological change is correlated with reductions on coal mine injuries. In another important field, debate continues over how much of the improvement in car safety is due to technological change and how much is the result of government regulation.

Summary

Dummy variables are commonly used in time series models to register the occurrence of particular events or the existence of particular policies which affect the value of the dependent variable. This section considered a fictional example and an actual example of the use of dummy variables in time series regressions. The next section explores another use for dummy variables in time series analysis.

21.4. Seasonal Adjustment

Workbooks: SeasonalTheory.xls; SeasonalPractice.xls

This section explains the basic mechanics of seasonal adjustment. Macroeconomic data that are measured more frequently than on an annual basis – that is, quarterly or monthly data – are often seasonally adjusted. For example, quarterly GDP figures are usually reported as "Seasonally Adjusted at Annual Rates."

The quarterly figures are "at annual rates" because this makes the quarterly production figures comparable to the annual figures. To express output in terms of annual rates, multiply quarterly output by four. (Remember that GDP is a flow variable; in a whole year the economy can produce four times as much as it can produce in 3 months.) In addition to reporting GDP in annual rates, the quarterly figures are also "seasonally adjusted." How exactly is the adjustment performed? Why are the data adjusted?

Consider a second example: monthly unemployment rates. The table in Figure 21.4.1 reports seasonally and not seasonally adjusted data. What is the adjustment being applied to the "not seasonally adjusted" data to get the "seasonally adjusted" figures? Which one should you use? This section addresses these questions about seasonally adjusted data.

Table A-1. Employment status of the civilian population by sex and age

Table A-1. Employment status of the civilian population by sex and age

(Numbers in thousands)

Employment status, sex, and age	Not seasonally adjusted			Seasonally adjusted(1)						
	Mar. 2001	Feb. 2002	Mar. 2002	Mar. 2001	Nov. 2001	Dec. 2001	Jan. 2002	Feb. 2002	Mar. 2002	
TOTAL										
Civilian noninstitutional population.	211,171	213,206	213,334	211,171	212,767	212,927	213,089	213,206	213,334	
Civilian labor force.	141,751	142,057	142,092	141,869	142,279	142,314	141,390	142,211	142,005	
Participation rate.	67.1	66.6	66.6	67.2	66.9	66.8	66.4	66.7	66.6	
Employed.	135,298	133,349	133,433	135,808	134,253	134,055	133,468	134,319	133,894	
Employment-population ratio.	64.1	62.5	62.5	64.3	63.1	63.0	62.6	63.0	62.8	
Agriculture.	2,921	2,878	2,882	3,163	3,154	3,246	3,273	3,246	3,126	
Nonagricultural industries.	132,377	130,472	130,551	132,645	131,099	130,809	130,195	131,073	130,768	
Unemployed.	6,453	8,707	8,659	6,061	8,026	8,259	7,922	7,891	8,111	
Unemployment rate.	4.6	6.1	6.1	4.3	5.6	5.8	5.6	5.5	5.7	
Not in labor force.	69,421	71,149	71,243	69,302	70,488	70,613	71,699	70,995	71,329	
Persons who currently want a job.	4,103	4,436	4,369	4,257	4,698	4,661	4,824	4,375	4,537	

Figure 21.4.1. CPS unemployment data.
Source: <www.bls.gov/cps/>.

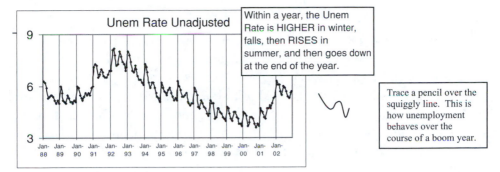

Figure 21.4.2. Not seasonally adjusted.
Source: <www.bls.gov/cps/>.

Comparing Graphs

Figure 21.4.2 shows monthly unemployment rates between January 1988 and December 2002. The series shows a marked pattern: Winters and summers seem to have high unemployment rates; spring and fall months show lower unemployment rates. Construction layoffs in January, February, and March help explain the winter increase. Students pouring into the labor market in June and July generate the summer increase. November and December consumer spending drives the fall decline in unemployment. Figure 21.4.3 depicts seasonally adjusted unemployment data for the same period.

Compare years such as 1989, 1995, and 2000 in the two figures. These years have a relatively stable seasonally adjusted unemployment rate over the entire year. The exaggerated, persistent pattern in Figure 21.4.2 has been largely removed in the seasonally adjusted graph.

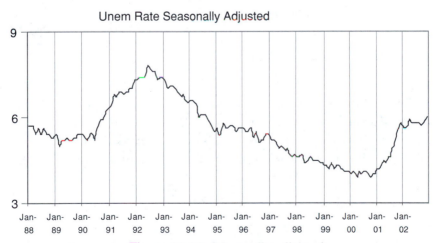

Figure 21.4.3. Seasonally adjusted.
Source: <www.bls.gov/cps/>.

Why Seasonal Adjustment?

Seasonal adjustment is designed to control for the persistent time patterns in economic data. Seasonal adjustment is an application of the general principle "Do not mislead your audience."

If the data come in units that exhibit systematic patterns over time and you want to make comparisons across time periods, seasonally adjusting the data usually makes for better comparisons. If you insist on comparing raw data that have strong seasonal patterns, you might make some rather silly statements.

For example, in 2002, we cannot say that the economy was improving because the unemployment rate was higher in July (5.9 percent) than December (5.7 percent) because July is usually high and December is usually low. In fact, the seasonally adjusted rate in July 2002, 5.8 percent, was lower than the seasonally adjusted December 2002 value of 6 percent. In the seasonally adjusted figures, July's rate was reduced somewhat to account for the usual flood of students into the labor market, whereas December's rate was increased to reflect the hiring of retail workers to help with the usual increase in fourth-quarter consumer spending. The unemployment rate, after removing the effect of seasonal variation, was actually worse in December than in July. Comparing seasonally adjusted rates in July and December is better than looking at unadjusted rates because we get an apples-to-apples comparison.

The Bureau of Labor Statistics says this about seasonal adjustment:

Question: What is seasonal adjustment?

Answer: Seasonal adjustment is a statistical technique which eliminates the influences of weather, holidays, the opening and closing of schools, and other recurring seasonal events from economic time series. This permits easier observation and analysis of cyclical, trend, and other nonseasonal movements in the data. By eliminating seasonal fluctuations, the series becomes smoother and it is easier to compare data from month to month.   Source:www.bls.gov/dolfaq/bls_ques25.htm

Seasonal Adjustment Theory

Open the Excel workbook SeasonalTheory.xls to see an implementation of a DGP with seasonal variation. The workbook is based on an extremely simply seasonal variation model. We augment a well-behaved classical econometric model DGP with an additive, stable seasonality component:

$$y_t^* = \beta_0 + \varepsilon_t$$
$$y_t^{\text{observed}} = y_t^* + y_t^{\text{s}}$$

The error term ε_t is just an independent, identically distributed draw from an error box. The seasonal component is y_t^{s}, which takes on one of four values

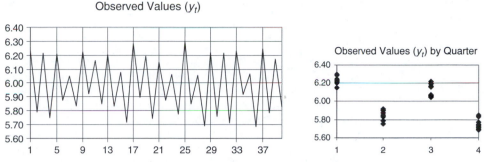

Figure 21.4.4. Observed *y* (with seasonal variation included).
Source: [SeasonalTheory.xls]Deconstruction.

as determined by the season of the year. These parameter values are given
in cells B10 to B13 of the *Deconstruction* sheet.

The resulting values for observed *y* look like those in Figure 21.4.4.

There is no doubt about it – we have a strong, seasonally varying series. Now
the question is, How can we remove the seasonality? There are many different
methods of seasonal adjustment. We demonstrate a relatively straightforward
three-step approach:

1. Regress the variable on dummies for the seasons (quarters or months).
2. Create a seasonal index.
3. Use the index to adjust the raw data.

Scroll right to column Q in the *Deconstruction* sheet to see how regression
can be used to create a seasonally adjusted series. After regressing observed
Y on three quarterly dummies (leaving Fall out as the base case), we obtain
the results shown in Figure 21.4.5. Your results will be somewhat different
because the sheet is live and new error terms are drawn every time you hit
F9. Notice that the three coefficients on the dummy variables are positive.
The interpretation is clear: Relative to Fall, the predicted values of the three
other seasons are higher, and Winter is the highest of all. This result reflects
the parameter values in cells B10:B13. Notice as well that the estimates are

y on Seasonal Dummies			
Summer	Spring	Winter	Intercept
0.355	0.082	0.491	4.758
0.019	0.019	0.019	0.013
0.962	0.042	#N/A	#N/A
299.949	36	#N/A	#N/A
1.583	0.063	#N/A	#N/A

Figure 21.4.5. Regression of *y* on Seasonal Dummies.
Source: [SeasonalTheory.xls]Deconstruction.

Quarter	Season	Predicted	Seasonal Index
1	Winter	5.232	0.229
2	Spring	4.876	−0.127
3	Summer	5.141	0.139
4	Fall	4.761	−0.242
	Average	5.002	

Figure 21.4.6. The seasonal index.
Source: [SeasonalTheory.xls]Deconstruction.

random variables. Chance error is at work here (the spread of the chance errors is controlled by the SD Error parameter in cell B15).

The next step is to create the seasonal index. The computations are shown starting in column AA. We first compute predicted values for each season (cells AC5 to AC8) based on the estimated coefficients from the dummy variable regression. To produce the seasonal index values, we subtract the predicted value for each season from the average of the predicted values for all four seasons. In effect, we have recentered the coefficients on the dummy variables (including the absent Fall dummy around zero). Figure 21.4.6 displays a typical result.

We know we are on the right track because the seasonal index reflects the seasonality in the series. Winter and Summer are higher than Spring and Fall just like the parameter values in cells B10:B13.

The final step is to use the seasonal index values to adjust the observed Y data. Column AJ shows that we simply subtract the seasonal index from the observed Y to obtain the seasonally adjusted value. Thus, Winter and Summer values are adjusted downward, whereas the other two seasons are nudged upward. The results, shown in Figure 21.4.7, are impressive.

Seasonal Adjustment in Practice

Unfortunately, seasonal adjustment in the real world is not as easy as in this example. The way in which seasonality affects a series may not be as simple

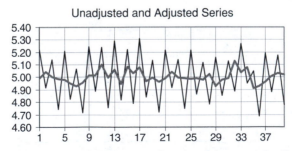

Figure 21.4.7. The results of regression-based seasonal adjustment.
Source: [SeasonalTheory.xls]Deconstruction.

Estimation of Seasonal Effects

From the BLS Handbook of Methods Bulletin 2490, April 1997 Chapter 17, The Consumer Price Index, "Estimation of Price Change", p. 192

Seasonal adjustment Seasonal adjustment removes the estimated effect of changes that normally occur at the same time every year (such as price movements resulting from changing climatic conditions, production cycles, model changeovers, holidays, sales, etc.). CPI series are selected for seasonal adjustment if they pass certain statistical criteria and if there is an economic rationale for the observed seasonality. Seasonal factors used in computing the seasonally adjusted indexes are derived using the ARIMA option of the X-11 variant of the Census Method II Seasonal Adjustment Program. In some cases, intervention analysis seasonal adjustment is carried out using X-12-ARIMA to derive more accurate seasonal factors. Consumer price indexes may be adjusted directly or aggregatively depending on the level of aggregation of the index, and the behavior of the component series.

Revision The seasonal factors are updated annually. BLS recalculates and publishes seasonally adjusted indexes for the previous 5 years.

Figure 21.4.8. Bureau of Labor Statistics discussion of seasonal adjustment. *Source:* <www.bls.gov/cpi/cpisameth.htm.>

as the additive process implemented in the workbook. (For a hint about the reason, see the *Trend* and *Q&A* sheets in SeasonalTheory.xls: If a series contains a trend, seasonal adjustment is more difficult.) In fact, as indicated in Figure 21.4.8, the Bureau of Labor Statistics uses a complicated method involving autoregressive integrated moving-average methods (ARIMA) used by econometricians to model autocorrelation in time series.

The Excel workbook SeasonalPractice.xls has a link to Bureau of Labor Statistics (BLS) unemployment data and compares the regression-based adjustment method with the BLS Adjusted Unemployment Rate series. The BLS method generates different adjustments than the simple regression-based approach just outlined. One reason for this is that we have estimated the monthly seasonal adjustments by running the regression over the entire period, which assumes that the seasonal pattern has not changed over the past 57 years. A second, more important reason is that the BLS method allows the size of the adjustment to vary. We plotted the differences between the raw, unadjusted unemployment series and the adjusted BLS series and the differences between the raw, unadjusted unemployment series and our dummy-variable-regression-adjusted series on the same graph against time in Figure 21.4.9. We are close, but our method does not exactly replicate the BLS series.

Seasonal Adjustment: To Do or Not To Do?

Most comparisons over time involving different months or quarters are better made with seasonally adjusted data because the adjustment removes recurring seasonal events. When you are using a variable in a regression equation, however, the decision to use unadjusted or adjusted data is not an obvious one. If the seasonal adjustment used by the BLS were easily replicated via

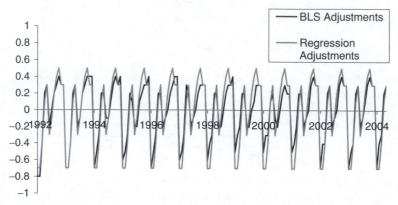

Figure 21.4.9. Comparing seasonal adjustments by the Bureau of Labor Statistics (BLS) and the dummy variable regression methods.
Source: [SeasonalPractice.xls]UnempAdjCompared.

regression, it would not matter if we used seasonally adjusted data or unadjusted data with seasonal dummies. Figure 21.4.9 shows, however, that we cannot rely on this easy solution. Ideally, the underlying economic theory would point to the way seasonality should be incorporated. Absent such a theoretical guide, the choice is a difficult one. One simple, but time-consuming step is to estimate the model both ways and to see how the results compare.

Summary

This section introduced the concept of seasonal adjustment. The basic purpose of seasonal adjustment is to facilitate the comparison of the values of economic variables over time. Seasonal adjustment ideally removes purely seasonal factors which affect a time series in the same regular way year after year. We saw how regressions with dummy variables for seasons (or months) can be used to measure the size of seasonal factors and how the time series can be adjusted via seasonal indexes based on the dummy variable coefficient estimates. In practice, seasonal adjustment can be a good deal more complicated, but the same fundamental ideas apply.

21.5. Stationarity

Workbook: Stationarity.xls

So far in this chapter we have introduced functional forms that help researchers do a better job of modeling economic variables that change over time. In the next two sections, we return to a more careful consideration of the data generation process for time series variables. We highlight the key ideas of stationarity and weak dependence. The distinctions between stationary

and nonstationary time series and between time series that are weakly dependent and those that are strongly dependent have important implications for
the properties of estimation methods like OLS. For example, if an economic
variable is not stationary or is strongly dependent, it generally must be transformed before OLS can have a hope of producing consistent estimates of
the parameters of interest. This section considers the issue of stationarity;
Section 21.6 introduces the notion of weak dependence.

We begin with a somewhat loose definition: If a sequence of random variables is a *stationary* time series process, then the joint probability distribution
(the expected values, SDs, and correlations) of the random variables is constant no matter at what point in the sequence one looks. This concept is best
appreciated through examples.

Trends

Suppose that the data generating process is

$$Y_t = \beta_0 + \beta_1 t + \varepsilon_t, \quad t = 1, \dots T,$$

where ε_t is a mean-zero draw from an error box. Then for any given time
period t the expected value of Y_t is given by

$$E(Y_t) = \beta_0 + \beta_1 t,$$

and the variance of Y_t is

$$Var(Y_t) = Var(\varepsilon),^8$$

where $Var(\varepsilon) = SD(\varepsilon)^2$ is the common variance of the error terms (they are
identically distributed – that is, drawn from the same box).

Open Stationarity.xls and go to the *Trend* worksheet to see an implementation of this DGP. Figure 21.5.1 shows the expected values of the random
variables in the time series (the straight line) and a single realization of the
time series when $\beta_1 = 2$ and $SD(v) = 5$.

Stationarity has to do with the joint distribution of different elements in
the time series. Key features of the joint distribution are the expected values
of each random variable in the series, their variances, and their covariances
(which are directly related to their correlations). Figure 21.5.2 makes it clear
that the expected values of different elements in the series are different as t
changes when $\beta_1 \neq 0$. Thus, for example, the joint distribution of Y_1 and Y_2 is
not the same as the joint distribution of Y_{11} and Y_{12}. When $\beta_1 \neq 0$, the Trend
DGP is not stationary. The numerical facts about the joint distributions of
these random variables are summarized in Figure 21.5.2.

---

[8] More precisely, this is the variance of Y_t conditional on the trend term, t.

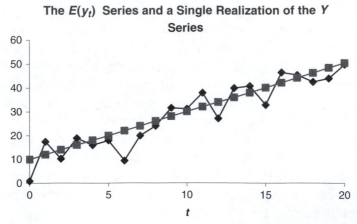

Figure 21.5.1. Comparison between single realization of time series of a trending random variable and its expected values.
Source: [Stationarity.xls]Trend.

Figure 21.5.2 requires some explanation. The expected values of the Y_t and ε_t random variables follow directly from the DGP. The expected values of the ε_t's are always zero because the error terms are draws from an error box with mean zero. If the true slope parameter is known, we can determine the expected values of the Y_t's. The variances refer to the spread of each Y_t around its own expected value. Thus, the table tells us that, when $\beta_0 = 10$ and $\beta_1 = 2$, Y_{12} is expected to equal 34 give or take 5 (the square root of the variance of 25). The variance of each Y_t is exactly the common variance of the ε_t's because each ε_t is what makes each Y_t move off of its expected value after taking into account the value of t. Similarly, the covariance between two Y_t's is related to whether a higher than expected value in, Y_1, for example, is correlated with a higher than expected value of Y_2. The covariances are zero because, for example, the existence of a positive ε_1 that makes Y_1 higher than expected tells us nothing about the expected value of ε_2 and therefore

Joint Distributions					
	Exp Value	Var		Exp Value	Var
Y_1	12	25	ε_1	0	25
Y_2	14	25	ε_2	0	25
Cov(Y_1,Y_2)	0		Cov($\varepsilon_1,\varepsilon_2$)	0	
	Exp Value	Var		Exp Value	Var
Y_{11}	32	25	ε_{11}	0	25
Y_{12}	34	25	ε_{12}	0	25
Cov(Y_{11},Y_{12})	0		Cov($\varepsilon_{11},\varepsilon_{12}$)	0	

Figure 21.5.2. Joint distributions of two pairs of random variables in the time series.
Source: [Stationarity.xls]Trend.

Parameters									
SD(v)	5								
β_0	10								
β_1	2			Correlations					
	Avg	SD		Y_1	Y_2	Y_3	Y_{11}	Y_{12}	Y_{13}
Y_1	12.0	5.0	Y_1	1					
Y_2	14.1	5.1	Y_2	0.00	1				
Y_3	15.9	5.1	Y_3	0.02	0.01	1			
Y_{11}	32.0	5.0	Y_{11}	0.02	0.05	0.04	1		
Y_{12}	34.2	4.8	Y_{12}	-0.02	0.00	-0.01	-0.04	1	
Y_{13}	35.9	4.9	Y_{13}	0.01	0.00	-0.04	-0.06	0.02	1

Figure 21.5.3. Monte Carlo approximation to expected values, SDs, and correlations of random variables in the trend time series.
Source: [Stationarity.xls]Trend.

what will happen to Y_2. The zero-valued covariances just signify that the draws from the error box are independent. Put another way, after taking into account the time trend, the Y's are uncorrelated with one another.

It is important to realize that Figure 21.5.1 depicts an entire series of random variables. Each time you hit F9, you will see another realization of 21 different random variables, each bouncing around its own respective expected value. Even though they are related to each other through the common intercept and slope parameters, the Y_t's are independent random variables. To drive this point home, we performed a Monte Carlo analysis of the Trend DGP. Click on the Go To Monte Carlo Simulation button to switch to the *MCTrend* sheet.

The *MCTrend* sheet runs 1,000 repetitions of the Trend DGP and displays the results for six different random variables in the series: Y_1, Y_2, Y_3, Y_{11}, Y_{12}, and Y_{13}. Then it computes correlations between each term. Figure 21.5.3 displays a typical outcome of the Monte Carlo experiment.

Click on cell L8; its formula reads "=CORREL(B6:B1005,A6:A1005)." This computes the empirical correlation between the 1,000 pairs of Y_1 and Y_2 from the 1,000 repetitions. This Monte Carlo experiment supports the claims we made about the trend series in Figure 21.5.2. Thus, Figure 21.5.3 is consistent with our assertions that the Y_t's have changing expected values but constant variance and are uncorrelated with one another. Of course the numbers in the table are not all exactly 5 (the SDs) or 0 (the correlations), but that is to be expected given that we took a finite number of repetitions. The scatter diagram to the right of the empirical autocorrelation table graphs the (Y_1, Y_2) pairs from the first 100 repetitions to make the point visually that there is no correlation between these random variables.

In summary, the Trend DGP is nonstationary only because the expected values of the Y_t's are changing. In all other aspects the joint distributions of

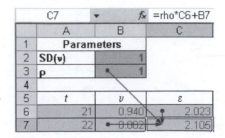

Figure 21.5.4. The data generation process for
the AR(1) series.
Source: [Stationarity.xls]AR(1).

the random variables in the series stay constant across time periods. Although the Y series is not a stationary time series, it is obvious how to convert it into a stationary one: simply remove the trend. This brings us back to a series with the same expected value (β_0) for each element in the series and leaves the variances and correlations unchanged. More generally, a *trend stationary process* is one that is stationary after taking the trend into account.

Autoregressive Process

We turn now to the autoregressive process:

$$\varepsilon_t = \rho\varepsilon_{t-1} + v_t,$$

where the v_t's are independent and identically distributed. This process is simulated in the *AR(1)* sheet of Stationary.xls. Go to that sheet now and make sure that the values of the parameters are set so that $\rho = 0.5$ and $SD(v) = 1$. Then click on cell C7. Figure 21.5.4 shows the data generation process in action for the random variable ε_{22}. We have added auditing arrows to make the data generation process clearer. The random variable ε_{22} equals ρ multiplied by ε_{21} (in cell C6) plus v_{22} (in cell B7). Is this a stationary process?

We can use Monte Carlo simulation to get a tentative answer. We focus on the six shaded observations: ε_{21}, ε_{22}, and ε_{23}, and ε_{38}, ε_{39}, and ε_{40}. (We explain later in this section why observations earlier in the series are not considered.) Hit F9 a few times, and you will see the series bounce around in the time series graph. We are interested in the expected values, variances (SDs), and correlations of the six random variables. Click on the [Go To Monte Carlo Simulation] button and then run a Monte Carlo simulation in the *MCAR(1)* sheet. We display a typical outcome of the Monte Carlo simulation in Figure 21.5.5.

This Monte Carlo experiment provides suggestive evidence that the AR(1) process we are studying is indeed stationary. Click on the various cells in the table (located in cells I5 to R12) to see how they are calculated. The table tells us the following. First, the empirical averages of the values of the six random variables from the 1,000 repetitions are all very close to zero, which is consistent with a claim that the expected value for every random variable in the series is zero. Second, the SD column is consistent with a

Parameters	
SD(v)	1
ρ	0.5

Reset Parameters

	Avg	SD			Correlations					
					ε_{21}	ε_{22}	ε_{23}	ε_{38}	ε_{39}	ε_{40}
ε_{21}	−0.01	1.12	ε_{21}		1					
ε_{22}	0.00	1.13	ε_{22}		0.52	1				
ε_{23}	0.03	1.18	ε_{23}		0.29	0.50	1			
ε_{38}	0.05	1.17	ε_{38}		−0.05	0.00	0.01	1		
ε_{39}	0.03	1.16	ε_{39}		−0.04	0.00	−0.02	0.49	1	
ε_{40}	0.00	1.15	ε_{40}		−0.01	0.01	0.02	0.28	0.5	01

Figure 21.5.5. Monte Carlo approximation to expected values, SDs, and correlations of random variables in the AR(1) time series.
Source: [Stationarity.xls]MCAR(1).

claim that the spread of the random variables is constant (though it seems to be somewhat greater than the spread of the underlying error term, $SD(v)$, which is 1 in this case). Third, the correlations display a definite, constant pattern. The correlation between a random variable and its counterpart in the next time period always appears to be about 0.5; the correlation between random variables and their counterparts shifted by two time periods always seems to be about 0.28 or so, whereas the correlation of variables separated by 15 time periods or more always seems to be close to zero. All of these observations suggest that the joint distribution of the random variables in the series stays constant over time.

In fact, this process is indeed, for all intents and purposes, stationary. (There is a slight caveat; see the discussion of initial conditions below.) We will not go through the algebra,[9] but it can be shown that, for all t (i.e., for every time period) and for $|\rho| < 1$,

(1) the expected value of each random variable in the series is zero,

$$E[\varepsilon_t] = 0,$$

(2) the spread of each random variable around its expected value stays constant,

$$SD(\varepsilon_t) = \frac{SD(v)}{\sqrt{1 - \rho^2}}, \text{ and}$$

(3) the correlations of two random variables separated a given distance (say h time periods) stay the same:

$$Corr(\varepsilon_t, \varepsilon_{t-h}) = \rho^h.$$

---

[9] Derivations are in most econometrics textbooks. For example, see Goldberger (1998, p. 165) or Wooldridge (2003, pp. 363–4).

As examples of the second and third items in this list, when $\rho = 0.5$ and $SD(v) = 1$,

$$SD(\varepsilon_t) = \frac{1}{\sqrt{1 - 0.5^2}} = 1.15$$

$$Corr(\varepsilon_1, \varepsilon_3) = Corr(\varepsilon_{21}, \varepsilon_{23}) = 0.5^2 = 0.25, \text{ and}$$

$$Corr(\varepsilon_1, \varepsilon_{18}) = Corr(\varepsilon_{21}, \varepsilon_{38}) = 0.5^{17} \approx 7.6 \cdot 10^{-6}, \text{ or essentially zero.}$$

These formulas are implemented in the "Asymptotic Values" table in columns T through AC of the *MCAR(1)* sheet.

We now address the caveat and some special cases. The caveat is that, in the example in the *AR(1)* sheet, these formulas are only approximately true and the time series is not quite stationary. The reason is related to the *initial conditions* (i.e., how we got the series started). To start the series off, we set $\varepsilon_1 = v_1$. Because $\varepsilon_1 = \rho\varepsilon_0 + v_1$, this implies that we arbitrarily set ε_0 equal to zero. This choice makes the first term in the series different in character from all subsequent terms. Owing to the autoregressive nature of the time series, the initial condition has ripple effects on all subsequent random variables in the series. When ρ is not too close to 1, however, the correlation between random variables that are far enough away is very small, and thus the ripples are of rapidly diminishing importance. That is why we let the series run for a while (to observation 21) before looking at its properties.

If you want to see the initial conditions still affecting the series, set ρ equal to 0.99 in the *AR(1)* sheet and then run a Monte Carlo simulation in the *MCAR(1)* sheet. In the empirical SD column (cells K7 to K12), you will observe that the approximate SDs of the earlier random variables ($t = 21$, 22, and 23) are substantially less than the SDs of the later random variables ($t = 38$, 39, and 40). What is happening is that, in this case of a very high autocorrelation coefficient, the initial condition exerts a constraining effect on the realizations of even random variables that are far away.[10]

Next we consider the special cases. First, let us make the series blow up. In the *AR(1)* sheet, set ρ equal to 1.1. Hit F9 several times. The time series plot will literally go off the chart (we have locked down the axes so that only values between -25 and $+25$ are displayed). Run a Monte Carlo simulation and verify that, although the empirical averages of the ε_t's are still close to zero, the SDs of the ε_t's are rapidly increasing as t rises. To see a different explosive pattern, return to the *Trend* sheet, set ρ equal to -1.1, and hit F9 several times.

---

[10] It is possible to get rid of the influence of the initial condition by setting ε_1 equal to v_1 plus an error term with a spread equal to the SD for the stationary series, $SD(v)/\sqrt{1 - \rho^2}$. This solution not coincidentally resembles the transformation we use for the first observation in the GLS and FGLS methods for dealing with first-order autocorrelation in the previous chapter. Go to cell A31 in the *Intro* sheet to see the Excel formula for implementing this change.

	Avg	SD				Correlations			
				ε_{21}	ε_{22}	ε_{23}	ε_{38}	ε_{39}	ε_{40}
ε_{21}	−0.04	4.63	ε_{21}	1					
ε_{22}	−0.07	4.77	ε_{22}	0.98	1				
ε_{23}	−0.02	4.84	ε_{23}	0.96	0.98	1			
ε_{38}	−0.11	6.27	ε_{38}	0.73	0.76	0.77	1		
ε_{39}	−0.14	6.41	ε_{39}	0.72	0.75	0.76	0.99	1	
ε_{40}	−0.12	6.48	ε_{40}	0.71	0.73	0.75	0.97	0.99	1

Parameters: SD(v) 1, ρ 1 — Reset Parameters

Figure 21.5.6. Monte Carlo approximation to expected values, SDs, and correlations of random variables in the AR(1) time series for random walk. *Source:* [Stationarity.xls]MCAR(1).

In both cases, when ρ is greater than 1 in absolute value, each deviation from 0 in one random variable is magnified in the next random variable in the series because they are multiplied by a number bigger than 1 in absolute value. On the other hand, when ρ is less than 1 in absolute value, deviations from 0 are damped down. This makes first-order autoregressive processes with $|\rho| < 1$ stationary and those with $|\rho| \geq 1$ nonstationary. Stationary autoregressive processes are also called *stable* processes for obvious reasons.

Random Walks

A very interesting and important special case occurs when $\rho = 1$, which is known as a *random walk*. The data generation process for the most basic kind of random walk is described by

$$\varepsilon_t = \varepsilon_{t-1} + v_t,$$

where the v_t's are independent and identically distributed. To learn about random walks, set ρ equal to 1 in the *AR(1)* sheet and run a Monte Carlo simulation. Figure 21.5.6 displays findings from our experiment.

We highlight three important results from the Monte Carlo simulation of a simple random walk. First, the empirical averages are consistent with the fact that the expected value of any given random variable in the series is still zero. Second, the spread of the random variables is increasing as t increases. In fact, the spread of the random variables increases without limit as time increases. This implies that a random walk is *not* stationary. Third, the correlations in the table are all very high. In fact, these correlations will increase as time increases. That is, if we could observe the series up to $t = 240$, for instance, we would find that the correlation between the two random variables ε_{221} and ε_{240} is greater than the correlation between two earlier random variables that are also 20 time periods apart (e.g., ε_{21} and ε_{40}).[11]

It is not difficult to work out the expected values, variances, and SDs algebraically for some versions of the random walk. In the *AR(1)* sheet, the initial value of the series is always

$$\varepsilon_0 = 0.$$

The $t = 1$ and $t = 2$ values are

$$\varepsilon_1 = \varepsilon_0 + v_1 = v_1, \quad \text{and}$$
$$\varepsilon_2 = \varepsilon_1 + v_2 = v_1 + v_2.$$

Repeatedly applying the basic formula of the data generation process, we arrive at, for any given time period T,

$$\varepsilon_T = (v_1 + v_2 + \cdots + v_T).$$

It now comes in extremely handy that all the v's are independent and have the same spread (variance or SD). Applying standard formulas for the expected value and variance of a sum of independent random variables,[12] we have

$$E(\varepsilon_T) = 0$$
$$Var(\varepsilon_T) = T \cdot Var[v]$$
$$SD(\varepsilon_T) = \sqrt{T} \cdot SD(v).$$

The last equation says that the spread of the random walk around its expected value increases proportionally to the square root of the time.

An important variation on the basic random walk is a *random walk with drift* whose data generation process

$$\varepsilon_t = \beta + \varepsilon_{t-1} + v_t,$$

where, as usual, the v_t's are independent and identically distributed. The β term is known as the drift because it determines the general course of the time series. The worksheet *RWDrift* illustrates such a process. The key difference vis-à-vis the basic random walk is that the expected values of the random variables in the series are now no longer constant at zero. Instead

[11] When a series Y follows a random walk and $SD(Y_0) = 0$ (as is the case in the *AR(1)* sheet), the formula for the correlation between two terms in the series separated by h time periods is $Corr(Y_t, Y_{t+h}) = \sqrt{\frac{t}{t+h}}$. Note that this correlation depends on what time period you start from (which violates one of the rules for a stationary series) and that the correlation increases asymptotically toward 1 as t increases toward infinity. See Wooldridge (2003, p. 374).

[12] The formulas say that the expected value of the sum of random variables is the sum of the expected values. The variance of the sum of independent, identically distributed random variables is just the number of random variables multiplied by the common variance.

the expected value is given by

$$E(\varepsilon_T) = \varepsilon_0 + \beta \cdot T.$$

The variance and SD however, are still the same as they are for the basic random walk:

$$Var(\varepsilon_T) = T \cdot Var(v)$$
$$SD(\varepsilon_T) = \sqrt{T} \cdot SD(v).$$

Monte Carlo experiments support these claims, as you can see for yourself by going to the *MCRWDrift* sheet.

Summary

This section introduced the important concepts of stationarity and random walks. Stationarity is crucial for time series because without it, ordinary statistical inference fails. First-differencing time series is a frequently used remedy used to restore stationarity to time series. Random walks, a special case of the AR(1) process, are a prime example of a nonstationary time series. Random walks with drift are quite commonly employed to model important economic time series, such as the movement of the stock market and of GDP. Section 21.9 returns to the topic of random walks in the context of forecasting time series.

21.6. Weak Dependence

Workbooks: Stationarity.xls; Spurious.xls

Throughout most of this book we have assumed that the X's are fixed in repeated sampling. This assumption, although false in most practical applications, has essentially the same statistical implications as a more realistic assumption that the X's are obtained via random sampling. In both cases, a crucial step in showing that OLS is unbiased involves the fact that the X's are independent of the error terms contained in the Y values. Time series models make the task of specifying the data generation process more complicated. This section discusses the assumption of weak dependence that econometricians use for time series data when it is no longer possible to claim that the X's are independent of the error terms.

A good example of this problem occurs in time series models in which lagged versions of the dependent Y variable show up as X variables. When this is the case, the X's are clearly not independent of the error terms (for example Y_{t-1} is correlated with the $t-1$ error term). This means that the crucial step in showing that OLS is unbiased fails, and, in fact, OLS slope estimates involving models with lagged Y's as regressors are generally biased.

Fortunately when the X and Y variables are no longer independent but are still weakly dependent, OLS estimators can be shown to be consistent: The bias goes away as the sample size increases. In general, a sequence of random variables is *weakly dependent* if the elements of the sequence become essentially independent at a sufficiently rapid pace as the distance between them grows. The alternative is a *strongly dependent* series. The prime example of a strongly dependent series is a random walk. The Stationarity.xls file showed that the correlations between different random variables in a random walk remain very high even when separated by long periods of time.

Unit root processes are a more general type of strongly dependent process than random walks. As is the case with a random walk, in a unit root process the previous value of the series is added to an error term to produce the current value; however, the error terms themselves can be autocorrelated.

We saw an example of consistent estimation of a parameter of interest involving weakly dependent series in the previous chapter: estimating ρ when the error terms follow an AR(1) process. In this case, the residuals are proxies for the unobserved error terms, which are correlated with one another. We regress the residuals on their one-period lagged counterparts. Suppose, to simplify the discussion, we knew the error terms and were trying to use them to estimate ρ. The equation we would estimate is the AR(1) process:

$$\varepsilon_t = \rho\varepsilon_{t-1} + v_t.$$

We know that OLS regression produces unbiased estimates when the X's are fixed in repeated samples, or more generally, when the X's are independent of all the error terms. But those assumptions about the data generating process do not hold in the case of our AR(1) process. Clearly, each ε_t in the series other than ε_1 is correlated with v_1. As a result, estimated ρ is biased. However because, the ε_t's are weakly dependent when $|\rho| < 1$, this bias goes away as the sample size increases. The correlation between regressors and error terms can be overcome when the errors are weakly dependent.

This is not true if the series is strongly dependent. In the simple random walk case, we have seen that the value of v_1 has a strong influence on the value of all subsequent ε_t's in the series. The correlation between regressors and error terms stays too high as the sample size increases to improve the bias. As an example, consider the following data generating process for two random variables:

$$Y_t = Y_{t-1} + \varepsilon_t, \quad t = 1, \ldots, T,$$
$$X_t = X_{t-1} + \delta + \eta_t, \quad t = 1, \ldots, T,$$

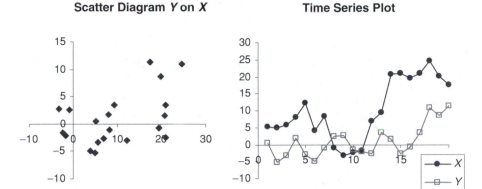

Figure 21.6.1. One realization of the two unrelated random walks. *Source:* [Spurious.xls]RandomWalks.

where both the ε's and the η's are draws from error boxes with mean 0. The two error terms are mutually independent. In other words, both X and Y are random walks and there is no connection between the two. If δ is nonzero, X also has a drift. This data generating process is represented in the *RandomWalks* sheet of Spurious.xls. One example of the resulting time series is contained in the two graphs of Figure 21.6.1.

In the *RandomWalks* sheet we run two regressions on samples with 20 observations: a short regression of Y on X and an intercept and a long regression of Y on X and the time period t. Set δ equal to 0 and the SD's of the two error terms, ε and η, equal to 5. Hit F9 repeatedly and examine the regression output. We are especially interested in the z-statistics, which can be used to test the null hypothesis that the slope of Y on X is equal to zero. You should observe that the corresponding P-values are very small all too often. We confirmed this to be the case by using the MCSim add-in to run a 1,000-repetition Monte Carlo experiment. Our experimental results are in the *MCSimRWPValues* sheet. Figure 21.6.2 shows the histograms of the 1,000 pairs of P-values.

That the histograms are very far from a uniform distribution tips us off that something is amiss. Further evidence comes from the point we highlighted in Figure 21.6.2. The height of the lower histogram – the one for the P-values from the long regression (cell H11 on the *RandomWalks* sheet) – is 252 at the point 0.025. This says that in 252 of the 1,000 repetitions we obtained a P-value of 0.025 or less. Thus, at the 2.5-percent level of significance, we would reject a true null hypothesis about ten times as often as we should. The height of the taller histogram, the one for the P-values from the short regression (cell H4 in the *RandomWalks* sheet), is 445: we would reject the true null almost half the time even when we chose a very cautious 2.5-percent level of significance to guard against the possibility of rejecting a true null!

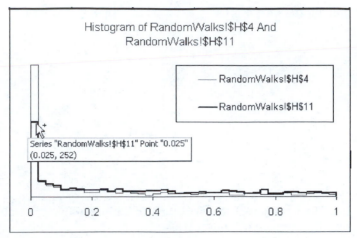

Figure 21.6.2. *P*-values for regression of unrelated random walks. *Source:* [Spurious.xls]MCSimRWPValues.

This is the spurious regression problem for random walks: One can easily be misled into believing that there is a statistically significant relationship between two unrelated economic variables if they follow random walks.

One might suspect the problem would go away if we were just to increase the sample size. Unfortunately, this is not the case. The RandomWalks 100 sheet extends the random walks for *X* and *Y* to 100 observations. The *MCSimRW100PValues* sheet gives the results of a Monte Carlo simulation approximating the sampling distributions of *P*-values from both the short and long regressions. In both cases more than 60 percent of the *P*-values are under 2.5 percent even though the null hypothesis is true. These results are strong evidence that the OLS slope estimate is inconsistent in this version of the data generating process.

What if anything can be done if you suspect the data you are working with are strongly dependent? A popular, and often effective, remedy is to *difference* the data. The first difference of a variable is its current value less its one-period lagged value:

$$\Delta Y_t = Y_t - Y_{t-1}.$$

The differencing remedy is to substitute first differences for the original variables in the regression equation. Chapter 20 presents a variation of this strategy in the GLS and FGLS estimators for AR(1) models.

In the *DifferencedRWs* sheet we apply the differencing strategy to the preceding example. There we set up two random walks using exactly the same data generating process outlined and implemented in the *RandomWalks* sheet. Figure 21.6.3 shows the results for the first three observations.

t	X	ε	Y	η	ΔY	ΔX
1	3.7	1.1	1.1	1.7		
2	5.3	−1.4	−0.3	−0.4	−1.4	1.6
3	7.4	−1.3	−1.6	0.1	−1.3	2.1

Figure 21.6.3. First differenced data.
Source: [Spurious.xls]DifferencedRWs.

For example, the first difference between Y_2 and Y_1 is

$$\Delta Y_2 = Y_2 - Y_1$$
$$= -1.6 - (-0.3)$$
$$= -1.3.$$

We ran a 10,000-repetition Monte Carlo simulation in which we regressed the first difference of Y on the first difference of X with an intercept term (this is the Short Regression in the *DifferencedRWs* sheet). The results are contained in the *MCSimDifferPValues* sheet and are displayed in Figure 21.6.4.

Using the z-test in 632 or 6.32% of the repetitions, we obtained a P-value below 5 percent. The Monte Carlo experiment demonstrates that first-differencing substantially alleviates the spurious regression problem.

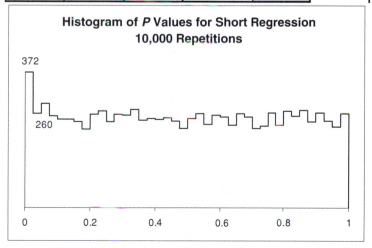

Summary Statistics			Notes	
Average	0.491		**Parameters**	
SD	0.2935		δ	0
Max	1.000		$SD(\varepsilon)$	5
Min	0.000		$SD(\eta)$	2

Figure 21.6.4. First differenced data.
Source: [Spurious.xls] MCSimDifferPValues.

Summary

In this section we have asserted that the weak dependence assumption is sufficient to ensure that OLS estimates in many time series models are consistent even if they are biased. We have also demonstrated that, when variables are strongly dependent, the consistency property does not necessarily hold. Finally, we have shown that first-differencing can restore consistency to OLS estimates involving strongly dependent time series.

In the next section we analyze a leading example of time series in which the weak dependence assumption is invoked: lagged dependent variable models.

21.7. Lagged Dependent Variables

Workbook: PartialAdjustment.xls

In this section we discuss the use of lagged dependent variables in time series models. Recall that a variable lagged one period is just a series containing the one-period previous values of the original variable. It is also common to see lags of two or more periods. Lagged variables can be either lagged independent variables or lagged dependent variables. Many models contain both. We address only models with lagged dependent variables. Our discussion serves merely as an introduction to some of the main issues in this area. We will give some reasons why lagged dependent variables are included in econometric models and explain the implications of including a lagged dependent variable for the short- and long-run impact of an independent variable on the dependent variable. In Section 21.8 we go on to present a leading example of the use of lagged dependent variables in econometrics. Finally, we discuss ways to test for the presence of autocorrelation when the regressors include a lagged dependent variable.

Partial Adjustment Models

Lagged dependent variables make frequent appearances in time series analyses. One common justification for the inclusion of a lagged dependent variable is the concept of *partial adjustment*. In a partial adjustment model, the researcher assumes that there is some level of the dependent variable economic agents desire but that there are costs of adjustment. This implies that, when the desired level changes, the actual level does not immediately and completely respond to the change in the desired level. Instead there is partial adjustment with the actual level moving closer and closer to the desired level over time.

A simple example can be used to illustrate the idea of partial adjustment. Assume that the initial value of an economic variable, call it Y, is 100. In

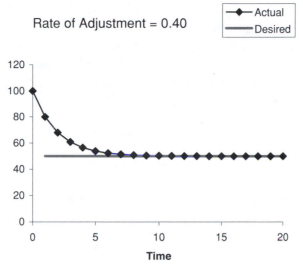

Figure 21.7.1. A simple partial adjustment process.
Source: [PartialAdustment.xls]Example.

the next period and every succeeding period, economic agents wish to set Y equal to 200. It is not possible, however, for agents to change the value of Y immediately to 200. Instead, in each time period they partially adjust to the new, desired level. The way they adjust is the following: Y in each period is equal to the previous period's Y plus some fraction of the distance between previous period's Y and the desired level of Y. In equation form,

$$Y_t = Y_{t-1} + \lambda(Y_t^* - Y_{t-1}).$$

In this equation, Y_t is the actual observed level of the variable in period t, Y_t^* is the desired level of the variable in period t, and λ is the rate of adjustment.

Open the file PartialAdjustment.xls and go to the *Example* sheet to see a concrete version of this adjustment process. We have set up the workbook so that the initial level of Y, Y_0 is 100, the new desired level is 50 in every period from $t = 1$ onward, and the rate of adjustment is 0.4. As you can see in Figure 21.7.1, this setup implies that, in each period, Y moves 40 percent of the distance between its previous value and the desired value. Thus, when we start with $Y_0 = 100$ and set the desired level at $Y_t^* = 50$ for every time period (t) greater than 0, in the first period we move 40 percent of the way from 100 to 50 or down to $Y_1 = 80$; in the next period we move 40 percent of the distance between 80 and 50 or down to $Y_2 = 68$, and so on.

You should experiment with the workbook to see how the adjustment process changes when the value of the adjustment parameter is changed. Two important special cases are $\lambda = 0$ (no adjustment) and $\lambda = 1$ (immediate adjustment). When λ is greater than 1, we have overshooting (the adjustment is too great); λ less than 0 makes little economic sense.

Next we show how the partial adjustment model leads to the inclusion of a lagged independent variable in the regression equation. Suppose that the desired level of a variable Y at time t is a linear function of some independent variable X at time t plus a time t error term. In equation form,

$$Y_t^* = \beta_0 + \beta_1 X_t + \varepsilon_t.$$

It is crucial to note, however, that we do not observe the desired level of Y; instead we observe the actual level, which depends on the adjustment process. If the partial adjustment process is as described above, observed Y is given by

$$Y_t = \lambda(Y_t^* - Y_{t-1}) + Y_{t-1}.$$

The key step in getting to the lagged dependent variable model is substituting the previous equation for Y_t^* into this partial adjustment equation:

$$Y_t = \lambda \left(\beta_0 + \beta_1 X_t + \varepsilon_t \right) - \lambda Y_{t-1} + Y_{t-1}$$
$$= \lambda \beta_0 + (1 - \lambda) Y_{t-1} + \lambda \beta_1 X_t + \lambda \varepsilon_t.$$

We can rewrite the second line as follows:

$$Y_t = \gamma_0 + \gamma_1 Y_{t-1} + \gamma_2 X_t + \nu_t.$$

In this formulation the parameters estimated by a regression are functions of the original parameters. Thus, $\gamma_0 = \lambda \beta_0$, $\gamma_1 = 1 - \lambda$, and $\gamma_2 = \lambda \beta_1$. Note especially that the slope on the lagged dependent variable Y_{t-1} is equal to one minus the adjustment parameter. This line of reasoning tells us that a partial adjustment model implies that a lagged dependent variable belongs in the regression equation for the observed Y variable.

Short- and Long-Run Impacts in Partial Adjustment Models

A natural question to ask in dealing with models involving partial adjustment is, How does a change in the value of an independent variable affect the value of the dependent variable over time? Actually there are two questions:

1. What is the immediate, next-period effect of a change in an independent variable?
2. What is the long-run effect, after all the adjustment has been made?

The *Short&LongRun* sheet in PartialAdjustment.xls provides helpful intuition into the algebraic answers to these questions. We work with the bivariate, partial adjustment model just derived but drop the error term in order to

	One Time Change in X		
t	X_t	Y_{t-1}	Y_t
0	0		12.5
1	0	12.5	12.5
2	1	12.5	15.5
3	0	15.5	14.3
4	0	14.3	13.58
5	0	13.58	13.148
6	0	13.148	12.889
7	0	12.889	12.733
8	0	12.733	12.64
9	0	12.64	12.584
10	0	12.584	12.55
11	0	12.55	12.53

Figure 21.7.2. Impact of a one-time change in X on the value of Y over time. *Source:* [PartialAdjustment.xls]Short&LongRun.

focus on the essential ideas. Thus, the lagged dependent variable model is

$$Y_t = \gamma_0 + \gamma_1 Y_{t-1} + \gamma_2 X_t.$$

In order to follow our discussion, in the *Short&LongRun* sheet make sure that the parameter values are set as follows: $\gamma_0 = 5$, $\gamma_1 = 0.6$, and $\gamma_2 = 3$. We first consider the impact of a one-time change in X on the value of Y. Figure 21.7.2 shows in tabular and graphical forms what happens to Y when X, which is usually 0, temporarily switches to a value of 1 in period 2.

The parameter $\gamma_2 = 3$ gives the short-run impact of a one-time change in X. In this case, a one-unit change in X leads to an immediate three-unit increase in Y. In period 3, X falls back to zero, but the sharp increase in Y is not immediately reversed. To see why, compare the equation determining the value of Y_3 with the equation determining Y_1. In both cases the X value is zero: $X_1 = X_3 = 0$, however, whereas in period 1 the previous value of Y was $Y_0 = 12.5$, in period 3, the previous value of Y was $Y_2 = 15.5$. Thus,

$$Y_1 = 5 + 0.6Y_0 + 3X_1$$
$$= 5 + 0.6 \cdot \mathbf{12.5} + 3 \cdot 0$$
$$= 12.5;$$
$$Y_3 = 5 + 0.6Y_2 + 3X_3$$
$$= 5 + 0.6 \cdot \mathbf{15.5} + 3 \cdot 0$$
$$= 14.3.$$

To clarify what exactly is the process driving observed Y, go to the *BehindTheScenes* sheet. In this worksheet we work out the implied original parameter values in the two-equation system that is the actual data generation process standing behind the model of the *Short&LongRun* sheet. Recall

t	X_t	Y_{t-1}	Y_t^*	Y_t
0	0		12.5	12.5
1	0	12.5	12.5	12.5
2	1	12.5	20	15.5
3	0	15.5	12.5	14.3
4	0	14.3	12.5	13.58
5	0	13.58	12.5	13.148
6	0	13.148	12.5	12.8888
7	0	12.8888	12.5	12.73328
8	0	12.73328	12.5	12.63997
9	0	12.63997	12.5	12.58398
10	0	12.58398	12.5	12.55039
11	0	12.55039	12.5	12.53023
12	0	12.53023	12.5	12.51814
13	0	12.51814	12.5	12.51088
14	0	12.51088	12.5	12.50653
15	0	12.50653	12.5	12.50392

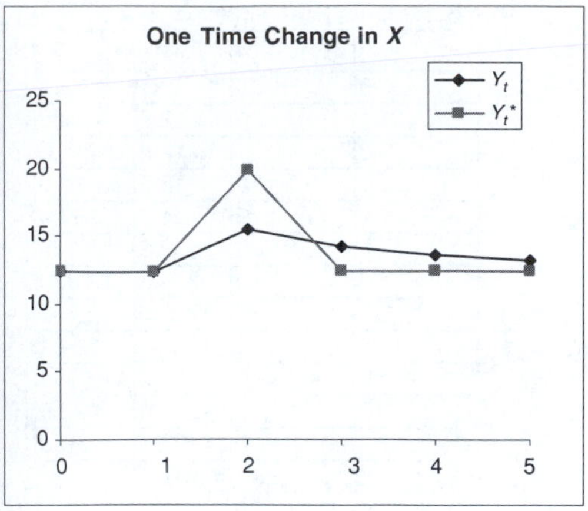

One Time Change in *X*

Figure 21.7.3. Impact of a one-time change in X on the value of Y and Y^* over time. *Source:* [PartialAdjustment.xls]BehindTheScenes.

that it was the two equations

$$Y_t^* = \beta_0 + \beta_1 X_t \,^{13}$$

and

$$Y_t = Y_{t-1} + \lambda(Y_t^* - Y_{t-1})$$

that produced the model we actually observe:

$$Y_t = \gamma_0 + \gamma_1 Y_{t-1} + \gamma_2 X_t.$$

Now, using the facts that $\gamma_0 = \lambda\beta_0$, $\gamma_1 = 1 - \lambda$, and $\gamma_2 = \lambda\beta_1$, we can solve for the parameters of the Y^* and partial adjustment equations:

$$\lambda = 1 - \gamma_1,$$
$$\beta_0 = \frac{\gamma_0}{\lambda}, \text{ and}$$
$$\beta_1 = \frac{\gamma_2}{\lambda}.$$

This means that from the observed values of γ_0, γ_1, and γ_2, we can infer the values of λ, β_0, and β_1. In the *BehindTheScenes* sheet the relevant formulas are in cells J3 through J5. We obtain these values for our three underlying parameters: $\lambda = 0.4$, $\beta_0 = 12.5$, and $\beta_1 = 7.5$. Figure 21.7.3 shows how Y_t and Y_t^* evolve over time. The figure makes clear that the move from $Y_1 = 12.5$ to $Y_2 = 15.5$ is actually a partial adjustment that goes 40 percent of the way to the new desired level, $Y_2^* = 20$. Furthermore, the gradual decline in Y in

---

[13] Note that we have removed the error term to simplify the exposition. This changes nothing essential in the argument.

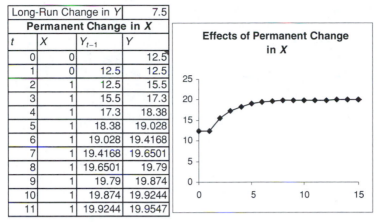

Long-Run Change in Y			7.5
Permanent Change in X			
t	*X*	Y_{t-1}	*Y*
0	0		12.5
1	0	12.5	12.5
2	1	12.5	15.5
3	1	15.5	17.3
4	1	17.3	18.38
5	1	18.38	19.028
6	1	19.028	19.4168
7	1	19.4168	19.6501
8	1	19.6501	19.79
9	1	19.79	19.874
10	1	19.874	19.9244
11	1	19.9244	19.9547

Figure 21.7.4. Impact of a permanent change in *X* on the value of *Y* over time. *Source:* PartialAdjustment.xls]Short&LongRunImpact.

periods 3 onward reflects a partial adjustment in each period back to the original desired level, $Y^* = 12.5$.[14]

The bottom line for the impact of a one-time change in an independent variable on the dependent variable is that its immediate effect is given by its coefficient in the observed *Y* equation and that its effects diminish over time as determined by the size of the adjustment parameter, which is equal to one minus the coefficient on lagged *Y*.

We now move to examining the long-run impact of a permanent increase in the value of an independent variable in a model with a lagged dependent variable. Return to the *Short&LongRun* sheet and look at the right-hand side display (in column I).

The second column in Figure 21.7.4 shows that *X* rises in value from 0 in period 1 to 1 in period 2 and remains at the new, higher level permanently, whereas the chart shows that *Y* responds by increasing with the rate of increase falling as it moves to the new long-run level of 20. We follow the process up to $t = 100$, which is our measure of the new long run solution. The "Long-Run Change in *Y*" cell computes the difference between Y_{100} and Y_1. With our parameter values, the impact of a permanent change of one unit in *X* is a change of 7.5 units in *Y*.

What determines the magnitude of the long-run impact of *X* on *Y*? There are two ways to think about this question: at the level of the lagged dependent variable model or in terms of the underlying partial adjustment data generation process. The lagged dependent variable story is this: At each step

---

[14] Notice that we have set Y_0 in such a way that it is in long-run equilibrium; unless *X* changes there is nothing to cause *Y* to change. See the formulas in cells D8 and L8 in the *Short&LongRun* sheet. We ask you to explain this algebraically in an exercise.

Long-Run Change in Y				7.5
Permanent Change in X				
t	X	Y_{t-1}	Y_t^*	Y
0	0		12.5	12.5
1	0	12.5	12.5	12.5
2	1	12.5	20	15.5
3	1	15.5	20	17.3
4	1	17.3	20	18.38
5	1	18.38	20	19.028
6	1	19.028	20	19.4168
7	1	19.417	20	19.65008
8	1	19.65	20	19.79005
9	1	19.79	20	19.87403
10	1	19.874	20	19.92442
11	1	19.924	20	19.95465
12	1	19.955	20	19.97279

Figure 21.7.5. Impact of a permanent change in X on the value of Y and Y^* over time.
Source: [PartialAdjustment]BehindTheScenes.

after period 1, each new Y depends on a different lagged Y; thus, Y keeps on changing. For example, in the calculations below, we have put the successive values of Y in boldface:

$$Y_2 = 5 + 0.6Y_1 + 3X_1$$
$$= 5 + 0.6 \cdot \mathbf{12.5} + 3 \cdot 1$$
$$= 15.5;$$
$$Y_3 = 5 + 0.6Y_2 + 3X_3$$
$$= 5 + 0.6 \cdot \mathbf{15.5} + 3 \cdot 1$$
$$= 17.3$$
$$Y_4 = 5 + 0.6Y_3 + 3X_1$$
$$= 5 + 0.6 \cdot \mathbf{17.3} + 3 \cdot 1$$
$$= 18.4;$$

$$\cdots$$

Because the model is stable, Y is moving toward a new equilibrium value – namely 20.

Go to the *BehindTheScenes* sheet to see the partial adjustment story. Figure 21.7.5 shows that in each time period Y is partially adjusting toward a permanently higher desired level of Y, $Y^* = 20$. In this version of the story, it is easy to work out the magnitude of the effect of a permanent change in X on Y; it is simply β_1, the coefficient on X in the desired Y equation. To work out the long-run impact in terms of the lagged dependent variable equation, recall that $\beta_1 = \frac{\gamma_2}{\lambda}$. Because the rate of adjustment is given by $\lambda = 1 - \gamma_1$, the long-run impact in terms of the parameters of the lagged dependent variable equation is $\beta_1 = \frac{\gamma_2}{1-\gamma_1}$.

Summary

This section introduced the concepts of lagged dependent variables and partial adjustment models. We tied partial adjustment models to costly adjustment by economic agents and demonstrated how partial adjustment models lead to regression specifications which include lagged dependent variables. In partial adjustment models, it is important to distinguish between the short and long-run impacts of changes in independent variables on the value of the dependent variable. The next section contains an actual example of the use of partial adjustment models.

21.8. Money Demand

Workbooks: MoneyDemand.xls; LaggedDepVar.xls

In this section we examine one prominent example of the use of partial adjustment models that leads to the use of lagged dependent variables, and we discuss tests for the presence of autocorrelation when there is a lagged dependent variable.

Partial adjustment models have been applied to many areas of empirical economics, including models of agricultural supply and investment behavior. A leading example of the use of the partial adjustment idea is econometric studies of the demand for money. In transactions theories of the demand for money, individuals and institutions want to hold some of their assets in the form of money (cash and checking accounts) to pay for goods and services. The greater the GDP, which is a measure of the volume of activity in the economy, the more money people need in order to buy goods and services. On the other hand, the greater the interest rate on alternatives to money, the greater the opportunity cost of holding money (cash earns no interest and checking accounts pay low rates of interest) and therefore the less money people will want to hold.

Thus, changes in GDP and interest rates cause people to revise their desired holdings of money. Economists argue, however, that changing the amount of money people hold is costly, and thus people do not adjust their money holdings completely and immediately in response to changes in the economic environment. This gives rise to the partial adjustment theory of money demand. In one version of the theory, the desired amount of money, M_t^*, is expressed in terms of real money balances, which is the nominal money stock divided by the price index.

Variable	Description
M	Natural log of the nominal money stock
y	Natural log of real GDP
P	Natural log of the price level (measured by the GNP deflator 1972=100)
RCP	Natural log of interest rate on commercial
RTD	Natural log of an average of interet rates on time deposits and similar interest-bearing assets.

Figure 21.8.1. Variable definitions for MacKinnon and Milbourne study used in MoneyDemand.xls.
Source: MacKinnon and Milbourne (1988).

The MoneyDemand.xls workbook contains quarterly data, obtained from MacKinnon and Milbourne (1988), on money demand, GDP, and interest rates between 1952 and 1973. The definitions of the variables they use are given in Figure 21.8.1.

The authors estimate many different equations, but we will concentrate on their equation (3):

$$M_t - P_t = \gamma_0 + \gamma_1 y_t + \gamma_2 RCP_t + \gamma_3 RTD + \gamma_4(M_{t-1} - P_{t-1}) + v_t.$$

One potentially confusing aspect of this equation is the use of logarithms. The difference between logs of two variables is equal to the log of the quotient of the two variables. Thus,

$$M_t - P_t = \ln\left(\frac{\text{Nominal Money Supply}_t}{\text{PriceLevel}_t}\right).$$

To be clear, the dependent variable in MacKinnon and Milbourne's Eq. (3) is the natural log of the real money supply, and the last independent variable is the log of the one-period lagged real money supply.

The *Equation(3)* sheet in MoneyDemand.xls estimates the model reports the Durbin–Watson statistic and an estimated ρ test, both of which point to autocorrelation in the error terms, and then reestimates the model, correcting for first-order autocorrelation. (These two tests are discussed later in this section.) The results from the FGLS procedure are given in Figure 21.8.2. We can use these estimates to compute short- and long-run effects of changes

Figure 21.8.2. Estimates from autocorrelation corrected version of Equation (3).
Source: [MoneyDemand.xls]Equation(3).

Variable	Estimate	SE
Intercept	−0.874	0.155
Y_t	0.179	0.033
RCP	−0.018	0.003
RTD	−0.044	0.010
M(t−1) − P(t−1)	0.678	0.070

in the independent variables on money demand. Because equation (3) is a double-log model, the slopes we compute are elasticities.

The short-run elasticities can be read straight from the regression results. According to the equation (3) estimates, a 1-percent increase in real GDP leads to roughly a 0.18-percent increase in money demand. The short-run interest rate elasticities are quite small: -0.018 and -0.044 for commercial paper and time deposits, respectively. For the long-run elasticities, we need to know the rate of adjustment. The estimated coefficient on lagged real money is $g_4 = 0.678$. Thus, our estimate of the rate of adjustment (call it l to stand for the roman letter version of lambda) is $l = 1 - 0.678 = 0.322$. The estimated long-run income elasticity of money demand is therefore as follows:

$$\text{Estimated Long-Run Income Elasticity} = \frac{g_1}{1 - g_4} = \frac{g_1}{l} = \frac{0.179}{0.322} = 0.55.$$

The estimated interest rate elasticities can be computed in the same way:

$$\text{Estimated Long-Run RCP Elasticity} = \frac{g_2}{1 - g_4} = \frac{g_2}{l} = \frac{-0.018}{0.322} = -0.055$$

$$\text{Estimated Long-Run RTD Elasticity} = \frac{g_3}{1 - g_4} = \frac{g_3}{l} = \frac{-0.044}{0.322} = -0.135.$$

These results are roughly in accord with economic theory. For example, the simple Baumol–Tobin model of the transactions demand for money predicts an interest rate elasticity of 0.5. The interest rate elasticities are of the correct sign, and care needs to be taken in interpreting them. The commercial paper rate and the time deposit rate averaged 4.3 percent and 3.0 percent, respectively, over the period 1952–1973; a one percentage point increase in interest rates would translate into roughly 25 percent and 33 percent increases in the levels of these interest rates. According to our results, if a 25-percent increase in both interest rates is assumed, the long-run response of money demand would be on the order of 0.19×25 percent or approximately a 5-percent decrease in money demand.

Before turning to a discussion of econometric issues relating to the detection of autocorrelation when lagged dependent variables are included among the regressor, we wish to explain why we estimated money demand using data that is over 30 years old – data originally reported in a paper published more than 15 years ago. There are good reasons for both facts, each of which sheds light on the difficulties faced by econometricians working with time series data.

The reason our example is based on such old data is that the parameters of the money demand function have changed drastically over time. Back in the early 1970s, results like the ones we have just reported were quite reassuring to monetary economists. The estimated elasticities were in accord with economic theory, and the somewhat low estimated partial adjustment parameter (32 percent per quarter) was still plausible. Since 1973 or so, several things have gone wrong with estimates of money demand. The most important factor, perhaps, is that the money demand function has changed owing to major innovations in financial markets. The increased availability of credit cards as a substitute for cash is just one example. This has made the money demand function quite unstable. Estimates on data from later periods using the model of Eq. (3) generally find that the rate of adjustments and the income and interest rate elasticities are all much lower than they were previously. The variability of underlying parameter values over time is a real challenge for all time series models.

The reason we obtained our data from a relatively old paper relates to the issue of replicating prior results. We had a great deal of difficulty replicating early 1970s estimates of money demand – in part because the M1 and GDP (formerly GNP) series have undergone significant revisions. This means that the numbers that economists were using back in the mid-1970s for the period 1952 to 1973 are different from the numbers pertaining to the same period available to us today in government data banks of historical statistics. Fortunately, a useful data archive, the Real-Time Data Set for Macroeconomists (RTDSM) maintained by the Federal Reserve Bank of Philadelphia, contains data as they were available to economists in the past. Even with data as they existed in 1973, however, we could not come close to replicating 1973 studies of money demand. We are not sure why, but we suspect that the lack of a series containing the rate on time deposits in the RTDSM archive doomed our efforts. For more on RTDSM, see the Basic Tools \ InternetData folder.

Replication of prior results has been a thorny problem in all areas of empirical economics – not just time series models.[15] In reaction, economics journals have begun to ask authors to make data sets publicly available. A leader in this effort has been the *Journal of Applied Econometrics*.[16] The earliest published paper that contributed to that journal's data archive was the MacKinnon and Milbourne paper on money demand used as the source of the data for this example. (As it happens, MacKinnon is the coordinator of the data archive for this journal as well as the coauthor of two excellent advanced econometrics texts.) MacKinnon and Milbourne in turn obtained data on interest rates on time deposits from one of the leading researchers on money demand, Stephen Goldfeld. They also used older data on income and money – not the updated series available to them in the late1980s.

---

[15] See, for example, Dewald and Thursby, et al. (1986).

[16] Other journals that have led the charge include the *Journal of Money Credit and Banking*, *Federal Reserve Bank of St. Louis Review*, and the *Journal of Business and Economic Statistics*.

Detecting First-Order Autocorrelation When There Is a Lagged Dependent Variable

We now return to an important issue that was glossed over a few pages ago. When the regression includes a lagged dependent variable and one wishes to test for first-order autocorrelation in the error terms, the Durbin–Watson statistic is unreliable. In this discussion we will first outline an alternate, simple test that is an extension of the estimated ρ test and then provide Monte Carlo evidence demonstrating that this augmented estimated-ρ test is superior to the Durbin–Watson test in these circumstances.

Recall the estimated ρ test for first-order autocorrelation initially involves estimating the main equation of interest and then regressing the residuals on one-period lagged residuals without an intercept term. Because the residuals are good estimates of the error terms, first-order autocorrelation, if present, should manifest itself as a nonzero slope. Therefore, a z-test is performed with the null hypothesis that the coefficient on lagged residuals is zero.

The estimated ρ test can easily be extended to handle a situation in which a lagged dependent variable is one of the regressors. All that is necessary is to regress the residuals against lagged residuals and all the X variables (including of course the lagged dependent variable). The idea is that including the lagged dependent variable in the estimated ρ regression is a way of handling the correlation between the residuals and the lagged dependent variable.[17] The test statistic is the same as in the original estimated ρ test: a z-statistic for the null that the parameter multiplying the lagged residual equals 0.

The Excel workbook LaggedDepVar.xls demonstrates the use of the augmented estimated ρ test and shows that it does a much better job than the Durbin–Watson test in detecting first-order autocorrelation in the presence of a lagged dependent variable. Go to the *LaggedEndogAR(1)* sheet. This sheet simulates the following simple version of a lagged dependent variable model:

$$Y_t = \beta_0 + \beta_1 Y_{t-1} + \varepsilon_t \quad \text{and}$$

$$\varepsilon_t = \rho \varepsilon_{t-1} + v_t.$$

We set parameter values in the upper-left-hand corner of the worksheet. To handle the problem of initial conditions, we set the process going at $t = -21$. We only begin observing the process at $t = 0$ after the initial conditions have had time to wear out. See cells M11 through Q12, which show initial values for Y_t, Y_{t-1}, ε_t, and v_t. We observe the data from $t = 0$ to $t = 60$. Figure 21.8.3 shows the setup of the worksheet.

---

[17] Note that the estimated ρ test can be extended to 2nd or higher order autocorrelation by including higher order lags of the residuals; in this case an F-test of the null that the parameters multiplying all the lagged residuals are all equal to 0 is required.

Parameters		b_1	b_0	Residual Test for AR(1)				
β_0	10	0.78	3.61	Resid $_{t-1}$	Y_{t-1}	Intercept		
β_1	0.5	0.08	1.75	0.164	−0.073	1.414	z-stat	0.99
ρ	0.5	0.60	8.93	0.166	0.105	2.032	P value	32.4%
SD(v)	10	88	58	0.017	8.792	#N/A		
DGP:		7038	4623	0.490	56	#N/A		
		DW	1.77	75.80	4329.06	#N/A		

$$Y_t = \beta_0 + \beta_1 Y_{t-1} + \varepsilon_t$$
$$\varepsilon_t = \rho \varepsilon_{t-1} + v_t$$

Figure 21.8.3. Detecting AR(1) errors in the presence of a lagged dependent variable. *Source:* [LaggedDepVar.xls]LaggedEndogAR(1).

In Figure 21.8.3 the OLS slope (b_1) and intercept (b_0) estimates of a regression of Y on lagged Y are in the center. We also compute the Durbin–Watson statistic, though not its P-value. On the right the augmented estimated ρ test is displayed in which the residuals are regressed on lagged residuals and the included X variable (lagged Y). The z-statistic is the test statistic for the null hypothesis that the parameter multiplying the lagged residuals is equal to zero. Hit F9 a few times to see the estimates bounce as new samples are drawn.

To compare the relative performance of the Durbin–Watson and estimated ρ test statistics in detecting first-order autocorrelation, we performed a few Monte Carlo simulations. We first examined the case in which there is no autocorrelation and then a case in which there is positive first-order auto-correlation. To replicate our work, set ρ equal to zero in cell B4 of *LaggedEndogAR(1)*. Click on the Go to Monte Carlo button. Once in the Monte Carlo sheet, click on the Run Monte Carlo button. You will next be asked to choose the number of observations in each sample. Then you will be asked to choose the number of repetitions. Warning: This is a very slow Monte Carlo simulation. The reason is that, for each sample (i.e., each repetition), we compute the exact P-value for the Durbin–Watson statistic, which is a computationally intensive task. You may wish to choose 10 repetitions before attempting a full-scale Monte Carlo experiment. Alternatively, choose a small number of observations (for instance, 10).

We chose the default options – 40 observations and 1,000 repetitions. After a quick coffee break, the output in Figure 21.8.4 was waiting for us. The broad picture is quite clear. If the test statistic is functioning as it ought to, the P-value histogram should be completely level when the null hypothesis is true as in this case. The histogram for the estimated ρ test is fairly level; that for the Durbin–Watson test rises steadily, meaning that high P-values are much more likely to be observed than low P-values. As a corollary, the graph tells us that the P-value for the Durbin–Watson statistic was below 5 percent in only two repetitions, whereas the P-value for the estimated ρ-test was below

Parameters				Experimental Setup	
β_0	10	ρ	0	nobs	40
β_1	0.5	SD(v)	10	reps	1000

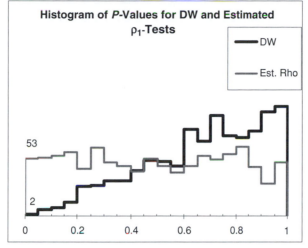

Figure 21.8.4. Monte Carlo results for Durbin–Watson and estimated ρ tests for first-order autocorrelation with a lagged dependent variable: Null hypothesis of no autocorrelation is true.
Source: [LaggedDepVar.xls]MCLaggedEndogAR(1).

5 percent in 53 or 5.3 percent of the repetitions. (These numbers are reported in the left portion of the histogram chart itself above the 0.05 level.)

The hasty student might conclude that the Durbin–Watson test is performing exceptionally well – after all, in this case, we know that the null is true, and so perhaps we ought to like a test that rejects the true null too rarely! One way to show that this reasoning is fallacious is to see what happens when the null is, in fact, false.

To that end, we next investigated how the two test statistics performed when the null is false. We set ρ equal to 0.5 and obtained the results depicted in Figure 21.8.5. This experiment provides strong evidence that the estimated ρ test does a better job of detecting first-order autocorrelation than the Durbin–Watson procedure when lagged dependent variables are included as regressors. In 425 of the 1,000 repetitions, the estimated ρ test rejected the null hypothesis at the 5-percent level of significance, whereas the Durbin–Watson test rejected the null hypothesis only 287 times. In light of the results obtained when the null was true, this is not surprising – with lagged dependent variables, the Durbin–Watson test is biased toward not rejecting the null. Notice that no test statistic is perfect; the risk of failing to reject the null even when it is false is always there.

Parameters				Experimental Setup	
β_0	10	ρ	0.5	nobs	40
β_1	0.5	SD(ν)	10	reps	1000

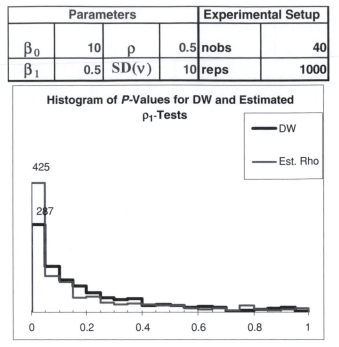

Figure 21.8.5. Monte Carlo results for Durbin–Watson and estimated ρ-tests for first-order autocorrelation with a lagged dependent variable: Null hypothesis of no auto-correlation is false; $\rho = 0.5$.
Source: [LaggedDepVar.xls] MCLaggedEndogAR(1).

Summary

This section has given an important example of the use of lagged dependent variables in empirical economics – estimating the demand for money – and discussed procedures for detecting autocorrelation when lagged dependent variables are included as regressors. The next section offers one final topic in time series analysis.

21.9. Comparing Forecasts Using Different Models of the DGP

Workbooks: AnnualGDP.xls; ForecastingGDP.xls

In this section we discuss basic issues pertaining to forecasting using time series models. Using the example of annual Real GDP in the United States, we contrast forecasts made from two different models of the data generation process: a trend with an AR(1) process for the errors and a random walk with drift.

Recall from Section 21.2 that in the *Data* sheet of AnnualGDP.xls we estimated a log-linear model for U.S. Annual GDP and obtained an estimate of 3.4 percent for the long-run growth rate of GDP. That model was fine for illustrating simple trends, but we ignored the possibility of autocorrelation in the error terms. For forecasting purposes, it is necessary to take into account autocorrelation, which we model in two different ways: as an AR(1) process and as a random walk with drift. In the *RandomWalkvsTrend* sheet we implement the two models: a log-linear trend with AR(1) errors and a logarithmic random walk with drift model. To avoid complications we will not worry about converting back to the level of GDP; instead we will discuss only the logarithmic series.

The trend AR(1) model for the data generating process is

$$\ln GDP_t = \beta_0 + \beta_1 t + \varepsilon_t,$$
$$\varepsilon_t = \rho \varepsilon_{t-1} + \nu_t.$$

The random walk model for the log of GDP is the following:

$$\ln GDP_t = \ln GDP_{t-1} + \delta + \eta_t.$$

We assume that the ν_t's and η_t's are independent, identically distributed error terms with mean zero. We estimated the trend AR(1) model in two steps, using our standard FGLS procedure. Details are in cells A1 through K7 of the *RandomWalkvsTrend* sheet. To estimate the random walk model, we took the first difference of the original series:

$$\Delta \ln GDP_t = \ln GDP_t - \ln GDP_{t-1} = \delta + \eta_t.$$

Upon regressing $\Delta \ln GDP_t$ against an intercept term, we obtained estimates of the drift parameter, δ, and, via the RMSE, the spread of the η_t terms, $SD(\eta)$.

Both models yield plausible results. The estimated slope of the trend is 0.0346, and the estimated drift is 0.0337; these translate into growth rates of 3.52 percent and 3.43 percent respectively. The value of estimated ρ in the AR(1) model is 0.822. The RMSEs, which are necessary for forecasting purposes, are 0.023 and 0.022 for the AR(1) trend and random walk models, respectively. The estimated residuals from the two models show very different patterns. Figure 21.9.1 shows the residuals from both models.

The dotted line in the Residuals from Trend chart represents forecasted future errors, which decline exponentially. Forecasted future errors are nonzero because of the first-order autocorrelation in the errors. We are assuming that the value of the last residual, for 2003 ($t = 57$), is a good estimate of the error for 2003. Specifically, the forecasted future value of the error-term h periods from 2003 (where h could be 1, 2, etc.) is the expected value of the error-term given our current knowledge about it.

$$\text{Forecasted}\varepsilon_{57+h} = (\text{Estimated } \rho)^h \text{ Residual}_{57}$$

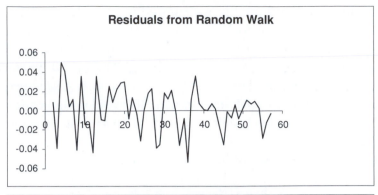

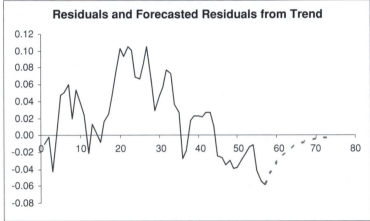

Figure 21.9.1. Residuals from the two models of GDP.
Source: [AnnualGDP.xls]RandomWalkvsTrend.

This equation follows directly from the AR(1) assumptions that $\varepsilon_t = \rho\varepsilon_{t-1} + v_t$ and that the expected value of the v_t's is zero. If we make the strong but convenient assumption that the parameters are known with certainty, then the year 2003 or fifty-seventh error is equal to the 2003 or fifty-seventh residual. In any case, if the model of the data generating process is correct, the residuals are good estimates of the errors; thus, this is not such a bad assumption.

On the other hand, forecasted future errors for the random walk model are zero. Again this follows from our assumptions about the random walk with drift data generating process.

Which model is best? It is very hard to tell.[18] Many economists believe that GDP is a random walk. Choosing a model, however, has important

---

[18] Wooldridge (2003, pp. 607–615), discusses tests that can be applied to distinguish unit root processes from other data generating processes.

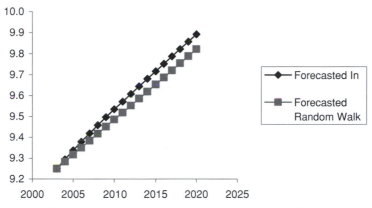

Figure 21.9.2. Two forecasts for the log of GDP.
Source: [AnnualGDP.xls]RandomWalkvsTrend.

implications for forecasts – in particular for the SE of the forecast error, which is a topic we turn to now.

Chapter 15 discusses the SE of the forecast error and explains that in forecasts there are two components to the forecast error – one due to chance error (modeled here as either an AR(1) process or a random walk) and a second due to estimation error (error in estimating the trend and drift parameters). We concentrate on the first component because the second one turns out to be fairly small (this is rather common for long time series in which the parameters are estimated quite precisely).[19] Note that future values of the trend term (*t*) are known with certainty in the AR(1) trend model so we do not need to worry about forecasting the values of the independent variables.

Let us first compare point forecasts. The random walk forecast is below the trend AR(1) forecast. In Figure 21.9.2 we take into account that the forecasted residual declines in absolute value, but this is hard to see; most of the differences in the forecast occur because the trend model predicts faster growth in GDP.

As emphasized in Chapter 15, point forecasts should be accompanied by interval forecasts to reflect the degree of uncertainty remaining even after it is assumed that one has the correct model of the data generating process and that the parameters will stay constant over the forecasted future of the variable of interest. To construct the interval forecasts we need to pay close attention to the way in which the forecast errors evolve.

Let us consider the AR(1) model first. Suppose we forecast one period out to period 58 (equivalent to year 2004). If we know the parameters, the

---

[19] To see the impact of the estimation error component, look at columns X through Z in AnnualGDP.xls and compare the overall forecast SEs in columns AA and AB with the forecast SEs due to chance error alone in columns U and V. We do not take into account estimation error for the estimated value of ρ.

forecast error is

$$\text{Forecast Error} = GDP_{58} - E(GDP_{58})$$
$$= (\beta_0 + \beta_1 58 + \varepsilon_{58}) - (\beta_0 + \beta_1 58 + \rho\varepsilon_{57})$$
$$= \rho\varepsilon_{57} + v_{58} - \rho\varepsilon_{57}$$
$$= v_{58}.$$

In other words, the forecast error arises solely from the v_{58} term. The spread (SE) of this forecast error is simply $SD(v)$. Let us forecast out one more period. The forecast error for GDP_{59} is given by

$$\text{Forecast Error} = GDP_{59} - E(GDP_{59})$$
$$= (\beta_0 + \beta_1 59 + \rho\varepsilon_{58} + v_{59}) - (\beta_0 + \beta_1 59 + \rho^2\varepsilon_{57})$$
$$= \rho^2\varepsilon_{57} + \rho v_{58} + v_{59} - \rho^2\varepsilon_{57}$$
$$= \rho v_{58} + v_{59}.$$

Now there are two components to the forecast error, one corresponding to the v_{58} error term and the other to the v_{59} error term. Because these are independent of each other, we can use a square-root law and the fact that ρ is a constant to derive the spread of the period 59 forecast error. It is

$$\sqrt{SD(v)^2 + \rho^2 SD(v)^2} = SD(v)\sqrt{1 + \rho^2}.$$

We will not bore you with additional terms in this series. The basic point behind the mathematics is that each additional v term contributes to the

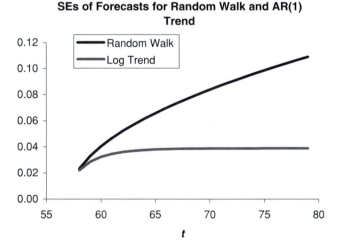

Figure 21.9.3. How the SE of the forecast error evolves for two models of log of GDP.
Source: [AnnualGDP.xls]RandomWalkvsTrend.

	Trend AR(1)			Random Walk with Drift		
	FE_1	FE_2	FE_5	FE_1	FE_2	FE_5
Avg	0.001	0.000	0.001	0.000	0.002	0.003
SD	0.022	0.029	0.035	0.023	0.033	0.052

Figure 21.9.4. Monte Carlo evidence on SE of the forecast error for two models of log of GDP.
Source: [ForecastingGDP.xls] MCTwoModels.

spread of the predicted ln GDP series, but the impact of each term diminishes over time because, when ρ is less than one, the error is damped away by the passage of time. Columns V and W in [AnnualGDP.xls]RandomWalkvsTrend carry out the detailed computations.

Matters are different with the random walk model. In this case, in essence $\rho = 1$, and so the impact of additional error terms is not worn down by the passage of time. The spread of the forecast error still obeys a square-root law, but it rises faster than the spread of the forecast errors from the AR(1) trend model. The exact formula for an h-period ahead forecast, implemented in column V of [AnnualGDP.xls]RandomWalkvsTrend is

$$SE(ForecastError) = SD(\eta) \sqrt{h}.$$

Figure 21.9.3 shows the difference between the two SEs.

Another way to think about the forecast errors is to create a Monte Carlo simulation that builds in the two data generating processes. Open the ForecastingGDP.xls workbook. On the assumption the parameters (derived from the regression estimates in AnnualGDP.xls) are known with certainty, we simulate the future path of the log of GDP for both models in the *RWDrift* and *ARTrend* sheets. Both sheets carefully set up the data generation process. The *ARTrend* sheet computes forecast errors for both models from simulations. The *MCTwoModels* sheet runs a Monte Carlo experiment that computes, 1,000 one-period, two-period, and five-period ahead forecasts errors for the two models. It then finds the empirical spread of the six different forecast errors. Representative results are shown in Figure 21.9.4. The results from the Monte Carlo simulation in ForecastingGDP.xls compare very well to the formula-derived forecast SEs in columns U and V of [AnnualGDP.xls]RandomWalkvsTrend. The SE of the random walk Forecast error increases faster than the SE of the trend Forcecast error.

Summary

This section has shown how to incorporate autocorrelation into a forecast and how the SE of the forecast error evolves over time. This discussion should have provided further insight into the data generating process of time series models but is only an introduction to a vast topic. To students interested in studying the subject further, we recommend Wooldridge's text for a serious discussion of econometric details and Diebold's book for a very clear introduction to the field of forecasting.

21.10. Conclusion

This chapter has covered several topics relating to time series models. Our purpose has been to give you an introduction to some of the main ideas in the field. We began the chapter by covering some of the basic tools for modeling economic variables that change over time. Many series trend upwards and there are many different functional forms for trends, though we discussed only two: the linear and the exponential (or log-linear) trends. Dummy variables can be used both to single out observations subject to special influences (e.g., wars or changes in government policy) and to model seasonal variation in a time series.

We then went on to take a closer look at the data generating process for time series variables. We made two crucial distinctions: between stationary and nonstationary time series and between series that are weakly dependent and strongly dependent. Very broadly speaking, OLS gives biased but consistent estimates when variables are stationary and weakly dependent; when variables are nonstationary, strongly dependent, or both, they must generally be transformed to make it possible for OLS to provide consistent estimates of the variables of interest. One popular transformation is simply to deal with the first differences of the variables rather than their levels.

Spurious regression is a major issue for time series models. We examined two types of spurious regressions. The first arises when a trend is incorrectly omitted from a regression involving economic variables; this is essentially an instance of omitted variable bias. The second type of spurious regression arises when both the X and Y variables are random walks.

In the last three sections of the chapter we introduced two important areas in time series. The first was lagged dependent variables. When a lagged dependent variable is present in a regression, it is necessary to distinguish between short- and long-run impacts of changes in independent variables on the dependent variable. The presence of a lagged dependent variable clearly violates the classical econometric model because the independent variables are of necessity correlated with the error terms. This is one of the reasons we discussed weak dependence: If variables are weakly dependent it is still possible to obtain consistent estimates using OLS. Finally, we noted that the presence of a lagged dependent variable invalidates the Durbin–Watson test for first-order autocorrelation in the errors; however, the estimated ρ test can be adapted to provide a consistent test.

The last topic covered was forecasting. We showed how to construct forecasts of future values of a time series using two very simple models – an autocorrelated trend and a random walk. This example gave us another opportunity to apply the techniques of Chapter 20 for estimating parameters under first-order autocorrelation. We noted that the assumed data generating process has important implications for forecasts – in particular for the SEs of the forecast error.

21.11. Exercises

1. Suppose we are considering two variables to measure trend in a study of U.S. population. The first five values of each variable are in Figure 21.11.1: We ran two regressions,

$$(1) \ Predicted \ U.S. \ Population = a_1 + b_1 Trend_1, \text{ and}$$

$$(2) \ Predicted \ U.S. \ Population = a_2 + b_2 Trend_2,$$

and obtained the results in Figure 21.11.2.
   a. What are the estimates of the constants (a_1 and a_2) and the slopes (b_1 and b_2) in each regression?
   b. Using Figure 21.11.3, write down the mathematical relationships between the constants and slopes from bivariate regressions using two different Trends. If you can, express the relationships in general terms rather than the particular numbers from this example.
2. (Creating Predicted Level Using Log-Linear Trend Model) To see why it is necessary to correct for the influence of the error term, make sure the MCSim add-in is installed and available; then open a blank Excel workbook and create 400 cells with the formula =NORMALRANDOM(0,1) in column A. In column B exponentiate the numbers in column A by entering the formula =EXP(A1) in cell B1 and then copying this formula down. Suppose that we wish to find the average value of the exponentiated numbers. Compute three separate estimates of the average of the exponentiated normally distributed random variables. In cell D2 type "=AVERAGE(A1:A400)." In cell E2, type "=EXP(AVERAGE(A1:A400))." In cell F2, compute the normal correction factor by typing the formula " =EXP(STDEV(A1:A400)2/2)." In cell G2, multiply Exp(Ave) by the correction factor by typing in the formula " =D2*F2." Figure 21.11.4 shows the setup. Of course we should use the result in cell D2 if we want to know the average of the exponentiated numbers, but how far off would we be if we used the number in cell E2 instead? How much can we improve matters by using the normal correction factor and therefore the number in cell G2?

Year	Trend1	Trend2
1970	0	20
1971	1	21
1972	2	22
1973	3	23
1974	4	24

Figure 21.11.1. The first five observations in the data.

Year	U.S. Pop (millions)	Predicted Pop Using Trend1	Predicted Pop Using Trend2
1970	205.05	202.52	202.52
1971	207.66	205.00	205.00
1972	209.9	207.48	207.48
1973	211.91	209.96	209.96
1974	213.85	212.45	212.45

Figure 21.11.2. The first five observations in the data.

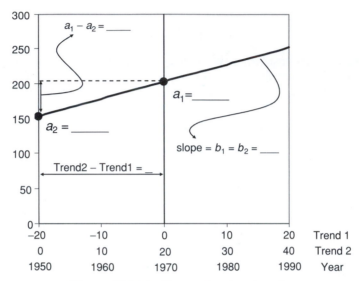

Figure 21.11.3. Comparing two trends.

	A	B	D	E	F	G
						Corr Factor *Exp(Ave)
1	=normalrandom(0,1)	=EXP(A1)	Ave(Exp)	Exp(Ave)	Correction Factor	
2	=normalrandom(0,1)	=EXP(A2)	=AVERAGE(B1:B400)	=EXP(AVERAGE(A1:A400))	=EXP(STDEV(A1:A400)^2/2)	=E2*F2

Figure 21.11.4. Setting up the problem.

To answer these questions, run two Monte Carlo simulations, one in which you compare the Exp(Ave) with the Ave(Exp) and a second in which you compare Ave(Exp) with the Corr Factor*Exp(Ave). Comment on your results.

On a separate sheet, create the same setup but use RANDOM() instead of NORMALRANDOM(0,1). How well does the normal correction work in this case?

3. (Dummy Variables) In the TimeSeriesDummyVariable.xls file we set up a "short regression" in which we regressed Ice Cream Sales on Price only, ignoring the Coupon dummy variable. Then we performed a Monte Carlo analysis; the average value of the estimated slope coefficient for Price in 1,000 repetitions was −742 and the SD was 42. This is fairly strong evidence of bias in the short regression. Explain why the short regression estimate for Price is biased.

4. In the coal mining example, a regression of the fatality rate on the regulation dummy variable gives the results in Figure 21.11.5, whereas a regression of the

Variable	Estimate
Intercept	1.233077
R	-0.07077

Figure 21.11.5. Coal mining regression results.

Variable	Estimate
Intercept	1.31714286
Trend	-0.01401099
R	0.11137363

Figure 21.11.6. Coal mining regression results with a trend term.

fatality rate on the regulation dummy variable and a trend term gives the results in Figure 21.11.6. Explain why the coefficient estimate for R changes. Be sure to discuss the relationship between R and Trend in your answer.

5. (Lagged Dependent Variables) In the *Example* sheet of PartialAdjustment.xls, we have set the initial value of Y as follows:

$$Y_0 = \frac{\gamma_0 + \gamma_2 \cdot X_0}{(1 - \gamma_1)}.$$

Bearing in mind the equation for the data generating process,

$$Y_t = \gamma_0 + \gamma_1 Y_{t-1} + \gamma_2 X_t,$$

use algebra to explain why this is an equilibrium value (i.e., a value such that if X does not change, then Y will not change).

References

This anthology includes a part of a quite readable paper by Yule on "nonsense correlations," which is related to the discussion of spurious regressions in Section 21.6. Yule used Monte Carlo experiments in this paper. This anthology also is the source of the epigraph of this chapter. The original citation for Jevons's paper is

Jevons, W. S. (1862 and 1884). "On the Study of Periodic Commercial Fluctuations," Read to the British Association in 1862, In Jevons, W. S., *Investigations in Currency and Finance*, London Macmillan, 1884, pp. 3–10 and plates.

Good books on time series and forecasting include: Stock and Watson (2003), Wooldridge (2003) and

Diebold, F. X. (2001). *Elements of Forecasting*. Cinncinnati: South-Western Thomson Learning.

Enders, W. (2004). *Applied Econometric Time Series*, 2nd ed., Hoboken, NJ: John Wiley & Sons.

Pindyck, R. S. and D. L. Rubinfeld (1997). *Econometric Models and Economic Forecasts*, 4th ed. New York: McGraw-Hill.

The data for the money demand example comes from

James G. MacKinnon and Ross D. Milbourne (1988). "Are Price Equations Really Money Demand Equations on their Heads?", *Journal of Applied Econometrics* **3**(4): 295–305.

The Web address of the *Journal of Applied Econometrics* data archive is
    <http://qed.econ.queensu.ca/jae/>.

An early article on replication of empirical economic results is

Dewald, W. G., J. G. Thursby, and R. G. Anderson, (1986). "Replication in
    Empirical Economics: The Journal of Money, Credit and Banking Project,"
    The American Economic Review **76**(4): 587–603.

The coal mining example is derived from

Andrews, W. H. and C. L. Christenson (1974). "Some Economic Factors Affecting
    Safety in Underground Bituminous Coal Mines," *Southern Economic Journal*
    40(3): 364–376.

22

Dummy Dependent Variable Models

Bliss invented a procedure he called "probit analysis." His invention required remarkable leaps of original thought. There was nothing in the works of Fisher, or "Student," or of anyone else that even suggested how he might proceed. He used the word probit because his model related the dose to the probability that an insect would die at that dose.

David Salsburg[1]

22.1. Introduction

In earlier chapters, we have created and interpreted dummy independent variables in regressions. We have seen how 0/1 variables such as Female (1 if female, 0 if male) can be used to test for wage discrimination. These variables have either/or values with nothing in between. Up to this point, however, the dependent variable Y has always been essentially a continuous variable. That is, in all the regressions we have seen thus far, from our first regression using SAT scores to the many earnings function regressions, the Y variable has always taken on many possible values.

This chapter discusses models in which the dependent variable (i.e., the variable on the left-hand side of the regression equation, which is the variable being predicted) is a dummy or dichotomous variable. This kind of model is often called a *dummy dependent variable (DDV), binary response, dichotomous choice*, or *qualitative response* model.

Dummy dependent variable models are difficult to handle with our usual regression techniques and require some rather sophisticated econometrics. In keeping with our teaching philosophy, we present the material with a heavy emphasis on intuition and graphical analysis. In addition, we focus on the box model and the source of the error term. Finally, we continue to rely on Monte Carlo simulation in explaining the role of chance. Although the material remains difficult, we believe our approach greatly increases understanding.

---

[1] Salsburg (2001, p. 76).

What Exactly Is a Dummy Dependent Variable Model?

That question is easy to answer. In a dummy dependent variable model, the dependent variable (also known as the response, left-hand side, or Y variable) is qualitative, not quantitative.

Yearly Income is a quantitative variable; it might range from zero dollars per year to millions of dollars per year. Similarly, the Unemployment Rate is a quantitative variable; it is defined as the number of people unemployed divided by the number of people in the labor force in a given location (county, state, or nation). This fraction is expressed as a percentage (e.g., 4.3 or 6.7 percent). A scatter diagram of unemployment rate and income is a cloud of points with each point representing a combination of the two variables.

On the other hand, whether you choose to emigrate is a qualitative variable; it is 0 (do not emigrate) or 1 (do emigrate). A scatter diagram of Emigrate and the county Unemployment Rate would not be a cloud. It would be simply two strips: one horizontal strip for various county unemployment rates for individuals who did not emigrate and another horizontal strip for individuals who did emigrate.

The political party to which you belong is a qualitative variable; it might be 0 if Democrat, 1 if Republican, 2 if Libertarian, 3 if Green Party, 4 if any other party, and 5 if independent. The numbers are arbitrary. The average and SD of the 0, 1, 2, 3, 4, and 5 are meaningless. A scatter diagram of Political Party and Yearly Income would have a horizontal strip for each value of political party.

When the qualitative dependent variable has exactly two values (like Emigrate), we often speak of *binary choice* models. In this case, the dependent variable can be conveniently represented by a dummy variable that takes on the value 0 or 1.

If the qualitative dependent variable can take on more than two values (such as Political Party), the model is said to be *multiresponse* or *multinomial* or *polychotomous*. Qualitative dependent variable models with more than two values are more difficult to understand and estimate. They are beyond the scope of this book.

More Examples of Dummy Dependent Variables

Figure 22.1.1 gives more examples of applications of dummy dependent variables in economics. Notice that many variables are dummy variables at the individual level (like Emigrate or Unemployed), although their aggregated counterparts are continuous variables (like emigration rate or unemployment rate).

The careful student might point out that some variables commonly considered to be continuous, like income, are not truly continuous because fractions

Topic	Dummy-Dependent Variable	Description
Labor Force Participation	Inlaborforce	0 if out of the labor force 1 if in the labor force
Choice of Occupation	Managerial	0 if not managerial 1 if managerial
Firm Location	Shoppingmall	0 if not in shopping mall 1 if in shopping mall
Union Membership	Union	0 if not a union member 1 if a union member
Retirement	Retired	0 if not retired 1 if retired
Use of Seat Belts	Seatbeltused	0 if does not use seat belt 1 if uses seat belt

Figure 22.1.1. Applications of dummy variables in economics.

of pennies are not possible. Although technically correct, this criticism could be leveled at any observed variable and for practical purposes is generally ignored. There are some examples, however, like educational attainment (in years of schooling), in which determining whether the variable is continuous or qualitative is not so clear.

The definition of a dummy dependent variable model is quite simple: If the dependent, response, left-hand side, or Y variable is a dummy variable, you have a dummy dependent variable model. The reason dummy dependent variable models are important is that they are everywhere. Many individual decisions of how much to do something require a prior decision to do or not do at all. Although dummy dependent variable models are difficult to understand and estimate, they are worth the effort needed to grasp them.

Organization

The next two sections provide intuition for the data generating process underlying the dummy dependent variable model. We emphasize the fundamental idea that a chance draw is compared with a threshold level, and this determines the observed 0 or 1 value of the dummy dependent variable. Section 22.4 continues working on the data generating process by drawing the box model that generates the observed values of 0 or 1. In Section 22.5, we introduce the linear probability model (LPM), which simply fits a line to the observed scatter plot of 0's and 1's. The LPM is easy to work with, but its substantial defects lead us to look for better methods. Section 22.6 uses nonlinear least squares (NLLS) to fit an S-shaped curve to the data and improve on the LPM. Nonlinear least squares is better than LPM but more difficult to interpret, and so we devote the next section to interpreting the results from the NLLS regression. We conclude the chapter with a real-world example of a dummy dependent variable that examines the issue of mortgage discrimination.

22.2. Developing Intuition about Dummy Dependent Variable Models

Workbook: Raid.xls

Suppose you wanted to know if a bug spray really works. You took 200 bugs and split them up into two groups (obeying random assignment rules and double-blinding; we note that blinding the subject, a bug, should not be a problem). One group is the treatment group, Sprayed with Raid[2] (SR) for 2 seconds, whereas the control group is dosed with a placebo for 2 seconds and called Sprayed with Water (SW). At the end of an hour, it is time to count them up. Figure 22.2.1 presents the results of our hypothetical experiment.

The research question is, Does Raid work? We can not simply argue that Raid obviously works because many more bugs died with Raid. The flaw in this argument is that some roaches died without the Raid (20 of them) and some roaches (16 of them) did not die with the Raid. In reality, the question is, Does Raid increase the odds of death and, if so, by how much?

As soon as you realize that Raid will not wipe out all bugs on contact, determining the efficacy of Raid becomes quite difficult. The problem is that Raid, to the extent that it works, merely increases the probability of death – it does not guarantee death. This line of thinking opens the door to the chance explanation – that the results of this single sample might be due to chance alone.

Once it is realized that observed deaths contain an element of randomness, we must confront the task of modeling the chance process generating the data. Unfortunately, this process is much more complicated than the classical econometric model.

For an individual bug, the chance process looks something like this:

- Dead if the draw from the error box is the same or less than the threshold value needed to kill the bug.
- Alive if the draw from the error box is more than the threshold value needed to kill the bug

The draw from the error box reflects the hardiness of the bug – its ability to withstand poison. The bug needs a draw greater than the threshold value in order to live. If Raid is effective, it increases the threshold value, meaning that the bug has to be more poison-resistant to survive. The problem is that we will see only if the bug is dead or alive; we cannot observe either the draw from the error box or the value needed to kill the bug.

---

[2] Raid is a popular insecticide made by SC Johnson & Sons.

Group	Number Dead	Number Alive
SR	84	16
SW	20	80

SR: Sprayed with Raid for 2 seconds
SW: Sprayed with Water for 2 seconds

Figure 22.2.1. Results of Raid experiment (hypothetical).

These ideas are implemented in the Excel workbook Raid.xls. Begin by reading the *Description* sheet. Make sure you scroll down and play around a bit with the sheet. When you are ready, go to the sheet *Single Bug*. The workbook facilitates understanding of what is going on by making clear that we observe only the *dichotomous outcome*, dead or alive, generated by a chance process. The crucial idea is that a random error term is compared with some threshold value, and this comparison determines whether or not the observed value is dead or alive.

Figure 22.2.2 displays the happy outcome for a single bug. She lived because her draw from the box (reflecting her hardiness to the environment) was bigger than the threshold level. Her draw was not particularly fortuitous, but it did not need to be because she only had a 20 percent chance of dying.

Click the ⟨Take a Draw⟩ button repeatedly to conduct the experiment on a single bug. Every click takes a draw and compares it with the threshold level. Sometimes the bug dies, but most of the time (80 percent of the time in the long run) the bug lives. Click the ⟨Instructions⟩ button and follow the directions.

Increase the value of the yellow-shaded cell to 50 percent and hit the F9 key a few times. In this case, a positive draw is needed for survival. If the probability of dying is increased to 90 percent, the outlook for the bug will be rather bleak. The effectiveness of an insecticide rides on its ability to push the threshold value very high so that there will be little chance for the bug to survive.

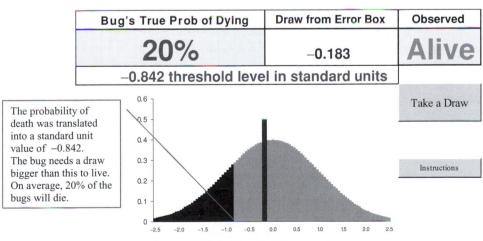

Figure 22.2.2. The DGP at work.
Source: [Raid.xls]Single Bug.

	Number Dead	Number Alive	%Dead
SR	84	16	84%
SW	20	80	20%

Figure 22.2.3. Results of Raid experiment restated (hypothetical).

This same chance process was carried out on our hypothetical experiment. In the case of the 200 bugs we observed, the odds favor Raid. Look at the odds of death from Raid versus water in Figure 22.2.3.

Raid appears to increase the threshold value for death by a large amount. The reason why we cannot simply conclude that Raid works is our old friend chance error. Rewind and replay the world, and you will obtain different numbers in Figure 22.2.3. Use the *Death by Raid* sheet in Raid.xls to demonstrate that the percentage dead varies as you resample. Clearly, the sample percentage dead is one realization of the chance process.

In other words, our fundamental problem is that the true increase in the probability of death from using Raid is not guaranteed to be what we observe from a single sample:

$$84\% - 20\% = 64\%.$$

The calculation above is merely the sample difference (for a sample we obtained). We do not know the true difference because it is not directly observable. Chance error, modeled by the draw from the error box, makes the observed sample differences bounce around.

The sheet *Death by Raid* in the Raid.xls workbook clarifies this concept. Every click of the Repeat the Experiment button draws a new sample in which 200 bugs are dosed and counted. Repeated clicking of this button convincingly demonstrates that the sample difference bounces around the True Effectiveness of Raid in cell F4. Click the Instructions button and follow the directions.

Although we have been pointing out that Raid cannot be said to work just because some bugs died, the same argument applies to those who would reject Raid even though it is not 100 percent effective. We cannot just say that Raid obviously does not work because 16 percent lived through the Raid.

Raid is effective because many more of the bugs died as the result of its use. That 16 bugs survived the Raid does not mean that it is ineffective. Your knowing someone 90 years old in perfect health who has smoked everyday since he was 7 does not clear smoking of causing lung cancer. What takes place is not like the law of gravity – that is, pencils always fall to the floor when dropped. If a pencil rose when dropped, you would have a major situation on your hands. Yes/No dependent variables are different. An issue of probability is involved. Raid can be said to "work" if it increases the probability of death. Of course, the more it increases the probability of death, the better it works;

however, it does not have to guarantee death for us to conclude that it is effective.

Summary

Keep the following two ideas in mind as you study dummy dependent variable models:

- Chance plays a role in the observed sample through a complicated box model. In this model, one takes a draw from an error box and compares it with a threshold value. If the draw is greater than the threshold value, the outcome is 0; if the draw is less than or equal to the threshold value, the outcome is a 1.
- Although we see only the outcome as Yes or No, we are interested in determining an underlying probability – that is, the threshold value with which the draw is compared.

22.3. The Campaign Contributions Example

Workbook: CampCont.xls

In this section, we turn to another, slightly more complicated dummy dependent variable example. We are still developing your intuition and proceeding slowly to get the details exactly right.

Research Question: What is the effect of campaign contributions on voting in the legislature?

Put more bluntly, can a special interest lobby buy the votes it needs?

One common theory says that the reason corporations and special interest groups donate money to a political candidate is simple: If you help a candidate win, he or she will be more likely to vote in ways beneficial to the donor. That is not to say that a particular vote will be guaranteed – only that it is more likely.

The problem for social scientists investigating this hypothesis is that the observed voting record on a particular bill will be Yes or No, whereas the *underlying, unobserved* probability of a particular vote may be sensitive to the amount of money received. This is not to say that as soon as a representative receives money he or she immediately votes one way or the other; rather, it is a matter of probability – of increasing the chances of a particular vote.

This is akin to the Raid example of the previous section. We only see the legislator's vote as 0 or 1. Taking a draw from an error box and comparing it with some unknown threshold value determines whether the vote is 0 (no) or 1 (yes). If the draw is less than or equal to the unknown threshold

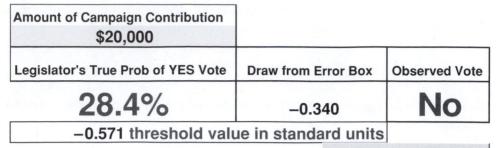

Amount of Campaign Contribution $20,000		
Legislator's True Prob of YES Vote	Draw from Error Box	Observed Vote
28.4%	−0.340	**No**
−0.571 threshold value in standard units		

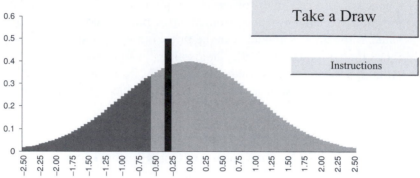

Figure 22.3.1. The DGP for observed voting behavior.
Source: [CampCont.xls]SingleLegislator.

value, we see a Yes vote (and thus the campaign contribution worked). The campaign contribution affects the unknown threshold value – it *increases* it (like Raid did), making it more likely, but not certain, that the legislator will vote Yes.

Although this example shares the same underlying box model as the Raid example, it also differs in an important way from the Raid example. Instead of a dummy *independent* variable (get water or Raid), the independent variable is continuous. The unknown threshold value with which the draw from the error box is compared is a function of the amount of money received.

The Excel workbook CampCont.xls demonstrates how the campaign contribution affects the threshold value of a Yes vote. Figure 22.3.1 displays the *SingleLegislator* sheet in CampCont.xls.

Click the Instructions button and follow the steps described to see how changing the amount of campaign contributions affects the threshold level and, thus, the observed voting response. Be certain you are comfortable with the idea that the threshold level is determined by the amount of campaign contribution. As the legislator receives more money, the chances of voting Yes rise.

When you are finished working with the *SingleLegislator* sheet, you should understand the following ideas. The dummy dependent variable, VotesYes is being determined in part by a chance process. When the draw from the error box is less than the threshold level, -0.571, in Figure 22.3.1, the legislator votes Yes (VotesYes=1). The legislator in Figure 22.3.1 voted No (VotesYes=0, even though he or she pocketed a \$20,000 contribution) because the draw from the box was greater than the threshold level. This is just like the Raid example in which some bugs sprayed with Raid lived.

The threshold level is a function of the amount of campaign contributions. The higher the campaign contributions, the greater the threshold level, which in turn makes it more likely that the legislator will vote Yes.

The Raid example could be made similar to this campaign contribution example if one were to allow for different doses or strengths of insecticide in Raid. As the dose strength increased, the threshold level would increase, making it more likely that the bug would die.

Finally, you should be aware that we are interested in estimating the parameters of the function driving the threshold level. We will want to know how much the probability of voting Yes increases when the campaign contribution goes up. This is a crucial concept.

Summary

This section extended the Raid example from Section 22.2 by incorporating continuous variation in the X variable. As X (the amount of campaign contribution) increases, so does the threshold level, making it more likely that we observe a Yes vote. The next sections will demonstrate how we can estimate the parameters of the function determining the threshold level. We will begin our explanation with a more formal description of the box model.

22.4. A DDV Box Model

Workbooks: Raid.xls; CampCont.xls

The Raid and Campaign Contributions examples have set the stage for a careful exposition of the way the ultimately observed 0 or 1 responses are generated in a dummy dependent variable model.

The data generation process underlying the Raid and Campaign Contribution examples is much more complicated than the classical econometric model, which is a continuous, dependent variable data generation process. The Raid and Campaign Contribution examples have a Y that is forced to be either 0 or 1. The observed 0/1 dependent variable value is generated by drawing a ticket from the error box and comparing it against the threshold level – if the ticket is greater, then we see a 0; otherwise, we observe 1.

The box model for this data generation process looks like Figure 22.4.1.

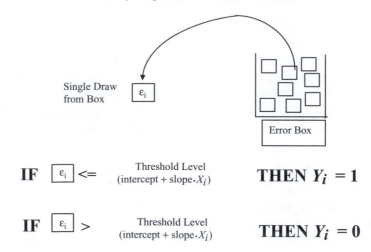

IF $\boxed{\varepsilon_i}$ <= $\begin{array}{c}\text{Threshold Level} \\ (\text{intercept} + \text{slope}\cdot X_i)\end{array}$ **THEN** $Y_i = 1$

IF $\boxed{\varepsilon_i}$ > $\begin{array}{c}\text{Threshold Level} \\ (\text{intercept} + \text{slope}\cdot X_i)\end{array}$ **THEN** $Y_i = 0$

Figure 22.4.1. Data generation process for bivariate binary choice model.

Figure 22.4.1 offers a visual box model statement of the data generation process. The Raid and Campaign Contribution examples were built with this box model in mind. The single draw from the box, the error ticket in Figure 22.4.1, is the blue vertical line in the Raid.xls and CampCont.xls workbooks. The process of comparing the error ticket with the threshold level is shown in Figure 22.4.1 via the if-then statements and is visually depicted in the two workbooks by a change in color. Finally, the resulting, mutually exclusive 0 or 1 value is what we observe.

In addition, it is important to understand that the threshold level is a function of a deterministic component, $\beta_0 + \beta_1 X$, whose parameters we will be trying to estimate from a single sample. The Campaign Contributions example has made it clear that increases in campaign contributions (the X variable) increase the threshold level, making it more likely that the resulting observed vote will be Yes.

This unusual box model has important implications for the way in which we interpret observed data in dummy dependent variable models. If we know enough about the contents of the box and the determinants of the threshold, we can compute the probability that a particular observation will take on a value of 1. This is done as follows: The probability that a given Y will equal 1 is equal to the probability that a ticket drawn from the box will have a value less than or equal to the threshold. Figure 22.4.2 shows an example taken from the campaign contributions example.

In this example, we see that a campaign contribution of \$20,000 leads to a threshold value of -0.571 in standard units and that a draw from the error box will fall below that threshold 28.4 percent of the time. More generally, in the campaign contributions example, the probability that a given vote will be Yes is the area under a standard normal curve to the left of the threshold.

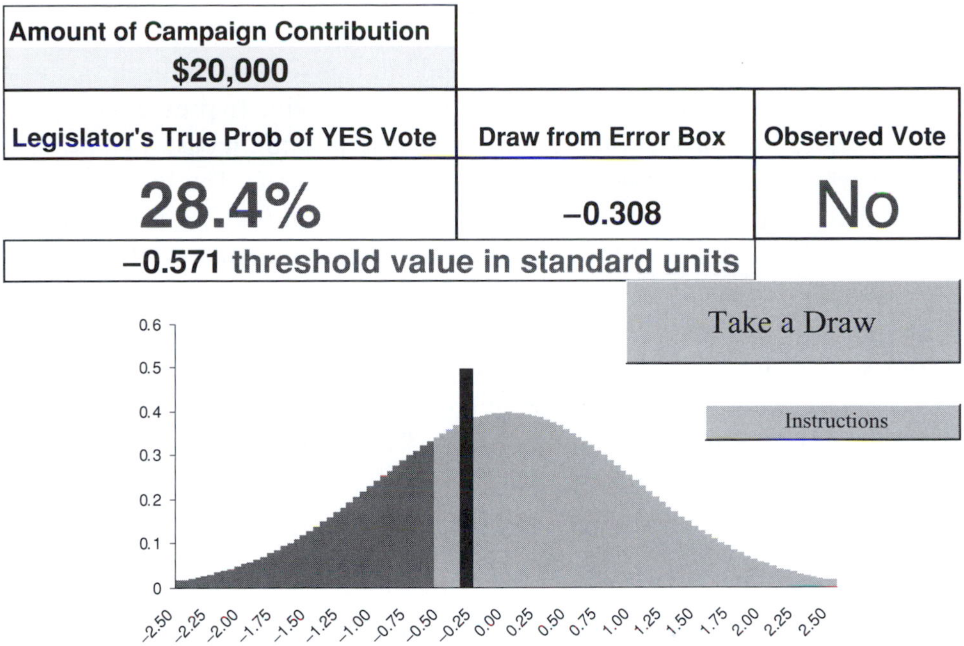

Amount of Campaign Contribution $20,000		
Legislator's True Prob of YES Vote	**Draw from Error Box**	**Observed Vote**
28.4%	**−0.308**	**No**
−0.571 threshold value in standard units		

Figure 22.4.2. The threshold model for campaign contributions. *Source:* [CampCont.xls]SingleLegislator.

For example, if we were to examine the votes of a large number of legislators, each of whom received a $20,000 contribution, we would expect to find that about 28 percent of them voted Yes. A group of legislators who received $30,000 would share a threshold value of 0.583, and we would expect that about 72 percent would vote Yes. In other words, the threshold model says that the probability that the dependent variable equals 1 is a function of the area under the distribution of the tickets to the left of the threshold value – a value that varies as the independent variable changes. More generally, in mathematical terms,

$$\Pr(Y_i = 1 \text{ given } X_i) = \Pr(\varepsilon_i < \text{Threshold determined by } X_i)$$
$$= \Pr(\varepsilon_i < \beta_0 + \beta_1 X_i).$$

We call the probability on the left a *conditional probability function* because the probability that Y equals 1 depends on (is conditional on) the value of X. Two further observations are in order. First, the distribution of the tickets matters in determining the probability. In most of what follows, we assume that the tickets are normally distributed. Second, in general, this model leads to a nonlinear relationship between the probability that the dependent variable equals 1 and the threshold – in other words, the conditional probability function is, in general, nonlinear.

Summary

Figure 22.4.1 holds the core idea developed in this section. It displays a new box model called the dummy dependent variable model. In previous chapters in this book, we have presented the coin flip, polling, measurement, and, most importantly, the classical econometric box models. The box model we are working with in this chapter shares many similarities with these models, especially the idea that chance is at work in determining observed outcomes. The dummy dependent variable model differs markedly, however, from the others in that it uses a threshold level to guarantee a binary response. In other words, the two values, 0 or 1, are the only possible outcomes. We are interested in estimating the function that determines the threshold level. The next section presents an obvious, easy, but flawed approach.

22.5. The Linear Probability Model (OLS with a Dummy Dependent Variable)

Workbooks: CampCont.xls; LPMMonteCarlo.xls

In this section we take a closer look at the hypothetical campaign contributions example. We extend the analysis to consider many legislators receiving varying amounts of campaign contributions. We estimate a model with OLS and point out the weaknesses of this approach.

Suppose that a special interest lobby has given campaign contributions varying from \$1 to \$50,000 to 500 representatives who subsequently voted on a piece of legislation very important to that lobby. The special interest lobby was hoping for enough Yes votes to pass the legislation.

We have records of how each legislator voted and the amount of campaign contributions each legislator was given by the special interest lobby. The data are in columns A and B of the *SingleSample* sheet of CampCont.xls. The relationship between the representatives' votes on the legislation and the campaign money they received is graphically depicted in Figure 22.5.1.

Figure 22.5.1 discloses the way each individual representative voted as a function of the campaign contributions received. A Yes vote is coded as a 1; a No vote is coded as a 0. There are 500 observations on the graph bunched up in the bottom-left and top-right corners. It is somewhat difficult to see this in this scatter plot because there is no histogram-like height to indicate how many observations fall in a certain range.

Even though the scatter diagram is difficult to read, it appears that something is going on. Sure, there are a few representatives who received substantial campaign money but still voted No (0) and a few who voted Yes (1) although they did not receive much money, but there is some obvious clumping at the bottom-left and top-right.

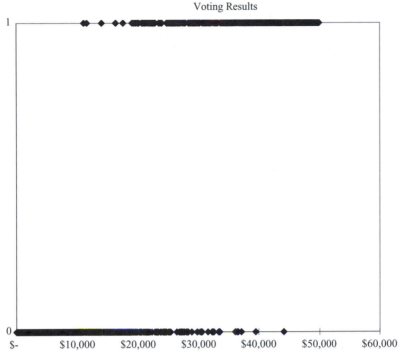

Figure 22.5.1. Observed vote as a function of campaign contribution.
Source: [CampCont.xls]SingleSample.xls.

The threshold model offers a coherent method for interpreting the data. The model focuses attention on the conditional probability function. In this case, that means the probability of a Yes vote given the level of campaign contributions. It is difficult to see that probability function in Figure 22.5.1. One way to visualize the probability function is to draw a graph of averages, as shown in Figure 22.5.2.

In Figure 22.5.2, we grouped the contributions into $1,000 intervals and showed the percentage of representatives in each interval who voted Yes. The data underlying Figures 22.5.1 and 22.5.2 are the same, but instead of 500 dots Figure 22.5.2 has only 50 dots. The vertical strip in the figure summarizes the votes of 10 representatives who received contributions averaging $28,500. Sixty percent of these representatives voted Yes. The graph of averages shows the empirical conditional probability that a representative will vote Yes given the amount of the campaign contribution he or she receives.

There are three different ways to estimate the conditional probability function: ordinary least squares (known as the Linear Probability Model), nonlinear least squares (NLLS), and maximum likelihood. We start with OLS in this section because it is the easiest method to understand. Econometricians commonly estimate a linear probability model before turning to

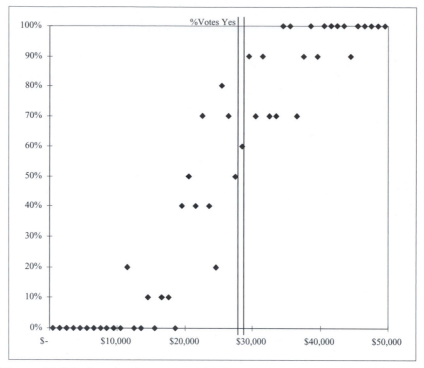

Figure 22.5.2. Graph of averages with a vertical strip centered on $28,500.
Source: [CampCont.xls]SingleSample.

more complicated estimation procedures. However, OLS has significant limitations that lead us to consider nonlinear least squares. The latter method is typically not employed to estimate dummy dependent variable models, but we spend time on it for two reasons. First, the application to dummy dependent variables is a good opportunity for us to introduce the concept of nonlinear least squares, which is widely used in other contexts. Second, the generally preferred estimator, maximum likelihood, is too complicated to explain fully in this introductory textbook. Maximum likelihood estimates, however, can be interpreted in exactly the same way as NLLS estimates. We have written two Excel add-ins that will enable you to produce both NLLS and maximum likelihood estimates for dummy dependent variable models.

Using the Linear Probability Model (LPM)

Our first attempt at estimating the effect of the probability that a representative votes Yes is simply to fit a straight line via ordinary least squares to the Y variable. The application of OLS to dummy dependent variable models is known as the linear probability model. Although we will soon be criticizing this model, remember that it does have the virtue of simplicity, making it easy to find the estimates and to interpret them.

OLS Model: VotesYes = $\beta_0 + \beta_1$CampCont + ε			
slope	2.69E-05	−0.171	intercept
estimated SE	9.78E-07	0.028	estimated SE
R^2	0.603	0.316	RMSE
F	756.601	498	df
RegSS	75.383	49.617	SSR

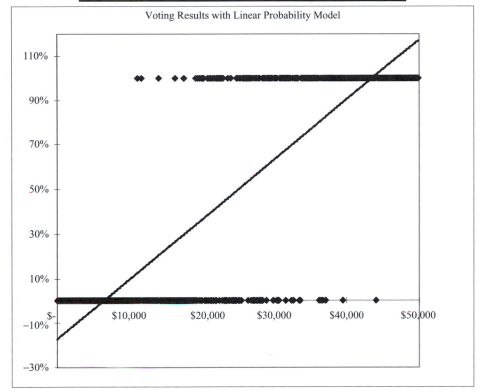

Figure 22.5.3. LPM results.
Source: [CampCont.xls]SingleSample.

Ordinary least squares estimation on a dummy dependent variable simply ignores the fact that the dependent variable takes on only two values and fits a line to the scatter plot (which has only two horizontal strips). The result is neatly captured in the usual OLS equation:

$$\text{Predicted } Y = b_0 + b_1 \text{CampaignContribution}$$

along with the usual estimated standard errors, RMSE, R^2, F-statistic, and so on. The interpretation of Predicted Y is the probability that the dependent variable equals 1 given the value of the X variable. The Predicted Y in the voting example is the predicted probability that a representative who receives a given amount of campaign contributions would vote Yes.

The *SingleSample* sheet in the CampCont.xls workbook displays the results, as shown in Figure 22.5.3.

Because Predicted Y is the predicted probability of voting Yes given a value for CampaignContribution, we can simply plug in a campaign contribution value and use the equation of the fitted line to compute the predicted probability of voting Yes. If the legislator received $25,000 in campaign contributions, we would compute: Predicted $Y = -0.18 + 0.0000269 \, (25,000) = 50.25$ percent. Thus, 50.25 percent is the predicted probability of voting Yes given a $25,000 campaign contribution.

We might also be interested in the increase in the predicted probability of voting Yes as the amount of campaign contributions rises. The slope estimate b_1 tells us exactly this. Thus, a $10,000 donation will buy you a 26.9 percent increase in the probability that a representative votes Yes because $0.0000269 \times 10,000 = 26.9$ percent. Note that what the LPM predicts is the same regardless of whether the increase is from 0$ to $10,000 or from $40,000 to $50,000.

Three Problems with the Linear Probability Model

There are three important difficulties with the linear probability model.

1. LPM Imposes a Linear Relationship

The assumption implicit in the linear probability model is that an additional dollar increases the probability of a Yes vote by the same amount for all levels of campaign contributions. We may, however, have theoretical reasons to believe that the slope changes with the level of contributions. After all, do we really believe that giving another $10,000 to representative A, who has already received $40,000, is going to have the same change on the probability of voting Yes as giving $10,000 to representative B, who has received only $15,000 thus far?

Figure 22.5.2 should convince you that this is unlikely. At the $40,000 mark, the probability of a Yes vote is quite high, and another $10,000 is not going to increase the probability of a Yes vote by much more. On the other hand, at $15,000, near the center of the scatter plot, there is much action. It looks as if $10,000 might really matter. The LPM cannot capture this kind of variability. It imposes a single, straight line on the scatter plot.

2. LPM Is an Unbounded Functional Form

The results of the LPM in this example violate the laws of probability. Look again at Figure 22.5.3. Many representatives have predicted probabilities of voting Yes of less than 0 or greater than 1. That is obviously nonsensical.

Now, you may argue that we have seen nonsensical results before. After all, in earnings functions regressions, predictions of wage at Education=0

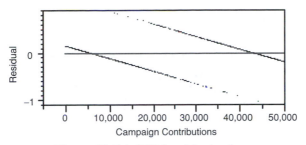

Figure 22.5.4. LPM residuals plot.

and Experience=0, for instance, are often negative (because the intercept estimate is less than 0). We have excused such results by pointing out that predictions "way outside the sample scatter of points" are not interesting. No one is interested in predicting the wage of a newborn infant! But the situation in the linear probability model is different because the unbounded estimates are often *in-sample*. In our case, representatives with campaign contributions under roughly $6,400 yield negative predicted probabilities, whereas those above roughly $43,500 lead to predicted probabilities greater than 100 percent. There are actual observations in these ranges. We know the LPM is giving us erroneous predictions for those ranges of the independent variable.

3. The LPM Suffers from Heteroskedasticity

The last difficulty is a more technical issue than the first two. Figure 22.5.4 is a plot of the residuals from our regression. It may be difficult to interpret exactly what is going on in that residual plot, but you have to agree that no "formless blob" is evident. The residuals, which are our estimates of the errors, are definitely not the same across the values of X. The heteroskedasticity in the linear probability model generates biased and inconsistent estimates of the estimated SE of the sample slope.[3]

Summary

Given these three problems (constant slope, unboundedness, and heteroskedasticity) with the linear probability model, econometricians have developed better ways of estimating the underlying probability of an observed outcome in a dummy dependent variable model. We consider one of these alternatives in the next section.

---

[3] To see this, explore the file LPMMonteCarlo.xls. Heteroskedasticity and its meaning and effect on the OLS estimator are covered in Chapter 19.

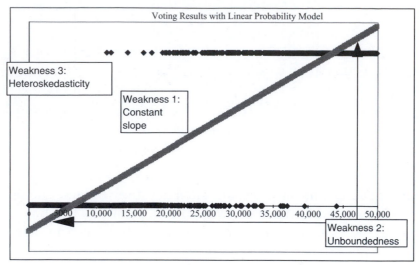

Figure 22.6.1. Three defects of the LPM.

22.6. Nonlinear Least Squares Applied to Dummy Dependent Variable Models

Workbooks: NLLSFit.xls; NLLSMCSim.xls

In the previous section, we used OLS to fit a line to a scatter plot of the voting decisions of 500 hypothetical representatives as a function of received campaign contributions. Figure 22.6.1 shows the OLS fitted line and highlights the three difficulties of the linear probability model.

We can do better by paying closer attention to the data generating process. In our earlier Raid and Campaign Contribution examples, we assumed the error box to be normally distributed. Econometricians call this a *Probit Model*. In the old days (before ubiquitous computing), for ease of calculation the errors were assumed to be logistically distributed.[4] If this assumption is invoked, the data generation process is called a *Logit Model*.

There is not much practical difference between the normal and logistic distributions. They both are symmetrical, bell-shaped curves with S-shaped cumulative distributions. The logistic has slightly fatter tails. The logistic "more closely resembles a *t* distribution with 7 degrees of freedom" Greene (2000, p. 815). The primary advantage of the logistic is that it has a closed-form cumulative distribution that can easily be derived (see previous footnote), whereas the normal distribution must be tediously calculated to figure out what fraction of the area lies up to a given value. Computers, however,

---

[4] The random variable x has a standard logistic distribution if its density function is $f(x) = e^x/(1 + e^x)^2$. The corresponding cumulative distribution function is $F(x) = e^x/(1 + e^x)$.

make the logistic's computational advantage almost irrelevant. We will work exclusively with the normal distribution and, thus, the probit model.

Having decided that we will model the errors as coming from a normally distributed box, we turn our attention to the method of estimation. Let us consider two nonlinear alternatives: (1) nonlinear least squares (NLLS) and (2) maximum likelihood (ML).

Nonlinear least squares is more complicated than the OLS algorithm used to estimate the linear probability model, but NLLS applied to a probit (or logit) model corrects two of the three defects inherent in the LPM via the OLS approach. Nonlinear least squares will fix the problems of constant slope (i.e., linearity of the functional form) and impossible predicted probabilities less than 0 and greater than 1 (i.e., unboundedness). This approach, however, will still suffer from heteroskedasticity (which means the estimated SEs are biased). In principle, NLLS can be corrected for heteroskedasticity with an appropriately weighted nonlinear least squares estimator, but, in practice, many investigators turn to maximum likelihood estimation.

We will use NLLS (uncorrected for heteroskedasticity) because its familiar least squares logic makes it easier to understand than the likelihood maximization approach. The Excel add-ins packaged with this book enable you to use the ML method. The references at the end of this chapter have several sources for learning about maximum likelihood.

Because it is easy to be confused by the terminology, we will use the flow chart in Figure 22.6.2 to present the various pieces involved. Although the errors can come from any distribution, the normal and logistic distributions are the most commonly used. Figure 22.6.2 also points out that the data generating process and the estimation approach are separate. You could have a probit model and estimate it via OLS (which would be called the LPM), NLLS, or ML.

To be clear, maximum likelihood is the preferred approach, but a careful explanation of this method is beyond the scope of the presentation in this introductory textbook. Of the familiar least squares approaches, we show in the next paragraphs that NLLS overcomes two of the three weaknesses of OLS. Unfortunately, the gain comes at a price – NLLS estimation is more difficult, and extra care is required in interpreting the computed estimates.

Why Nonlinear Least Squares?

We know from Figure 22.5.3 that OLS has a major weakness in fitting dummy dependent variables models. The LPM forces a straight line fit to an S-shaped pattern of dots. We want to fit some kind of a curve to the data,

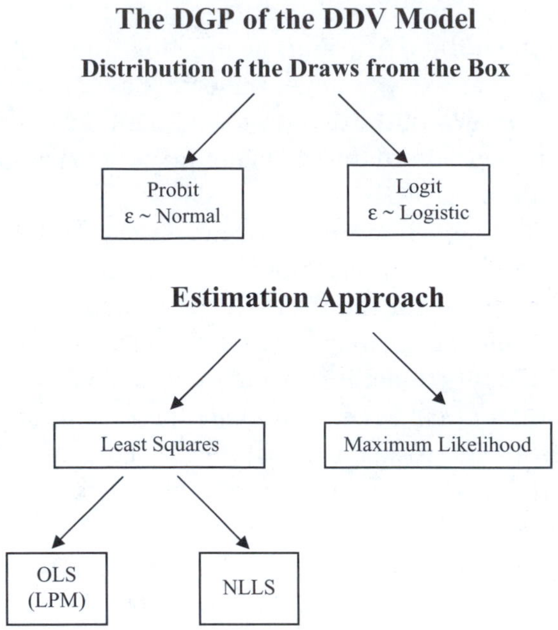

The DGP of the DDV Model

Distribution of the Draws from the Box

| Probit
ε ~ Normal | Logit
ε ~ Logistic |

Estimation Approach

| Least Squares | Maximum Likelihood |

| OLS
(LPM) | NLLS |

Figure 22.6.2. The terminology of the DDV model.

not a straight line, like OLS does. Figure 22.6.3 dramatically illustrates the difference between LPM and NLLS estimates of the conditional probability function.

Although much of the material in this chapter – from the box model to the estimation techniques and interpretation of results – is admittedly quite difficult, Figure 22.6.3 speaks volumes about the intuition and basic idea of NLLS. Notice especially how the constant slope and unboundedness defects of OLS are avoided by NLLS.

So, why should we use NLLS? The answer is easy – NLLS allows us to fit an S-shaped curve to an obviously S-shaped scatter diagram. Ordinary least squares restricts us to a straight line. What if the vertical strips were in a straight line? That would not pose a problem – a straight line is a particular type of S-shaped curve! In other words, the S-shape can be quite pronounced or almost indistinguishable from a line. This will be demonstrated next.

Which S Shape?

Although there are many S-shaped functional forms available, we are going to use the S-shaped functional form provided by the normal distribution. Open the NLLSFit.xls workbook and proceed to the *NormalDist* sheet to see how the normal's cumulative distribution function provides a flexible S-shaped fit. You will see a display like that shown in Figure 22.6.4.

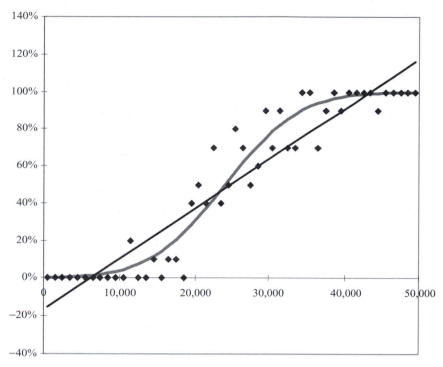

Figure 22.6.3. NLLS versus LPM fits for the campaign contributions data set. *Source:* [NLLSFit.xls]Fitting.

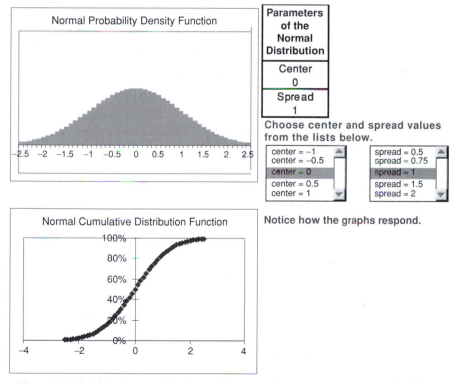

Figure 22.6.4. Understanding how the normal curve generates an S shape. *Source:* [NLLSFit.xls]NormalDist.

From the standard normal distributions's probability density function (in visual terms, the bell-shaped curve), we know that about 16 percent of the area lies between minus infinity and -1.[5] What, however, if we plotted the area under the curve *up to* each standard unit? We would be adding up or accumulating the areas. Then we would have what is called the *cumulative distribution function*.

As Figure 22.6.4 shows, the normal's cumulative distribution function is clearly an S shape. For values in the left tail, such as -2.5, there is little area, and thus the cumulative distribution function is near zero. At a standard unit of 0, 50 percent of the area under the curve is from negative infinity to zero; thus, the *y*-intercept of the cumulative distribution function is 50 percent. Finally, for high values of the standard unit, the area under the normal curve approaches 100 percent and so does the cumulative distribution function. It is clear that as the value of the standard unit rises, so does the area under the curve up to the value of the standard unit; however, the upward rise is not constant. The cumulative distribution function has a pronounced S shape.

Furthermore, you can manipulate the location and S shape by changing the center and spread of the distribution. This can be demonstrated by selecting different center and spread values in the lists.

If the Normal's S Shape Can Be Altered, How Is a Particular S Shape Determined?

Different values of the b_0 and b_1 parameters alter the S shape. Figure 22.6.5 shows part of the *Fitting* sheet of the NLLSFit.xls workbook. Your natural reaction should be that Figure 22.6.5 displays a poor fit. The S shape should be shifted over to the right so that it predicts better. After all, right now it says that $20,000 of campaign contributions almost guarantees a Yes vote, and this is clearly not true.

You can change the value in cell E2 of the *Fitting* sheet to adjust the position of the S-shaped curve. Try 0.0005, 0.001, and 0.00005 in cell E2. Keep your eye on the fitting table (top-left corner in cell H23) below the chart in the *Fitting* sheet as you change the value of the slope in cell E2. The fitting table makes clear how the S shape is being generated. For example, the S shape in Figure 22.6.5 was generated with E2 = 0.00025. The fitting table shows how the predicted probabilities are created.

Cells L23:L28 show that the formula for Std Units is simply the intercept + slope*X. Cells M23:M28 show that the Std Units value is then fed into

---

[5] Because 68 percent of the area lies from -1 to 1, 32 percent must lie outside of that interval. Because the normal curve is symmetric, we can divide 32 percent by two to get the area from minus infinity to -1.

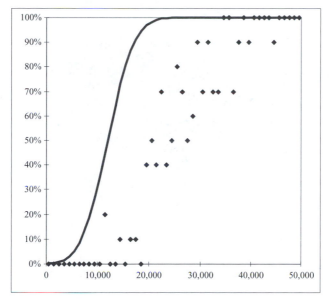

Fitting Table: Uses the b_0 and b_1 values in cells E1 and E2

b_0	b_1	X	Std Units	Pred Prob Yes
−3.008949	0.00025	$0	−3.00895	0.13%
−3.008949	0.00025	$10,000	−0.50895	30.54%
−3.008949	0.00025	$20,000	1.99105	97.68%
−3.008949	0.00025	$30,000	4.49105	100.00%
−3.008949	0.00025	$40,000	6.99105	100.00%
−3.008949	0.00025	$50,000	9.49105	100.00%

Figure 22.6.5. Determining the S shape.
Source: [NLLSFit.xls]Fitting.

Excel's NORMDIST function (with parameters 0 and 1 for the center and spread) to find the probability of a Yes vote (by computing the area under the curve up to the Std Units value).

Of course, you can only do so much by eye to fit the curve. Actually fitting an S-shaped curve to a set of data requires an objective function. The obvious choice is to minimize the sum of squared residuals. Just as with OLS, a residual is defined as actual minus predicted, and squaring penalizes equally for being above or below the predicted value. Thus, the fitting algorithm is similar to OLS: Choose an intercept and slope to fit the S shape so as to minimize the SSR.

Before describing the actual process of finding the optimal intercept and slope combination, we take a quick look at the surface under consideration, as shown in Figure 22.6.6.

The *3DSurface* sheet in NLLSFit.xls contains the data used to create Figure 22.6.6. Each intercept and slope pair generates an SSR value. We

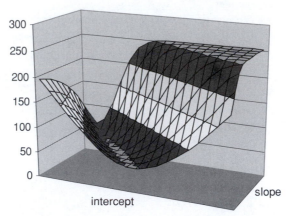

Figure 22.6.6. A 3D view of the SSR surface.
Source: [NLLSFit.xls]3DSurface.

are trying to find the intercept and slope that lead to the lowest point on the SSR surface. The *3DSurface* sheet allows you to rotate the chart and change the range of the slope coefficient.

Now that it is clear a minimization problem is being considered, we are ready to deal with a difficult question: How can we find the coefficients that solve the minimization problem? It turns out that there is only one alternative. To fit the S shape of the normal cumulative distribution, you need a numerical method.

Chapter 4 demonstrates several ways to fit a least squares line. We can use Solver to minimize the sum of squared residuals or apply Excel's LINEST function (which underlies the Data Analysis: Regression approach). The LINEST function uses an algebraic solution to the minimization problem. In fact, there are many shortcuts that have been developed specifically for finding the OLS estimates. When you hit F9 to draw a new sample, Excel's LINEST formula is able to use the algebraic solution to quickly and easily compute the values of the intercept and slope estimates that minimize the sum of squared residuals.

Fitting the S shape with the normal curve, however, is more complicated. The problem of minimizing the sum of squared residuals from the S shape based on the normal distribution has no closed-form solution. This means that the parameter estimates must be derived through a process of *iteration*. Basically, initial values are posited, the sum of squared residuals is evaluated at those initial values, and then the values are changed and the SSR re-evaluated. This procedure of repeated evaluation is called iteration, and it continues until little improvement can be made in the SSR. At that point, the solution is found.

Ordinary least squares estimates can be found iteratively (which is what Excel's Solver does), but it is much more convenient (and exact) to use the simple algebraic solution. The point is that the S shape based on the normal cumulative distribution function can be found only through numerical methods.

In the case of the dummy dependent variable model, the optimization problem is to choose the values of b_0 and b_1 (estimates of intercept and slope parameters) of the underlying threshold function $b_0 + b_1$ Campaign Contributions so as to minimize the sum of squared residuals.

It is easy to see why a computer is needed. Although it is technically possible for a human being to zoom in iteratively on the solution by hand, it is so time-consuming and cumbersome that it is not feasible.

The bad news is that the S shape of the normal cannot be represented in a simple equation. The good news, on the other hand, is that we do have a computer at our disposal and Excel has a built-in optimization algorithm called Solver; thus, the iterative procedure that must be employed is well within our means.

Using Excel's Solver to Fit the S Shape

The *Fitting* sheet in the NLLSFit.xls workbook shows how Excel can be used to find the parameter estimates for the 500 observed votes based on the S-shaped normal cumulative distribution function. Execute Tools: Solver and note how the Target Cell, Equal To, and Changing Cells have been chosen. Click the Solve button.

Solver offers the S shape shown in Figure 22.6.7 as the best one.

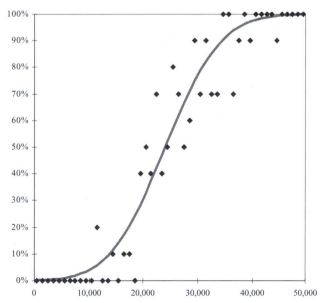

Figure 22.6.7. Finding the optimal S shape.
Source: [NLLSFit.xls]Fitting.

There are an infinite number of other cumulative normal S shapes from which to choose. Each combination of b_0 and b_1 establishes a particular S shape (as we demonstrated earlier in the *Normal Dist* sheet).

The particular combination of b_0 and b_1 in Figure 22.6.7 is the best solution to the minimize-the-sum-of-squared-residuals optimization problem. Excel iteratively cranked through combinations of b_0 and b_1 and evaluated the SSR for each combination until it found one for which the SSR could not be lowered by changing b_0 and b_1. Excel then reported this combination, and we used those values of b_0 and b_1 to draw the graph.

The Sample-Based S Shape Bounces

Proceed to the *NLLSvLPM* sheet. It attempts to make the usual point that the sample coefficients are random variables. This is more difficult to see for NLLS than for OLS, however, because the S-shaped NLLS fit for each sample cannot be immediately displayed as you hit F9.

Follow the instructions in the sheet to convince yourself that the sample coefficients are indeed random variables. Scroll right to see the different graphs displayed. Notice that there is a true S-shaped curve based on the β_0 and β_1 parameter values (in cells B1 and B2).

Each new sample generates an estimated curve that differs from the previous result and from the true relationship. This is the result of chance error in our observed sample. Rewind and replay the world, giving 500 new legislators exactly the same amounts of campaign contributions, and the estimated S-shaped curve will move because the observed pattern of Yes and No votes will change. An observed sample is merely one outcome of the many possible outcomes. The S-shaped curve bounces in the same way as the OLS-fitted line!

In Graphs 4 and 5 in the *NLLSvLPM* sheet, compare the NLLS S shape and the OLS/LPM line. Notice how the line bounces around when you hit F9 but the estimated S shape does not. Why does the estimated S shape not bounce? For our answer, see the text box under Graph 5 (top left corner is cell AU50).

Monte Carlo Simulation

Getting the b_0 and b_1 values to minimize the sum of squared residuals for a particular sample is important, but once we realize there is only a single outcome of the chance process generating the data, we must find a measure of the variability in the estimates. We can obtain a reading of the SEs of the estimates via the Monte Carlo methods used throughout this book.

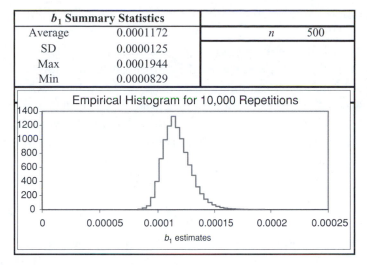

b_1 Summary Statistics			
Average	0.0001172	n	500
SD	0.0000125		
Max	0.0001944		
Min	0.0000829		

Figure 22.6.8. Monte Carlo simulation of b_1.
Source: [NLLSMCSim.xls]MCSim (*MCSim* sheet available only after clicking Show MCSim button in *Data* sheet).

Open the Excel workbook NLLSMCSim.xls to run your own Monte Carlo simulation. The *Intro* sheet explains the setup, and the *Data* sheet implements it. Be careful about the number of repetitions you request. Because the Monte Carlo algorithm has to get a new sample and use Excel's Solver to find the optimal coefficients, the process may take a while. Hit the ESC key if you think this activity is taking too long. If the Monte Carlo is the middle of Solver's routine, it will ask if you want to continue. Keep hitting ESC until you get to a dialog box that asks if you want to End or Debug. Choose End. You could also let the Monte Carlo run over night. Figure 22.6.8 shows the results for one Monte Carlo experiment (that ran all night).

Notice how the sampling distribution of b_1 is not especially normal even though we have a large sample of 500 observations. This problem is inherent to this model, for DDV models require extremely large sample sizes before large sample (or asymptotic) properties come into play.

We know the true parameter value of 0.000115 and can thus conclude that the NLLS b_1 estimator is biased because the average of the 10,000 repetitions does not equal the true parameter value. The good news is that the bias is not large and, more importantly, it diminishes as the sample size increases. Thus, the NLSS b_1 estimator, though biased is in small samples, is a consistent estimator.

As usual, the empirical SD is an approximation to the true, exact SE of the estimator. It tells us by how much the sample estimate bounces. Just as with conventional OLS estimation, we are going to want a give-or-take number that signals the variability of our estimate.

We included Excel's Solver in the algorithm running the Monte Carlo simulation in the NLLSMCSim.xls workbook to make it easy for you to explore the sampling distributions of the coefficients via Monte Carlo methods. The Excel add-in, MCSimSolver.xla (explained in more detail in Chapter 9), enables you to run Monte Carlo simulations that utilize Solver in each repetition. It uses a nonvolatile random number function, RANDOMNV(), that allows Solver to converge to the optimal solution without redrawing random numbers with each trial solution. You can use the Monte Carlo Simulation with Solver add-in on your own nonlinear regression models.

Summary

This section has explained the estimation of a dummy dependent variable model via an S-shaped curve with NLLS. It is clear that the intercept and slope coefficients determine the S shape and that, by using the usual least squares criterion (i.e., min SSR), we can compute the values of b_0 and b_1 that generate a best-fit S shape. Unfortunately, we cannot derive an analytical formula for the optimal solution; thus, we must rely on numerical optimization algorithms (such as Excel's Solver). Finally, because each sample contains chance error, the estimates are random variables with sampling distributions.

Although much has been accomplished, we still need to learn how to obtain and interpret the estimates in practice. This is the subject of the next section.

22.7. Interpreting NLLS Estimates

Workbooks: NLLSFit.xls; DDV.xla (Excel add-in)

Before we interpret the estimates, we have to get them! Although it is possible to set up a worksheet to do this (as in the previous section), we have developed an Excel add-in that does a great deal of the work for you. Use the DDV.doc instructions in the Basic Tools\ExcelAdd-ins folder of the CD-ROM packaged with this book to install the DDV.xla software in Excel and then run the add-in on the dead data in the *Fitting* sheet of the NLLSFit.xls workbook.[6] The *Y* values are in $D$4:$D$504, and the *X* data range is $A$4:$A$504. Check the Probit NLLS box and click OK. See the *ProbitNLLS10* sheet to check your answers, which should look something like Figure 22.7.1.

---

[6] This book has a second DDV model add-in called DDV Gauss–Newton (filename DDVGN.xla). The DDV.xla add-in uses Excel's Solver and will help you understand the optimization problem involved in the DDV model. DDVGN.xla does not need Excel's Solver and is faster and more flexible. Full documentation on both add-ins can be found in the Basic Tools\ExcelAddins folder. Because they use different methods, they give slightly different answers.

	A	B	C	D	E
1	SSR	Predicted	Residual²	Analysis Options	
2	45.34816841	0.001275	1.63E-06		
3	Intercept	0.001329	1.77E-06		
4	-3.017343318	0.001385	1.92E-06		
5	Campaign Cor	0.001442	2.08E-06		
6	0.000125314	0.001503	2.26E-06		
7		0.001565	2.45E-06		
8		0.00163	2.66E-06		

Figure 22.7.1. DDV.xla results.
Source: [NLLSFit.xls]ProbitNLLS10.

Interpreting the Estimates

Although the NLLS S-shaped curve can be a vast improvement on the OLS straight line in terms of the fit to the data, when it comes time to interpret the estimates, NLLS is much more difficult than OLS. In particular, unlike OLS estimates that easily and quickly convey information (e.g., $b_1 = -1.34$ means that a unit increase in X_1 leads to a 1.34 decrease in Y), a *transformation* of NLLS estimates is required.

We repeat: You cannot easily interpret the NLLS estimates as you do in OLS regressions. Transformation is required. The standard procedure for interpreting NLLS coefficients is to use the coefficients to determine the predicted probabilities at given values of the independent variables. A table of predicted probabilities can be augmented by a column for the change in predicted probability as an independent variable changes as well as a graph.

Figure 22.7.1 shows that the slope estimate is 0.000125314. This most certainly does not mean that an additional $1,000 of campaign contributions leads to a 12.5-percent increase in the predicted probability of voting Yes. That would be an OLS-like, untransformed interpretation of the estimate, which is wrong.

Clearly, the NLLS parameters are not acting directly on observed voting behavior. Instead, the parameters are used to determine the value in standard units up to which we will compute the area under the normal curve (this area is the actual probability of voting Yes). Thus, to determine the effect of campaign contributions on the predicted probability of voting Yes, we must transform the parameter estimates into standard units (multiplying by the given X) and then report the predicted probability as the area under the normal curve. Figure 22.7.2 depicts the procedure for one value of X.

The area under the normal curve up to a standard unit value is a nonlinear function of the standard unit value. For a standard unit value of -2, we know the area under the normal curve from negative infinity to -2 is about 2.5 percent. If the standard unit value is increased to -1, the area up to -1 will rise to 16 percent – a gain of 13.5 percentage points. If the standard unit

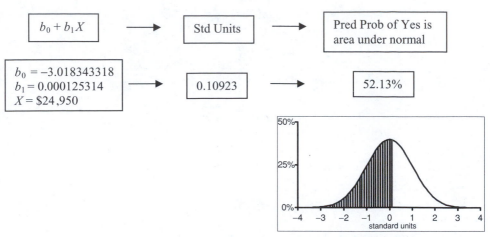

Figure 22.7.2. Transformation of NLLS estimates.

value is again increased by one unit to 0, the area will be 50%. From -1 to 0, the area increases by 34 percentage points.

This means that, unlike the LPM, we cannot simply and easily say that a given increase in campaign contributions will yield a particular change in the predicted probability of observing a Yes vote. The predicted probability of a Yes vote is the area up to the standard unit value, and this relationship is nonlinear – it depends on the value of campaign contribution from which the increase is taking place. Thus, we need a table to display the effect of increasing campaign contributions from a variety of starting values for campaign contributions.

The Dummy Dependent Variable Analysis add-in does this. After estimating the Probit Model via NLLS, click on the [Analysis Options] button and check both boxes to get approximate SEs and a predicted probability table (click on cell A5 when prompted). The latter is crucial for interpreting estimates, whereas the former tells us the variability in our estimates. An example of the output from the [Analysis Options] button is shown in Figure 22.7.3.

The predicted probability table output helps you interpret the estimates. The table converts the coefficients into predicted probabilities for different levels of Campaign Contributions. Other independent variables are evaluated at their means, but in this example there are no other X variables. Notice that the table cells for the predicted probabilities are formulas. This means the table is alive and can be easily changed to compute predicted probabilities for other X variable values.

Now it is time to clean up the results. The DDV add-in computes predicted probabilities for a range of the chosen X variable from 2.5 SDs below the average to 2.5 SDs above the average. In some cases, as in this one, some of the values make no sense and should be deleted. In this example, negative

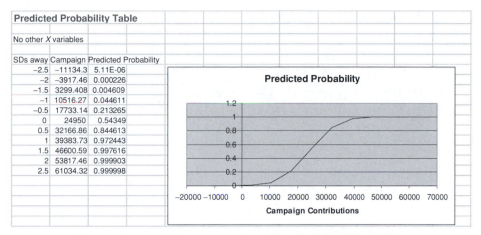

Predicted Probability Table

No other X variables

SDs away	Campaign	Predicted Probability
−2.5	−11134.3	5.11E-06
−2	−3917.46	0.000226
−1.5	3299.408	0.004609
−1	10516.27	0.044611
−0.5	17733.14	0.213265
0	24950	0.54349
0.5	32166.86	0.844613
1	39383.73	0.972443
1.5	46600.59	0.997616
2	53817.46	0.999903
2.5	61034.32	0.999998

Figure 22.7.3. Initial results of predicted probability table.
Source: [Analysis Options] button applied to a ProbitNLLS output sheet.

campaign contributions are not reasonable, and so we would delete the first three rows of the predicted probability table. Although the initial output is based on the values of the chosen X variable in standard units, the table is alive and any values of the X's can be used to compute the predicted probability. In this case, it seems natural to let campaign contribution values range from $0 to $50,000 by $10,000 increments.

Because the change in predicted probability is often of interest, we can add a new column that computes this change as the given X variable changes. Finally, we format the cells to make the table easier to read.

Our cleaned up version can be seen in the *ProbitNLLS10* sheet. It looks like Figure 22.7.4. Clearly, it is impossible to state the magnitude of the effect of an increase in Campaign Contributions on the Predicted Probability of voting Yes unless you know the initial amount of Campaign Contributions

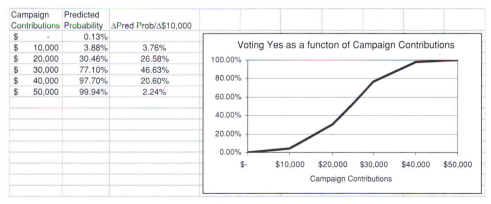

Campaign Contributions	Predicted Probability	ΔPred Prob/Δ$10,000
$ -	0.13%	
$ 10,000	3.88%	3.76%
$ 20,000	30.46%	26.58%
$ 30,000	77.10%	46.63%
$ 40,000	97.70%	20.60%
$ 50,000	99.94%	2.24%

Figure 22.7.4. Cleaning up the results.
Source: [NLLSFit.xls]ProbitNLLS10.

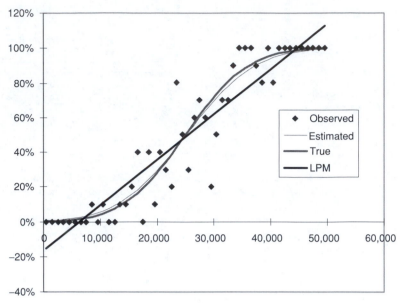

Figure 22.7.5. LPM versus NLLS.

from which the increase takes place. This is another way of saying that the predicted probability is nonlinear in campaign contributions. Where does the contributor get the biggest bang for the buck? This occurs right around the middle of the campaign contribution distribution. An extra $10,000 in contributions increases the predicted probability of a Yes vote by 46 percentage points from $20,000 to $30,000. The same $10,000 does very little at either end of the campaign contribution range.

LPM versus NLLS with a Probit DGP

We conclude this section by examining Figure 22.7.5, which is a graph that compares the two estimation procedures presented in this chapter. The figure is quite busy. The dots represent the percentage of those voting Yes in $1,000 intervals. The straight line is obviously the OLS fit for this particular sample. There are two S shapes. The thicker one is the true relationship between the probability of voting Yes and the amount of campaign contributions. The thinner one is the fit for this particular sample.

There is no doubt about it – NLLS entails much more work than OLS, but it does a much better job when the DGP follows the probit model. Not only are the predicted probabilities always safely bounded between 0 and 100 percent, but the NLLS approach does not force the predicted probability to be a linear function of the amount of campaign contributions.

We point out, however, that NLLS still suffers from heteroskedasticity. Therefore, in practice, most econometricians would use maximum likelihood to estimate the parameters of a probit model.

Summary

Although NLLS in the dummy dependent variable setting is much more difficult to estimate and interpret than OLS, it is important to recognize that the same framework is being applied. We use a sample to get estimates (b_0 and b_1) of the true, unknown parameters (β_0 and β_1) of interest. We use the reported SE of the coefficient estimate as a give-or-take number on the estimate that provides information on its variability. Estimation procedures and presentation of results may vary, but the idea that the observed sample is merely one outcome of the chance process that generated the data (and that therefore we need to determine the variability of the sample estimate) will always remain the crux of inferential econometrics.

22.8. Is There Mortgage Discrimination?

Workbooks: MortDisc.xls; MortDiscMCSim.xls; DDV.xla(Excel add-in);DDVGN.xla(Excel add-in)

This section uses mortgage discrimination as another example of a binary response model. After introducing the example, including summary statistics on the real-world data, we use hypothetical data to demonstrate the data generation process and to show the behavior of binary response estimators via Monte Carlo simulation. We then return to the real world and look at the results of an important paper.

The Research Question

To obtain a home mortgage loan, one fills out an application and then the lender decides whether to grant the loan. The research question focuses on discrimination. Are minorities more likely to be denied loans solely because of racial discrimination?

Home Mortgage Disclosure Act (HMDA) data show that, in fact, minorities are rejected for home mortgage loans more often than whites. In Figure 22.8.1, you can see that in 1998 blacks had a 38.42-percent mortgage denial rate compared with an 18.16-percent rate for whites. Can we conclude that there is racial discrimination in the home mortgage market?

Unfortunately, we cannot answer the question on racial discrimination in mortgage loans on the basis of the difference in denial rates alone just as

Summed across income categories

April 2000: http://www.ffiec.gov/hmda_rpt/aggnat_98.htm, selected 5-2 and clicked Retrieve by Table

AGGREGATE TABLE 5-2: DISPOSITION OF APPLICATIONS FOR CONVENTIONAL HOME-PURCHASE LOANS,

1 to 4 FAMILY HOMES, BY INCOME AND RACE OF APPLICANT, 1998

FINAL 1998 NATIONAL
AGGREGATES

Number of Loans

Race 4, 8	Apps. Received 14	Loans Originated	Apps. Approved But Not Accepted	Apps. Denied	% Apps. Denied	Apps. Withdrawn	Files Closed as Incomplete
AMERICAN IND/ALASKAN NATIVE	18251	8997	1918	5837	31.98%	1246	253
ASIAN/PACIFIC ISLANDER	149748	109887	10898	15697	10.48%	10949	2317
BLACK	291135	124544	28465	111849	38.42%	21579	4698
HISPANIC	278535	142549	26959	86139	30.93%	18738	4150
WHITE	3289082	2235747	249557	597184	18.16%	176157	30437
OTHER	46969	28709	4543	9540	20.31%	3428	749
JOINT (WHITE/MINORITY) 5	88852	61346	6541	14611	16.44%	5384	970
RACE NOT AVAILABLE 6	441773	205055	47910	112001	25.35%	63988	12819

Figure 22.8.1. Conventional mortgage dispositions.
Source: [MortDisc.xls]HMDAConv.

we cannot conclude that there is gender discrimination in wages by simply comparing male and female average wages. There are many omitted variables that may be correlated with race (credit history, loan to value ratio, and so on). It may be these variables that are responsible for the higher observed black denial rates. This is another example of the persistent, fundamental issue of confounding in an observational study.

In their paper, Munnell et al. (1996) painstakingly extracted the individual data from each loan application to include many potentially confounding variables in a dummy dependent variable model. Their goal was to test for racial discrimination in home mortgage lending. We first work with a hypothetical data set in order to understand the model and then turn to the real-world results.

Mortgage Discrimination as a Dummy Dependent Variable Model

In our hypothetical example we will ignore real-world complications surrounding empirical analyses of mortgage lending in order to use mortgage lending as an example of a dummy dependent variable model. We use a simple, single-equation, three-independent-variable specification to generate the latent probability of loan denial for each individual:

$$\text{Threshold} = \beta_0 + \beta_1 \text{Loan to Appraised Value Ratio} + \beta_2 \text{Years on Job} + \beta_3 \text{Black}$$

Each individual who applies for a loan has an error term reflecting other characteristics that influence that person's credit worthiness. The loan is denied if ε_i, individual i's draw from the credit-worthiness error box, is less than the threshold value. The parameter on the dummy variable Black, β_3, is the crucial coefficient in the analysis.

We created an Excel workbook, MortDisc.xls, that puts this hypothetical model into action. Open MortDisc.xls and proceed to the *BoxModel* sheet displayed in Figure 22.8.2. Notice that the two individuals being compared have the same Loan to Appraised Value Ratio and Years on Job, but the first person is black and the second is not. $\beta_3 = 0.7$ reflects discrimination because its positive value means that blacks have to cross a higher threshold of credit worthiness to secure a home mortgage loan. We assume that the tickets in the error box are normally distributed. Thus we use a probit model for estimation.

We explain the formulas in each cell and how the graphs are constructed. Then we illustrate the data generation process. Follow along in the *BoxModel*

Hitting the F9 key recalculates the sheet.

Cell C7 determines if there is discrimination.
Change cell C7 to 0 and hit F9. What happened?

Intercept (β_0)		–6.5
β_1	β_2	β_3
8	–0.02	0.7

Loan-to-Appraised-Value Ratio	Years on JobB	lack	Threshold	Probability Loan Denied	Normal Random Draw	Loan Denied
75.00%	10	1	0.00	50.0%	–0.5888	1

Loan to Appraised Value Ratio	Years on JobB	lack	Threshold	Probability Loan Denied	Normal Random Draw	Loan Denied
75.00%	10	0	–0.70	24.2%	–0.3102	0

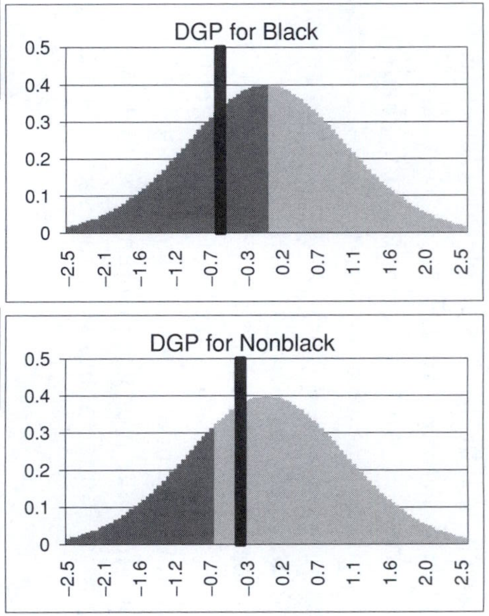

Figure 22.8.2. Understanding the DGP in a mortgage loan binary choice model.
Source: [MortDisc.xls]BoxModel.

698

sheet in the MortDisc.xls workbook. Click on cell D11 (or D21) to show that the threshold for loan denial is determined by the following formula:

$$\text{Intercept} + \text{beta1}^*\text{A11} + \text{beta2}^*\text{B11} + \text{beta3}^*\text{C11}.$$

We named cell D11 ThresholdBlack and cell D21 ThresholdNonBlack. Because $\beta_3 = 0.7$, when Black is 1, the threshold for blacks works out to 0, whereas that for nonblacks is -0.7. The cells immediately to the right, E11 and E21, compute the probability of loan denial based on the threshold value. The Excel function NORMDIST returns the normal cumulative distribution function. The first person's probability of denial evaluates to 50 percent, whereas the second person has only a 24.2-percent probability of loan denial. The pink area (or left side) in each graph represents the probability of loan denial, and the green area (or right side) is the probability of loan acceptance (1 – probability of denial).

Click on cell F11 (or F21) to display the formula used to generate the independently, identically, normally (probit) distributed random error term in the model,

$$= \text{NORMALRANDOM}(0, 1).$$

The blue vertical lines on the graphs indicate the random errors drawn for each person. A logistic, or any other, distribution could be implemented by using a random number generator corresponding to the desired distribution.

The last cells to be explained are G11 and G21. Their formulas are

$$\text{G11}: = \text{IF}(\text{F11} < \text{ThresholdBlack}, 1, 0) \text{ and}$$
$$\text{G21}: = \text{IF}(\text{F21} < \text{ThresholdNonBlack}, 1, 0).$$

Excel's IF function returns a 1 in cell G11 when F11 is less than Threshold Black and 0 when F11 is greater than or equal to ThresholdBlack. This generates the observed 0/1 outcome that is the essential characteristic of a dummy dependent variable model.

Figure 22.8.2 illustrates how two observations in a sample would be generated. The first person has been denied a loan because the value of the normally distributed error term is less than the threshold level. The nonblack loan applicant, with exactly the same Loan to Value and Years on Job characteristics, has been approved because the realized error term value exceeds the threshold level. Figure 22.8.2 shows that the random draw of the nonblack applicant would have resulted in a loan denial for a black applicant because the threshold to be crossed to yield a loan acceptance is greater for the black applicant.

By hitting the F9 key on your keyboard, it is possible to bring Figure 22.8.2 to life. Using the F9 key recalculates the sheet, drawing new random numbers and reevaluating all cells. Hit F9 again and again to reveal a variety of situations. The black loan applicant is not always rejected: If the blue vertical line falls in the green area, then the random draw is above the threshold level and the loan is not rejected. Similarly, the nonblack applicant is not always accepted. You may have to hit the F9 key a few times, but you should quickly see a draw for the nonblack loan applicant less than the threshold level of -0.7 in standard units, which leads to the blue vertical line's falling in the pink area signifying that the loan application is denied.

Having completed the exploration of the DGP in this dummy dependent variable model using the initial coefficient values, we invite you to change the parameter coefficients to see how the model responds. Of particular interest is β_3 in cell C7. By changing this value to 2, for example, and hitting F9 several times, you can see how the threshold level is affected. There is less discrimination at $\beta_3 = 0.7$ than at $\beta_3 = 2$. The threshold level, in standard units, increases as β_3 rises. Of course, no discrimination implies $\beta_3 = 0$, making the two graphs identical. Were this to be true, any observed differences in black and nonblack loan-denial rates in a sample would be due to chance alone.

Using the DDV.xla Add-in on a Sample

With the data generation process well understood and implemented in Excel, you are ready to draw a sample and use the Dummy Dependent Variable Analysis add-in. Go to the *Live* sheet in the MortDisc.xls workbook to see the 1,000-observation data set. The X's (Loan to Appraised Value Ratio, Years on Job, and Black) are fixed in repeated sampling. Each observation is generated according to the DGP presented in the *Intro* sheet. Click the `Draw a Sample on THIS sheet` button to draw new normal random errors (in column F), resulting in a new series of observed loan denial values (column G). The Pivot Table reports the number of Loan Denials by Black for this sample. Because the workbook opens with cell C7 = 0, cells M17 and M18 which contain sample loan-denial rates usually are close to each other.

Set the discrimination coefficient β_3 in cell C7 to 0.7. Click the `Draw a Sample on THIS sheet` button repeatedly and watch cells M17 and M18. There is a marked difference in loan denial rates now. Black denial rates have soared. By changing β_3 from zero to 0.7, you have increased the threshold value that blacks must cross to obtain a loan. Their denial rates are now much higher than those of nonblacks.

With the discrimination coefficient $\beta_3 = 0.7$, click the `Draw a Sample in a NEW book` button to have a new sample generated and displayed in a separate workbook. This sample follows the same data generating process as that of the *Live* sheet in

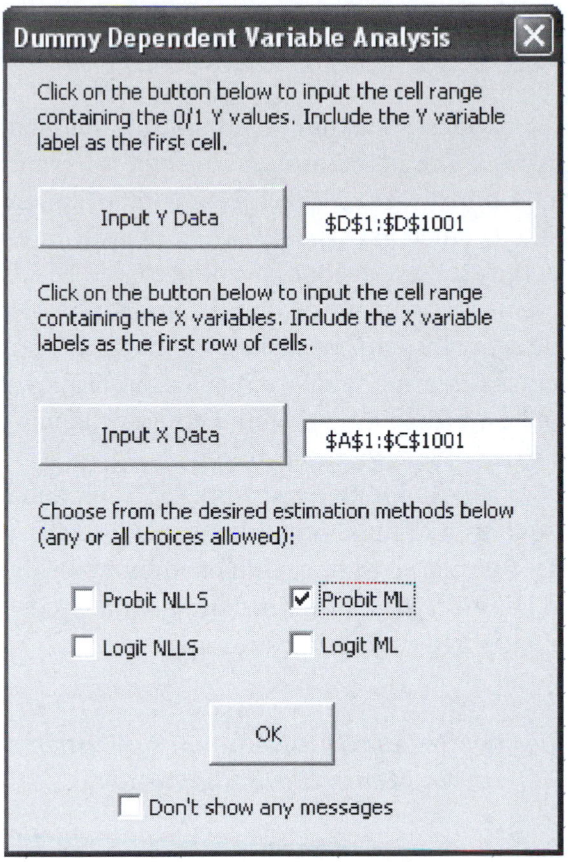

Figure 22.8.3. DDV Add-in applied to your sample.

the MortDisc.xls workbook, but it differs from the *Live* sheet in two respects. First, the underlying probability of loan denial, threshold level, and normal random draw information is not displayed. Second, the observed loan denial is a "dead" 0 or 1 instead of a "live" formula. This sample will be used to demonstrate the Dummy Dependent Variable Analysis add-in.

The next step is to make sure the DDV.xla add-in is available. If not, instructions are provided in the file DDV.doc, entitled "Installing and Using the Dummy Dependent Variable Excel Add-in" in the Basic Tools\ExcelAddins folder of the CD-ROM packaged with this book.

With the DDV.xla add-in properly installed, use it to estimate a Probit ML model on your sample data. Figure 22.8.3 shows how to configure the DDV add-in's dialog box.

When finished, the DDV add-in displays a few messages and inserts a new sheet in your workbook. Click on the cells in columns A, B, and C to see the formulas. Execute Tools: Solver to see that Solver is used to solve the least squares minimization problem.

Using the [Analysis Options] button makes quick work of creating a predicted probability table. Because the results are presented as formulas on the spreadsheet,
you are easily able to see the source of displayed numbers, quickly edit cells,
and make new calculations. For example, computing marginal probabilities or
making comparisons of predicted probabilities for different sets of independent variables are routine tasks in Excel. This is important in binary response
models because the coefficient estimates are not easily interpreted.

In our sample, the estimated slope on the variable Black, b_3, was 0.7391.
This slope represents an estimate of the discrimination level, but it cannot
be interpreted directly. Instead, predicted probabilities must be computed
for a variety of cases. Creating tables and charts to display the effects of the
coefficients is the best way to interpret and convey the information from an
estimated dummy dependent variable model.

The add-in also makes it possible to compare Probit and Logit models via
nonlinear least squares and maximum likelihood. See the references at the
end of this chapter for sources that explain maximum likelihood. You can use
the DDV.xla and DDVGN.xla add-ins to compare the predicted probabilities
from different models and estimation strategies.

Understanding the SE and Sampling Distribution
via Monte Carlo Simulation

Because your sample has its own set of realized random error values and,
therefore, observed 0/1 values, it will have its own set of estimated coefficients.
The sampling distribution of the estimated coefficient is often of interest.
We want the expected value, or center, of the sampling distribution of an
estimated coefficient, $E(b_k)$, to be equal to the true coefficient value, β_k. We
also would like to know the spread of the sampling distribution, or standard
error, in order to determine the variability of the estimate.

The software you use to estimate a DDV model will report an estimated
SE. In our sample, the estimated slope on the variable Black, b_3, was 0.7391,
and the estimated SE of b_3 was 0.1016. Your results will be different.

Because the sample was cooked from known parameters (especially
$\beta_3 = 0.7$), Monte Carlo simulation can be used to confirm that the reported
SE is reasonably accurate and to understand the SE itself. Open the MortDis-
cMCSim.xls workbook and click the [Show Monte Carlo Simulation] button (in the *Data* sheet)
to reveal a new worksheet from which to run Monte Carlo simulations. Notice
that the workbook uses the method of Maximum Likelihood (ML) instead
of NLLS. Because you will undoubtedly come across papers that use ML, we
thought it would help you to see that it is simply another way to estimate the
coefficients.

b_3 Summary Statistics			
Average	0.7055	n	1000
SD	0.1023	Average Estimated SE	0.1028
Max	1.1084		
Min	0.2954		

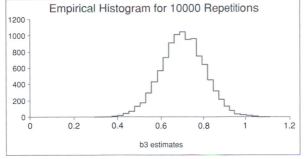

Figure 22.8.4. Monte Carlo simulation of maximum likelihood estimation of b_3.
Source: [MortDiscMCSim.xls]MCSim.

By generating 10,000 samples and estimating b_3 in each sample, Monte Carlo simulation provides an approximation of the sampling distribution. Your Monte Carlo will differ slightly from that reported in Figure 22.8.4.

The standard deviation of the 10,000 b_3 coefficients, 0.1023, which is an approximation to the exact SE, substantially agrees with the average estimated SE of 0.1028 reported by the Monte Carlo simulation. You are invited to change the number of observations from 1,000 to 100 to see the effect on the sampling distribution and average estimated SE of b_3.

Mortgage Discrimination in the Real World

We conclude this section by returning to reality. We used cooked data to explain the data generating process involved in the mortgage discrimination question, and now we are ready to see what the real-world results show. In their paper, Munnell et al. (1996) highlight a list of variables that compare groups. Table 22.8.1 shows a few of these comparisons.

As you can easily see in the first row of Table 22.8.1, blacks and hispanics have a 28-percent mortgage denial rate in their sample, whereas only 10 percent of white loan applications are denied. This 18-percentage point gap is the crux of the analysis. Is it due to discrimination by lenders or can other variables plausibly explain the gap? For example, lenders would be more likely to reject applicants with unstable work histories. Table 22.8.1 says that whites have an average of 23 years in the same line of work and 19 years on the job.

Table 22.8.1. *Selected Differences between Applicant Groups*

Applicant Characteristic	Total	White	Black/Hispanic
Percent rejected	15	10	28
Mean age	37	36	37
Mean years of school	15	16	14
Percent of applicants married	59.9	61.8	53.6
Mean number of years in line of work	20	23	13
Mean number of years on job	17	19	10
Mean base monthly income	$4,109	$4,407	$3,132
Mean purchase price	$186,000	$197,000	$150,000
Mean value liquid assets	$85,000	$99,000	$41,000
Mean value total assets	$316,000	$373,000	$128,000
Percent meeting credit history guideline for approval	89.8	93.6	77.4
Percent with delinquent consumer credit accounts	16.8	13.9	26.6
Percent with public record defaults	7.9	5.9	14.7
Percent of loans in special programs (MHFA)	7.3	3.3	20.2
Percent single-family type of property	60.9	67.9	38.1

Note: Percentage base for each item does not include applicants for whom information was missing.
Source: Munnell et al. (1996), p. 32.

Their black and hispanic counterparts, however, have only 13 and 10 years, respectively.[7] There are clear differences in other relevant variables such as the applicant's assets, credit history, and the type of property being purchased.

The question remains, however, Can these differences account for the entire 18-percentage point gap? By estimating a dummy dependent variable model, this question can be answered. Of course, we have several regression specifications to choose from, including the linear probability, probit, and logit models. For the latter two, we can choose NLLS or ML estimation approaches.

Munnell and her colleagues used a variety of models and estimation approaches and decided to report a logit model via ML and the LPM (with OLS, of course) as their first results (see Table 22.8.2). They point out a claim we made while explaining the linear probability model: "One benefit of OLS estimates is the ease with which one can interpret the coefficients. The OLS coefficient on race implies that the rejection rate of minority applications is 7 to 8 percentage points higher than the rejection rate of applications by whites with similar characteristics" (Munnell et al. 1996, p. 33).

They further point out that interpreting the logit coefficients is much more difficult. To aid the reader, they created a Percentage Point Impact column

---

[7] We should note that given the mean applicant ages, all of these job tenure figures appear too high.

Table 22.8.2. *Selected Determinants of Probability of Mortgage Loan Application Denial*

Variable	Logit Base (1)	Logit Percentage Point Impact (2)	OLS Base (3)
Constant	−13.69		−0.22
	(12.62)		(−1.47)
Risk of Default:			
Housing expense/income	0.63	4.6	0.06
	(2.76)		(3.56)
Consumer credit history	0.51	4.1	0.04
	(9.16)		(9.46)
Cost of default:			
Denied private mortgage insurance	6.16	65.0	0.65
	(8.55)		(16.06)
Personal characteristics:			
Race (Black/Hispanic = 1)	1.00	8.2	0.07
	(3.73)		(2.57)
Percent correctly predicted	95.3		
Adjusted R^2			0.32
Number of observations	2,925		2,925

Notes: Numbers in parentheses are *t* statistics.
Not all variables included in the regression are displayed in this table.
Source: Munnell et al. (1996), p. 34.

[column (2) in Table 22.8.2] in addition to reporting the Logit estimates. For continuous variables, the authors computed the change in the predicted probability from a 1 SD increase (with all other variables held constant). Thus, for example, the housing expense to income ratio has a logit estimate of 0.63. This cannot be interpreted as a 63-percent increase in the probability of rejection. Instead, the authors computed the probability of rejection for the mean housing expense to income ratio and then found the probability of rejection for a 1-SD increase in the housing expense to income ratio with the other included variables held constant. The percentage point difference resulting from the 1-SD increase in the housing expense to income ratio is reported as the Percentage Point Impact.

For dummy independent variables, such as Race (which is 1 if you are a minority applicant), they simply calculated the change in the predicted probability of loan denial for an applicant with a particular characteristic. The Percentage Point Impact reported in Table 22.8.2 for Race is 8.2 percentage points. In other words, Munnell and her coauthors found that, with all of the included variables held constant, the rejection gap between minority applicants and whites falls from 18 percentage points to 8.2 percentage points.

From this analysis they concluded that there is evidence of discrimination, but not as much as the raw, unadjusted comparison would have you believe.

Unfortunately, this is an observational study. The authors are well aware that there may be subtle, hidden confounding factors that have not been accounted for. The remainder of the paper tries alternative models while focusing on the Race variable. Because Race keeps popping up as significant, the authors wrote "that a serious problem may exist in the market for mortgage loans" (Munnell et al. 1996, p. 51).

Summary

As we have done in previous chapters, we devoted the last section of this chapter to a real-world application of the theoretical ideas presented in earlier sections. There are countless examples of dummy dependent variable models in the literature and we merely scratched the surface of the issues surrounding mortgage discrimination. We like the example because mortgage discrimination is an important issue. Table 22.8.2 is a nice model for how to present results from Logit or Probit estimations.

22.9. Conclusion

Dummy dependent variable or binary response models are common because many individual decisions are simply yes or no ones. Labor force participation, union status, voting, and attending college are a few of the many examples of dichotomous choices. Unfortunately, the data generation process underlying the observed 0 or 1 dependent variable makes estimating parameters and interpreting results quite difficult.

We used a live, interactive display in three separate examples – Raid, Campaign Contributions, and Mortgage Discrimination – to emphasize that the 0 or 1 binary response is generated by comparing a draw from an error box to a threshold level. This idea is difficult to understand in the abstract but easy to grasp once seen on your computer screen. Similarly, the fact that the normal distribution has a flexible, S-shaped cumulative distribution function that responds to values of the coefficients is much easier to understand once you see a visual demonstration.

Although you will probably use sophisticated commercial statistical analysis software to actually estimate a DDV model, the two add-ins packaged with this book, DDV.xla and DDVGN.xla, provide a user-friendly, simple way to fit a dummy dependent variable model, including standard errors and a table of predicted probabilities. The latter is crucial because one drawback of NLLS or ML estimation of binary response models is that the coefficients

cannot be interpreted as easily as the usual OLS coefficients. Transformation is required.

Finally, as is done throughout this book, we employ Monte Carlo simulation to explain the concept of the SE and the sampling distribution. As with any fitting procedure or estimator, a new sample will generate new coefficients. By repeatedly resampling and examining the resulting estimated coefficients, you have learned, once again, the idea behind the sampling distribution of a coefficient. It is worth remembering that dummy dependent variable DGPs require large sample sizes before the sampling distribution of the estimators begins to resemble the normal curve.

22.10. Exercises

1. Open the Raid.xls workbook and go to the *Death By Raid* sheet. The initial default parameters were A2 = 18 percent and G2 = 78 percent. Could these parameters have produced the results in Figure 22.2.1?
2. Repeatedly clicking the `Repeat the Experiment` button offers convincing evidence that the sample effectiveness of Raid is bouncing. That means it has a sampling distribution. Determine and report its center and spread. Describe your procedure.
3. Change the probability of dying by Raid to 18 percent. Resample by hitting the F9 key. What kinds of results do you get? Does Raid ever seem to be effective (even though it really is not)?
4. Open the NLLSMCSim.xls workbook. Click the `Get a 100 Obs Sample` button in the *Data* sheet and use your sample to estimate the model via OLS and Probit NLLS. Create a graph that compares the predicted probabilities of the two estimation techniques.
5. Open the MortDisc.xls workbook. With a positive level of discrimination, use the MCSim.xla add-in to make sure the model is responding as expected. In other words, track both Loan Denial cells and check to make sure the probability of loan denial rates are correct. Take a picture of your results and report on the results of your testing.
6. From the MortDisc.xls workbook, set $\beta_3 = 2$ and follow the instructions in Section 22.8 to create your own sample and estimate it via NLLS. Report your results. Do you find evidence of discrimination in mortgage lending from your sample?

References

The mortgage discrimination example is from Munnell, A.G., M. B. Tootell, L. E. Browne, and J. McEneaney (1996). "Mortgage Lending in Boston: Interpreting HMDA Data," *The American Economic Review* **86**(1): 25–53. An introductory econometrics book that uses mortgage discrimination as an example and discusses maximum likelihood is Stock and Watson (2003).

For more mathematical but still introductory presentations of the DDV model, we recommend Greene, W. H. (2000). *Econometric Analysis*, 4th ed. (Englewood Cliffs, NJ: Prentice-Hall, Inc.) and Amemiya, T. (1994). *Introduction to Statistics and Econometrics* (Cambridge, MA: Harvard University Press).

There are many books focused solely on the DDV Model. See, for example, Maddala, G. S. (1983). *Limited-Dependent and Qualitative Variables in Econometrics* (Cambridge, UK: Cambridge University Press).

The chapter's opening quotation is from Salsburg, D. (2001). *The Lady Tasting Tea: How Statistics Revolutionized Science in the Twentieth Century* (New York: Henry Holt and Company).

Chester Bliss, an entomologist, may have independently derived the probit method. However several researchers preceded him in the field, including, most prominently, Gustav Fechner, a psychophysicist, Charles Peirce, a philosopher and logician, and John Gaddum, a pharmacologist. See

Finney, D. J. (1947) *Probit Analysis: A Statistical Treatment of the Sigmoid Response Curve.* (Cambridge, UK: Cambridge University Press), Chapter 3, and

Stigler, S.M. (1978) "Mathematical Statistics in the Early States," *The Annals of Statistics*, **6**(2): 239–265.

23

Bootstrap

I also wish to thank the many friends who suggested names more colorful than *Bootstrap*, including *Swiss Army Knife*, *Meat Axe*, *Swan-Dive*, *Jack-Rabbit*, and my personal favorite, the *Shotgun*, which to paraphrase Tukey, "can blow the head off any problem if the statistician can stand the resulting mess."

Bradley Efron[1]

23.1. Introduction

Throughout this book, we have used Monte Carlo simulations to demonstrate statistical properties of estimators. We have simulated data generation processes on the computer and then directly examined the results.

This chapter explains how computer-intensive simulation techniques can be applied to a single sample to estimate a statistic's sampling distribution. These increasingly popular procedures are known as bootstrap methods. They can be used to corroborate results based on standard theory or provide answers when conventional methods are known to fail.

When you "pull yourself up by your bootstraps," you succeed – on your own – despite limited resources. This idiom is derived from *The Surprising Adventures of Baron Munchausen* by Rudolph Erich Raspe. The baron tells a series of tall tales about his travels, including various impossible feats and daring escapes. Bradley Efron chose "the bootstrap" to describe a particular resampling scheme he was working on because "the use of the term bootstrap derives from the phrase *to pull oneself up by one's own bootstrap* ... (The Baron had fallen to the bottom of a deep lake. Just when it looked like all was lost, he thought to pick himself up by his own bootstraps.)" [Efron and Tibshirani (1993), p. 5].

In statistics and econometrics, bootstrapping has come to mean to resample repeatedly and randomly from an original, initial sample using each

---

[1] Efron (1979, p. 25).

bootstrapped sample to compute a statistic. The resulting empirical distribution of the statistic is then examined and interpreted as an approximation to the true sampling distribution.

The tie between the bootstrap and Monte Carlo simulation of a statistic is obvious: Both are based on repetitive sampling and then direct examination of the results. A big difference between the methods, however, is that bootstrapping uses the original, initial sample as the population from which to resample, whereas Monte Carlo simulation is based on setting up a data generation process (with known values of the parameters). Where Monte Carlo is used to test drive estimators, bootstrap methods can be used to estimate the variability of a statistic and the shape of its sampling distribution.

There are many types of bootstrapping because there are many ways to resample, and there are a variety of ways to use the bootstrapped samples. The next section introduces the bootstrap by returning to the free-throw shooting example used to explain Monte Carlo simulation. We then apply the bootstrap with regression analysis, using data presented by Ronald Fisher. Section 23.4 demonstrates how the Bootstrap Excel add-in can be used on your own data to obtain bootstrapped SEs. We conclude our introduction to bootstrapping by exploring how the bootstrap can be applied to get a measure of the variability of the R^2 statistic.

23.2. Bootstrapping the Sample Percentage

Workbook: PercentageBootstrap.xls

We introduce the bootstrap with a simple example. Suppose you had a single sample of 100 free throws and computed the percentage made. If you did not know the true, underlying accuracy of the free-throw shooter, your best estimate of the shooter's probability of making a free throw would be the sample percentage made.

Of course, there is variability in the percentage made out of 100 free throws. The standard error of the sample percentage can be estimated via conventional methods by dividing the sample SD (an estimate of the unknown population SD) by the square root of the number of free throws. This is not the exact SE because the true SD is unknown.

With the estimated SE of the sample percentage and taking advantage of the central limit theorem, we can generate confidence intervals and compute P-values. This relies on the sampling distribution being approximately normal.

A bootstrapping approach to the problem of estimating the SE and finding the sampling distribution of the sample percentage treats the original sample as a population from which to sample, with replacement, 100 free throws. By repeatedly sampling 100 free throws from this artificial population, we generate a list of bootstrapped sample percentages. The length of the list is equal to the number of bootstrap repetitions. Each number in the list is the percentage of 100 free throws made from a bootstrapped sample. Just as in a Monte Carlo simulation, the spread in the list approximates the SE of the sampling distribution, and the empirical histogram of the repetitions mirrors the probability histogram of the sample percentage.

The PercentageBootstrap.xls workbook puts these ideas into action. From the *Introduction* sheet, click the Draw a Sample button. A new sheet, called *OriginalSample*, appears in the workbook. Columns A and B contain the results of 100 free-throw attempts. The workbook is set up so that the shooter will have a true probability of success between 65 and 75 percent. The best estimate of this unknown probability is the sample percentage. Cell D15 reports the estimated SE using the conventional approach, and cells D17 and D18 display the lower and upper bounds of a 95-percent confidence interval (relying on the normal distribution).

To understand how the bootstrap method works, click the Draw One Bootstrap Observation button several times. Each click draws a new observation for the bootstrapped sample (from the 100 free throws in the original sample) and places it in columns H and I. The sampling is done with replacement, and each observation in the original sample is equally likely to be drawn. To obtain a complete bootstrapped sample, we need 100 observations, the same size as the original sample.

Instead of drawing the bootstrapped sample one observation at a time, you can simply click the Draw One Bootstrap Sample button to draw 100 observations. Click the Draw One Bootstrap Sample button repeatedly. Each click draws a bootstrapped sample. The bootstrapped sample percentage is displayed in cell I1. Each new bootstrapped sample generates a new bootstrapped sample percentage.

A particular observation may appear more than once in a bootstrapped sample, whereas another may not be drawn at all. Cell K1 displays the number of times a particular observation, number 27 in the original sample, appears in the bootstrapped sample. Click the Draw One Bootstrap Sample button repeatedly and keep your eye on cell K1. Sometimes observation number 27 does not appear at all, but usually it is drawn at least once. As you repeatedly draw a new bootstrapped sample, you will probably see it appear between zero and three times.

The bounce in the bootstrapped sample percentage is the sampling variation we want to capture. We need to resample repeatedly, keeping track of the sample percentage in each bootstrapped sample. Click the Bootstrap Simulation button to access a new sheet, *Bootstrap*, from which a bootstrap analysis can be carried out.

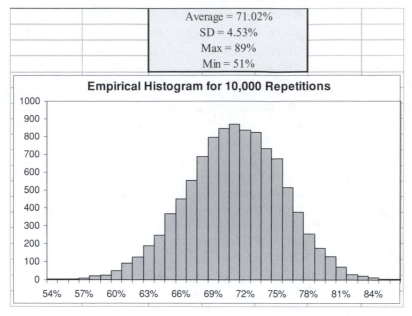

| Average = 71.02% |
| SD = 4.53% |
| Max = 89% |
| Min = 51% |

Figure 23.2.1. Bootstrapping the sample percentage.
Source: [PercentageBootstrap.xls]Bootstrap.

When we drew a sample, our Original Sample had 71 free throws made. Using conventional methods – that is, the sample SD divided by the square root of *n* (the number of observations)– the estimated SE is 4.56 percentage points. Our bootstrap results are displayed in Figure 23.2.1. The bootstrapped SE, the estimate of the exact SE based on bootstrapping, is 4.53 percentage points. How did you do?

When estimating the SE of the sample percentage of 100 free throws, the bootstrap and conventional approaches are in substantial agreement. This makes sense because both are using the same information from the original sample. The conventional approach uses the sample SD to construct the estimated SE via a formula. The bootstrap treats the sample as a population and resamples from it. The bootstrap converges to the conventional result as the number of repetitions increases.

The two methods differ in estimating the sampling distribution itself. Instead of relying on the normal distribution to approximate the unknown shape of the sampling distribution, the bootstrap uses the empirical histogram from the simulation as an estimate of the sampling distribution. Brownstone and Valleta clearly stake out the issues:

This bootstrap method described above will only give accurate estimates if the original sample is large enough to reflect the true population accurately. The traditional analytic approach approximates the sampling distribution by a normal distribution centered at the sample mean with variance equal to the sample variance. This traditional approximation requires that the sample be large enough for the central limit theorem to apply to the sample mean. If the sample size is small and the true population is not normally distributed, then the bootstrap approximation should be more accurate.   Brownstone and Valleta (2001, p. 130).

In other words, the bootstrap will do a better job of answering questions that involve the shape of the sampling distribution when its profile is not normal. Suppose, for example, that we wanted to know the chances that a 95-percent free-throw shooter will make 16 or less out of 20 free throws. The standard approach will fare badly because the sampling distribution of the sample percentage for this case is not very normal.

Summary

This section has introduced the bootstrap by showing how it can be used to estimate the SE and sampling distribution of the sample percentage. By sampling with replacement from an original sample, we generate an artificial sample. We use the artificial, or bootstrapped, sample to compute a statistic of interest. By repeating this procedure many times, we obtain an approximation to the sampling distribution of the statistic. The next section shows how the bootstrap can be applied to regression analysis.

23.3. Paired XY Bootstrap

Workbook: PairedXYBootstrap.xls

In the 1940s, "although digitalis had been a standard medication for heart disease for more than a century, there were still no reliable methods for evaluating its potency. Biological assays (bioassays) were performed on frogs, pigeons, and cats, but none were totally satisfactory" (Scheindlin, 2001, p. 88). In too high a dose, digitalis is deadly. Doctors needed to know the right dosage for different patients. Experiments on laboratory animals were undertaken in an attempt to determine toxicity levels.

In 1947, Ronald Fisher published an article that analyzed the data from digitalis assays from 144 cats. The data set had the sex, heart weight (in grams), and body weight (in kilograms) of each cat. Fisher's Table 1 (see Figure 23.3.1) displayed salient summary characteristics.

Fisher noted that the "heart as a fraction of the entire body" was remarkably similar for female and male cats. Could the optimal digitalis dose be determined simply as a function of the patient's body weight? After all, if given body weight, heart weight is simply a constant fraction, then from body weight we can infer heart weight and administer the correct dosage.

Fisher's Original TABLE 1					
				Females	Males
Number				47	97
Total Body Weight				110.9 Kg.	281.3 Kg.
Total Heart Weight				432.5 g.	1098.2 g.
Heart as fraction of entire body				.3900%	.3904%

Figure 23.3.1. Fisher's cat data for digitalis study.
Source: [PairedXYBootstrap.xls]Data.

Unfortunately, closer inspection revealed that the correspondence between body and heart weight broke down. Fisher reported that the slope coefficients from regressions of heart weight on body weight for each sex differed: "namely .2637% for females and .4313% for males." A 1-kg increase in body weight led, on average, to a 4.313-g increase in heart weights for males but only a 2.637-g increase in heart weights for females. Figure 23.3.2, which Fisher did not include in his published article, shows the two individual regressions.

Fisher suspected that male and female cats in his sample had different relationships between body and heart weight. The next step required a decision on whether this difference was real. It could be that the difference observed in the sample was simply due to chance error in the selection of the particular cats chosen for the study.

Fisher used the data to illustrate how the analysis of covariance method can be used to determine if the coefficient estimates from the two regressions are statistically significantly different from each other. He concluded that "the close agreement between the sexes in the average percentage of the body taken up by the heart seems to mask a real difference in the heart weight to be expected for a given body weight" (Fisher 1947, p. 68).

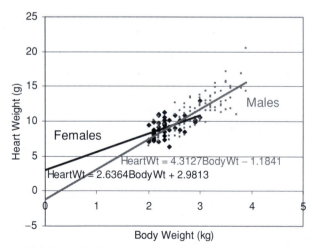

Figure 23.3.2. Individual regressions on female and male cats.
Source: [PairedXYBootstrap.xls]Data.

	Dependent Variable: Heart Weight (g)			
	Model 1	Model 2	Model 3	Model 4
	Females	Males	Both	Both
Intercept	2.981	−1.184	−0.497	−1.184
	(1.485)	(0.998)	(0.868)	(0.925)
Body Weight (kg)	2.6364	4.3127	0.082	4.313
	(0.625)	(0.340)	(0.304)	(0.315)
Female			4.076	4.165
			(0.295)	(2.062)
Female*BodyWeight (kg)				−1.676
				(0.837)
N	47	97	144	144
RMSE	1.162	1.557	1.457	1.442
R^2	0.28	0.63	0.65	0.66
	SEs in parentheses			

Figure 23.3.3. Uncovering gender differences via regression.
Source: [PairedXYBootstrap.xls]Data.

Although he chose to use the analysis of covariance method, Fisher could have explored the effect of sex on the relationship between heart and body weight with multiple regression analysis. Figure 23.3.3 compares the results from four models. Models 1 and 2 treat females and males separately. Model 3 is a multivariate model that forces the slopes to be equal but allows the intercepts to be different for female and male cats. The interaction term, Female*BodyWeight (kg), in Model 4 relaxes the restriction on the slopes. The coefficient on the interaction term has a *P*-value of 4.7% when testing the null that it is 0. We would conclude that the slopes are statistically significantly different from each other.

The hypothesis test of the null that the coefficient on Female*Body Weight (kg) is zero relies heavily on the estimated SE. In turn, the computation of the estimated SE is based on the estimate of the spread of the errors, the RMSE. Ordinary least squares regression requires homoskedastic errors and uses a single number to estimate the spread of the errors. Unfortunately, the RMSEs from the individual regressions are worrisome because it looks like the male cats have much greater spread around the regression line (RMSE = 1.557) than the female cats (RMSE = 1.162). This is evidence of heteroskedasticity. Fisher was aware of this problem and ended the paper with the following observation: "It may be noted that the estimated variance of heart weight for given body weight in males, 2.424 g.^{2}, is considerably greater than the value for females, 1.351 g.^{2} The greater residual variance for males possibly was related to their larger size. The heaviest female weighed 3.0 Kg. while nearly 40 percent of the males exceeded this weight" (Fisher 1947, p. 68).

Heteroskedastic errors pose serious problems for OLS regression analysis. Although estimates remain unbiased, OLS is no longer the best linear unbiased estimator, and the reported OLS estimated SEs cannot be trusted.

Regression Statistics for Heart Weight (g)				
Number of observations	144	Number of missing observations = 0		
Mean of Dep Var	10.631			
RMSE	1.442			
Coefficient Estimates				
Variable	Estimate	SE	Robust SE	
Intercept	−1.184	0.925	1.166	
Female	4.165	2.062	1.854	
Female*BodyWeight (kg)	−1.676	0.837	0.735	
Body Weight (kg)	4.313	0.315	0.414	

Figure 23.3.4. Robust SEs of regression coefficients.
Source: [PairedXYBootstrap.xls]Data.

Because we use the estimated SE to compute the *t*-statistic and *P*-value, the hypothesis test conducted on the Female*Body Weight (kg) coefficient is flawed.

The conventional solution is to estimate SEs that are robust to the presence of heteroskedasticity. Figure 23.3.4 shows the results of this approach (using the OLS Regression add-in described in detail in the chapter on heteroskedasticity). The estimated SE falls by 12 percent from 0.837 to 0.735. The *P*-value on the null that the slope is zero falls by half from 4.7 to 2.4%.

Another approach to estimating the SE is to use the bootstrap. For regression analysis, several different resampling schemes are possible. We will demonstrate the most popular one, called paired XY or case resampling. Using the original sample with 144 observations, three independent variables (Female, Female*Body Weight, and Body Weight), and the dependent variable (Heart Weight), we generate each bootstrap sample by randomly drawing 144 rows from the data.

Scroll over to column AK in the *Data* sheet of PairedXYBootstrap.xls. Click the `Draw One Bootstrap Observation` button several times. Each click draws a new observation for the bootstrapped sample and places it in columns AK, AL, AM, and AN. Each click takes an entire row or record (which accounts for the names paired XY or case resampling). The sampling is done with replacement, and each observation in the original sample is equally likely to be drawn. To get a complete bootstrapped sample, simply click the `Draw One Bootstrap Sample` button to draw 144 observations. Click the `Draw One Bootstrap Sample` button repeatedly. Each click draws a bootstrapped sample. Regression results for the artificial bootstrapped sample are displayed in cells AP2:AS6 of the *Data* sheet. Each new bootstrapped sample generates a new bootstrapped regression line. The cell highlighted in yellow (AQ2) is the coefficient for the interaction term.

The bootstrapped SE of the slope of Female*Body Weight (kg) is the standard deviation from the list of coefficients generated by repeatedly resampling. The *Bootstrap* sheet enables you to run your own analysis by simply clicking the `Run Bootstrap` button. Figure 23.3.5 shows our results.

Slope Female*BodyWt Estimates		Average - Original Sample Slope Female*BodyWt Estimate
Average	−1.6903	−0.0140
SD	0.7224	
Max	0.9250	
Min	−4.7243	

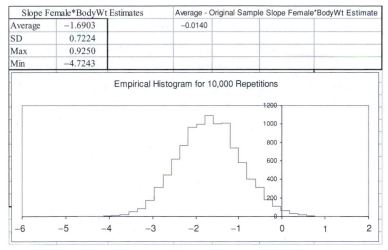

Figure 23.3.5. Bootstrapping the interaction term.
Source: [PairedXYBootstrap.xls]Bootstrap.

The bootstrapped SE, the spread of the 10,000 bootstrapped coefficients, is about 0.72 or 0.73. This agrees with the estimated SE via robust methods, 0.735. By resampling the entire row, or case, the paired XY bootstrap correctly handles the heteroskedasticity.

To construct a confidence interval or conduct a test of significance via the bootstrap, we have the possibility of two approaches. First, one can simply use the bootstrapped SE as the estimated SE in a conventional computation. For example, for a hypothesis test of the null that the coefficient on the interaction term is zero, we use the bootstrapped SE to compute the *t*-statistic:

$$\frac{\text{observed} - \text{expected}}{\text{estimated SE}} = \frac{-1.676 - 0}{0.722} = -2.32.$$

This *t*-stat produces a *P*-value of about 2.2 percent.

There is an alternative to marrying the SE generated via the bootstrap to the conventional approach. By directly using the bootstrapped approximation to the sampling distribution, we can compute confidence intervals and conduct hypothesis tests. A 95-percent confidence interval for the interaction term coefficient is simply the 2.5th to the 97.5th percentile of the 10,000 bootstrap repetitions. Scroll over to column AJ of the *Bootstrap* sheet to see that this interval is from roughly −3.0 to −0.2. Because the interval does not cover 0, you would reject the null that the true parameter value is 0.[2]

---

[2] Efron and Tibshirani (1993) discuss the connection between confidence intervals and hypothesis tests. The simple approach to bootstrapping canfidence intervals presented here, the percentile method, is not used very often. For a review of better alternatives, see DiCiccio and Efron (1996).

It appears Fisher was right. There is a statistically significant difference in the relationship between body and heart weight for male and female cats. Using the usual estimated SEs from OLS, however, is an inappropriate way of obtaining the variability in the estimated coefficients because heteroskedasticity is present. Robust SE methods and the bootstrap are two alternative, better approaches.

Summary

In the previous section, we bootstrapped the SE of the sample percentage by generating an artificial sample, finding the sample percentage for the artificial sample, and repeating the procedure many times. This section has done the same thing. From an original sample, we generated a pretend sample, ran a regression on the pretend sample, and repeated the procedure 10,000 times. The heart of bootstrapping is to generate artificial samples and construct the same statistic on each sample as the statistic of interest in the original sample.

In both examples thus far, the spreadsheet has been set up for you. Can you run a bootstrap analysis on your own data? Yes, you can, and the next section shows you how.

23.4. The Bootstrap Add-In

Workbooks: PairedXYBootstrap.xls; Bookstrap.xla (Excel add-in)

The previous sections introduced bootstrapping using workbooks especially designed for that purpose. This section shows how to use an Excel add-in packaged with this book that enables you to run a bootstrap from any Excel workbook. Thus, the add-in allows you to use bootstrapping methods on your own data and your own statistic of interest.

The first step is to install the Bootstrap add-in. The software is in the Basic Tools\ExcelAddIns\Bootstrap folder. Open the Bootstrap.doc file in that folder for instructions on how to install and use the add-in.

Having installed the Bootstrap.xla file, open the PairedXYBootstrap.xls workbook to test drive the Bootstrap simulation add-in. The *Female* sheet shows the OLS estimated SE on Body Weight is about 0.625. Let us use the Bootstrap add-in to find the Paired XY bootstrap SE of Body Weight.

Begin by inserting a sheet into the workbook (Insert: Worksheet) and renaming it *BootFemale* and then go to the *Data* sheet and copy the body and heart weight data for the female cats (cell range C1:D48) to the A1:B48 range of the *BootFemale* sheet. We use the data in the *BootFemale* sheet as our original sample and the same range as the place in which we will write our bootstrapped resamples. This will destroy the original sample in

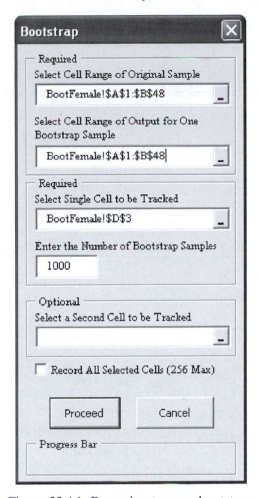

Figure 23.4.1. Preparing to run a bootstrap.

the *BootFemale* sheet, but we have it in the *Data* sheet and thus this is not a problem.

We need, however, to compute the statistic of interest (the OLS estimated SE of Body Weight) for each bootstrapped sample. We can use Excel's LINEST function for this. In the *BootFemale* sheet, select a 5 × 2 cell range and use LINEST to regress Heart Weight on Body Weight. With the data in the *BootFemale* sheet in cells A1:B48, the LINEST formula should look like this: "= LINEST(B2:B48,A2:A48,1,1)." The LINEST results (especially the OLS estimated SE for Body Weight) should be exactly equal to the regression results in the *Female* sheet.

With LINEST available to recompute the slope coefficients as we repeatedly put down new samples in the worksheet, we are ready to bootstrap. Execute Tools: Bootstrap . . . to bring up the bootstrap dialog box.

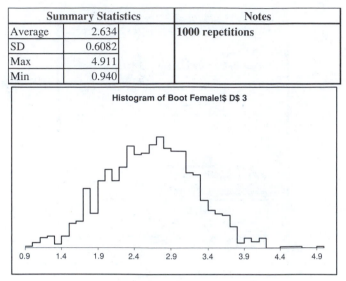

Summary Statistics		Notes
Average	2.634	**1000 repetitions**
SD	0.6082	
Max	4.911	
Min	0.940	

Figure 23.4.2. Results from the bootstrap add-in for the heart weight coefficient.

Enter the same cell range for the Original and Bootstrap Sample input boxes and select the coefficient on Body Weight as the cell to be tracked. Figure 23.4.1 shows how the dialog box should look. The BootFemale! $A\$2:\$B\$48$ range contains the data, and we selected cell D3 as the tracking cell because we put Excel's LINEST array function in cells D3:E7, which reports the slope coefficient in cell D3. We obtain a bootstrapped approximation of the slope coefficient's sampling distribution by repeatedly resampling and keeping track of the slope coefficient from each bootstrapped sample.

When you click the Proceed button, the add-in immediately warns you that the original sample data will be overwritten. The Bootstrap add-in reads the original sample, samples from it (with replacement), and then writes the bootstrap sample (temporarily) to the spreadsheet. It records the tracked cell and then repeats this procedure for as many repetitions as you request. Because the original sample is used as the place in which bootstrapped samples are written, a warning is issued. In this case, we can safely proceed because the original female cat data is in the *Data* sheet.

When the bootstrap simulation finishes its last repetition, a worksheet is added to the workbook that displays the first 100 repetitions along with summary statistics and a histogram of the complete results (see Figure 23.4.2).

For female cats, the paired XY bootstrapped SE and OLS estimated SE on Body Weight are almost the same. This is not true for the male cats (as the *Q&A* sheet in the PairedXYBootstrap.xls workbook asks you to show).

Summary

You may have noticed that the bootstrap built into the workbook is much faster. Unlike the simulations in the *Bootstrap* sheet, the Bootstrap add-in spends a great deal of time writing each sample to the spreadsheet. Using this add-in on a large data set may be impractical (although the authors have let the Bootstrap add-in run over night).

The Bootstrap add-in is ideal, however, for exploring problems on your own. Any statistic you can compute on the spreadsheet, no matter how complicated, can be bootstrapped. The next section shows how to apply bootstrap methods to a statistic for which no conventional method exists for estimating its sampling distribution.

23.5. Bootstrapping R^2

Workbook: BootstrapR2.xls

In this section, we apply the bootstrap to a statistic for which there is no standard analytical means of estimating its variability. We also introduce a new resampling scheme called the residuals bootstrap.

The coefficient of determination, commonly abbreviated and reported simply as R^2, is often used as a measure of the overall goodness of fit of a regression. This coefficient ranges from 0 to 1: 0 signifies that the regression explains none of the observed variance in the dependent variable, and 1 denotes a perfect fit. Chapter 5 explains the R^2 statistic in detail and shows how it is calculated. Excel reports R^2 through its Data Analysis: Regression add-in and in the third row and first column of the LINEST array function.

Like the sample slope, estimated SE, and other sample-based statistics, R^2 is a random variable. If you draw a new sample, a new R^2 will result. Ohtani (2000) points out that the sampling properties of R^2 have been investigated. Researchers, however, rarely, if ever, report a measure of the precision of the R^2 value because the sampling distribution of R^2 is complex and depends on the particular values of the X variables. Thus, although we know R^2 is a random variable, without an SE, confidence intervals and hypotheses tests using R^2 are simply ignored.

The bootstrap offers a way to estimate the SE of R^2 and its sampling distribution. The bootstrap, in this case, is conducted by repeatedly resampling from the original sample and keeping track of the R^2 of each artificial sample. Just like any other sample-based statistic, we can approximate the sampling distribution of R^2 via the empirical histogram generated by the bootstrap simulation and use the SD of the bootstrapped R^2 values as an estimate of the exact SE of R^2.

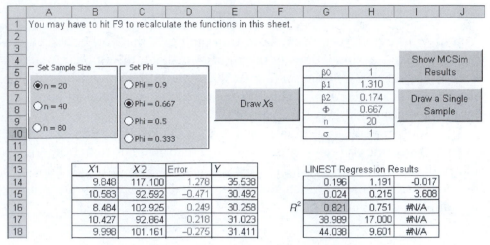

Figure 23.5.1. The data sheet.
Source: [BootstrapR2.xls]Data

Open the Excel workbook BootstrapR2.xls and go to the *Data* sheet. Both the Monte Carlo Simulation and Bootstrap add-ins will be applied to this workbook, and so you need to have them available.

Let us begin with a tour of the *Data* sheet, a portion of which is displayed in Figure 23.5.1. Hit F9 to recalculate the sheet and confirm that R^2 is a random variable.

The data generation process meets all of the classical model's requirements. The *X's* are fixed in repeated sampling (and thus do not change when you hit F9); the errors are independently and identically distributed (and, in addition, drawn from a normal distribution); and each Y is generated by $\beta_0 + \beta_1 X_1 + \beta_2 X_2 + \varepsilon$.

The *Data* sheet allows you to control two crucial parameters, the sample size and Φ, by clicking on the buttons. The Greek letter Φ is the parent coefficient of determination. This parameter controls the position and shape of the sampling distribution of R^2. In Figure 23.5.1, and on the spreadsheet in cell G16, notice that Φ (set at 0.667) does not equal the R^2 obtained from the 20 observation sample. This is due to chance error, which is also responsible for the deviation of the sample coefficients (in the first row of the LINEST Regression Results table) from their respective parameter values (the betas in cells H5:H7).

Unlike the sample slope coefficients, whose expected value is equal to the parameter value, R^2 is a biased estimator of Φ. The R^2 statistic is consistent, however, and thus, as the sample size increases, its expected value does converge to its parent parameter value (and the SE converges to 0). You can quickly get a sense of the sampling distribution of R^2 by running a Monte Carlo simulation. Execute Tools: MCSim . . . and select cell G16 as the tracking variable. The average of your Monte Carlo repetitions is an approximation to the expected value, and the SD is an estimate of the exact SE. Your results should be similar to the *MCSimN20Phi0.667* sheet (available by clicking the [Show MCSim Results] button). Note the bias of R^2 as an estimator of Φ (the average of the 10,000 R^2 values is not close to 0.667) and the nonnormal shape of the histogram.

Now that the properties of the sampling distribution for R^2 for this data generation process are known, we are ready to proceed to the bootstrap. Instead of using the paired XY Bootstrap, we introduce a different resampling scheme. The residuals bootstrap uses the residuals as a stand-in for the errors and produces a bootstrapped sample by shuffling the residuals and creating a bootstrapped Y observation according to the equation

$$\text{Bootstrapped } Y = b_0 + b_1 X_1 + b_2 X_2 + residual.$$

Note that the coefficients are not the β's (because the true parameter values are unknown) but the original sample-estimated coefficients.

Some preparatory work is needed to run the residuals bootstrap, but we have set up the spreadsheet for you. Click the [Draw a Single Sample] button in the *Data* sheet to obtain an Original Sample and regression results. Click on the Y data cells in column AE to see that the cells contain numbers (not formulas) that represent a single realization from the data generation process. Column AD is blank because you cannot observe the errors.

Cell range AG14:AI18 of the *Data* sheet reports the regression results for your Original Sample. Cell AG16 displays the R^2 value for which we want to find the SE. In column AK, we have computed the residual for each observation. Click on cell AK14 to see the usual actual minus predicted formula for the residual.

The data next to the residuals column are labeled "Adj residuals." By multiplying the residuals by an adjustment factor, we improve the performance of the bootstrap.[3] The Adj Residuals represent the errors and are our artificial population. By sampling with replacement from the Adj Residuals, we can create artificial dependent variables and bootstrapped regression results. Click on one of the Boot Y cells in column AQ and examine the formula. It uses the Original Sample coefficients along with a randomly sampled Boot Residual to form Boot Y.

We will use the Bootstrap add-in to write the Boot Residuals in column AP and track the R^2 for each bootstrapped sample in cell AS16. Figure 23.5.2 shows how the Bootstrap add-in should be configured.

Click Proceed to obtain a bootstrap estimate of the variability of R^2 and the shape of its sampling distribution. You now have Monte Carlo and Bootstrap

---

[3] For more on rescaling the residuals, see Wu (1986, p. 1281).

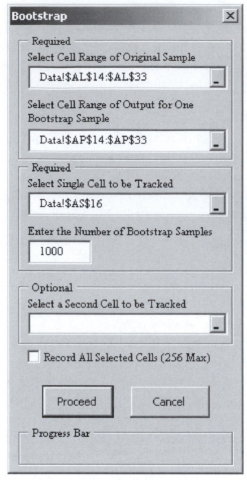

Figure 23.5.2. Setting up the bootstrap.
Source: Bootstrap.xla add-in.

simulation results. It is time to figure out what all of this means. Figure 23.5.3 compares the Monte Carlo with the Bootstrap for $n = 20$ and $\Phi = 0.667$.

The Monte Carlo results, on the left, are a good approximation to the true sampling distribution of R^2. The average of the 10,000 repetitions is 0.706, which is close to the exact expected value (reported by Ohtani) of 0.7053. Similarly, the SD of the 10,000 repetitions, 0.0945, is a good approximation to Ohtani's exact SE of 0.0955. The Monte Carlo simulation is based on knowing the data generation process and simply repeating it and directly examining the results. Your Monte Carlo results should be quite close to ours. It should not be surprising that the Monte Carlo with 10,000 repetitions does a good job of reflecting the true sampling distribution.

The Bootstrap results, the right panel in Figure 23.5.3, are not as good as the Monte Carlo results. With 1,000 bootstrap repetitions, we had an average R^2 of

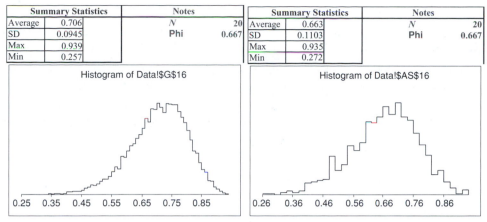

Figure 23.5.3. Monte Carlo and bootstrap simulation results.
Source: [BootstrapR2.xls]Data.

0.663 with an SD of 0.1103. Your bootstrap results may be markedly different from ours (available by clicking the $\boxed{\text{Show Bootstrap Results}}$ button). To understand the inferiority of the bootstrap compared with the Monte Carlo, remember that the latter is based on knowing and running the true data generation process. The bootstrap, however, takes one Original Sample – one realization of the DGP – and treats it as a population from which to resample. The bootstrap relies on the premise that the Original Sample will closely mirror the population. The sample size, however, is merely 20 in this case, and so it is quite possible that the Original Sample differs substantially from the true population.

In fact, seen in this light, it is actually quite remarkable that the bootstrap does as well as it does. After all, the bootstrapped and Monte Carlo sampling distributions are reasonably similar, and our bootstrap approximate SE (0.1103) is not that far off the true mark (0.0955).

Of course, to run a full test of the bootstrap, we would have to nest simulations. In other words, take an Original Sample, bootstrap it (like we did), then take another Original Sample, bootstrap it, and repeat this many times. The $\boxed{\text{Advanced Thinking}}$ button allows you to do exactly this, but Ohtani (2000) has done the hard work for us. His experiments show that the Residuals Bootstrap has an expected value of 0.7089 with a spread of 0.0899. This shows that, for this case, the Residuals Bootstrap does a good job of approximating the sampling distribution of R^2.

Once a bootstrap approximation of the variability of the statistic has been obtained, we have two options: (1) use the Bootstrapped SE in conventional ways to construct confidence intervals and conduct tests of significance or (2) use the bootstrapped values themselves for these purposes. Note that we are using the bootstrap to estimate the variability of R^2, not the statistic itself.

Could we have used the paired XY instead of the residuals bootstrap on this problem? Yes, and the *Q&A* sheet in BootstrapR2.xls invites you to do so. Remember that, unlike Fisher's cat data, the DGP in the BootstrapR2.xls workbook exactly follows the classical econometric model. If you know that the errors are identically, independently distributed, then the Residuals Bootstrap is appropriate. On the other hand, if the DGP is based on sampling X and Y from a population, then use the paired XY Bootstrap. In general, the bootstrap procedure adopted should mimic the DGP as closely as possible.

Unlike the paired XY Bootstrap, if the residuals bootstrap is applied to Fisher's cat data (in PairedXYBootstrap.xls), you will not correctly estimate the sampling distribution. You could use a modified residuals bootstrap, tying the size of the residual to whether the cat was male or female.

As Efron and Tibshirani make clear, "perhaps the most important point here is that bootstrapping is not a uniquely defined concept" (Efron and Tibshirani 1993, p. 113). In other words, within the realm of "resample from an original sample," there are a great many possibilities in the resampling scheme. Research in bootstrapping methods focuses on the properties of alternative resampling plans.

Summary

Unlike previous sections in this chapter where we used bootstrapping methods to reproduce results obtained with conventional techniques, this section showed how the bootstrap can be used to estimate the variability of R^2, a statistic with a sampling distribution whose analytical solution is beyond the reach of traditional statistical practice. This example also allowed us to introduce the idea that there is more than one way to resample. The next section concludes our introduction to the bootstrap by highlighting a few of the points in the debate about the role of bootstrap methods.

23.6. Conclusion

The heart of the bootstrap is not simply computer simulation, and bootstrapping is not perfectly synonymous with Monte Carlo. Bootstrap methods rely on using an original sample (or some part of it, such as the residuals) as an artificial population from which to randomly resample.

Because the bootstrap utilizes resampling, advances in computing power have facilitated the development of the bootstrap. Bradley Efron is recognized as the inventor of the bootstrap – not because he was the first to conceive of replacing an unknown population with a single sample but because he realized that the explosion in computing would permit a wide variety of resampling schemes.

The method, however, is still in its infancy, and many questions remain unanswered.

Grand claims sometimes have been made for bootstrap analysis. For instance, Efron and Tibshirani (1993) and Vinod (1998) envision the bootstrap as part of a strategy to find universally applicable methods for estimation and inference, which can be implemented with very little effort or analysis by researchers. This vision is tempting, especially given the ease and speed with which bootstrap estimates for many models can be obtained using modern desktop computers. However, Manski (1996) argues that this vision is flawed due to the inherent ambiguity of statistical theory in comparing alternative estimation procedures.

Brownstone and Valleta (2001, p. 139)

The fundamental requirement of the bootstrap is that the resampling be faithful to the data generation process. This can be difficult to do in practice. Consider the two bootstrap methods used in this chapter: paired XY and residuals bootstraps. These are two of many possible resampling schemes. The paired XY Bootstrap handled the heteroskedasticity in Fisher's cat data, but it is not always clear which resampling strategy is best for a particular case.

But critics have not been able to slow the advance of bootstrap methods. Modern data analysis software includes commands for bootstrapping, and the latest research papers report bootstrap results. Econometrics textbooks increasingly devote space to explaining the bootstrap.

The allure of the bootstrap is due to the weakness of its competition as much as its own inherent advantages. Remember that conventional statistical theory relies heavily on large-sample asymptotic theory. With finite sample sizes, we know for a fact that using the limiting distribution (for example, the normal distribution for a regression coefficient) is merely an approximation to the exact sampling distribution. Research is showing that bootstrapping outperforms the conventional approach in areas in which the shape of the sampling distribution is crucial such as confidence intervals.

In addition, bootstrap methods force you to confront the data generation process directly. You must describe the way the dependent variable is generated and the role of the X's (for example, fixed or stochastic) to construct a resampling scheme that mimics the DGP. Once so described, the bootstrap can quickly approximate the sampling distribution of complicated statistics that would require difficult (and sometimes impossible) mathematical derivations.

Finally, no restrictive distributional assumptions are required to use the bootstrap. The sample data simply are what they are. Are the errors normally distributed? This is a crucial question for anyone wishing to apply a conventional *t*-test correctly, but the answer is irrelevant for a bootstrap analysis.

"Bootstrap methods, and other computationally intensive statistical techniques, continue to develop at a robust pace.... The twenty-first century may or may not use different theories of statistical techniques, but it will certainly be a different, better world for statistical practitioners" (Efron and Tibshirani 1993, p. 394).

23.7. Exercises

1. In Section 23.2, the text claims that, "in other words, the bootstrap will do a better job of answering questions that involve the shape of the sampling distribution when its profile is not normal. Suppose, for example, that we wanted to know the chances that a 95-percent free throw shooter will make 16 or less out of 20 free throws. The standard approach will fare badly because the sampling distribution of the sample percentage for this case is not very normal."
   a. Use the normal approximation to estimate the chances that a 95-percent free-throw shooter will make 16 or less out of 20 free throws. Describe your procedure and show your work. HINT: You need to find the SE of the sample percentage and use the endpoint correction (calculating the area under the normal curve up to 16.5, instead of just 16).
   b. Suppose you had an original sample of 19 out of 20 free throws made. Use the Bootstrap add-in to find the chances that the shooter will make 16 or less out of 20 free throws. Describe your procedure and take a screenshot of your results.
   c. Given your work in parts a. and b., what do you conclude about the claim that the bootstrap will do better than the standard approach (using the normal approximation)?
2. Suppose you had an original sample from a 95-percent free shooter in which he or she made all 20 free throws. How would the bootstrap work in this case?
3. Use the *Bootstrap* sheet in PairedXYBootstrap.xls to estimate the SE and sampling distribution of the coefficient on BodyWeight in Model 4. Take a screenshot of your bootstrap results.
4. The OLS estimated SE for the coefficient on BodyWeight in Model 4 is 0.315. Does your bootstrap SE substantially agree with the OLS estimated SE? Explain the reason for the difference or agreement.
5. Use the Bootstrap add-in to run a residuals bootstrap of the coefficient on BodyWeight in Model 4. Take a screenshot of your bootstrap results.
6. Compare the paired XY and residuals bootstraps for this case. Which one do you prefer? Why?

References

For general introductions into bootstrapping methods, we recommend the following:

Brownstone, David and Robert Valleta (2001). "The Bootstrap and Multiple Imputations: Harnessing Increased Computer Power for Improved Statistical Tests," *Journal of Economic Perspectives* **15**(4): 129–141.
Chernick, Michael (1999). *Bootstrap Methods: A Practitioner's Guide* (New York: John Wiley & Sons). This includes an extensive bibliography.

Davison, Anthony C. and David V. Hinkley (1997). *Bootstrap Methods and Their Application* (Cambridge, UK: Cambridge University Press). Part of the cat data from Fisher (1947) is also used in an exercise in this book.

Efron, Bradley and Robert Tibshirani (1993). *An Introduction to the Bootstrap* (New York: Chapman and Hall).

Leisch, Friedrich and A. J. Rossini (2003). "Reproducible Statistical Research" *Chance* **16**(2): 41–45. This easily accessible article is critical of bootstrap methods because each simulation leads to different results. This article cites Fisher (1947) and provided the inspiration for our use of Fisher's data in Section 23.3.

More advanced articles on bootstrapping include the following:

Andrews, Donald W. K. and Moche Buchinsky (2000). "A Three Step Method for Choosing the Number of Bootstrap Repetitions" *Econometrica* **68**(1): 23–51.

DiCiccio, Thomas J. and Bradley Efron (1996). "Bootstrap Confidence Intervals," *Statistical Science* **11**(3): 189–212.

Ohtani, Kazuhiro (2000). "Bootstrapping R^2 and Adjusted R^2 in Regression Analysis," *Economic Modelling* **17**(4): 473–483.

The following are early works in the bootstrapping literature:

Efron, Bradley (1979). "Bootstrap Methods: Another Look at the Jackknife," *The Annals of Statistics* **7**(1): 1–26. This is Efron's original article on the bootstrap.

Freedman, David (1981). "Bootstrapping Regression Models," *The Annals of Statistics* **9**(6): 1218–1228.

Wu, C. F. J. (1986). "Jackknife, Bootstrap and Other Resampling Methods in Regression Analysis," *The Annals of Statistics* **14**(4): 1261–1295.

Additional sources for this chapter include:

Fisher, R. A. (1947). "The Analysis of Covariance Method for the Relation between a Part and the Whole," *Biometrics* **3**(2): 65–68.

Project Gutenberg at <www.gutenberg.net/> has the full text of *The Surprising Adventures of Baron Munchausen* by Rudolph Erich Raspe.

Scheindlin, Stanley (2001)."A Brief History of Pharmacology," *Modern Drug Discovery* **4**(5) <pubs.acs.org/subscribe/journals/mdd/v04/i05/html/05timeline.html>.

24

Simultaneous Equations

The method of two stage least squares (2SLS or TSLS) is second in popularity only to ordinary least squares for estimating linear equations in applied econometrics.

Jeffrey M. Woolridge[1]

24.1. Introduction

Throughout this book, we have used regression analysis in a variety of ways. From the simplest bivariate regression to consideration of the effects of heteroskedasticity or autocorrelation, we have always worked with a single equation. This chapter introduces you to *simultaneous equations models* (SEM). As the name makes clear, the heart of this class of models lies in a data generation process that depends on more than one equation interacting together to produce the observed data.

Unlike the single-equation model in which a dependent (y) variable is a function of independent (x) variables, other y variables are among the independent variables in each SEM equation. The y variables in the system are jointly (or simultaneously) determined by the equations in the system.

Compare the usual single-equation DGP,

$$y = \beta_0 + \beta_1 x_1 + \varepsilon,$$

with a simple, two-equation SEM:

$$y_1 = \alpha_0 + \alpha_1 y_2 + \alpha_2 x_1 + \varepsilon_1$$
$$y_2 = \gamma_0 + \gamma_1 y_1 + \varepsilon_2.$$

Notice that the first equation in the system has a conventional x variable, but it also has a dependent variable (y_2) on the right-hand side. Likewise, the second equation has a dependent variable (y_1) as a right-hand side variable. In a simultaneous equations system, variables that appear only on the

---

[1] Wooldridge (2003, p. 484).

right-hand side of the equals sign are called *exogenous* variables. They are truly independent variables because they remain fixed. Variables that appear on the right-hand side and also have their own equations are referred to as *endogenous* variables. Unlike exogenous variables, endogenous variables change value as the simultaneous system of equations grinds out equilibrium solutions. They are endogenous variables because their values are determined within the system of equations.

A natural question to ask is, What happens if we just ignore the simultaneity? Suppose, for example, we are interested only in the effect of y_1 on y_2. Could we simply toss out the first equation and treat the second one as a standalone, single equation, using our usual ordinary least squares regression to estimate the coefficients? In fact, this is what most single-equation regressions actually do – they simply ignore the fact that many x variables are not truly exogenous, independent variables. Unfortunately, it turns out that closing your eyes to the other equations is not a good move: the single-equation OLS estimator of γ_1 is biased. This important result, called *simultaneity bias*, occurs because y_1 is correlated with ε_2, as we will show in Section 24.3.

Fortunately, there are ways to consistently estimate the coefficients in the system. The most common approach is called the method of instrumental variables or IV. When several instrumental variables are available, they are combined via regression (the first stage) and then used in a second regression. This procedure is called two-stage least squares, 2SLS (or TSLS).

We cannot hope to cover this wide and complex area of econometrics completely in this introductory text, but we can convey the essentials of SEMs. As we have done with other topics, we will focus on fundamental concepts, using concrete examples to illustrate key points.

The next section introduces a simple example used throughout the chapter. Section 24.3 shows how OLS on a single equation pulled from a simultaneous system of equations is hopelessly flawed. With OLS out of the picture, we then turn to a demonstration of how IV estimation via 2SLS works.

24.2. Simultaneous Equations Model Example

Workbook: SimEq.xls

The hoary example of simultaneous equations in econometrics is supply and demand. Every first-year student in economics is taught that quantity demanded depends on own price, prices of other goods, and consumers' income. On the other hand, quantity supplied depends on own price, prices of goods related in production, and firms' expectations. Together, supply and demand interact to generate an equilibrium price and quantity combination.

Because there is a solid foundation of theory and intuition behind the joint determination of price and quantity, it is not surprising that almost every introduction of SEM utilizes supply and demand. Illustrating simultaneity via supply and demand can be found in countless econometrics texts and is so clichéd that we will rely on a different example.

Our hypothetical SEM example is built on a simple, two-equation model of the crime rate and law enforcement spending.

$$EnforcementSpending_i = \gamma_0 + \gamma_1 CrimeRate_i + \varepsilon_i^{ES}.$$

$$CrimeRate_i = \beta_0 + \beta_1 EnforcementSpending_i + \beta_2 Gini_i + \varepsilon_i^{CR}.$$

Each error term is independently and identically normally distributed with mean zero and a given, constant SD. In a simultaneous equations model, each y variable has its own structural equation describing how the variable is generated.

The first structural equation says that enforcement spending by the state, measured in dollars per person per year, is a function of the number of crimes per 100,000 people. The Bureau of Justice Statistics (available online at <www.ojp.usdoj.gov/bjs/>) reports that, in the United States, enforcement spending is about $500 per person and the crime rate is about 4,000 per 100,000 people. Suppose that the parameter of special interest in this example, gamma1 (γ_1), is positive; increases in the crime rate lead to more police officers, prison guards, and so forth.

The second structural equation flips enforcement spending and the crime rate. People deciding how many crimes to commit are influenced by the locality's law enforcement expenditures. Communities with high levels of enforcement will enjoy lower crime rates ceteris paribus. In addition, the distribution of income, measured by the Gini coefficient,[2] also affects the crime rate. Higher Gini values mean more income inequality and higher crime rates. Unlike enforcement spending, Gini is a truly exogenous variable in this model.

As Wooldridge (2003) points out, "the most important point to remember in using simultaneous equations models is that each equation should have a ceteris paribus, causal interpretation" (p. 525). Our model meets this requirement because government policy makers allocate resources to enforcement spending based on the amount of criminal behavior, whereas criminals decide how many crimes to commit depending on the perceived probabilities of conviction and severity of punishment, which are determined by enforcement spending.

---

[2] The Gini coefficient, or index, ranges from 0 (perfect equality) to 1, or 100 percent (meaning one person has all of the income). The *GiniData* sheet in SimEq.xls has values for a few countries from the 1990s and sources for learning more about this measure of income inequality.

The model also contains an equilibrating force that characterizes most simultaneous equations models. An increase in the crime rate, for example, leads to more enforcement spending, which, in turn, lowers the crime rate, which lowers enforcement spending, and so on, until the model settles to its equilibrium solution. We assume that only the equilibrium enforcement spending and crime rate pairs are being observed.

The interaction between crime rate and enforcement spending can be mathematically expressed by solving the two structural equation system for the reduced-form equations of crime rate and enforcement spending. We begin by substituting the Crime Rate equation into the Enforcement Spending equation.

$$EnforcementSpending_i = \gamma_0 + \gamma_1 \left[\beta_0 + \beta_1 EnforcementSpending_i + \beta_2 Gini_i + \varepsilon_i^{CR}\right] + \varepsilon_i^{ES}.$$

We obtain the reduced form for enforcement spending by solving for Enforcement Spending as follows:

$$EnforcementSpending_i - \gamma_1\beta_1 EnforcementSpending_i$$
$$= \gamma_0 + \gamma_1\beta_0 + \gamma_1\beta_2 Gini_i + \gamma_1\varepsilon_i^{CR} + \varepsilon_i^{ES}.$$

$$EnforcementSpending_i = \frac{\gamma_0 + \gamma_1\beta_0}{1 - \gamma_1\beta_1} + \frac{\gamma_1\beta_2}{1 - \gamma_1\beta_1}Gini_i + \frac{\gamma_1\varepsilon_i^{CR} + \varepsilon_i^{ES}}{1 - \gamma_1\beta_1}.$$

By similar algebra, we can find the reduced-form expression for the crime rate as follows:

$$CrimeRate_i = \beta_0 + \beta_1\left[\gamma_0 + \gamma_1 CrimeRate_i + \varepsilon_i^{ES}\right] + \beta_2 Gini_i + \varepsilon_i^{CR}.$$

$$CrimeRate_i - \beta_1\gamma_1 CrimeRate_i = \beta_0 + \beta_1\gamma_0 + \beta_2 Gini_i + \beta_1\varepsilon_i^{ES} + \varepsilon_i^{CR}.$$

$$CrimeRate_i = \frac{\beta_0 + \beta_1\gamma_0}{1 - \gamma_1\beta_1} + \frac{\beta_2}{1 - \gamma_1\beta_1}Gini_i + \frac{\beta_1\varepsilon_i^{ES} + \varepsilon_i^{CR}}{1 - \gamma_1\beta_1}.$$

These two reduced-form expressions represent the equilibrium solution to the simultaneous equations model. Given parameter values and a Gini value, draws of chance errors (ε^{CR} and ε^{ES}) generate observed enforcement spending and crime rate.

The *Data* sheet in SimEq.xls brings this DGP to life. Figure 24.2.1 shows part of the sheet.

By hitting F9, you recalculate the workbook, drawing new error terms in columns E and F, which result in new observed values for Crime Rate and Enforcement Spending in columns G and H. Click on the dependent variable cells (e.g., G23 or H24) to see the formulas being used to generate the values. The formulas are simply the reduced-form expressions for each variable.

Data Generation Process

$$EnforcementSpending_i = \gamma_0 + \gamma_1 CrimeRate_i + \varepsilon_i^{ES}$$

γ_0	275
γ_1	0.02
SDErrorES	10

$$CrimeRate_i = \beta_0 + \beta_1 EnforcementSpending_i + \beta_2 Gini_i + \varepsilon_i^{CR}$$

β_0	6000
β_1	–15
β_2	75
SDErrorCR	1

Hypothetical Data. Cross section. Each observation is a geographic area (e.g., county or state) at a given time.

Average -->	43.95	–0.04	–4.37	4028.27	351.20
Observation	Gini	Crime Rate Error	Enforcement Spending Error	Crime Rate	Enforcement Spending
1	49	–1.15	–16.07	4454	348
2	47	–0.01	–16.90	4349	345
3	46	0.49	3.71	4054	360

Figure 24.2.1. The DGP in action.
Source: [SimEq.xls]Data.

Summary

With this constructed example, we know that $\gamma_1 = 0.02$. In other words, if the crime rate increases by 1,000 (per 100,000 people per year), enforcement spending will rise by \$20 per person per year. But what if we were trying to estimate γ_1? The next section shows that using OLS on a single equation is not a good way to estimate the effect of crime rate on enforcement spending.

24.3. Simultaneity Bias with OLS

Workbook: SimEq.xls

The previous section has described a simple, two-equation model of the crime rate and law enforcement spending:

$$EnforcementSpending_i = \gamma_0 + \gamma_1 CrimeRate_i + \varepsilon_i^{ES}.$$

$$CrimeRate_i = \beta_0 + \beta_1 EnforcementSpending_i + \beta_2 Gini_i + \varepsilon_i^{CR}.$$

This section shows what happens if we simply ignore the second equation and estimate the parameter of interest, γ_1, directly from the first equation using conventional ordinary least squares regression. Figure 24.3.1 displays the results, which are available starting in cell M21 of the *Data* sheet in SimEq.xls.

The problem with ignoring the second equation is immediately clear – our estimate from a single sample, $g_1 = -0.008$, says that enforcement spending will *fall* when the crime rate *rises*. That makes no sense at all. Of course, we

Single-Equation OLS Estimation of Enforcement Spending

g_1	
−0.008	386.048
0.0072	28.6966
0.068	6.5938
1.305	18
56.7	782.6

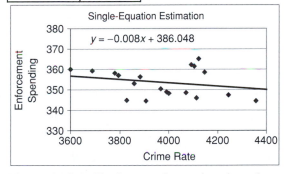

Figure 24.3.1. Single-equation estimation of γ_1.
Source: [SimEq.xls]Data.

Summary Statistics		Notes
Average	−0.008	
SD	0.0073	
Max	0.020	
Min	−0.028	

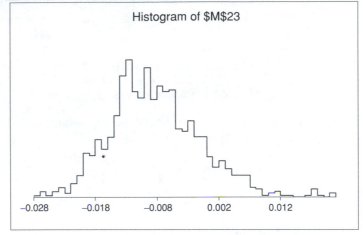

Figure 24.3.2. Monte Carlo simulation of g_1.
Source: MCSim add-in applied to cell M23 in [SimEq.xls]Data.

have looked at just one sample. Hit F9 to recalculate the sheet, drawing a new sample and new estimated coefficients. As you would expect, g_1 bounces.

Use the Monte Carlo simulation add-in (Chapter 9) to explore the sampling distribution of g_1. Our results, shown in Figure 24.3.2, reveal that the OLS estimator of γ_1 is hopelessly biased. It is centered around −0.008, whereas the true parameter value is 0.02.

Because the sampling distribution of g_1 is not centered on γ_1, we say that the OLS estimator is biased. The bias is caused by ignoring the fact that the crime rate is actually an endogenous variable in a second equation and is therefore called *simultaneity bias*. Furthermore, OLS is inconsistent – the bias will not go away as the sample size increases.

The source of the poor performance of the OLS estimator lies in the fact that the SEM data generation process fails to meet the requirements of the classical DGP. In particular, regressing Enforcement Spending on the Crime Rate violates the requirement that the x variable be independent of the error term. The reduced-form expression for the crime rate shows quite clearly that it depends on the enforcement spending error (ε^{ES}):

$$CrimeRate_i = \frac{\beta_0 + \beta_1 \gamma_0}{1 - \gamma_1 \beta_1} + \frac{\beta_2}{1 - \gamma_1 \beta_1} Gini_i + \frac{\beta_1 \varepsilon_i^{\text{ES}} + \varepsilon_i^{\text{CR}}}{1 - \gamma_1 \beta_1}.$$

Consider what happens when the error term for a particular observation on enforcement spending (ε^{ES}) is high. In the crime rate equation, enforcement

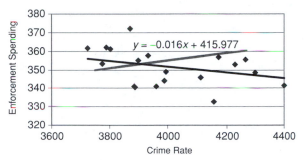

Figure 24.3.3. Understanding simultaneity bias.
Source: [SimEq.xls]Data.

spending is multiplied by $\beta_1 = -15$, and so the error term in the reduced form expression for the crime rate will likely be negative, which means that the crime rate for that observation will now be relatively low. Of course, when ε^{ES} is negative and large in absolute value, the crime rate will be relatively large. This is what is causing the negative relationship in Figure 24.3.1 and the bias in estimating γ_1.[3]

Understanding the source of simultaneity bias is important. We can use our concrete example to create a graph that shows exactly where OLS runs into problems. Figure 24.3.3 shows an OLS regression of Enforcement Spending on Crime Rate. In addition, Figure 24.3.3 depicts the true relationship between these two variables (the upward sloping line).

The top left corner of the live version of Figure 24.3.3 is in cell S28 of the *Data* sheet. Hit F9 to recalculate the sheet and refresh the graph. The points are obviously bouncing, but they do not bounce vertically around the upward sloping line that captures the true relationship between enforcement spending and crime rate. In fact, it is difficult to see what is going on in this graph.

Scroll down a bit in the *Data* sheet to see the live version of Figure 24.3.4 titled "Tracing the Movement of One Observation." Click the ┌Trace One Observation┐ button and accept the default value (1) in order to see how the first observation bounces.

Notice by glancing at the Obs Number and Gini table to the left of the graph that observation number 1 has a Gini value of 49. Hit the F9 key a few times to recalculate the sheet. The observation is bouncing, but it stays on the traced line.[4] The slope of the line on which the observation is moving is $1/\beta_1$ (the coefficient on Enforcement Spending in the Crime Rate structural equation). All of the observations follow this pattern. Click the ┌Trace One Observation┐

---

[3] The sharp reader will note that we cooked the example to exaggerate this effect and to facilitate our explanation. After all, the error term on enforcement spending has an SD of 10, whereas the SD of $\varepsilon^{CR} = 1$.

[4] In fact, to be exactly correct, it does vary a bit because ε^{CR} is low but not zero. If you are interested, you can change the value of ε^{CR} later to explore the effect it will have on the scatter plot and OLS fit.

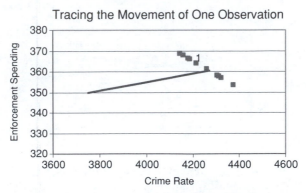

Figure 24.3.4. Focusing on the bounce of a single observation.
Source: [SimEq.xls]Data.

button and experiment with a few other observations. Include observation 19, which has the lowest Gini, 40, in your trials.

Scroll down again to see a graph that tracks the movement of two observations at once. Figure 24.3.5 displays an example of this graph. Once again, notice the behavior of the observations as you hit the F9 key. The two observations are clearly tied to the downward-sloping lines. In Figure 24.3.5, observations 2 and 3 will never leave their respective tracks. Each new sample generates a new pair of equilibrium values of enforcement spending and crime rate that move in a patterned way. The bigger the draw in the error term, the farther the observations move from the red line – but always along the track line. Click the [Trace Two Observations] button and enter a pair of observations to track. Try observations 5 and 12. Because these two observations have the same value of the fixed exogenous variable (Gini = 43), they bounce along the same line.

Having visually demonstrated that the observations are moving along prescribed tracks, we are ready to see the full scatter plot in motion. Figure 24.3.6 is the same as Figure 24.3.3 but with one crucial addition – we have added the tracks along which all of the observations bounce.

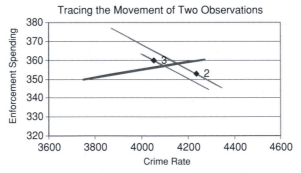

Figure 24.3.5. Focusing on the bounce of two observations.
Source: [SimEq.xls]Data.

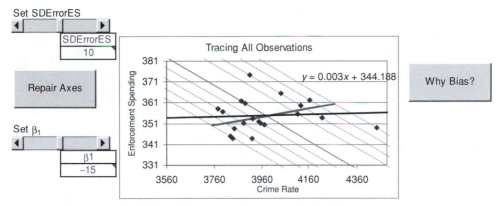

Figure 24.3.6. Focusing on the bounce of all of the observations.
Source: [SimEq.xls]Data.

Go to cell S80 of the *Data* sheet and hit F9 a few times. With the aid of the track lines, you should be able to see that the observations are not bouncing vertically around the upward-sloping (true) line. Instead, they are moving with a tilt. This tilt is responsible for the bias in the OLS estimator of the slope of the enforcement spending on crime rate relationship.

Click the [Why Bias?] button to display a new sheet called *Bias*. The scroll bar will enable you to see why the tilt causes bias. For OLS to work as advertised, the variation in the dependent variable must be in truly vertical strips. Figure 24.3.7 shows two situations. The left graphic in Figure 24.3.7 shows that the variation in *y* is vertical and that OLS estimates the true relationship well. On the right, however, the variation in *y* is tilted, and thus the fitted line is way off the true relationship.

Now that we know that this phenomenon of tilted strips is exactly what is causing the simultaneity bias in our model, return to the *Data* sheet to see how the bias depends on two factors. Use the Set SDErrorES scroll bar to set the SDErrorES to zero. That means there is no chance error in enforcement

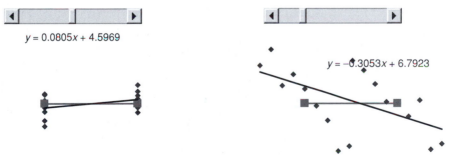

Figure 24.3.7. OLS needs vertical strips.
Source: [SimEq.xls]Bias.

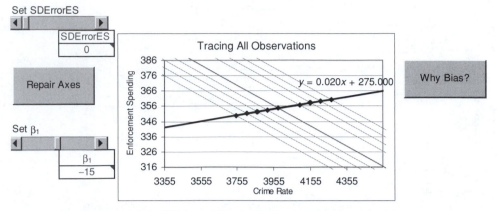

Figure 24.3.8. SDErrorES=0 eliminates simultaneity bias.
Source: [SimEq.xls]Data.

spending. Hit F9 a few times to recalculate the sheet. The simultaneity bias should disappear. Figure 24.3.8 shows this result.

Return the SDErrorES to its initial value of 10 and set the value of β_1 to 0 (by dragging the scroll box all the way to the right).[5] Use the Repair Axes button to reset the axes in the graph. Hit F9 to see that the OLS-fitted line is now dancing around the true relationship. Figure 24.3.9 shows this result. Of course, when $\beta_1 = 0$, we no longer have a simultaneous equations model because the link between enforcement spending and crime rate is broken.

In general, when an endogenous variable (determined by a system of equations) is included as an explanatory variable in a single-equation OLS regression, the result will be misleading because the OLS-fitted line will not capture the true relationship. In our example, the single-equation OLS estimate of γ_1 is confounded by the interaction of crime rate and enforcement spending. By carefully tracing the variation in expenditure spending given crime rate, we have demonstrated that the fundamental source of the simultaneity bias, from a geometrical point of view, lies in the way the points bounce in a tilted pattern.

As long as there is a positive spread in ε^{ES} and a nonzero β_1, there will be simultaneity bias. The reduced form for crime rate makes this clear because the correlation between crime rate and the enforcement spending error term depends on the $\beta_1\varepsilon^{ES}$ term:

$$CrimeRate_i = \frac{\beta_0 + \beta_1\gamma_0}{1 - \gamma_1\beta_1} + \frac{\beta_2}{1 - \gamma_1\beta_1}Gini_i + \frac{\beta_1\varepsilon_i^{ES} + \varepsilon_i^{CR}}{1 - \gamma_1\beta_1}.$$

[5] Actually, because the track lines have slope $1/\beta_1$, you cannot set $\beta_1 = 0$. Dragging the scroll box to the right sets $\beta_1 = 0.000001$. This is small enough to make the lines appear (almost) vertical.

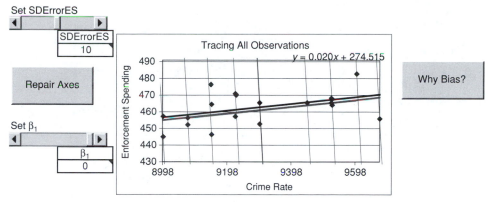

Figure 24.3.9. $\beta_1 = 0$ eliminates simultaneity bias.
Source: [SimEq.xls]Data.

Under the conventional OLS assumptions, the value of the error term should have no effect at all on the value of the right-hand-side x variables. When an included x variable is correlated with the error term, OLS estimators are biased. Omitted variable bias occurs when an included variable is correlated with an omitted variable. Simultaneity bias arises when the included x variable is actually a y variable in a simultaneous system of equations and, by virtue of the interaction between the equations, the right-hand-side y variable is correlated with the error term in the equation.

The commonality between omitted variables and simultaneity enable us to point out that there are other forms of bias in the endogeneity problem family. Selection bias and bias from measurement error in included x variables (called errors-in-variables) are two other manifestations of the endogeneity problem. In every case, the problem is that the right-hand-side variable is not independent of the error term. This causes tilt in the data strips and guarantees that OLS will fail.

Summary

Simultaneity bias means that, on average, our OLS estimate of γ_1 is wrong. Can we do better? Yes, by using instrumental variables and two-stage least squares, we can correctly estimate γ_1. The next section shows how.

24.4. Two-Stage Least Squares

Workbook: SimEq.xls

The previous section described how single-equation OLS estimation of a simple, two-equation model of the crime rate and law enforcement spending results in simultaneity bias.

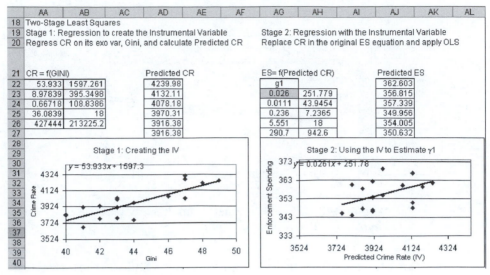

Figure 24.4.1. Running 2SLS to estimate γ_1.
Source: [SimEq.xls]Data.

This section shows how a variation on the familiar methodology of least squares regression can be used to recover unbiased estimates of some of the parameters of the structural equation. By taking two steps, one to create a new variable called an instrumental variable (or instrument) and another step to actually estimate the parameter of interest, two-stage least squares (2SLS) succeeds where simple OLS fails.

The 2SLS approach, discovered independently by H. Theil and R. L. Basmann in the 1950s, is a clever idea that shows how flexible regression analysis can be. The first stage uses OLS regression to generate predicted values that serve as the explanatory variable in the second-stage OLS regression.

Scroll over to cell AA1 in the *Data* sheet of SimEq.xls to see how 2SLS can be applied to estimate γ_1. Figure 24.4.1 has a screenshot of this area of the spreadsheet. Remember that the workbook itself is alive; therefore, hit the F9 key to see the bounce in the graphs and click on cells to reveal their formulas. It is a good idea to click the Reset button to return the parameter values to their initial values.

Cell AA22 contains the top-left corner of the first-stage regression results. Crime Rate is regressed on Gini because the reduced form expression dictates that crime rate depends on Gini. The coefficients from this regression (in cells AA22 and AA23) are then used to create Predicted Crime Rate values for each observation (see cells AD22:AD41). Note that this simple example uses only one instrument, Gini, instead of combining several available instruments in a multiple regression with Crime Rate as the dependent variable. Two

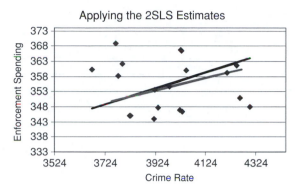

Figure 24.4.2. The results of 2SLS estimation of γ_1.
Source: [SimEq.xls]Data.

stage least squares typically involves the use of multiple instruments and, often, multiple endogenous variables. In such cases, in the first step each endogenous variable is regressed on every instrument.

Once the Predicted Crime Rate instrumental variable is available, we are ready for the second stage. The shaded cell, AG23, contains the 2SLS estimate of γ_1. It is the slope on the regression of Enforcement Spending on Predicted Crime Rate. Notice the crucial substitution of Predicted Crime Rate (created in the first-stage regression) for Crime Rate. This is the secret to the success of 2SLS.

In Figure 24.4.1, $g_1 = 0.026$. That is not a bad estimate of $\gamma_1 = 0.02$. Recalculate the sheet (by hitting the F9 key) several times to draw new samples and generate new 2SLS g_1's. You cannot do a full-scale Monte Carlo simulation by hitting the F9 key a few times, but it should be enough to convince you that 2SLS is in the ballpark.

Scroll down a bit to see the chart titled "Applying 2SLS Estimates" (depicted in Figure 24.4.2). This chart shows the original data on Enforcement Spending and Crime Rate (on the x-axis) along with the true relationship between these two variables (with slope $\gamma_1 = 0.02$). Instead of the usual OLS-fitted line, we used the coefficient estimates from the second-stage regression (in cells AG23 and AG24) to create 2SLS Predicted Enforcement Spending. The cells in AJ22:AJ41 have formulas that show how to create the fitted line for the 2SLS estimator from the sample coefficients. Hit F9 a few times to see strong visual evidence in favor of 2SLS. Click the Add OLS Line button (below the chart) to add the usual OLS fitted line to the chart. The button is a toggle, and thus you can remove the OLS line when you wish. Although the OLS-fitted line is persistently downward sloping (it is the least squares fit for the data displayed in the chart), the 2SLS seems to be bouncing around the true relationship.

Data!$M$23		Data!$AG$23		Notes	
Average	−0.008	Average	0.023	γ_1	0.02
SD	0.0076	SD	0.0165	SD ErrorES	10
Max	0.023	Max	0.114	$\beta 1$	−15
Min	−0.030	Min	−0.007		

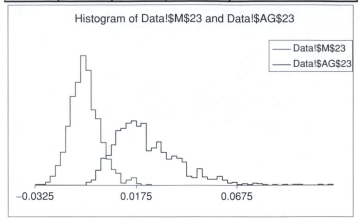

Figure 24.4.3. Racing OLS and 2SLS estimators of γ_1.
Source: [SimEq.xls] MCSimOLS2SLS.

You can conduct a definitive, final demonstration of the superiority of 2SLS over OLS by running a Monte Carlo simulation. Use the Monte Carlo simulation add-in (Chapter 9) to track the OLS estimate of γ_1 in cell M23 and the 2SLS estimate of γ_1 in cell AG23. Our results are contained in the *MCSimOLS2SLS* sheet and displayed in Figure 24.4.3. The 2SLS estimator is somewhat biased, but it is vastly superior to the OLS estimator.

Notice that the sampling distribution of the 2SLS estimate of γ_1 in this example is most decidedly not normally distributed. As is often the case, the small sample properties of 2SLS estimators are the source of a great deal of research interest. We can report that 2SLS is consistent, and it is an important tool in applied econometrics.

You probably would not perform 2SLS estimation by manually running the first stage, computing predicted values, and then running the second regression. Most modern statistical packages have commands through which you simply list the endogenous and exogenous variables in the system and the software handles all of the computations for you.

Besides ease, there is one important additional reason for not running 2SLS in two separate regressions: Getting the estimated SEs for the coefficients (and any other statistic that relies on an estimate of the SD of the errors) requires an adjustment. Scroll over to column BB if you want to see how the adjustment factor is computed and applied to the estimated SEs from the second-stage regression.

Summary

Two stage least squares and instrumental variable regression techniques in general rely on the availability of truly exogenous instruments for the endogenous variables other than the variables already included in the regression equation. The term instrument, or instrumental variable, refers to a variable which is uncorrelated with the error term in an equation determining the endogenous variable, but correlated with the endogenous variable itself. Both Gini and the Predicted Crime Rate (a linear function of Gini alone) can be called instruments for the Crime Rate variable in the enforcement spending equation. In our example, the Gini variable meets the requirements of being uncorrelated with the enforcement spending error term and being correlated with Crime Rate. Furthermore, the Gini variable is not present in the enforcement spending structural equation.

On the other hand, 2SLS fails when no truly exogenous instrument is available. For the task of estimating the coefficients in the crime rate equation, 2SLS is not a viable approach. In the technical language of simultaneous equations models, the crime rate equation is not identified. Identification means the ability to obtain a consistent estimate of the parameters in question. The discussion starting in column BU in the *Data* sheet of SimEQ.xls demonstrates why the parameters of the crime rate equation are not identified. The second stage of the 2SLS procedure encounters perfect multicollinearity because the only potential instrument available, Gini, is already present in the crime rate equation.

24.5. Conclusion

This chapter has introduced an important but complicated class of estimation problems: simultaneous equations models. Even at the introductory level, a good student of econometrics should be aware of the pitfalls associated with simply ignoring that an explanatory variable is actually a dependent variable in another equation.

We demonstrated, via concrete example and Monte Carlo simulation, that the OLS estimate of a structural parameter in a SEM is, in general, biased. Ordinary least squares is also inconsistent – that is, the bias does not go away as the sample size increases. We also showed, through a careful examination of the source of the variation in the dependent variable, that the problem with OLS arises because the errors cause the y variable to bounce along nonvertical strips. This throws the OLS line off its intended mark. This will happen whenever the data generation process is such that an included x variable is not independent of the error term in the equation.

By constructing an artificial exogenous variable, called an instrumental variable, in the first stage, and using it in place of the problematic right-hand-side y variable in the second stage, 2SLS provides consistent estimates of some of the parameters in the structural equation.

Our simple cooked example has neatly illustrated a few basic points, but there is much more to discuss in the world of simultaneous equations models. We have given just enough information to make you aware of the issue of simultaneity bias and the most popular solution to the problem. To learn more, turn to one of the readings we recommend in the References section.

We started this book by using the demand for cigarettes as an interesting example to introduce the idea of regression analysis. We returned to the cigarette data to illustrate the problems associated with using aggregate data (Chapter 2), to demonstrate tests of significance (Chapter 16), and as an example of autocorrelation (Chapter 20). We have pointed out, several times, that fitting a line to a cloud of price and quantity points is a poor way to estimate a demand curve. With a single independent variable, price, the estimated coefficient is sure to be biased by the omission of other factors that influence quantity demanded and are correlated with price.

This chapter explained how simultaneous equations bias is a second fundamental difficulty in estimating a demand curve. Throughout this book, we have tried to follow explanations of theoretical concepts that use hypothetical data with real-world examples. We could have used our cigarette data to show how the instrumental variables technique can be used to estimate the demand for cigarettes in a simultaneous system of demand and supply. A careful, clear presentation of this very example is in Stock and Watson (2003), Section 10.4, however, and we highly recommend it.

If you read Stock and Watson (2003) or, another book that we recommend, Wooldridge (2003), you may find the level of presentation challenging at first. We hope, however, that the fundamental ideas you have learned from our strong emphasis on simulation and visual display will enable you to understand more sophisticated presentations of econometrics.

24.6. Exercises

Let us explore the ideas in the chapter using the supply and demand SEM in the *Q&A* sheet of SimEq.xls.

1. Use the equations for quantity demanded and quantity supplied to find the reduced-form expressions for Q and P.
2. Use LINEST to regress Q on P in order to find the single-equation OLS estimate of α_1. Show the results from a single sample.
3. Run a Monte Carlo simulation to approximate the sampling distribution of a_1. Is OLS biased? Explain.
4. Use the data to find the 2SLS estimate of α_1. Describe your procedure and explain your results.

5. Run a Monte Carlo simulation to approximate the sampling distribution of 2SLS a_1. Is 2SLS biased? Explain.
6. Suppose we were interested in estimating δ_1. Can 2SLS be used? Explain.

References

For a history of the discovery of 2SLS, see Mary Morgan (1990). *A History of Econometric Ideas* (New York: Cambridge University Press). For an interesting perspective from one of the founders, see R. L. Basmann (1993). "'Discovery' of Two-Stage Least Squares: The Predicament of a Living Primary Source," Ch. 9 of *Perspectives on the History of Economic Thought*, Vol. 9, edited by R. F. Hebert (Aldershot: Edward Elgar).

Introductory explanations of instrumental variables and 2SLS that go beyond this book can be found in a variety of places. With a little work, the explanations in the textbooks below should be accessible to you.

We recommend these three books as a good starting place: Wooldridge (2003), Stock and Watson (2003), and Dougherty, Christopher (2002). *Introduction to Econometrics* 2nd ed. (Oxford: Oxford University Press).

For an interesting article that attempts to break the endogeneity circle between the crime rate and enforcement spending, see Klick, J. and A. Tabarrok (2005). "Using terror alert levels to estimate the effect of police on crime." *Journal of Law and Economics*. 48(1): 267–279.

A popular book which discusses a variety of fascinating empirical studies based on instrumental variables techniques is Levitt, S. and S. Dubner, (2005) *Freakonomics*, (New York: William Morrow).

Glossary

Algebra of expectations: A set of rules for computing expected values of random variables.

Alternative hypothesis: In a hypothesis test, a claim made about a parameter or parameters which contradicts the null hypothesis. According to this claim, differences between the estimated and hypothesized values of a parameter or parameters reflect real differences.

AR(1) process: A first-order autoregressive process, i.e., one in which a variable is determined by a regression on a one-period lag of itself.

Autocorrelation: The correlation of values of a variable with lagged values of itself.

Autoregression: A linear regression of a variable on lagged values of itself. The number of lags determines the order of the autoregressive process.

Auxiliary regression: A regression used as a diagnostic or supporting analysis. See also *omitted variable rule* and *Breusch–Pagan test*.

Best linear unbiased estimator (BLUE): A set of criteria for choosing an estimator that excludes biased and nonlinear estimators, while defining best as that which has minimum variance (or spread).

Bias: The difference between the expected value of an estimator and the true value of the parameter being estimated.

Biased estimator: An estimator whose expected value is not equal to the value of the population parameter being estimated. See also, *unbiased estimator*.

Bivariate regression: A regression using only two variables, a dependent variable and an independent variable.

Bootstrap: Computer-intensive, simulation techniques that are applied to a single sample in order to estimate a statistic's sampling distribution. See also, *paired XY bootstrap* and *residuals bootstrap*.

Box model: A description of a data generation process that includes the role of chance via the metaphor of draws from a box.

Breusch–Pagan (BP) test: A procedure in which the squared residuals are regressed on the independent variables in order to determine if the errors are heteroskedastic.

Central Limit Theorem: A theorem from probability theory which says that the distribution of the standardized average of independent random variables tends to the standard normal distribution as the number of random variables in the average increases.

Classical econometric model (CEM): A standard model of the data generation process for economic data.

Coin flip box model: A box model in which the data are generated according to a chance mechanism, like flipping a coin. See also *polling box model*.

Conditional mean function: A function that produces the average Y for a given value of an X variable or given values of more than one X variable.

Conditional median function: A function that produces the median Y for a given value of an X variable or given values of more than one X variable.

Conditional probability function: In a dummy dependent variable model, a function that expresses the probability of observing a value of 1 for the dependent variable given values of the independent (X) variables.

Confidence interval: An interval constructed from a sample parameter estimate and an estimated SE, designed so that the procedure will cover the true parameter a specified percentage of the time in repeated sampling

Controlled experiment: An experiment in which the investigator assigns subjects into treatment or control groups at random. See also, *observational study*.

Correlation coefficient: A measure of the linear association between two sets of data or random variables. Bounded between -1 and 1.

Covariance: A measure of the degree to which two random variables move together, taking into account their expected values. Related to the *correlation coefficient*.

Critical value: In hypothesis testing, a number against which the test statistic is compared in order to determine whether to reject the null hypothesis. For confidence intervals, a value which determines the width of the interval.

Cross-sectional data set: A data set that is a slice of information gathered at one point in time across different units of observation. See also *panel data set* and *time series data set*.

Cross tab: Short for cross tabulation; a table that displays results (e.g., a count or average) for one variable for given values of another variable. For example, average income given level of education. Also known as a contingency or cross classification table. See also *PivotTable*.

Data generation process (DGP): A description of how each observation in the sample was produced, often including the source of chance error.

Degrees of freedom: In regression, the number of observations minus the number of parameters estimated.

known as an ent**e**: A variable that is determined by other variables, also variable includes a chance variable. In econometric theory, the dependent onent. By convention, a dependent variable is denoted by the letter Y.

Distributed lag model: A model that includes effects from the past via lagged variables. See also *static model*.

Dummy dependent variable: A dependent variable that is not continuous and can take on only two values.

Dummy dependent variable (DDV) model: A model for the data generation process of a dummy dependent variable. Also known as a binary response model.

Dummy variable: An indicator variable that reveals (indicates) whether an observation possesses a certain characteristic. The value of the dummy variable is 1 if the observation possesses the characteristic and 0 if it does not.

Durbin–Watson test: A statistical test that uses the residuals and independent variables (X's) in order to determine if there is first-order autocorrelation in the errors.

Ecological correlation: The practice of using correlation coefficients based on grouped or aggregated data.

Elasticity: The percentage change in a dependent (Y or endogenous) variable for a given percentage change in an independent (X or exogenous) variable.

Glossary

Empirical histogram: In contrast to a *probability histogram*, a histogram based on data.

Endogeneity: A general term to describe a situation in which a right-hand side variable is not independent of the error term, e.g., simultaneity bias.

Error term: An element of a linear regression equation which encapsulates the effects of measurement error, omitted variables, and luck.

Estimate: The outcome of applying an estimator to sample data; a data-based guess at the value of a population parameter.

Estimated ρ-test: A regression of residuals on lagged residuals in order to test for autocorrelation.

Estimator: A recipe for producing estimates of the value of a population parameter.

Expected value: The long-run average value of a random.

Feasible generalized least squares (FGLS): A procedure based on generalized least squares, but using estimated values of parameters determining the distribution of the errors.

First difference: The first difference of a variable is its current value less its one-period lagged variable.

Forecast error: The actual, realized value of the dependent variable (Y) minus the forecasted value.

Gauss-Markov theorem: This theorem states that if the data generation process follows the classical econometric model, then ordinary least squares is the best linear unbiased estimator.

Generalized least squares (GLS): A procedure in which the original model is transformed before running ordinary least squares in order to deal with heteroskedasticity or autocorrelation in the errors. See also *feasible generalized least squares*.

Gini coefficient: A measure of inequality in the distribution of income.

Heteroskedasticity: A situation in which the residuals (in the context of descriptive statistics) or errors (in the context of inferential statistics) have differing amounts of spread.

Homoskedasticity: A situation in which the residuals (in the context of descriptive statistics) or errors (in the context of inferential statistics) have the same amount of spread.

Hypothesis test: A procedure for using sample data to determine whether a claim about a population parameter is true.

Identification: In a simultaneous equations model, the ability to consistently estimate the parameters of an equation.

Independent variable: In a regression model, a variable which helps to determine the value of the dependent variable. By convention, an independent variable is denoted by the letter X.

Inference: The process of using sample evidence to reach conclusions about the values of population parameters.

Initial conditions: In an autoregressive process, assumptions made about starting values for the process.

Instrument: An instrument for an endogenous variable, also called an instrumental variable, refers to a variable which is uncorrelated with the error term in an equation determining the endogenous variable, but correlated with the endogenous variable itself. See also *two stage least squares*.

Interval forecast: A confidence interval for a forecast, typically centered on the point forecast.

Iteration: A procedure based on repeated recalculation until convergence or little improvement is found.

Joint confidence region: Analogous to a confidence interval, a multi-dimensional region constructed from sample estimates, estimated SE's, and estimated covariances in such a way that the region covers the coordinates for the true parameters a specified percentage of the time in repeated sampling.

Joint sampling distribution: A sampling distribution for two or more random variables, which takes into account the correlation between the random variables.

Lagging: Reading a previous value of a variable: Z_t lagged one period is Z_{t-1}.

Linear estimator: An estimator that is a linear function of the dependent variable (Y's); an estimator that can be written as a weighted sum with each observation on Y raised to the first power.

Linear functional form: A regression equation in which the dependent variable (Y) is a linear function of the independent variable(s) (X's), such as $Y_i = b_0 + b_1 X_i$. There are no terms involving X raised to a power other than one or zero.

Linear probability model (LPM): A linear regression applied to a dummy dependent variable model.

Linear regression: A fitting procedure in which the equation for the regression line is a linear function of the parameters. The dependent and independent variables can be nonlinearly transformed as long as the equation remains linear in the coefficients. See also *nonlinear least squares*.

LINEST: An array function in Excel that returns regression results.

Logit model: A dummy dependent variable regression model in which the errors are logistically distributed.

Long regression: A regression of Y on all of the X's, instead of a subset of the X's (termed the *short regression*).

Maximum likelihood (ML): An estimation technique that chooses coefficients that maximize the likelihood of observing a given sample. This advanced method is not presented in this book, but the DDV add-ins compute maximum likelihood estimates of probit and logit models as one option.

Measurement error: Variation in measurements of the dependent variable due to inherent randomness in the process of observing and taking readings. In more advanced texts and the econometrics literature, measurement error often refers to the situation in which the values of the independent variables are incorrectly measured.

Missing value: An unobserved value for a variable, which is properly indicated by a period, not a blank in Excel.

Monte Carlo simulation: A method of analysis based on artificially recreating a chance process, running it many times, and directly observing the results.

Multicollinearity: Refers to the correlation among independent variables in a regression. As the degree of multicollinearity increases, estimates remain unbiased, but the SE increases. See also *perfect multicollinearity*.

Multiple regression: A regression model with more than one independent variable. Also called multivariate regression (although in advanced econometrics, this refers to models with more than one dependent variable).

Nonlinear least squares (NLLS): Regression analysis applied to a function that is nonlinear in the parameters. See also *linear regression*.

Normal approximation: A procedure in which the normal curve is substituted for the exact histogram in order to determine a particular area of the histogram; often used for computing P-values of statistics known to converge to the normal curve as sample size increases.

Null hypothesis: In a hypothesis test, a claim made about a parameter or parameters. According to this claim, any difference between the estimated and hypothesized values of the parameter(s) is (are) due to chance.

Observation: All the information about a single unit in a collection of data.

Observational study: In an observational study, one gathers data by directly observing decisions and behaviors in a natural environment. Individuals self-select into the group (e.g., smoker versus non-smoker) they are in. See also *controlled experiment*.

Omitted variable: An independent (X) variable not included in the regression.

Omitted variable bias: A situation in which an estimator's sampling distribution is not centered on the true parameter value because the regression omits a relevant independent (X) variable that is correlated with one or more of the included independent variables.

Omitted variable rule: A set of equations which relates the value of a parameter estimate in a short regression to the corresponding estimate in a long regression, which produces a measure of the level of bias in the short regression. The rule involves an auxiliary regression of the omitted X variable on the included X variable.

Ordinary least squares (OLS): A linear regression technique in which the regression estimates are that set of coefficients which minimize the sum of squared residuals.

Paired XY bootstrap: A bootstrap procedure that samples entire rows (or observations). See also *residuals bootstrap*.

Panel (longitudinal) data set: A data set that combines time series and cross-sectional data, following different units of observation over time. These data sets are not discussed in this book.

Parameter: A numerical fact about a population that typically is unknown and must be estimated from a sample.

Perfect multicollinearity: A special case of multicollinearity, perfect multicollinearity occurs when there is an exact linear relationship among the Xs. There is no unique solution to the least squares problem and software will often zero out one of the variables.

PivotTable: An interactive table produced by Excel, which can be used to create cross tabs. Execute Data: PivotTable to begin.

Point forecast: The single best guess as to the future value of a variable of interest.

Point of averages: In a scatter diagram of a bivariate data set, the point whose x-coordinate is the average value of the X's and whose y-coordinate is the average value of the Y's.

Polling box model: A box model in which the contents of the box represent characteristics of an existing population. See also *coin flip box model*.

Population: A class of individuals, whose characteristics we wish to learn about.

Probability histogram: A histogram which represents the chances of a random variable taking on different values. The probability histogram gives the exact, long-run probability of obtaining a particular outcome to a chance process. Also known as the sampling distribution.

Probit model: A dummy dependent variable regression model in which the errors are normally distributed.

Population regression function: A linear functional relationship which best summarizes the relationship between a dependent variable and one or more independent variables for the entire population. The goal of regression analysis is to estimate the population regression function from a sample.

R^2: A statistic which measures the improvement in prediction gained by using the regression line instead of the average value of the dependent variable.

Random number generation (RNG): An algorithm used to produce pseudo-random number sequences by a computer.

Random variable: In a chance process, a function that ties a numerical value (probability) to every possible outcome.

Random walk: A first-order autoregressive (AR(1)) process in which $\rho = 1$. Each term in the series is equal to the previous term plus a random error and, possibly, a drift parameter.

Random X's model: A box model in which the independent variables (the X's) are randomly generated, unlike the fixed-X's-in-repeated-sampling data generation process that underlies the classical econometric model.

Reduced-form equation: An equation from a simultaneous equations model which expresses the value of the dependent variable (Y) as a function of independent (X) variables alone. See also *structural equation*.

Regression line: Summarizes the relationship between two variables as a line that optimizes an objective function. The prime example is ordinary least squares, which minimizes the sum of squared residuals.

Regression sum of squares: The total sum of squares minus the sum of squared residuals; also known as the explained sum of squares.

Regression through the origin: A regression in which the intercept is forced to be zero. In Excel, the third parameter in the LINEST function is set to zero as in this formula: "=LINEST(A1:A10,B1:B10,0,1)."

Residual: The actual (or observed) value minus the predicted value; the vertical distance of the actual, observed Y from its predicted Y value.

Residual plot: A scatter plot of the residuals on the y-axis against the independent variable or one of the independent variables on the x-axis.

Residuals bootstrap: A bootstrap procedure that samples from the residuals. See also *paired XY bootstrap*.

Robust SE: An estimated SE that takes into account heteroskedasticity. (There are also serial-correlation robust SE's, but those are not discussed in this book.)

Root mean square error (RMSE): A measure of the dispersion of the data around the regression line. If the classical econometric model applies, the RMSE is an estimate of the common SD of the error terms.

Sampling distribution: See *probability histogram*.

Seasonal adjustment: A method of adjusting a time series in order to control for persistent time patterns in the data. The purpose is to facilitate comparisons across time periods.

Short regression: A regression of the dependent variable on a subset of the independent variables, instead of all the independent variables. See also *long regression*.

Simultaneity bias: Occurs when an estimate's sampling distribution is not centered on the true parameter value because it was obtained by estimating a single equation which is actually part of a simultaneous equations model (SEM). The bias is due to correlation between endogenous right-hand-side variables and the error term.

Simultaneous equations model (SEM): A model with more than one equation in which dependent variables (Y's) appear as regressors (in the right-hand side of the equations).

Spurious regression: Comes in two types, both of which produce biased estimates of the slope of Y on X. The first type occurs when both X and Y variables are trending. In this case, a regression of Y on X which does not include a trend term typically gives biased estimates. The second type occurs when both X and Y variables are random walks.

Stable process: An autoregressive process which does not "blow up". For an AR(1) process, this means that the absolute value of ρ is less than one.

Standard deviation (SD): A measure of the spread of a list of numbers. See also *standard error*.

Standard error (SE): A measure of the spread (SD) of the values of a random variable, typically a sample statistic. The standard error of a regression estimate can be exact (if the SD of the errors is known), estimated (when the SD of the errors must be estimated) or approximate (when we use the SD from a Monte Carlo simulation). See also *standard deviation*.

Standard normal distribution: The normal distribution with mean 0 and SD 1.

Static model: A time series model that deals with a contemporaneous relationship between a dependent variable and one or more independent variables. See also *distributed lag model*.

Stationary time series: Loosely speaking, a time series is stationary if the joint probability distribution of the random variables in the time series is constant at every point in the sequence.

Structural equation: One of the equations in a simultaneous equations model (SEM). The typical structural equation includes dependent (endogenous variables) on both sides of the equation. See also *reduced-form equation*.

Test statistic: A statistic based on the sample data which can be used to conduct a hypothesis test.

Threshold: In DDV models, the deterministic component to which a random draw is compared in order to produce the observed zero or one variable.

Time series data set: A data set that follows the same observational unit over different periods of time. See also *cross-sectional data set*.

Total sum of squares: The sum of squared deviations of the Y variable from its average.

Trend stationary process: A time series which is stationary after taking into account the trend in the series.

***T*-statistic:** a test statistic which follows the *t* distribution. Computed in exactly the same way as the z-*statistic*.

Two stage least squares (2SLS): A regression procedure used to estimate coefficients in a simultaneous equations model in which the first stage regression is run to create predicted values of the endogenous variables, which are then used in a second stage regression to estimate the coefficients.

Unbiased estimator: An estimator whose expected value is equal to the value of the population parameter being estimated. See also *biased estimator*.

Variance: The square of the standard deviation.

Wage discrimination: The practice of paying otherwise identical workers different amounts based on a characteristic (such as gender or ethnicity) that is unrelated to productivity.

Weak dependence: A sequence of random variables is weakly dependent if the elements of the sequence become essentially independent at a sufficiently rapid pace as the distance between them grows.

Whole model *F*-test: A hypothesis test in which the null is that all of the slope coefficients, jointly, are equal to zero.

Z-statistic: A test statistic which approximately follows the standard normal distribution in large samples. Formed by taking the observed value, subtracting the hypothesized value, and dividing the result by the appropriate SE.

Index